Keyboard Shortcuts for Excel Commands (continued)

Command	*Shortcut*
Format Number (general)	Ctrl-~
Format Number (#,##0.00)	Ctrl-!
Format Number (h:mm AM/PM)	Ctrl-@
Format Number (d-mmm-yy)	Ctrl-#
Format Number (($#,##0.00_);($#,##0.00))	Ctrl-$
Format Number (0%)	Ctrl-%
Format Number (0.00E+00)	Ctrl-^
Format Font (default)	Ctrl-1
Format Font (bold)	Ctrl-2
Format Font (italic)	Ctrl-3
Format Font (underline)	Ctrl-4
Format Font (strikeout)	Ctrl-5
Format Border (outline)	Ctrl-&
Format Border (no border)	Ctrl-_
Format Row Height (hide)	Ctrl-F9
Format Row Height (unhide)	Ctrl-Shift-F9
Format Column Width (hide)	Ctrl-0
Format Column Width (unhide)	Ctrl-Shift-0
Options Display (formula display)	Ctrl-`
Options Display (outline symbols)	Ctrl-8
Options Display (placeholders or hiding)	Ctrl-6
Options Calculate Now	F9 or Ctrl-=
Options Calculate Document	Shift-F9
Window Show Info	Ctrl-F2

Computer users are not all alike. Neither are SYBEX books.

We know our customers have a variety of needs. They've told us so. And because we've listened, we've developed several distinct types of books to meet the needs of each of our customers. What are you looking for in computer help?

If you're looking for the basics, try the **ABC's** series. You'll find short, unintimidating tutorials and helpful illustrations. For a more visual approach, select **Teach Yourself**, featuring screen-by-screen illustrations of how to use your latest software purchase.

Mastering and **Understanding** titles offer you a step-by-step introduction, plus an in-depth examination of intermediate-level features, to use as you progress.

Our **Up & Running** series is designed for computer-literate consumers who want a no-nonsense overview of new programs. Just 20 basic lessons, and you're on your way.

We also publish two types of reference books. Our **Instant References** provide quick access to each of a program's commands and functions. SYBEX **Encyclopedias** provide a *comprehensive reference* and explanation of all of the commands, features and functions of the subject software.

Sometimes a subject requires a special treatment that our standard series doesn't provide. So you'll find we have titles like **Advanced Techniques**, **Handbooks**, **Tips & Tricks**, and others that are specifically tailored to satisfy a unique need.

We carefully select our authors for their in-depth understanding of the software they're writing about, as well as their ability to write clearly and communicate effectively. Each manuscript is thoroughly reviewed by our technical staff to ensure its complete accuracy. Our production department makes sure it's easy to use. All of this adds up to the highest quality books available, consistently appearing on best-seller charts worldwide.

You'll find SYBEX publishes a variety of books on every popular software package. Looking for computer help? Help Yourself to SYBEX.

Mastering Excel 3.0 for Windows

Mastering Excel 3.0 for Windows™

Carl Townsend

San Francisco • Paris • Düsseldorf • Soest

Acquisitions Editor: Dianne King
Developmental Editor: Christian T.S. Crumlish
Editor: Stefan Grünwedel
Project Editor: Janna Hecker
Word Processors: Scott Campbell, Ann Dunn, and Lisa Mitchell
Chapter Art and Production: Eleanor Ramos
Screen Graphics: Cuong Le
Typesetters: Stephanie Hollier and Bob Myren
Proofreaders: Lisa Haden, Patsy Owens, and Dina Quan
Indexer: Ted Laux
Cover Designer: Thomas Ingalls + Associates
Cover Photographer: Mark Johann

Library of Congress Card Number: 91-65109
ISBN: 0-89588-643-X

Manufactured in the United States of America
10 9 8 7 6 5 4 3 2 1

To Sandy

for helping to keep the ship on course as the book was written.

ACKNOWLEDGMENTS

I would like to express my appreciation to many people who helped make this book possible. A special thanks to Tanya van Dam and Christy Gersich at Microsoft for supplying Excel and support during the writing of the book. Thanks also to Jack Sullivan for his help and advice.

At SYBEX, thanks to Stefan Grünwedel for editing the book. Thanks also to Janna Hecker for her editorial assistance, and to Christian Crumlish for helping me develop the manuscript.

Contents at a Glance

Table of Contents

INTRODUCTION

There are corporate executives, wholesalers, retailers, and small-business owners who talk about their business lives in two time periods: before and after the electronic spreadsheet.

—Steven Levy

BACKGROUND

Before the invention of the personal-computer spreadsheet program, it was not unusual for a financial vice-president of a company to spend the night manually preparing the company's financial projections for an annual meeting, using nothing more than a hand calculator. If even a small error was made, it would ripple through all subsequent calculations on the entire spreadsheet. Spreadsheet programs did exist for large main-frame computers, but they were often cumbersome to use, and the computers were not very accessible to most employees.

The VisiCalc spreadsheet program, invented by Robert Frankston and Dan Bricklin in 1978 for the Apple II computer, suddenly changed all this. For the first time, a business manager could set up an entire financial model and analyze any number of scenarios quickly, accurately, and inexpensively.

The popularity and capabilities of personal-computer spreadsheet programs grew at a rapid rate. Sorcim's SuperCalc (1980), Microsoft's Multiplan (1982), and Lotus's 1-2-3 (1983) each added new features, capabilities, and integrated tools. These products represented important milestones in the evolution of the spreadsheet, but spreadsheet users wanted still more capabilities.

Users wanted more cells in their spreadsheets to build larger models, and they wanted to be able to link spreadsheets to form hierarchical relationships. They also wanted to be able to produce WYSIWYG ("what you see is what you get") displays and make presentation-quality charts and worksheets. Users found macros to be the most powerful feature in spreadsheet programs, yet they were cumbersome to use in the products that included them, and they were not included at all in some spreadsheet programs marketed as late as 1985.

Excel changed all this. In 1985, Microsoft released Excel for the Macintosh, the first spreadsheet program designed specifically to address the needs of users who manage many types of data—those frustrated by the limitations of the numerical-analysis products currently available. In 1987, Microsoft introduced a version of Excel for the PC/AT, PS-2, and compatibles.

THE PHILOSOPHY OF EXCEL

Before you begin using Excel, it is important to understand some of the philosophy that went into the design of the product. It is not, like many spreadsheet products, intended to be integrated software that combines many applications. Rather, Excel is limited to three applications—spreadsheet (or worksheet), database, and graphics—and it does each to a depth that is not available in competitive products.

Excel is an example of a *contextually integrated* product. That is, it combines the applications that are frequently used in the same context by users whose primary task is analyzing and processing numerical data. This contextual integration permits a user to move quickly from one application to another to see the results of an analysis.

Because Excel is designed specifically for users working with data in a large variety of numerical-analysis contexts, it supports the data-processing application more thoroughly than any other personal-computer software product. However, Excel users are not restricted by the program's narrow range of applications. Windows 3.0 offers the capability of interfacing Excel data and objects seamlessly with word processors, communication programs, and presentation programs, such as Microsoft PowerPoint.

BOOK ORGANIZATION

This book is divided into seven sections. After a brief introduction (Part I), you learn the basic principles of working with Excel (Part II). Part III covers database management. Part IV describes special features of Excel. Part V covers charting and graphics.

Part VI includes five chapters on application design and the Excel utilities. Using specific applications, such as invoicing, financial management, and trend analysis, you will gain some understanding of how to use Excel to solve specific problems.

Finally, Part VII describes macros and how to use them. This section is primarily tutorial, but you will find a few examples to help you design your own macros.

Appended to this book are a glossary and an exhaustive list of macro language function commands. You will also find some tips to help you gain more speed from Excel and some notes on installing the software.

Throughout this book, you will be given many tutorial examples that show how Excel can meet a variety of needs. I encourage you to try these examples. Each of them will give you valuable insights into the special features of Excel.

VISUAL ELEMENTS OF THIS BOOK

Several features of which you should be aware are included in the text and margins of this book.

TEXT ELEMENTS

Any data or keystrokes that you type appear in **boldface.** For example, you might read, "...and enter the formula **=C1+C3**."

Alternatively, words, data, or instructions that you read *directly* from the screen appear in program font. For example, you might read, "...either of the following displays $123.00..."

3.0

MARGIN ELEMENTS

This is a note.

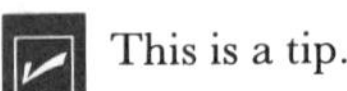

This is a tip.

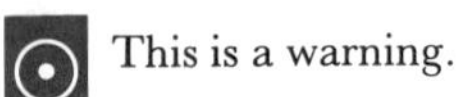

This is a warning.

Features that are new to Excel 3.0 are highlighted for your information with an icon in the margin, shown here.

There are also three types of margin notes that appear in this book: Notes, Tips, and Warnings. Their symbols are shown in the margin here as well.

Finally, pictures of various pull-down menus are shown in the margins whenever a new menu selection is being discussed. This is to make you sure that you're on the right track when following instructions, as well as to show you how the menu looks, should you be reading the book while away from your computer.

An Overview of Excel

PART I OF THIS BOOK IS FOR THOSE WHO WOULD like to start using Excel quickly without learning many commands and instructions. You'll find out how to install Excel, explore Windows 3.0, and be guided through the creation of a simple worksheet and chart.

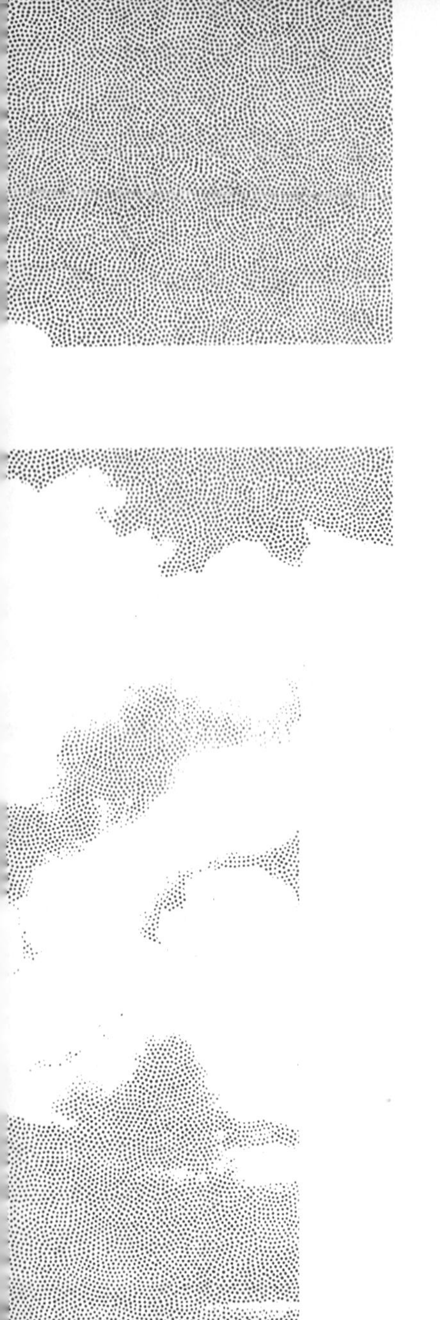

1 Introduction to Excel

EXCEL IS AN ADVANCED WORKSHEET (OS SPREADsheet) product for IBM AT or PS/2 compatibles that also supports database and graphic functions. A *worksheet program* is essentially a replacement for the ledger sheet, pencil, and calculator. The computer displays a two-dimensional worksheet, divided into rows and columns. Each intersection of a row and a column is called a *cell*. An Excel worksheet may look very similar to a paper one, but it has several advantages:

- It can be much, much larger than its paper counterpart. In fact, one of Excel's outstanding features is the number of worksheet cells available—over 4 million cells in 256 columns of 16,384 rows
- You can edit and change it quickly: changing one number immediately affects all calculations based on that number
- The printed worksheet is presentation-quality and can be used for published reports or overhead projectors

- The Excel worksheet is more accurate than the paper one, as it performs some level of self-checking

FEATURES OF EXCEL

There are two types of features of Excel. *Analysis features* perform various calculations on data in the worksheet. *Presentation features* display information to the user.

ANALYSIS FEATURES

Excel offers several analysis features that many competing worksheets do not offer:

- Excel is easy to learn and use. The Windows 3.0 interface includes windows, pull-down menus, dialog boxes for input, and mouse support
- Excel can link worksheets and develop hierarchical relationships among them. For example, department managers can develop marketing and production worksheets independently, and then link their component worksheets to the larger corporate worksheet
- Excel's problem-solving capabilities are extensive. Approximately 424 functions are provided with Excel—and you can create other functions of your own
- Excel supports arrays and tables
- Using "what-if" analysis, you can define an output value and then see what input values you need to reach this goal
- When calculating, Excel includes only those cells that have changed since the last calculation. This provides quick worksheet updating
- Users will find that repetitive tasks can be automated with Excel's easy-to-use macros and user-definable functions
- Excel users can make extensive use of data already created using other worksheet software, even from other

computers. Excel offers two-way file capability with Multiplan, dBASE IV, and Lotus 1-2-3, as well as any program using the Microsoft SYLK format

- Excel includes integrated, full-featured graphing and charting capabilities
- Excel supports on-screen databases with querying, extracting, and sorting functions
- Excel permits you to add, edit, delete, and find database records
- Excel provides extensive auditing control. You can give cells names, even name a range of cells with one name or give one cell several names. You also can add notes to cells or show the attributes (format, formula, value) of active cells
- Macros can be used for two-way communication with other programs, and you can even use macros to add your C routines within Excel

PRESENTATION FEATURES

Excel produces presentation-quality worksheet documentation and offers you a wide selection of fonts and formats. Its presentation features include the following:

- Individual cells and chart text can be formatted to any font and font size supported by Windows
- Variations in font style (normal, boldface, underline, strikeout, and italic) and alignment control (left, center, right, and fill) can be determined at the cell level
- There are five border styles, as well as shading and shadow capability
- Extensive pattern control is available for printing worksheets and charts with black and white printers
- There are 64 predefined cell pictures
- User-definable pictures are supported

- There are 68 built-in chart formats, including 24 three-dimensional formats
- You can add legends, text, arrows, patterns, scaling, and symbols to charts
- Global zero suppression, which prevents the printing of zero values, is available
- Worksheets can be printed horizontally (landscape) or vertically (portrait)
- Outline control is available for printing summary worksheets

MICROSOFT WINDOWS AND EXCEL

Excel is a Microsoft Windows application program, which means it requires Windows 3.0 or later. Windows is a software shell that resides in memory with DOS. It provides windows, icons, pull-down menus, multitasking and other features to application programs running under it (see below), while providing a common user interface with other Windows application programs.

FEATURES OF WINDOWS

Windows provides you with the following features:

- The Excel program can be used with other programs, such as word processors or database managers that run under Windows
- You can use the Clipboard to move data between Excel and other programs
- The size of the spreadsheet is not limited by the conventional memory limit of 640K. Using Windows 3.0, Excel can take advantage of any extended memory installed. This means you can build much larger worksheets with Excel than you can with other programs

- The graphical user interface is very easy to learn and is rapidly becoming the standard for many application programs
- Access to peripheral devices from Excel is logical rather than physical; that is, Excel does not write to any specific type of printer or plotter. To install a new printer for all Windows application programs on the system, it is only necessary to add the new printer driver to Windows
- The use of the mouse is integrated with both Windows and Excel. This makes it easier to move around in worksheets and to make selections than with nonmouse worksheet programs or programs in which the use of the mouse was designed after the fact
- Windows includes math coprocessor support for the 8087, 80287, and 80387
- Networking is supported if the network is compatible with the Microsoft Networks (Microsoft Corporation)

NEW FEATURES OF EXCEL 3.0

3.0

If you are already using Excel and upgrading to version 3.0, you will find many new features that extend the analysis and presentation capabilities of Excel. These are marked in this book with the icon to the left, but here is a quick summary of the new features.

NEW WORKSHEET FEATURES

Here are Excel's new worksheet features:

- Text in cells can be formatted in any manner supported by Windows 3.0. Any number of formats can be used in the worksheet simultaneously
- Charts can be drawn on the worksheet

- Using a new tool bar, you can draw graphic objects on the screen and type comments in text boxes
- There is a more versatile array of colors, patterns, and shading available
- Objects from other programs can be embedded in the worksheet
- You can define style sheets for a worksheet
- A new Formula Goal Seek command is included that enables you to find which input value is needed for a specified output value
- You can undo more format changes
- You can outline your worksheets and control the display and printing of detail levels

NEW CHARTING FEATURES

Below are Excel's new graphing or charting capabilities:

- Excel supports 68 chart formats, 24 of them three-dimensional
- Data series markers can be graphics, enabling you to create picture charts.
- You can edit data series more easily
- You can drag data series markers and change the underlying worksheet
- You can place legends anywhere on your charts
- Excel handles presentation features such as patterns, colors, and graphics better than before

NEW MACRO FEATURES

Excel's new macro features are as follows:

- The new version has a better user-defined dialog box capability, with drop-down lists and grayed-out items

- You can automate the loading of macro sheets upon starting. This makes it easy to add a macro library
- The new version has improved debugging features

NEW UTILITIES

Finally, Excel 3.0 includes the following new features:

- A Q+E Utility for using external databases
- A Solver utility for doing what-if analysis
- A Dialog Editor for creating user-defined dialog boxes (see Chapter 28)

WHAT CAN I DO WITH EXCEL?

Anyone who works with numerical data processing can take advantage of Excel's extensive worksheet capabilities. For administration and record-keeping purposes, you can use Excel to check registers, expense reports, annual reports, and five-year forecasts. Excel's financial applications include amortization schedules, cash-flow projections, general ledgers, accounts receivable, accounts payable, comparative investment analyses, personal net-worth statements, balance sheets, and tax planning. Some examples of sales and marketing applications are sales comparisons, marketing analyses, and product-line summaries as well as sales-forecast and linear-regression analyses. For operations, you can use Excel for inventory-management systems, material-requirement planning, inventory-rate-of-turnover analyses, and last-in-first-out analyses.

Here are some examples of how users might apply their Excel systems:

- Donald, a building contractor involved in competitive bidding, puts all his cost factors into an Excel worksheet. Then he alters each factor to see how it affects his final proposed bid. He can then study and analyze each factor that controls his cost to produce a final bid that is as low as possible

- Susan is trying to conserve energy in her home. She creates a model of her house on an Excel worksheet. This model includes factors that control heating and cooling costs, such as attic insulation, window caulking, and a high-efficiency furnace. She also can calculate the cost of installing each of these energy-saving features. By doing this, she can analyze the results to see how long it would take her to recover the costs of each energy-saving idea
- Carol invests in stocks, commodities, and bonds. She uses Excel worksheets to create investment models and to perform what-if analyses to find the best investment opportunities
- George is in charge of labor negotiations for his company. Every few years, the union contracts are renegotiated. George has to be able to study proposals from the unions quickly and determine how they would affect the company's earnings on both short-term and long-term bases. Using a worksheet, he can create a financial model of the company and quickly see how the union proposals will affect profits
- John likes to do a little real-estate business from his home. He manages several rental properties and needs to be aware of costs, such as upkeep, taxes, and depreciation. He also has to know when to buy and sell the properties that he manages. The Excel worksheet gives him instant information on his profits as these factors change
- Widget Manufacturing creats an entire model of their financial operation on Excel, using a collection of interlinked worksheets. The first sheet is the source and application of funds worksheet. The last worksheets are the balance sheet and income statements. These worksheets are interlinked, and if an update is made in the source and applications of funds, all subsequent worksheets change automatically

All of these applications can be grouped into one of two broad classifications: reporting on what has happened (analysis) or forecasting what could happen (what-if analysis). In the first case, the user takes data that describe something that has happened in the past (such as the sales of a product in three areas of the country during the last three months) and puts them into a form that can be analyzed (such as a pie chart). From this, the user can make a decision (such as the marketing strategy for next month). In the second case, the user changes one or more variables and sees how these changes will affect a specific goal (for example, modifying various cost factors to see how each change would affect the bid on a project).

Now that you have some idea of what Excel is and what it can do, it's time to get started using Excel!

2 Getting Started

BEGINNING TO USE EXCEL IS, WITHOUT DOUBT, AN exciting adventure. Before starting, however, you should be sure that you have everything you need. You also should take certain initial precautions, as you would when beginning to use any new computer program.

This chapter provides step-by-step instructions on how to get started with Excel. It also includes a brief review of Microsoft Windows, and how to get help if you need it.

WHAT DO I NEED?

As with any program, there is some specific hardware and software you need to run Excel. Excel 3.0 is available for DOS 3.2 or later (with the Windows 3.0 environment or later). You also can use it with OS/2 and Macintosh System Software 7.0 operating systems. Excel 3.0 is also supported by the Hewlett-Packard NewWave and IBM OfficeVision/2 environments with DOS. This book assumes you have Excel 3.0 for the Windows 3.0 environment, running on

DOS 3.2 or later. Be sure you are using a version of Excel for this environment. Almost all the examples in this book will work with any flavor of Excel 3.0, but the user interface instructions (keystrokes and short-cut keys) and screens may differ.

HARDWARE RESOURCES

The following is the minimum recommended hardware for using Excel 3.0 with Windows:

- An IBM AT, PS/2, or 386 computer that is DOS compatible. You also should have enough memory in your computer to run Windows in the standard or 386-enhanced mode. You can find out what mode your Windows is using by selecting About Program Manager from the Help menu of Windows's Program Manager. Excel will not run in the real mode
- A hard-disk drive
- A Windows-compatible printer
- A VGA, EGA, Hercules, or other Windows-compatible monitor

Excel will run on slower PC compatibles, but for maximum efficiency you should run Excel in a Windows 386-enhanced mode with a 386 processor and have two or more megabytes of extended memory, as well as a math coprocessor.

Excel will run on slower PC compatibles, but for maximum efficiency you should run Excel in a Windows 386-enhanced mode with a 386 processor and have two or more megabytes of extended memory, as well as a math coprocessor.

SOFTWARE RESOURCES

You need the Excel program disks, extra disks, and the documentation that came with Excel. You also will need a copy of DOS 3.2 and Windows 3.0. Later releases of either of these can also be used.

CREATING BACKUP COPIES

Before starting to use Excel, you should create backup copies of the Excel disks. The Excel disks are not copy-protected, so you can copy them with any conventional copy program, such as the DOS COPY (or XCOPY) program.

INSTALLING EXCEL

The installation program makes Excel easy to install:

1. Place a copy of the Excel Setup disk in drive A.
2. Start Windows.
3. Select Run from the File menu.
4. In the dialog box type **A:SETUP** and press Enter.

Follow the installation directions of the setup program. You will first need to enter your organization's name. Then you will be asked for the directory to which you wish to install Excel. A dialog box is then displayed from which you can choose your installation options.

STARTING EXCEL

Excel can be started from Windows or from the DOS prompt.

STARTING EXCEL FROM THE DOS PROMPT

To start Excel from the DOS prompt, first enter the directory you wish to use for your worksheets (the default is C:\EXCEL). Then type **WIN EXCEL** and press Enter. This will start Excel and display an empty worksheet, as shown in Figure 2.1.

You can start Excel another way if you know the file name of a worksheet you wish to edit. Again, first be sure you are in the

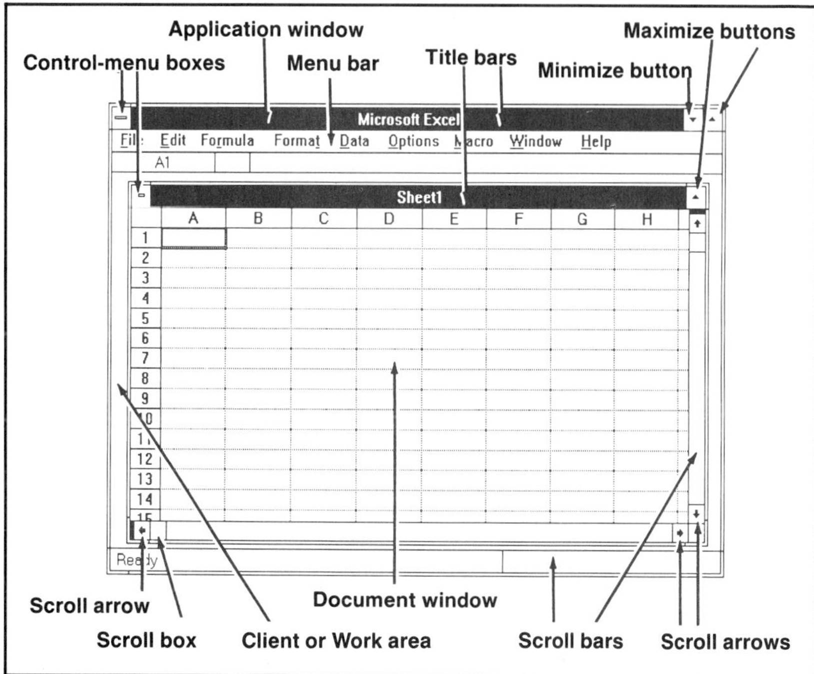

Figure 2.1: The Excel menu bar and worksheet

directory containing the worksheet you wish to use (or the directory where you will create it). Then enter **WIN** and the worksheet name:

```
WIN WORKSHEET.XLS
```

Be sure to include the extension .XLS as a part of the file name. This will start Excel and load the worksheet.

STARTING EXCEL FROM WINDOWS

3.0

If Windows is already running, you can start Excel from it using any of the methods for starting Windows programs. The easiest method is generally to use the Program Manager and switch to the Microsoft Excel 3.0 group. Double-click the Excel icon (or use the direction keys and press Enter). This will start Excel with an empty worksheet.

If you have trouble starting Excel with a worksheet name, Excel is not installed properly.

To start Excel with a worksheet, use the Windows File Manager and double-click the worksheet name. A second method is to use the Run command on the Program Manager's File menu and enter the worksheet name, including its path, in the Run dialog box (be sure to use the worksheet file-name extension). A third method is to put the data file in a group and double-click the data-file icon.

THE MOUSE

The cursor on the screen is controlled by the mouse. To move the pointer, simply move the mouse on any flat surface. If you run out of room, pick the mouse up and put it back down elsewhere on the surface. The pointer moves only when the mouse is moved. To click with the mouse, you usually press only the left mouse button. (You can change this to the right button, if you wish, with the Control Panel program with Windows.)

If you are left-handed and move the mouse with your left hand, you can make the right button the mouse action button with the Windows Control Panel program.

The primary mouse techniques are pointing, clicking, dragging, and double-clicking:

Pointing: Move the mouse until the cursor is at the desired cell or spot

Clicking: Press and release the left mouse button

Dragging: Position the pointer over an object and select it by holding the left mouse button down. Move the object to a new position and release the mouse button

Double-clicking: Press the left mouse button twice in rapid succession

USING WINDOWS

Excel is much like any other Windows program. It has the same elements and user interface as other Windows programs.

THE WINDOW ELEMENTS

Now let's look at the individual elements of the windows on-screen. The Excel program has its own single *application window*. Within the work area of this window are any number of *document windows* for the application. In Figure 2.1 a single document window, called Sheet1, is displayed. Multiple applications can be opened at a time, each with its own application and document windows. These windows will overlay each other on the desktop, but can be rearranged. Document windows must always remain inside the application window's work area.

Although many application windows may be open, only a single application can be active (in use) at a time. Its title bar will be shown in a dark color. Several document windows also can be open at a time, but only one document window can be the *focus* of the keyboard, so that data typed at the keyboard will be placed in this window. The document window with the current focus is called the *active document window.*

Here is a summary of the basic application window elements:

Title bar: Shows the window title. Currently displays the name of the application program, Microsoft Excel

Control-menu box: Changes the size of the window, quits the program, and does other system-level operations. The box contains a horizontal bar

Menu bar: Contains the names of the available command menus for the application program. The Excel menu bar options will vary depending on the mode in which Excel is running (e.g., the menu options for a worksheet are different from those for editing a chart)

Minimize buttons: Reduce a window to an icon at the bottom of the page. They contain a downward-pointing arrowhead

Maximize button: Zooms the window to full-screen size. It contains an upward-pointing arrowhead. When a window is maximized to the fullest extent, the arrowhead changes to a double-headed arrow

Client or Work area: Displays the worksheets, charts, or macros in Excel

Each document window contains some of the same elements:

Title bar: Shows the name of the open file, if any files are open.

Control-menu box: Changes the size of the document window, closes the document file (worksheet, chart, etc.), and performs other document operations. It contains a horizontal bar

Maximize button: Zooms the document window to the full size of the application window work space. It contains an upward-pointing arrowhead

Chapter 3 will describe document window features that are specific to Excel.

THE CONTROL-MENU BOX

The *Control-menu box* is a small box containing a horizontal bar in the upper-left corner of the window. Notice that Figure 2.1 contains two Control-menu boxes—one on the application window and another on the document window. Pressing Alt–Spacebar (application), Alt–Hyphen (document), or clicking the corresponding Control-menu box will display the Control menu. The Control menu provides options for moving, sizing, minimizing, maximizing, restoring, and closing the application or document window. You can either type the underlined letter or use the mouse to activate any command in the menu. Notice that the menus are slightly different. Close the menu by pressing Esc or clicking anywhere in the window outside the menu.

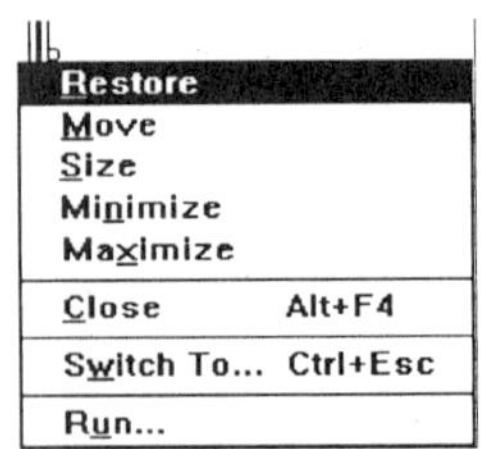

MULTITASKING WITH WINDOWS

Windows permits you to keep several programs in memory at a time. They can be Window application programs or non-Windows applications. This is important, as you may wish to run Excel while you run other programs.

To start another program, switch to the Program Manager (Alt–Tab) and start the program from its program group, or use the Run command from the File menu and enter the program name with its path. The new program will start and its application window will overlay Excel's.

You can use Alt–Tab to switch between the programs in memory, or Ctrl–Esc to see the Task Manager, from which you can select programs currently in memory.

APPLICATION AND DOCUMENT WINDOWS

Now let's explore how to activate, resize, move, enlarge, and close windows.

Making Windows Active

Although Windows permits you to load several programs into memory at once, only one of these can be *active* or available to the keyboard at a time. To make another application or document window active with the mouse, just click anywhere in it. You also can use the keyboard to change the active window. This is best used if the window you want to make active is not visible. Alt–Tab switches between applications windows and Ctrl–F6 switches between document windows.

Alt–Tab is really a preview mode: it activates all the programs (including the inactive programs represented as icons) in the order in which they were loaded. Hold down the Alt key and press Tab until the desired title bar or icon is highlighted. The highlighted application will then become active. For any hidden window or icon, you will see the title bar during the preview. Alt–Shift–Tab rotates through the available windows in the order opposite to Alt–Tab. This works for all programs, whether they are Windows applications or not.

Alt–Esc is a third method of switching between programs that have active windows. A fourth method is to use Ctrl–Esc to see the Task Manager window and select the desired task to make active.

Resizing and Moving Windows

By resizing and moving windows you can place multiple windows side by side for comparing or doing related functions. You can resize and move windows with either the mouse or the keyboard.

You cannot resize or move a window if it is maximized.

To resize windows using the mouse, move the mouse pointer to the right or bottom border of the window until the pointer changes to a double-arrow. Click the (left) button. Drag the border to a new position, making the window either larger or smaller. As you drag the border, both the old and new window sizes are shown. When you release the mouse button, the window appears in its new size. If you wish to change two borders at once, select the lower-right corner of the window. The cursor will now become a two-headed arrow pointing to the upper left and lower right. Drag the corner to create the new window size.

To move a window with the mouse, drag the title bar to the new location.

To change the size of a non-maximized application window from the keyboard, first press Alt–Spacebar to display the Control menu. Type **S** to select Size from the Control menu. The mouse cursor will now look like a four-headed arrow in the window. Select a new border location by hitting the → or ← keys. You also can press both keys to select the lower-right corner and change both borders simultaneously. The selected borders are now highlighted. Use the direction keys to move the borders to their desired location. Press Enter to lock the location, or press Esc to abort the resizing. (Esc will not work after you've pressed Enter.)

To move a non-maximized application window from the keyboard, first make it active, then press Alt–Spacebar. Type **M** to select Move from the menu. Then use the direction keys to move the window to the new location. As you move a window, Windows shows you both the old and new locations. Press Enter. Press Esc before pressing Enter if you need to abort a move operation.

Maximizing Windows

Maximizing a window, or zooming it, enlarges the window so that it occupies the entire screen. This reduces clutter by temporarily eliminating other windows and icons from the screen. It also gives you a larger display for viewing more of a worksheet.

You will generally want to maximize Excel to get the maximum working area. Appendix H describes how to maximize a program automatically upon loading.

To maximize a window with the mouse, click the Maximize icon (the upward-pointing arrowhead) at the upper right of the window or double-click the title bar. The window will immediately fill the screen.

To maximize a window with the keyboard, first make it active. Then press Alt–Spacebar if it is an application window, or Ctrl–Spacebar if it is a document window, and type **X** for Maximize.

To restore a maximized window to its former size, make the window active and click the Restore icon (double-arrow) in the upper-right corner or double-click the title bar.

Restore a window from the keyboard by making the window active and pressing Alt–Spacebar. Type **R** for Restore. To restore a document window, you can use Ctrl–F5.

Minimizing Windows

Minimizing an application window clears the program from the screen, but keeps it in memory only a few clicks or keystrokes away. To minimize an application, select Minimize from Control menu or click the Minimize button in the upper-right corner. This will close the application's window and place an icon, representing the window, at the bottom of the screen. Minimizing can help unclutter your screen. You cannot minimize a document window.

To restore the window, double-click the icon or click it once and choose Restore from the displayed Control menu. Or, from the keyboard, press Alt–Spacebar and choose Restore. The program will come back, looking just as it did before it was minimized.

Try the following experiments to see how the windows change:

1. Resize the worksheet window by clicking the lower-right corner of the document window and moving the corner up and to the left.
2. Click the scroll boxes and arrows and scroll your worksheet window over the blank document.
3. Open a second worksheet by clicking the File menu and choosing New. Choose Worksheet in the dialog box and click OK.
4. Click the Minimize button to reduce the active application window to an icon at the bottom of the screen. Then double-click the icon to restore the worksheet window.
5. Click the Maximize button of the worksheet window to zoom the worksheet to its maximum size. This button will then become the Restore button. Click it to return the worksheet to its smaller size.
6. Close the topmost document by double-clicking the Control-menu box of the document.

Closing a Window

To close a window (application or document) with the mouse, double-click its Control-menu box. This will remove the window from the desktop. To close an application window with the keyboard, make the window active, press Alt–Spacebar, and type **C** for Close. To close an active document window, press Ctrl–Spacebar and type **C**. (See "Keyboard Shortcuts" for a faster way.)

If an application window or document window is requested to be closed and document files are open and changed, Windows will query about each and ask if you wish these saved.

THE SCROLL BARS

Excel worksheet and macro windows have scroll bars at the right or bottom that can be used to scroll the window over a larger area (see Figure 2.1). The scroll bar has arrows at the ends and a *scroll box* inside it, also called a *thumb box* or *elevator.*

To scroll with the mouse, use the following techniques:

- Drag the scroll box in the bar to scroll the window to a desired place in the worksheet
- Click either arrow at the top or bottom of the right scroll bar to scroll the window a line at a time
- Click either arrow at the left or right of the bottom scroll bar to scroll the window a column at a time
- Click anywhere between the arrows to scroll through a windowful of rows or columns at a time
- Click on an arrow and hold the mouse button down to scroll continuously, until the rows or columns you wish to see are visible

You also can scroll with the keyboard. Scroll in the desired direction by pressing any of the direction keys: ↑, ↓, ←, or →. Press PgUp and PgDn to move up and down a windowful of rows, respectively. Press Ctrl–PgUp and Ctrl–PgDn to move left and right a windowful of columns, respectively. Finally, from wherever you are in the workspace, press Home to move to column A (or Ctrl–Home to go to the first cell in the workspace, A1). Press End to move to the last column that contains data (or Ctrl–End to go to the last cell that contains data). If you notice that Ctrl–PgUp or Ctrl–PgDn does not work, then open the Options menu and select Workspace. In the dialog box that appears, you'll see that the Alternate Navigation Keys option is selected. Click on the × in the □ (or press **K**) to unselect that option.

THE MENUS

Excel's commands are stored in the menus listed across the top of the screen. There are two ways to select a command with the mouse:

- Click on the menu name and drag the mouse down while *keeping the mouse button depressed.* When you highlight the command of interest, just release the button to select it
- Click once on the menu name. The menu will remain open while you move the pointer to the command of interest. Click the mouse button again to select it

Excel, like most Windows applications, provides keyboard access to commands as well by assigning each menu name and command a keyboard character, usually a letter in the name. These underlined letters are called *mnemonics.* To activate a command from the keyboard, press Alt and type the mnemonic for the desired menu option name while holding down the Alt key. Once the menu is open, type the mnemonic for the command. For example, to print a file, press Alt–FP. (To cancel a command keystroke sequence while the menu is open, press Esc.)

If there is no character underlined in a menu option, you can still use the keyboard to access a command. Press F10 to highlight the first menu name on the left. Press → or ← until you've highlighted the menu you want to open. Press Enter or ↓ to open it. Press ↓ or ↑ to highlight the menu option and press Enter (or just type that command's mnemonic).

Menu commands can be any one of three types: direct command, state setter, or extended (see Table 2.1). A direct command initiates an action immediately, such as the Save command of the File menu. State setters are toggles, and the command name in the menu is preceded by a check (✓) if the toggle is on. State setters permit the user to select from a list. An example would be selecting the chart type on Excel's Gallery menu when creating a chart. Finally, extended commands are always followed by three periods: they bring up a dialog box. An example would be the Printer Setup command under the File menu.

Table 2.1: Menu Command Types

TYPE	DESCRIPTION
Direct command	Initiates a command immediately
State setter	Changes the program state or selects an item of a list
Extended command	Displays a dialog box for user input

Menu items may be enabled or disabled. Items that are enabled can be selected and are shown in black. Disabled menu items can't be selected in the program's current state and are shown in gray (or "grayed out") lettering.

KEYBOARD SHORTCUTS

Menu commands may have short-cuts, or *accelerator keys*. Accelerator keys permit you to initiate the command quickly from the keyboard without using the mouse. If an accelerator key exists for a command, it is generally faster to use it than handle the mouse or normal keyboard commands.

There are also keyboard shortcuts for the Control menus. Notice that all the application Control menu shortcuts start with the Alt key. Excel contains only one: Alt–F4 closes the application.

All the document window shortcuts start with the Ctrl key. Pressing Ctrl–F4, for example, closes the current document window. Here is a full set of the document window shortcuts:

OPERATION	*SHORTCUT*
Restore maximized window	Ctrl–F5
Move document window	Ctrl–F7
Resize document window	Ctrl–F8
Maximize document window	Ctrl–F10
Close document window	Ctrl–F4
Switch to next document window	Ctrl–F6

The quickest way to close a document window is to press Ctrl–F4. The quickest way to close an application is to use Alt–F4.

THE DIALOG BOXES

Excel uses dialog boxes to request information from you and to output information that is not a part of the normal data display. Another type of box, the message box, is used when displaying error messages and warnings to the user. If a menu item has an ellipsis (. . .) after a command, that means it displays a dialog box.

Dialog boxes contain one or more special features, or *controls*. Dialog boxes can support any of five types of controls. Figure 2.2 shows an example of some of them.

Command button: A command button looks like a labeled button. Examples include the OK and Cancel buttons. If the label ends with an ellipsis, clicking the button will activate another dialog box. If the button contains an underlined letter, it can be activated from the keyboard using the combination Alt–*Letter*

Option buttons: A round button (or "radio button") that permits you to select only one item from a group. The button is

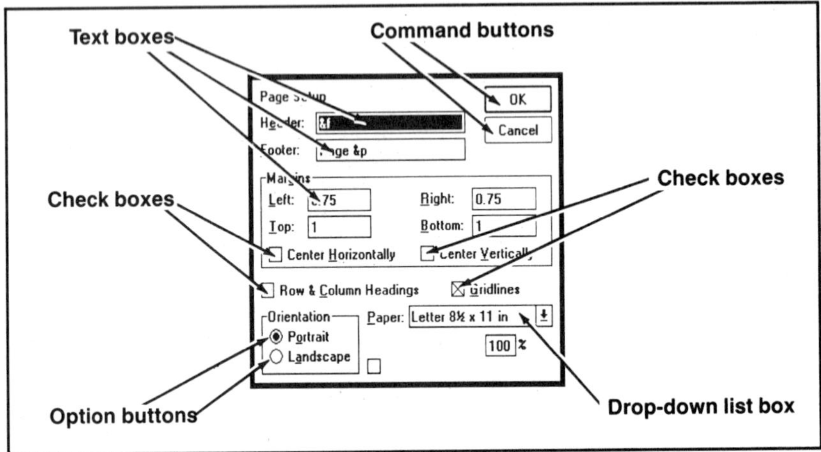

Figure 2.2: A dialog box showing the five types of controls

displayed as a small circle. You can select the desired button with a mouse or use the direction keys and the Spacebar

Check box: A toggle that turns a feature or state either on or off. The toggle is displayed as a small square with an × in it. It can be toggled by clicking the mouse or pressing the Spacebar

List box: A box showing multiple choices, such as the file list with the Open command. With a list box, use the mouse or direction keys to highlight your selection and then double-click, press Enter, or click the OK button. You also can press any letter to move the highlight to the first selection starting with the letter. For long lists, the control has a vertical scroll bar at the right that simplifies movement to the item. If the list allows multiple selections, you can use the direction keys and the Spacebar to select other items after the first. In small dialog boxes with long lists, a drop-down list box is used to conserve space. The list is opened from a single-line list box with an arrow in a square box at the right (see Figure 2.2). Click the arrow to open the box. Then select with a mouse. From the keyboard, press Alt–↓ to open the box. Then select the option with the direction keys and press Alt–↓ again

Text box: A box for entering text data. When it is selected, an insertion point appears in the box. You can enter or edit the text before pressing Enter or clicking on OK.

You can use either the mouse or keyboard to move about in a dialog box and choose controls. The dialog box displays default settings. To select a control with a mouse, click it. To select a control with the keyboard, use Tab or Shift–Tab to move to the desired control. After the control is selected, use the list above as a guide for setting it. Close the box by clicking on OK or Cancel.

Most Excel dialog boxes can't be moved or resized. Some dialog boxes are a little different. For example, look at the Define Name dialog box under the Formula menu. This box has a title bar and can be moved like any other window by dragging its title bar around. It also has a Control menu that permits some normal control options such as closing and moving. The controls work the same as with any other dialog box.

SETTING THE DEFAULTS

The first time you use Excel you will want to set some default values if they are not already set:

1. Select Options from the menu bar. Examine this menu and be sure the last selection is Short Menus. If the selection is Full Menus, choose the Full menus option so that Excel displays longer menus.
2. Select Options from the menu bar and choose Workspace. When the Workspace dialog box shown in Figure 2.3 is displayed, be sure the following options are marked with an ×:

   Status Bar

   Scroll Bars

   Formula Bar

   Note Indicator

   Tool Bar

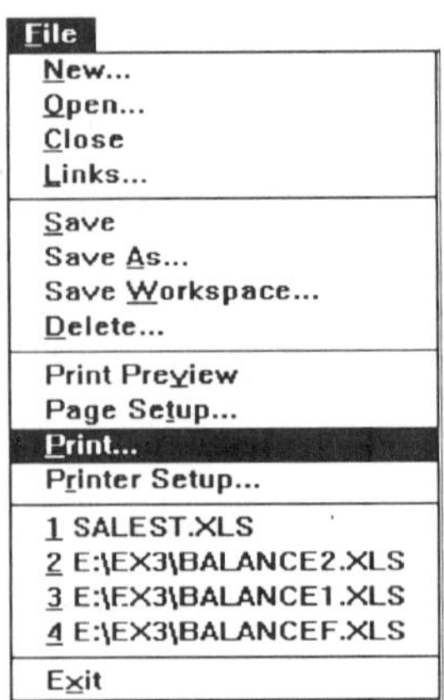

If any are not marked, click them to mark them. Then click OK. Be sure Alternate Navigation Keys is not selected.

3. Set the printer type by selecting File (to get the File menu), and choosing Printer Setup. When the Printer dialog box is displayed (Figure 2.4), select the printer type you are using in the list box, then click on Setup. In the message box displayed, choose OK. In the next dialog box, shown in Figure 2.5, set all the options for your printer. This dialog box will vary with the printer you are using. Then select OK to return to the Printer dialog box and choose OK again.

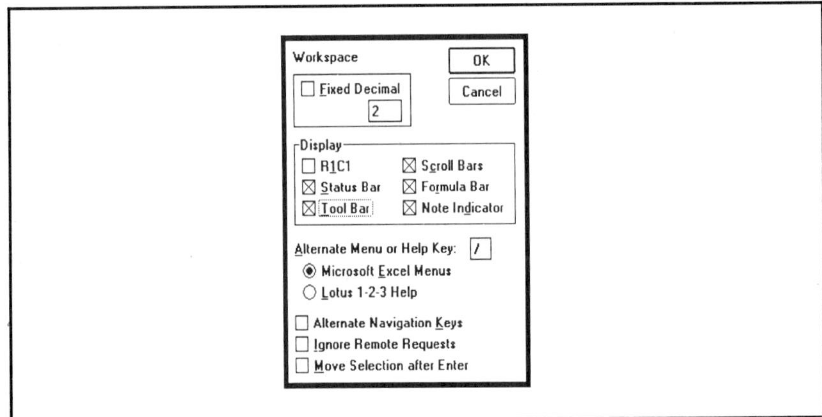

Figure 2.3: The Workspace dialog box

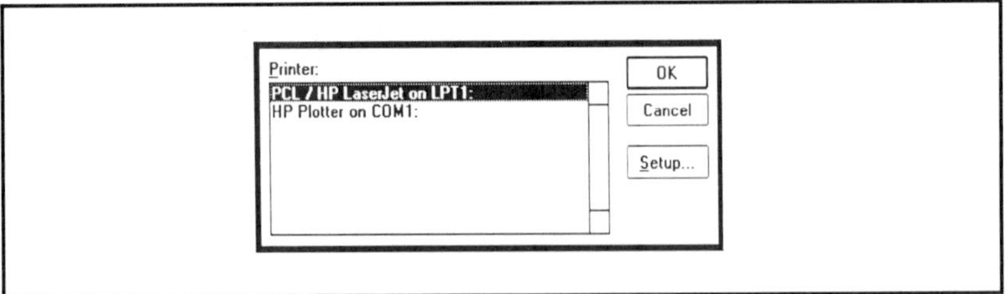

Figure 2.4: The Printer dialog box

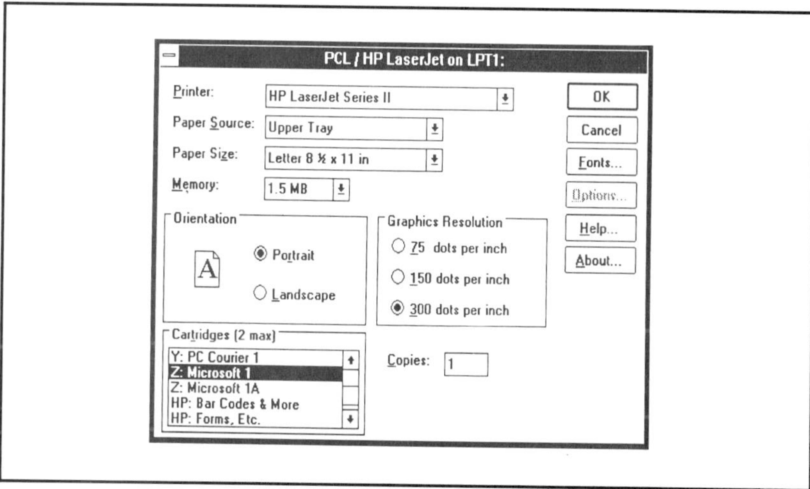

Figure 2.5: The Printer Setup dialog box

USING THE CLIPBOARD

Microsoft Windows contains a Clipboard. You can use it as a common area of memory for all programs. The Clipboard permits you to move and copy data within Excel, between Excel and other programs, or even to or from some non-Windows applications.

The Clipboard is accessed using the Edit menu of Excel or other Windows applications. For non-Windows applications, use the Control menu. The Edit menu on most Windows applications usually shows the Copy, Cut, and Paste commands. The Cut command removes the selected data from the current location and places it in the Clipboard. The Copy command creates a copy of the selected data in the Clipboard. The Paste command copies data from the Clipboard to a specified location in the same or another application program. These commands have the following keyboard shortcuts:

Cut	Shift-Del
Copy	Ctrl-Ins
Paste	Shift-Ins

The Clipboard can only store a single item at a time. Putting something else in the Clipboard will delete whatever was already there. You can do multiple pastes from the Clipboard, however, as pasting does not clear the Clipboard. Once you close Windows, the contents of the Clipboard are lost.

You can look at the contents of the Clipboard at any time using the Windows Clipboard program. Just start it from the Program Manager. Minimize or close the Clipboard window after viewing its contents.

GETTING HELP

If you need help while you're using Excel, there are two ways to obtain it: the Help menu and F1.

THE HELP MENU

Excel, as with many Windows applications, has a help system only a few keystrokes away. To see how it works, click Help on the menu bar or press Alt–H. This will display the Help menu.

The Help menu has six options on it:

Index displays a list of topics from which you can choose to get information

Keyboard displays a list of the Excel shortcut keystrokes. These can speed up many Excel operations and improve your productivity

Lotus 1-2-3 helps you find the Excel equivalents of Lotus 1-2-3 commands. Use this if you have been using Lotus 1-2-3 and need help learning Excel

Multiplan helps you find the Excel equivalents of Multiplan commands. Use this if you have been using Multiplan and need help learning Excel

Tutorial is a computer-based training system for learning Excel. It covers six topics: Introduction, Worksheets, Charting,

Macros, Help, and Lotus 1-2-3. (This option temporarily removes the worksheet from the screen, giving you a full screen for the tutorial. The screen is restored when you exit it.)

About gives you an information screen containing the current memory allocation. Use this when working on large worksheets to see the status of your memory resources

You can select any of these from the Help menu by clicking it or pressing the underlined letter of the menu item. This will open a Help window. The window can be resized or moved like any other window. In fact, with some options you can (and may wish to) leave the Help window open on the screen or minimized as you work with your worksheet for quick help.

Many Help windows have a menu bar. You can use the print option from it to print the entire help file for that option. For example, if you wish to have a printed list of the keystrokes, display them and choose Print Topic from the File menu.

To close the Help window, double-click its Control-menu box or press Alt–F4 with the Help window active.

THE HELP INDEX

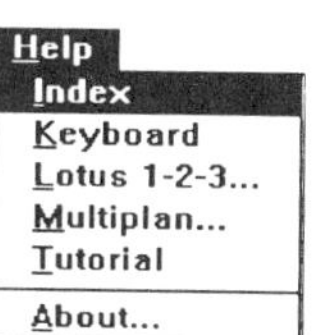

The Index option on the Help menu is probably the most useful. If Excel is in the Ready mode (**Ready** displayed in the lower left), you can use F1 or the Index option under the Help menu to display the help index in a window (Figure 2.6).

Once this window is displayed you can choose your topic by clicking the title or by using the Tab key to highlight the topic of interest and pressing Enter. The window has buttons for returning to the index, moving back, browsing, and searching.

PRESSING F1 FOR HELP

You also can use the system for finding context-sensitive help. For example, highlight Copy under the Edit menu and press F1. The Help window will open with help on the Copy command.

If you need help frequently for an application, keep the help window open and switch to it as necessary. An alternative is to minimize it: this will keep the window out of the way while keeping it in memory.

If you press Shift–F1, the mouse pointer becomes a question mark. Move the question mark to an element of the screen that you need help on (such as the tool-bar icons), click, and the help system will open with a window that can help you.

Press F1 to get the Help dialog box and select the Search icon. When the Search dialog box appears (see Figure 2.7), select the desired topic and choose Search. Topics found are displayed at the bottom of the dialog box. Select the desired topic and then choose GoTo to go to the topic.

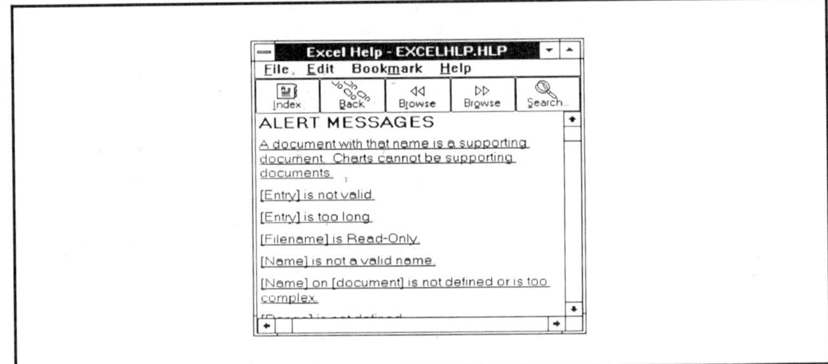

Figure 2.6: The Help index

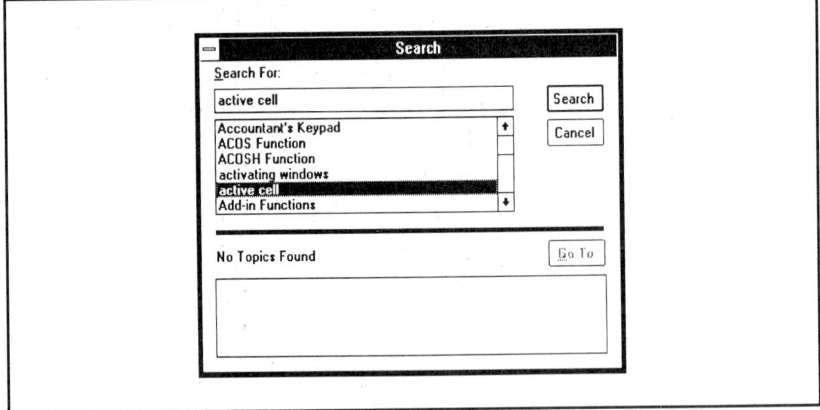

Figure 2.7: Searching for help

EXITING EXCEL

To quit Excel at any time, you can use any one of these methods:

- Double-click the Control-menu box of Excel (not the document) in the upper left
- Click the Control-menu box, then choose Close
- Click the File menu, then choose Exit
- Press Alt–F (to get the File menu) and then type **X** (for Exit)

3 A Quick Tour of Excel

ALTHOUGH EXCEL CAN SOLVE VERY COMPLICATED problems, it is actually quite easy to use. You'll discover this for yourself right now if you follow along with the exercises in this chapter. Here, you will use Excel to do the following:

- Create a worksheet, complete with formulas
- Format the worksheet
- Save the worksheet
- Print the worksheet
- Create a chart using the worksheet

These exercises will give you a feel for Excel and let you learn what it can do. Don't worry too much about how or why you do things—you'll learn the details in later chapters.

WORKSHEET WINDOW FEATURES

Start the Excel program (see Chapter 2). It should display an empty worksheet window, as shown in Figure 3.1.

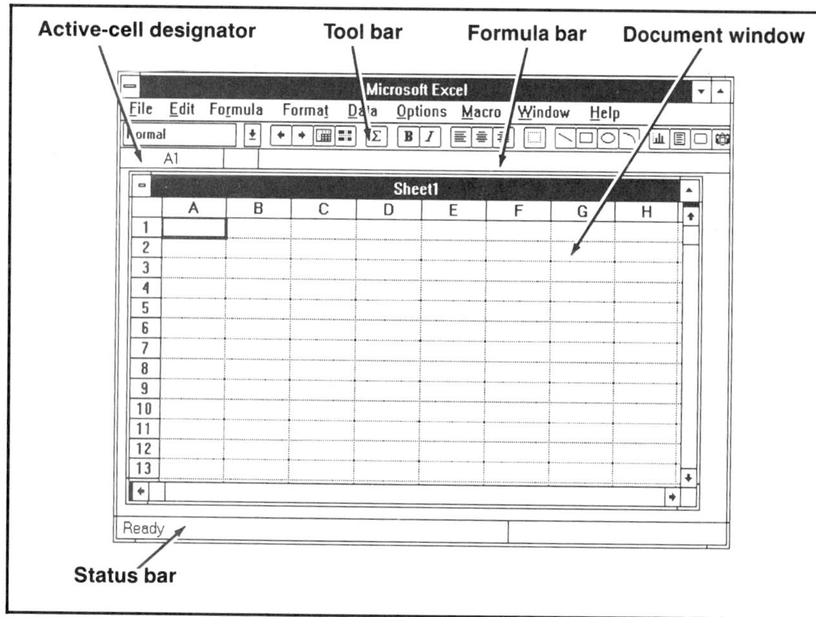

Figure 3.1: The worksheet window

Notice the elements of the Excel application window:

- The common application window elements: title, Control-menu box, menu bar, Minimize button, and Maximize button
- A *status bar* at the bottom of the screen for displaying messages. At the present time it shows that Excel is in the Ready mode
- A *tool bar* below the menu bar for doing some basic operations with the mouse
- The *active-cell designator* below the tool bar and to the left. This indicates the location of the currently active cell

- A *formula bar* to the right that displays the contents of the active cell. It is empty now
- A single document, a worksheet called Sheet1

The document window also has certain features (see Figure 3.2):

- A title: Sheet1. The title is the name of the file to which the worksheet will be saved
- A partial view of the underlying worksheet. The window can be scrolled over the worksheet
- The common document window elements: title, Control-menu box, Maximize button, and scroll bars
- Columns indicated by letters, rows by numbers. Each cell is shown as a box. Cells are designated by the column letter and row number. For example, cell B4 refers to the intersection of the second column with the fourth row
- The first cell, A1, highlighted with bold lines. This is the *active cell.* The cell name is also in the active-cell designator box

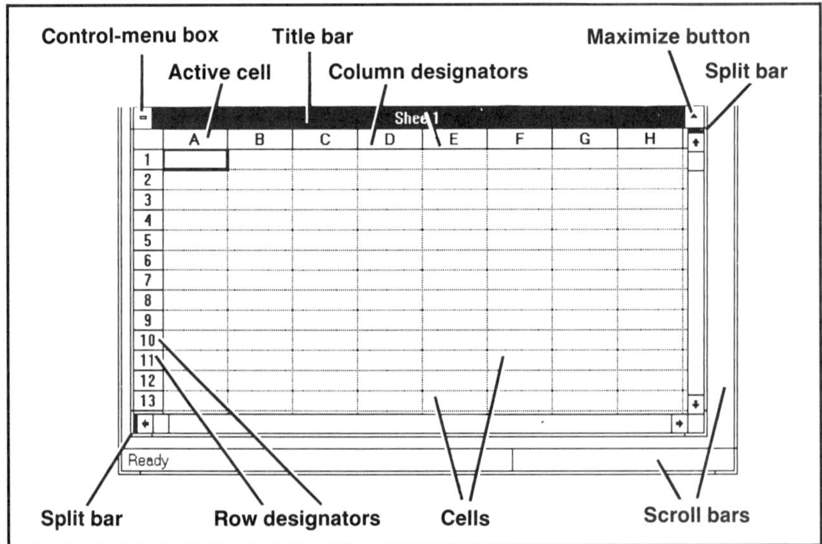

Figure 3.2: An Excel document window for a worksheet

- The scroll bars. To the upper right and lower left of the scroll bars are some split boxes for creating panes (see Chapter 7)
- Although the figure does not show it, a mouse cursor in the shape of a cross when it is on the worksheet cell area

Move the mouse about and you will see the mouse cursor move around the worksheet on-screen. The highlighted cell does not change and neither does the active-cell designator on the display line under the menu bar.

THE TOOL BAR

The tool bar (Figure 3.3) is a useful feature that is new to Excel Version 3.0. It permits you to do some operations with the click of a mouse. It does, however, require the mouse. It also takes the space of a row. You can turn it off or on with the Workspace option under the Options menu.

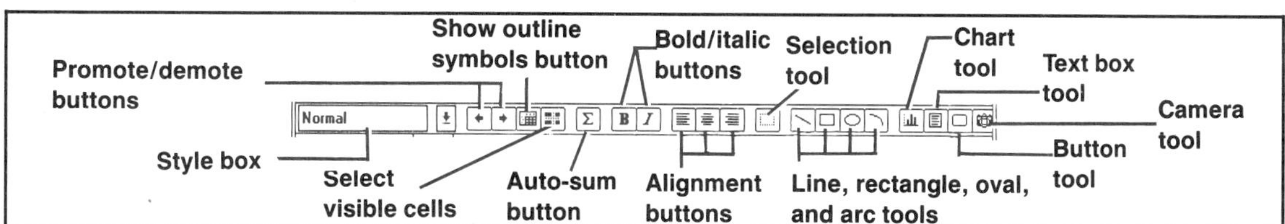

Figure 3.3: The tool bar

Here is a brief description of the tool bar areas, from left to right:

Style box—used to apply a style sheet to a selected range.

Promote and demote buttons—control the current outline level displayed

Show outline symbols button—turns outline symbols on the worksheet on or off

Select visible cells button—selects all visible cells on the worksheet

Auto-sum button—enters a sum formula in the active cell for the contiguous cell range above or below the active cell

Bold and italics button—formats the selected cells to bold or italic

Alignment buttons—aligns selected cells to left, center, or right

Selection tool—used to select objects to move, size, or format

Line, rectangle, oval, and arc tools—create the corresponding graphic object on document

Chart tool—creates a chart on the worksheet from a selected range

Text box tool—creates a text box on worksheets or macros

Button tool—creates a button on the worksheet. You can then use the button to initiate a macro execution

Camera tool—takes a picture of the selected worksheet or macro area and places it in the Clipboard. You can then paste it to another application. A link is maintained to the picture so that if the data changes, the picture changes

SCROLLING WITH EXCEL

Place the mouse cursor in the scroll bar at the right of the window. The cursor is now in the shape of an arrow. Click and drag the scroll box downward. Notice that the designator box in the upper left now shows the current row, rather than the active cell. When you release the mouse button, the row number shown will become the first row displayed at the top of the worksheet window. The designator box reverts to showing the current active cell.

Drag the scroll box again to the top of the scroll bar so that row 1 is at the top of the worksheet (or just press Ctrl–Home). Now drag the scroll box in the scroll bar at the bottom of the window towards the right. Watch the designator box show the current column letter. Release the mouse button and see that the column letter shown becomes the first column at the left. Finally, drag the scroll box all the way to the left so that column A is the first column (or press Ctrl–Home).

ENTERING ITEMS TO THE WORKSHEET

The basic procedure for entering items to the worksheet is as follows:

1. Move and click the mouse pointer or press direction keys to select the cell or range of cells in which you wish to enter data. The active cell for the keyboard entry is highlighted.
2. Enter the data, text, or formula.
3. Press Enter or click the ✓ in the formula bar. This locks the data or formula to that cell.

ENTERING TITLES

Your general worksheet strategy usually is to create the labels first, then enter the numbers, followed by any formulas. Finally, format the worksheet.

Now let's use this procedure to enter data to the worksheet.

Move the cursor to cell C1 and click on it. Cell C1 is now highlighted, and the active-cell designator on the display line reads C1. Use the keyboard to type the title for your worksheet as **INCOME ANALYSIS**.

Notice that, as you enter your data, two new boxes appear to the left of the formula bar: the Enter box with a check (✓) and a Cancel box with an ×, as shown in Figure 3.4. The entire title appears in the formula bar, whereas only a portion of it appears in cell C1. After you type in the title, press the Enter key or click the Enter box to complete the entry. You will now see the entire title on the worksheet. (The entire title is displayed only if the cell to the right (D1) is empty, as here. Excel always remembers the entire title, however, whether or not D1 is empty.)

Enter the titles for the rows next:

1. Click cell A5 and drag to cell A12 (see Figure 3.5).
2. Type **Sales** and press Enter.
3. Type **Cost of Goods Sold** and press Enter twice (to skip one row).
4. Type **Gross Margin** and press Enter twice.

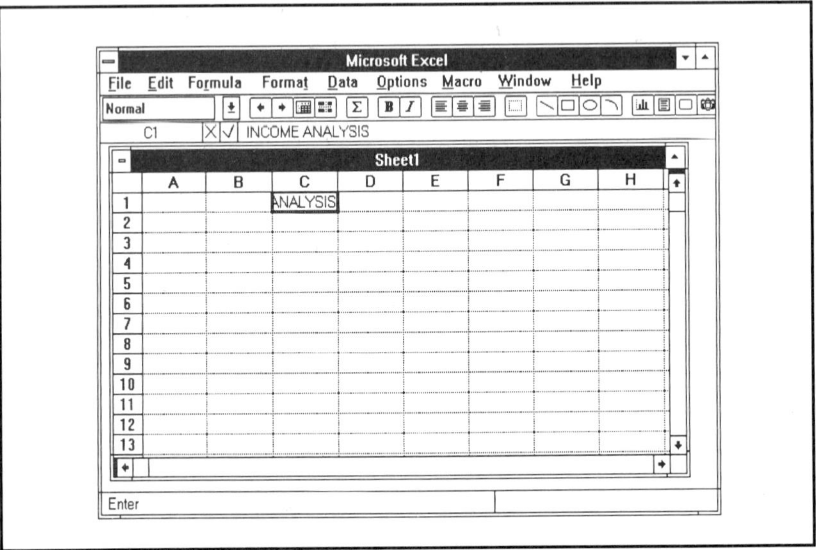

Figure 3.4: Entering the title

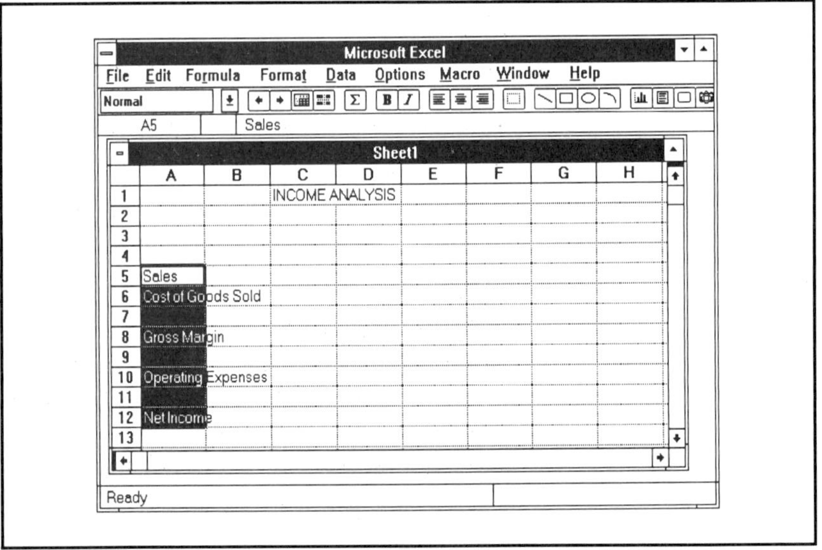

Figure 3.5: Entering the row headings

5. Type **Operating Expenses** and press Enter twice.
6. Type **Net Income** and press Enter.

If you make a mistake in typing any title before you press Enter, you can use the Backspace key to erase the error. If you notice a mistake after you've pressed Enter, go ahead and finish entering the row titles, then click the cell to be corrected and reenter the title.

After you have entered the row headings, you will notice that column A is not wide enough for three of the row titles. To widen the column:

1. Click once on cell A6.
2. Open the Format menu and choose Column Width.
3. You will now see the Column Width dialog box shown in Figure 3.6. Click the Best Fit button, then OK.

You will see column A widen to accommodate your titles, as shown in Figure 3.7.

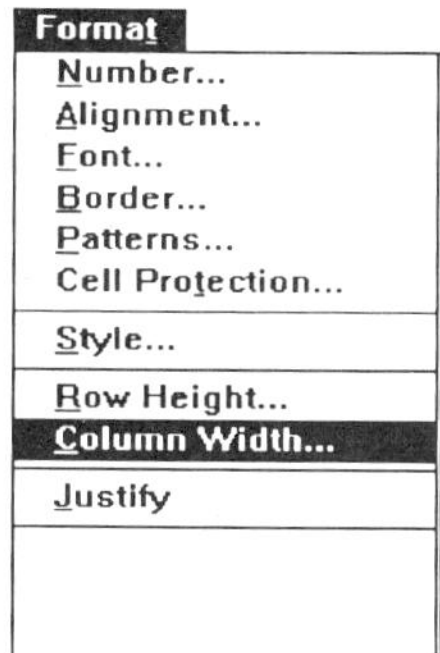

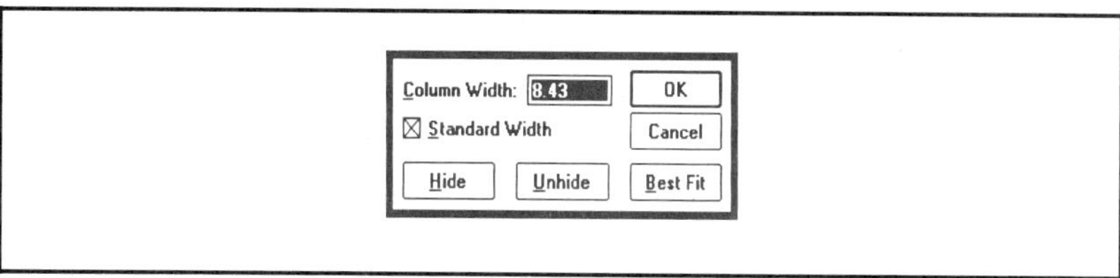

Figure 3.6: Setting the column width

Now enter the column titles:

1. Click cell B4 and drag to cell D4.
2. Type **1989** and press Enter.
3. Type **1990** and press Enter.
4. Type **1991** and press Enter.

ENTERING DATA

Now click cell B5 and enter the numbers shown in Figure 3.8 into rows 5, 6, and 10. (Do not enter data into rows 8 or 12.) You can

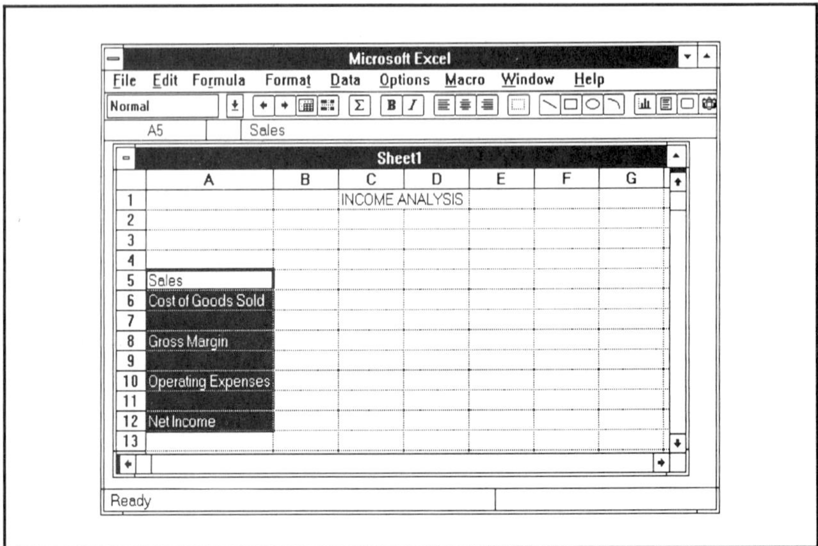

Figure 3.7: Column widths adjusted

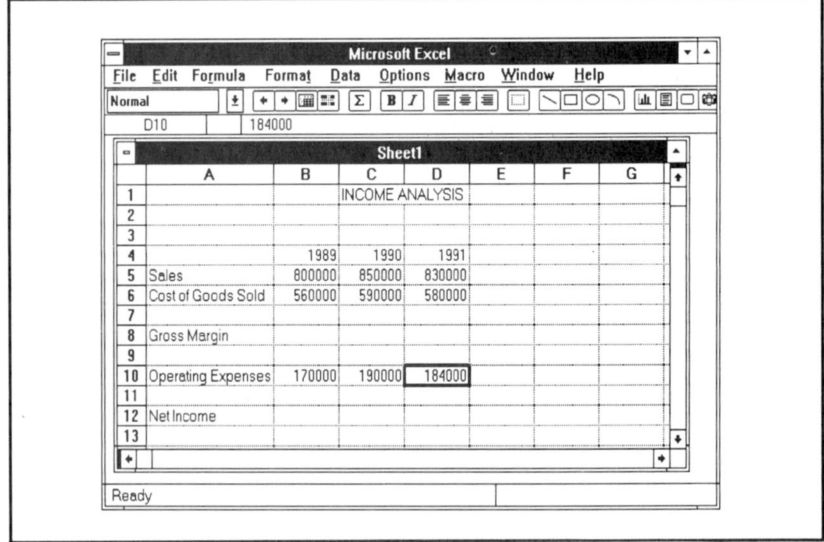

Figure 3.8: Entering the data

include commas in the numbers if you wish, but they will disappear each time you press Enter.

ENTERING FORMULAS

Enter the first formula by clicking cell B8 and typing **=B5 – B6**. Remember to type the equal sign first. This tells Excel to subtract the amount in B6 from the amount in B5. After you type out the formula, press Enter. The gross margin, **240000**, will appear in cell B8. If you make a mistake, select cell B8 and try entering the formula again.

Now you can try a slightly different approach for entering the formula into cell B12:

1. Click cell B12 and enter an equal sign (=).
2. Click cell B8 and enter a minus sign (–).
3. Click cell B10 and press Enter.

The net income, **70000**, will appear in cell B12.

To enter the formulas in rows 8 and 12, you can use a faster method:

1. Select cell B8 and drag to cell D8.
2. Open the Edit menu and choose Fill Right.

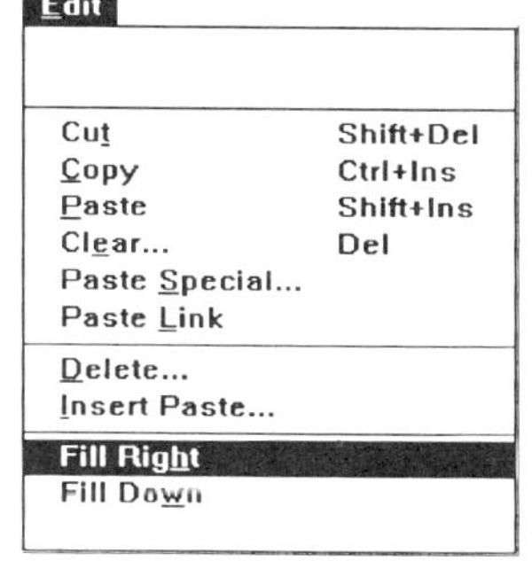

The correct totals will appear in row 9. Repeat this procedure for cell B12 to copy the formula to cells C12 and D12. In both cases, as the formula is copied, the referenced cells are automatically changed to reflect the new columns. Select cell C8 and examine the formula in the formula bar. Compare this with the formula shown when you select cell B8.

After you've entered all the formulas, your worksheet should look like Figure 3.9.

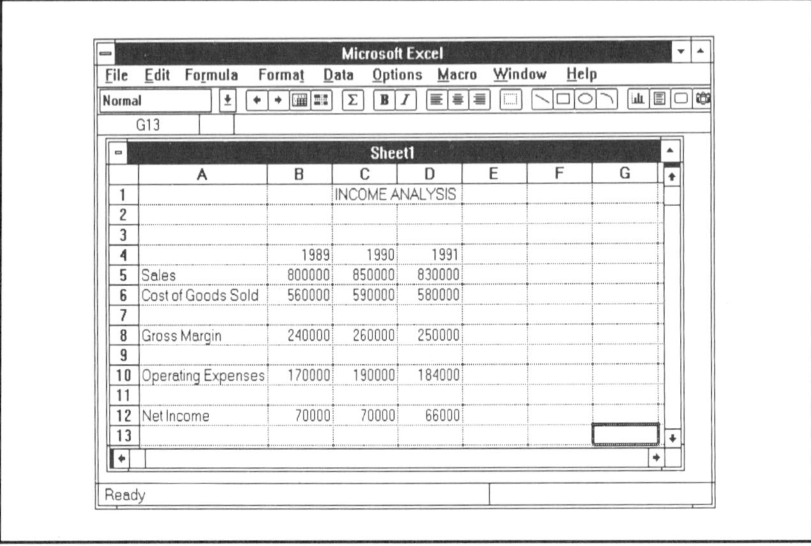

Figure 3.9: Worksheet after the formulas are entered

FORMATTING THE WORKSHEET

Now you can format the worksheet. Excel remembers three things for each cell in the worksheet: the value (constant or formula), information on how the value is to be displayed, and any attached notes. Data are now displayed with text left-justified and numbers right-justified. That is the default "picture" and alignment. Place the cursor on cell B5 and drag to cell D12. Open the Format menu and choose Number. The Format Number dialog box shown in Figure 3.10 will appear. Choose the first currency format (the one highlighted in the figure) and select OK. The screen now shows all numeric values in the selected range with a dollar sign and a comma every third digit.

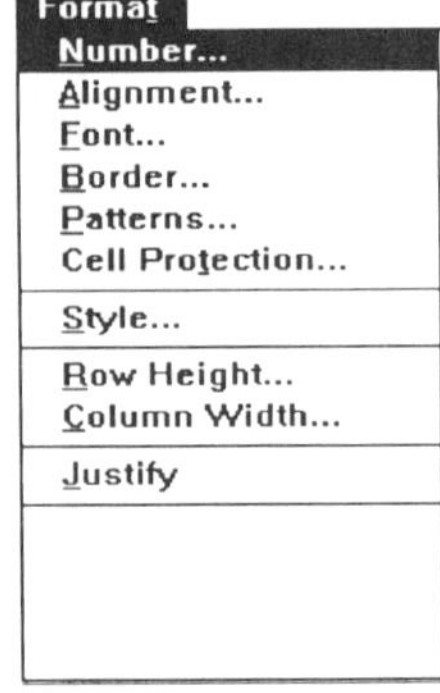

You can do a few more things to make the worksheet more readable. First, put the title in bold print:

1. Select cell C1.
2. Open the Format menu and choose Font.
3. The Font dialog box shown in Figure 3.11 appears. Choose the Bold selection and select OK.

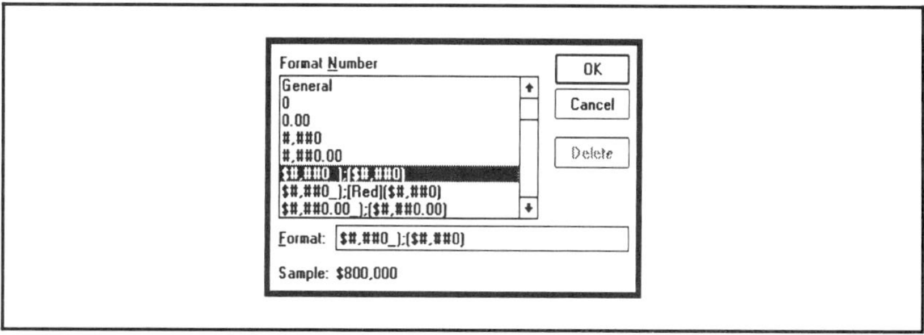

Figure 3.10: Formatting the numbers

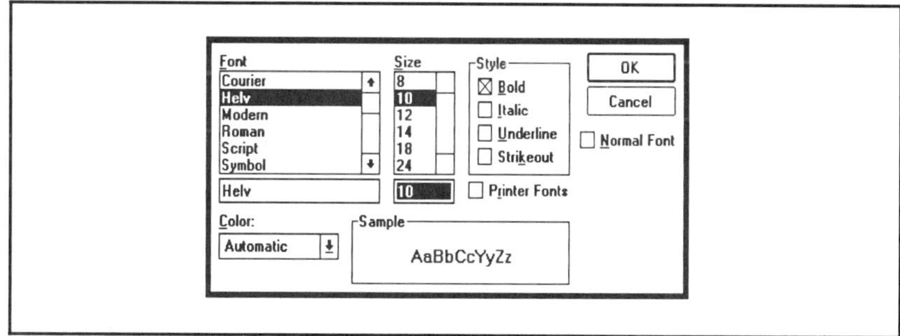

Figure 3.11: Putting the title in boldface print

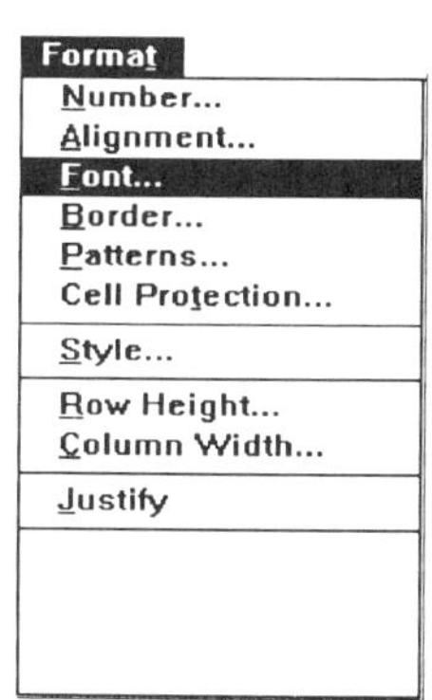

Next, center the column titles:

1. Select cell B4 and drag to cell D4.
2. Open the Format menu and choose Alignment.
3. The Alignment dialog box appears. Choose Center, then OK.

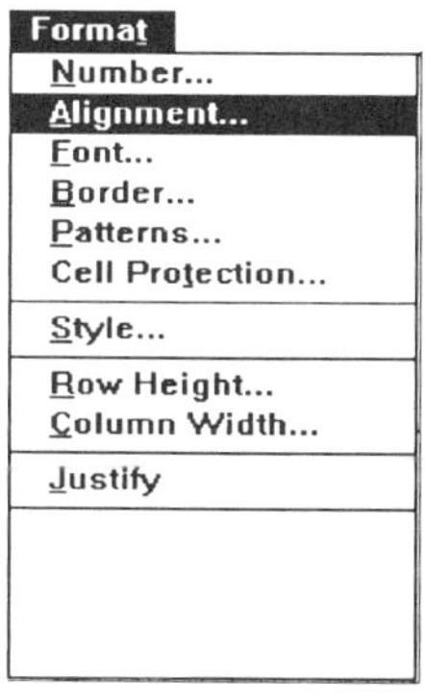

Finally, you can add some lines to separate the totals from the other numbers:

1. Select cell B7 and type one hyphen. Press Enter.
2. Open the Format menu and choose Alignment.
3. When the dialog box is displayed, choose Fill, then OK.
4. Select cell B7 and drag to cell D7.
5. Open the Edit menu and choose Fill Right.

6. Select B7.
7. Open the Edit menu and choose Copy.
8. Select B11 through D11.
9. Open the Edit menu and choose Paste. This should complete the entry of hyphens (making lines) in the six cells.

Your final worksheet should look like the one shown in Figure 3.12.

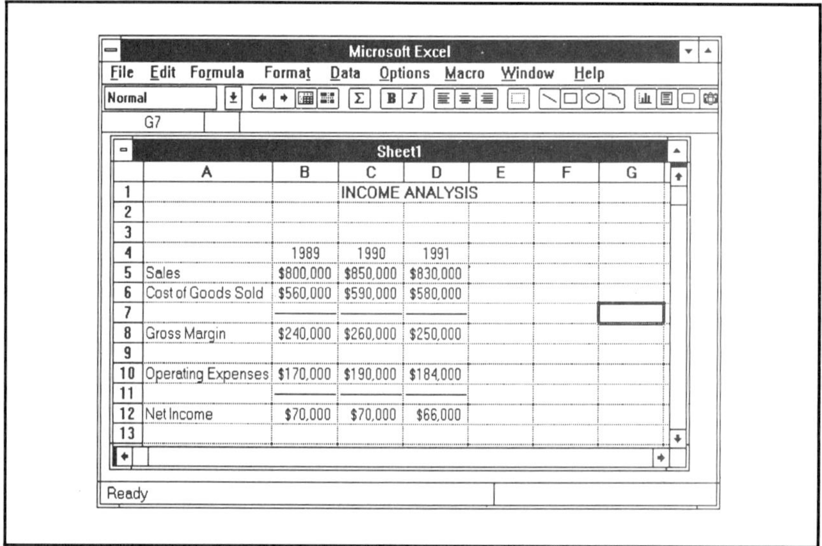

Figure 3.12: The final worksheet

You can now experiment by changing the values in rows 5, 6, and 10. You'll see that the numbers in rows 8 and 12 automatically change to reflect the new values.

SAVING THE WORKSHEET

Before quitting Excel, you should save the worksheet. If you save the worksheet at this time under its default name, it will become the starting worksheet each time you load Excel. You must save the worksheet under a new name.

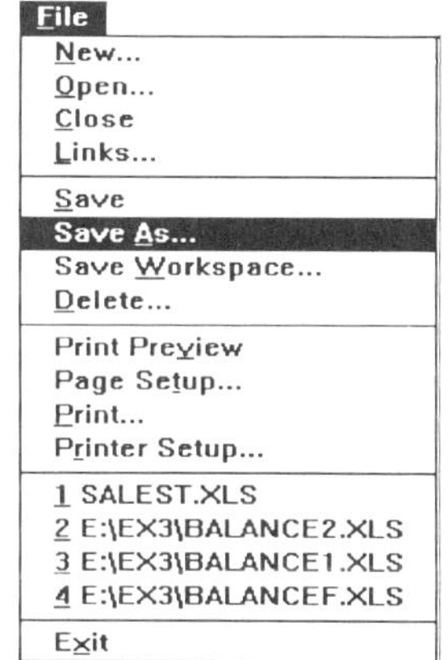

First, always check the worksheet over before saving. Be sure that the data in rows 5, 6, and 10 are correct. Open the File menu and choose Save As. The current path is displayed under the first text box in the dialog box, shown in Figure 3.13 (e:\ex3 here). Use the list box to change the path as necessary, selecting a new disk drive or directory. When the correct path is displayed, type the file name in the text box and click OK.

Figure 3.13: Saving the document

PRINTING THE WORKSHEET

When using a serial printer, always save the worksheet before printing. This is a good general rule, in fact, with any printer to prevent the loss of the spreadsheet, should there be an inadvertent lockup during printing. You should, however, do a printer and page setup before saving, so that these parameters are saved with the worksheet.

Before printing the worksheet, you should first turn off the row and column designators. Open the File menu and choose Page Setup. The dialog box shown in Figure 3.14 appears. If either the Print Row & Column Headings or the Gridlines option is marked,

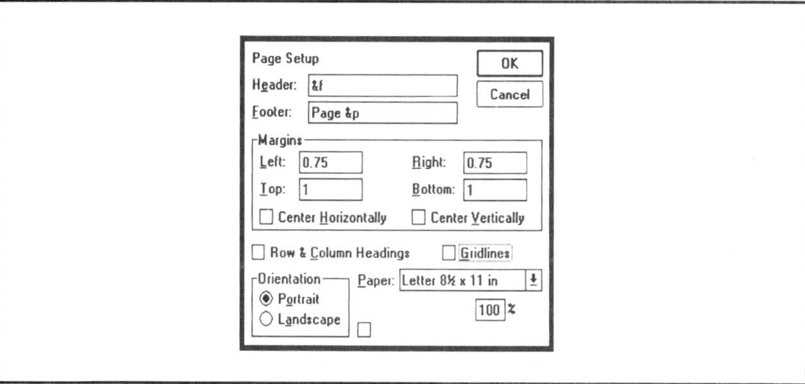

Figure 3.14: Turning off the grid lines and designators

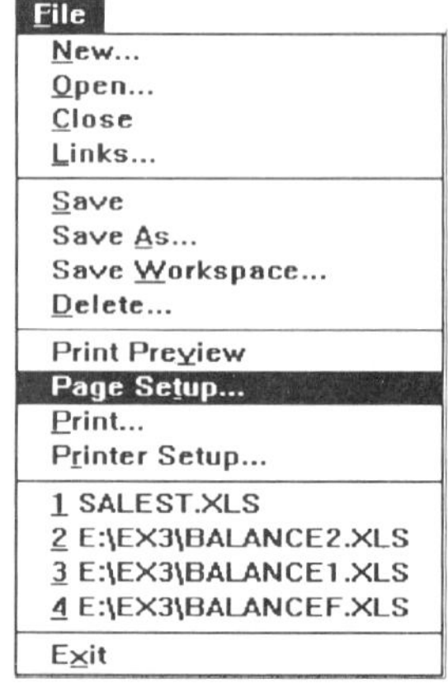

click it to turn it off, then choose OK. Gridlines are still displayed on the screen, but will not print.

Now print the worksheet. Open the File menu and choose Print. Be sure that the printer is on and ready. When the Print dialog box is displayed, choose OK. The final output is shown in Figure 3.15.

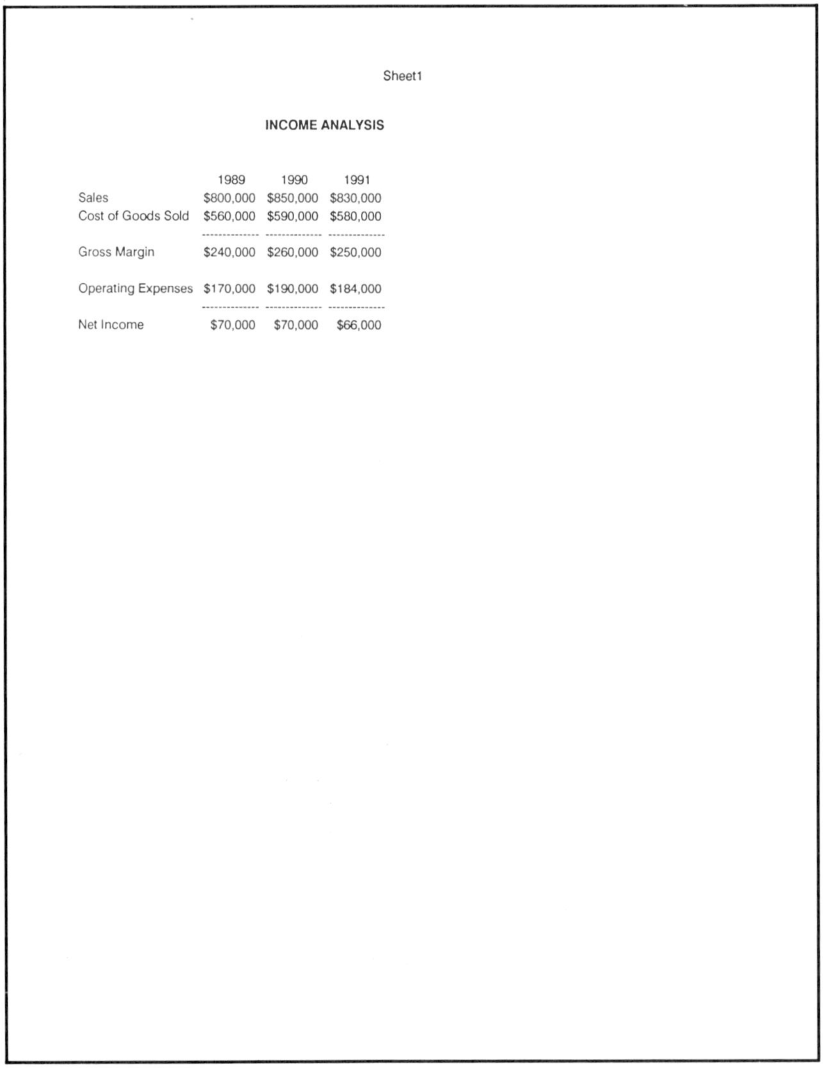

Sheet1

INCOME ANALYSIS

	1989	1990	1991
Sales	$800,000	$850,000	$830,000
Cost of Goods Sold	$560,000	$590,000	$580,000
	-------------	-------------	-------------
Gross Margin	$240,000	$260,000	$250,000
Operating Expenses	$170,000	$190,000	$184,000
	-------------	-------------	-------------
Net Income	$70,000	$70,000	$66,000

Figure 3.15: The printout

CREATING A GRAPH

Suppose you want to create a graph (or chart) from the sales figures on your Income worksheet. You will find that this takes only a few clicks of the mouse.

Follow these steps:

1. Highlight A4 to D5 to indicate the data and headings to use for the graph, as shown in Figure 3.16.
2. Open the File menu and choose New.
3. When the dialog box shown in Figure 3.17 is displayed, choose Chart, then select OK.

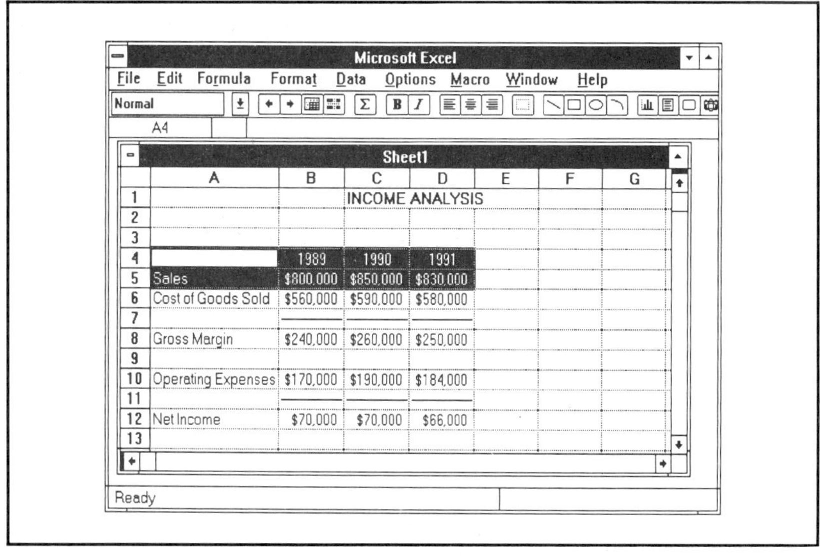

Figure 3.16: Selecting the data for the chart

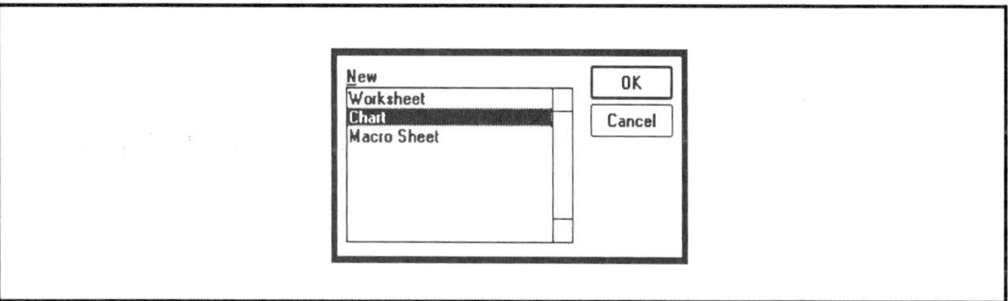

Figure 3.17: Opening a new chart document

Excel will draw the chart shown in Figure 3.18 in a new window on the screen. Notice that a different menu bar for charts is displayed as well. If you wish to view the worksheet and graph together on the screen, choose Arrange All on the Window menu.

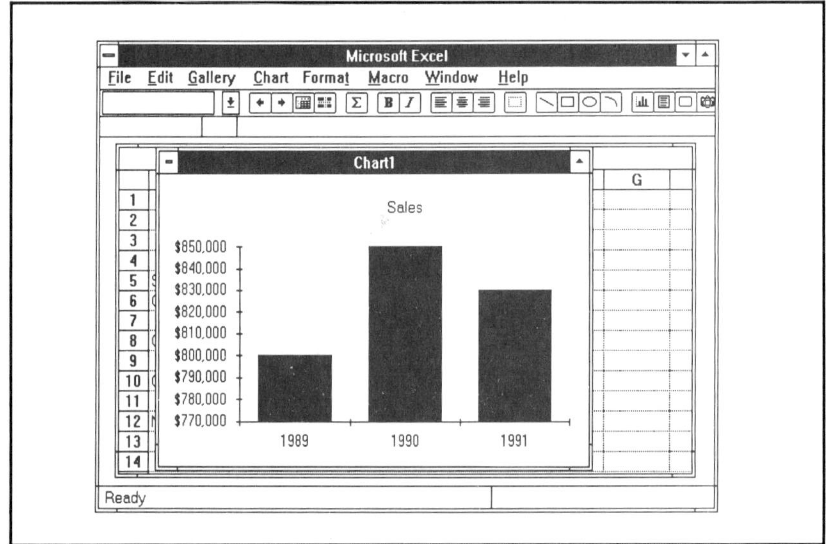

Figure 3.18: The chart

You can print this chart by following the steps that you used to print the worksheet: Open File and choose Print. As the chart is a graphic, it will take longer to print than the worksheet.

When you are finished with the chart, double-click the Control-menu box in the upper left of the chart window or press Ctrl–F4. When the dialog box shown in Figure 3.19 appears, choose No to indicate that you do not want to save the chart.

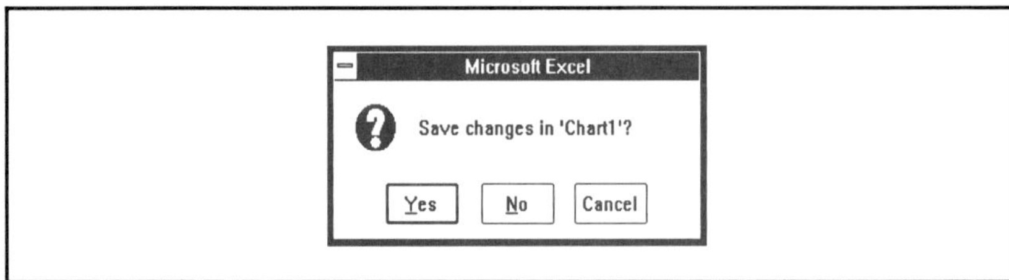

Figure 3.19: Closing the chart document

QUITTING EXCEL

If you forget to save your document before quitting, Excel will catch this and prompt you with a message box, giving you another chance. Your best insurance, however, is always to save your document before quitting Excel.

When you wish to leave Excel, there are only two simple steps: save your work and exit. After using Save or Save As to save the document, double-click the Control-menu box in the upper left of the application window or press Alt–F4.

You have now created a simple worksheet of data and formulas, and a chart using some of the data. You also learned how to do some formatting, how to print the worksheet, and how to save it to disk. In the next chapter, you will learn how to design a worksheet and use additional features.

Getting Right to Work with Excel

THE PROCESS OF MAKING A WORKSHEET IS DIVIDED into four steps: creating, editing, formatting, and printing. For each of these steps, there are several rules and procedures that you must be aware of and follow to work with any type of worksheet. Part II introduces you to the basic rules by teaching you how to create, edit, format, and print a simple balance sheet. Even if you have created worksheets before, take the time to work through these exercises. You will be surprised at how much easier it is to do them with Excel than with any other spreadsheet program you have used.

After you've created and printed the basic worksheet, we go on to introduce you to a few other basic features: window control, formulas and functions, and naming cells.

4 Creating the Worksheet

IN THIS CHAPTER, YOU WILL LEARN HOW TO CREATE a worksheet. Do not be too concerned about any errors that you make when entering data. In the next chapter, you will learn how to correct those errors. First, let's review the basic parts of a worksheet and the techniques used in creating one.

WORKSHEET DESIGN STRATEGIES

When creating a worksheet, you should have a specific goal in mind. It may be to show that a company's sales are better in a specific region, or to show that the profit is better than in previous years, or perhaps to show the relationship between literacy and infant mortality in a given area. Whatever it is, the conclusion should stand out so that a busy reader can see it quickly.

Often a chart is the best method for presenting the result: it catches the reader's attention quickly and can convey information better than words. In other cases, the more detailed numbers of a worksheet may be better. In either case, you are telling a story.

The basic rule of worksheets is that form follows function: what the worksheet or chart is supposed to convey should determine how it looks. Shadow boxes, arrows, and three-dimensional charts are great, but only if they help the reader see the conclusion.

The following are some general guidelines for creating useful worksheets:

- **Work out the general worksheet idea on paper before using Excel.** What is the objective of the spreadsheet? Who will use it? What type of input is required?
- **Partition large worksheets into blocks.** There should be four blocks on most worksheets: assumptions, input, calculations, and conclusions. Label the blocks. Data are entered to the input block, which is then used by the calculation block. The assumption block defines parameters that may vary in the future (interest rates, principal, etc.). This permits you to do what-if simulations by simply changing the assumptions. The results are in the conclusion block. If you have many input parameters, use several input blocks (which could even be on separate worksheets). Then feed the results into a master calculation block. Excel permits you to put the blocks on separate worksheets and link them together if you wish. For example, you could put all the company assumptions in a single assumption worksheet and use them with several worksheets
- **Use multiple worksheets instead of one large worksheet**. Consider using several worksheets and linking them together, such as putting the assumptions in a separate worksheet. This permits data to be shared by other worksheets, reduces worksheet loading time, and makes each worksheet easier to manage
- **Enter labels first.** The general worksheet strategy is to enter labels first to define the framework, then the numbers, and then any formulas. Finally, format the worksheet
- **Identify assumptions.** Be sure any assumptions are well documented. Specify the sources using notes, text boxes, or footnote text on the worksheet

- **Use a header.** Use a header and add date and time stamps. To help when tracking different versions of the worksheet, add the worksheet version number
- **Explain the purpose.** Use a subhead, the title, or some beginning comments to explain the purpose of the worksheet
- **Add notes to cells.** Use the notes to explain complex formulas
- **Give instructions.** Somewhere on the worksheet you should include instructions for using it. They should be in a language that the intended user can understand
- **Use more formulas to link cells and avoid using absolute values unless necessary.** For example, the worksheet may have a price that affects several cells and periodically changes. Put the price in a separate block on the page and use a formula to reference it in other cells in the worksheet. This will enable you to update all references from a single cell, improving accuracy
- **Keep formulas short.** Break formulas over several cells, if necessary, to make them easier to read and use
- **Use blank rows, columns, and cells liberally to improve worksheet readability.** White space and borders, when used properly, make the worksheet easier to read. If possible, use report formats with which the user is familiar. For example, on a large table of numbers leave every fifth or sixth row blank. This will make the numbers easier to read
- **Use cell names.** With Excel, you can label cells or cell ranges. Naming cells and cell ranges enables you to go quickly to a specific area of the worksheet. For example, naming the assumption area enables you to move quickly to this area by name to check or edit it. Names also improve the readability of the worksheet and, as a result, its accuracy
- **Check the worksheet over carefully before printing it.** People have used electronic worksheets to make major decisions

based on incorrect data. If the input data are wrong or if a formula is wrong, the results will be wrong. The computer can only do what you tell it to do. Don't assume it is correct just because there are no error messages

- **Test the worksheet.** Try some example data you have already used and be sure the conclusions are what you expect

BASIC WORKSHEET TECHNIQUES

To enter data to a cell, you must do three things:

1. Make the cell active.
2. Enter the data with the keyboard.
3. Lock the data to the cell.

In its simplest form, the procedure involves making the cell active by clicking on the desired cell, entering the data from the keyboard, and locking the data to the cell by pressing the Enter key.

With Excel, however, you have plenty of flexibility in entering data. The basic techniques for entering data into a worksheet are described in the next three sections. You will then use these techniques to begin to create a more complex worksheet than the simple one you set up in Chapter 3.

MAKING THE CELL ACTIVE

The *active cell* is the cell in which data are entered when you start typing on the keyboard. You may select one or more cells (such as a cell range), but only one cell can be active at a time. The active cell is indicated by a heavy border. Other cells in the selected range will be in reverse video. The name of the active cell always appears in the active-cell designator area.

When you want to enter data or do an operation on a cell or cell range, you must first select that cell or range. Each time you select a new cell or range, the previous selection will be canceled. You can tell which cell(s) are selected at any given time because they are highlighted. You can select a single cell, a row of cells, or a column—indeed, any rectangular block of cells. You also can select discontinuous ranges.

Selecting a range of cells does not change the contents of the cells. The cell contents will be changed only if you enter data from the keyboard or choose some operation (such as Clear or Cut from the Edit menu) after the cell is selected.

Selecting Cells and Ranges

There are several ways to select a cell or cells in Excel:

Select a single cell by placing the cursor on it and clicking the left mouse button once. From the keyboard, you can select a single cell by using the direction keys to highlight it. A border will appear around the cell and the cell's address will appear in the active-cell designator.

Select a cell range by placing the cursor on the first cell in the range and dragging it to the last cell in the range. If the range occupies several rows or columns, start the selection in the upper left and drag to the lower right. If the final cell of the desired range is beyond the window border, keep on dragging: the window will automatically scroll as you drag the cursor beyond the border. To select a range from the keyboard, use the direction keys to select the first cell of the range and extend the range with the direction keys while holding down the Shift key.

When you select a range of cells, the first cell from which you define the range becomes the active cell. The range is shown in inverse video, while the active cell remains in white. While defining a range, the active-cell designator displays the size of the range. When the mouse button is released, the designator displays only the active cell. (If you select a row or column, its first cell will be the active cell.)

Select an entire row by placing the cursor on the row designator at the left of the window and clicking once (or pressing Shift–Space from any cell in the row).

Select an entire column by placing the cursor on the column designator and clicking once (or pressing Ctrl–Space from any cell in the row).

Select the entire worksheet by clicking the small box to the left of the column headings and above the row headings (or pressing Ctrl–Shift–Spacebar).

Select a range of rows by clicking a row designator and dragging to another row. In the same way, you can select a range of columns by selecting a column designator and dragging to another column.

Select a large block of cells by clicking on the first cell and pressing F8. The status bar changes to show the EXT indicator. This indicates you are in an extended mode. Now click the cell at the opposite end of the block. Press F8 again to turn the status indicator off. Another way to select a range is to click the upper-left cell, hold down the Shift key, and click the lower-right cell of the range. To do this with the keyboard, select the first cell with the direction keys, press F8, extend with the direction keys and press F8 again.

Make multiple range selections by defining the first range and pressing Shift–F8. The ADD indicator appears in the status bar. Then select additional cells or cell ranges. Press Shift–F8 again to turn the indicator off. You can do this with a mouse by selecting the first range and holding down the Ctrl key while you select additional ranges. Multiple ranges selected in this way are called *discontinuous ranges.*

Before continuing, you should practice making each type of selection listed above.

To move the active cell around the worksheet, use the direction keys—or else Tab to move it one cell to the right and Shift–Tab to move it one cell to the left. If a range is selected, these keys will still work, but the active cell will move only within the range. In addition, you can use the Enter key to move the active cell downwards within a range.

Table 4.1 summarizes the mouse selection methods. Table 4.2 is a complete list of the keyboard selection commands. To move the active cell within a selected range with the mouse, hold down the Ctrl key and click the cell you wish to make active. Table 4.3 summarizes how to move the active cell in a range with the keyboard.

Here is another method of selecting a range that is useful when the range is large and the entire range won't fit on the screen. First, make the upper-left cell of the range active. Then press F8 to extend the range. The EXT designator should appear in the status bar. Now choose Goto from the Formula menu or press F5. In the dialog box, enter the address of the cell at the lower right of the range and press Enter. Press F8 to release the extended selection mode.

Table 4.1: Selecting Cells with the Mouse

ACTION	MOUSE
Select single cell	Click cell
Select range	Drag over range
Select row	Click row heading
Select column	Click column heading
Select range of rows	Drag over row headings
Select range of columns	Drag over column headings
Select entire array	Hold down Ctrl–Shift and double-click in array
Select entire worksheet	Double-click rectangle at top of row headings
Select multiple ranges	Select the first range and hold down the Ctrl key while selecting others

Table 4.2: Keyboard Call Selection Keys

ACTION	KEYSTROKES
Select cell	Use appropriate direction key to move active cell
Extend range by one adjacent cell	Use Shift with appropriate direction key
Move active cell to start of row	Home
Extend selection to start of row	Shift–Home
Move active cell to end of row	End
Extend selection to end of row	Shift–End
Select entire current row	Shift–Spacebar
Extend row selection to other rows	Shift–↑ or Shift–↓
Select entire current column	Ctrl–Spacebar
Extend column selection to other columns	Shift–← or Shift–→

Table 4.2: Keyboard Call Selection Keys (continued)

ACTION	KEYSTROKES
Select cell at upper left of worksheet	Ctrl-Home
Extend selection to A1	Ctrl-Shift-Home
Select cell at lower right of worksheet	Ctrl-End
Extend selection to last cell	Ctrl-Shift-End
Select entire worksheet	Ctrl-Shift-Spacebar
Collapse selection to single cell	Shift-Backspace

Table 4.3: Moving within a Range

ACTION	KEYSTROKES
Move down one cell in range	Enter
Move up one cell in range	Shift-Enter
Move right one cell in range	Tab
Move left one cell in range	Shift-Tab
Move to next corner of range	Ctrl-.
Move to next range	Ctrl-Tab
Move to previous range	Ctrl-Shift-Tab

Another way to select a large range is to select the first cell (upper left), press F5, and in the Goto dialog box enter the last cell (lower right). Hold down the Shift key and press Enter.

ENTERING DATA

Once an active cell is selected, the next step is entering data in the cell. You can enter either a constant value or a formula. There are four basic types of constant values that can be entered: text, numbers, dates and times, and logical values.

You also can enter data into a selected cell or cell range by pointing the mouse at other cells or cell names that you have defined. You will learn more about this technique later in this chapter.

When entering data in a range of cells, highlight the entire range and enter the data for each cell. Use the Enter or Tab key, as appropriate, to lock the data and move to the next cell in the range. (The Enter key moves down a column and the Tab key moves across a row.)

3.0

As soon as you start entering data in a cell, a flashing vertical bar appears in the formula bar. It acts as a cursor and is called the *insertion point.* Later you will learn how to move it for editing purposes.

When the insertion point appears, the Enter-box (✓) and Cancel-box (×) icons appear on the formula bar. The Enter box can be used, like the Enter key, to lock the data to the cell after you've typed them in. The Cancel box can be clicked, if you wish, to clear the typed-in data without locking the data to the cell. The Cancel box doesn't work (and even disappears) after pressing Enter or clicking the Enter box.

Entering Numbers

You can enter numbers in one of three formats:

FORMAT	*EXAMPLES*
Integer	1, 45, –45
Decimal fraction	43.5, –56.75
Scientific notation	25E +23, 4E –3

Use a minus sign or parentheses to enter negative numbers. Dollar signs, percent signs, the letter *E*, and commas also can accompany numeric entries. Unless you select otherwise, numbers are right-justified in a cell. If a number has too many characters to fit in a specific cell, Excel will display pound signs (######) in that cell to signify an overflow, or use scientific notation. Regardless of how numbers are displayed, they are always stored to 15 digits of accuracy.

Enter fractions as decimal numbers, then use the Numbers command under the Format menu to select either of the fraction formats, **# ?/?** or **# ??/??**. Entering a fraction in fractional form (such as **1/4**) will confuse Excel; it will be formatted as though it were a date. If you want to enter a fraction that does not have a finite decimal value (such as $^1/_3$), enter a leading zero and a space, as in **0 1/3**.

Entering Dates and Times

Excel stores both dates and times as serial numbers. The serial number for a date represents the number of days since January 1, 1900. Thus Excel can calculate the number of days between two

This is different from the Macintosh Excel, in which dates are measured from January 1, 1904. You can convert serial numbers from one format to another with the Options Calculate command.

dates by subtracting the earlier date from the later one. The serial number for a time represents the number of hours elapsed since midnight. A date or time is converted into a serial number as soon as it is entered.

You can enter dates in the *mm/dd/yy* format using slashes or hyphens. Alternatively, you can use the general date-entry format, as in **September 1, 1987**. You also can enter dates in any of three other formats: *dd/mm/yy* (25/May/85), *dd/mm* (25/May), or *mm/yy* (May/86). If you enter a date in any other format, Excel will not display an error message; it will simply store it as text rather than as a serial number.

You can enter time values in either standard (3:30:30 PM) or military (13:15:45) format. The seconds entry is optional, and you can use *A* or *P* instead of *AM* or *PM*. You can enter both a date and a time into a single cell. Be sure to use a space between the time and its AM/PM indicator.

If you need to use a date or time as text, enter it as text (i.e., inside quotation marks). The date will then remain as text. Excel will convert any date in a valid date format into a serial number when it evaluates the formula.

As a shortcut for entering dates, use Ctrl–; to paste in the current date and Ctrl–: to paste in the current time. These are fixed values and do not change, so this is a good way of date-stamping a worksheet. The next time the worksheet is changed, you must repeat the stamping to get the new time or date.

Entering Logical Values

You can enter logical values as either TRUE or FALSE. The use of logical values is discussed in Chapter 8. The logical value TRUE or FALSE can be entered in upper- or lowercase, but is always stored and displayed as uppercase in Excel.

Entering Text

Any characters that Excel cannot interpret as a number, date, time, logical value, or formula are considered text. Unless you select otherwise, text data are always left-justified in a cell. You can enter up to 255 characters in a cell.

If any part of a numeric string is nonnumeric, Excel will assume the entire string is text. For example, *234 Fox Drive* is assumed to be a text string, even though it begins with a number. You can enter text in formulas by enclosing the text in quotation marks.

For long text strings, you may wish to word-wrap them. To do so, choose Alignment under the Format menu and select Wrap Text. This will automatically increase the row height as necessary for the wrapped text.

Entering Formulas

The real power of Excel lies in its ability to calculate the value of a cell based on values in other cells. This is accomplished by *formulas*. Formulas tell Excel exactly how to calculate a cell value from data in other cells, even from formulas in other cells. A worksheet, then, can become a very complex system of interwoven formulas and values. Changing one value on the worksheet can initiate a complex chain of calculations that will change cells in the entire worksheet.

Creating Formulas To create a formula, first select the cell or cell range that you want to contain the value calculated by the formula. You can enter the formula into the cell in one of three ways:

- Type the formula from the keyboard. First type an equal sign, then the formula. Complete the entry by clicking the Enter box on the formula bar or pressing the Enter key
- Click the cells that are referenced by the formula. For example, to enter "cell B5 minus cell B7," type an equal sign, place the cursor on cell B5 and click, type a minus sign, and then place the cursor on cell B7 and click. To complete the formula, click the Enter box or press the Enter key. You can use this method only with relative cell referencing (see Chapter 8)
- Type or paste the name that you assigned to a cell or range of cells. Once you've defined names for cells (see Chapter 9), you can use the Paste Name command on the Formula menu to enter the formula (Excel will automatically begin the formula with an equal sign). Alternately, you can type

an equal sign and then type in the formula using the names. Again, click the Enter box or press the Enter key to complete the formula

Remember to begin each formula with an equal sign and complete the entry by clicking the Enter box on the formula bar or pressing the Enter key. If you make a mistake while you're typing a formula, click the Cancel box on the formula bar or backspace through the error. After entering data, you can usually correct it with the Undo command (see Chapter 14). Methods for building and using formulas are discussed in detail in Chapters 8 and 9.

Formula Operators In creating a formula, you use mathematical operators to show how Excel is to do the calculation. These operators are as follows:

OPERATOR	*FUNCTION*
+	Addition
–	Subtraction
*	Multiplication
/	Division
^	Exponentiation

You also can use an ampersand (&) as an operator to join two text values to create a new text value. For example = *"Mr. "&"Smith"* becomes *Mr. Smith.* You also can concatenate text to data or the contents of a cell in the same way, such as in = *"The total is: "&D5.*

You also can use a formula to compare cell values. The result of using comparison operators is always a logical value—TRUE or FALSE. The following comparison operators are available:

OPERATOR	*FUNCTION*
=	Equal to
<	Less than
< =	Less than or equal to

OPERATOR	*FUNCTION*
>	Greater than
> =	Greater than or equal to
<>	Not equal to

Reference operators are used to refer to two or more cells in formulas and function arguments. There are three reference operators available:

OPERATOR	*NAME AND FUNCTION*
:	Range—references all cells in the given range
,	Union—includes two references
space	Intersection—includes cells common to two references

For example, to show the range from cell A1 to cell A10, you could type **A1:A10**. You also can use these operators with the names that you assign to a cell or range of cells (see Chapter 9).

LOCKING THE ENTRY

Once data are typed to a cell, you must lock the data in it. There are three basic ways to lock data:

Plan your data entry so that the cursor moves to the next cell in the range.

- Press the Enter key. If only a single cell was selected, the active cell will remain highlighted. If a range was selected, the active cell will move down one cell
- Press any key that moves the active cell: Tab, Shift-Tab, or an arrow key. Each of these will lock the data in the cell and highlight the adjacent cell
- Click the Enter box. If only a single cell was selected, the active cell will remain highlighted. If a range was selected, the active cell will move down one cell

THE CELL DATA DISPLAY

An Excel cell can hold up to 255 characters. However, you will probably never display so many digits. (The default is 8.43 characters.)

The true cell value and the displayed value may be two different things. Excel always remembers whatever you typed into a cell, exactly as you typed it. This is the true cell value. If you type a 50-character text string into a cell eight characters wide, Excel will show the entire text string, provided the cells to the right are blank. If not, the active cell (with the long text string) will display only eight characters of the text. However, the formula bar will show the 50-character string.

If you enter a large number into a cell that is not large enough to display all the characters, Excel will try to display the number in exponential notation. If this fails, Excel will display pound signs (#). The number is always stored to 15 digits of accuracy, regardless of how it is displayed. You also can use the Format Number command to alter what is shown, as you will learn later. For example, if you enter the number 14.3245, you can format the cell to display **14.32**. The entire number, though, is still stored as the true cell value and will be used in calculations.

A displayed calculation on a cell range may not appear to be the right answer, as the displayed values are not necessarily the true cell values. If you wish to insure that totals reflect the displayed cell values instead of the true cell values, choose Calculation from the Options menu and select Precision as Displayed. For example, enter **3.7** in A1 in a worksheet and the same value in A2. In A3, enter **=A1+A2**. The total is 7.4, which is what you would expect. Now select all three cells, select Picture from the Format menu, and set the picture to the fourth picture in the list box. A1 and A2 now show **4**, and A3 shows **7**—which is not what you would expect. Select Calculation from the Options menu and choose Precision as Displayed. A3 changes to **8**, but is now less precise. Be sure to set Precision as Displayed off before continuing. A3 won't change back.

SPECIAL WORKSHEET TECHNIQUES

When creating a worksheet, there are several special worksheet techniques that are important to learn. These include clearing the worksheet, finding the active cell, filling a range of cells, moving and copying, and changing column widths.

CLEARING THE WORKSHEET

If you have some practice entries in your worksheet and you want to start over with a clean worksheet, you can clear it by following these steps:

1. Select the entire worksheet (see "Basic Worksheet Techniques" towards the beginning of this chapter).
2. Open the Edit menu and choose Clear. Select All and OK. (Alternatively, you can press Del and Enter with the entire worksheet selected.)

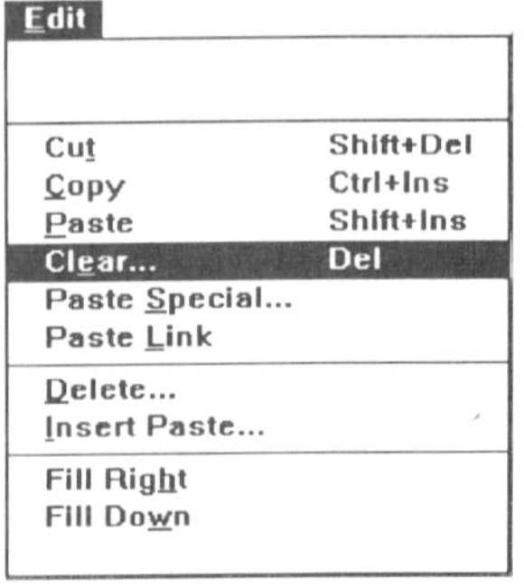

To clear a specific range, select the range and use the Edit Clear command. For even faster clearing, press Ctrl–Del or Del–Enter after selecting the range.

FINDING THE ACTIVE CELL

If you are entering data into a large worksheet and lose track of the active cell, press F7 to scroll the worksheet so that it brings the active cell back on-screen.

FILLING A RANGE OF CELLS

You can enter the same value into all the cells in a horizontal or vertical range by using the Fill commands:

1. Select the range, including the cell that already contains the value.
2. Open the Edit menu and choose Fill Right or Fill Down, as appropriate.

Excel will copy the value into each selected cell and adjust formulas that contain relative addresses automatically. (More on that in Chapter 8.)

You also can fill upwards or towards the left. To use one of these *reverse fills,* select the range, hold down the Shift key, and open the Edit menu. The menu will now show Fill Up and Fill Left as options. Select the desired fill.

MOVING AND COPYING DATA

When you copy, you take a value or a formula in one cell and copy it into a cell or range of cells. Moving is similar, except that the original cells are cleared. (When you use the Fill Right or Fill Down command, you are copying.)

When moving, save time by designating the destination range by a single cell—the upper-left corner of the destination range. The entire range will still be moved.

To move data, select the source cell range, open the Edit menu, and choose Cut (Shift-Del). This moves a copy of the current range data to the Clipboard. Select the entire destination range. The source range will remain marked with a dotted line. Open the Edit menu and choose Paste (Shift-Ins). The source cells will clear and the destination cells will then contain the data. Source and destination ranges can overlap if necessary.

When copying you can designate the destination range by selecting the upper-left corner of the range as a single cell. You also can specify a destination range that is an integer multiple of the source cells and create multiple copies. The destination range should be a single cell or an integer multiple of the source range. For example, if the source range is two cells, the destination range should contain two, four, six, or another even number of cells. Do not use overlapping copy ranges.

To copy data, select the source range. Open the Edit menu and choose Copy (Ctrl-Ins). This creates a copy of the source range data in the Clipboard. Select the destination range. Again, the source range remains marked. Open the Edit menu and choose Paste (Shift-Ins). The destination range will then contain the same data as the source range. The data are still in the Clipboard. You can do more pastes with the same source range without reusing the Copy command.

When formulas are copied into other cells, the formula references change to reflect their new position. This default method is called *relative addressing*. It is possible to prevent this adjustment with *absolute addressing*. You will learn more about relative and absolute addressing in Chapter 8.

CHANGING COLUMN WIDTHS

In creating a worksheet, you will often need to change the width of a column to display the entire cell contents or to improve the appearance of the worksheet. You can change column widths either by using the Column Width command under the Format menu or by dragging the column separator with the mouse.

Changing the Column Width with a Command

To change the width with a command, open the Format menu and choose Column Width. When the Column Width dialog box appears, type in the new width from the keyboard and click OK. The

You can use both methods to enter fractional column widths (for example, 20.5 characters). The mouse method, however, is less precise.

column width will change to reflect the value entered. The contents of the cells in that column will not be changed. You can have Excel automatically define a new width by clicking the Best Fit button, as long as the active cell contains the longest number, text string, or formula of that column.

Changing the Column Width with the Mouse

To change the width with the mouse, move the cursor to the line between the column-heading designators. The shape of the cursor will change to a vertical line with two arrows (←|→). Click and drag the cursor to the right or left. The width of the column on the left will follow the cursor. Release the mouse button at the desired width.

THE BALANCE WORKSHEET

In this and the next two chapters, you will create the worksheet shown in Figure 4.1. In this chapter you will use the techniques described so far to enter the worksheet data and formulas. At the end of this chapter the worksheet should look like Figure 4.2. In comparing the two figures, notice the difference in the quality of presentation that is achieved by formatting. Formatting is described in Chapter 6.

CREATING THE WORKSHEET

To start the worksheet, follow these steps:

1. Select cells A8 through A42 by selecting A8, pressing F5, and typing **A42**.
2. Hold down the Shift key and press Enter to highlight the column.
3. Enter the row titles shown in Figure 4.2. Press the Enter key after you've typed each title. Press the Enter key twice to skip a line. At the end, press Ctrl-. to return to A8.
4. Expand the width of column A by opening the Format menu and choosing Column Width. The dialog box shown in Figure 4.3 appears. Enter **25** and click OK.

ACME MANUFACTURING COMPANY

Balance Sheet for 1991
(Figures in Thousands of Dollars)

	Qtr 1	Qtr 2	Qtr 3	Qtr 4
Current Assets				
Cash	$28,653	$42,894	$64,882	$91,053
Accounts Receivable	$35,700	$44,150	$48,450	$55,230
Inventory	$11,400	$12,930	$14,500	$16,490
Total Current Assets	$75,753	$99,974	$127,832	$162,773
Fixed Assets				
P,P, and E				
Furniture, Fixtures	$12,100	$12,100	$12,100	$12,100
Equipment	$6,500	$16,600	$21,100	$42,300
Office Equipment	$4,100	$4,100	$4,100	$4,100
Gross P, P, and E	$22,700	$32,800	$37,300	$58,500
Accumulated Depreciation	$6,600	$8,700	$11,400	$13,400
Total Fixed Assets	$16,100	$24,100	$25,900	$45,100
Total Assets	**$91,853**	**$124,074**	**$153,732**	**$207,873**
Current Liabilities				
Accounts Payable	$17,340	$41,000	$42,300	$75,200
Income Taxes Payable	$4,043	$6,132	$7,301	$9,245
Total Current Liabilities	$21,383	$47,132	$49,601	$84,445
Non-current Liabilities				
Long-term debt	$22,000	$20,000	$18,000	$16,000
Total Liabilities	$43,383	$67,132	$67,601	$100,445
Capital				
Acme Capital	$48,470	$56,942	$86,131	$107,428
Total Liabilities & Equity	**$91,853**	**$124,074**	**$153,732**	**$207,873**

Figure 4.1: The final balance worksheet

In this and the following data entries, do not be too concerned about mistakes. If you make a mistake, continue to create your worksheet, working around the mistakes. In the next chapter, you'll learn how to edit the worksheet and correct your mistakes.

5. Drag the cursor from cell B6 to cell E6 and enter the column headings shown in Figure 4.2. Press Enter after each entry.

	A	B	C	D	E
1		ACME MANUFACTURING COMPANY			
2					
3		Balance Sheet for 1991			
4		(Figures in Thousands of Dollars)			
5					
6		Qtr 1	Qtr 2	Qtr 3	Qtr 4
7					
8	Current Assets				
9	Cash	28653	42894	64882	91053
10	Accounts Receivable	35700	44150	48450	55230
11	Inventory	11400	12930	14500	16490
12		------------	------------	------------	------------
13	Total Current Assets	75753	99974	127832	162773
14					
15	Fixed Assets				
16	P,P, and E				
17	Furniture, Fixtures	12100	12100	12100	12100
18	Equipment	6500	16600	21100	42300
19	Office Equipment	4100	4100	4100	4100
20		------------	------------	------------	------------
21	Gross P, P, and E	22700	32800	37300	58500
22	Accumulated Depreciation	6600	8700	11400	13400
23		------------	------------	------------	------------
24	Total Fixed Assets	16100	24100	25900	45100
25					
26	Total Assets	91853	124074	153732	207873
27					
28	Current Liabilities				
29	Accounts Payable	17340	41000	42300	75200
30	Income Taxes Payable	4043	6132	7301	9245
31		------------	------------	------------	------------
32	Total Current Liabilities	21383	47132	49601	84445
33					
34	Non-current Liabilities				
35	Long-term debt	22000	20000	18000	16000
36		------------	------------	------------	------------
37	Total Liabilities	43383	67132	67601	100445
38					
39	Capital				
40	Acme Capital	48470	56942	86131	107428
41					
42	Total Liabilities & Equity	91853	124074	153732	207873

Figure 4.2: The balance worksheet before formatting

Format Data Optio
Number...
Alignment...
Font...
Border...
Patterns...
Cell Protection...
Style...
Row Height...
Column Width...
Justify

Column Width: 25 OK
Standard Width Cancel
Hide Unhide Best Fit

Figure 4.3: Changing the column width

6. Add a title to the worksheet by selecting cell B1 and entering **ACME MANUFACTURING COMPANY** from the keyboard. Select cell B3 and enter **Balance Sheet for 1991**. Select cell B4 and enter **(Figures in Thousands of Dollars)**.

7. To enter the horizontal separators, first place one hyphen in the leftmost column (as in B12). Then open the Format menu and select Alignment and Fill. Copy B12 to E12 to the Clipboard and paste to B20, B23, B31, and B36. This will create the other rows of hyphens.

8. Enter the numbers shown in Figure 4.2 into the worksheet. Enter the data for rows 9–11, 17–19, 22, 29–30, 35, and 40. Do not enter the values for rows 13, 21, 24, 26, 32, 37, and 42. You'll use formulas to fill these in, as described below.

9. Enter the following formulas into column B:

INTO CELL	*ENTER THE FORMULA*
B13	= B9 + B10 + B11
B21	= B17 + B18 + B19
B24	= B21 – B22
B26	= B13 + B24
B32	= B29 + B30
B37	= B32 + B35
B42	= B37 – B41

10. Fill the cells with the formulas. Select cell B13 and drag to cell E13. Open the Edit menu and choose Fill Right. Repeat this procedure for all the rows that contain a formula.

Edit

- Cut Shift+Del
- Copy Ctrl+Ins
- Paste Shift+Ins
- Clear... Del
- Paste Special...
- Paste Link
- Delete...
- Insert Paste...
- **Fill Right**
- Fill Down

In Figure 4.4, columns B through E show the values that should appear on your worksheet after you've entered the formulas for row 13.

SAVING THE WORKSHEET

After you have created the worksheet, you will need to save it on your disk. Although the worksheet is displayed on-screen, it is stored cnly in the computer's memory. If you were to turn the computer off or reboot without saving the worksheet, the worksheet would be lost.

The File menu contains two commands you can use to save your worksheet: Save and Save As. The Save command saves the worksheet under the name currently displayed in the worksheet title bar.

Microsoft Excel

File Edit Formula Format Data Options Macro Window Help

Normal

B13 =B9+B10+B11

SHEET1.XLS

	A	B	C	D	E	F	G
1		ACME MANUFACTURING COMPANY					
2							
3		Balance Sheet for 1991					
4		(Figures in Thousands of Dollars)					
5							
6		Qtr 1	Qtr 2	Qtr 3	Qtr 4		
7							
8	Current Assets						
9	Cash	28653	42894	64882	91053		
10	Accounts Receivable	35700	44150	48450	55230		
11	Inventory	11400	12930	14500	16490		
12							
13	Total Current Assets	75753	99974	127832	162773		
14							
15	Fixed Assets						
16	P,P, and E						

Ready

Figure 4.4: The worksheet after entering a formula

This default name is Sheet1. The Save As command lets you save the worksheet under any name. The first time you save the new worksheet, use Save As and specify the name for the worksheet. The title bar will then change to reflect this new name. On all subsequent saves, you can use Save.

Try this now with your worksheet. Choose Save As under the File menu. A dialog box will appear (see Figure 4.5). Change to the directory to which you wish to save the worksheet and enter the worksheet name **BALANCE**. You can use upper- or lowercase letters. Choose OK and it will be saved under the file name you specify, with a .XLS extension added. For more information on saving a worksheet, see Chapter 7.

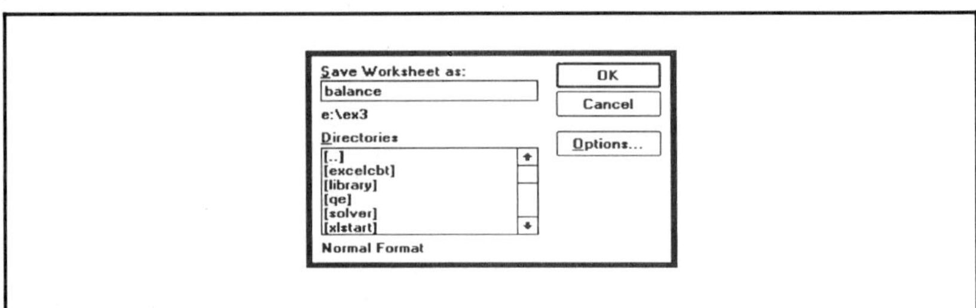

Figure 4.5: Saving a worksheet

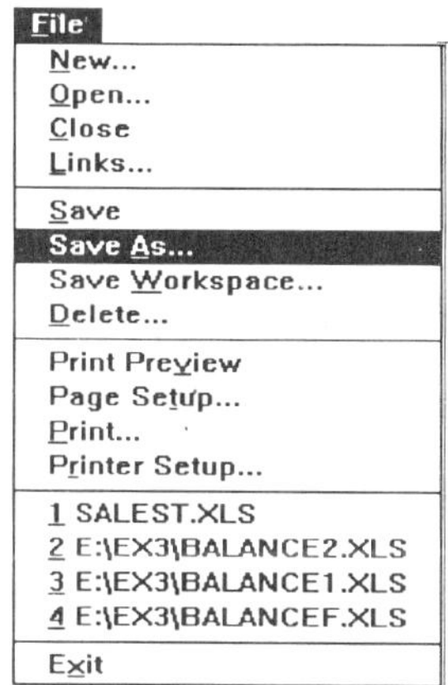

As a rule, while you're creating a worksheet you should save it approximately every 20 minutes. This will protect your work against power failures, hardware failures, or inadvertent user mistakes. Again, use Save As only the first time you save your file. On subsequent saves, choose Save. With Save, Excel won't display the dialog box. It saves the worksheet under the existing name.

EXPERIMENTING WITH THE WORKSHEET

Edit
Cut Shift+Del
Copy Ctrl+Ins
Clear... Del
Delete...
Insert...
Fill Right
Fill Down

Now you can try some different techniques. First, try copying a formula. Instead of entering the formulas for cells C13, D13, and E13 with the Fill Right command, copy the formula from cell B13 into the rest of the row:

1. Make cell B13 active.
2. Open the Edit menu and choose Copy (Ctrl–Ins). Notice that the highlighting on cell B13 changes.
3. Select cell C13 and drag to cell E13. Although cells C13, D13, and E13 are now selected, cell B13 is still marked to show the cell range for the copy.
4. Open the Edit menu again and choose Paste (Shift–Ins). The correct totals will immediately show in the rest of the row.

Edit
Cut Shift+Del
Copy Ctrl+Ins
Paste Shift+Ins
Clear... Del
Paste Special...
Paste Link
Delete...
Insert Paste...
Fill Right
Fill Down

Notice that the totals in cells C13, D13, and E13 are correct. The formula in cell C13 was automatically adjusted for the new columns when it was copied. To check this, select cell C13 and look at the formula in the formula bar at the top of the page (see Figure 4.6).

Now try a move. Just for practice, move row 42 to row 43:

1. Select A42 to E42.
2. Open the Edit menu and choose Cut (Shift–Del). Notice that the entire range is marked.
3. Place the cursor on A43.
4. Open the Edit menu again and choose Paste (Shift–Ins). Row 42 will move to row 43 (row 42 will be cleared). Notice that the formulas are automatically adjusted.

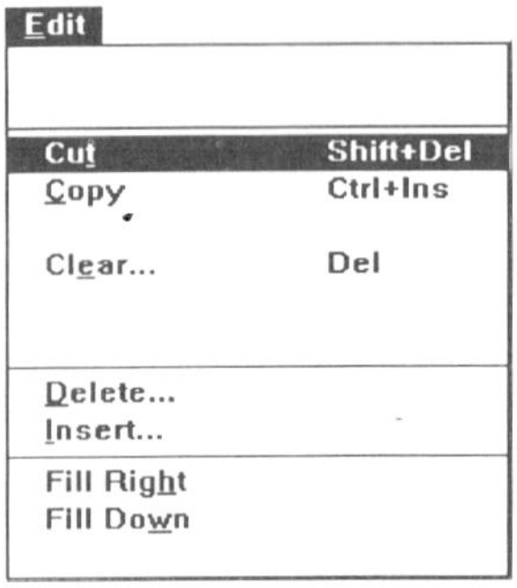

Edit

Cut	Shift+Del
Copy	Ctrl+Ins
Clear...	Del
Delete...	
Insert...	
Fill Right	
Fill Down	

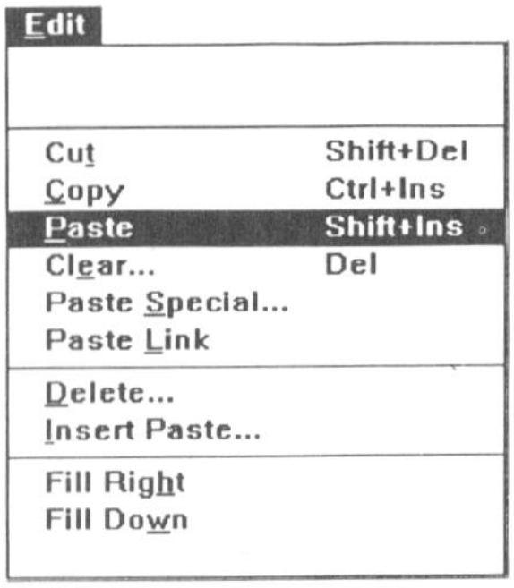

Edit

Cut	Shift+Del
Copy	Ctrl+Ins
Paste	Shift+Ins
Clear...	Del
Paste Special...	
Paste Link	
Delete...	
Insert Paste...	
Fill Right	
Fill Down	

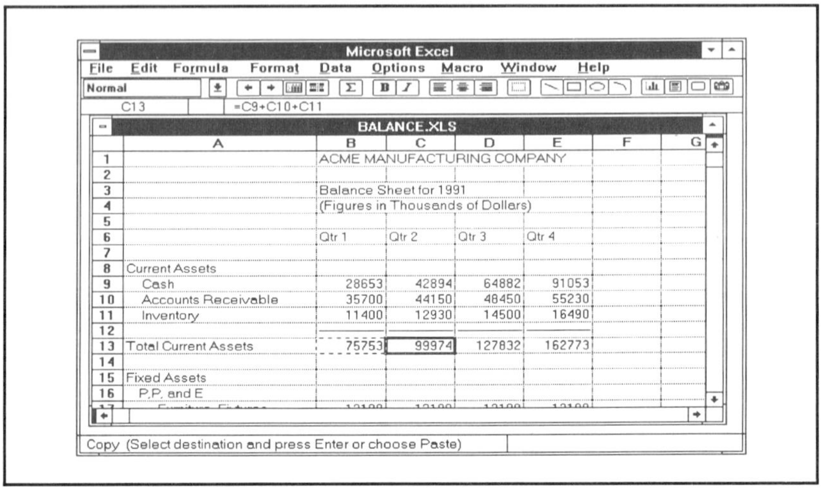

Avoid copying entire rows or columns using the row or column designators to select, unless necessary. It will use a lot of Clipboard memory and is slow.

Microsoft Excel

File Edit Formula Format Data Options Macro Window Help

Normal

C13 =C9+C10+C11

BALANCE.XLS

	A	B	C	D	E	F	G
1		ACME MANUFACTURING COMPANY					
2							
3		Balance Sheet for 1991					
4		(Figures in Thousands of Dollars)					
5							
6		Qtr 1	Qtr 2	Qtr 3	Qtr 4		
7							
8	Current Assets						
9	Cash	28653	42894	64882	91053		
10	Accounts Receivable	35700	44150	48450	55230		
11	Inventory	11400	12930	14500	16490		
12							
13	Total Current Assets	75753	99974	127832	162773		
14							
15	Fixed Assets						
16	P,P, and E						

Copy (Select destination and press Enter or choose Paste)

Figure 4.6: Examining a formula created by the Copy command

5. Recover the former worksheet immediately by selecting the Edit menu and choosing Undo Paste (or press Alt–Backspace). The worksheet should be restored. (If something goes wrong here, remember that you have already saved the worksheet. You can use the Open command under the File menu to reload it.)

Use the Clipboard for both cutting and copying. You can watch the Clipboard change during a cut and paste operation. First, click the application Control-menu box. Choose Run, then select Clipboard (see Figure 4.7). The Clipboard window will open and become the active window, as shown in Figure 4.8. It displays the size of the last cut or copy.

The Clipboard can be moved, scrolled, and closed, like any other active window. Do a cut or copy operation and watch the window.

To get back to the worksheet, minimize the Clipboard from its Control menu. This will put the Clipboard as an icon at the bottom of the screen. You can then double-click it to see the Clipboard if you need it again. Clipboard and Excel remain in memory unless closed from their Control menus.

In the next two chapters, you will be changing the worksheet you created in this chapter. When you leave Excel (double-click the Control-menu box or press Alt–F4), you will see a message box. The box indicates that the document has been changed and asks if you wish to save the new document. If you do not wish to save the altered document, choose No. If you do, choose Yes.

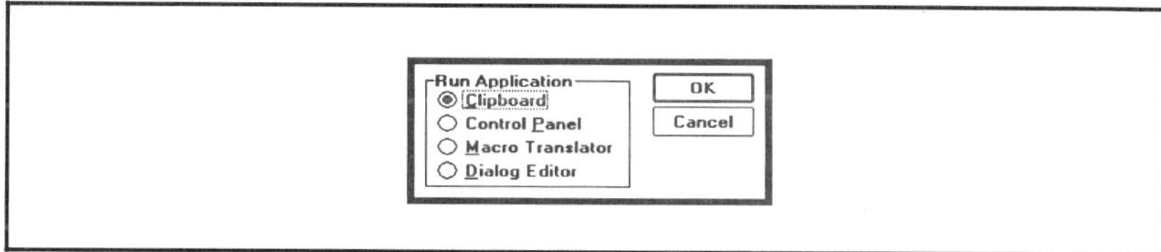

Figure 4.7: Running the Clipboard program

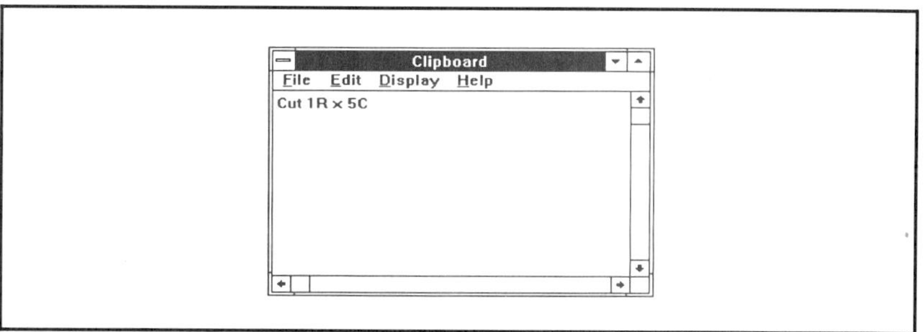

Figure 4.8: The Clipboard window

5 Editing the Worksheet

EXCEL HAS MANY EDITING FEATURES THAT CAN make your work easier. You can clear a cell or cell range, recover from an accidental deletion, and insert or delete rows and columns. You also can use standard Windows 3.0 editing techniques (cut, move, and paste) to edit any data in the formula bar.

In this chapter, you will learn the basic editing skills and techniques to use with Excel worksheets. These will enable you to correct any mistakes that you might have made in the exercises of the last chapter. Even if your worksheet does not have any mistakes, take the time to learn some of the editing techniques described here.

This chapter also includes information about adding comments to worksheets, using other commands for editing, and saving your edited worksheet. More advanced editing techniques are discussed in Chapter 14.

EDITING TECHNIQUES

Excel offers you a variety of worksheet editing techniques, which make it easy for you to keep your worksheets up to date and accurate, as well as use one basic worksheet structure for many purposes.

Let's examine how you can edit a worksheet. The techniques discussed in this section include:

- Clearing cells
- Undoing various operations
- Repeating a command
- Editing cells
- Editing formulas
- Inserting and deleting rows and columns
- Using templates

LOADING THE WORKSHEET

To begin editing, start Excel and load the worksheet, if you have not already done so. To open the worksheet, choose Open from the File menu. In the dialog box displayed (see Figure 5.1), switch to the directory containing the worksheet by using the Directories list box. Choose the file name BALANCE.XLS (double-click it or use the direction keys to highlight it and press Enter). (See Chapter 7 for more help on opening worksheets.)

Here are a few tips for loading and saving worksheets:

3.0

- Excel remembers the last few worksheets loaded. If the worksheet name you wish to load is on the File menu, choose the name from the File menu and bypass the Open command

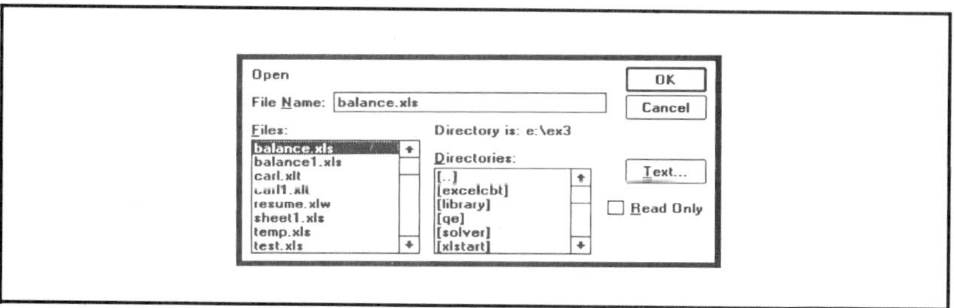

Figure 5.1: Opening the worksheet

- You can open Lotus 1-2-3 spreadsheets, dBASE files, and Multiplan documents from the Open dialog box shown in Figure 5.1. Excel is smart enough to figure out most spreadsheet formats and loads them automatically
- As a document loads, the format and percentage loaded is displayed in the upper left of the window
- When saving, you can specify the format by choosing Options on the Save As dialog box. Try to use the normal Excel format as much as possible, since it makes saving and loading faster. When exchanging worksheets with other environments (such as Macintosh Excel or Multiplan), try to use the SYLK format. This will save as much of the formulas and formats as possible

CLEARING A CELL OR CELL RANGE

You can clear or delete any cell or cell range. *Clearing* removes the contents, format, and notes of a cell or cell range without removing the cell itself. This is done with the Clear command under the Edit menu or by using the Del key. *Deleting* "physically" removes the cell or cell range from the worksheet. Rows and columns are adjusted as necessary to recover the space. Deleting is done with the Delete command under the Edit menu.

The simplest way to clear a cell or cell range is to select the cells and press Ctrl–Del. This will clear the cells (data, formulas, format, and notes) without so much as a query.

For selective clearing, choose the range and press Del. This is the same as choosing Clear from the Edit menu. The Clear dialog box shown in Figure 5.2 appears. (The dot in the circle next to Formulas indicates that values and formulas will be cleared, but not the cell format.) Click OK and the cell or cell range will be cleared.

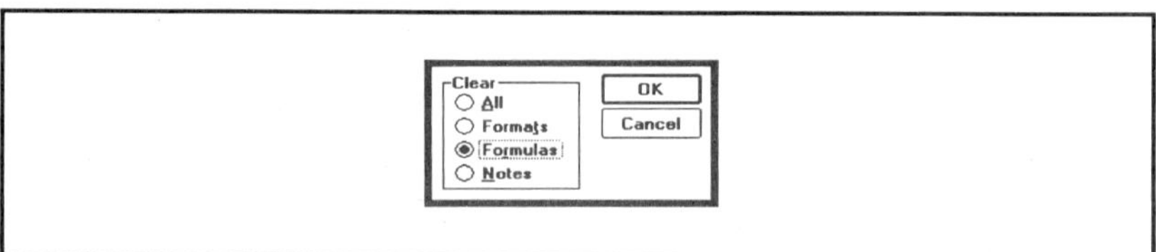

Figure 5.2: Clearing a cell or cell range

Edit
Cut Shift+Del
Copy Ctrl+Ins
Paste Shift+Ins
Clear... Del
Paste Special...
Paste Link
Delete...
Insert Paste...
Fill Right
Fill Down

You can try this now with your Balance worksheet. Select cells C13 to E13. Open the Edit menu and choose Clear. Click OK. The cells will clear. You also will notice that two totals in row 26 change, as you have just deleted data that were used to compute these totals. Before going on to anything else, open the Edit menu and choose Undo Clear (undoing is discussed below).

To clear an entire worksheet, select the entire worksheet and press Ctrl-Del.

The Clear dialog box also has options for clearing only formulas and only format. Clearing a format puts the cell(s) in the default *General* picture. (Text is aligned left, numbers are aligned right). Clearing formulas clears the data in the cell(s), but not the format. Clearing notes clears any notes associated with the cell(s) (see "Adding a Note to a Cell" in Chapter 9). Choosing All clears the format, data, and notes.

UNDOING

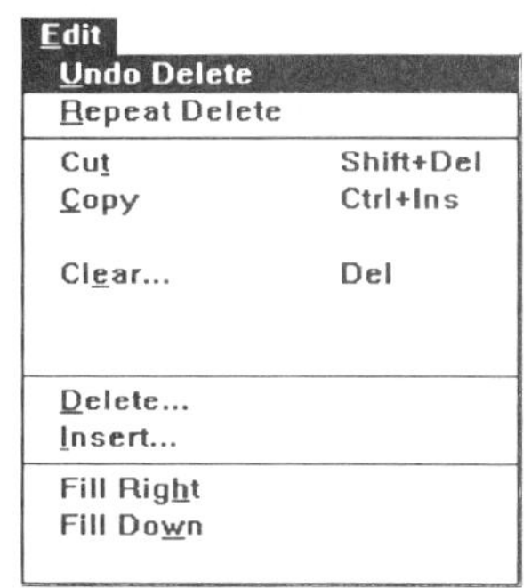

If you make a mistake while you're changing a worksheet, you can recover the previous version with the Undo command. The Undo command applies to most types of operations: inserting, deleting, moving, copying, pasting, formatting, etc. However, only the last operation can be undone—once you have gone on to something else, the undo capability is lost. Each time you open the Edit menu the Undo command will be shown highlighted, if available, and the function that you can undo will be the second word (such as **Undo Delete** or **Undo Paste**). You can press Alt-Backspace as a shortcut.

You can undo the Undo command as well, restoring what you had inserted, deleted, moved, copied, pasted, formatted, etc.

Edit
Undo Paste
Cut Shift+Del
Copy Ctrl+Ins
Clear... Del
Delete...
Insert...
Fill Right
Fill Down

You saw how this worked just above. Now move row 13 to row 14 and undo the operation:

1. Select A13 to E13.
2. Open the Edit menu and choose Cut.
3. Select A14.
4. Open the Edit menu and choose Paste. Row 13 has now moved to row 14.
5. Open the Edit menu and choose Undo Paste (or press Alt-Backspace). Row 14 is now moved back to row 13.

REPEATING A COMMAND

Sometimes you may wish to repeat a command that you have used. Rather than reselect the command and click OK on a dialog box again, simply choose Repeat from the Edit menu or press Alt-Enter. For example, you may be formatting multiple ranges to the same format. Select the first range and format it. Then select each additional range and press Alt-Enter.

EDITING A CELL VALUE

To edit a cell, first select it (make it active). The current value will appear in the formula bar. You can edit cell values that appear there in three ways: by reentering the entire value, editing the current contents, or copying something into the cell from another cell.

To reenter an entire value, simply type the new data into the formula bar, and press Enter or click the Enter box. The new data will replace the old. Try this now with cell B10 of your Balance worksheet. Select the cell. The current value (**35700**) is displayed in the formula bar. Reenter the same value. After you type the first number, the formula bar clears and you will see a **3**.

If the entry is long, your best approach is generally to edit the current value. For shorter entries, you may save time by simply retyping the entire value.

To edit the current contents, move the cursor into the formula bar and click at any point on the value. (Notice that the cursor changes to an I-beam.) As you type characters from the keyboard they will be inserted at the cursor position. You also can use the Backspace key to remove characters before the insertion point. Another way to delete characters is to click anywhere in the formula bar and drag the cursor over the characters you wish to delete. Then open the Edit menu and choose Cut. The Cut, Copy, and Paste commands work with characters in the formula bar in the same way that they work with cell contents. You also can drag the mouse over characters and then reenter new characters. The new characters will replace those you selected.

EDITING FORMULAS

You can edit formulas that appear in the formula bar in the same way that you edit cell values; that is, reentering the entire formula or editing the current formula. Copying and pasting from a cell that contains the correct entry is another way to edit a cell. If a formula is wrong, for example, it is often easier to copy the correct formula to the cell from another cell where it is already correct than to edit the formula bar or reenter the entire formula from scratch.

Whenever the formula bar is active, you can click the cell you want to include in a formula instead of typing its address from the keyboard. To use this technique, first click the cursor in the formula bar where you want the reference to be inserted, then click on the cell in the worksheet.

Any time you use the formula bar, the Cancel (×) and Enter (✓) boxes are displayed with the contents of the active cell. Click the Enter box to enter the edited formula or click the Cancel box to revert to the original formula. You also can undo any editing if you make a mistake.

INSERTING AND DELETING ROWS AND COLUMNS

3.0

When you are creating a worksheet, you may find that you need to add or delete rows and columns. With Excel, this is as easy as two clicks. For example, you can add a blank row between rows 12 and 13. Since new rows are always inserted *before* the selected row, you need to select row 13. Select any cell in that row, open the Edit menu, and choose Insert. In the dialog box (see Figure 5.3), choose Entire Row to insert a row. Choose OK. Excel will create a new row 13 and move the old row 13 and all rows below it down one row, as shown in Figure 5.4. Formulas throughout the worksheet are adjusted for the moved data.

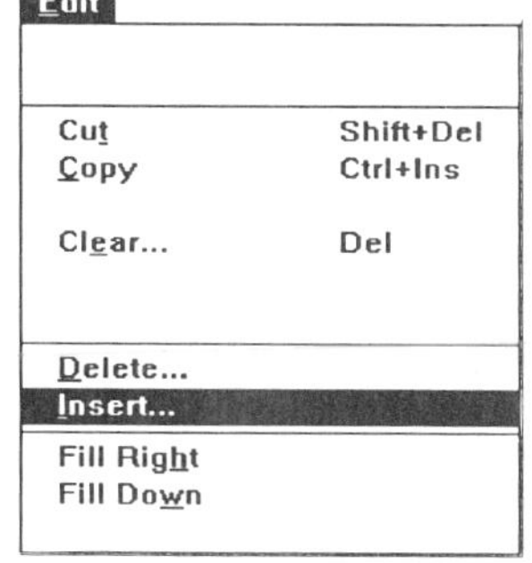

You can use the same procedure to add a column by choosing Entire Column in the Insert dialog box. The column is then inserted to the left of the selected column. You also can add a row or column

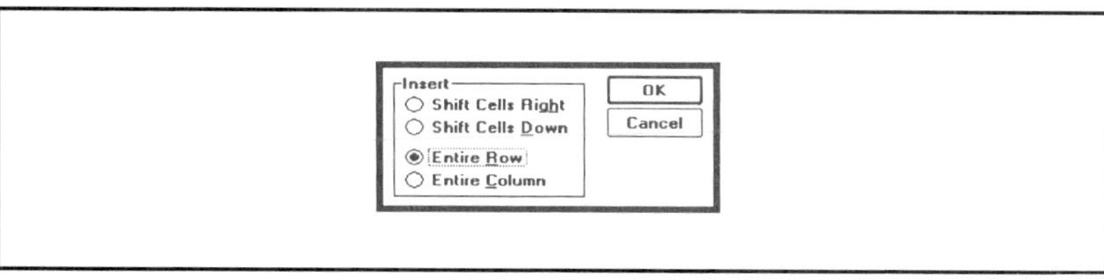

Figure 5.3: Inserting a row

Microsoft Excel

File Edit Formula Format Data Options Macro Window Help

Normal | A13

BALANCE.XLS

	A	B	C	D	E	F	G
8	Current Assets						
9	Cash	28653	42894	64882	91053		
10	Accounts Receivable	35700	44150	48450	55230		
11	Inventory	11400	12930	14500	16490		
12							
13							
14	Total Current Assets	75753	99974	127832	162773		
15							
16	Fixed Assets						
17	P.P. and E						
18	Furniture, Fixtures	12100	12100	12100	12100		
19	Equipment	6500	16600	21100	42300		
20	Office Equipment	4100	4100	4100	4100		
21							
22	Gross P. P. and E	22700	32800	37300	58500		
23	Accumulated Depreciation	6600	8700	11400	13400		

Ready

Figure 5.4: The worksheet with an inserted row

without calling up a dialog box by clicking any row or column designator and choosing Insert from the Edit menu.

To delete a row, use the Delete command under the Edit menu. Delete the row you just added. Select any cell in row 13, open the Edit menu, and choose Delete. Choose Entire Row in the dialog box and click OK. The rows will move up and the worksheet will be as it was before. You also can select the row designator and choose Delete from the Edit menu to delete a row without the dialog box. This works for columns as well.

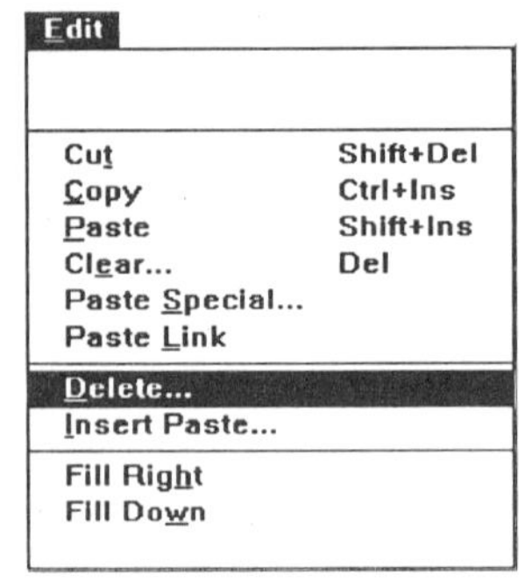

You also can insert or delete portions of columns or rows. To do this, select a cell or cell range. Then choose Insert or Delete on the Edit menu. The dialog box will ask whether other cells or rows should be shifted right or down to adjust for the insertion or deletion (see Figure 5.3). Choose the appropriate response and click OK.

Try this with your Balance worksheet:

1. Select cells A17 through E19.
2. Open the Edit menu and choose Delete.
3. When the dialog box appears, choose Shift Cells Up (if not already selected), and click OK.
4. The cells will be shifted and several error messages will appear on your worksheet. (Can you guess why?)

5. To recover the deleted cells, open the Edit menu and choose Undo Delete. The delete cells reappear and error messages disappear.

If you delete a cell or range of cells on which the values of other cells depend (because they are based on a formula that uses the deleted cell), the dependent cells will display **#REF!**. This shows that the cell's formula references a cell that has been deleted. You will then need to correct the formula. You can see how this works by deleting row 21 from the Balance worksheet. Because the values in what will be rows 23 and 25 after the deletion depend on the values that were in row 21, you will see **#REF!** in rows 23 and 25, as shown in Figure 5.5. Now restore row 21 by opening the Edit menu and choosing Undo Delete.

	A	B	C	D	E	F	G
14							
15	Fixed Assets						
16	P.P. and E						
17	Furniture, Fixtures	12100	12100	12100	12100		
18	Equipment	6500	16600	21100	42300		
19	Office Equipment	4100	4100	4100	4100		
20							
	Accumulated Depreciation	6600	8700	11400	13400		
22							
23	Total Fixed Assets	#REF!	#REF!	#REF!	#REF!		
24							
25	Total Assets	#REF!	#REF!	#REF!	#REF!		
26							
27	Current Liabilities						
28	Accounts Payable	17340	41000	42300	75200		
29	Income Taxes Payable	4043	6132	7301	9245		

Figure 5.5: Deleting cells on which other cells depend

Now try one more experiment. Add a new column before the first column. Notice that the new column is standard width. The former column A becomes B and remains wide. Now delete the column A that you added.

If you like, experiment some more with some of the techniques you've learned in this chapter, before reading on. Try inserting and deleting more rows and columns, and editing cell entries (formulas and values). When you are through, either save the worksheet under a different name (using the Save As command under the File menu) or close the document window without saving the changes you made since you loaded it earlier (using the Close command under the File menu, or by clicking the Control-menu box).

USING TEMPLATES

A basic worksheet structure that has many applications is called a *template.* For example, you might have a worksheet form that you use each quarter for a report. It might contain titles, row headings, some formatted cells, and other common features that are used for each report. Figure 5.6 shows a template you could use for creating the balance sheet.

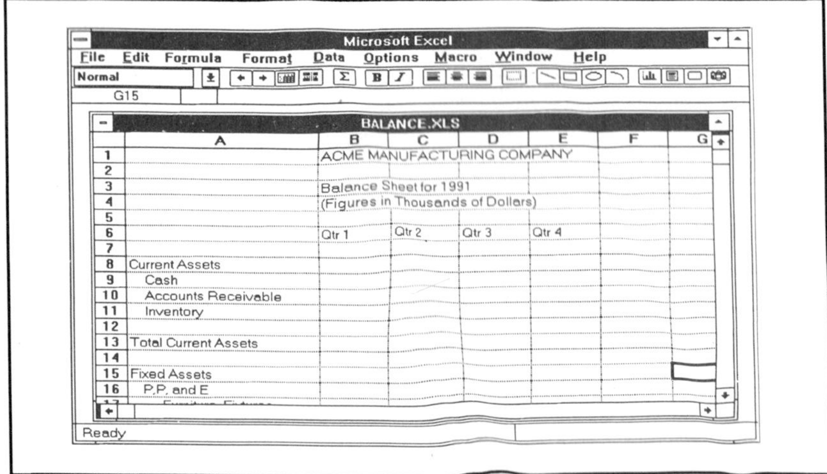

Figure 5.6: An example template

A template offers several advantages:

- **Saves time.** You don't have to reenter text, data, and formats that are common to several worksheets
- **Improves consistency.** By defining a set of templates for your company, you can ensure that your organization's worksheets have a consistent appearance

- **Improves accuracy.** By reducing data entry, you improve accuracy. Using templates and macros to input new data to the basic worksheet, you can enable users with a minimum of Excel experience to do productive work

One method of creating a template is to create a master worksheet that contains the starting formats and data. This is then saved and used each time as a beginning form.

3.0 There is an even better way with Excel, however. You can create true templates. This gives you an added degree of control and protection for your templates.

To create a template, you begin as if you were creating a worksheet:

1. Enter the basic data and formats, then choose Save As from the File menu.
2. Choose Options in the dialog box to display a second-level dialog box (see Figure 5.7).
3. Choose **Template** from the list box.
4. Click OK to return to the Save As dialog box and click OK again. This saves the worksheet form as a template with an .XLT extension.

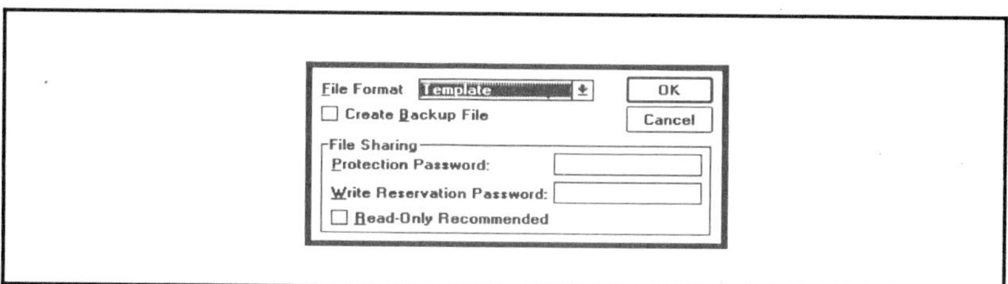

Figure 5.7: Saving a worksheet as a template

If you wish to edit the template, open the template file by selecting the file, then holding down the Shift key while you choose OK.

To change a template to a standard worksheet, use the Options button when saving to save it as a Normal worksheet. To delete a template, use the Delete command of the File menu and delete it as when deleting worksheets.

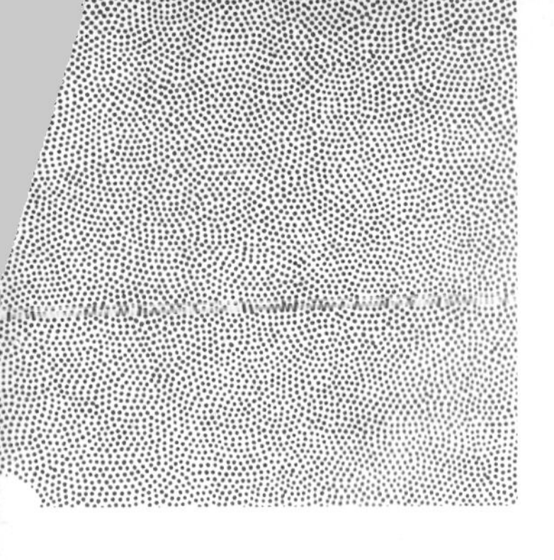
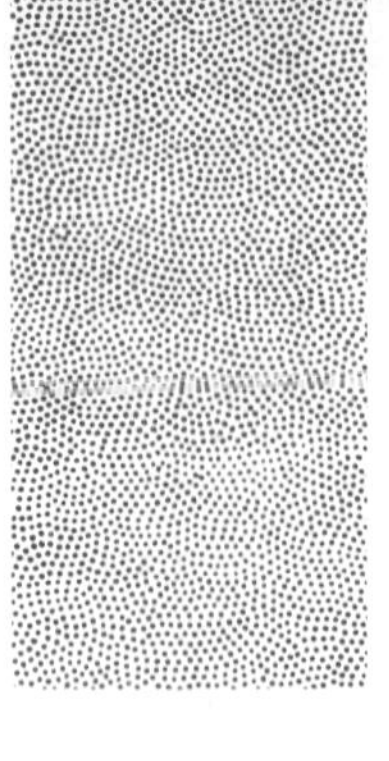

6 Improving the Worksheet's Appearance

IN THIS CHAPTER, YOU'LL LEARN HOW TO CONTROL the appearance of your worksheets. There are two things that Excel knows about each cell in a worksheet: its value (whether a constant or variable formula) and its formatting information. The latter, which determines the appearance of a cell's display, includes the following:

- How numbers are to be displayed (the cell's picture)
- The alignment of the cell's display (left, center, or right)
- The font used in the cell's display. This includes the font family (Helvetica, Times Roman, Courier, and so on) as well as style (regular, boldface, underline, strikeout, or italics), size, and color

In addition, you can control the display of the worksheet's grid lines and add borders around the whole worksheet or just certain areas.

Formatting is important for three reasons:

- It makes a presentation-quality document

- It makes the worksheet easier to read and understand
- It emphasizes the conclusions you wish to portray so they stand out from the rest of the worksheet

Excel offers you extensive formatting control, so you can exercise your creativity in setting up your worksheets.

FORMATTING YOUR WORKSHEET

Formatting defines the appearance of a cell or range. As you would expect, you will find most of the formatting commands on the Format menu. The other commands are either in the Display or Page Setup dialog boxes.

The rule is simple: formatting aspects that apply to a cell or cell range are on the Format menu, those that apply to the entire display of the worksheet are in the Display dialog box, and those that apply to the entire printed worksheet are in the Page Setup dialog box. There is an exception to this: if you use the Display command to change the appearance of a formula, you will also affect its appearance when it prints.

Let's first look at formatting cells or cell ranges. Here is the general procedure for using the Format menu: select the cell or cell range to format, open the Format menu, and choose the desired command. The three basic format controls are the picture (number), alignment, and font (font family, size, and style).

The format of a cell is copied with its value when you copy, fill, or use the Series command. Take advantage of this fact by formatting the source cell before you copy it.

You can define the format before or after a cell entry. If you define a format before making a cell entry, there will be no visible indication, of course, until a cell value or formula is entered. Once you format a cell, the format remains the same even if you change the value or formula in the cell. The format will change only if you select a new format.

To clear a format (i.e., return it to its default setting) without erasing the cell value, open the Edit menu and select Clear. Choose Formats in the dialog box. To erase the values from a cell or cell range without changing the format, choose Formulas in the dialog box instead. To clear both content and format, choose All.

THE CELL PICTURE

Pictures are the choices you have for displaying numbers, dates, or times in your worksheet. For example, the picture **0.00** indicates that the value is to be displayed with two places to the right of the decimal. If necessary, the number is rounded off for the display. This does not affect the way the number is stored in the computer's memory, however.

Excel includes 23 predefined pictures for cell display: the general format (default), 13 for numeric displays, and 9 for dates and times. In addition, you can define as many as 43 new pictures. Custom pictures are useful for worksheets that involve special values, such as foreign currency, social security numbers, or telephone numbers.

Plan your worksheet ahead and format before data entry as much as possible. Format by range to save formatting time. Because numeric pictures do not affect text cells, you can often apply a single numeric picture for a whole worksheet.

You can change the default format by creating a *template* with the formats you wish to use. You also can use the style box on the tool bar to select quick formats for a range of cells.

Predefined Pictures

Excel's predefined pictures give you the following choices:

- How many digits appear to the right of the decimal
- Whether commas are used in numbers
- Whether a dollar sign appears
- Whether a percent sign is used
- Whether dates and times appear with hyphens, dashes, or colons

In the default mode (when you first start Excel), Excel displays all cells using the *General picture.* The General picture shows all numbers as precisely as possible. In other words, if you enter *123,* the cell will display **123**; if you enter *123.23,* the cell will display **123.23**. If a number with a General picture is too large for the current column width, Excel will display the number in exponential notation. For example, the default cell width is 8.43 characters. If you enter *100000000,* a nine-digit number, the cell will display 1E+08.

Now let's format a worksheet. Open the Balance worksheet you created in Chapter 4. To open it, choose Open from the File menu. Select BALANCE.XLS in the list box and choose OK. You may need to change directories to find the file name (see Chapter 7).

Choose a predefined picture for a cell or range of cells:

1. Select B9, press F5, and type **E42**. Hold down the Shift key and press Enter.
2. Open the Format menu and choose Number.
3. The Format Number dialog box appears. The highlight will be on General, as that is the default picture. Choose the first currency picture (see Figure 6.1). If need be, you can click the scroll arrows, drag the scroll box, or use the direction keys to see the picture code you need.
4. Click OK and the cell or cell range will be formatted according to the picture that you selected.

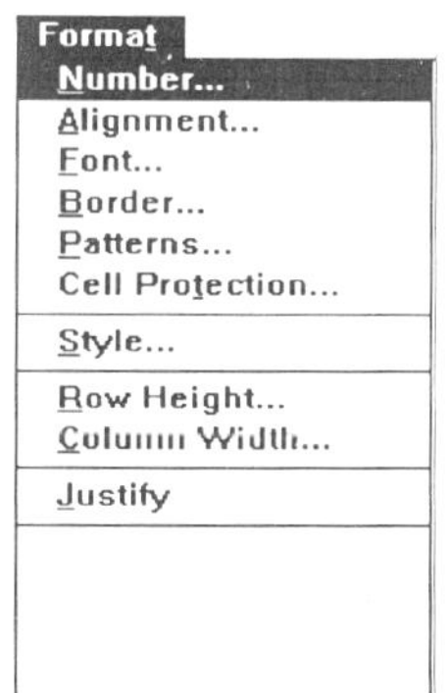

Now try a little experiment. Although B14 has no data in it, the cell has been formatted. Enter some data and press Enter. The number is displayed in the new format. Clear the cell before continuing.

Here are some examples of how the predefined pictures can be used to format a particular display:

ENTRY	*PICTURE*	*DISPLAY*
123	0.00	123.00
123.67	0	124

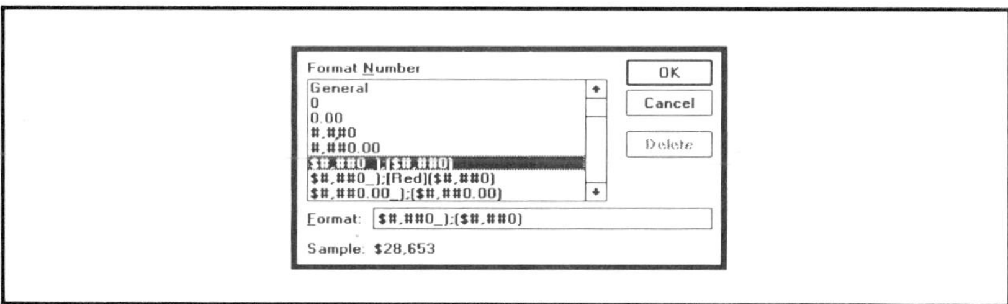

Figure 6.1: Selecting a picture

ENTRY	*PICTURE*	*DISPLAY*
123	$#,##0.00	**$123.00**
.1534	0.00%	15.34%

Most of the pictures are self-explanatory. The only confusing ones are perhaps the percentage picture, which multiplies the entered value by 100; that is, if you enter *.1534* for a picture of **0.00%**, it will be displayed as **15.34%**.

Numeric pictures will not affect the display of a text cell.

3.0

Excel also contains two pictures for displaying fractions: # ?/? and # ??/??. The first allows only single-digit numerators and denominators; the second allows double-digit ones as well. For example, if you were to enter *0.53* in a cell that was formatted as # ?/?, the cell would read 1/2; but if it were formatted as # ??/??, it would read 44/83, a more accurate approximation of 0.53.

Defining New Pictures

Instead of using a predefined picture, you can create your own. For example, if you need to enter social security numbers, you can define a picture that automatically puts in the dashes. Other uses for custom pictures include telephone numbers and foreign currencies. You can even create a picture that uses text (such as lbs).

As an example, you can set up a picture that puts No. in front of any number entered into a cell. Follow these steps:

1. Select a blank cell or cell range on the screen, such as C14.
2. Open the Format menu and choose Number. Clear the text box at the bottom of the dialog box.
3. In the text box, enter **"No."####** (include the quotation marks). Then choose OK.

Enter a few numbers to the cell and see what happens. Remember that only the cell that you selected has been formatted.

Now that you have defined this new picture for the Balance worksheet, it will appear as one of your choices in the Format Number dialog box that is displayed when this worksheet is active. You can easily format other cells using the new picture by simply selecting it from the dialog box. However, the new picture that you define for *this* particular worksheet will not be available for other worksheets unless you either enter it into the Format Number dialog box when you're formatting that worksheet or make it part of a template.

You can use an asterisk in a picture to define a repeating character, following it with a character that you want to be repeated as often as necessary to fill the blank space in the cell. For example, the picture ##,##0.00*@ would display $123.23 as 123.23@@, with the @ symbol filling the rest of the cell. This is useful for printing a check in which the entire check-amount box must be filled.

Table 6.1 lists the symbols that you can use for creating your pictures. You can delete pictures from the Format Number dialog box by selecting the format you want to remove and clicking the Delete button.

Table 6.1: Symbols Used for Creating Pictures

SYMBOL	MEANING
0	Picture for a single numeric digit. If the entry has fewer digits on either side of the decimal point than the picture does, Excel displays the extra zeros. If the entry has more zeros to the right of the decimal than the picture does, Excel rounds the entry to the number of places in the picture. If the entry has more digits to the left of the decimal than the picture does, the extra digits are displayed. Example: Picture: 0.0; Entry: .8; Displayed: 0.8
#	Picture for a single numeric digit. Follows the rules for 0 above, except extra zeros are not displayed to the right and left of the decimal. Example: Picture #.#; Entry: .8; Displayed: .8
.	Decimal point. Use in conjunction with either the 0 or # symbol

Table 6.1: Symbols Used for Creating Pictures (continued)

SYMBOL	MEANING
%	Multiply by 100 and add a percent sign
,	Thousands separator. Thousands are separated by commas if this is included in the picture surrounded by #s or 0s. A comma following a # or 0 scales the number by a thousand; two commas by a million
E –, E +, e –, e +	Scientific format notation
?	Display numeric digit, omitting zeros
:, $, –, +, (,), /, *space*	Display the character. To display a character not shown here, precede it with a backslash (\)
@	Text placeholder. Text entered in the cell is placed in the format wherever the @ appears. Example: Picture: @ + @; Entry: *text*; Displayed: *text* + *text*
_ (underline)	Skip width of next character
*	Repeat next character to fill column width
m, mm, mmm, mmmm	Display the month in number format without leading zeros
d, dd, ddd, dddd	Display the day without leading zeros
yy, yyyy	Display the year
h, hh	Display the hour without leading zeros
m, mm	Display minutes without leading zeros (must be after hours)
s, ss	Display seconds without leading zeros (must be after minutes)
AM, PM, A, P	Display hour using 12-hour clock with AM or PM

Table 6.1: Symbols Used for Creating Pictures (continued)

SYMBOL	MEANING
dddd	Display day of week
text	Displays *text*
[*color*]	Displays all contents in *color* (black, blue, cyan, etc.)

Notes:
1. Two pictures can be entered for a cell separated by a colon(s). With one colon, the first applies to positive numbers and the second to negative. If you use two colons, the third picture will be applied to numbers equal to zero.
2. If you do not want negative numbers displayed, enter the format for positive numbers followed by a semicolon. If you do not want any numbers displayed, use two semicolons.

You also can create new pictures from existing ones. When the dialog box is displayed, the current picture is shown in the Format box. You can click in it and edit the format as you wish. When you choose OK, the cell or range will be formatted to the new picture. The new picture will be added to the end of the picture list as well, for use later on. For example, you could add a new fraction format by highlighting # ??/?? and editing it to show # ???/???. (In that case, 0.53 would be formatted in the cell as 53/100.)

To delete a custom picture, highlight it and click Delete in the Format Number dialog box. You cannot delete a predefined picture.

If you examine the pictures in the list box, you will see that some of them consist of multiple pictures that are separated by a semicolon, such as:

```
$#,##0.00_);($#,##0.00)
```

These are conditional pictures. Here the first picture ($#,##0.00_)) is used for positive numbers and the second for negative numbers (see Table 6.1). You also can create conditional custom pictures.

Another way to format cells is to use a shortcut command. Here are the keys for the common formats:

PICTURE	*KEYSTROKE*
General	Ctrl-~
#,##0.00	Ctrl-!
h:mm AM/PM	Ctrl-@
d-mmm-yy	Ctrl-#
$#,##0.00_);($#,##0.00)	Ctrl-$
0%	Ctrl-%
0.00E+00	Ctrl-^

Select the cell or cell range and enter the keystroke to format it instantly.

ALIGNMENT

Alignment refers to the position of the value in a cell. Excel offers you a choice of five alignments:

- **General,** which left-justifies text and right-justifies numbers
- **Left,** which left-justifies all entries (numbers, dates, and text)
- **Right,** which right-justifies all entries
- **Center,** which centers each entry
- **Fill,** which repeats the entry until the cell is filled

To align row headings (text) with the data below them (numbers), keep the numbers right-aligned and realign the text. If necessary, insert spaces for column alignment.

When you first start Excel, all cells are set to General alignment. To change the alignment of text or numbers, first select the cell or cell range that you want to realign, open the Format menu and choose Alignment. The dialog box shown in Figure 6.2 appears. Choose the alignment that you want and click OK.

In the default mode, if a long text string doesn't fit in a cell the cell will show only a small portion of the text if the cells to the right (when left-justified) or left (when right-justified) are in use. If you select

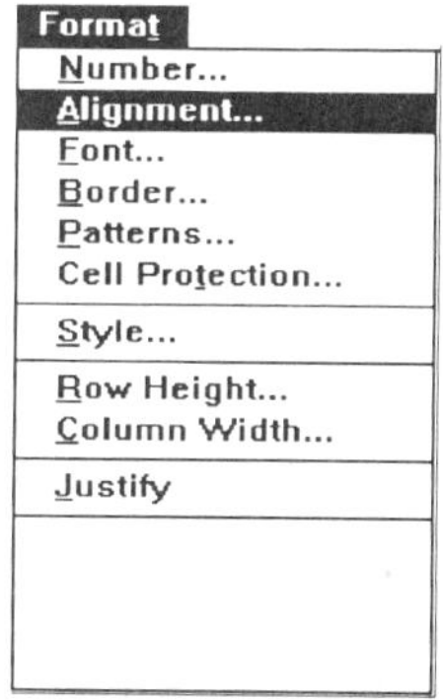

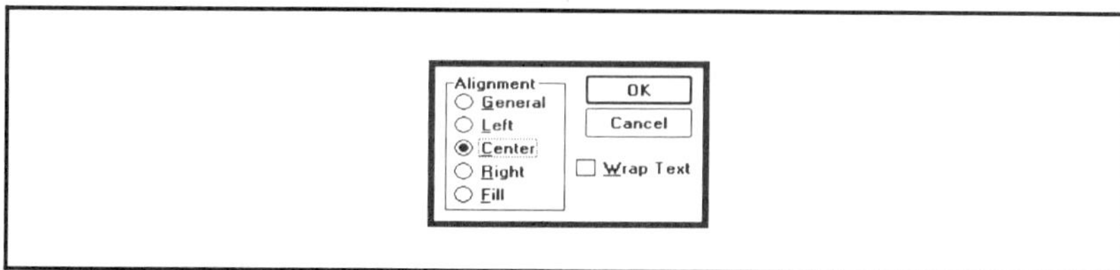

Figure 6.2: Choosing the alignment

Wrap Text in the Alignment dialog box, the entire text string will be displayed: it will be wrapped over adjacent lines to fit in the cell, and the row height will increase to accommodate the wrapped text.

To center the information at the top of your Balance worksheet, follow these steps:

1. Select cells A1 through E6 by dragging.
2. Open the Format menu and choose Alignment.
3. Choose Center and click OK.

All the text in the selected cell range is now centered.

CHOOSING THE FONT

The term *font* refers to four aspects of the cell display: family, size, style, and color. The first is the actual design of the characters, which is known as the family. Typical family names include Helvetica, Times-Roman, Prestige, and Courier. The second aspect, size, is the actual height of the characters measured in points. An inch is 72 points. Courier is normally 12 points and Prestige is 10 points. The third aspect is the style, whether the character is displayed as normal, bold-faced, or in italics. Color is the color of the text.

Fonts for Printing and Displaying

Which families, sizes, and styles are available depends on your printer and how it is installed (see Chapter 17). Excel permits you to select up to 255 fonts (i.e., family/size/style combinations) for any one worksheet. Moreover, you can define these fonts at the cell level.

Remember that printing and displaying are controlled from Windows, not from Excel. For example, to add large-size soft fonts, you have to use the Control Panel of Windows.

Changing the Font

For very small text (6 points on a Hewlett-Packard LaserJet), use the Modern font.

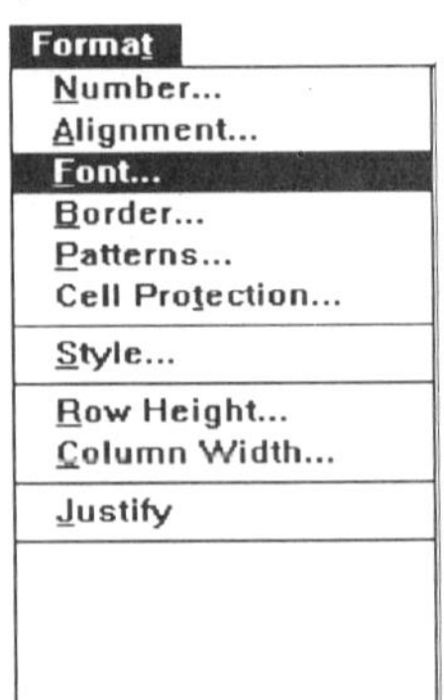

Cells or cell ranges can be displayed in any installed font if it is available to your printer. To change the font, select the cell or cell range that you want to display in the different font. Open the Format menu and choose Font. The Font dialog box shown in Figure 6.3 appears. Choose the desired font, style, and color. An example of the highlighted font appears in the Sample box. If Printer Fonts is selected, the list shows only those fonts currently available for your printer. If this is not selected, the list shows the display fonts available. Clicking Normal Font sets the default font, currently Helvetica, at 10 points. When you've made your selection, click OK.

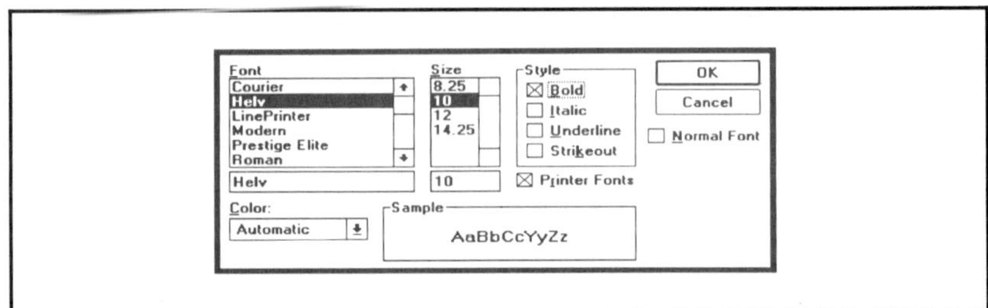

Figure 6.3: Changing the font

Choose Repeat Font under the Edit menu (Alt–Enter) to repeat a font setting in another cell or range, or select Undo Font under the Edit menu (or Alt–Backspace) to reverse a font selection. Save font settings as styles and select them from the tool bar or the Style option under the Format menu (see "Using Styles" below).

Setting Up Your Worksheet

Now you can change the fonts on part of your Balance worksheet. The title should be in boldface, as well as the Total Assets and Total Liabilities & Equity rows. Follow these steps:

1. Select cell B1 to select the title.

2. Open the Format menu and choose Font.
3. Select Helvetica, size 10, and style Bold. Then click OK.
4. Select A26 to E26. Press Shift–F8 and click A42 to E42. Press Shift–F8 again. Both rows are now highlighted.
5. Open the Format menu and choose Font.
6. Select Helvetica, size 10, and style Bold, then click OK.

When formatting, remember that the format information requires memory space. Instead of formatting an entire row, from column A to IV, format only the cells in use.

After the formatting, the totals in row 42 may overflow (depending on your monitor). If they do, change the column width to 10 by selecting columns B to E, opening the Format menu, choosing Column Width, and entering **10**. Choose OK.

The total assets on your Balance worksheet now stand out from the rest of the entries, as shown in Figure 6.4.

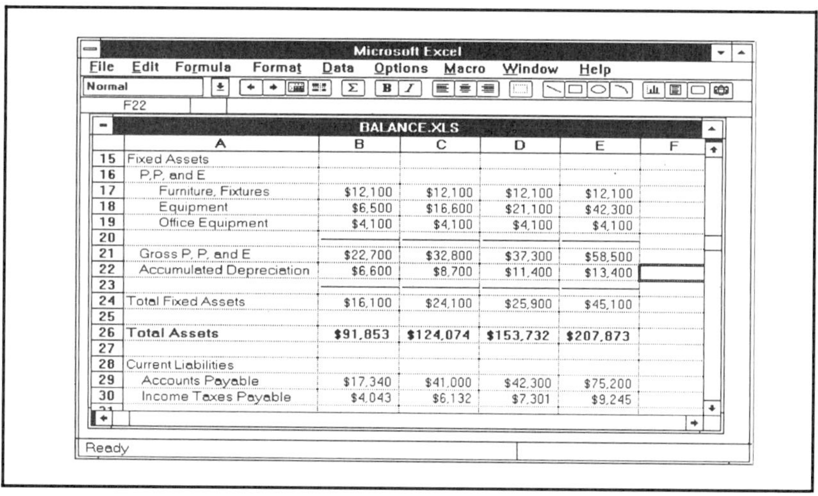

Figure 6.4: Boldfacing the total assets

DEFINING THE ROW HEIGHT

Excel defaults to an automatic row height that is slightly more than the height of the largest font used on the line. As you change the size of your text, the row height will automatically change. For example, if you type a worksheet title in a 16 point font, the cell height will increase accordingly to accommodate it.

Excel will maintain a minimum height to accommodate row headings.

You also can set this height directly. For example, small rows are useful for adding white space between rows when improving the image of the worksheet. Try this on the Balance worksheet:

1. Select row 5.
2. Choose Row Height from the Format dialog box (Figure 6.5).
3. Type in **16** as the new height (16 points) and click OK.

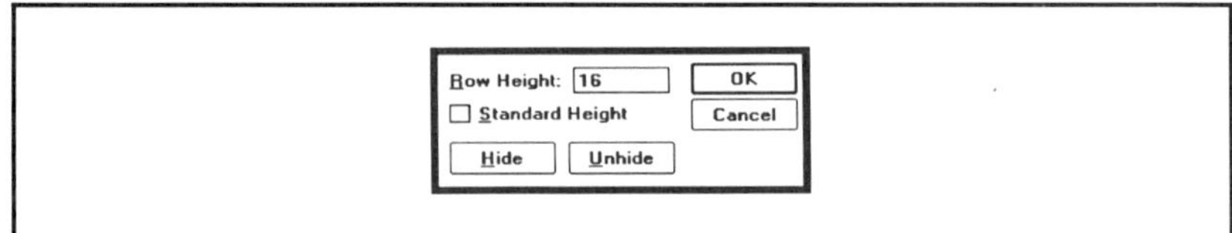

Figure 6.5: Changing the row height

ADDING BORDERS

You may wish to add a border to parts of the worksheet display or printout to make it easier to read. To add a border, first turn off the grid lines using the Display command on the Options menu, as described in "Displaying Grid Lines" below. (If the grid lines are not turned off, you will have a hard time seeing the borders on the display.) Next, select the cell or range of cells that you want to border. Open the Format menu and choose Border. When the Border dialog box shown in Figure 6.6 appears, select one or more options, then

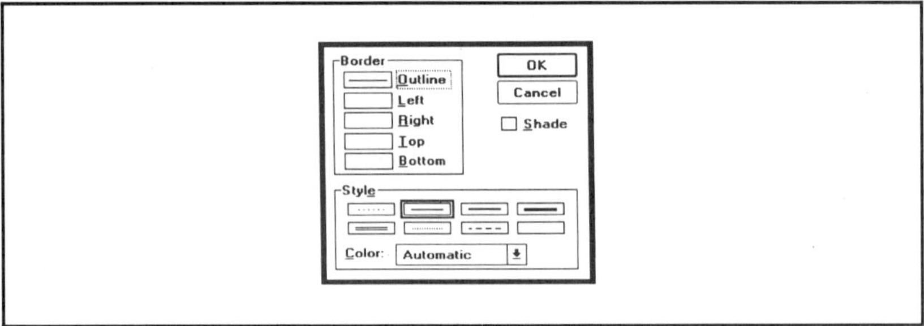

Figure 6.6: Selecting a border

click OK. Notice that you can select which edges of the range to border, the style, and the color. You also can choose to shade the cell range.

Excel offers these choices for borders:

- **Outline** outlines the entire range with a border
- **Left** draws a vertical line at the left of each cell
- **Right** draws a vertical line at the right of each cell
- **Top** draws a horizontal line at the top of each cell
- **Bottom** draws a horizontal line at the bottom of each cell
- **Shade** shades every cell in the range
- **Style** sets the style for the border line
- **Color** sets the color of the border

3.0

You can choose one or more of these border options for the selected cells. The added borders appear on both the screen display and the printed worksheet. By using a combination of styles and borders, you can emphasize any value on your worksheet. Figure 4.1 in Chapter 4 shows how bordering can be used effectively.

Now you can put the borders shown in Figure 4.1 on your Balance worksheet (be sure that the grid lines are turned off, or you will not be able to see them):

1. Select cell A8.
2. Open the Formula menu and choose Goto (or press F5). Enter **E42** into the Reference box. Hold down the Shift key and choose OK. You have selected cells A8 through E42.
3. Open the Format menu and choose Border. In the dialog box, choose Outline. Click OK.
4. In the same way, select cells A26 to E26 and put a border around them using Outline and Shade. (Some check boxes on the Format Border dialog box will be shaded now before you check them. This indicates that some cells in the range already have some type of border.)

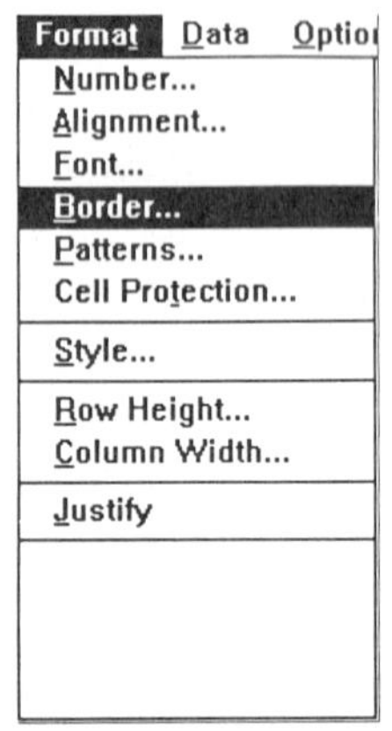

5. In the same way, put a border around cells A42 to E42 using Outline and Shade.
6. Select the range B8 to E42 and put a border around it using Left (but no Shade).

Your worksheet should now show borders and shading.

Borders are useful for dividing your worksheet into areas to draw attention to specific cell ranges. You also can use them to create tables, calendars, and forms.

To create a double underline under a row, first insert a blank row under the row you wish to underline. Put top and bottom borders on the blank row. Use the Row Height command under the Format menu to set the height of the blank row as desired. Another alternative is to select the double-underline style from the Border dialog box.

USING STYLES

Excel provides another option for quickly setting styles. A *style* is a collected set of attributes with a defined name. Each style has six attributes: picture, font, border, pattern, alignment, and protection. Once you have defined a style, it's easy to use: simply click it from the style box in the tool bar or choose Style from the Format menu. All six attributes of the style are then applied to any cell or range selected. Excel has four default styles.

Styles are attached to worksheets. You can, however, save styles in templates or copy them from one worksheet to another.

3.0

DEFINING A STYLE

You can create additional styles, if you wish, by using any of three methods: by example from an existing cell, by defining it from the Style command, or by copying it from another worksheet.

To define a style by example, first make active the cell that contains the style attributes you wish to use. If you have a mouse and are using the tool bar, move the cursor to the style box and enter the name you wish to assign to the style. An alternative after selecting the cell is to choose Style from the Format menu and enter the name to assign to the style (see Figure 6.7). It will now appear on the pull-down list for use with other cells.

To create a style by definition, select the cell to format and choose Style from the Format menu. Then click the Define button in the dialog box. In the next dialog box (see Figure 6.8), enter the name for the style. You also will see six buttons at the bottom, one for each attribute: number (picture), font, alignment, border, pattern, and protection. Choose from any of these buttons to open the appropriate dialog box to define that attribute. Define each attribute as you wish and click OK to close the dialog box. If you are adding several styles, keep the dialog box open by clicking Add after defining each one.

To copy a style from one document to another, first open both documents and make the destination document active. Choose Style under the Format menu. Select Define in the dialog box and Merge in the next. From the displayed list box, select the source document name. Choose OK, then Close.

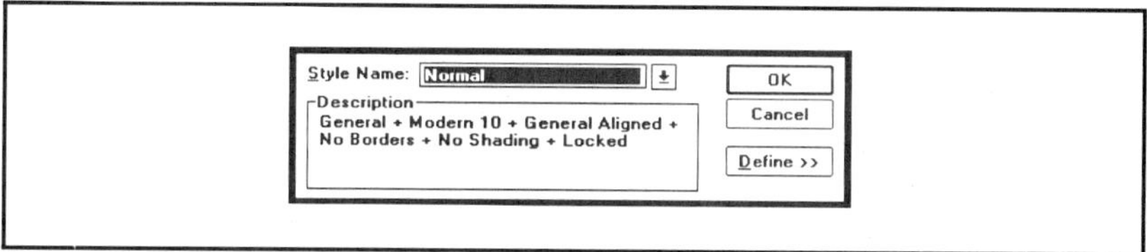

Figure 6.7: Defining a style

Figure 6.8: Naming a style

EDITING A STYLE

You can edit a style by example or definition. To edit by example, select the cell to contain the new format, format it, and reapply the style name from the tool bar (or the Style command under the Format menu). In the prompt box, answer Yes. To edit by definition, select the Style command, choose Define in the dialog box, and edit the appropriate attribute.

DISPLAYING WORKSHEET FEATURES

The Display command under the Options menu is used to display grid lines, column and row designators, and formulas.

DISPLAYING GRID LINES

On the worksheet, cells are separated by vertical and horizontal grid lines. However, you may want to turn these off to see how a worksheet looks without them.

To turn off the grid lines on-screen:

1. Open the Options menu and choose Display. The Display dialog box shown in Figure 6.9 appears.
2. Select Gridlines to remove the × in the box next to it, then click OK.

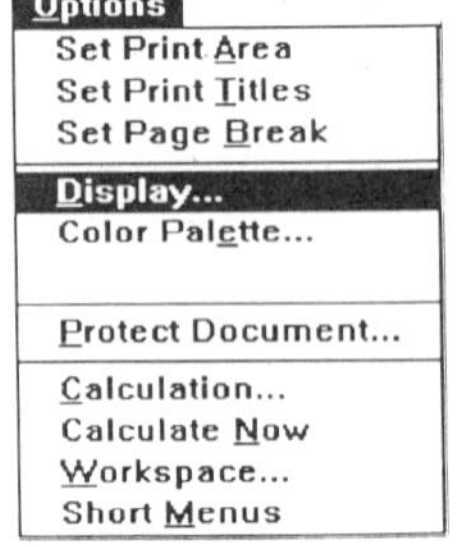

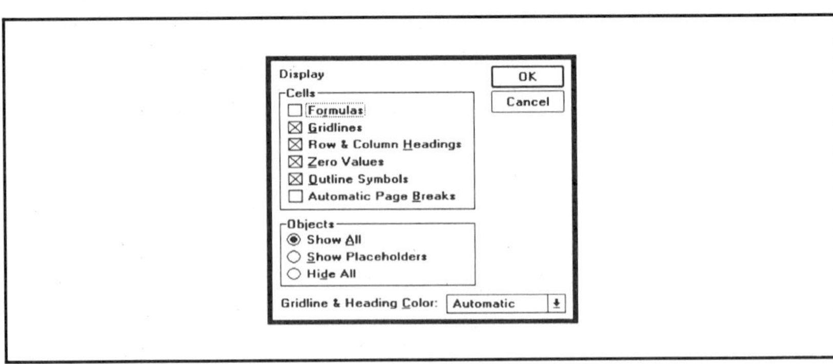

Figure 6.9: The Display dialog box

The Gridlines option is a toggle that switches the grid-line display on and off. (If there is an × next to it, the option is on; if not, it is off.) However, even if you toggle the Gridlines option off, the grid lines will still be printed. This dialog box controls only the *screen display* of the grid lines, not the printed display.

To print a worksheet without grid lines, you have to use the Page Setup command on the File menu. Follow these steps:

1. Open the File menu and choose Page Setup.
2. The Page Setup dialog box shown in Figure 6.10 appears. Click Gridlines to remove the × in the box next to that option, if it is there (it isn't by default).
3. Click OK.

Grid lines may still appear on the screen while you work with the worksheet (depending on whether you turned them on as detailed above), but they will not show on the printed copy.

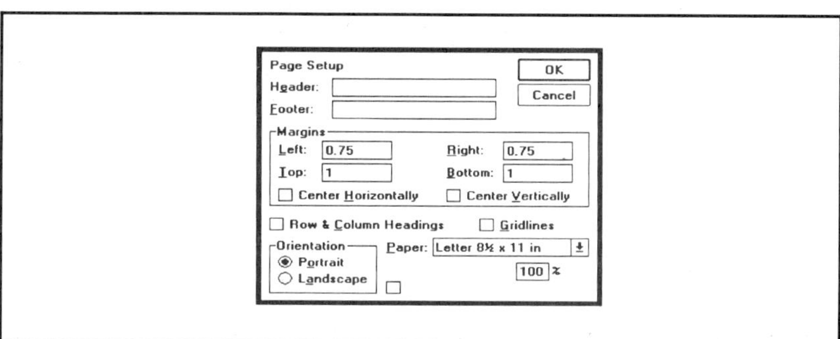

Figure 6.10: The Page Setup dialog box

DISPLAYING DESIGNATORS

At the top of each column is a column designator—A, B, C, and so on to IV. At the left edge are the row designators, numbered from 1 to 16,384. As with the grid lines, you can turn these off so that they don't appear on the worksheet on-screen. To do so:

1. Open the Options menu and choose Display.

2. When the Display dialog box appears (see Figure 6.9), choose Row & Column Headings (another toggle) and click OK.

This removes the × in the box next to that option. Remember, the Display dialog box options control only the screen display, not the printed output.

To eliminate the designators from the printed worksheet, you must use the Page Setup command on the File menu. Follow these steps:

1. Open the File menu and choose Page Setup.
2. When the Page Setup dialog box appears (see Figure 6.10), choose Row & Column Headings. This removes the × in the box next to that option. Click OK.

Row and column headings may still be displayed on the screen, but you won't see them on the printed worksheet.

DISPLAYING FORMULAS

There may be times when you need to see the formulas associated with a particular worksheet. To display formulas:

1. Open the Options menu and choose Display.
2. When the Display dialog box (see Figure 6.9) appears, choose Formulas and then click OK.

The screen display will then show the formulas. Each column will now be twice as wide as it was in your normal display to permit room for the formulas. You can switch the display off by repeating this operation.

If the formulas appear on-screen, they will print out as well.

HIDING A COLUMN OR ROW

There may be times when you want to hide a column on a worksheet so that it is not displayed or printed. This reduces visual clutter and can hide temporary work-area cells.

HIDING A COLUMN

To hide a column, first select it. Then choose Column Width from the Format menu. Choose Hide. The column will disappear from the worksheet.

To recover a column, select a column on either side of where it used to be. Select Column Width again from the Format menu and choose Unhide.

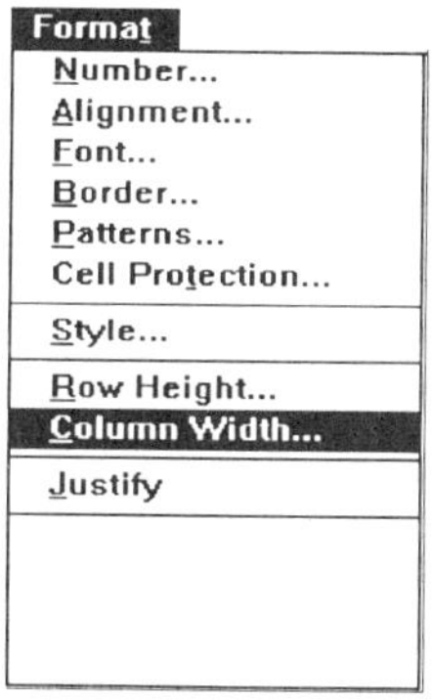

Format
Number...
Alignment...
Font...
Border...
Patterns...
Cell Protection...
Style...
Row Height...
Column Width...
Justify

HIDING A ROW

To hide a row, follow the same procedure as above, but choose the Row Height command under the Format menu. Click the Hide button on this dialog box. To recover the row, select a row on either side of where it used to be and click the Unhide button.

WORKING WITH GRAPHIC OBJECTS

If you have a mouse, you can add graphic objects to a worksheet or macro sheet to improve its appearance. You can create graphic worksheet documents such as calendars, forms, and organization charts with Excel graphic objects. Use the underlying cells as a grid.

CREATING OBJECTS

The basic strategy for creating graphic objects is to define the object to be created using the tool bar, draw it on the worksheet, edit it, and format it.

Let's add a text box for the title of the Balance worksheet and put it in a shadow box:

1. Delete the current title by clearing B1 to D4. Insert two more rows before row 1 to give more working space.
2. Create a text box by clicking the text-box tool in the tool bar. Click the cursor near the upper-left corner of cell B1 and drag it to the lower-right corner of cell E6.
3. Move the box to center it. Be sure the box is selected. To select an object, move the tip of the mouse cursor over the

object and click it. When an object is selected it has handles on it, which are small black rectangles attached to an invisible frame. The object identifier is also displayed in the active-cell designator.

4. Drag the box so the left edge is halfway into column A (see Figure 6.11).
5. Create the title text by placing the cursor near the upper left of the box. Press Enter (to make a space at the top) and type the first title line (see Figure 6.12). Press Enter twice, then enter the next two title lines.
6. Click and drag the cursor to highlight all three lines, then select the Center Alignment button from the tool bar. Highlight the first line and select the Bold button from the tool bar.
7. Add the shadow: select the box and choose Pattern from the Format menu. Choose Shadow and click OK.

You now have the title in a text box.

As you have seen, creating graphics involves selecting the object tool from the tool bar and creating the object on the worksheet. Here

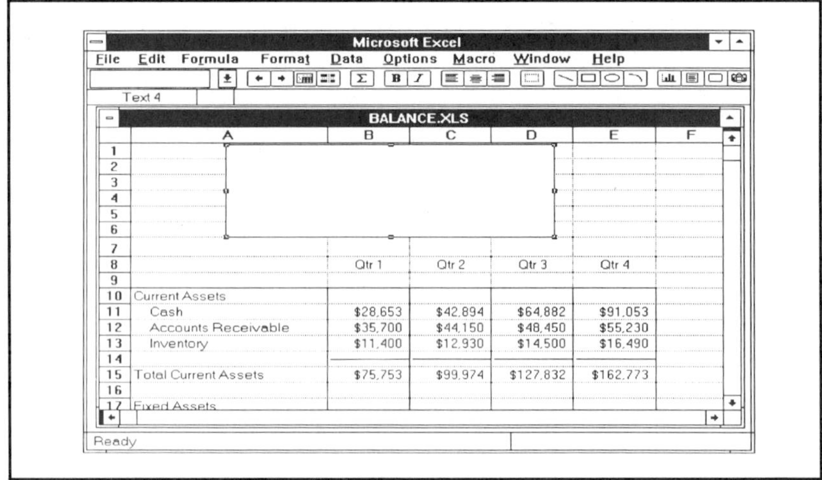

Figure 6.11: Positioning the text box

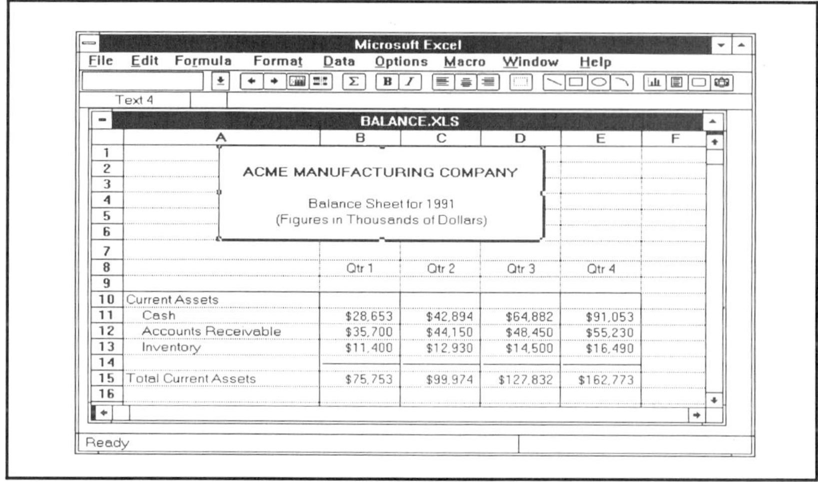

Figure 6.12: The final title box

are the basic rules:

- Select the tool. You can choose from lines, rectangles, ovals, arcs, and text boxes. Choose the tool you wish to use from the tool bar and move the cursor to the worksheet
- Click and drag the cursor to create the object. When you release the mouse button, the graphic is marked with handles for moving and sizing, and the mouse pointer changes. The tool bar icon returns to normal. To create multiple objects with the same tool, hold down the Ctrl key as you click the tool. Click the tool again when you are through
- To align a graphic object with the grid lines, hold down the Ctrl key as you draw, move, or resize an object
- When you use the arc tool, Excel draws a curve that is a quarter of an oval
- If you hold down the Shift key while drawing, lines are restricted to being vertical, horizontal, or at a 45-degree angle. The Oval button makes circles and the Rectangle button makes squares
- You can create complex objects by combining simple ones. Select the set of objects and choose Group from the Format menu; then you can resize or move the objects as a group.

To release a group, highlight it and choose Ungroup from the Format menu

- You can hide or show the tool bar by pressing Ctrl–7
- You can import graphic objects for pasting using the Clipboard. Copy the object to the Clipboard from another program, and paste it into the worksheet. You also can use the Paste Link command, found under the Edit menu, to paste objects. With this command, the object remains linked to the supporting document and changes when editing it (see Chapter 16)
- You can cancel a task at any time by pressing Esc

EDITING OBJECTS

To edit an object, first select it. To select multiple objects, hold down the Shift key and select the objects. Another way to select multiple objects is to use the selection tool. Click the tool, then draw a rectangle that completely encloses all the objects you wish to select.

To select all objects in the worksheet, choose Select Special from the Formula menu, choose Objects, and click OK.

The following commands can be used after selecting an object:

- To change the order of objects so that you can work with covered objects, use the Bring to Front or Send to Back commands on the Format menu
- To release objects from their underlying grid, use the Object Placement command on the Format menu
- To deselect an object in a group, hold down the Shift key and click the object
- To move an object, place the pointer on the object so that it is an arrow. Then drag to the new position. You also can group objects and move them as a group using the Group command on the Format menu
- To resize an object, drag a handle. The pointer must be a crosshair. To keep the object proportional, hold down the Shift key when dragging

- To align to grid, hold down the Ctrl key while dragging. You also can group objects and resize as a group using the Group command
- You also can use the Edit menu to cut or copy a graphic, even to another program
- You can change the pattern of a selected object with the Pattern command on the Format menu
- You can format the object (including fill and foreground colors) using the Patterns command. For example, you can add arrowheads to lines or shadows to boxes
- You can lock an object with the Object Protection command so that it cannot be selected, moved, resized, or formatted
- You can speed up your worksheet work by hiding objects. To hide an object, use the Display command in the Options menu and select Hide All, or use Ctrl-6 as a shortcut. Ctrl-6 toggles among showing Objects, Placeholders, and Hide All

DELETING OBJECTS

To delete an object, select the object and use the Cut command under the Edit menu (which places it on the Clipboard). Another method is to use the Del key.

THE FINAL BALANCE WORKSHEET

If you followed along with the examples in this chapter, you have done the following with your Balance worksheet:

- Put the first line of the title in boldface print
- Centered all column headings
- Put rows 26 and 42 in boldface

- Turned off the grid lines and row and column designators in the printout
- Added borders, shading cells in rows 26 and 42

Your final printout should look like Figure 4.2.

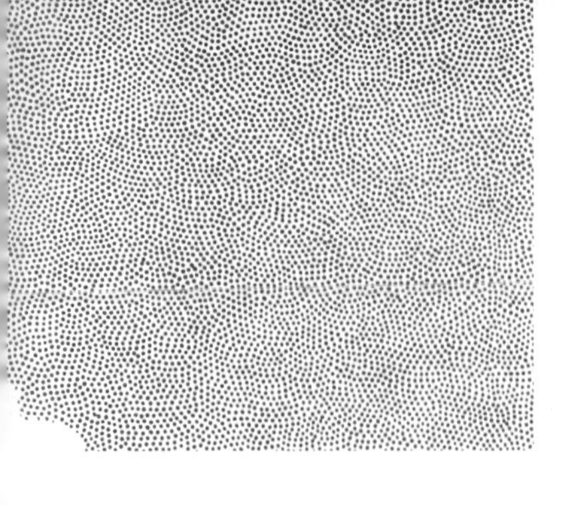
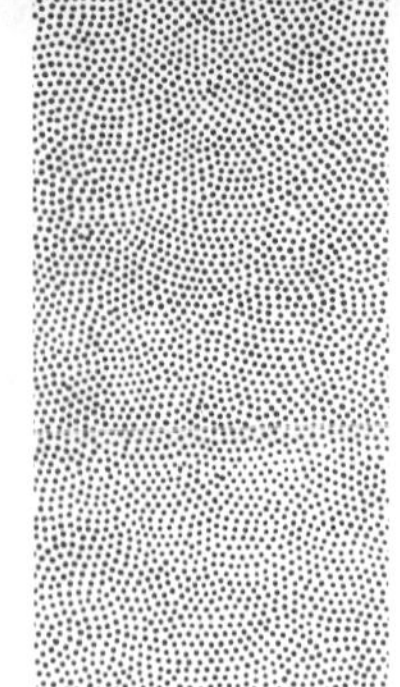

7 Managing Documents and Windows

THE WORKSHEET DOCUMENT IS ALWAYS DISPLAYED AS a window. With Excel, you can have several windows displayed simultaneously. Because you create and edit all documents in their respective windows, learning how to control windows is an important part of managing your worksheets. In this chapter, you will learn some special Excel file and window-management techniques. You will learn more about:

- Opening, closing, renaming, and deleting document files
- Setting up workgroups
- Setting up workspaces
- Using automatic startup files
- Protecting document files
- Switching between windows
- Opening additional windows in the same document
- Creating panes in a window for entering data into large worksheets

- Tiling windows
- Hiding windows
- Customizing window colors

Besides worksheets, windows display almost any type of Excel data: charts, databases, templates—even macros. The basic window-management commands apply to any type of Excel document. You can scroll a window using the scroll bars, move a window by dragging its title bar, and resize a window by dragging the lower-right corner of the window. Experiment with some existing worksheets for the next few sections.

CONTROLLING DOCUMENTS

As you are working with Excel, you will need to open, close, and delete documents. Worksheets, templates, charts, and macro sheets are saved as document files.

OPENING DOCUMENT FILES

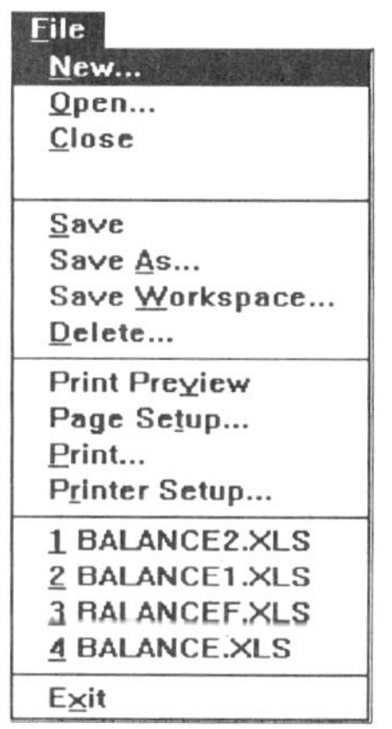

To create a new document, open the File menu and choose New. The New dialog box shown in Figure 7.1 will appear. As this figure shows, Worksheet is already selected as the type of document. To create a new worksheet, choose OK. Excel displays a blank worksheet titled "Sheet1". (If a worksheet with this title is already open, the new document will be called "Sheet2".)

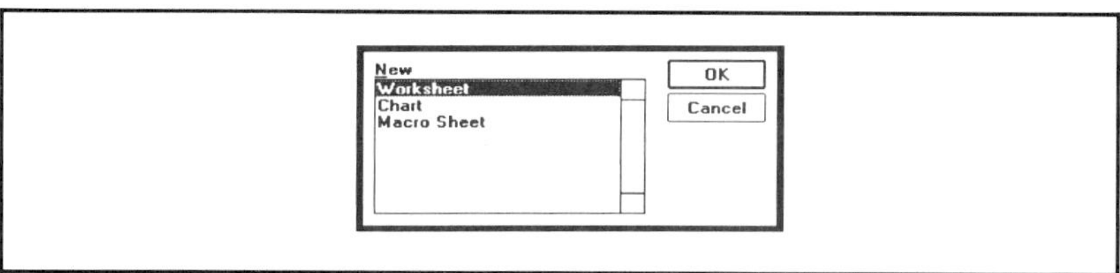

Figure 7.1: Creating a new worksheet

The following shortcuts can be used when creating a new document:

DOCUMENT TYPE	*SHORTCUT*
Worksheet	Shift–F11
Chart	F11
Macro sheet	Ctrl–F11

To open a document that you have already created and stored on disk, open the File menu and choose Open (or press Ctrl–F12). The dialog box shown in Figure 7.2 will appear. The left list box shows the names of the documents currently on the directory. If you highlight one of these, its name will be shown in the text box next to **File Name**. You can use the scroll bar to list additional documents in the same directory. The name of the current disk and directory is under the text box.

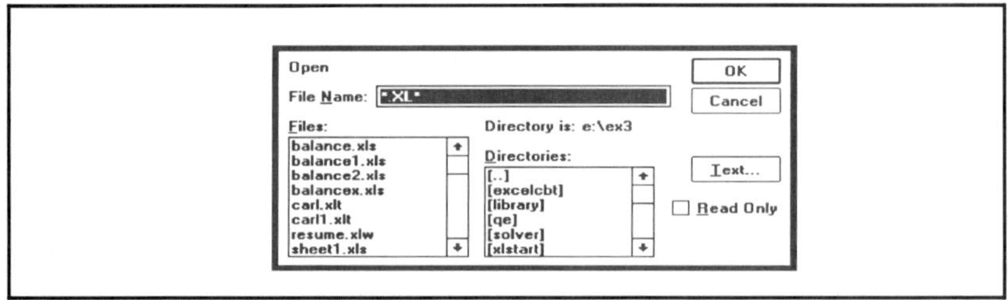

Figure 7.2: Opening an existing worksheet

If the desired document name is displayed, you can complete the command either by double-clicking the document name or by highlighting the name and clicking OK.

If the document name is not in the current directory, you must switch to the correct disk drive and directory in the right list box that contains the file:

- To change the drive, choose the corresponding drive letter in the Directories list box and click OK (or double-click the drive name)

- To change to a subdirectory, choose the corresponding subdirectory name in the Directories list box and click OK (or double-click the name)
- To move up the directory tree, choose the double-periods at the top of the Directories list box and click OK (or double-click them)

The Files list box always displays the files in the directory selected at right. Choose the file and click OK, or double-click the file name.

Alternatively, if you wish to specify the file name directly, you can click within the text box. The cursor will change to indicate an insertion point. Enter the name of the file, including its path name and extension.

Notice that you can use wildcard file names in the text box to control the file list display. The default text box contains *.XL*, which limits the display to Excel document files (worksheets, charts, macro sheets, templates, and workspaces). To load a foreign file (Lotus 1-2-3, dBASE IV, Multiplan, etc.), simply edit the text box so that the foreign file can be listed, select it, and click OK. Excel will load that file and convert it to its own native format (see Chapter 21). Use an asterisk (*) to represent any group of characters and a question mark (?) to represent any single character.

3.0

There is another quick way to load recently used documents. Excel always maintains the names of the latest four documents that have been opened on the File menu, even if you leave Excel. To open any of these again, open the File menu and choose the document name.

Excel allows you to have more than one document open at once. If you are working on a worksheet and need to open another document, open the File menu and choose New or Open. Select the type of document and you will then see the windows for both documents on the screen. The latest loaded window will be on top and active. If you wish to view the windows side-by-side, choose Arrange All from the Window menu.

SAVING AND CLOSING DOCUMENT FILES

Saving a document means saving it on disk. *Closing* a document refers to removing it from the computer screen. When you are finished working with an Excel document, you should close it. Before closing it, however, you may wish to save it so you can use it again. Whenever you close a document that has been changed, Excel will ask whether you wish to save the changes.

Saving Documents

To save a document under the displayed name at the top of the window without exiting Excel:

- Open the File menu and choose Save. The window will remain active. This method is useful for saving the worksheet periodically as you work on it
- Press Alt–Shift–F2 (or Shift–F12). This is the same as using Save

Use any of these methods if you wish to save the document under a *new* name:

- Open the File menu and choose Save As. You will see a dialog box with the current worksheet name, as shown in Figure 7.3. Enter the name you wish to assign to the document. Be sure that the directory assignment shown below the name area is correct. Then click OK. When you create a document, this is normally the way you save it the first time
- Press Alt–F2 (or F12). Enter the name you wish to assign to the document. Be sure that the directory assignment is correct. Then click OK
- Open the File menu and choose Save Workspace. This will save all windows that are currently opened. You will be prompted for a file name, to which the extension .XLW will be added (see "Setting Up Workspaces" later in this chapter). Windows that were displayed will be closed. This is the best way to end a session if you have several windows open and wish to resume with all of them later on

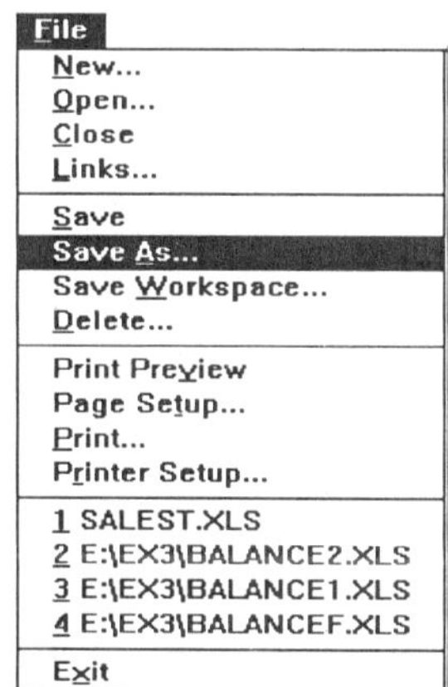

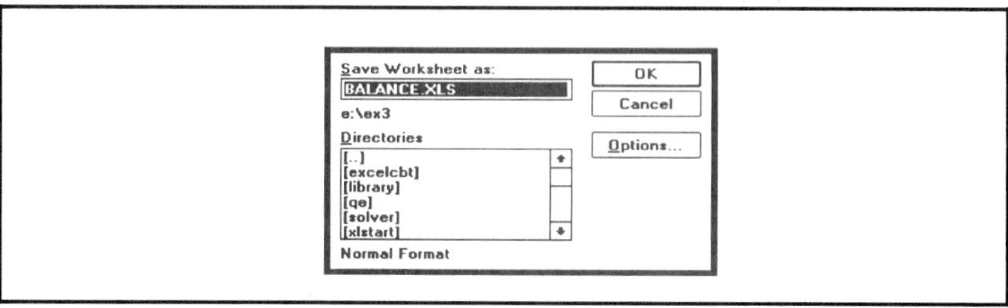

Figure 7.3: Saving a document file

Closing Documents

To close a document and remain in Excel, use any of these methods:

- Double-click the Control-menu box at the left end of the document's title bar. (Be sure to use the *document* Control-menu box, not the Control-menu box of Excel.)
- Press Ctrl–F4
- Open the Control-menu box of the document and choose Close

If the document has been changed in any way since you opened it, Excel will ask whether you wish to save the changes.

You can have several documents open at a time, closing them when you are through. When you close the last document from the document Control menu, or with the Ctrl key, you do not automatically exit Excel. After closing the last window, a short menu bar is displayed with only the File and Help options available. You can use the commands on the File menu to open or create another document. This method is useful if you have finished working with one document and you wish to work on another.

Saving All Documents and Exiting

To save all documents under their current names and exit Excel, use any of these methods:

- Double-click the Excel Control-menu box
- Press Alt–F4

- Open the Excel Control-menu box and choose Close
- Open the File menu and choose Exit

Saving in Other Formats

To save in a database format, you must first define a database range on the worksheet.

You also can save a document under other formats for use with other spreadsheet and database management programs (see Chapter 21). To save in another format, click the Options button in the Save As dialog box. Select the desired format from the pull-down list box (see Figure 7.4). Click OK to return to the Save As dialog box. Click OK again to save the document.

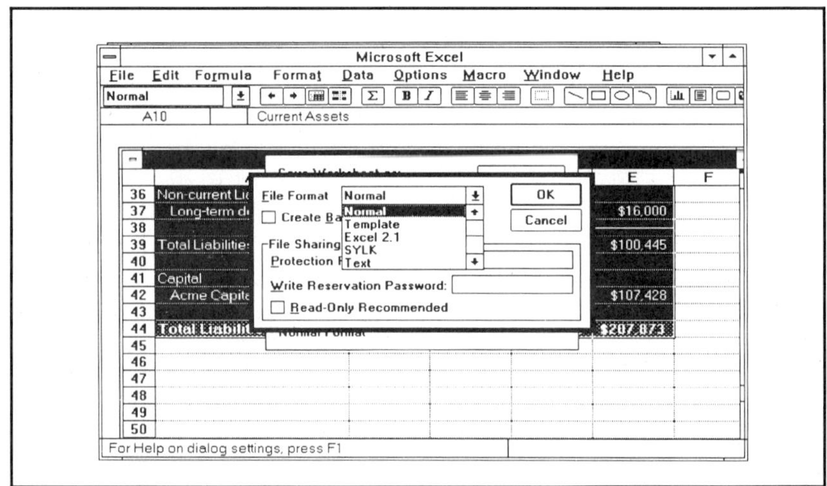

Figure 7.4: Choosing the format

RENAMING DOCUMENT FILES

You cannot change the name of a document that you have already saved using any of the commands under the File menu. To rename a document, you must first exit Excel (double-click the Excel Control-menu box) or minimize Excel to an icon (choose Minimize under the Excel Control menu). Then use the DOS RENAME command (REN for short) or the Windows File Manager to rename the document.

If you inadvertently save a document under a wrong or misspelled name, there is another way to rename it that is quicker than exiting Excel. Use the Save As command under the File menu to save the document under the correct name. Then use the Delete command on the File menu to delete the old document with the incorrect name (see below).

DELETING DOCUMENT FILES

You can't use Excel to undo a file delete. Be sure you really wish to delete the file before clicking that OK button. If you accidently delete the wrong file, exit Excel immediately without saving anything and use an unerase utility (such as Norton Utility by Symantec Corp.) to recover the file.

To delete a document from the disk, open the File menu and choose Delete. You will then see the Delete Document dialog box shown in Figure 7.5. If necessary, scroll to the document that you wish to delete, select its name, and click OK.

Proceed with caution, because you can't undo it. In the default mode (no file name selected), it deletes all files on the current directory (*.*). It's a pretty dangerous command.

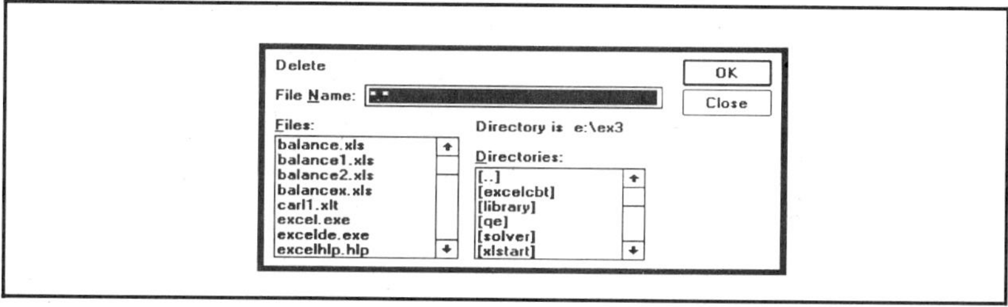

Figure 7.5: Deleting a document file

USING WORKGROUPS

3.0

There may be occasions when you wish to enter the same data or perform the same operation on a set of worksheets. Excel permits you to define the worksheets as a *group* and then use them as if they were a single worksheet.

For example, you might be setting up a group of year-end worksheets and using the same titles and headings for each. You plan to format them differently, and some details of each will differ. You could then create a workgroup out of the worksheets, enter the common data, then release them as individual worksheets for more detailed entry.

To define a workgroup, first load all the worksheets you plan to group. Make the worksheet to which you wish to enter the data active. Choose Workgroup from the Window menu. In the Select Workgroup dialog box, all worksheets that you loaded are selected (see Figure 7.6). If you wish to deselect some of them with the mouse, hold down the Shift key and click each selection. (To deselect from the keyboard, hold down the Ctrl key, press the ↑ and ↓ keys to choose each worksheet, and press the spacebar to toggle the selection in the workgroup off.) Click OK or press Enter.

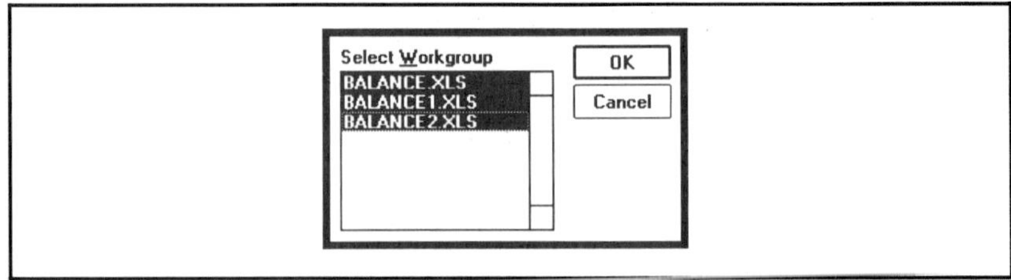

Figure 7.6: Creating a workgroup

To see all worksheets in the group, choose Arrange Workgroup from the Window menu. Only the workgroup is displayed. The title bars indicate the name of the workgroup.

To add or delete a worksheet from a workgroup, repeat the procedure with the Workgroup command again. This is a toggle: selecting a worksheet again will remove it from the group. Whenever you delete or add another file to the workgroup, you have to choose Arrange Workgroup either to get rid of or make room for the window on-screen.

Now enter data to the active worksheet. The same data will be added *at the same place* to each worksheet in the workgroup. If you perform any operation (such as formatting a range), it will be repeated on each worksheet in the workgroup.

To cancel the workgroup press Ctrl–F6.

SETTING UP WORKSPACES

Workspaces permit you to save a set of documents under a specified name. If you are working on several documents at a time, using workspaces is a good way to save the group as a unit and reload the entire set of documents. A workspace differs from a workgroup in that all documents are edited independently. You can define certain options (such as whether to have the tool bar or status bar on or off) and they will be saved with the workspace and restored to that setting when you restart it. You also can hide certain worksheets of the group, which will remain hidden when you load the workspace.

Here are some ways to use workspaces:

- When you are working with a set of documents (worksheets, charts, macro sheets) that support a given application and you wish to define these as a unit
- For linking worksheets (see Chapter 16) so that you don't have to remember the linkages
- When you wish to stop working temporarily on an application with several documents
- As a startup document to set the options for your particular configuration (windows, display mode, calculation mode, etc.)
- To enable someone with no Excel experience to start Excel quickly and use it with a particular application. (This also could require some macros.)

The workspace can be configured by choosing Workspace from the Options menu. This displays a dialog box (see Figure 7.7), which has several available options:

Fixed Decimal determines the number of decimal places in numbers that you enter

R1C1 changes the way that rows and columns are labeled and cells are addressed (so A1 becomes R1C1)

Status Bar displays the status bar

Tool Bar displays the tool bar

Scroll Bars displays the scroll bars

Formula Bar displays the formula bar

Note Indicator displays a dot in the upper-right corner of cells that have notes attached

Alternate Menu or Help Key specifies the key you have to type to activate the Excel menu bar or the Lotus 1-2-3 help system

Alternate Navigation Keys provides an alternate set of keystrokes for navigating the spreadsheet

Ignore Remote Requests controls the response to direct data exchange (DDE) requests (see Chapter 21)

Move Selection after Enter determines whether the cursor moves to the next cell down after you enter a value in a cell

When the desired options are set, click OK. The workspace settings are saved with the document when you save it.

Figure 7.7: Configuring the workspace

If you don't have a mouse, turn the tool bar off. Turning options off leaves more room for the document window (i.e., more rows for the worksheet), but limits editing options.

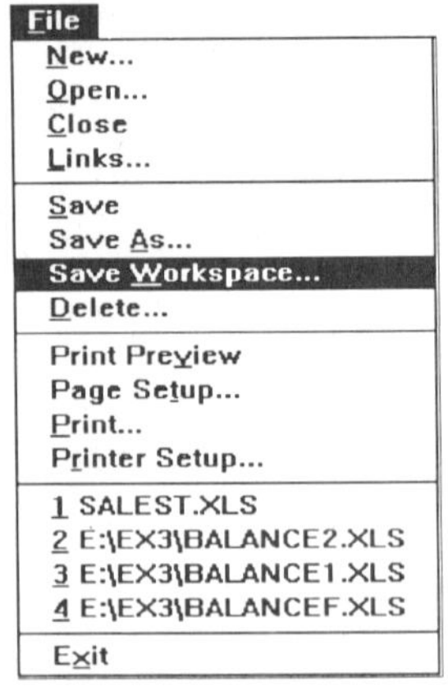

To save a set of worksheets and options as a workspace, choose Save Workspace from the File menu. Enter the document name and click OK. The workspace file is saved with an .XLW extension. Since this also saves the documents, it supersedes the Save command: you will be prompted before saving each document that has been changed. The "workspace" file is really a list of documents. In addition, it saves the following information about each document:

- Position and size of each window
- Options defined by the Workspace command

- Options defined by the Display command
- Menu style (short or full)
- Info window settings shown by the Show Info command
- Global calculation settings (automatic/manual and iteration)
- Preferred chart type (for chart documents)

To restore a workspace, choose Open under the File menu. Choose the file name on the file list (with its .XLW extension) and click OK. All documents that were a part of the workspace will be opened.

You can set up workspaces to open automatically with Excel (see below) or use a macro to start a workspace.

USING STARTUP DOCUMENTS

Excel always opens with Sheet1. This can be modified to start with any document, set of documents, macro, template, or workspace. For example, a bank could write a very complex set of linked documents that are started automatically with Excel. A clerk at a branch office could then use the workspace with very little training, since it would start automatically with Excel and run itself from a macro, prompting as necessary when data needed to be entered.

3.0

Place startup documents in the startup directory called XLSTART (by default), a subdirectory of the Excel directory. For example, if you want the Balance worksheet to open automatically upon starting Excel, place BALANCE.XLS in the startup directory by copying it there with the DOS COPY command. If you place more than one file in the startup directory, they will all come up when you load Excel.

You can change the startup directory using Excel's Setup program. Insert Excel's Setup disk in your drive. Start Setup from the Run command on Windows's File menu, then choose Install Microsoft Excel Using Options. Click the Alternate Startup Directory check box, then click OK. In the Alternate Startup Directory dialog box, type the path name of the desired startup directory. Click OK, then close the Setup program. When you restart Excel, it will start with any document in the new startup directory.

To cancel a startup setup, move the document from the startup directory or delete it altogether.

PROTECTING DOCUMENTS

Excel provides several alternatives for protecting documents from unauthorized access or editing. This prevents someone from using proprietary macros and formulas or editing important worksheets.

PREVENTING UNAUTHORIZED OPENING OR SAVING

To protect a document from unauthorized opening, save the document with a protection password:

1. Make the document activc.
2. Choose Save As on the File menu.
3. Click the Options button in the dialog box.
4. In the Protection Password text box (see Figure 7.8), enter a password.
5. Click OK.
6. In the next dialog box, reenter the password to confirm it.
7. Click OK.

Remember the password. If you forget it, you will never be able to open the document again!

The document is now saved in protected form and can only be opened with the password. If a user tries to open the document, he or she will be prompted for the password.

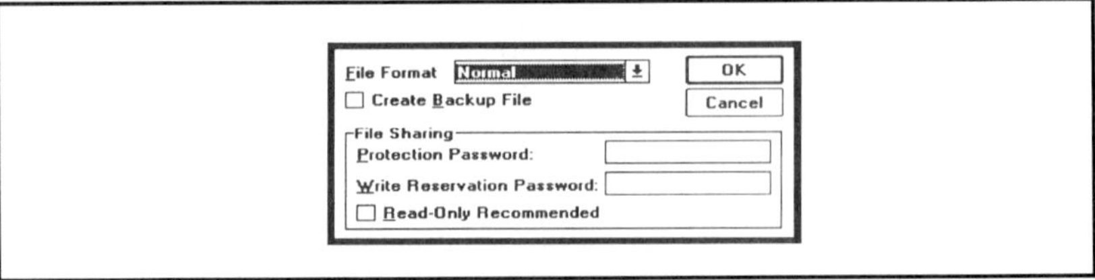

Figure 7.8: Entering a password

If you later wish to remove this protection, use the Save As command again and click the Options button. Delete the password and click OK, then click OK again to close the first dialog box.

PREVENTING UNAUTHORIZED EDITING

There may be times when you wish to make a document available to users without the need for a password, but you wish to protect against unauthorized editing or changes of the document.

To protect against editing:

1. Make the document active.
2. Choose Save As under the File menu.
3. Click the Options button to open the Options dialog box.
4. In the Write Reservation Password text box, enter a password (capitalization counts).
5. Click OK.
6. In the next dialog box, reenter the password to confirm it.
7. Click OK.

To use the document without entering a password, the Read Only box must be checked in the Open dialog box. If it is not, Excel will assume that the user wishes to edit the document and will prompt for the password.

You can cancel this protection by using the Save As command and deleting the password.

There is another read-only mode that is sometimes useful on a network. It recommends to the user who has entered the password that the file should be opened on a read-only basis, unless changes need to be saved. To set this mode, click the Read-Only Recommended box in the Options dialog box described above.

OTHER PROTECTION METHODS

You also can lock or hide individual cell or cell ranges, and protect graphic objects. This is discussed in Chapter 14.

MANAGING DOCUMENT WINDOWS

There may be times when you need to open more than one document window on your screen. Excel's multiple-window feature permits you to view two or more documents at once and to move data from one document to another. The other windows may show other documents or the *same* document, as described later in this section.

The commands under the Edit menu are still available when you have more than one window open, so you can easily move data and formulas between windows. Use the Copy and Paste or Cut and Paste commands, just as if you were working with a single window.

(The linking of worksheets in different windows is discussed in Chapter 16.)

OPENING WINDOWS OF OTHER DOCUMENTS

Any time you are using one window and want to open a second document window, open the File menu and choose Open, just as you did to open the first document. The new document will appear in a new active window. Only one window can be active at a time. You can change the active window by clicking anywhere on the window that you wish to make active. Another way to switch between windows is to open the Window menu and choose the name of the window that you want to make active. The Window menu always lists all the open documents.

OPENING WINDOWS OF THE SAME DOCUMENT

There may be times when you need to open a second window of the same worksheet. Multiple windows are primarily useful with large worksheets in which one part of the worksheet is dependent on another. If you look at both parts at once, you can edit or change values in one part of the worksheet and immediately see the effect in the other window. This reduces the need to scroll through the worksheet excessively. Each window can be controlled independently by using the scroll bars on that window.

Try this now with your Balance worksheet:

1. Open the Balance worksheet with the Open command on the File menu.

2. Make the window smaller (see Figure 7.9) by dragging the lower-right edge of the window.
3. Open the Window menu and choose New Window.
4. When the new window opens, make it smaller, too, as shown in Figure 7.10.

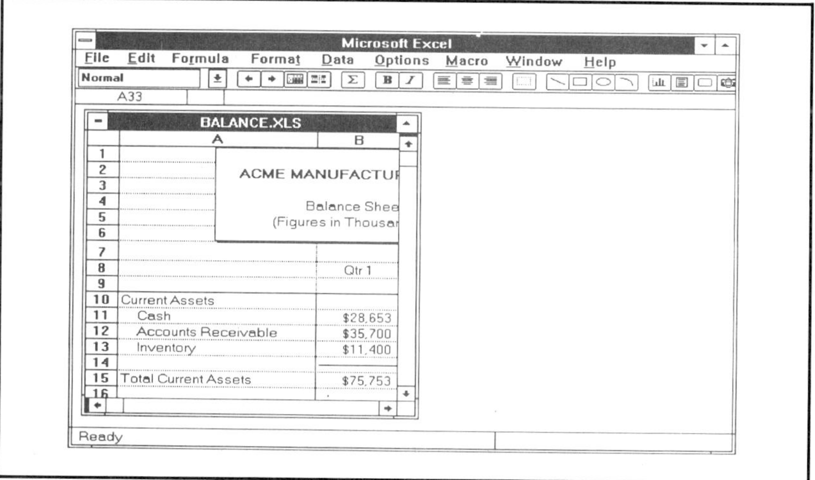

Figure 7.9: Making the window smaller

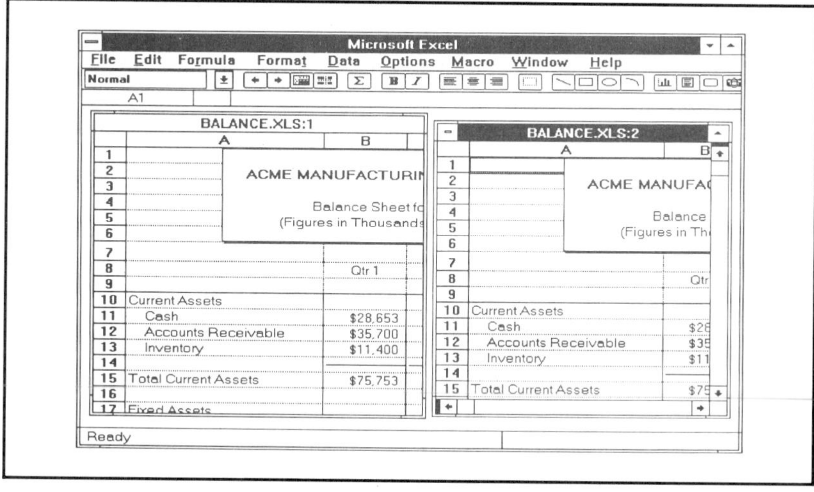

Figure 7.10: Opening another window of the same document

The New Window command opens an additional window of the *same* worksheet. No new worksheet is created. Any change made in an open window affects the entire underlying worksheet.

Notice that the new window is titled BALANCE.XLS:2 and your original window has become BALANCE.XLS:1. You now have two windows of the same worksheet. If you scroll one window, the other remains stationary.

If you have more than one document open on-screen and you choose New Window, Excel will create a new window of the worksheet that is currently active.

You can restore a window to full size using the Restore command under the document Control menu (or pressing Ctrl–F5) or by clicking the document Maximize box.

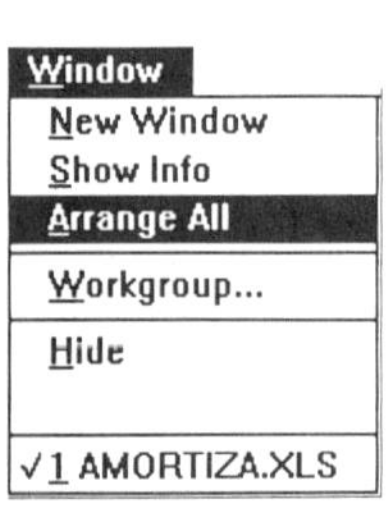

TILING WINDOWS

Multiple windows are viewed like sheets of paper on a desk, with the most recent window on top. Often you may prefer to *tile* the windows, that is, put the windows side-by-side on the screen. To tile windows, open the Window menu and choose Arrange All.

As an exercise, tile the two Balance worksheet windows that are displayed. Notice that only the active window has scroll bars.

CLOSING WINDOWS

To close a window when more than one window of the same document is on-screen, simply double-click the close box of the window. This deletes that window and renumbers the remaining windows. Closing a window does not cause the loss of any worksheet data, nor does it save the worksheet. The underlying worksheet remains in memory. If you try to delete the last window for a document, Excel will assume you wish to close the file; it will display a dialog box that asks whether you want to save the file.

SPLITTING WINDOWS

In the next two sections, you will learn some strategies for working with a large worksheet. For instance, look at the Balance worksheet. Resize the window horizontally so that column E is not visible (see Figure 7.11). Notice how hard it is now to enter data and check formulas. Entering the data for the first few rows is easy, but what happens when you try to enter the data in the last rows? As Figure 7.12 shows, you no longer see the row headings. What happens when you enter the last part of the data for any particular column? You will not be able to see the column headings. If the worksheet is very large with many rows, you can quickly become lost in the worksheet.

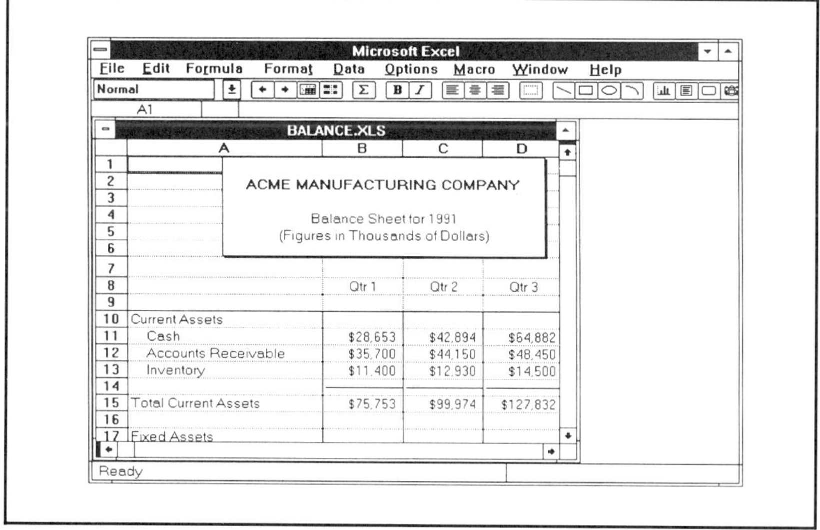

Figure 7.11: The Balance worksheet in a small window

With Excel, you can solve this problem by splitting the window into different *panes*. Panes let you view multiple parts of the same worksheet and scroll them together.

Creating Panes

Let's see how this works with your Balance worksheet. First, be sure cell A8 is in the upper-left corner of the window. Place the cursor on the small black bar at the left end of the horizontal scroll bar. The cursor will change into the shape of two vertical bars. Click and drag it to the right until this split bar is between columns A and B. Release the mouse button.

When using panes, start with the column-heading row at the top and the row headings at the far left.

You now have two panes in a single window. Each pane has its own horizontal scroll bar, but there is only one vertical scroll bar. Leave the left pane as it is. Scroll the right pane so that only the three columns are visible, as shown in Figure 7.13.

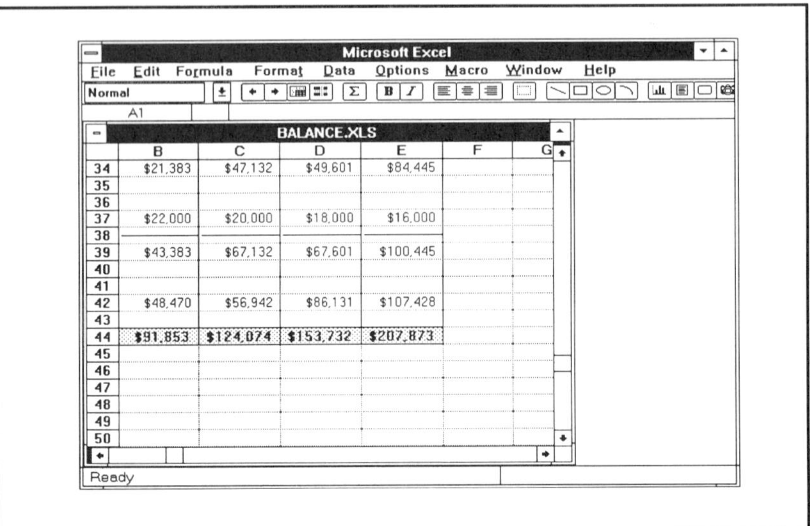

	B	C	D	E	F	G
34	$21,383	$47,132	$49,601	$84,445		
35						
36						
37	$22,000	$20,000	$18,000	$16,000		
38						
39	$43,383	$67,132	$67,601	$100,445		
40						
41						
42	$48,470	$56,942	$86,131	$107,428		
43						
44	$91,853	$124,074	$153,732	$207,873		
45						
46						
47						
48						
49						
50						

Figure 7.12: Getting lost in a worksheet

	A	C	D	E
8		Qtr 2	Qtr 3	Qtr 4
9				
10	Current Assets			
11	Cash	$42,894	$64,882	$91,053
12	Accounts Receivable	$44,150	$48,450	$55,230
13	Inventory	$12,930	$14,500	$16,490
14				
15	Total Current Assets	$99,974	$127,832	$162,773
16				
17	Fixed Assets			
18	P,P, and E			
19	Furniture, Fixtures	$12,100	$12,100	$12,100
20	Equipment	$16,600	$21,100	$42,300
21	Office Equipment	$4,100	$4,100	$4,100
22				
23	Gross P, P, and E	$32,800	$37,300	$58,500
24	Accumulated Depreciation	$8,700	$11,400	$13,400

Figure 7.13: The Balance worksheet with two panes

Now you can create four panes. Be sure the column headings (Qtr1, Qtr2, and Qtr3) are at the top of the window. Split the window again by placing the cursor on the small black bar at the top of the vertical scroll bar. Click and drag the mouse down so that the split bar is just under the top row that displays the column headings (row 8). Release the mouse button. Scroll the lower-right pane one row so that the column headings are shown only once, as shown in Figure 7.14.

Microsoft Excel

File Edit Formula Format Data Options Macro Window Help

Normal

A1

BALANCE.XLS

	A	B	C	D
8		Qtr 1	Qtr 2	Qtr 3
9				
10	Current Assets			
11	Cash	$28,653	$42,894	$64,882
12	Accounts Receivable	$35,700	$44,150	$48,450
13	Inventory	$11,400	$12,930	$14,500
14				
15	Total Current Assets	$75,753	$99,974	$127,832
16				
17	Fixed Assets			
18	P,P, and E			
19	Furniture, Fixtures	$12,100	$12,100	$12,100
20	Equipment	$6,500	$16,600	$21,100
21	Office Equipment	$4,100	$4,100	$4,100
22				
23	Gross P, P, and E	$22,700	$32,800	$37,300
24	Accumulated Depreciation	$6,600	$8,700	$11,400

Ready

Figure 7.14: The Balance worksheet with four panes

Use panes to lock row and column headings when working with a large worksheet.

Now there are four panes, each with its own set of scroll bars. The only pane that you *must* scroll vertically and horizontally for data entry is the one at the lower right. You will see that the row and column headings are always displayed in the adjacent panes.

Remember that you are looking at only a single window of the same worksheet. If you select a cell in any pane and enter new data, the corresponding cells in the other panes will also show the new data.

The black bars in the scroll boxes that separate the panes are called *split bars.* You can close any pane by dragging the split bar. In the Balance worksheet, for example, dragging the lower split bar all the way back to the left closes both left panes; dragging the split bar in the right scroll bar back to the top closes the top panes.

A quick way to set panes is to use the document's Control menu. Starting with a single pane, scroll the worksheet so that the headings are at the top and left of the window. Choose Split from the document's Control menu and move the marking lines to define a single column to the left and a single row above. Then click OK or press Enter.

A quick way to restore the original worksheet without panes is to select Split under the Control menu and then press Home–Enter.

Handling a Large Worksheet

With the Balance worksheet, panes would have helped some, but on a full window you really only need to split the column headings. With other worksheets, however, full panes can save you much time and improve the accuracy of the worksheet.

Look at the worksheet in Figure 7.15. This example illustrates how the use of panes can help you to work with a large worksheet. Don't try to enter it (unless you like challenges), just examine the figures. By using panes, you could lock column and row headings, permitting you to scroll around the rest of the worksheet while the headings remain displayed.

HIDING WINDOWS

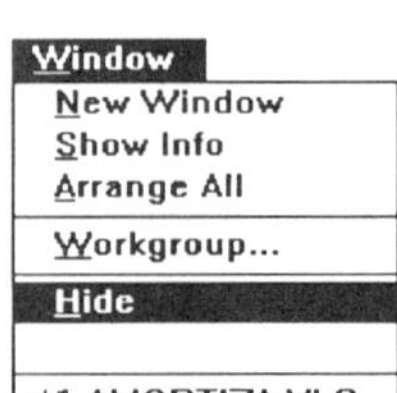

There may be times when you wish to hide a window or document, yet leave it open. Hiding a window reduces clutter on the screen and helps prevent accidental edits. It does not, however, protect against viewing or unauthorized access. Macros and cell links are still active. For example, if you have a macro sheet with a library of common macros that you use, you can open it in a workspace and hide the macro sheet. You can then still use all the macros on the sheet by unhiding it as needed.

To hide a window, make the window active and choose Hide on the Window menu. To make it visible again, open the Window menu and choose the Unhide command. Then choose the window from the list that you wish to unhide and click OK.

CUSTOMIZING COLORS

An Excel document can display up to 16 colors at a time from a specified palette that you can customize. Customized palettes can be copied between documents.

	A	B	C	D	E	F	G	H	I	J	K	L	M	N
1							WIDGET MANUFACTURING							
2							CASH FLOW ANALYSIS - 1991							
3								Assump:	Interest Rate			9%		
4									Cost of Goods/Sale of Goods			0.55		
5									Advertising/Sales			0.1		
6														
7		Jan-91	Feb-91	Mar-91	Apr-91	May-91	Jun-91	Jul-91	Aug-91	Sep-91	Oct-91	Nov-91	Dec-91	Totals
8														
9	CASH ON HAND	$43,000	$34,236	$63,507	$80,761	$162,282	$176,211	$179,147	$179,754	$224,074	$255,279	$271,356	$286,063	
10														
11	INCOME													
12	Sale of Goods	$83,394	$110,237	$114,563	$117,239	$123,291	$108,345	$98,234	$132,874	$143,819	$132,764	$123,127	$131,872	$1,419,759
13	Sale of Services	$6,432	$10,234	$11,784	$76,123	$10,523	$11,239	$9,272	$11,555	$10,234	$12,812	$13,916	$14,123	$198,247
14	Total Sales	$89,826	$120,471	$126,347	$193,362	$133,814	$119,584	$107,506	$144,429	$154,053	$145,576	$137,043	$145,995	$1,618,006
15	Interest Income	$323	$323	$257	$476	$606	$1,217	$1,322	$1,344	$1,348	$1,681	$1,915	$2,035	$12,845
16		---------	---------	---------	---------	---------	---------	---------	---------	---------	---------	---------	---------	----------
17	Total Income	$90,149	$120,794	$126,604	$193,838	$134,420	$120,801	$108,828	$145,773	$155,401	$147,257	$138,958	$148,030	$1,630,851
18														
19	EXPENSES													
20	Cost of Goods	$45,867	$45,867	$60,630	$63,010	$64,481	$67,810	$59,590	$54,029	$73,081	$79,100	$73,020	$67,720	$754,205
21	Rent	$11,543	$8,923	$8,923	$8,923	$8,923	$8,923	$8,923	$8,923	$8,923	$8,923	$8,923	$8,923	$109,696
22	Salaries	$19,894	$15,234	$15,234	$15,234	$15,234	$15,234	$15,234	$15,234	$15,234	$15,234	$15,234	$15,234	$187,468
23	Taxes	$1,204	$1,094	$1,094	$1,094	$1,094	$1,094	$1,094	$1,094	$1,094	$1,094	$1,094	$1,094	$13,238
24	Supplies	$2,050	$2,050	$2,050	$2,050	$2,050	$2,050	$2,050	$2,050	$2,050	$2,050	$2,050	$2,050	$24,600
25	Repairs	$2,873	$2,873	$2,873	$2,873	$2,873	$2,873	$2,873	$2,873	$2,873	$2,873	$2,873	$2,873	$34,476
26	Advertising	$8,983	$8,983	$12,047	$12,635	$19,336	$13,381	$11,958	$10,751	$14,443	$15,405	$14,558	$13,704	$156,184
27	Insurance	$734	$734	$734	$734	$734	$734	$734	$734	$734	$734	$734	$734	$8,808
28	Utilties	$2,345	$2,345	$2,345	$2,345	$2,345	$2,345	$2,345	$2,345	$2,345	$2,345	$2,345	$2,345	$28,140
29	Emp. Benefits	$1,234	$1,234	$1,234	$1,234	$1,234	$1,234	$1,234	$1,234	$1,234	$1,234	$1,234	$1,234	$14,808
30	Dues, Subscriptions	$254	$254	$254	$254	$254	$254	$254	$254	$254	$254	$254	$254	$3,048
31	Travel	$1,432	$1,432	$1,432	$1,432	$1,432	$1,432	$1,432	$1,432	$1,432	$1,432	$1,432	$1,432	$17,184
32	Miscellaneous	$500	$500	$500	$500	$500	$500	$500	$500	$500	$500	$500	$500	$6,000
33		---------	---------	---------	---------	---------	---------	---------	---------	---------	---------	---------	---------	----------
34	Total Expenses	$98,912	$91,522	$109,350	$112,317	$120,491	$117,864	$108,221	$101,452	$124,197	$131,179	$124,251	$118,097	$1,357,854
35														
36	Net Income	($8,764)	$29,271	$17,253	$81,521	$13,929	$2,937	$606	$44,320	$31,205	$16,078	$14,707	$29,933	$272,996
37	Net Cash on Hand	$34,236	$63,507	$80,761	$162,282	$176,211	$179,147	$179,754	$224,074	$255,279	$271,356	$286,063	$315,996	

Figure 7.15: A huge cash-flow analysis worksheet

Options
Set Print Area
Set Print Titles
Set Page Break
Display...
Color Palette...
Protect Document...
Calculation...
Calculate Now
Workspace...
Short Menus

To customize a palette for a worksheet, choose Color Palette from the Options menu. To customize a palette for a chart, choose Color Palette from the Chart menu. In the Color Palette dialog box, choose the color you wish to change. Click the Edit button. Select the new color you wish to use. Press F1 if you need help in using the palette. Click OK. Edit other colors as you wish, then click OK on the first dialog box.

To copy a palette to another document, make the windows with the destination document active and choose Color Palette from the Options menu (for a worksheet) or Color Palette from the Chart menu (for a chart). In the Copy Colors From box, enter the name of the document with the palette you wish to import. Click OK.

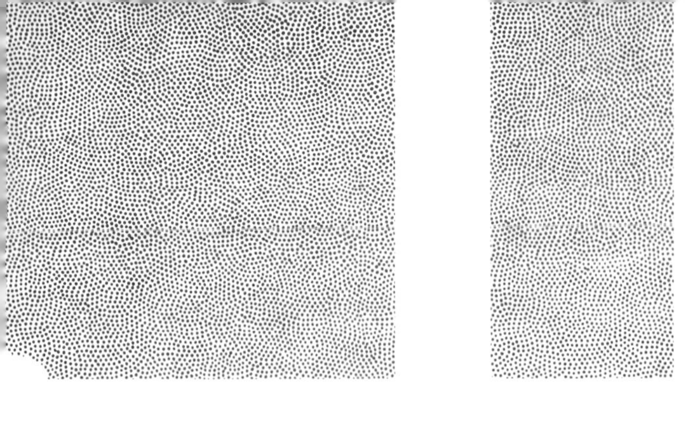

8 Calculating with Formulas and Functions

FUNCTIONS ARE ABBREVIATIONS OF FORMULAS THAT enable you to perform a task quickly that would take much longer (or could not be done at all) using other operations. Excel provides a total of 146 worksheet functions. In most worksheets, you will want to use one or more of these to calculate cell values.

In this chapter, you will use some of Excel's functions to create a very useful amortization schedule. Amortizing something means, literally, to put it to death. That is what you do when you pay off a car loan or house mortgage. In amortizing a loan, you make a series of equal payments for a fixed period of time. During this time, however, the proportion that you pay for the principal increases while the proportion that you pay for the interest decreases. If you are purchasing anything on credit, you may need to evaluate your loan consistently to calculate your taxes or to plan for refinancing. In this chapter, you will learn how Excel can help you to perform this evaluation.

However, before you can use this example and Excel's functions, you need to understand some basics of cell addressing and how functions work. The first part of this chapter provides that information.

Later you will find an overview of Excel's functions and a summary of how to use each one.

CELL ADDRESSING

With formulas and functions, you can use either relative, absolute, or mixed cell addressing.

RELATIVE CELL ADDRESSING

The Income worksheet that you created in Chapter 3 and the Balance worksheet that you created in Chapters 4–6 both used relative cell addressing. In Chapter 3, you created the following formula for cell B8:

= B5 – B6

What you really stored in cell B8 was a formula that said, "Subtract the value in the cell two cells up from the value in the cell three cells up." This is why you could copy the formula to other cells, without having to retype it. *Relative cell addresses* refer to other cells by their position in relation to the current cell's location.

You can enter a relative cell address into a formula by typing it at the keyboard or by clicking the appropriate cell on the worksheet.

ABSOLUTE CELL ADDRESSING

There may be times when you want to make a permanent reference to a cell that will not change with a copy, move, or fill operation. In other words, if you used B5 in a formula and then copied it into another cell, you would still want it to reference B5. The concept of making a specific cell reference is called *absolute cell addressing.*

To indicate this kind of addressing, you must insert a dollar sign before both the row and the column designators of the referenced cell, as in

= $B$5 – $B$6

If you copied or moved this formula, cells B5 and B6 would still be referenced in the new cell. Absolute cell references are generally entered from the keyboard. (Chapter 14 describes an alternative method.)

The large cash-flow analysis worksheet in Chapter 7, shown in Figure 7.15, uses absolute cell addressing. Near the title, in column L, is a list of assumed parameters that were used in computing the projected interest, cost of goods, and advertising costs. The formulas in column C used these assumptions. When these formulas were copied into the other columns, it was important that the referenced cell(s) in column L were still referenced after the fill or copy operations. Thus, these formulas used absolute cell referencing. For example, advertising costs in column C were $L$5*B14—the advertising/sales ratio (a fixed number) times the total sales of the previous month (a variable).

MIXED CELL ADDRESSING

There may be times when you need to use a combination of absolute and relative cell addressing in a single cell. Excel allows you to make either the row or the column relative and the other absolute. For example, B$5 refers to a relative column B and an absolute row 5, and $B5 refers to an absolute column B and a relative row 5. This is called *mixed cell addressing*. Mixed cell references are generally entered from the keyboard.

WHAT IS A FUNCTION?

A *function* is an abbreviation of a formula. It provides a quick way to calculate the value of a cell that would often require a long expression. For example, in a worksheet you might use the following formula to find the sum of many cells:

```
= B5 + B6 + B7 + B8 + B9
```

Instead, you could use the SUM function and specify a range of cells as its input:

```
=SUM(B5:B9)
```

See how much shorter the entry has become?

A *function statement* is a function whose arguments (see below) are in parentheses. An *expression* is an entire equation entered in a cell. For example,

=SUM(B5:B9) + ABS(B5)

is an expression: it contains two function statements, SUM and ABS. (SUM adds the values in cells B5–B9 together and ABS returns the absolute value of the number in cell B5.)

Functions also allow you to perform calculations that would be impossible with a formula, such as the square-root function SQRT.

FUNCTION ARGUMENTS

Arguments are the data that a function uses in its calculation. With the SUM function, for example, you can have as many as 14 cells or cell ranges as arguments. The number of arguments used by a particular function depends on the function. Some functions do not use any arguments.

Every function expects each of its arguments to be of a certain type. For example, the SUM function expects all its arguments to be numeric. There are ten argument types that can be used by Excel functions. These are listed in Table 8.1.

Table 8.1: Types of Excel Arguments

ARGUMENT	DEFINITION
Number	Anything that produces a number: numeric value, numeric formula, or a reference to a cell with a numeric value
Numbers	Anything that produces one or more numbers
Text	Anything that produces text: text, a text formula, or a reference to a cell containing text
Logical	Anything that produces a logical value
Logicals	Anything that produces one or more logical values

Table 8.1: Types of Excel Arguments (continued)

ARGUMENT	DEFINITION
Ref	Anything that produces a reference
Value	Anything that produces a value
Values	Anything that produces one or more values
Array	Anything that produces an array
Vector	Anything that produces a one-dimensional array
Note: Text arguments must be enclosed in quotation marks.	

The arguments of an Excel function must be in a certain order, which is determined by the function. This ordering of arguments is detailed in the library of functions listed later in this chapter. Be sure to check the appropriate order, because Excel's argument order may be different from that of other worksheet programs, such as Lotus 1-2-3. Some functions may use one or more optional arguments as well.

ENTERING FUNCTIONS INTO CELLS

The following general rules apply for entering functions in your worksheet:

- Always begin an expression entry with an equal sign. This informs Excel that you are entering a function, not a text string
- Function names are not case-specific
- Referenced cells can contain other functions, making it possible to create hierarchies of calculations
- Separate arguments with commas
- A function can have up to 14 arguments

- An expression can contain a maximum of 255 characters (the cell limit)
- You can use any of the three reference operators (see Chapter 4) to define the input for a function. For example,

  =SUM(A3:A5,B6)
- calculates
- A3 + A4 + A5 + B6
- Arguments can be constants. For example,

  8 = SUM(100 + B5)
- Stores the value of 100 plus the contents of cell B5 in cell B8
- Arguments can be functions. For example,

  =SUM(ROUND(A3,0),ROUND(C1,0))

If you enter the function by typing the name manually, use lowercase to check spelling. If a valid function name is spelled correctly, Excel will capitalize it automatically.

There are two ways to enter a function into a cell. One is to type the function as a part of your formula. The second way is to paste the function name into the formula and then enter the arguments from the keyboard or by clicking:

- To enter a function manually, simply type the name. For example, find a blank cell on a worksheet and enter

  =ROUND(2.34,1)
- Notice that the cell displays **2.3**, the first argument rounded to one decimal place
- To paste a function name into a formula, use the Paste Function command. Try the previous example this way. Select a blank cell, open the Formula menu, and choose Paste Function. Scroll to the ROUND function name, double-click the function, and enter the arguments from the keyboard. (Notice that it was not necessary to enter the equal sign.)

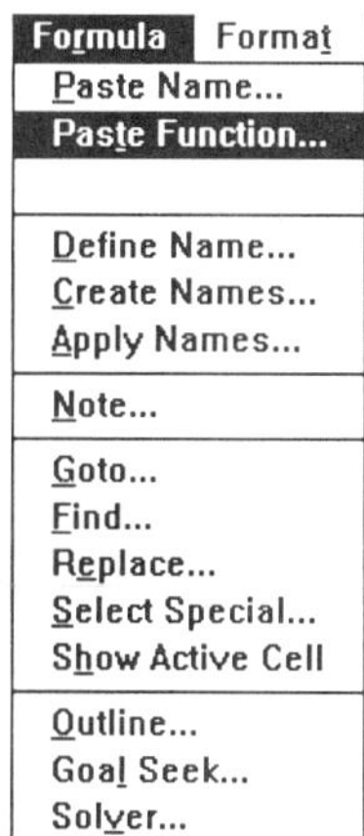

If you know the name of the function you want to paste, you don't have to scroll through all the functions. When the list box is displayed, just press the first letter of the function you want. For example, press **R** to get to the first function name beginning with *R*. Then double-click on ROUND.

USING THE SUM TOOL

3.0

The sum tool on the tool bar is useful for adding the sum function to a cell. Simply click on an empty cell at the end of a column or row of numbers and then click on the Σ button. Excel will mark the cells it thinks you are trying to sum with dotted lines. If this is correct, press Enter. If not, edit the entry in the formula bar.

CREATING A WORKSHEET WITH FUNCTIONS

Figure 8.1 shows a part of a worksheet that you can use to experiment with functions. In this example, $8,000.00 is borrowed at 12 percent interest, and Excel is used to calculate the monthly payments, the total amount paid, and the amortization schedule. This example makes extensive use of both the PMT (periodic payment) and PV (present value) functions, which are used frequently for financial analyses. Once you create the worksheet, you can change the amount borrowed, the interest, and the term to see how it affects the schedule. This makes the example much more than a simple tutorial—you can save it and use it to calculate the schedule whenever you purchase something on credit. (You will find more information on the PMT and PV functions in Chapter 23.)

Note that the data-entry area for the user, marked in the upper left of the worksheet, has only three cells: B6, B7, and B8. Normally, you would want the rest of the worksheet protected, so that a user could change only those three cells (protecting cells is described later in Chapter 14).

Begin the Amortization worksheet by entering the titles in cells C1 and C2. Create the data-entry area in cells A5 through B8 (enter labels and asterisks) and enter the input values shown in Figure 8.2 into this area. Remember to enter a percent sign each time you insert a value for cell B7; this identifies the cell value as a percent.

	A	B	C	D	E	F	G
1			AMORTIZATION SCHEDULE				
2			*Amortization Payment Schedule by Month*				
3							
4	**********	***********	***********	**			
5	Data Entry Area			*			
6	Principal	$8,000.00		*			
7	Interest	12.00%		*			
8	Term	48	Months	*			
9	**********	***********	***********	**			
10	Payment:	$210.67					
11	Total Paid	$10,112.19					
12							
13	Month	Beginning	Ending	Payment	Total Paid	Tot. Princ.	Tot. Interest
14		Balance	Balance			Paid	Paid
15	1	$8,000.00	$7,869.33	$210.67	$210.67	$130.67	$80.00
16	2	$7,869.33	$7,737.35	$210.67	$421.34	$262.65	$158.69
17	3	$7,737.35	$7,604.05	$210.67	$632.01	$395.95	$236.07
18	4	$7,604.05	$7,469.42	$210.67	$842.68	$530.58	$312.11
19	5	$7,469.42	$7,333.45	$210.67	$1,053.35	$666.55	$386.80
20	6	$7,333.45	$7,196.11	$210.67	$1,264.02	$803.89	$460.14
21	7	$7,196.11	$7,057.40	$210.67	$1,474.69	$942.60	$532.10
22	8	$7,057.40	$6,917.31	$210.67	$1,685.37	$1,082.69	$602.67
23	9	$6,917.31	$6,775.81	$210.67	$1,896.04	$1,224.19	$671.84
24	10	$6,775.81	$6,632.90	$210.67	$2,106.71	$1,367.10	$739.60
25	11	$6,632.90	$6,488.55	$210.67	$2,317.38	$1,511.45	$805.93
26	12	$6,488.55	$6,342.77	$210.67	$2,528.05	$1,657.23	$870.82
27	13	$6,342.77	$6,195.53	$210.67	$2,738.72	$1,804.47	$934.24
28	14	$6,195.53	$6,046.81	$210.67	$2,949.39	$1,953.19	$996.20
29	15	$6,046.81	$5,896.61	$210.67	$3,160.06	$2,103.39	$1,056.67
30	16	$5,896.61	$5,744.90	$210.67	$3,370.73	$2,255.10	$1,115.63
31	17	$5,744.90	$5,591.68	$210.67	$3,581.40	$2,408.32	$1,173.08
32	18	$5,591.68	$5,436.93	$210.67	$3,792.07	$2,563.07	$1,229.00
33	19	$5,436.93	$5,280.63	$210.67	$4,002.74	$2,719.37	$1,283.37
34	20	$5,280.63	$5,122.76	$210.67	$4,213.41	$2,877.24	$1,336.18
35	21	$5,122.76	$4,963.32	$210.67	$4,424.08	$3,036.68	$1,387.40
36	22	$4,963.32	$4,802.28	$210.67	$4,634.76	$3,197.72	$1,437.04
37	23	$4,802.28	$4,639.63	$210.67	$4,845.43	$3,360.37	$1,485.06
38	24	$4,639.63	$4,475.36	$210.67	$5,056.10	$3,524.64	$1,531.46
39	25	$4,475.36	$4,309.44	$210.67	$5,266.77	$3,690.56	$1,576.21
40	26	$4,309.44	$4,141.87	$210.67	$5,477.44	$3,858.13	$1,619.30
41	27	$4,141.87	$3,972.61	$210.67	$5,688.11	$4,027.39	$1,660.72
42	28	$3,972.61	$3,801.67	$210.67	$5,898.78	$4,198.33	$1,700.45
43	29	$3,801.67	$3,629.01	$210.67	$6,109.45	$4,370.99	$1,738.46
44	30	$3,629.01	$3,454.63	$210.67	$6,320.12	$4,545.37	$1,774.75
45	31	$3,454.63	$3,278.51	$210.67	$6,530.79	$4,721.49	$1,809.30
46	32	$3,278.51	$3,100.62	$210.67	$6,741.46	$4,899.38	$1,842.09

Figure 8.1: First page of the Amortization worksheet

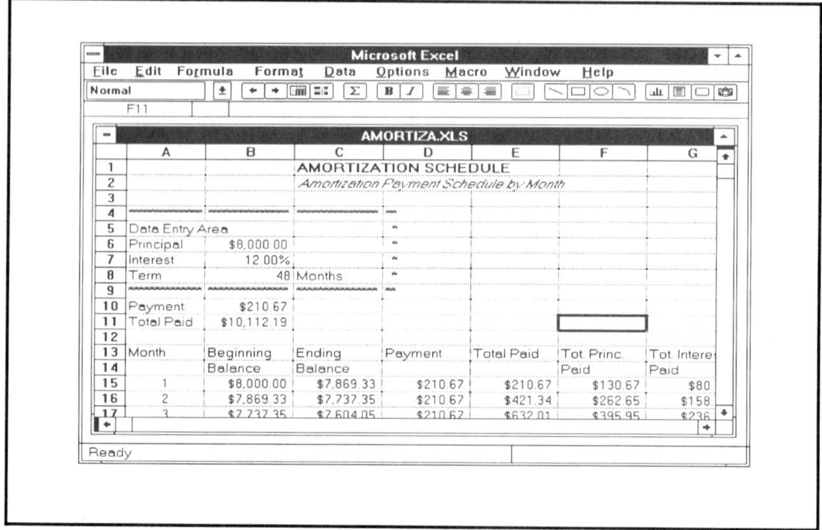

Figure 8.2: Creating the Amortization worksheet

> If you have been using Lotus 1-2-3, you will notice that the order of the arguments in Excel is slightly different from the Lotus convention. Excel's financial functions follow the HP-12C Financial Calculator's conventions.

Enter **Payment:** into cell A10 and **Total Paid** into cell A11. Enter the following function and formula according to the list below:

CELL	*ENTRY*
B10	= PMT($B$7/12,$B$8, –$B$6)
B11	= ($B$8 * $B$10)

Enter the column headings into cells A13 through G14. Then enter the month numbers sequentially into column A. (There are 48 payments.)

Enter these formulas for the values for the first row:

CELL	*ENTRY*
B15	=$B$6
C15	= –PV($B$7/12,($B$8 – A15),$B$10)
D15	=$B$10
E15	=D15
F15	=B15 – C15
G15	=E15 – F15

Copy cell C15 to C16 and enter the following into the row for Month 2:

CELL	*ENTRY*
B16	=C15
E16	=E15 + D16
F16	=F15 + B16 − C16

Now you can have Excel calculate the remainder of the amortization schedule by using the Fill Down command under the Edit menu for each column, except the first. For columns B, C, E, and F, you will need to fill from the second row down. On the remaining rows, fill from the first row down. The resulting values should be the same as those shown in Figure 8.1.

Format the worksheet, set up the alignments, and set the styles for the titles, as shown in Figure 8.1. Refer to Chapter 6 if you need help. Format B7 as a percent.

Once you have set up the worksheet, save it using the name *Amortiza.* Then prepare a copy for printing by opening the File menu and choosing Page Setup. Set the options you wish and click OK. Now print the worksheet.

You can try changing any of the values in the data-entry area to see what happens to the amortization schedule. Remember to use the percent sign when you enter a different interest rate. Notice how fast Excel calculates the entire schedule.

This is a valuable worksheet. Save it for calculating the schedule whenever you purchase something on credit—a house, automobile, computer, or whatever. It calculates the proper interest for income-tax purposes, also giving you the status of the principal in case you wish to refinance a loan.

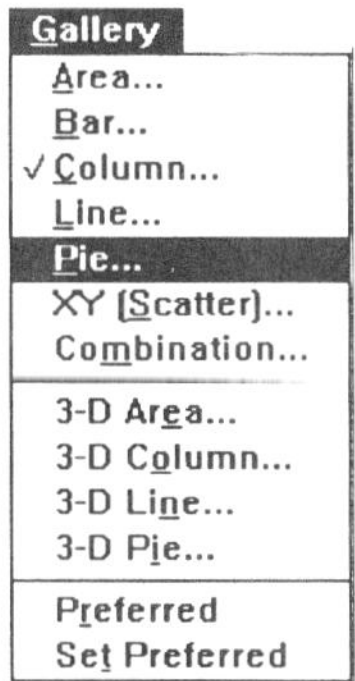

If you are the adventurous type, you can try to create a pie chart from your amortization worksheet, showing the relative percentages of principal and interest paid on a 48-month loan. Select only cells F62 and G62, which contain the final totals. Open the File menu, choose New, and double-click Chart in the dialog box. A column graph appears. Open the Gallery menu and choose Pie to change the column chart that was automatically created into a pie chart. Choose pie chart style #6. Now select Arrange All from the Window menu to show both the chart and worksheet. Change the interest on the worksheet and watch the chart change. (If you get stuck, refer to Chapter 18.) When you are done, close the chart window.

CHANGING FORMULAS TO VALUES

When you paste an expression into a cell, the cell value becomes dependent upon values in other cells, other variables (such as the date or time), or even values in other worksheets. There may be occasions, however, when you wish to lock the results of an expression into a cell; that is, you wish the current results of the expression to be a *value*, no longer dependent on other cells.

A quick way to store a date value is to press Ctrl-;. To store the time press Ctrl-:.

As an example, you might use the function =NOW( ) as an expression in a worksheet to enter the current date in a cell, thus date-stamping the cell. Enter this function in F4 of the amortization schedule worksheet. Set the date format using Number on the Format menu. The next time you open the worksheet, however, the cell date (or time) will read the new date (or time). That's not exactly what you wish. To convert the result of an expression to a fixed value, follow this procedure:

1. Select the cell or cell range you wish to convert to values. Select F4 in this case.
2. Open the Edit menu and choose Copy. The cell or cell range is marked.
3. Open the Edit menu and choose Paste Special.
4. In the Paste Special dialog box, choose Values (see Figure 8.3).
5. Click OK.

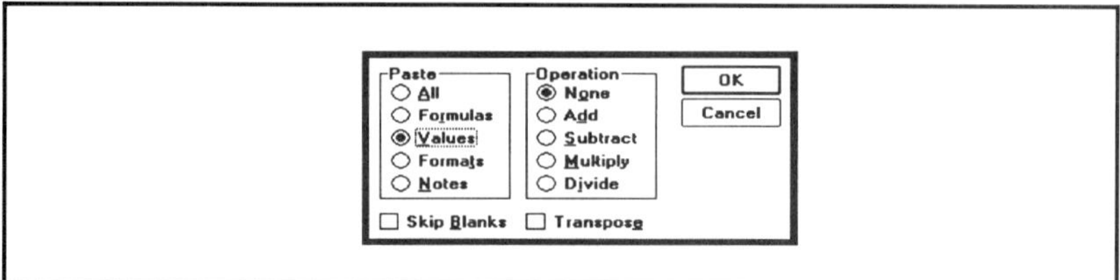

Figure 8.3: Converting an expression result to a value

You can also convert a formula to a value in the formula bar using this method:

1. Select the cell and highlight all the characters in the formula bar.
2. Open the Options menu and choose Calculate Now.

Both methods convert the date to a value, and the value (not the equation) is stored in the worksheet.

TYPES OF FUNCTIONS

There are 146 functions available to the Excel user. These can be classified into nine types: mathematical, statistical, database, trigonometric, logical, text, financial, date, and special-purpose. Each function is described by type in the remainder of this chapter.

MATHEMATICAL FUNCTIONS

The following are Excel's mathematical functions:

ABS(*number*): returns the absolute value of *number*

EXP(*number*): returns *e* raised to the power of *number.* EXP is the reverse of the LN (natural logarithm) function. To calculate the power to other bases, use the exponentiation operator

FACT(*number*): returns the factorial of *number*

INT(*number*): returns the largest integer less than or equal to *number*. For example: INT(7.6) is 7

LN(*number*): returns the natural logarithm of *number,* which must be positive. LN is the inverse of EXP

LOG(*number, base*): returns the logarithm of *number* to *base*

LOG10(*number*): returns the base 10 logarithm of *number*

MOD(*number, divisor number*): returns the remainder after *number* is divided by *divisor number*

PI( ): returns the value of π. There is no argument

PRODUCT(*number 1, number 2, . . ., number n*): returns product of *numbers*

RAND( ): returns a random number between 0 and 0.999. . . . The value changes each time the worksheet is recalculated. There is no argument

ROUND(*number, number of digits*): returns *number* rounded to *number of digits*

SIGN(*number*): returns 1 if *number* is positive, 0 if it is 0, and −1 if it is negative

SQRT(*number*): returns the square root of *number,* which must be positive

TRUNC(*number, number of digits*): returns integer part of *number*

The RAND function is useful for creating random data when testing worksheets. The value changes with each recalculation, so sometimes you may wish to convert the expression result to a value to save time in iterative calculations.

STATISTICAL FUNCTIONS

Excel has the following statistical functions:

AVERAGE(*number 1, number 2, . . ., number n*): returns the average of the numeric arguments

COUNT(*number 1, number 2, . . ., number n*): returns the number of numbers in a list of arguments. Example: COUNT(A1:A5,A8) equals 6

COUNTA(*number 1, number 2, . . ., number n*): returns the number of nonblank values in a list of arguments

GROWTH(*Y array, X array, new x's, const*): returns an array with the *y* values as the exponential curve of regression *y* = *b***m*^*x* for two variables represented by *X array* and *Y array*

LINEST(*Y array, X array, const, stats*): returns the horizontal array of two elements, the slope and *y* intercept of the line of regression for $y = mx + b$, for two variables, X and Y, represented by *X array* and *Y array*

LOGEST(*Y array, X array, const, stats*): returns a horizontal array of two elements, the parameters of m and b in the exponential curve of regression $y = b*m\hat{}x$, for two variables represented by *X array* and *Y array*

MAX(*number 1, number 2, . . ., number n*): returns the largest number in a list of arguments

MEDIAN(*number 1, number 2, . . ., number n*): returns the median of a list of arguments

MIN(*number 1, number 2, . . ., number n*): returns the minimum number in a list of arguments

STDEV(*number 1, number 2, . . ., number n*): returns the standard deviation of the numbers in a list of arguments

SUM(*number 1, number 2, . . ., number n*): returns the sum of the numbers in a list of arguments

TREND(*Y array, X array, x array*): returns an array, the y values on the line of regression $y = mx + b$, for the two variables X and Y represented by *X array* and *Y array*

VAR(*number 1, number 2, . . ., number n*): returns the estimate of variance of the numbers in the sample

VARP(*number 1, number 2, . . ., number n*): returns the variance of the population

The SUM and AVERAGE functions ignore cells with blanks, logical values, or text. COUNT returns the number of cells with numbers. COUNTA, in contrast, tells how many cells include text, logical values, numbers, and error values. Both also do not count blank cells.

To enter the SUM function quickly from the tool bar for simple applications, click the sum button in the tool bar. This will enter an expression that sums the cells above or to the left of the active cell into the first blank cell.

For more information on using the statistical functions, see Chapter 23.

DATABASE FUNCTIONS

The following are Excel's database functions:

DAVERAGE(*database, field name, criteria*): returns the average of the numbers in a particular field of a database that meet the specified criteria

DCOUNT(*database, field name, criteria*): returns the count of the numbers in a particular field of a database that meet the specified criteria

DCOUNTA(*database, field name, criteria*): returns the count of the nonempty cells in a particular field of a database that meet the specified criteria

DGET(*database, field name, criteria*): extracts single record that matches criteria

DMAX(*database, field name, criteria*): returns the maximum of the numbers in a particular field of a database that meet the specified criteria

DMIN(*database, field name, criteria*): returns the minimum of the numbers in a particular field of a database that meet the specified criteria

DPRODUCT(*database, field name, criteria*): returns the product of the numbers in a particular field of a database that meet the specified criteria

DSTDEV(*database, field name, criteria*): returns the estimate of the standard deviation of a population based on a sample of a particular field of a database that meets the specified criteria

DSTDEVP(*database, field name, criteria*): returns the standard deviation of a population based on the entire population, using a particular field of a database that meets the specified criteria

DSUM(*database, field name, criteria*): returns the sum of the numbers in a particular field of a database that meet the specified criteria

DVAR(*database, field name, criteria*): returns the estimate of the variance of a population using a sample in a particular field of a database that meets the specified criteria

DVARP(*database, field name, criteria*): returns the variance of a population using numbers in a particular field of a database that meet the specified criteria

For more information on using the database functions, see Part III of this book.

TRIGONOMETRIC FUNCTIONS

Excel has the following trigonometric functions:

ACOS(*number*): returns the arccosine of *number*

ACOSH(*number*): returns inverse hyperbolic cosine of *number*

ASIN(*number*): returns the arcsine of *number*

ASINH(*number*): returns inverse hyperbolic sine of *number*

ATAN(*number*): returns the arctangent of *number*

ATAN2(*x number, y number*): returns the arctangent of *x number* and *y number*

ATANH(*number*): returns inverse hyperbolic tangent of *number*

COS(*number*): returns the cosine of *number*

COSH(*number*): returns hyperbolic cosine of *number*

SIN(*number*): returns the sine of *number*

SINH(*number*): returns hyperbolic sine of *number*

TAN(*number*): returns the tangent of *number*

TANH(*number*): returns hyperbolic tangent of *number*

Excel measures angles in radians rather than degrees. To convert, use the following equation:

Angle in degrees = Angle in radians * (180/PI( ))

LOGICAL FUNCTIONS

The following are Excel's logical functions:

AND(*logical 1, logical 2, . . ., logical n*): returns TRUE if all logical values in the list of arguments are true. If any of the values are FALSE, the function will return a value of FALSE

FALSE( ) returns the value of FALSE. Useful as an argument in the CHOOSE function

IF(*logical, value if true, value if false*): returns *value if true* if *logical* is true, otherwise returns *value if false*

ISBLANK(*value*): returns TRUE if *value* is blank

ISERR(*value*): returns TRUE if *value* is any error except #N/A

ISERROR(*value*): returns TRUE if *value* is any Excel error value

ISLOGICAL(*value*): returns TRUE if *value* is a logical value

ISNA(*value*): returns TRUE if value is #N/A (number not available)

ISNONTEXT(*value*): returns TRUE if *value* is not text

ISNUMBER(*value*): returns TRUE if *value* is a number

ISREF(*value*): returns TRUE if *value* is a reference or reference formula

ISTEXT(*value*): returns TRUE if *value* is text

NOT(*logical*): returns FALSE if *logical* is TRUE, TRUE if *logical* is FALSE

OR(*logical 1, logical 2, . . ., logical n*): returns TRUE if any of the logical values in the list of arguments is TRUE. If all logical values in the list are FALSE, it returns FALSE

TRUE( ) returns a logical value of TRUE. Used with the CHOOSE function. There is no argument

Logical expressions return a value of TRUE or FALSE. For example, look at the following expressions:

=(5*4)*7>480/4

=C4>D10

=D5 ="No"

Each of these is really a question. The answer, either TRUE or FALSE, is placed in the cell containing the expression. The first reads "Is (5*4)*7 greater than 480/4?". The answer is yes, or TRUE. The available operators are listed in Chapter 4.

Use the ISERROR and ISNA functions to trap errors in your worksheet. This is especially useful in macros (see Part VII), since error conditions will terminate a macro execution. Using these functions, you can test for an error condition and, if you get one, edit the macro so that it runs smoothly.

TEXT FUNCTIONS

Text strings must be enclosed in double quotes.

The following are Excel's text functions:

CHAR(*number*): returns ASCII character of *number*

CLEAN(*text*): removes control characters from *text*

CODE(*text*): returns ASCII code of first character in *text*

DOLLAR(*number, number of digits*): rounds *number* to *number of digits,* formats it to currency format, and returns a text result

EXACT(*text 1, text 2*): returns TRUE if *text 1* = *text 2*

FIND(*find text, within text, start*): finds *find text* in *within text,* starting at *start.* You can use wildcards

FIXED(*number, number of digits*): rounds *number* to *number of digits,* formats to a decimal format with commas, and returns a text result

LEFT(*text, number of characters*): returns left-most *number of characters* in *text*

LEN(*text*): returns a number equal to the length of *text*

LOWER(*text*): converts *text* to lowercase

MID(*text, start position, number of characters*): extracts *number of characters* from *text,* starting with *start position*

PROPER(*text*): returns *text* with first letters of each word in capitals

REPLACE(*old text, start, number, new text*): replaces *number* of characters of *old text* with *new text* starting at *start*

REPT(*text, number of times*): repeats *text* for *number of times*

RIGHT(*text, number of characters*): returns right-most *number of characters* of *text*

SEARCH(*find text, within text, start*): searches for *find text* within *within text* from *start.* You can use wildcard characters

SUBSTITUTE(*text, old text, new text, num*): replaces *old text* with *new text* in *text. Num* indicates which occurrence of *old text* to replace

TEXT(*number, format text*): formats *number* to *format text* and returns it as text

TRIM(*text*): removes spaces from *text*

UPPER(*text*): converts *text* to uppercase

VALUE(*text*): converts *text* to a number. (Not necessary to use in a formula, as Excel converts it automatically if necessary.)

The TEXT function is useful for displaying numeric text in a special format or alignment. For example,

=TEXT(C1,"##0.00")

would display 123.3 in cell C1 as **123.30**. Unlike a right-aligned number, however, the value would be left-aligned. Text always has a default left alignment. You can use most of the formatting symbols (see Chapter 6), but you cannot use the asterisk in the format to force a repeating symbol to fill a cell. For example,

=TEXT(230,"""Please remit: ""$#,##0.00")

would display

Please remit: $230.00

Because the second argument contains a text string within a text string, two sets of double quotation marks enclose the internal string. This is analogous to the convention in English of using single quotation marks to enclose a quotation within a quotation.

The DOLLAR and FIXED functions are often better alternatives in displaying currency values. For example, either of the following displays **$123.00**:

=DOLLAR(123,2)

=TEXT(123,"$#,##0.00")

But which is easier to enter? Both DOLLAR and FIXED automatically round the displayed value.

You should remember that the ampersand (&) is available for text operations. You can combine text strings, text with data, or text with the contents of a cell (see Chapter 4).

FINANCIAL FUNCTIONS

The following are Excel's financial functions:

DDB(*cost, salvage, life, period, factor*): returns depreciation of asset using double-declining balance method

FV(*rate, nper, pmt, pv, type*): returns the future value of an investment (see PV for a description of the arguments)

IPMT(*rate, per, nper, pv, fv, type*): returns interest payment for an investment

IRR(*values, guess*): returns internal rate of return of a series of cash flows, represented by *values*. *Guess* is an optional argument, specifying the starting point for the iteration. If *guess* is omitted, it is assumed to be 0.1 or 10%. *Values* should be an array or reference that contains numbers

MIRR(*values, safe, risk*): returns a modified internal rate of return on a series of case flows, represented by the numbers in *values*, given *safe* and *risk*. *Safe* is the rate returned by the investment that will finance the negative cash flows. *Risk* is the rate at which the positive cash flows can be reinvested

NPER(*rate, pmt, pv, fv, type*): returns the number of periods of an investment involving constant cash flows (see PV for a description of the arguments)

NPV(*rate, value 1, value 2, ..., value n*): returns net present value of a series of future cash flows, represented by the numbers in the list of values, discounted at a constant interest rate specified by *rate*

PMT(*rate, nper, pv, fv, type*): returns the periodic payment on an investment involving constant cash flows (see PV for a description of the arguments)

PPMT(*rate, per, nper, pv, fv, type*): returns payment on the principal for an investment

PV(*rate, nper, pmt, fv, type*): returns the present value. The arguments are as follows:

rate: interest rate per period

nper: number of periods

pmt: periodic payment

fv: future value

type: indicates whether payments occur at the beginning or end of the period. If *type* = 0, first payment is due after the first period. If *type* = 1, payment is at beginning. If the argument is omitted, it is assumed to be 0

RATE(*nper, pmt, pv, fv, type, guess*): returns the interest rate per period of an investment involving constant cash flows. (See PV for a description of the arguments.) *Guess* is an optional argument that specifies the starting value for the iteration. If omitted, it is assumed to be 0.1 or 10%

SLN(*cost, salvage, life*): straight-line depreciation of an asset

SYD(*cost, salvage, life, per*): sum of years' digits depreciation for an asset

VDB(*cost, salvage, life, start period, end period, factor, no switch*): returns depreciation of an asset for a specified or partial period using a declining balance method

The functions PV, FV, NPER, PMT, and RATE are all interrelated; you can calculate one given the values of the others. For more information on the financial functions, see Chapter 23.

DATE AND TIME FUNCTIONS

The following are Excel's date functions:

DATE(*year, month, day*): returns the serial number of the specified day. If *day* is 0, it returns last day of previous month. If *month* is 0, it returns last month of previous year

DATEVALUE(*date text*): returns the serial number of *date text*. Use this to import dates from other worksheets if they are labels

DAY(*serial number*): converts *serial number* to the day of the month

DAYS360(*start date, end date*): returns the number of days between two dates based on a 360-day year

HOUR(*serial number*): converts *serial number* to the hour of the day

MINUTE(*serial number*): converts *serial number* to the minute

MONTH(*serial number*): converts *serial number* to the month of the year

NOW( ): returns the serial number of the current date and time. There is no argument

SECOND(*serial number*): converts *serial number* to the second

TIME(*hour, minute, second*): returns the serial number for the specified time

TIMEVALUE(*time text*): returns the serial number of *time text*

TODAY( ): returns the serial number of today's date. There is no argument

WEEKDAY(*serial number*): converts *serial number* to the day of the week (Sunday = 1)

YEAR(*serial number*): converts *serial number* to the year

For dates in the twenty-first century, use a three-digit year number; e.g., =DATE(101,4,1) is April 1, 2001. You can use any year up to 2040 with this method.

You can enter a date in a cell using the DATE function. For example, =DATE(92,04,15) stores the equivalent serial number for April 15, 1992 in the cell. If you enter an illegal date, Excel will try to calculate a serial date based on the number. For example, if you enter a day of 32 for a month with 31 days, the serial number returned will be for the first day of the next month. You will get no error message.

Once a date is entered, use the Number command under the Format menu to format the serial number to the desired date form.

You also can enter a date by clicking the cell and typing the date in the desired format. The cell will be formatted automatically. You can use custom date pictures by entering them with the Number command.

You can write formulas to calculate the number of days between any two dates. (The calculations will be performed on the serial date numbers.) The result will be the true difference in days; to get the difference in weeks, divide by 7.

If the number of seconds is not important, you can omit the third argument. Be sure to keep the comma, though. Example: =TIME(7,15,)

The TIME function works in a similar way. For example, =TIME(3,15,10) becomes **3:15 a.m.** You can enter a time and then format it. You also can enter a time in any valid time format and it will be formatted automatically. The time is stored as a fractional number and represents the fraction of the day that has elapsed. For example, 8:00 a.m. is stored as 0.333.

You also can take the difference of two times. The difference, when multiplied by 24, will give you the true difference in hours. (Remember that the fraction represents the fractional part of 24 hours that has elapsed.) To convert a fractional hour to minutes, multiply by 60. Use the INT function to extract the fractional part of a date or to get the fractional part of an hour.

The NOW( ) function is useful for time-stamping your worksheets. Use the special format that includes both the date and time: *m/d/yy h:mm*. This will be wider than a standard cell width, so put it in a wide cell. The date and time will be updated each time you calculate the worksheet (see *Changing Formulas to Values* earlier in the chapter).

Using the techniques of Chapter 6, you can create custom date and time formats.

SPECIAL-PURPOSE FUNCTIONS

Excel's special-purpose functions are the following:

ADDRESS(*row, column, abs, ref style, worksheet*): returns reference as text to a single cell

AREAS(*ref*): returns the number of areas in *ref. Ref* can refer to multiple areas. Example: AREAS(A1:A5,B1) equals 2

CELL(*type of info, reference*): returns information on cell. Use this when writing macros to get information on cell

CHOOSE(*index, value 1, value 2, . . ., value n*): returns the value from the list of arguments based on the value of *index.* If *index* is 1, *value 1* is returned

COLUMN(*ref*): returns the column number of *ref.* If *ref* is omitted, it returns the column number of the current cell. *Ref* cannot refer to multiple areas

COLUMNS(*array*): returns the number of columns in *array*

HLOOKUP(*lookup value, compare array, index number*): searches the first row of *compare array* for the largest value that is less than or equal to *lookup value.* The function moves down the column by the amount specified by *index number* and returns the value found there

INDEX(*array, row, column*): returns the value of a single element within *array,* selected by *row* and *column*

INDEX(*ref, row, column, area*): returns the cell that is defined in *ref* by *row* and *column.* If *ref* refers to multiple areas, *area* defines the areas from which the cell is to be obtained

INDIRECT(*ref, type of ref*): returns contents of cell from its *ref*

INFO(*type number*): returns information on the current operating environment

LOOKUP(*lookup value, compare array*): searches first row or column of *compare array* for largest value that is less than or equal to *lookup value.* The function returns the corresponding value in the last row or column of *compare array.* Whether the first row or column is searched depends on the size of the array. If it is square or has more rows than columns, LOOKUP searches the first column and gives a value from the corresponding last column. If there are more columns than rows, the first row is searched and LOOKUP gives the value of the corresponding cell in the last row. The values in the array can be text, numbers, or logical, but they must be in ascending order

LOOKUP(*lookup value, compare vector, result vector*): searches *compare vector* for largest value less than or equal to *lookup value.* The function returns the corresponding value of *result vector.* The values in *compare vector* can be text, numbers, or logical, but they must be in ascending order. Microsoft recommends using this version of LOOKUP rather than the next one

MATCH(*lookup value, compare vector, type*): returns the corresponding number of the comparison value in *compare vector* that matches *lookup value.* Example: If the lookup value matches the second comparison value, MATCH returns a **2**

MDETERM(*array*): returns determinant of *array*

MINVERSE(*array*): returns inverse of *array*

MMULT(*array 1, array 2*): returns product of two arrays

N(*value*): returns numeric value of *value*

NA( ): returns the error value of #N/A (value not available). There is no argument

ROW(*ref*): returns the row number of *ref* if *ref* references a single cell. If *ref* refers to a range of cells, a vertical array is returned. If the argument is omitted, the row of the current cell is returned. ROW cannot refer to multiple areas

ROWS(*array*): returns the number of rows in *array*

SUMPRODUCT(*array 1, array 2*): multiplies corresponding components of the specified arrays and returns sum of those products

T(*value*): returns text representation of *value*

TRANSPOSE(*array*): returns an array that is the transpose of *array;* that is, the rows become columns and the columns rows

TYPE(*value*): returns a code defining the type of *value:* 1 for number, 2 for text, 4 for logical, 16 for error, and 64 for an array. This is useful in user-defined functions to determine the type or argument passed to it

VLOOKUP(*lookup value, compare array, index number*): identical to HLOOKUP, except that it searches the first column of *compare array,* moving right in that row the amount specified by *index number*

For more information on the lookup functions, please refer to Chapter 13.

SOLVING FOR X

3.0

Excel permits you to define a goal and work backward to find data values that will give you this goal. This is called solving for *x,* the variable. There are two ways of doing this: using the Goal Seek command on the Formula menu and using the Solver utility provided with Excel. The utility is described in Chapter 25.

For now, let's see how to use the simple Goal Seek command. Use the amortization schedule worksheet and assume you are purchasing a car and can only afford $175 a month on the payments. How much of a loan can you assume if the interest remains constant?

With the amortization schedule loaded, make the cell active that contains the payment value. Open the Formula menu and choose Goal Seek. Figure 8.4 shows the dialog box, which you can move by dragging the title bar if you need to see certain worksheet cells. The Set Cell text box contains the goal cell, or B10 here. This defines the cell for the payment. The To Value text box contains the goal value, or $175 here. The By Changing Cell text box contains the cell that can be changed to meet the goal. Enter **B6**, the cell containing the principal. Click OK.

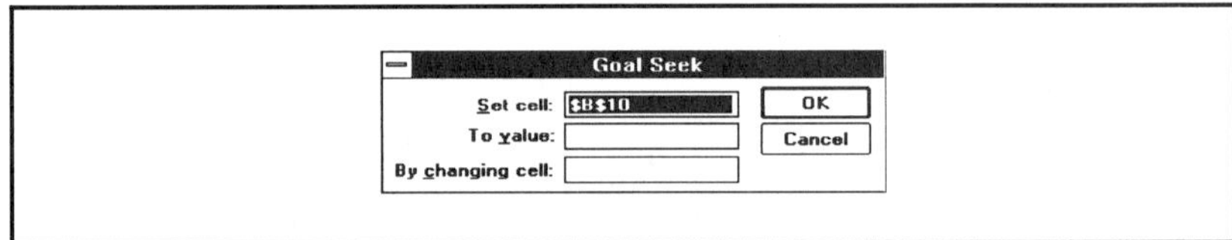

Figure 8.4: Defining the parameters

Excel performs iterative calculations to find the correct value and then displays the worksheet with the new principal ($6645.44) for this payment. Click OK to keep the new principal and payment in the cells or Cancel to return to the unaltered worksheet.

For more complex simulations involving several cells, use the Solver (Chapter 25).

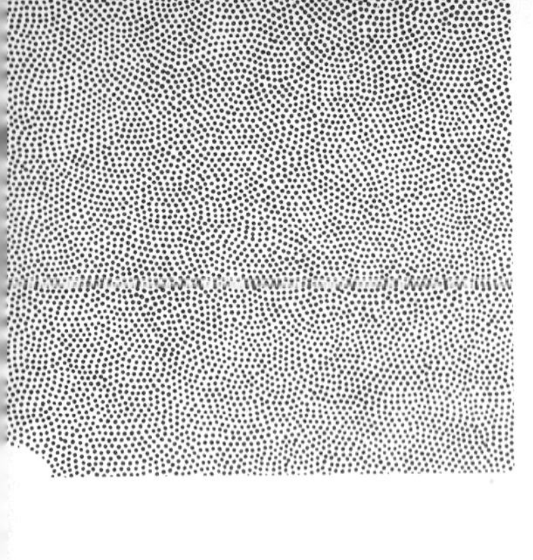
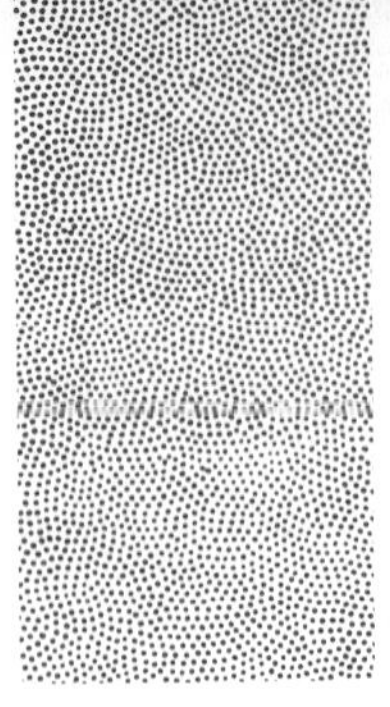

9 Organizing and Documenting Worksheets

HOW YOU ORGANIZE AND DOCUMENT YOUR WORKsheets is important, as this makes the worksheet easier to read and improves its accuracy. In this chapter you will learn the following:

- How to name cells and cell ranges
- How to use the outline feature of Excel
- How to add comments to a cell
- How to audit your worksheets

While working with this chapter, you will be working with both the Income and Balance worksheets you have already created. You will be changing these, but avoid saving either of these worksheets with the changes. We also will be referring to some data in the cash-flow worksheet of Chapter 7. You do not need to create this worksheet; simply refer to Figure 7.15.

NAMING CELLS

When you are creating a worksheet, you may often find it advantageous to identify a cell or cell range. Names make worksheets and formulas easier to work with and read. They also reduce the likelihood of writing an incorrect formula, because you reference a cell's name, not its address. You can name areas of a worksheet to make it easy to go quickly to that area, such as an assumption area, for editing. Another use of naming is to name a constant, such as an interest rate. This makes it easier to understand what the constant represents.

Once you have defined a name, you can use it in functions and formulas, just as you would use a cell or cell-range reference. For example, you could name a cell range and use the range name in a SUM function. You also can use names with the Goto command to simplify moving to a cell or cell range.

You can use names for absolute, relative, or mixed cell references, although names are generally used for absolute references. For example, the cash-flow analysis worksheet shown in Chapter 7 used a series of constants in column L (near the top of the page). These were part of the worksheet calculations for each month (see Figure 7.15). You could give the names *Interest, Cost_of_Goods_Ratio,* and *Advertising _Ratio,* to the three cells in column L. The formula for cell C26, the advertising cost for February, would then be

=Advertising_Ratio*B14

where B14 is January's total sales. You also could give cell B14 a name. You would, however, have to use relative cell addressing in defining that name if you wanted to use a Copy or Fill command to copy the formula into other cells.

DEFINING NAMES

There are two ways that you can name a cell or cell range:

- Use the Create Names command on the Formula menu (or Ctrl-Shift-F3) to designate row or column titles as names
- Use the Define Name command on the Formula menu (or Ctrl-F3) to create a name for any cell, cell range, or constant

Using an Existing Name

The easiest way to define a name for a row or column is to use the row or column title:

1. Select the entire row or column.
2. Open the Formula menu and choose Create Names (or press Ctrl-Shift-F3). The Create Names dialog box shown in Figure 9.1 appears.
3. Select Top Row if you wish to use column titles as names; select Left Column if you wish to use row titles as names. Notice that you also can name upward from a bottom row or to the left of a right column. You can use both row and column titles by choosing both Top Row and Left Column.
4. Click OK.

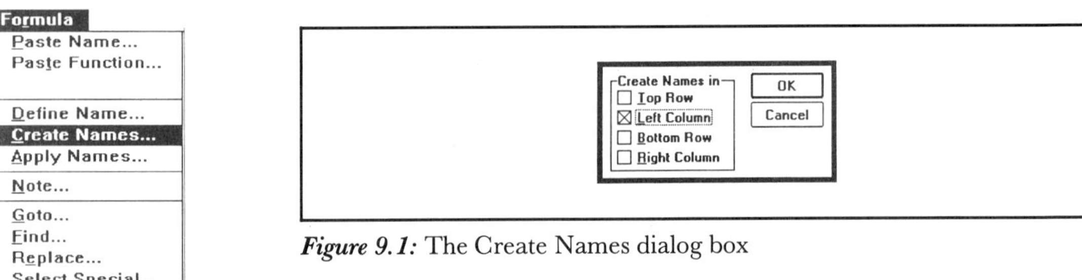

Figure 9.1: The Create Names dialog box

As an example, let's use the simple Income worksheet that you created in Chapter 3, shown in Figure 9.2.

Now try the following exercise:

1. Select rows 5–12 by selecting the range A5 to D12.
2. Open the Formula menu and choose Create Names (or just press Ctrl-Shift-F3).
3. When the Create Names dialog box shown in Figure 9.1 is displayed, select Left Column, then click OK.
4. Select cell B8. The cell's current formula is displayed in the formula bar, as shown in Figure 9.3.

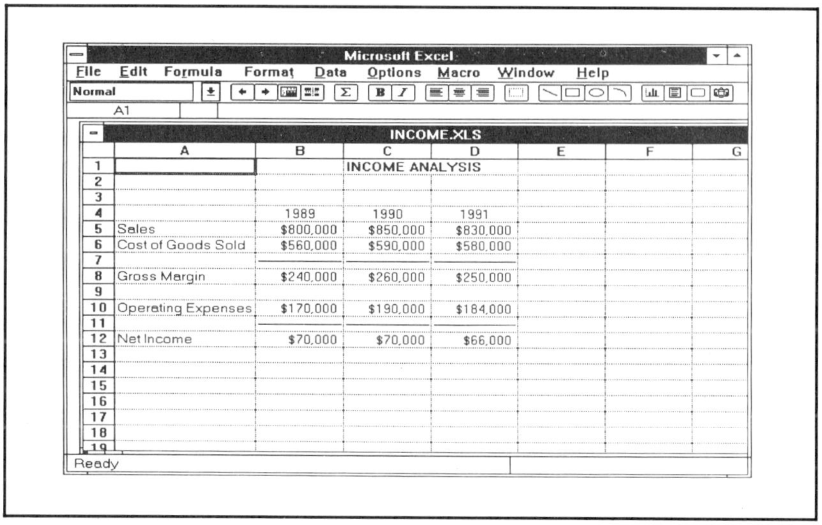

Figure 9.2: The Income worksheet

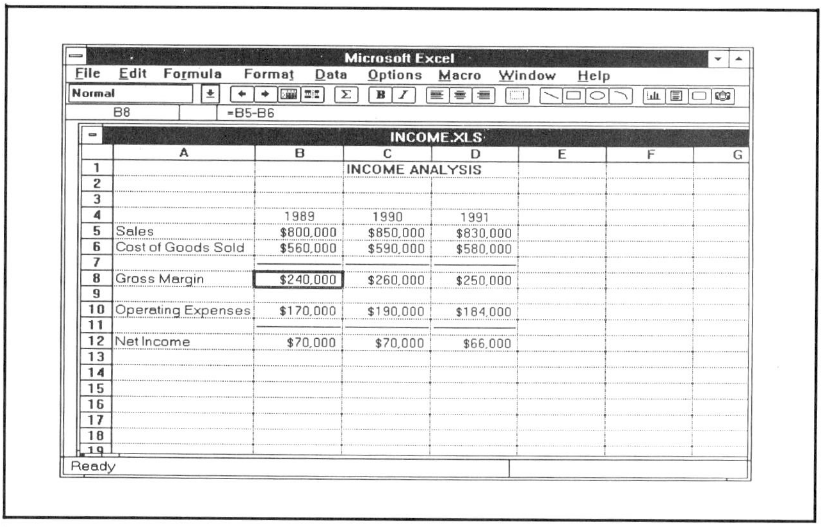

Figure 9.3: The selected cell's current formula displayed in the formula bar

5. Open the Formula menu again and choose Paste Name (or just press F3). The Paste Name dialog box shown in Figure 9.4 appears. It lists the names that are currently available. These names are the row titles that you selected in Step 1. Notice that Excel automatically converted all the

spaces that were in the names into underlines. This is because you cannot use spaces in names.

6. Double-click Sales. The dialog box clears and an equal sign as well as the name **Sales** are entered in the cell (and formula bar), as shown in Figure 9.5.
7. Enter a minus sign after the name.
8. Open the Formula menu again and select Paste Name (or just press F3). When the Paste Name dialog box appears, double-click Cost_of_Goods_Sold. This name will appear in the formula bar as part of the expression, as shown in Figure 9.6.
9. Press Enter or click the Enter box (the ✓) in the formula bar and the correct total will appear in cell B8.

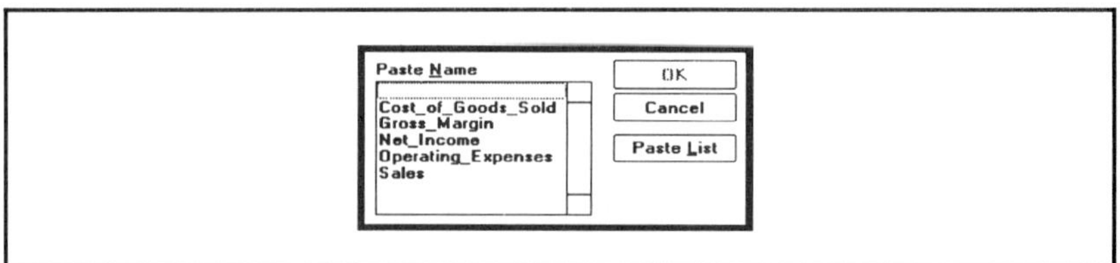

Figure 9.4: The names available for pasting

	A	B	C	D
1			INCOME ANALYSIS	
4		1989	1990	1991
5	Sales	$800,000	$850,000	$830,000
6	Cost of Goods Sold	$560,000	$590,000	$580,000
8	Gross Margin	=Sales	$260,000	$250,000
10	Operating Expenses	$170,000	$190,000	$184,000
12	Net Income	$70,000	$70,000	$66,000

Figure 9.5: Pasting a name in a formula

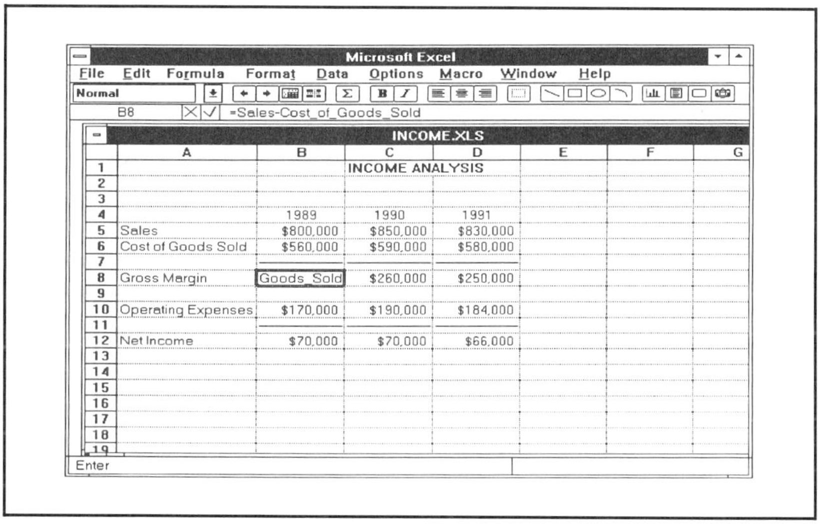

Microsoft Excel

File Edit Formula Format Data Options Macro Window Help

B8 =Sales-Cost_of_Goods_Sold

INCOME.XLS

	A	B	C	D	E	F	G
1			INCOME ANALYSIS				
2							
3							
4		1989	1990	1991			
5	Sales	$800,000	$850,000	$830,000			
6	Cost of Goods Sold	$560,000	$590,000	$580,000			
7							
8	Gross Margin	Goods_Sold	$260,000	$250,000			
9							
10	Operating Expenses	$170,000	$190,000	$184,000			
11							
12	Net Income	$70,000	$70,000	$66,000			

Enter

Figure 9.6: The formula bar after the second name is pasted

You do not assign the name with the Create Names command. The name is simply taken from the first cell in the row or column. Spaces are converted to underlines. If you wish to assign your own name, see the next section.

Now select B8 to D8 and use the Fill Right command in the Edit menu to copy the new equation to the other columns.

Creating a Name

You also can assign a name to a cell or cell range that is not a row or column title by using the Define Name command on the Formula menu. You can choose a name and assign it to any type of worksheet range, even a discontinuous range.

Try creating a name for row 8 of your Income worksheet:

1. Select the cell range you want to name by selecting A8 to D8.
2. Open the Formula menu and choose Define Name (or press Ctrl-F3).
3. The Define Name window shown in Figure 9.7 is displayed. It lists the names that are currently active and shows the cell range that you just selected in the Refers To box. Enter Gross_Sales at the cursor location in the text box, then press Enter or click OK. Use an underline instead of a space to separate the two words. Notice which letters are in capitals. Names are case-sensitive, so maintain consistency here.

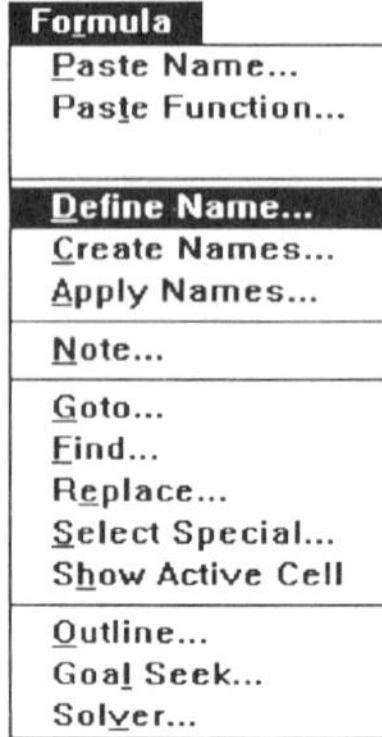

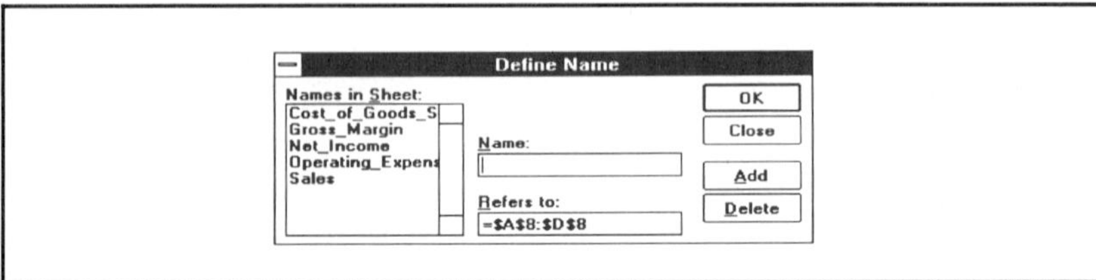

Figure 9.7: Defining a name

The following rules are applicable to creating names:

- The first character must be a letter
- Spaces are not allowed
- Except for the first character, letters, digits, periods, and underlines can be used
- Names can be up to 255 characters long
- Uppercase and lowercase letters are distinguished from each other
- The name cannot look like an absolute, relative, or mixed cell reference, such as *$B$2*
- Text and dates can be used to define a name
- You can use discontinuous ranges to define a name, such as *H1:H3,H7:H12*

If you try to use a name that breaks any of these rules, Excel will display an illegal-name message.

You can define more than one name at a time by clicking the Add button in the dialog box after each entry.

Using the Define Name Window

Instead of selecting a cell or cell range, you can use the Refers To box on the Define Name window to define the range to which a name refers. You can even enter formulas or other names as part of the reference.

Any cell(s) that you select before you invoke the Define Name command will appear in the Refers To box when the window is displayed. You can change that entry and your new cell or cell range will replace the previous selection. You can also clear the entry in the Refers To box by selecting the entire contents and pressing the Backspace key.

You can enter the cell or cell range in the Refers To box either by typing it from the keyboard or by clicking the cell you want to reference in the worksheet before choosing Define Name. If you click a cell, its address will be entered as an absolute cell reference. (The opposite is true when you click a cell to enter it to the formula bar—then it is a relative cell reference.) You can, of course, enter a cell address from the keyboard as an absolute, relative, or mixed cell reference.

The commands on the Edit menu are not available for editing the Define Name window. Although you can mark a portion for cutting or moving, you will not be able to execute any operation.

WORKING WITH NAMES

Once you have named a cell or cell range, you can use that name in many ways. You can perform cut, copy, and fill operations in the same way that you did with other types of cell referencing. You can enter names into formulas, which you did earlier in this chapter, and you can use names with the Goto command.

Names and the Goto Command

Using names with the Goto command moves you directly to any specific cell or cell range. Try this with your Income worksheet. Open the Formula menu and choose Goto (or just press F5). When the Goto dialog box shown in Figure 9.8 is displayed, double-click Net_Income. The cursor will move to this row on the screen right away.

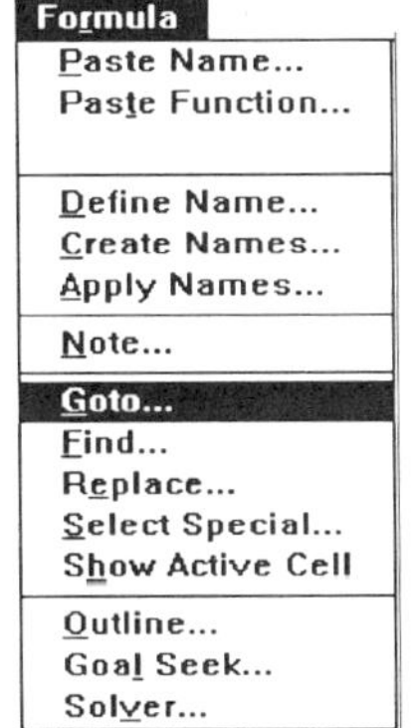

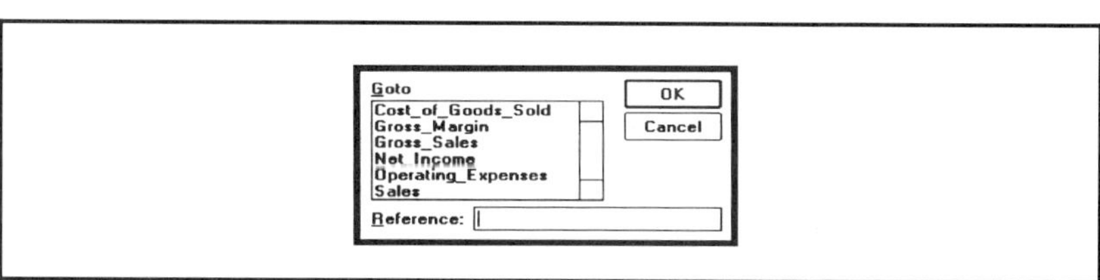

Figure 9.8: The Goto dialog box

EDITING AND DELETING NAMES

To edit a name that you have already defined, open the Formula menu and choose Define Name (or press Ctrl–F3). The Define Name window (see Figure 9.7) will be displayed. Scroll until the name that you want to edit is visible, then select it. The current name will be displayed in the Name box and the current reference will be in the Refers To box. The contents of either box can be edited. Click OK when you have completed your editing.

Excel does not delete the old name when you edit the spelling of a name. Formulas change correctly, but you should take the time to delete the old name and double-check your formulas.

If you want to delete a name that you previously defined, first edit any cell references in the worksheet that use the name so that they no longer use it. If you don't do this, all cells referencing that name will display an error message.

Invoke the Find command in the Formula menu to locate all references to the name. When the dialog box is displayed, type the name you will delete in the Find What field. Check Formulas and Part in the Find dialog box and select either option in the Look By column. (Choose Part if the name is part of a whole name—such as *SALES* in 91SALES and 92SALES; otherwise choose Whole.) When you click OK, the first occurrence will be displayed. Press F7 to find successive occurrences. As an exercise, delete the Gross_Sales name that you defined earlier:

1. Open the Formula menu and choose Define Name (or press Ctrl–F3).
2. When the Define Name window is displayed, choose Gross_Sales.
3. Select Delete.

PRECAUTIONS IN NAMING CELLS

Keep the following precautions, notes, and tips in mind when naming cells:

- Deleting a cell name that is used in worksheet cells will invoke error messages. Edit the cells first so that they no longer use the name
- When you insert a row or column anywhere within a named range, the definition will change accordingly.

- If you cut and paste an entire named range, the definition will be changed accordingly
- Avoid using relative references when naming cell ranges. The result will depend on the active cell when the name is defined. The name definition will also change if you copy or move the cell in which the name is used. Excel defaults to absolute references

APPLYING NAMES TO EXISTING FORMULAS

Composing a formula out of cell names, rather than normal cell references, makes the formula easier to read. As you can see, the formula

=Total_Sales*Tax_Rate

calculates the tax on a sale more intuitively than

=B4*A7

does. To create a formula that uses cell names, you first have to give the relevant cells names, then you have to apply the names to the formula. Naming a cell that a formula references will not automatically rewrite that formula. For instance, in the example above, giving cell B4 the name *Total_Sales* and cell A7 the name *Tax_Rate* will not automatically change the formula =B4*A7 to =Total_Sales*Tax_Rate. But once those cells *are* named, it is easy to rewrite the formula.

Try this:

1. Select the cell containing the formula.
2. Open the Formula menu and choose Apply Names. The list box will show the active names in the worksheet (see Figure 9.9).
3. Select the names you wish to substitute for references in the existing formula. You can select multiple names by hold-ing downthe Shift key and clicking with the mouse.
4. Make other selections as necessary (see below) and click OK.

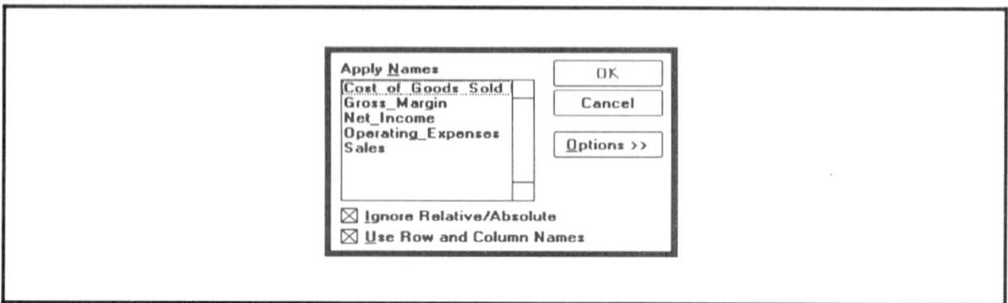

Figure 9.9: The Apply Names dialog box

At the bottom of the dialog box are two options: one determines whether to ignore relative/absolute references; the second whether to use row and column names. When the first option is turned on, Excel ignores relative/absolute references and replaces absolute references with absolute names and relative references with relative names. Leave this option turned on, unless you plan to copy cells to a new location and need to preserve the reference styles of the formulas. The second option, when selected, permits the Apply Names command to rename cell ranges defined by row and column headings.

Additional options are available when you click the Options button in this dialog box (see Figure 9.10). This dialog box permits you to omit a column name in the same column, omit a row name in the same row, and control the name order (by row or column).

MAKING A NAME LIST

It's a good idea to make a list of named cells and their corresponding addresses on the worksheet, so that you have a handy record of what is

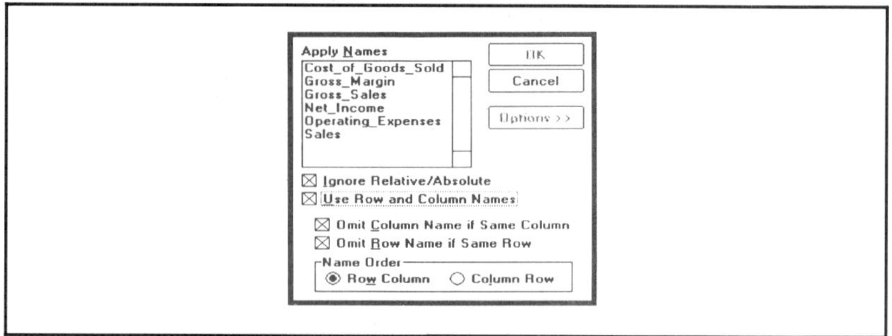

Figure 9.10: Advanced Apply Names options

what. It takes up two columns and can be as long as necessary to list all the names. Find a worksheet area that this will not erase and select the top two cells for the list. Open the Formula menu and choose Paste Name (or press F3). When the dialog box is displayed, choose Paste List. This will paste the current names and their references in the two selected columns of the worksheet (see Figure 9.11).

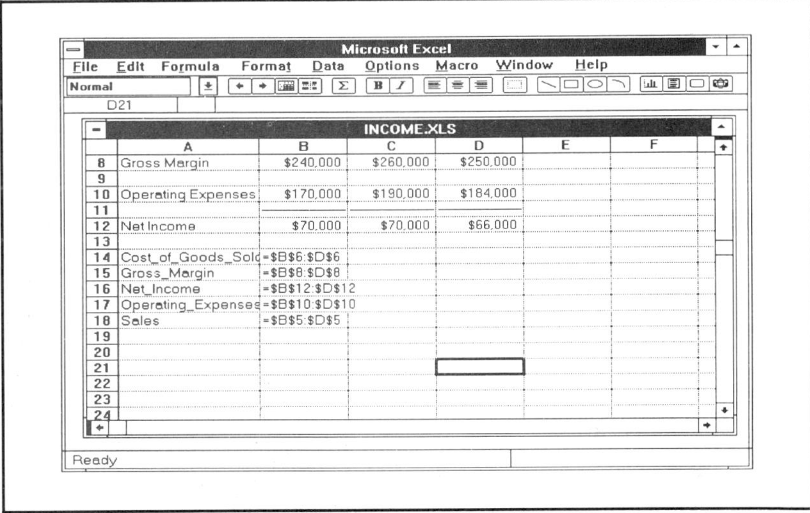

Figure 9.11: Pasting a name list to a worksheet

This table will overwrite any data in the columns it fills. If you overwrite worksheet data by mistake, select Undo from the Edit menu immediately.

This list is static: if you edit the names later you must repaste the list to update it.

You have now defined and pasted names using a simple worksheet. The same techniques can be applied to any type of document. You probably will use names quite often to clarify your worksheet formulas and function arguments.

OUTLINING WORKSHEETS

3.0

Outlining a worksheet is a rather useful feature of Excel. You can:

- Compress the worksheet to show summary information only, making it easier for people to see the relevant data without wading through the details

- Outline when charting to eliminate detail data. For example, if you have weekly sales figures and monthly summary data, you can ignore the weekly data and plot just the monthly totals

Excel can outline rows or columns. To simplify things we will limit the discussion to outlining rows.

Outlining involves grouping rows based on a hierarchy. Moving a row up a level is called *promoting* that row. Moving a row down a level is called *demoting* that row. Excel accepts up to seven outline levels.

Excel does its outlining automatically, based on these factors:

- **Indentation**: blank cells at the beginning of a row are used to define levels
- **Formulas**: Excel can determine from the types of formulas where the levels should break
- **Row headings**: these are used as level headings for the outline breaks
- **Formula reference direction**: Excel uses the *direction* in which the formulas reference to determine level breakings. You should use a consistent referencing direction. Typical directions are bottom to top and right to left. In the Balance worksheet, for instance, references always refer to rows above the current cell

You can manually promote or demote rows (or columns) in the outline from this, but it is helpful when first designing the worksheet to understand how the outlining works. Design your worksheet to support, as much as possible, Excel's automatic outlining feature.

You can outline from the tool bar or the menu bar. Figure 9.12 shows the buttons on the tool bar that are used in outlining.

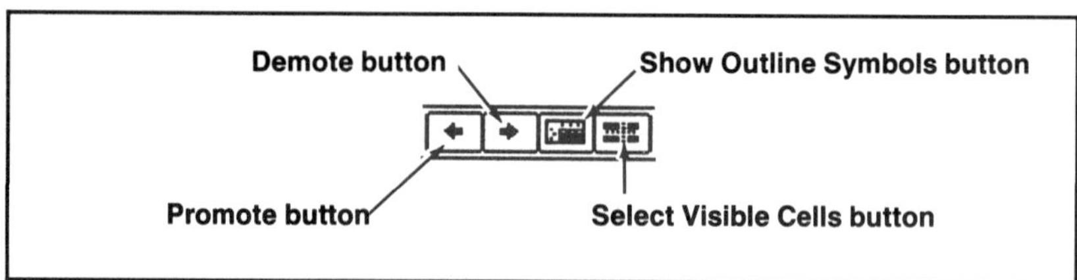

Figure 9.12: The tool bar buttons for outlining

- **Promote button:** raises selected rows or columns to a higher level
- **Demote button:** moves selected rows or columns to a lower level
- **Select Visible Cells button:** selects only visible cells in an outline. Useful for charting or copying
- **Show Outline Symbols button:** toggles the display of the outline symbols or, if no outline exists, creates an outline

CREATING THE OUTLINE

To see how outlining works, let's create an outline from the Balance sheet. Open the Balance worksheet and follow these steps:

1. Select the range to outline: A10 to E44.
2. Choose Outline from the Formula menu.
3. In the dialog box (Figure 9.13), specify whether summary columns are to be included. Click the Summary Rows Below Detail check box and be sure Summary Columns To Right of Detail is not checked.
4. Click the Create button.

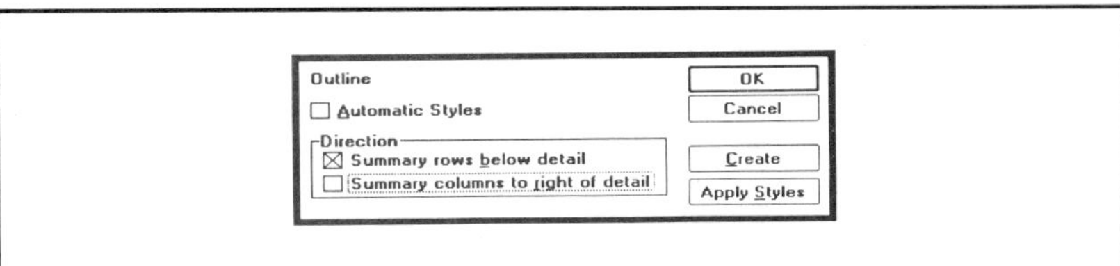

Figure 9.13: The Outline dialog box

Another way to create an outline is to select the range and click the Show Outline Symbols button on the tool bar. Then fill out the dialog box in the same way.

Excel outlines the worksheet and automatically displays the outline symbols. Excel includes some built-in cell styles for summary rows and columns. If you wish to apply these automatically, be sure Automatic Styles is turned on. The summary row here is already formatted, so this is not selected.

Figure 9.14 shows the outlined worksheet. Notice the following features in the worksheet window (columns are not outlined in this example):

- **Row Level buttons:** indicates the number of row levels in an outline
- **Collapse Button (minus sign):** collapses rows or columns under this item
- **Expand button (plus sign):** expands rows or columns under this item
- **Row Level bars:** indicates that all detail data are displayed

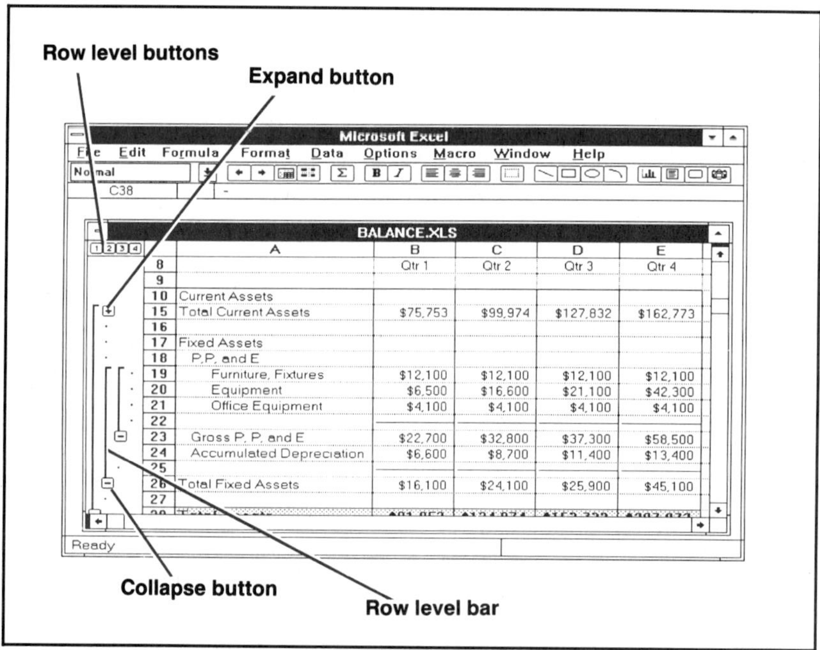

Figure 9.14: The outlined worksheet

If you wish to hide the outline buttons, open the Options menu and select Display, toggle the Outline Symbols option off, and click OK. Toggling the check box on will display them again. Another way to toggle the outline symbols display is to click the Show Outline Symbols button on the tool bar.

If you make a mistake in creating an outline and wish to start over, the easiest method may be to clear the outline from the worksheet. Clearing an outline does not affect the worksheet data. To clear an outline, first select the outlined area. Then click the Promote button, or press Alt-Shift-←, to promote all rows and columns to level one. The symbols will disappear.

EDITING THE OUTLINE

If you fail to select an entire row or column, Excel will ask you to specify whether you are promoting or demoting an entire row or column.

You can edit the outline so that rows (or columns) are correctly aligned by level. Do this by promoting and demoting the rows:

- To demote a row (i.e., move it to a lower level), select the entire row and click the Demote button on the tool bar, or press Alt-Shift-→.
- To promote a row (move it to a higher level), select the entire row and click the Promote button on the tool bar, or press Alt-Shift-←.

Columns are demoted and promoted in the same way.

CONTROLLING THE LEVELS DISPLAYED

You can control the levels displayed by expanding or collapsing them. For example, you could create a summary worksheet by collapsing the worksheet around the summary totals.

- To collapse a level, select the row (or column) to collapse and press Alt-Shift-=. You also can click the collapse buttons to collapse portions of the outline
- To expand a level, select the row (or column) to expand and press Alt-Shift--. You also can click the expand buttons to expand portions of the outline
- To display a specific level of the outline, click the corresponding row- or column-level button
- To quickly select a row or column with all detail levels, hold down the Shift key and click the collapse or expand button of the row or column. This is a fast way to select ranges for charting

Figure 9.15 shows the same worksheet after collapsing many rows.

Before continuing, clear the outline by selecting the outlined area and pressing Alt-Shift-← as necessary to promote and clear all symbols.

ADDING COMMENTS TO A WORKSHEET

There are three ways in which Excel allows you to add comments to a worksheet:

- You can place them as text directly on the worksheet. You can refer to it with asterisks or other special symbols from other cells in the worksheet
- You can add them as notes attached to cells. This type of comment is not directly visible, but is attached to the cell and can be viewed or printed using menu commands
- You can place them in a text box and use arrows to point to the cells to which they refer

The first method is easy. Let's look at the other two.

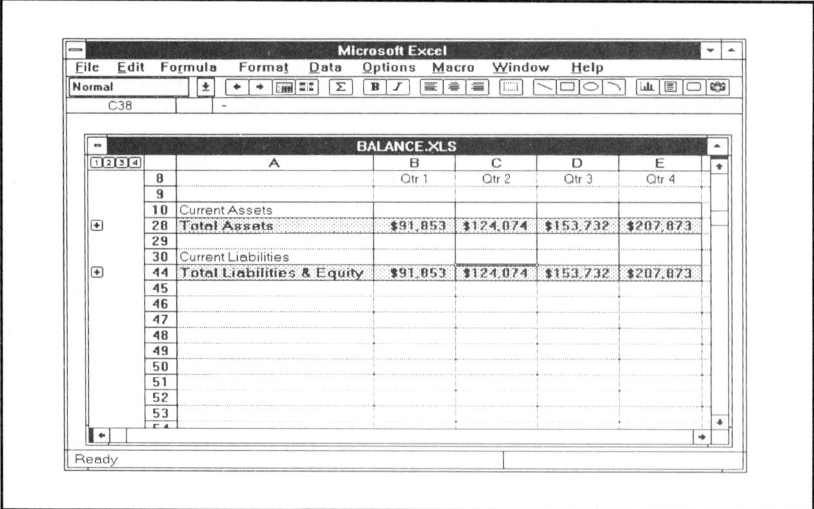

Figure 9.15: The worksheet after collapsing rows

ADDING A NOTE TO A CELL

Sometimes you may wish to add a comment about a cell that will be useful to someone entering data into the worksheet. You do not, however, want the comment to show on the worksheet at all times. Here is a way to add such a comment with Excel. Try this with the Balance worksheet:

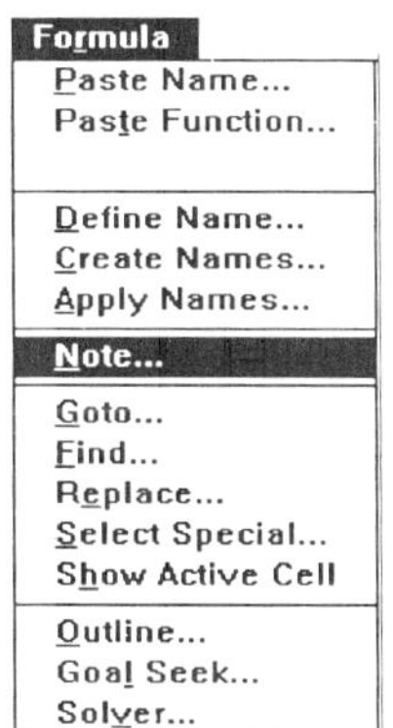

1. Select the cell to which you wish to add the note, in this case cell B13.
2. Open the Formula menu and choose Note.
3. Type the note within the Note box, as shown in Figure 9.16. Word-wrapping is automatically activated—do not use the Enter key at the end of a line.
4. When you have typed the complete note, press Enter or click OK. The Note box will disappear and you will be back at the worksheet. The cell will be marked to show it contains a note.

To add multiple notes, click the Add button on the dialog box.

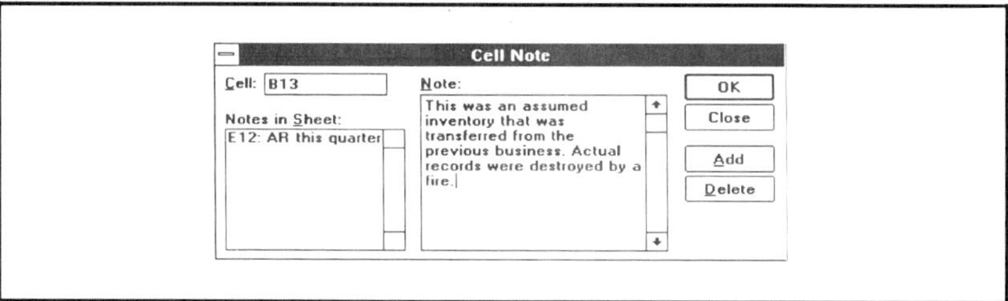

Figure 9.16: Adding a note

To view the note:

1. Select the cell to which the note is attached.
2. Open the Formula menu and choose Note. The note will appear in the Note box.

The Notes in Sheet list box contains available notes on the current worksheet. You can choose any of these to see the corresponding note in the Note box.

To view all notes in the worksheet, choose Show Info from the Window menu. Then choose Arrange All on the Window menu to display the Info window tiled with the worksheet. Activate the worksheet and choose Select Special from the Formula menu. Select the Notes option and click OK (see Figure 9.17). You can now move from cell to cell and see each note.

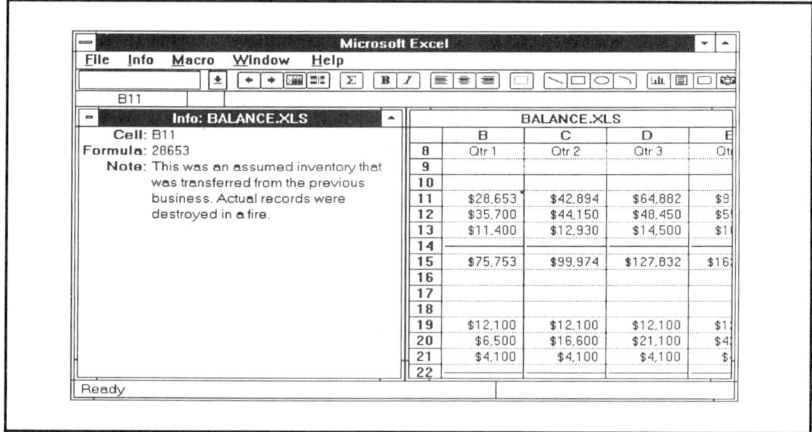

Figure 9.17: Using the Show Info window to view a note

To print all notes in the worksheet, choose Show Info from the Window menu, then choose Print from the File menu. Another method is to select Print and then select the Notes option in the dialog box.

To delete notes, select the cell or cell range from which you wish to clear notes. Choose Clear from the Edit menu and select the Notes option. Another method is to select the cell with the note, choose Note from the Formula menu, and select Delete.

ADDING A NOTE IN A TEXT BOX

Adding a note in a text box is easy with a mouse. Figure 9.18 shows the buttons on the text bar you will need for this.

To add a note in a text box:

1. Click the text-box tool in the tool bar. (To draw multiple text boxes at a time, hold down the Ctrl key and click the tool.)

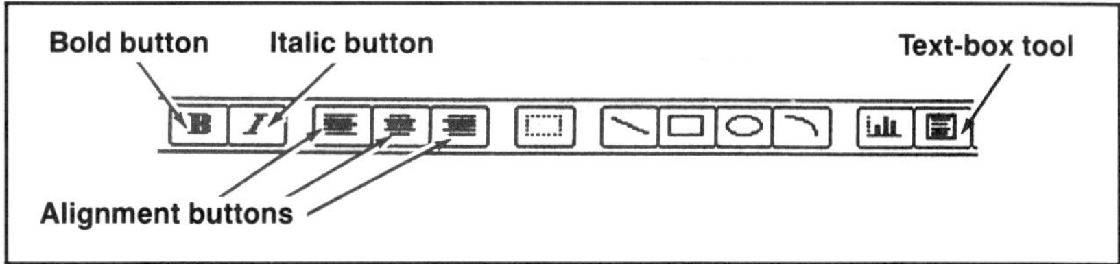

Figure 9.18: The tool bar buttons for creating text-box notes

2. Click the mouse pointer at the upper-left corner of where you wish the text box to sit.
3. Drag the mouse to create a text box of the size you wish. If you wish the text box to be anchored to the underlying grid, hold down the Ctrl key while dragging.
4. Type the desired comment in the text box. Word-wrapping is active, so don't use the Enter key at the end of a line. You also can use the Edit menu to copy to the text box, as when copying a formula.
5. If drawing multiple text boxes, draw the next box and click the text-box tool again when you are finished. If drawing a single text box, click outside the text box when you are finished.
6. You can edit the text in the box using the Edit menu or format it using the Format menu (see Chapter 6).
7. To draw an arrow, click the line tool on the tool bar and drag to create the line in the direction you wish the arrow to point. Open the Format menu and select the Patterns command. Choose a style in the dialog box with an arrowhead (see Figure 9.19). Set the width and length as desired and click OK.

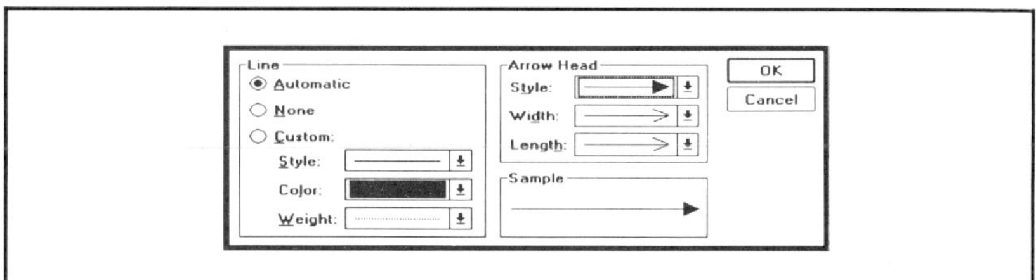

Figure 9.19: Formatting an arrow

Figure 9.20 shows the worksheet with a text box.

To delete a text-box note, select the line and box. Then choose Clear on the Edit menu or press Ctrl–Del.

AUDITING WORKSHEETS

Once a worksheet is created, you should always take the time to check, or audit, the worksheet. There are several techniques you can use in creating a worksheet to minimize errors and related problems:

- Plan the worksheet before starting. Where will the different types of data (assumptions, input, etc.) be placed?
- Use names for cells and cell ranges, and use the names in any expressions. Put the name list on the worksheet.
- Add comments. Use cell notes liberally
- Avoid complex expressions. When writing an expression, break it down over several cells so that the expression in each cell is not complex
- Test the worksheet with data for which you know the results
- Use the Print Preview command in the File menu to see how the resulting worksheet will look before printing it

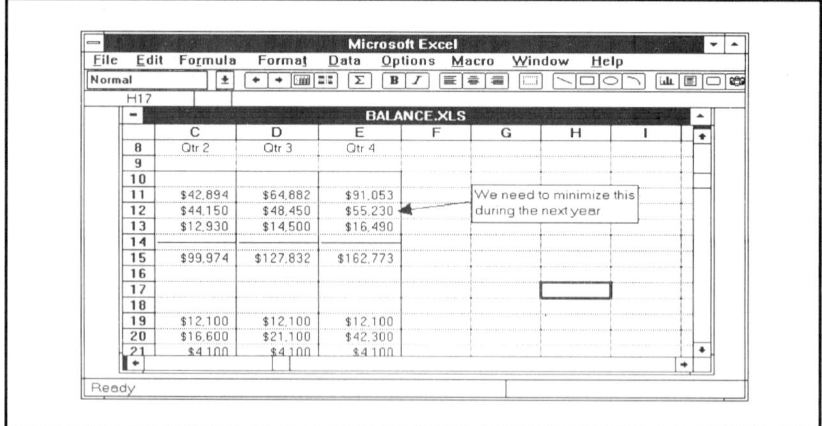

Figure 9.20: Worksheet with a text-box note

In spite of all precautions, however, you will still need to audit each worksheet. Excel provides a variety of tools to help you. Take the time to use them to ensure that the worksheet is accurate and works correctly. Some of these tools work automatically: others you will need to discipline yourself to use.

There are two automatic tools:

- **Circular reference checking**: Excel automatically checks the worksheet for circular references—i.e., cell formulas that directly or indirectly reference the cell containing the formula (see Chapter 14)
- **Formula checking**: Excel checks to be sure that data types are consistent in formulas and issues error messages when it finds a problem. For example, a numeric equation should not reference a cell with text, or an expression should not include division by zero

There are also a few manual tools available for auditing. Here are a few of the types of auditing tasks and the tool you should use for each:

- **Finding cells with error values**: Use Select Special or Find in the Formula menu and search for cells starting with #
- **Finding cells that are "different"**: Use Select Special and choose Row Differences or Column Differences
- **Debugging circular references**: Use the status bar for more specific information
- **Finding detail cell information**: Select Show Info in the Window menu

GETTING CELL INFORMATION

To get specific information on a cell, use the Show Info command in the Window menu. Once you select a cell and this command, a new Show Info window is displayed with its own menu bar. You can resize or move the window on the screen; you also can use Arrange All in the Window menu to tile it on the screen with the worksheet.

As you click the mouse over the worksheet, the Show Info window displays the information about the active cell (see Figure 9.21). Use the Print command on the File menu to print this information. You can preview the printout with the Preview command, just as with a worksheet.

You can control what type of information is displayed by opening the Info menu when the Show Info window is active. You can check to show cell addresses, values, formulas, formats, protection status, names, precedents, dependents, and notes.

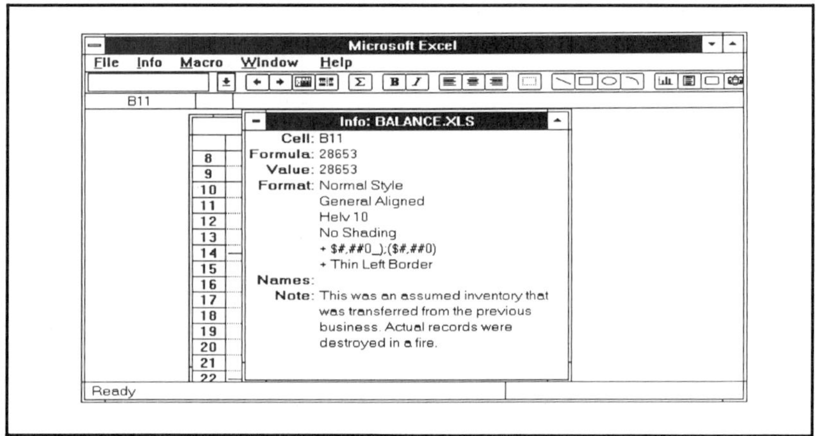

Figure 9.21: Using the Show Info window for auditing

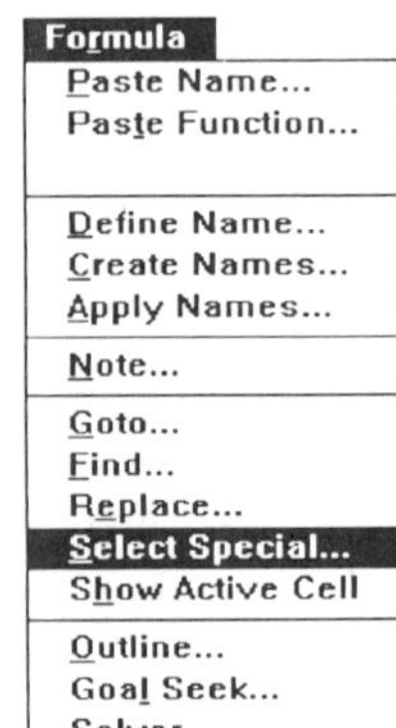

SELECTING CELLS BY CONTENT

Another way to check cells is to select cells by content. This type of auditing is done by using the Select Special command in the Formula menu.

For example, let's try this with our Balance worksheet:

1. Select cells A10 to E44.
2. Create names from the row headings using Create Names on the Formula menu (or by pressing Ctrl-Shift-F3).
3. With the same range selected, apply the names to the entire worksheet using Apply Names (see Figure 9.22) on the Formula menu. All names are selected by default. Click OK.

Check a few formulas, and you will see that names are used in all of them now.

4. Now delete a name using Define Name (or press Ctrl–F3). Delete the name Cash. Choose Delete, then click OK. This will create several error messages in the worksheet, since formulas now reference a name that no longer exists.
5. Choose Select Special from the Formula menu. Select Formulas in the dialog box (see Figure 9.23), and be sure Errors is the only option checked. Choose OK.
6. All cells with the error messages are selected.

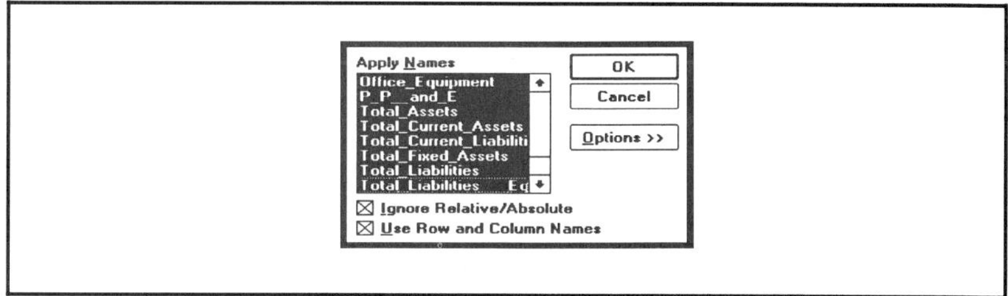

Figure 9.22: Applying names to the entire worksheet

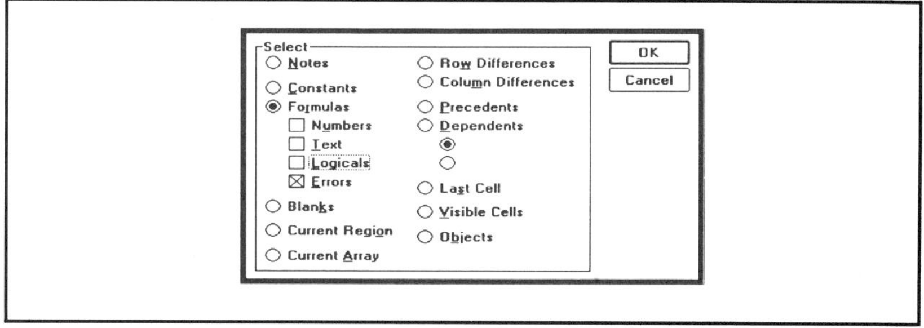

Figure 9.23: Searching for cells with error values

You can use this method to find cells with formulas, cells with notes, cells with constants, cells with no data, row differences, column differences, and cells changed since the last update. For example, you might expect a certain cell to contain a formula and discover that it contains a constant value. This typically happens when formulas are converted to values for one reason or another. For example, if you paste a table value (see Chapter 13) to a cell, it is pasted as a value. It won't change as the table value changes (unless Linked as described in Chapter 16).

LEAVING THE WORKSHEET

The Balance worksheet has been modified in this chapter with various experiments. Don't save the Balance worksheet at this point (or else save it under a different name). In the next chapter you will start building a new worksheet to illustrate database management, tables, and charting.

Effective Database Management

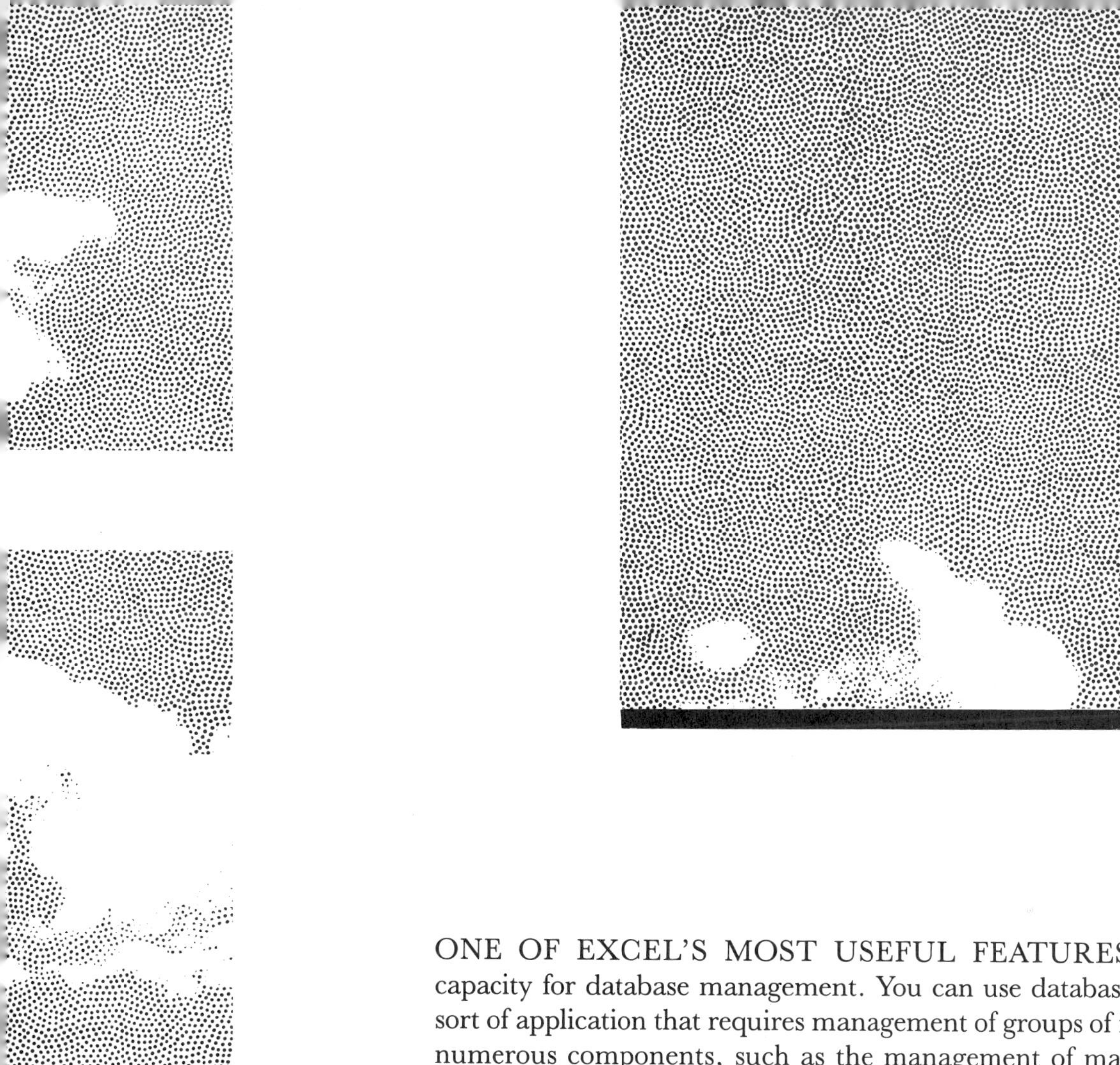

ONE OF EXCEL'S MOST USEFUL FEATURES IS ITS capacity for database management. You can use databases for any sort of application that requires management of groups of items with numerous components, such as the management of mailing lists, prospect lists, census data, a video tape library, or an organization's membership roster. In the case of a mailing list, for example, each database record is an address that includes the name, street address, city, state, zip code, and telephone number.

Excel's on-screen database-management capability allows you to create a database as part of a worksheet and use it to calculate cell values in other parts of the worksheet.

Part III consists of three chapters. Chapter 10 discusses the fundamentals of database management. You will create a database and learn how to add, edit, and delete records in it. In later chapters, this same database will be used to create complex reports and charts. Chapter 11 discusses how to find records in the database that meet specific criteria. Chapter 12 discusses the techniques of sorting and ordering your database.

10 Creating and Editing a Database

YOU CAN LOOK AT THE EXCEL ON-SCREEN DATABASE-management system much as you would an electronic filing system. A database is a structured collection of data. The data may be about people, products, events—in short, anything that you would like to store information about. The primary use of a database is to manage the collection of data for reporting and making decisions.

DATABASE APPLICATIONS

You probably use one or more databases every day, although they are perhaps not electronic. Your address book, the telephone book, the recipe box, and the dictionary are all examples of commonly used databases. Each is a collection of data. In each case, the database is ordered so you can find the information you want quickly. Because none of these are electronic, however, they are relatively cumbersome to update.

Excel, however, permits you to create electronic databases that are easy to use and update. Here are some typical applications for an Excel database:

- Financial: general ledgers, accounts-receivable, payroll and accounts-payable systems
- Sales and marketing: contract management, sales projections, expense accounts, and prospect lists
- Business: personnel registers, telephone-extension directories, inventory listings, low-inventory reports, and material-requirement planning
- Home: cataloging of books and audio recordings, nutrition analyses, and recording of addresses

For example, Widget Manufacturing has a staff of sales representatives in each of four areas of the country. Each representative has a sales target, and the sum of the targets for the representatives in each area represents the sales target for that particular area. Widget also tracks sales performance by representative during each three-month cycle. These data are recorded in a database and used for a variety of reports. Management uses these reports to track the sales performance of each representative and the performance of each sales area.

THE DATABASE COMPONENTS

Figure 10.1 shows a sample Excel database. Notice that it is really nothing more than a rectangular range of worksheet cells. In Excel, a *database* is two or more rows of cells that span at least one column.

Each row represents a single item, or *record.* In this case there are 15 records visible in the database. Each piece of data that you store about an item is called a *field.* In this sample database, the fields are LAST, FIRST, TARGET, and REGION. The first row of the database is used to define the field names. In the worksheet analogy, the records are rows and the fields are columns.

The sales target for each sales representative is shown as part of the Excel database. Notice that the records do not have titles, but each

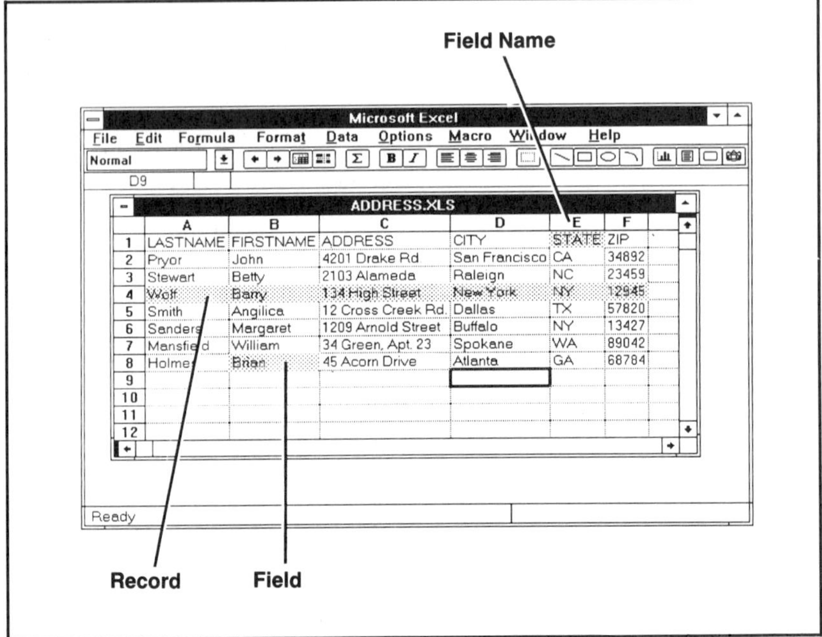

Figure 10.1: The database components

field, including the first, has a name. You can put as many as 16,383 records in an Excel database (the top row must contain the field names).

WORKING WITH DATABASES

The fact that an on-screen database looks very much like a worksheet makes the Excel database so easy to use. There are only two primary differences between the database and the worksheet: in a database, the rows no longer have a title and each column (including the first) has a name (a field name).

The features and commands that are available for working with worksheets are the same as those available for databases. The menu bar at the top of the screen also remains the same. You can define any part of a worksheet for a database and use the remainder for worksheet functions, or you can define the entire worksheet as a database. You can add, edit, and delete records and fields in a database in the same way that you work with cells in a worksheet. You can move data from a database to somewhere else on the worksheet (or from somewhere else on the worksheet to the database) using the familiar Copy, Cut, and Paste commands.

An Excel database can be sorted so that the records are in any desired order. For example, the database in Figure 10.1 could be sorted by name or region. You also can extract information based on a particular criterion; for example, from this database you could extract all the entries for the western region. In this chapter, you will learn the basics of creating a database. In later chapters you'll learn how to extract information (Chapter 11), how to sort the database in any order (Chapter 12), and how to create charts from databases (Chapter 19).

CREATING AN EXCEL DATABASE

Let's create the Sales database shown in Figure 10.2. There are four steps involved in creating and using a database:

1. Defining the fields.
2. Entering the data.
3. Formatting any data as necessary.
4. Defining the database range (that part of the worksheet that will be used as the database).

	A	B	C	D
13	LAST	FIRST	TARGET	REGION
14	Adams	Chuck	$118,000	South
15	Allen	Ellen	$90,000	East
16	Atkins	Lee	$113,000	East
17	Conners	Paul	$142,000	West
18	Ford	Carl	$191,000	Midwest
19	Glenn	John	$80,000	South
20	Harris	Ken	$176,000	West
21	Ellis	Nancy	$122,000	East
22	Jackson	Robert	$112,000	East
23	Keller	Janet	$105,000	West
24	Kennedy	Sandra	$135,000	East
25	Linn	Vera	$80,000	Midwest
26	Parker	Greg	$196,000	South
27	Peterson	Tom	$98,000	Midwest
28	Stevens	Carle	$110,000	East

Figure 10.2: Widget sales targets

DEFINING THE FIELDS

You start creating a database exactly as you would begin a worksheet. Open a new worksheet for the database by opening the File menu and choosing New. You will see the New dialog box, as shown in Figure 10.3. Leave Worksheet selected (because a database is a part of a worksheet) and click OK. Excel displays an empty worksheet.

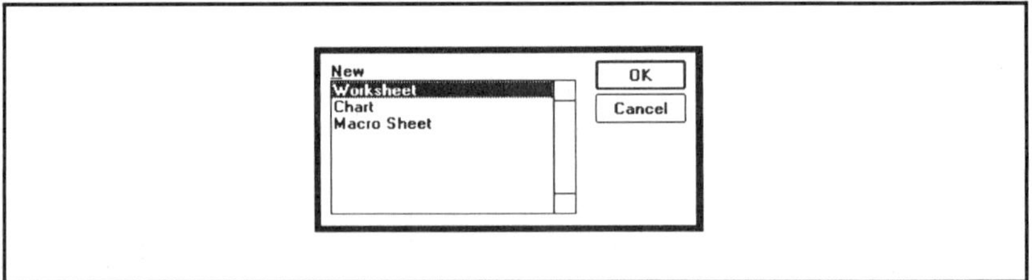

Figure 10.3: Opening a worksheet window for a database

Enter the field names shown in Figure 10.2. Start in row 13, because you will need some working space at the top later. You may use any text (to a maximum of 255 characters) for field names, but it is a good idea to keep the names short to simplify searches. You also can use functions that produce text to create field names; however, you cannot use numbers or functions that produce numbers as field names.

You should plan your database before entering the fields. Usually you will want separate fields for first and last names. This permits you to treat each part of the name as a separate component. You could then use the FIRST field in a form letter (for example, *Dear Vera*). Any piece of data you might use for a search criterion or for sorting should be put in a separate field.

You can use text, numeric values, or logical values for fields. You also can use calculated fields if you wish. For example, for an inventory database you might have a QOH field (Quantity-on-hand) and a COST field. You could then define an extended cost field as QOH*COST (see Chapter 22 for an example).

ENTERING THE DATA

When using formulas in calculated fields, use absolute references or names to refer to cells outside the database range and relative references to refer to cells inside the database range.

Now enter the worksheet data shown in Figure 10.2. The best way to enter a large amount of data like this is record by record, because it follows the way we read: left to right and line by line. Select the entire entry area, then use the Tab key after each entry to move to the next cell.

FORMATTING THE DATA

To save time, format databases column by column, as all cells in a column are formatted the same. The column width should normally be equal to or greater than the longest cell entry in that field.

You can format any data in a database, just as you would any other cell or cell range in a worksheet. Set the picture by selecting Number in the Format menu. For any field width change, use the Column Width option. For any alignment changes, use the Alignment option. Fonts and styles are set with the Font option.

DEFINING THE DATABASE RANGE

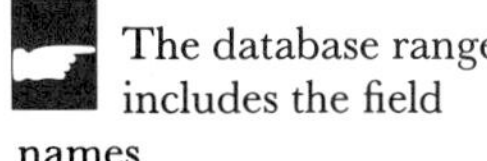

The database range includes the field names.

Now you must define the area of the worksheet that will serve as your database:

1. Select cell A13.
2. Hold down the Shift key and click cell D28. You have now selected the entire database area (see Figure 10.4).
3. Select the Data menu and choose Set Database. This assigns the name *Database* to the worksheet area that you have defined. You can now use this name in commands and formulas.

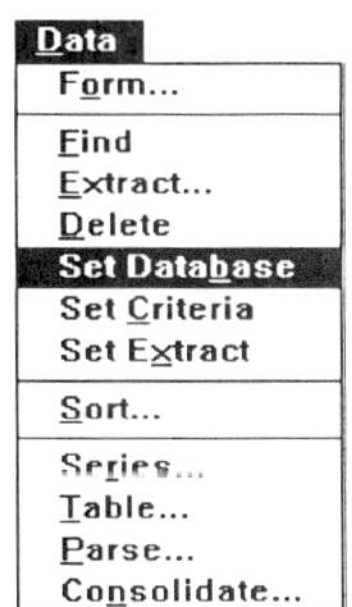

There is really nothing special about what you have just done. You simply defined a range and then named that range Database. You also could have done it with the Define Name command, but the Set Database command is easier. If you open the Formula menu and choose Paste Name, you will see **Database** listed as an available name. This name is used by the commands on the Database menu and the database functions to determine which area of the worksheet to operate on.

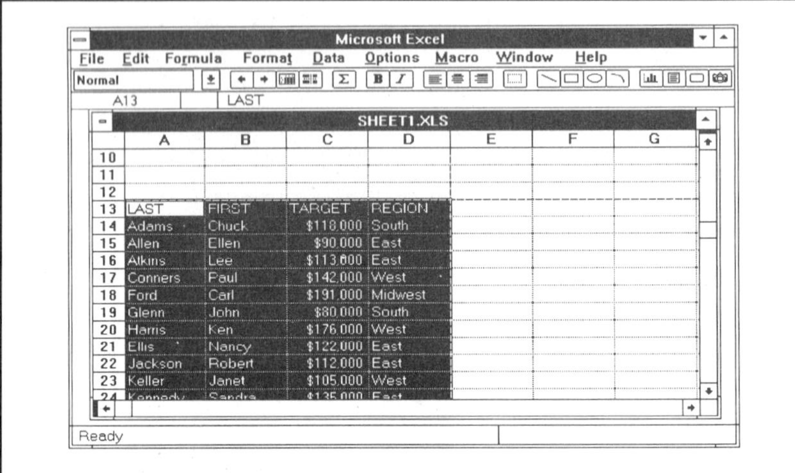

Figure 10.4: Selecting the database range

EDITING A DATABASE

Editing a database involves adding, deleting, editing, and moving records and fields. These operations are described in the following pages. Excel provides two methods of editing the records of a database: using menu commands or using a data form. You can use either method at any time. Choose the one that is the easiest for you.

ADDING A RECORD USING A MENU COMMAND

To add a record to the database using a menu command, first select the row designator where you wish to enter the record. Open the Edit menu and choose Insert. A blank row will be inserted above the selected row (see Figure 10.5). Enter the data in the new record. It is not necessary to reset the database range or to format data entered to any cells: the database range is updated automatically to include the new record and the new record is formatted to match existing records.

There is one exception to the above rule. If you add a record to the end of the database, the database range must be reset (using the Set Database command in the Data menu), and the new record must be

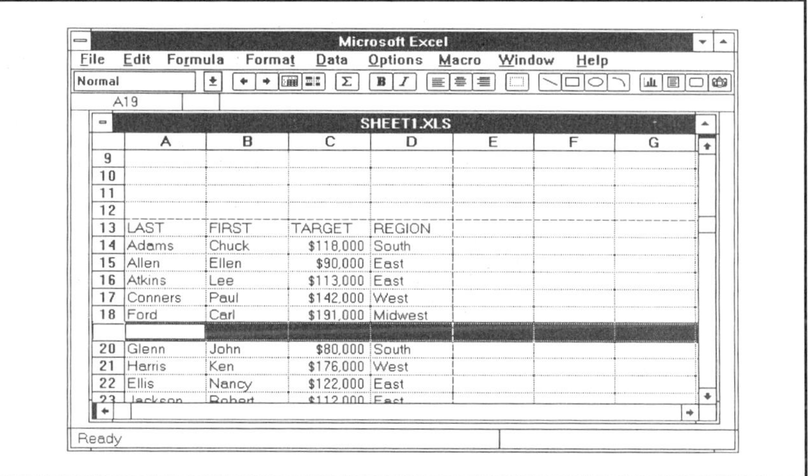

Figure 10.5: Adding a record with a menu command

formatted. To eliminate the need to update the database range and format new data, put a dummy record as the last record that always stays at the end after any sort. The dummy record also should be formatted correctly. Any records inserted before the dummy end-record will automatically extend the range and be formatted. Name the last row so that you can use the Goto command to get to this row quickly.

ADDING A RECORD USING A DATA FORM

To add a record using a data form, open the Data menu and choose Form. A dialog box will be displayed with the fields to the left of a scroll bar and pushbutton selections to the right of the scroll bar, as shown in Figure 10.6. Click the New button. The scroll box moves to the bottom of the scroll bar and an empty record is displayed. Enter the values for the cells in that record. Press the Tab key to move between fields. (Don't press Enter, as it closes the dialog box.) When the record entry is completed, click Close or press Enter, and the new record will be entered at the end of the database. You also can close the dialog box by double-clicking its Control menu or by pressing Alt-F4. The database will be extended automatically and the new fields formatted.

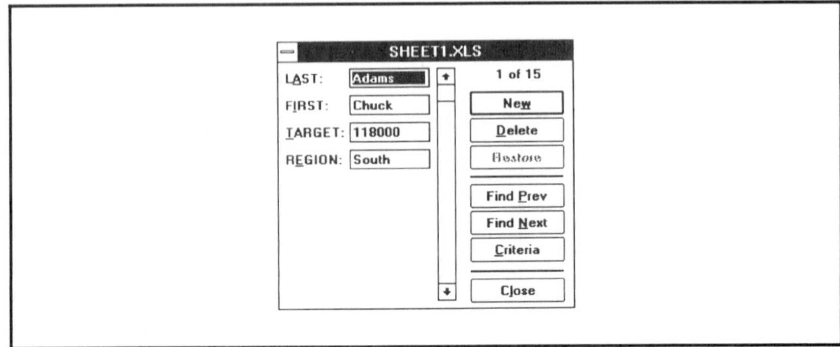

Figure 10.6: Adding a record using a data form

ADDING A FIELD

You can add a field to the database using menu commands, just as when you add records. (You cannot add a field using a data form.) To add a field to the right of the current fields, type the field name at the top of the column and enter the data for each record (see Figure 10.7). You will then have to redefine the database range to include the new field, as well as format the new field.

To eliminate the necessity of updating the database range, add new fields within the current database range instead of beyond it.

You also can insert a field by adding a blank column with the Insert command in the Edit menu. Enter the field name at the top of the new blank column, then enter the data for each record. If you insert a field between other fields, the database range definition is updated automatically, but you probably still have to format the new field column. Fields often have different formats from adjacent fields.

DELETING A RECORD USING A MENU COMMAND

To delete a record from a database using a menu command, select the row designator for the record you wish to delete. Open the Edit menu and choose Delete. The record will be deleted and the records below will move up to recover the space. Be sure there are no data on the row to the right or left of the database area before deletion, or they will be deleted as well. If there *are* other data on the row, only delete the database cells on that row.

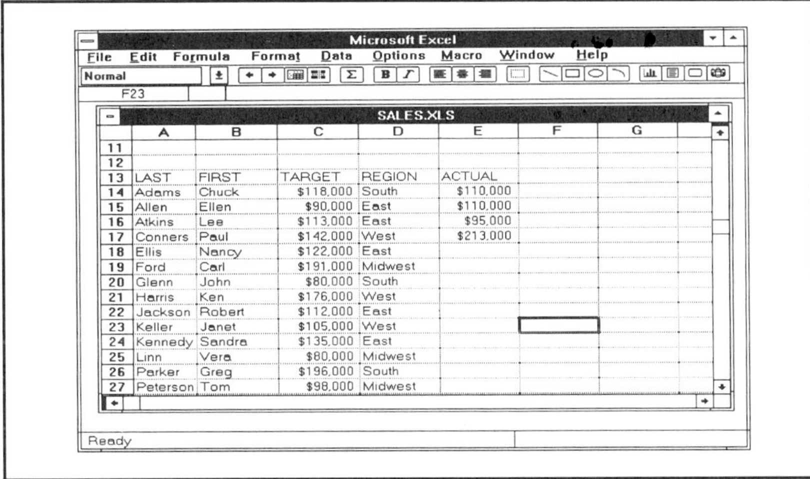

Figure 10.7: Adding a new field

You won't see a warning message or a dialog box when you delete a record using menu commands. If necessary, you can recover the delete with the Undo command on the Edit menu if you do it immediately after deletion.

To delete a field, follow the same procedure. Select the column designator for the field to delete. Then open the Edit menu and choose the Delete command to delete the field. When either records or fields are deleted, the range definition is adjusted automatically and the database size decreased. Remember that any other data in the column outside the database area will also be deleted. If other data are in the column, select only the database portion of the column for deletion.

DELETING A RECORD USING A DATA FORM

Unlike with the menu commands, when you delete a record using the data form, the record is permanently deleted and cannot be recovered with Undo. So be sure you have selected the correct record before deleting.

To delete a record with a data form, open the Data menu and choose Form. When the Data Form dialog box is displayed, move the scroll box until the record you wish to delete is displayed, as shown in Figure 10.8. Click Delete. A message will be displayed verifying the deletion. Click OK. Then choose Close.

At this point, delete any additional records you have added to the database that are not in Figure 10.2.

EDITING RECORDS

You can edit existing records either by editing the cells directly or by using a data form. To use a data form, open the Data menu and

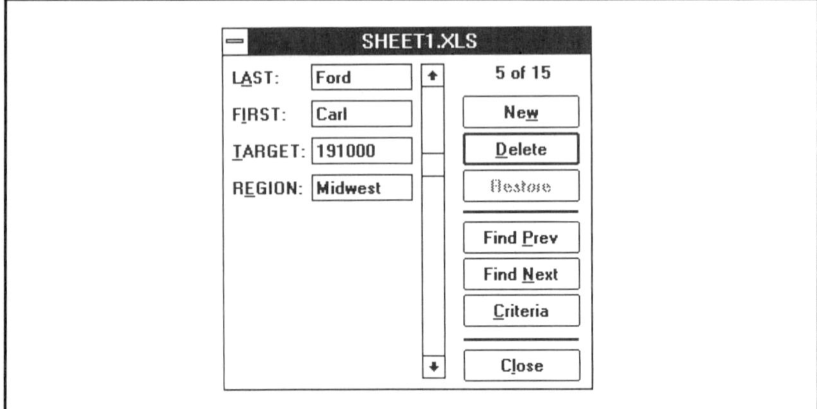

Figure 10.8: Deleting a record with a data form

choose Form. Select the desired record by moving the scroll box. Tab to or click on the desired cell and edit it. Then click Close. You can click the Restore button to restore a field to its original value, just as you click the Cancel box in the formula bar to restore a cell.

MOVING RECORDS

To rearrange the order of records and fields in your database, follow the rules for moving cell ranges. Select the cells to move. Open the Edit menu and choose Cut. Select the new location, then choose Paste.

SAVING THE DATABASE

Before leaving this example, be sure the database is saved. Open the File menu, choose Save As, assign the name SALES to the database, then click OK.

You've now learned the basics of managing a database. The database is really nothing more than a named area of the worksheet, and as a result, is accessible to the options on the Data menu and the database functions.

EXCEL VERSUS OTHER DATABASE PRODUCTS

Excel is an excellent program for managing databases, but is not designed to replace any single-application database management system you may be using, such as dBASE IV, FoxPro, or R:BASE.

Single-application database-management systems are designed to support database management only, and do it well. The data are stored on and listed or extracted from the disk. The amount of data that can be stored in the database is limited only by the size of the disk storage area. As a result, you can create very large databases and perform very complex operations on them. These systems also support programming, linked files (relational databases), report generation, and more.

When you are working with a database in Excel, *all* the database data are stored in the computer memory at the same time. As a result, the size of the database that you can create is limited by the amount of computer memory available. (When the database is not in use, data are stored in a file on the disk, just as in a single-application system.) Because of this storage system, the entire database is in memory at once and database operations are much faster than in comparable single-application products. This limits the size of the database, but with Excel and extended memory you can still work with large databases. You also can use the database information in calculations in other areas of the worksheet directly, without having to import it.

If you have a database that is very large and requires complex reporting and processing, you might consider using an external database-management system to store the data as well as using Excel to manage a portion of the database. For example, suppose that you are managing a pension fund for a company. You could keep the annual data for each employee in an Excel database and use an Excel worksheet to calculate the earnings for the year for each employee. After you've done this, you could transfer the results to an external database (using the procedure described in Chapter 21), which would store all the historical information and produce summary reports.

Another option is to use the Q+E utility with Excel to manage external databases (see Chapter 25).

Here is a specification comparison of an Excel database with a dBASE IV database:

SPECIFICATION	*EXCEL*	*dBASE IV*
Maximum number of records	16,383	1 billion
Maximum number of fields per record	256	255
Maximum field size (characters)	255	254

11 Using Databases Efficiently

SO FAR YOU'VE LEARNED HOW TO CREATE DATA-bases and edit them, but database management is far more than this. In this chapter you will learn how to use your Excel database to find records that meet specific criteria and how to use the Excel statistical functions to calculate statistics for the records that match the criteria you have defined.

USING CRITERIA

Criteria are rules or tests by which records are judged. If a record meets the rule (or passes the test), it is accepted, or said to match. Here are some typical applications that use criteria:

- Finding all the addresses with a specified zip-code range in a database of addresses
- Finding all the members with a membership expiration date equal to or earlier than a specified date in an organizational membership list

- Finding all the salespeople with sales exceeding a specified value in a sales database
- Finding all prospects that match a specified call-back date ("tickle date") in a prospect list, indicating when they should be contacted again

Notice the single word used in each of these applications: *specified.* You are defining a specification, and you wish to find all records in the database that match it. The specification is called the *criterion.*

You also can create complex test relationships. For example, a record can be accepted if it passes Criterion A *or* Criterion B, Criterion A *and* Criterion B, or Criterion A *and not* Criterion B.

FINDING RECORDS BASED ON CRITERIA

As with adding or editing records, you can use either of two methods to find records based on criteria: a data form or menu command.

USING A DATA FORM TO FIND RECORDS

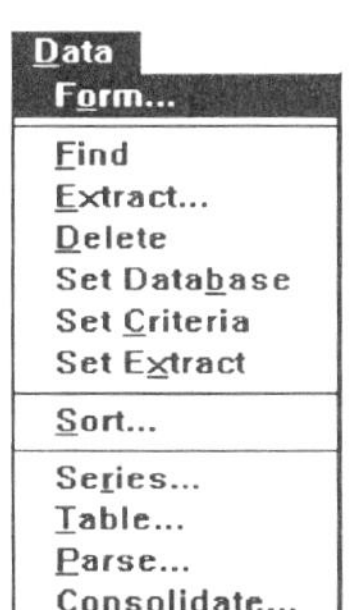

Often the easiest method to find a desired record is to use a data form. Try this now with the Sales database. Open the database you used in the last chapter, then open the Data menu and choose Form. A form will be displayed. Click the Criteria button. The Criteria button changes to a Form button, and the Delete button changes to a Clear button, as shown in Figure 11.1.

Enter the desired criteria into the fields of the form. In this example, the form specifies to find all records with a sales target of less than $100,000. Click on the Find Next button. The cursor will move to the first record with a sales target of less than $100,000.

To find additional records matching the criterion, choose Find Next again. To search backward, choose Find Previous. When you are finished, select Close.

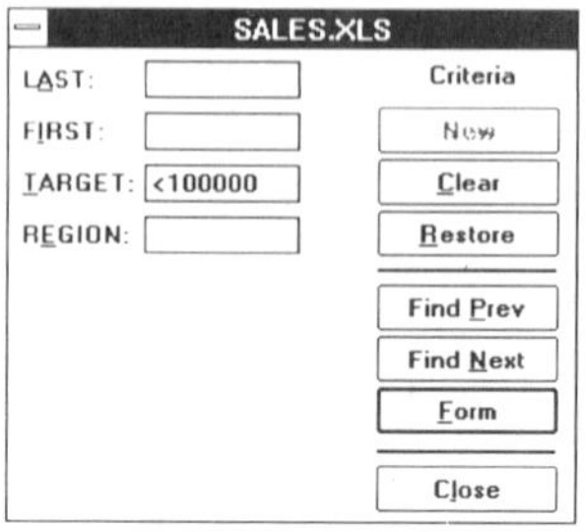

Figure 11.1: Finding records using a data form

You use a data form only with limited criteria specifications. You cannot use computed criteria (see the section titled "Computed Criteria" later in this chapter) and can use only exact text comparisons, though you can use wild-card specifications (* and ?). All text strings have an implicit asterisk appended, so **Rob** will match on *Robert* and *Roberta.*

For more complex criteria specifications, use the menu-commands method described below.

USING MENU COMMANDS TO FIND RECORDS

Finding records using menu commands is a three step process: defining the criteria range, entering the specification, and initiating the action. It's more time consuming than simply using a form, but allows for more complex operations.

Defining a Criteria Range

Before you can define your criteria, you must create a range on the worksheet that can be used to specify the criteria. This is called the *criteria range.* You can create this range by copying the field names of interest as headers to this new range.

Create this range for the worksheet you used in the last chapter:

1. With the SALES.XLS worksheet open, copy all the field names you will use for the criteria by clicking A13 and dragging to cell D13.

You can enter the field names to the criteria area from the keyboard, but using the Copy command to create the criteria range eliminates the possibility of misspelling the field names.

2. Open the Edit menu and choose Copy (or press Ctrl–Ins).
3. Copy the field names to a blank area of the worksheet, A3 to D3, by selecting cell A3, opening the Edit menu, and choosing Paste (or press Shift–Ins). The field names are now copied to a new area of the worksheet.
4. Select the criteria range. Select cell A3 and drag to cell D4. Notice that you have selected a range that includes *two* rows, as shown in Figure 11.2. You will enter criteria for searches in the second row.
5. Name this range. To do this, open the Data menu and choose Set Criteria. This assigns the name *Criteria* to the worksheet area that you just defined. You can use this name later in formulas and commands

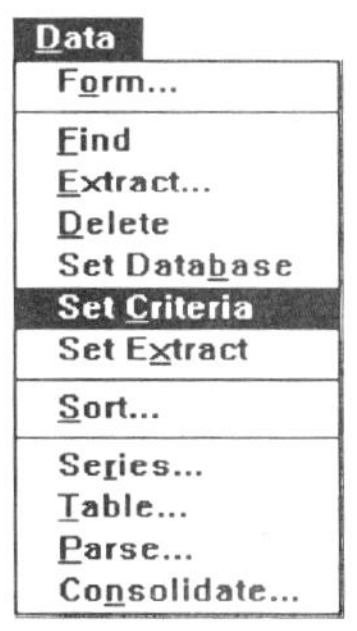

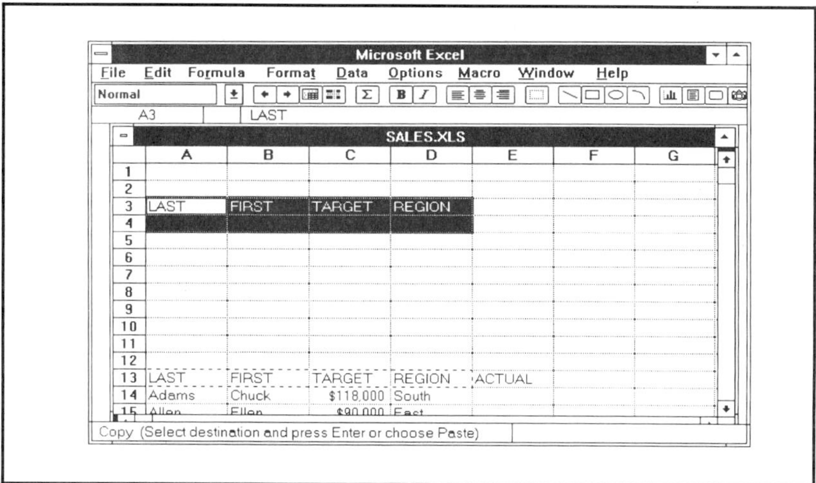

Figure 11.2: Creating a criteria range

The criteria range must always include at least two rows. The first row contains the field names, and the following row is used to enter values (or value ranges) for the fields. However, you may need three or even more rows in some cases. Allow as many as necessary. You will see an example using more rows later in this chapter.

In defining the criteria range, it is not necessary to copy all the field names. Copy only those you will need for your searches. Field names must be identical with those in the database, but case is ignored—you can use upper- or lowercase in specifying the field names.

You also can redefine the criteria range at any time. Simply select the new range and issue a new Set Criteria command.

Entering the Specification

The next step is to enter the desired specification for the criteria. Enter **West** in cell D4 under the word REGION in cell D3, as shown in Figure 11.3.

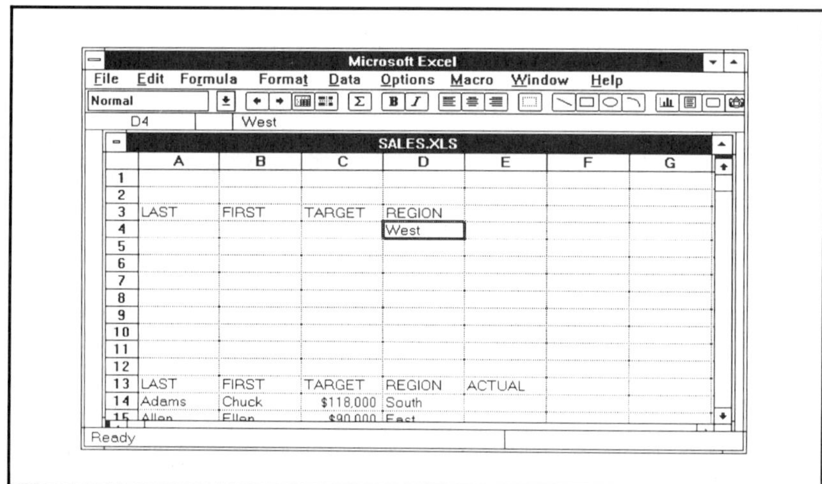

Figure 11.3: Specifying a criterion

Use the Clear command on the Edit menu or Ctrl–Del to clear a criteria cell.

When entering criteria, keep the following rules in mind:

- The criteria you enter are not case sensitive. You can enter *WEST* or *West*
- You can use numbers, labels, or formulas to define the criteria. The criteria must always be positioned directly below the field name to which they correspond
- Be sure there are no rows left entirely blank in the criteria range. A blank row is like a wild card and will match any

database record; therefore it will cause the search to stop on the first record. As long as at least one cell in the row contains a criterion, the search will work, since cells in the same row will combine their criteria specifications

Initiating the Action—The Find Command

Once the criteria are specified, you can use them to initiate any of three actions: find, delete, or extract. As an illustration, try the example below.

To find the first record that meets our REGION = West specification, open the Data menu and choose Find. Excel will then display the first record in the database that meets the specified criterion, as shown in Figure 11.4. Notice several changes. The scroll boxes are now striped. The number of the record in the database is displayed in the upper left where the active-cell designator normally is. The Data menu has changed and no longer contains the Find option; it contains an Exit Find option instead.

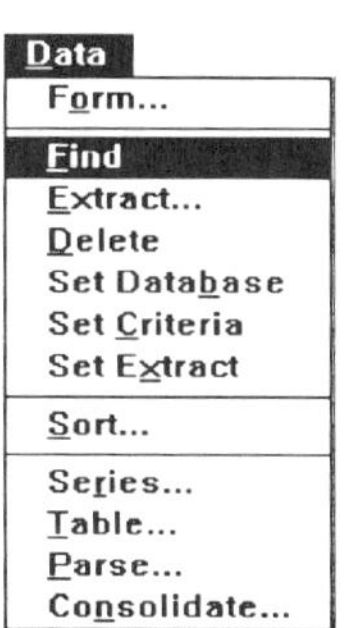

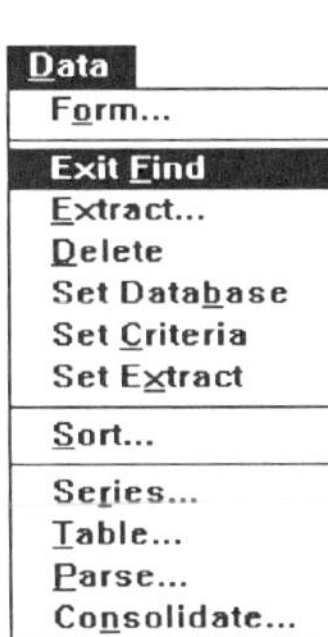

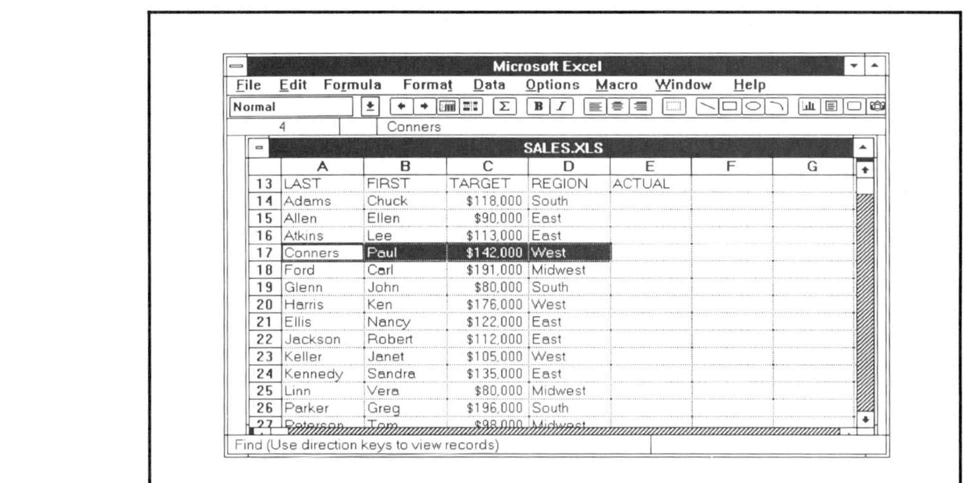

Figure 11.4: Finding the first record that matches the criterion

To find the next match, click the scroll arrows or press ↓. They permit you to move through the database to the next or previous record that meets the specified criterion. If you move the scroll box at the right all the way to the end of the scroll bar, Excel will display the last record in the database that matches the criterion. While in this search mode, the Edit commands (Copy, Cut, and so on) are still active. This allows you to edit the records once you find them. You also can use Delete in the Data menu to delete all records matching the criterion.

To exit the search, open the Data menu and choose Exit Find or press Esc. The scroll boxes return to normal. You also could exit by clicking any cell in the worksheet outside the database range. You can now specify another criterion and search the database again.

When the Find command is activated, it starts from the beginning of the database if no cell in the database is active. If any database cell is active, the search starts after that cell's record.

COMBINING SEARCH CRITERIA

Now try to combine two search conditions. Enter **176000** in cell C4 under TARGET (leaving West in cell D4) and repeat the find operation. Notice that the two conditions are combined; Excel looks for the first record where the region is West *and* the target is $176,000. It is not necessary to click Set Criteria again. As long as the cell range used for criteria entry is not changed, you can continue to repeat searches using other criteria. When you have more than one entry in a row, Excel will find only cells that fit *all* the specified criteria. This is called an AND condition.

To clear a criteria cell, always use Clear on the Edit menu or press Ctrl–Del. If you try to clear a cell by entering a space, all you will do is enter a space as a part of the search criteria.

Now clear cell C4 (press Ctrl–Del), leave West in D4, and enter **East** in D5. Expand the criteria range to A3 through D5 (Set Criteria in the Data menu). Initiate a find, and Excel will stop on the first record in which the region is West *or* East. As you can see, more than one entry in a criterion column tells Excel to find records containing any one of the criteria. This is called an OR condition. If you are using both AND and OR conditions together, you can create complex Boolean operations. The next section describes methods of creating special criteria specifications.

Remember, if you use multiple rows for criteria, you must include them all in your criteria range. Issue a new Set Criteria command if necessary. If you clear some criteria rows, reset the criteria to exclude those rows; otherwise, Excel will search for either a blank record or the existing criteria, and the search will stop on the first record in the database.

Notice that you now have two areas on the worksheet: the database area and the criteria area. You can use the remainder of the worksheet for normal worksheet applications: formulas, text, or whatever you wish.

COMPLEX CRITERIA SPECIFICATIONS

Excel criteria specifications can be divided into three broad categories: simple, comparison, and computed. In any given single search, you can mix these as necessary. You have already seen an example of simple criteria where a single value is entered in the criteria range. Now let's look at comparison and computed criteria.

If you have a large database or a large criteria range, use two windows to simplify access (New Window in the Window menu): one for the database, another for the criteria range.

NUMERIC COMPARISON CRITERIA

You can use any of the relational operators listed in Chapter 4 to specify a numeric comparison criterion. For example, enter **>150000** in cell C4 under TARGET, clear D5, and be sure D4 still contains West. Reset the criteria range to A3 through D4. Initiate a find, and Excel will stop on the first salesperson in the western region whose target is greater than $150,000.

You can tell Excel to search for records with field values within a range by setting up two columns in the criteria-name row that have the same field name. Put one limit under one and the second limit under the other. For example, let's set up a criterion to find records within a target range of $100,000 to $150,000:

1. Enter the word **TARGET** in E3 and set the criteria range as A3 to E4 (see Figure 11.5).
2. Enter **>100000** in C4 to define the lower limit of the range.
3. Enter **<150000** in E4 to define the upper limit of the range.
4. Select Find from the Data menu. Excel will stop on the first record with a target value within this range (C14 in this case).

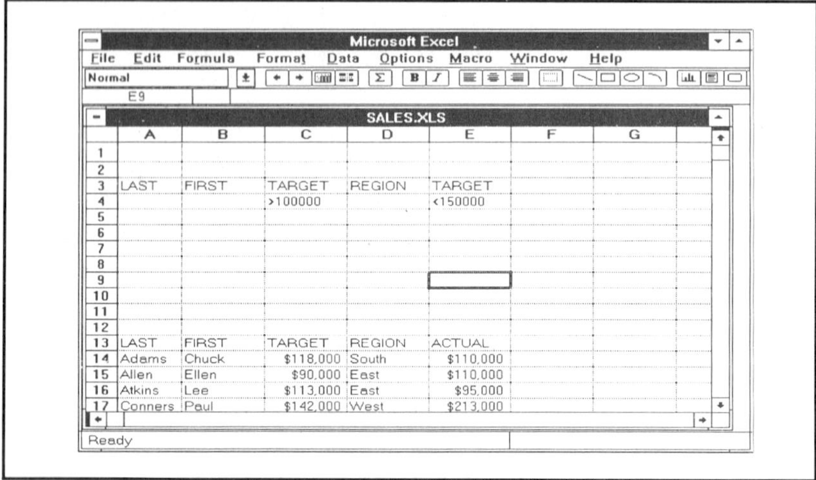

Figure 11.5: Using a criteria range

TEXT COMPARISON CRITERIA

You can use the relational operators to compare text fields as well. In this system, *A* is "less than" *B,* and *F* is "less than" *m.* Upper- and lowercase letters are considered equivalent (i.e., *D* "equals" *d*).

You also can use a question mark (?) to match a single character or an asterisk (*) to match a group of characters. For example, **J?dy** will match *Judy* and *Jody,* and **rob*** will match *Robert Jackson.*

In finding exact text matches, use extra care with Excel. Both **Rob** and **="Rob"** in B4 would match *Robert Jackson.* In both cases, B4 would show only Rob. If you wanted to find only people with the first name Rob and not Robert, you would have to use an equal sign with the text inside a quotation:

="=Rob"

This would put =Rob in B4 and would match only the first name *Rob.*

COMPUTED CRITERIA

You also can use formulas to create criteria. There are, however, some precautions you must be aware of. Suppose you use the formula

>E4 in C4 and put a value of 120,000 in E4. You might think this would match any record with a target greater than $120,000. But actually Excel would look for a text entry that matched **>E4** in a cell. Entering =E4 also wouldn't work; you would get an error message.

To make this comparison work, you must first expand the criteria range to A3 through E4. Always remember to extend the criteria range to contain the calculation. Make cell E3 blank (you don't need a header in the column for a calculated criterion in the criteria range). Clear C4 and E4.

Now put the following equation in E4:

Note the absolute reference to cell E7. Any reference to a cell outside the database range must be absolute because it will always refer to that specific cell. Now put the value for comparison, **120000**, in E7. If you have followed this correctly, you should see **FALSE** in E4, as shown in Figure 11.6. You now have created a computed criterion in E4 in which the target value (C14 in the first record) is compared with the value in E7. The result of any computed criterion (a condition) is either true or false. Initiate the find, and Excel should stop on the first target greater than $120,000. Press ↓ to find the next targets that match the criterion. When you've reached the end, press ↑ to review the matched target values.

Figure 11.7 shows another example. A few actual sales figures have been added to compare with the targets. Format by copying the format from column C: copy a cell from column C to the clipboard, then open the Edit menu and select Paste Special to paste the format only to column E.

The criteria area includes the formula **=(E14/C14)>=1** in A2. The criteria range is A1 to A2. This is requesting a match if the actual sales equal or exceed the target value.

You also can use functions in computed criteria. For example, you could compare the square root of a list of fields to a fixed value with:

Be sure the database includes column E.

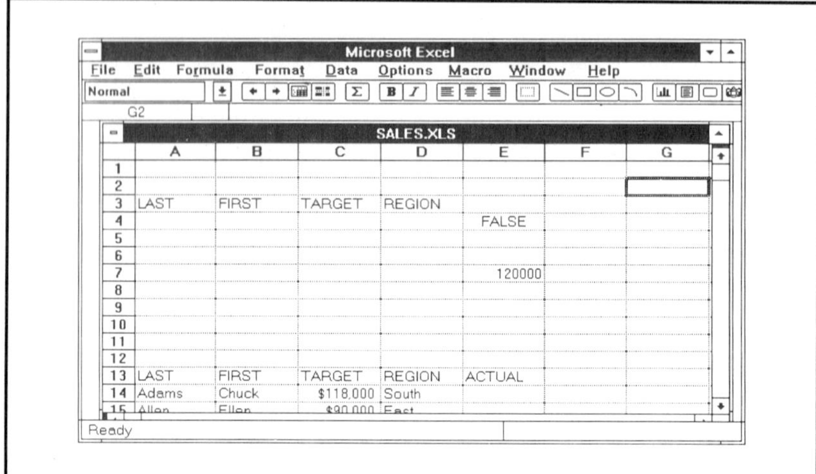

Figure 11.6: A criteria calculation

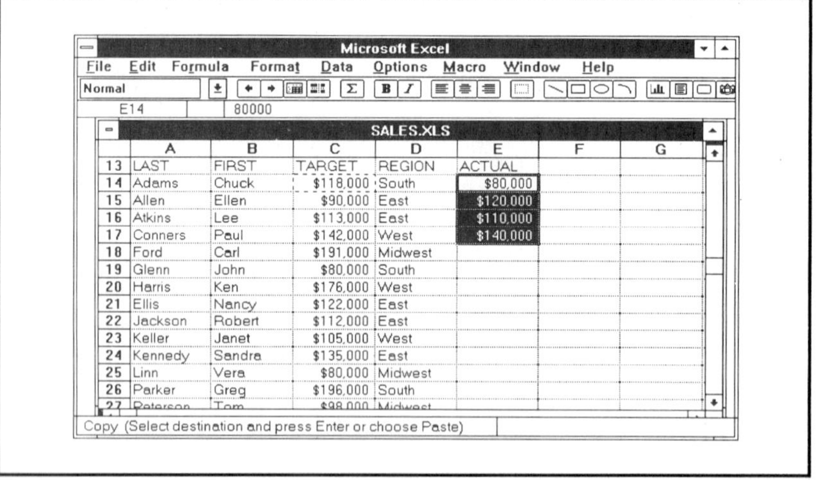

Figure 11.7: Using a formula in a criterion

DATABASE STATISTICAL FUNCTIONS

You use database functions in the same way that you use worksheet functions. Let's experiment with your original Sales database.

As a goal, we wish to find the sum of the eastern sales targets:

1. Set the criteria range from A3 to D4. Enter **East** into cell D4 (the criterion). Be sure that cells A4, B4, and C4 are clear.
2. Click cell E6 to select it. This will be the working cell for the answer.
3. Open the Formula menu and choose Paste Function (or press Shift–F3).
4. The Paste Function dialog box shown in Figure 11.8 appears. Scroll through this dialog box until **DSUM( )** is displayed. Be sure Paste Arguments is off. Select DSUM ( ) (double-click or highlight and press Enter). The function name is now entered into the formula bar with an equal sign before it, as shown in Figure 11.9. The cursor is in the formula bar ready for you to enter the first argument.
5. Open the Formula menu and choose Paste Name (or just press F3). When the Paste Name dialog box shown in Figure 11.10 appears, double-click Database (the name of your database). It is now entered into the formula bar.

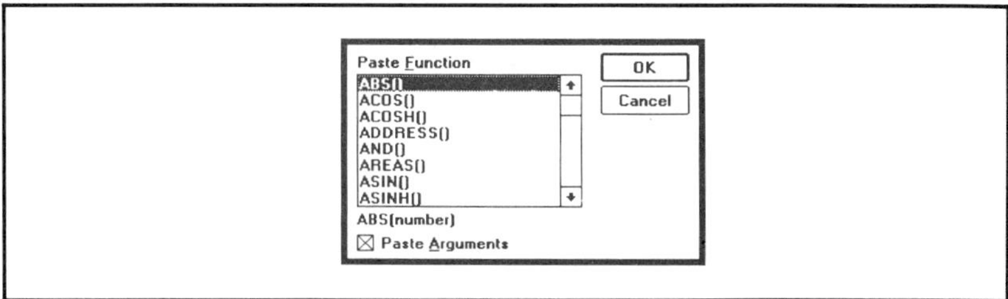

Figure 11.8: Pasting a function name

6. Type a comma and "**Target**" (with quotation marks) in the formula bar.
7. Type another comma, open the Formula menu again, and choose Paste Name.
8. Double-click Criteria, and what you've typed is entered into the formula bar.

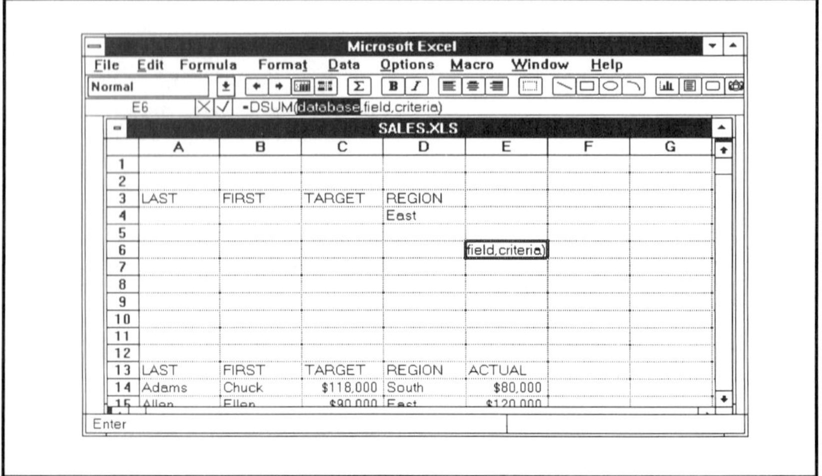

Figure 11.9: Starting the formula entry

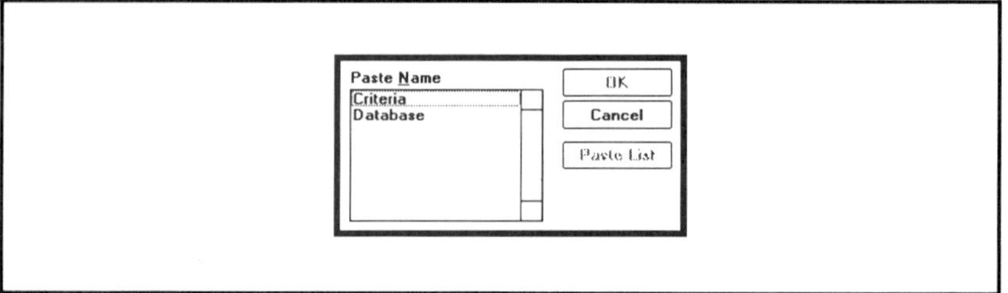

Figure 11.10: Pasting a name

9. Click the Enter box (✓) or press Enter to complete the entry.

You now have a complete formula:

=DSUM(Database,"Target",Criteria)

This matches the general form for this function: DSUM(*database, field name, criteria*). The sum of the eastern sales targets is now displayed in cell E6: **$682,000**. Enter **West** into cell D4, and the sum changes to **$423,000**, the sum of the western sales targets. You can specify any region, and cell E6 will automatically change to reflect those target totals.

Although you created this formula by pasting the function and name, you could have entered the entire formula from the keyboard. If you need to review the database functions, see Chapter 8.

At this point, you should save the database again, as you will need it in the current form for the next chapter. Clear A1 to A2, set the criteria to A3 to D4, and select Save in the File menu.

SOME DATABASE MANAGEMENT TIPS

Database functions are a valuable asset in building your worksheets. Here are a few tips:

- Use the CHOOSE and MATCH functions with your databases. For example, in the database of this chapter you had to enter the full region name for each region. To simplify entry and to eliminate misspellings, you could create a new field in column F called REGION CODE. Then you could put the equation

  CHOOSE(F14,"South","East","Midwest","West")

  in D14 and copy it down the column. You would then enter a region code for each REGION CODE field (1, 2, 3 or 4), and the corresponding region would be entered into the REGION field
- You can use the database functions on any continuous range of cells in the worksheet. Enter the continuous range as the database in the function and the range for the criteria. It is not necessary to define any database or criteria. For example, if you have a set of grades and wish to do some statistical calculations, you can use the statistical database functions, entering the database range for the database argument in the function. You still need a criteria range, but you don't have to define it with Set Criteria; just enter the cell addresses in the database function
- You can set up multiple criteria on the worksheet. Although only one can be active at a time, you can have several criteria set up ready to use. Just use Set Criteria to select

the one you wish to use, leaving the others still on the worksheet

- You can use the field index number instead of the field name in the database function's second argument. The field index number is the order of the field in the record. For example, in the DSUM example of the previous section you could have used the number *3* (to refer to the third field) instead of the word *Target* as the second argument. You also can use a reference in the database to the field header. Just click on the field name to enter it into the database function
- Don't confuse the Find command in the Data menu with the search capabilities of the Find and Replace commands on the Formula menu. The Find and Replace commands work on the entire worksheet, including the database. The Find on the Data menu works only within the current database, and searches are based on a criterion. If a QOH (Quantity-on-Hand) is 15 and needs to be changed to 19 in a database, using the Formula menu could change other 5s or 15s that shouldn't be changed. Using the Data menu gives you more control

OTHER OPERATIONS THAT USE CRITERIA

You have already seen how you can find records based on specified criteria. You also can extract or delete records based on criteria.

EXTRACTING RECORDS USING CRITERIA

You can extract the part of your database that matches specified criteria and place it in another area of the worksheet or in another worksheet. As an example here, extract all the western salespeople from the database.

Extraction is a three-step process: defining the criteria, defining the extraction destination range, and initiating the extraction.

Defining the Criteria

You define criteria for extraction just as you would define them for a search. Define A3 to D4 as the criteria range and enter **West** in D4 (See Figure 11.3).

It is often helpful to do a find before extraction to define how many rows will be needed.

Defining the Extraction Range

To define the extraction area, copy the cells that contain the field names into a new area of the worksheet or into another worksheet, as shown in Figure 11.11. The extracted database will be placed below these field names. Be sure there is sufficient room for the extracted database. You may delete any field names that are not needed in the extracted database.

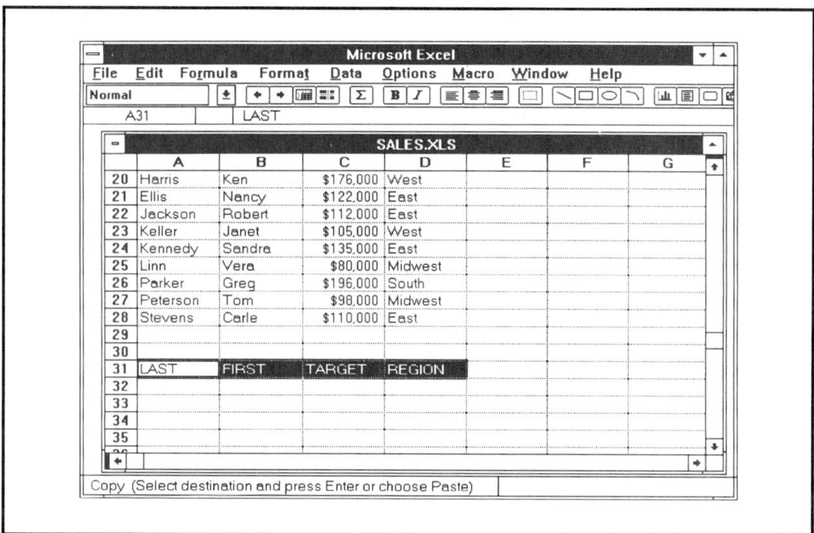

Figure 11.11: The extracted database

Next, select the field names in the destination area in which you want to copy the extracted records. If you want to copy all the fields of the matching records, select all the field names of the destination range. If you want only a partial extraction, select the field names and one or more additional rows of the destination range. Only those rows will be filled. This is useful if you don't know how many records will match the criteria, and you are afraid the extraction might destroy (write over) other data.

Initiating the Extraction

Select A31 to D31. Open the Data menu and choose Extract. You will then see the Extract dialog box shown in Figure 11.12. Click Unique Records Only, because you don't want the extracted file to contain any duplicates. Click OK. The extracted records will be copied into the new worksheet area, as shown in Figure 11.13.

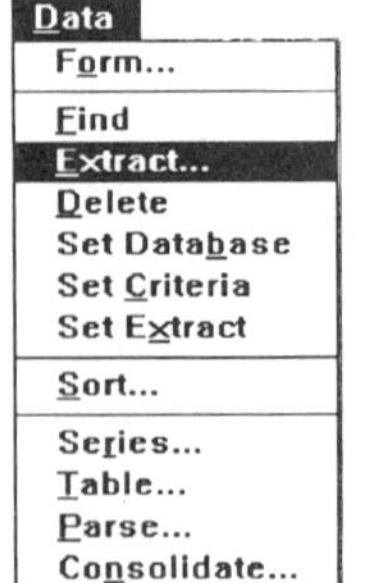

Figure 11.12: The extract dialog box

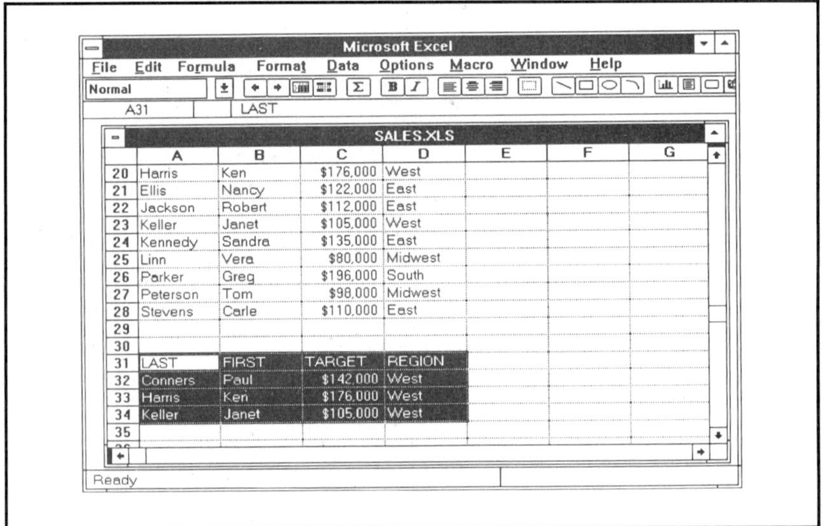

Figure 11.13: The new extracted database

An alternative is to select A31 to D31 (the destination field headings), choose Set Extract on the Data menu, and then choose Extract.

You should understand the following characteristics of extractions:

- The extracted database will contain only values. Formulas are extracted as values, not formulas
- The extracted database is not linked to the master. If the master is updated, the extracted database will not be updated
- If the destination range is defined by selecting one or more fields, all records in the original database that match the desired criteria will be transferred. Transferred records can overwrite existing cell data without Excel giving you a precautionary message. Select a cell range for the destination range, or be sure that many cells under the destination field headers are cleared of data

DELETING RECORDS USING CRITERIA

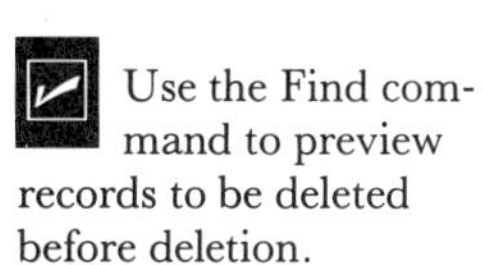

Use the Find command to preview records to be deleted before deletion.

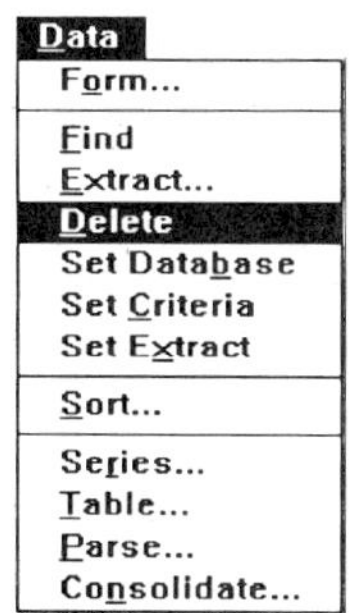

To delete records from a database using criteria, first select the criteria for deletion. Next, open the Data menu and choose Delete, then click OK. Excel automatically deletes the selected records and moves the remaining records up to close the space. You will see an alert message when you delete records. Be sure that the database is saved before you delete any part of it, because a database deletion cannot be undone.

12 Sorting Data

WITH EXCEL, YOU CAN SORT YOUR DATABASE quickly in any desired sequence. Sorting is useful for many types of databases: you can sort a mailing list in either name or zip-code order, an inventory file in part-number order, or a prospect list in name or date order.

Usually, when you enter records into a database, you do so in a random order (as most records come to you). When you finish entering the data, you can sort the records in whatever order you want. If you enter new records at a later time, you can either add them in their correct position (using the Insert command in the Edit menu) or add them to the end of the database and resort the database.

You can sort a database's rows or columns, with any number of fields, called *keys,* controlling the sort. Each field can be sorted in ascending or descending order. Usually you will want to sort rows; a columnar sort will rearrange the field order.

It is also important to understand that you can sort any data. They don't have to comprise a database. In fact, the Sort command, although on the Data menu, has no relationship to the database commands. Any area of the worksheet can be sorted at any time.

SORTING BY A SINGLE FIELD

Let's try sorting the sales projections database by the region field:

1. Open the Sales worksheet. Select the range of cells to sort, A14 to D28. (Notice that you do not include the row containing the field names.)
2. Open the Data menu and choose Sort. The Sort window shown in Figure 12.1 appears. This is actually a window, not just a dialog box, and it can be moved (but not resized).
3. Click any cell in column D (to sort by region), and this cell reference will be entered into the Sort window as the first key. Click OK. The items are now sorted alphabetically by region, as shown in Figure 12.2.

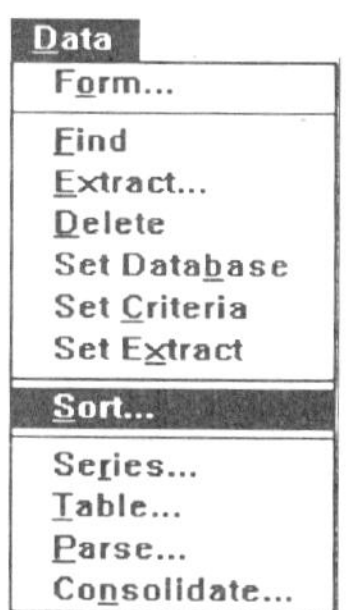

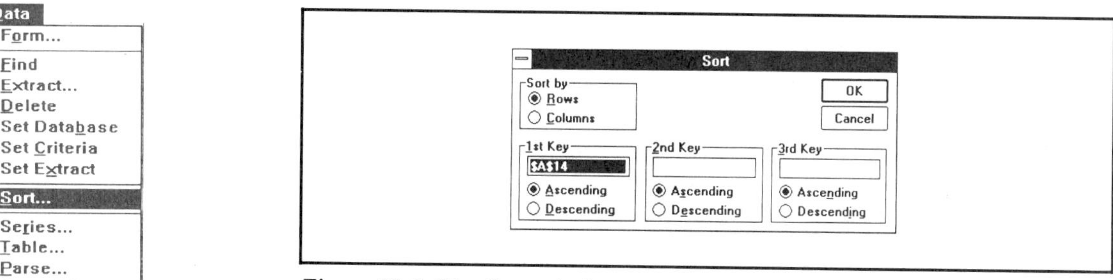

Figure 12.1: The Sort window

Here are some tips on sorting:

- After selecting the sort range and choosing Sort, select the key by clicking on a cell in the sort column. (Note that you can click any cell in the column to define the sort key, including the field name.)
- You can undo a sort by immediately selecting Undo Sort in the Edit menu. (After any other command is initiated, you cannot undo it.) If you think you might need to recover the original order, add a new field (column) that contains the database's record (row) numbers before you sort the database. Use the Series command to assign a sequential number to each record (see Chapter 14). After you've sorted the

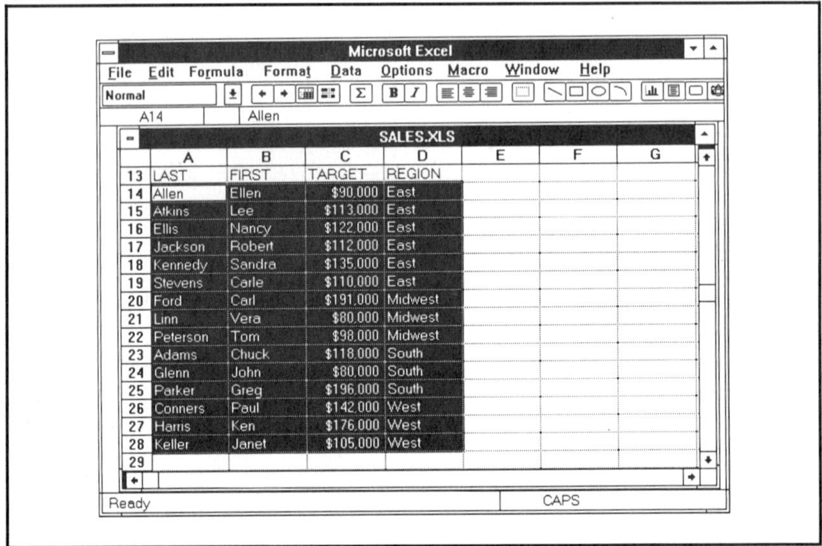

Figure 12.2: The database after sorting

database, you can recover the previous order easily by sorting the database with the record-number field as the key

- When defining the sort range, be sure all fields of all records are selected—i.e., the entire database range *excluding* the field names. You cannot use the Goto command with the database name to select the database range for sorting, because it will include the field names
- If you plan to sort the database often, name the sort range using Define Name in the Formula menu. Then you can use the Goto command to select this range
- You can use range names or formulas to define the sort keys. For example, in the previous sort exercise you could have used any named cell in column D as the key
- If you use calculated fields, be sure to use absolute references for cells outside the database and relative references for cells inside the database. Otherwise, a sort will scramble the formulas
- Numeric characters are sorted before alphabetic characters

- Sorting a database will of course lose the order of entry. Include a field that shows a date (and perhaps time) of entry if you want to keep track of when a particular record was entered
- You can use macros (see Part VII) to time-stamp, identify, and sort entries
- You can sort by any type of range. It does not need to be defined as a database
- As an added precaution, save before sorting

SORTING BY TWO OR THREE FIELDS

You can sort by two or three fields easily. Suppose, using the previous example, you want the database sorted by region, by last name within the region, and by first name if the last name is the same (there are no duplicate last names here, but we will assume that this could happen).

1. Select the range to sort.
2. Select Sort from the Data menu. The Sort window will be displayed.
3. Click anywhere in column D, the first field by which the database will be sorted. *Do not* press Enter or click OK yet.
4. Click anywhere in column A, the column for the last name, for the second key.
5. Click anywhere in column B, the column for the first name, for the third key.
8. Click OK or press Enter.

The database will be sorted by region and by name within the region.

Keep in mind that sorting with multiple keys in this way is not the same as doing multiple sorts. If you try multiple sorts, each sort will rearrange the order of the previous sort. For example, if you sort the above database by region and then again by last name, the database will end up in last-name order only. Using multiple keys ensures that the second sort does not invalidate the first sort; that is, the database remains sorted by region after the sort on the last name is completed. Last names are then sorted only within the same region.

SORTING BY MORE THAN THREE FIELDS

Sometimes you may wish to sort by more than three keys. This can be done easily if you use the following procedure. The sorting makes an assumption that the most important keys are unique. For example, in a database of addresses you could sort by last name and first name, then by zip code and last name to get a database in zip-code, last-name, and first-name order. Assume the database is to be sorted by six fields, with key 1 as the most important and key 6 as the least:

1. Initiate one sort using the three least important keys; that is, key 4 (first key), 5 (second key), and 6 (third key).
2. Initiate another sort using the three most important keys: key 1 (first key), 2 (second key), and 3 (third key).

This method will work with any number of keys. Start with the least important keys, using the most important of these as the first key in the Sort window. If the number of fields is not divisible by three, use a two- or one-key sort the first time with the two least or single least important key(s).

FINDING SALES TOTALS BY REGION

You can use these sorting techniques to find the sales totals for each region in the Sales database. Sort the database by region and add a small worksheet area under the criteria area. In cell B6, enter the sum of the eastern regions as **=SUM(C14:C19)**. Continue with the other sums:

REGION	*CELL*	*FORMULA*
East	B6	**=SUM(C14:C19)**
Midwest	B7	**=SUM(C20:C22)**

South	B8	**= SUM(C23:C25)**
West	B9	**= SUM(C26:C28)**

Add the row titles **East**, **Midwest**, **South**, and **West** in cells A6 through A9, as shown in Figure 12.3. In Chapter 15, you will learn a better way to create this worksheet. For now, save the Sales worksheet for exercises in other chapters.

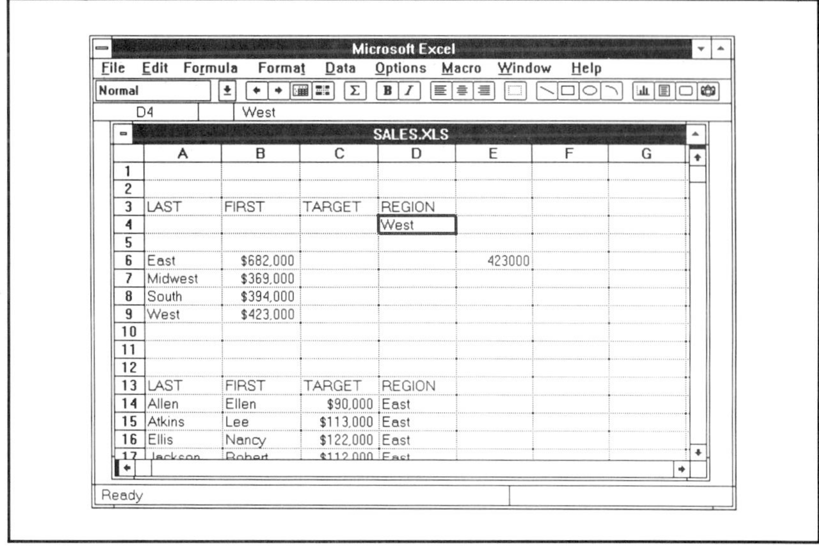

Figure 12.3: Showing the regional sums

SORTING WITHOUT A DATABASE

The Sort command does not require any defined database or criteria. It can be used on any worksheet range. For example, Figure 12.4 shows a worksheet (not a database) that indicates the sales of various salespeople for a four-year period. The sales are shown here in descending year order. Assume that for presentation purposes you need to rearrange this in ascending year order.

To do this, use a columnar sort instead of a row sort. Select C3 to F7 as the range to sort. Open the Data menu and choose Sort. Select a column sort, and for the first key click anywhere in row 3. Figure 12.5 shows the resulting worksheet, sorted in increasing year order.

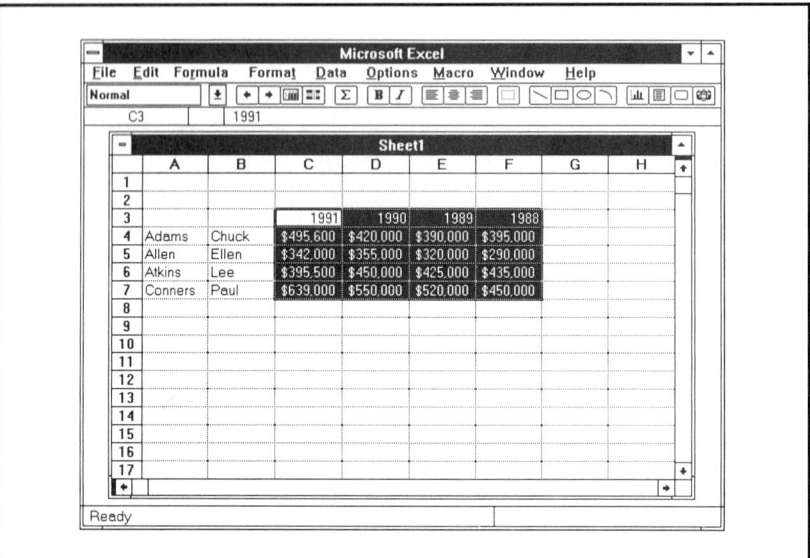

Figure 12.4: Sorting a worksheet

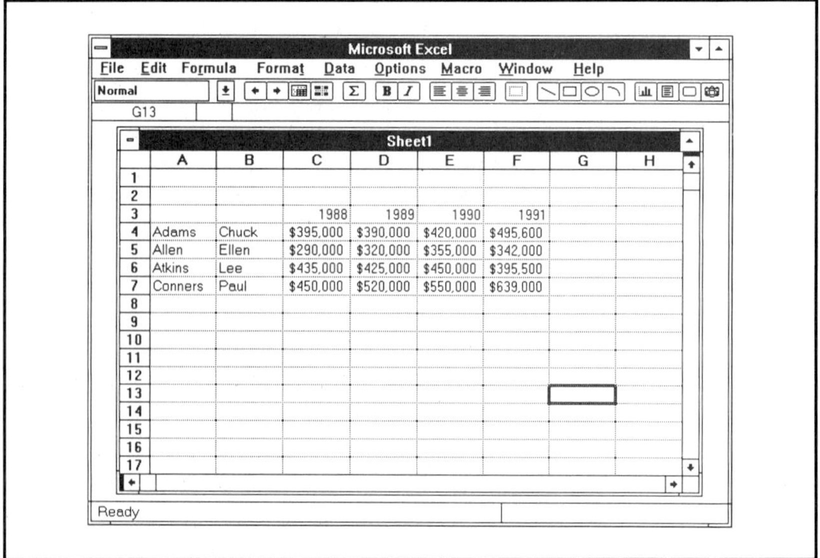

Figure 12.5: After a columnar sort

A columnar sort is seldom used for databases. Sorting by columns is generally not useful even for rearranging the field order because the Sort command can sort the columns with the field names only in ascending or descending order. To rearrange fields, use the edit commands instead, inserting a blank column and then moving the desired field column to the new position.

In summary, the Sort command can be used to sort any area of a worksheet in the ascending or descending order of one or more specified columns or rows.

IV

Using Excel Productively

EXCEL PROVIDES MANY SPECIAL TECHNIQUES THAT are often not supported by competing products. Part IV introduces you to many of these techniques with application examples you can use in your own work. You will learn how to use arrays and tables, how to link documents, and how to use the special printing features of Excel.

13 Producing Tables

THERE MAY BE TIMES WHEN YOU WANT TO CHANGE certain values on a worksheet to see how it affects the rest of the worksheet. For example, in Chapters 10–12, you created a database of sales targets. You then searched this database using various criteria. You could use only one criterion at a time, which is somewhat cumbersome if you want to use a series of criteria and then create a table or chart showing the results of each analysis. You did create a short worksheet portion showing the totals for each region, which were calculated using the SUM function. However, the calculations were only correct if the database was sorted by region. Entering the equation for each region was laborious and you were required to adjust the equations as you added or deleted records in the database.

In this chapter, you will learn how to use the Table command to avoid these problems. You will take the same example (the Sales database and worksheet) and use the Table command to search the database based on a series of criteria. You will see that tables are useful for what-if analyses with worksheets because they allow you to perform multiple analyses with a series of input values.

You also will learn how to use look-up tables. These types of tables work with the LOOKUP, VLOOKUP, and HLOOKUP functions, rather than with the Table command. They provide a quick way to find certain values in your worksheet.

USING THE TABLE COMMAND

The Table command should be used whenever you change one or two cells in a worksheet to create a series of output values in one or more columns or rows.

ONE-INPUT TABLES

You use a one-input table to see how changes in one cell affect the values calculated by one or more formulas. To design a one-input table, you need three things:

- A single input cell containing the value that you wish to change
- A column or row containing the values that will be applied successively to the input cell
- One or more columns or rows to contain the resulting values, with formulas used as headings for each column or row. You can use formulas that refer directly to the input cell or to other cells on the worksheet. The formulas do not show on the worksheet

Creating a One-Input Table

So that you can understand the basics of how a one-input table is used, let's experiment with the Sales database that you created in Chapters 10–12. You'll set up a one-input table to search the database using a series of criteria.

First, open the Sales database and worksheet, as shown in Figure 13.1. Notice that the DSUM example used in Chapter 11 is still in E6. Be sure the criteria are defined correctly (A3:D4).

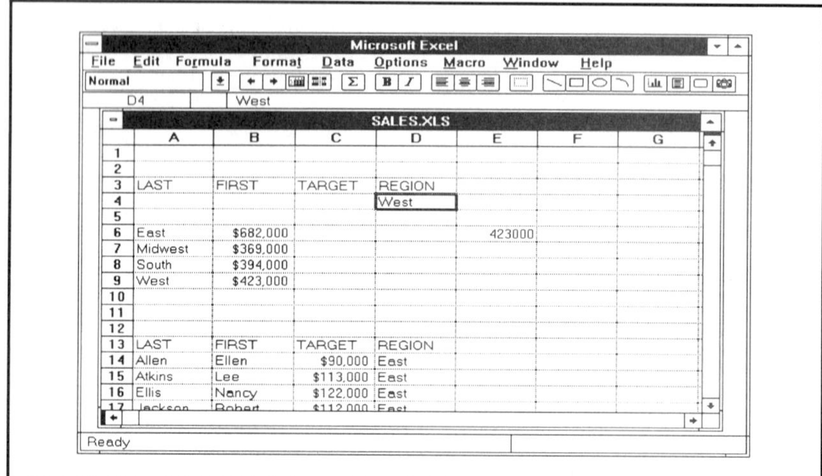

Figure 13.1: The Sales projections database and worksheet

Our particular area of interest is the worksheet portion, rows 6–9, which contain the sales totals by region. These totals were obtained previously with the SUM function, which required the database to be sorted by region. Editing the database or sorting it can cause these totals to change and be incorrect.

To see this, sort the database (refer to Chapter 12 if you need help) so that the database is alphabetized by name. The totals in the worksheet cells B6 through B9 will also change, becoming incorrect, as shown in Figure 13.2. This is because the formulas in these cells, which reference absolute cells that move as a result of the sort, do not change to reflect the new order.

Notice, however, that the total in cell E6 does not change when you sort the database. This is because it is calculated using the DSUM function and a criterion—target sales in the West. Examine the formula for this cell, and you will see that the total is based on the formula

=DSUM(Database,"Target",Criteria)

Although the DSUM function gives the correct value, you can only use a single criterion at a time. With a table, however, you can use multiple criteria.

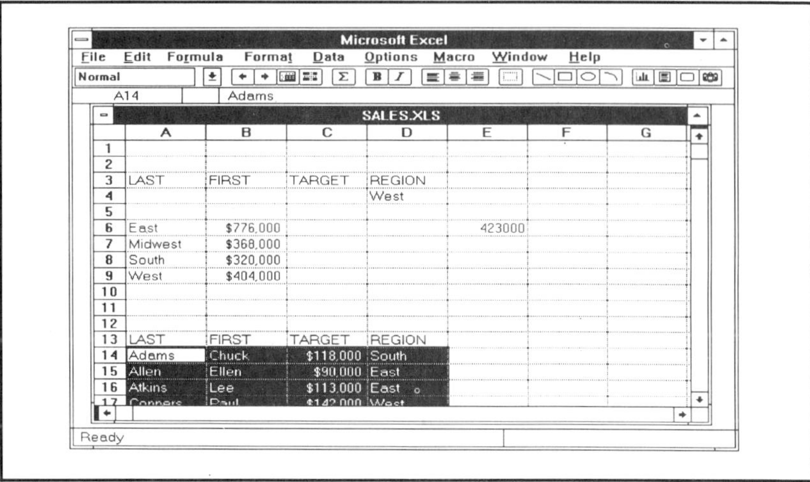

Figure 13.2: The database after sorting, with incorrect worksheet totals

Now let's change the formulas in cells B6 through B9, so that the values are calculated using a table and the DSUM function. Follow these steps:

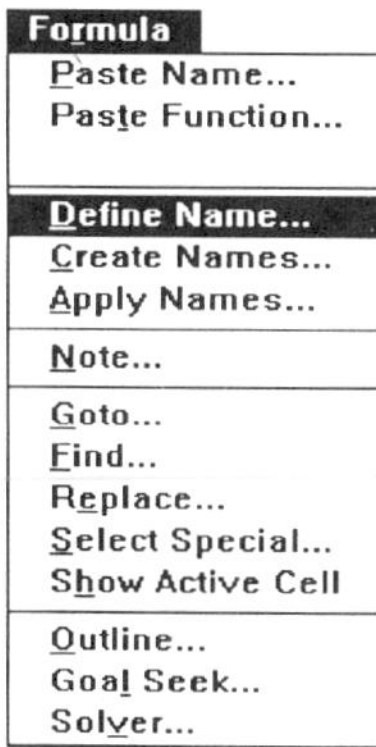

1. Sort the Sales worksheet by region again so that the data are correct, and clear cell D4.
2. Be sure that the database and criteria range are defined. Open the Formula menu and choose Define Name. You should see both **Database** and **Criteria** listed in the window. (If they are not, refer to Chapter 10.) Click Close to close the window.
3. Create a heading cell containing the formula that will be used for the table by copying cell E6 into cell B5. The formula must be in the first row of the table. Cell B5 is the heading cell for the column that will contain the results of the formula in B5.
4. Select the table area with the formula in the first row by clicking cell A5 and dragging to cell B9.
5. Open the Data menu and select Table. The Table dialog box (see Figure 13.3) will be displayed. Move the box so that cell D4 is visible, if necessary.

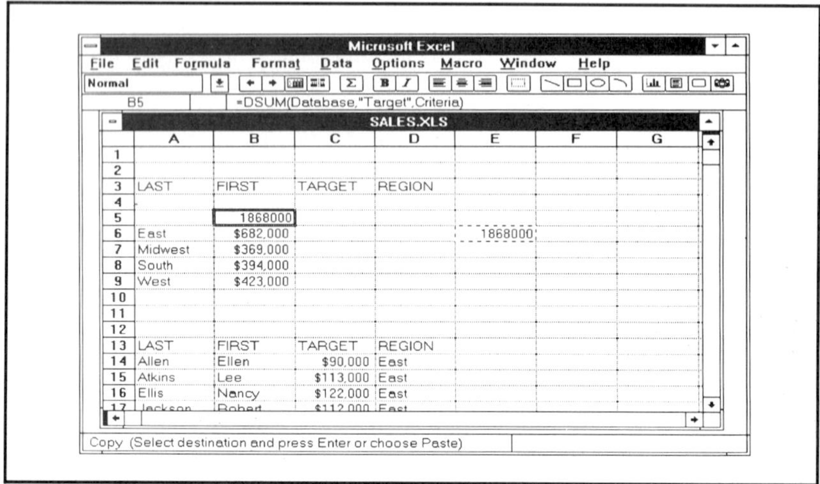

Figure 13.3: The Table dialog box

6. Click Column Input Cell on the dialog box, because the criteria will be from the Region column.
7. Select cell D4. This is the single input cell that will contain each input value from the table. This indicates that the selected values in column A (cells A6 through A9) will be applied sequentially as a value in cell D4. The value **$D$4** is now displayed in the Table dialog box.
8. Click OK.

The totals for cells B6 through B9 remain the same, but the formula for each cell is now different. Show them by opening the Options menu and selecting the Display command (see Figure 13.4). What has happened? Each title in cells A6 through A9 was applied successively to cell D4. The formula in cell B5, the first row of column B in the selected range, was then used to evaluate the cell in column B across from the cell in column A. Figure 13.5 shows the results. Compare these numbers with Figure 13.1 and the erroneous Figure 13.2.

Now sort your database again by name:

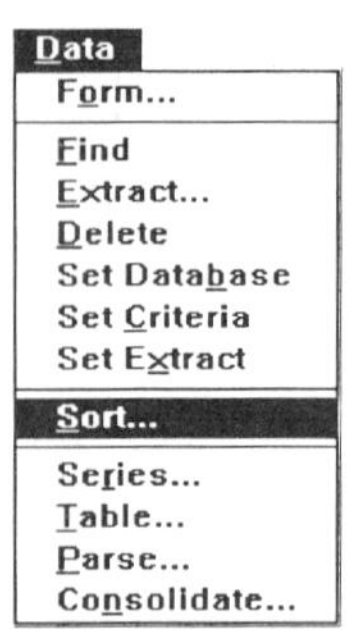

1. Select A14 to D28, but be careful not to select row 13, which contains the database field names.
2. Open the Data menu and select Sort.

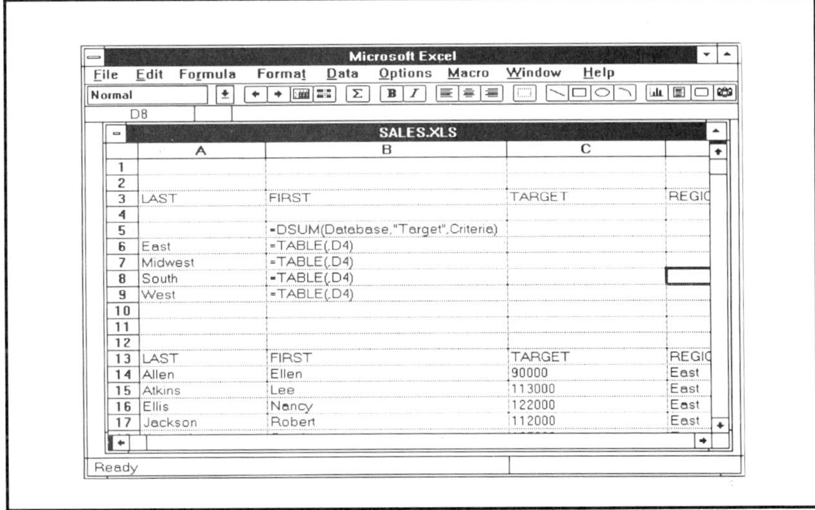

Figure 13.4: The formulas revealed

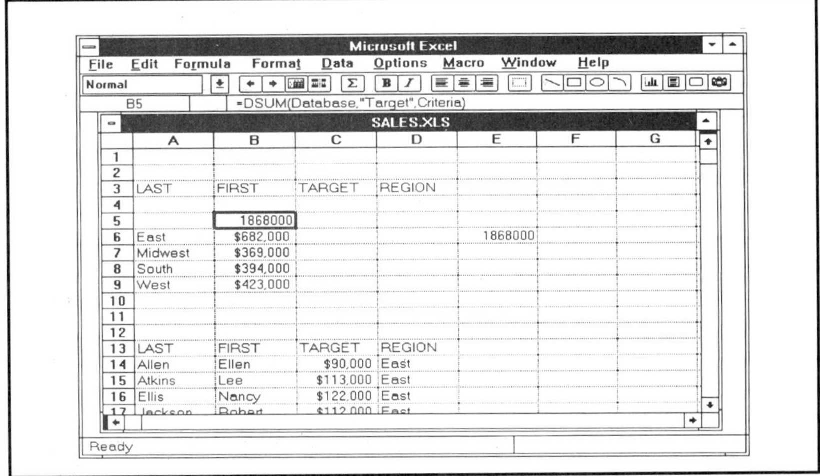

Figure 13.5: The worksheet values calculated with the Table command

3. The Sort dialog box shown in Figure 13.6 is displayed. With column A (the last name) defining the key field, click OK.

This time, the totals did not change. You can edit, resort, or otherwise modify the database, and the worksheet totals will always remain accurate.

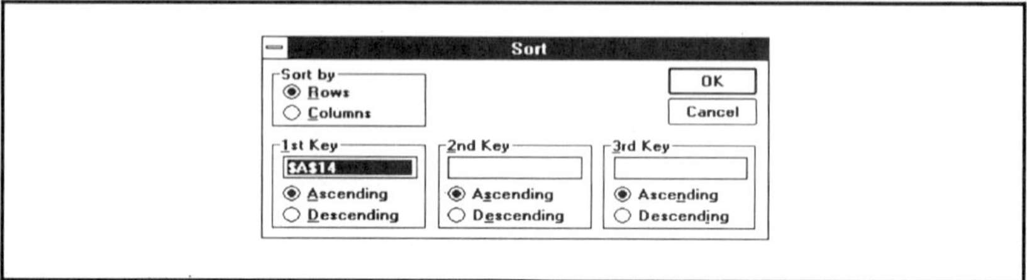

Figure 13.6: The Sort dialog box

Now look again at the three areas that we said earlier must be defined:

- The single input cell for all values that are to be changed is D4
- The column or row that contains the values that will be supplied successively to the input cell is A6 to A9 (this is the criterion)
- The column that will contain the output values (with the formula as the heading) is B6 to B9. The formula is the heading for this column

Calculating Two Columns

If you add or insert rows within the database range, your entries will be formatted correctly and the database totals will be updated to reflect the changes. The table definition has not changed. If you add data to the *end* of the database, however, you will need to redefine the database area in order for the totals to be correct. You also will need to format the new entries at the end of the database (by opening the Format menu and choosing Number).

Using the Table command, you can use multiple formulas to calculate the values for more than one column or row.

Let's try an example with a two-formula table. Assume that you now have a few actual sales figures and you want to create a separate field for them in your database. Then you want to recalculate the worksheet total values using the Table command. First sort the Sales database by region and save it. Then follow these steps:

1. Add a new field to your database titled **ACTUAL**, as shown in Figure 13.7.
2. Enter the values shown in the figure into this field and format them.
3. Redefine your database area by selecting the range with the field names (A13 to E28), opening the Data menu, and choosing Set Database.

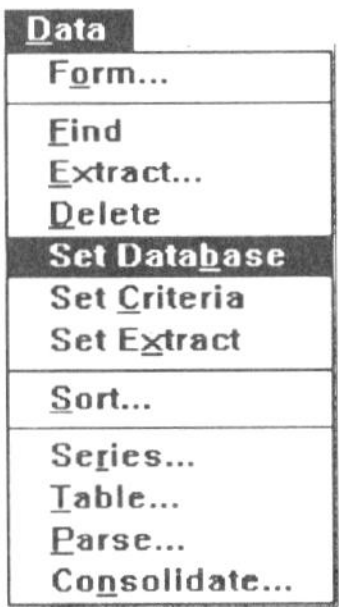

4. Add the new field to your criteria area in E3.
5. Redefine your criteria area by selecting the range (A3 to E4), opening the Data menu, and choosing Set Criteria.
6. Copy the formula in cell B5 into cell C5 using Fill Right from the Edit menu, then change the word TARGET to ACTUAL in C5.
7. Select cells A5 through C9.
8. Open the Data menu and choose Table.
9. Click the Column Input Cell box in the Table dialog box and click cell D4, just as you did before. Then click OK.

Now both columns will be calculated and the results will be displayed. Format the results, as shown in Figure 13.8. Figure 13.9 shows the formulas.

Microsoft Excel
File Edit Formula Format Data Options Macro Window Help
Normal
F20
SALES.XLS

	A	B	C	D	E	F	G
13	LAST	FIRST	TARGET	REGION	ACTUAL		
14	Allen	Ellen	$90,000	East	$110,000		
15	Atkins	Lee	$113,000	East	$95,000		
16	Ellis	Nancy	$122,000	East	$80,000		
17	Jackson	Robert	$112,000	East	$165,000		
18	Kennedy	Sandra	$135,000	East	$115,000		
19	Stevens	Carle	$110,000	East	$185,000		
20	Ford	Carl	$191,000	Midwest	$95,000		
21	Linn	Vera	$80,000	Midwest	$190,000		
22	Peterson	Tom	$98,000	Midwest	$110,000		
23	Adams	Chuck	$118,000	South	$110,000		
24	Glenn	John	$80,000	South	$125,000		
25	Parker	Greg	$196,000	South	$65,000		
26	Conners	Paul	$142,000	West	$213,000		
27	Harris	Ken	$176,000	West	$95,000		
28	Keller	Janet	$105,000	West	$120,000		

Ready

Figure 13.7: The actual-sales field

Hide the numbers in B5 and C5 by defining a custom picture as ;;. Select B5:C5, open the Format menu and choose Number. In the Format Number box, delete the entry and enter ;;. Click OK. Set the picture for B5 and C5 to this.

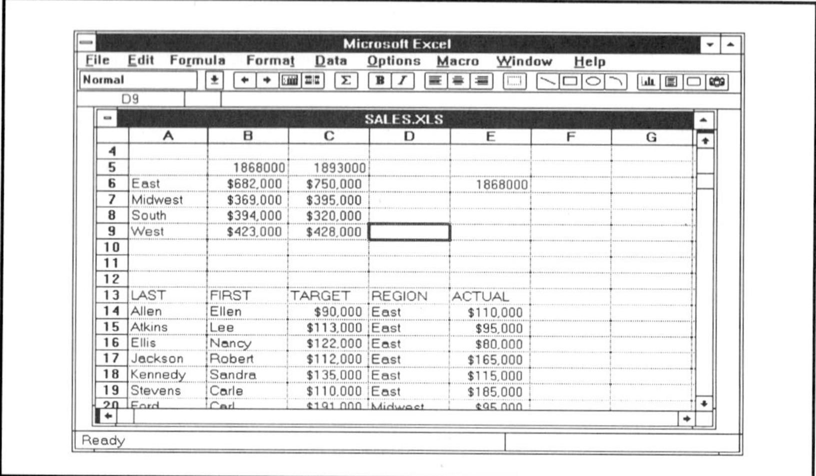

Figure 13.8: The worksheet showing actual-sales results by region

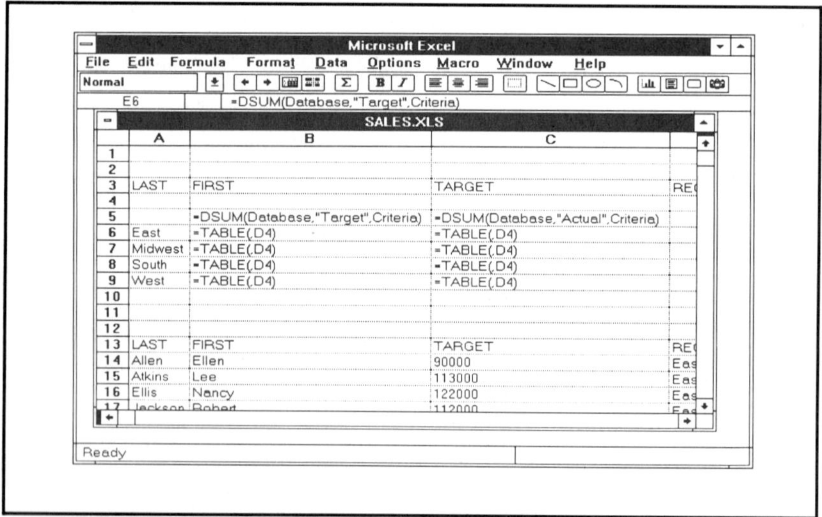

Figure 13.9: Formulas for two-column, one-input table

TWO-INPUT TABLES

In a one-input table, a single input cell is used to calculate the values for one or more columns or rows. In a two-input table, as its name implies, two input cells are used to calculate the values for one or more columns or rows.

Designing a Two-Input Table

To design a two-input table, you need to define the following four areas on your worksheet:

- Two input cells to contain the values that you wish to change
- A row containing the values that will be applied successively to one input cell
- A column containing the values that will be applied successively to the other input cell
- One or more columns or rows to contain the resulting values, with formulas used as headings for each column or row. You can use formulas that refer directly to the input cell or to other cells on the worksheet

Creating a Two-Input Table

You create a two-input table by following the same procedure that you used to create a one-input table, except that you will have both a row input cell and a column input cell.

Let's try an example. Figure 13.10 shows a method of using a two-input table to calculate monthly payments for a variety of interest rates and time periods on an $8000 loan. The interest rates are placed in column B and the period values (in months) in row 6. Two input cells must be defined: one for the interest values (B3) and one for the periods (C3). The following formula is placed at the intersection of the row and column (B6):

=PMT(B3/12,C3, –8000)

Don't worry about the **#DIV/0!** in B6; it's there because the two input cells are empty. Select B6 to F12. Open the Table menu and click cell C3 for the Row Input Cell. For the Column Input Cell, click B3. Format the table and it should look like Figure 13.10. Notice that no database or criteria are defined; they are not needed to create a table.

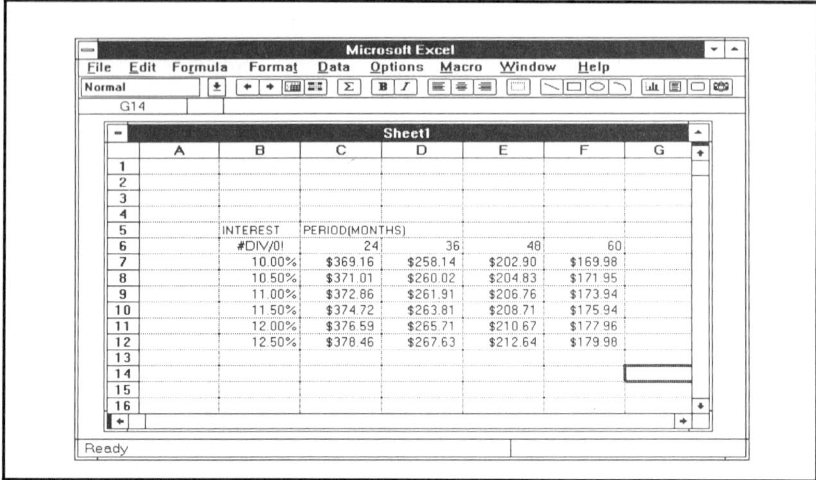

	A	B	C	D	E	F	G
1							
2							
3							
4							
5		INTEREST	PERIOD(MONTHS)				
6		#DIV/0!	24	36	48	60	
7		10.00%	$369.16	$258.14	$202.90	$169.98	
8		10.50%	$371.01	$260.02	$204.83	$171.95	
9		11.00%	$372.86	$261.91	$206.76	$173.94	
10		11.50%	$374.72	$263.81	$208.71	$175.94	
11		12.00%	$376.59	$265.71	$210.67	$177.96	
12		12.50%	$378.46	$267.63	$212.64	$179.98	
13							
14							
15							
16							

Figure 13.10: A two-input table

A database is not needed to use the Table command.

To improve the table's appearance, hide cell B6 by following the instructions in Chapter 14, or by creating a custom picture (the Number command in the Format menu) ;; and using it (see "Calculating Two Columns" above).

This worksheet will not be used in my further examples, but you can save it if you wish.

EDITING TABLES

A table must always be edited as a unit. You can't edit an output cell in a table.

You can edit the values used for input cells or the formulas of a table by using the commands on the Edit menu. The table will be updated automatically after you make any changes. However, you *cannot* edit the output columns or rows of a table (such as cells B6 through B9 in the Sales database and worksheet example).

For example, reload the Sales worksheet and try changing Midwest to Europe on the worksheet: select cell A7 and enter **Europe**. Because there are no records that match this criterion, the value in cell B7 becomes zero. You can't edit the individual cells B6 through B9 or even clear them. You also cannot clear a portion of a table; you must clear the entire table.

If you copy a value from an output row or column into another cell of the worksheet, the new cell will contain only the value, not the formula.

When you select cells in the output columns or rows, the formula bar will display the table reference. For example, for cells B6, B7, B8, and B9, the formula bar shows:

{ = TABLE(,D4)}

(D4 is the input cell for the table.) The braces indicate that the formula is part of a table.

To delete a table or redefine it, select the entire table and use the Clear command on the Edit menu.

NOTES FOR USING THE TABLE COMMAND

The following notes apply to using the Table command:

- You enter the formula for the output into the first cell in each column or row that will contain the output values
- Once you have defined a range as a table, the entire range must be cleared or edited as a unit—tables cannot be partially cleared
- There is no limit to how many tables you can have active at one time

USING TABLES FOR LOOKUP ACCESS

Tables can substitute for formulas to produce an output value from an input value. Here you are using table functions, not the Table command. You can create such tables, called *lookup tables,* anywhere on a worksheet. Here are some typical applications for them:

- Looking up the number of days in a month
- Looking up a tax rate for a particular income
- Looking up a category value for a product or employee
- Looking up a price for a particular category value

In each of these cases there is no easy way to use a formula to get the desired value. A lookup table, however, provides a simple alternative.

THE CHOOSE FUNCTION

The simplest and easiest type of lookup table to use employs the CHOOSE function. The CHOOSE function has the following syntax:

=CHOOSE(*index, value 1, value 2,. . ., value n*)

The table, in this case, is the linear list of arguments within the function call. The value of *index* determines which item of the list the CHOOSE function chooses and returns.

For example, the following command will return the current name of the day of the week:

=CHOOSE(WEEKDAY(NOW( ))"Sun","Mon",
"Tue","Wed","Thu","Fri","Sat")

THE MATCH FUNCTION

The MATCH function is used to return the position of the item in a list that most closely matches a lookup value. The general form is

=MATCH(*lookup value, lookup range, type*)

For example, assume the following cell values are in Row 1: A1 =22, B1 =43, and C1 =54. The function

=MATCH(43,A1:C1)

returns the value 2.

The general form of the function is:

=MATCH(*lookup value, compare vector, type*)

The third argument is optional but, if used, defines the rules for the search. A value of 1 causes the function to return the largest value in the range equal to or less than *lookup value.* A value of 0 directs the function to accept only an exact match. If *type* is −1, the function returns the smallest value that is greater than or equal to *lookup value* in the range. If the argument is omitted, a default value of 1 is assumed. If nothing in the range matches the test condition, the error value #N/A is returned.

If you want to omit the type argument or specify it as 1, the table must be in ascending order. If you want the type to be −1, the table must be in descending order. If you want the type to be 0, the table may be in any order.

THE INDEX FUNCTION

The general form of the index function is as follows:

=INDEX(*index range, row, column, area*)

This function returns the address of a cell, not its value. The cell containing the function displays the value from the specified cell in the table, as the following example illustrates.

To use the function, you must first create a table in a separate area of the worksheet. The table must be a rectangular range that includes at least four cells. The *index range* argument is used to define the range of the table. The next two arguments define the *row* and *column* for the retrieval. Each must be greater than zero. For example, if

A1 = INDEX(C1:E3,A5,A6)

A5 = 2

A6 = 3

returns the value of E2 to A1 (that is, row 2 and column 3 in the table defined by the first argument), A1 would display the contents of E2.

As an example, Figure 13.11 shows a worksheet for determining the percent a bank might charge for a loan, based on the credit risk. The risk categories are 1, 2, and 3 in column B. Row 5 shows the years of the loan. The formula in B11 to calculate the percent for the specified risk is

=INDEX(C6:F8,D1,D2)

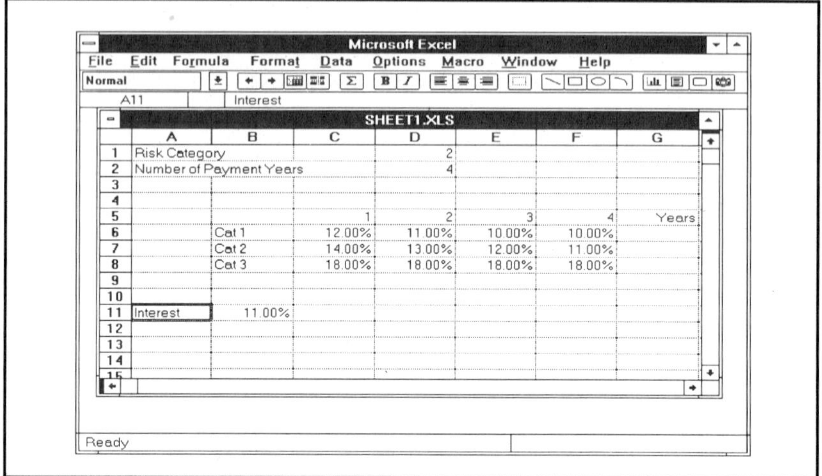

Figure 13.11: An example using the INDEX function

The row and column headings are not used in the formula and are for labeling only. The actual table displacements are in cells D1 and D2.

You also can use multiple areas, using the fourth argument to tell Excel which area to use:

=INDEX((C1:E3,F1:H3),2,3,2)

Here, the fourth argument value of 2 forces the use of the second table range, F1:H3.

The number of arguments is limited to 13, as with other functions. The expression width is limited to 255 characters.

THE LOOKUP FUNCTIONS

You also can access lookup tables in a separate area of the worksheet using the LOOKUP, VLOOKUP, and HLOOKUP functions (see Chapter 8). These functions permit you to locate a value in a table based on the value of a *test variable* (the first argument in a function). The second argument defines the lookup table as an array (see Chapter 15 on arrays).

The LOOKUP, VLOOKUP, and HLOOKUP functions search the first row or column of the table and return the largest value that is equal to or less than the test value. The table values must be in ascending order. For example, suppose cells D1 through D3 contain a table with the values 10000, 20000, and 40000, and cells F1 through F3 contain the values 5.00%, 6.00%, and 7.00%, as shown in Figure 13.12. If you entered the function *LOOKUP(25000,D1:F3)* in A1, it would return *6.00%*. The general form of LOOKUP is:

=LOOKUP(*value, array*)

The function searches the first row or column of *array* for *value* and returns the value of the corresponding cell of the last column or row. The LOOKUP function is identical to that of other worksheet programs.

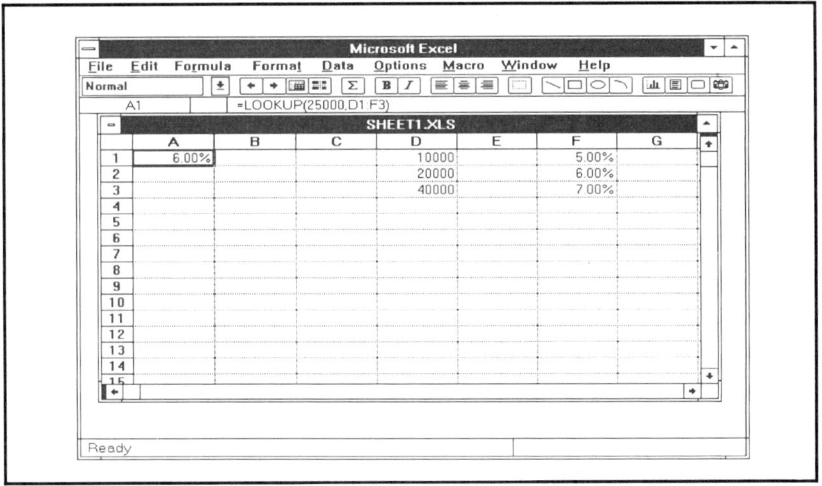

Figure 13.12: The LOOKUP function

The third argument is used the same way, but has a different value than in many competing worksheet programs. Remember that Excel counts the first column as column 1, while many other programs count it as column 0, and that table values must be in ascending order to work.

The HLOOKUP and VLOOKUP functions contain a third argument. HLOOKUP defines how far to move into the column, and VLOOKUP defines how far to move in the row for example. In the lookup table described above, the function *VLOOKUP(25000,D1:F3,3)* would return *6.00%*, and the function *VLOOKUP(25000,D1:F3,1)* would return *25000*, as the first column is 1, and the value is returned from that column.

Lookup tables are useful for obtaining a value that cannot be calculated directly from other cells on the worksheet using a formula, such as a loan risk rating based on two specified variables.

You have now learned how to create two types of tables: what-if tables (using the Table command) and lookup tables (using the LOOKUP functions). What-if tables are used to apply a series of input values to one or more cells to create a series of output values. Lookup tables are used as substitutes for formulas for certain types of worksheet calculations.

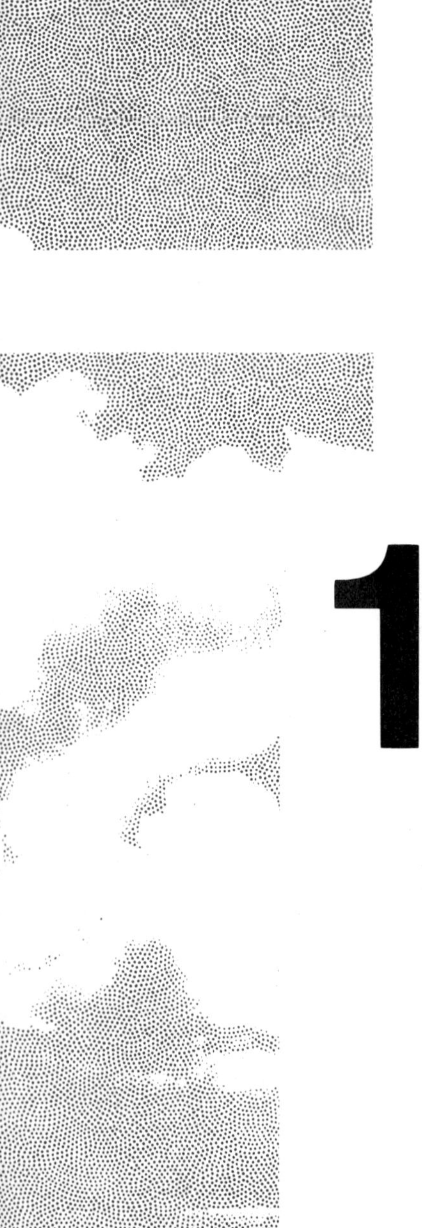

14 Exploring Special Features

ALTHOUGH YOU'VE CREATED SEVERAL WORKSHEETS, you have mainly used the standard features only: moving, copying, formatting, and using functions.

In this chapter, you will be introduced to some of Excel's special features that make it even easier for you to create worksheets. These include copying and clearing only specific information, entering a series of values, controlling when calculations are done, protecting cells, and performing iterative calculations. You will try those various operations on worksheets you have already created. (Note that you don't need to bother to save these changes for future operations.)

EDITING SELECTIVE PARTS OF CELLS

Excel stores three types of data about each cell: its value or formula, its format, and its notes. Excel's Clear and Paste Special commands allow you to work selectively with the values, formulas, or formats of the selected cells.

SELECTIVE CLEARING

The Clear command on the Edit menu can be used to selectively delete the formulas, formats, or notes of specified cells as well as of an entire worksheet. Excel's default selection in the Clear dialog box is Formulas, which clears the formulas and values in the selected cells but retains the format. If you select Formats on the dialog box, the selected cells will revert to the General template format but no data or formulas will be cleared. If you choose Notes, any notes assigned to that range will be cleared. If you choose All, the values, formulas, formats, and notes of the selected cells will be cleared.

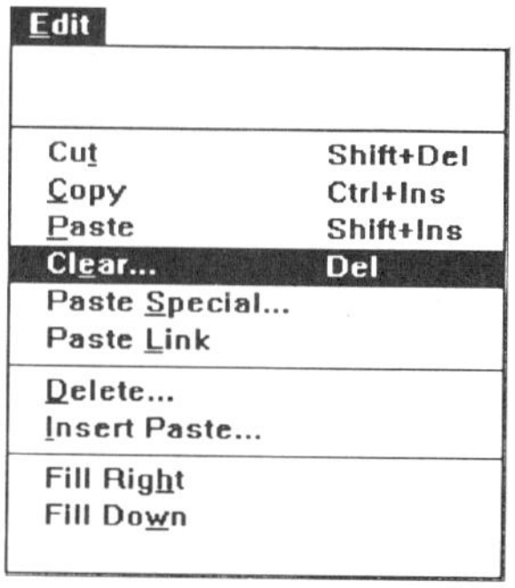

Edit

Cut	Shift+Del
Copy	Ctrl+Ins
Paste	Shift+Ins
Clear...	Del
Paste Special...	
Paste Link	
Delete...	
Insert Paste...	
Fill Right	
Fill Down	

Here are a few tips on clearing cells:

- Clearing a cell puts the cell value at zero. Formulas in the rest of the worksheet referring to that cell will assume that the cell has a zero value. By contrast, when you are deleting a cell (Delete command), the cell is removed from memory. Formulas referring to the cell will return the error value #REF
- For a fast method of clearing formulas, values, and notes from a cell or cell range, select the range and press Ctrl-Del
- Clearing a cell or cell range does not alter the column width or row height

As an example, open your Sales worksheet and select a few target values in column C of the database. Open the Edit menu and choose Clear. Then select Format and click OK. The format of the cells that you cleared returns to the General picture—the dollar signs and commas disappear. Reformat the cells to their previous format before you continue.

SELECTIVE COPYING

The Paste Special command on the Edit menu lets you control what you copy into another cell. You can copy just the values, formulas, formats, or notes of a cell instead of copying all the data from one cell or cell range to another. Excel's default selection in the Paste Special dialog box is All.

The Transpose option switches the rows and columns of the pasted data (see "Transposing Lists" at the end of this chapter). The Skip Blanks option blocks the pasting of blank cells.

The Operation part of the dialog box permits you to perform operations between cells as part of the copy process. This is particularly useful for combining data from several worksheets into a single summary worksheet. For example, a sales manager may receive worksheets from several sales areas. She could use the Add option in the Operation part of the Paste Special dialog box to combine the totals when she copies them into a summary worksheet.

Let's see how the Paste Special command works. First, add a name to the end of your Sales database. Notice that the value for TARGET is not formatted correctly. You could use the Format command to reformat the entry, but an easier method would be to use the Paste Special command to copy only the format. Follow these steps:

1. Open the Sales worksheet and be sure the last name is in row 28. Sort to last-name order if the order is by region.
2. Enter the values for the new salesperson in row 29, as shown in Figure 14.1.
3. Select cell C28, as it contains the cell format to copy.
4. Open the Edit menu and choose Copy.

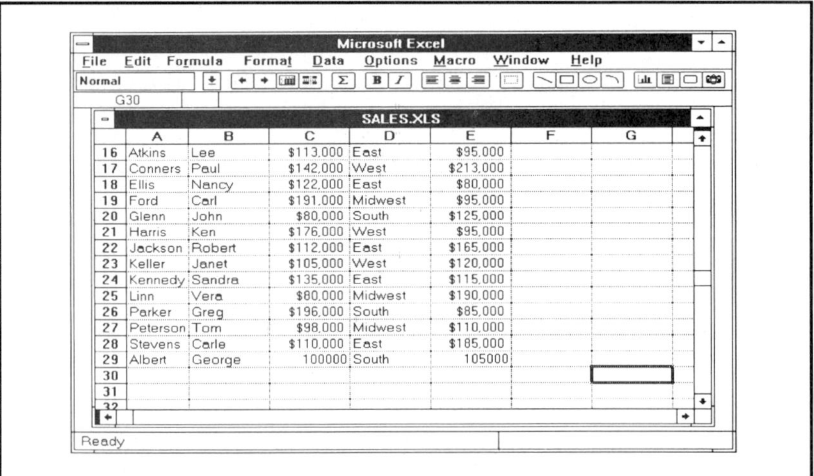

	A	B	C	D	E	F	G
16	Atkins	Lee	$113,000	East	$95,000		
17	Conners	Paul	$142,000	West	$213,000		
18	Ellis	Nancy	$122,000	East	$80,000		
19	Ford	Carl	$191,000	Midwest	$95,000		
20	Glenn	John	$80,000	South	$125,000		
21	Harris	Ken	$176,000	West	$95,000		
22	Jackson	Robert	$112,000	East	$165,000		
23	Keller	Janet	$105,000	West	$120,000		
24	Kennedy	Sandra	$135,000	East	$115,000		
25	Linn	Vera	$80,000	Midwest	$190,000		
26	Parker	Greg	$196,000	South	$85,000		
27	Peterson	Tom	$98,000	Midwest	$110,000		
28	Stevens	Carle	$110,000	East	$185,000		
29	Albert	George	100000	South	105000		
30							
31							

Figure 14.1: Adding a new salesperson

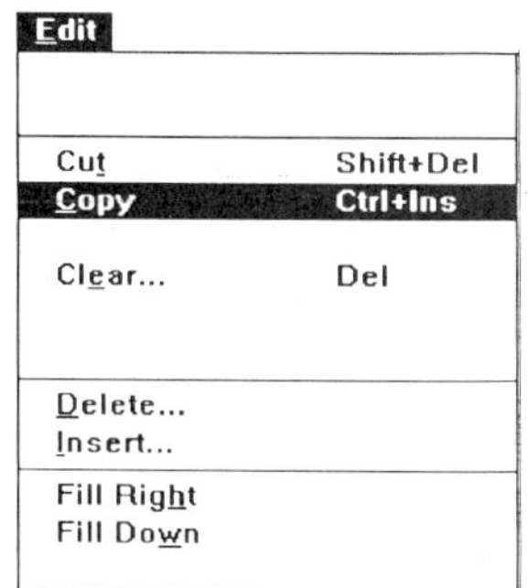

5. Select cells C29 and E29 as the destination cells. (Select C29, then hold down Ctrl and select E29.)
6. From the Edit menu, choose Paste Special.
7. When the Paste Special dialog box appears, choose Formats, then click OK.

The new entries in cells C29 and E29 are now formatted correctly, as shown in Figure 14.2.

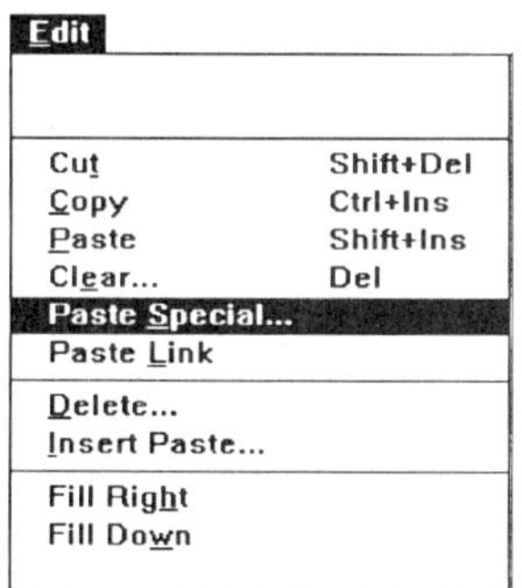

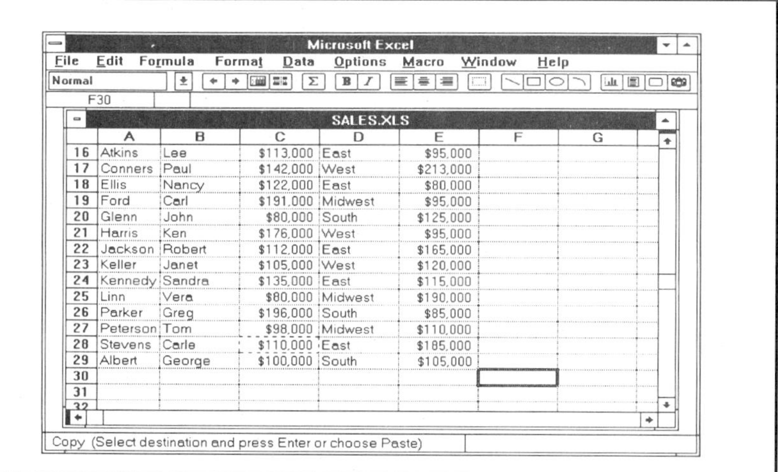

	A	B	C	D	E	F	G
16	Atkins	Lee	$113,000	East	$95,000		
17	Conners	Paul	$142,000	West	$213,000		
18	Ellis	Nancy	$122,000	East	$80,000		
19	Ford	Carl	$191,000	Midwest	$95,000		
20	Glenn	John	$80,000	South	$125,000		
21	Harris	Ken	$176,000	West	$95,000		
22	Jackson	Robert	$112,000	East	$165,000		
23	Keller	Janet	$105,000	West	$120,000		
24	Kennedy	Sandra	$135,000	East	$115,000		
25	Linn	Vera	$80,000	Midwest	$190,000		
26	Parker	Greg	$196,000	South	$85,000		
27	Peterson	Tom	$98,000	Midwest	$110,000		
28	Stevens	Carle	$110,000	East	$185,000		
29	Albert	George	$100,000	South	$105,000		
30							
31							
32							

Figure 14.2: The result of using the Paste Special command

To see how an Operation option works, select C28 and then choose Copy from the Edit menu. Select C29 and choose Paste Special. When the Paste Special dialog box appears, leave All selected and choose Add in the Operation box. The contents of cell C28 will be added to the contents of cell C29 in the copy process, and C29 will read $210,000.

Here are a few copying tips:

- As described in Chapter 5, use the Clipboard and the Edit menu to do your copying and moving. Invoke the Copy and Paste commands whenever possible to enter data into new columns and rows in a worksheet. This saves entry time and helps prevent mistakes

- Use the Paste Special command when you need to copy only the contents, format, or notes of a cell
- You also can move or copy cells or cell ranges using the Cut, Copy, and Insert commands. If you cut or copy a cell or cell range, **Insert** on the Edit menu changes to **Insert Paste**. You can then paste the cells in the Clipboard to another area of the worksheet
- When copying cells, the column width or row height is not copied
- You can use Repeat on the Edit menu to repeat a command (copy, paste, etc.)
- You can do multiple pastes from a single copy
- You can use Ctrl–` to copy from the cell above to the current cell. (Be careful not to use Ctrl–' here, as this toggles the Formula Display mode and displays the worksheet formulas.)
- You can copy or cut entire rows or columns by selecting the row or column designator, but this will require a lot of Clipboard space. For example, you can clear a record from a database by selecting an entire row and then deleting the row. The safer (in case there are data to the right of the database) and faster method is to select the record cells and then delete these. You can simplify this by using a relative name reference that includes the entire record and select Goto from the Edit menu (or press F5) to get the entire record

SPECIAL EDITING TECHNIQUES

Here are two helpful editing techniques to keep in mind:

- You can use the Edit menu to edit a formula in the formula bar as well as to move or copy cell contents. The Cut and Copy commands enable you to delete a portion of a formula or copy a portion to another part of the formula

- Use caution with the Paste Special command. If the Add option is selected, new values will replace the old ones in the range selected. You have no audit trail or track of what was there before. You can, however, undo the command (see next section). It would be better to create a new range, keeping the values in the new range that is added. The Paste Special command is very useful, however, for adding a constant in one cell to a range of cells

THE UNDO COMMANDS

If you make a mistake in editing, you can recover the original worksheet quickly by using the Undo command on the Edit menu (or pressing Alt–Backspace). For example, suppose you clear a range of cells accidentally. To recover the range, simply open the Edit menu and choose Undo Clear (or press Alt–Backspace). In the same way, if you are editing in the formula bar, you can use the Undo Typing command to restore the original contents of the cell. (If you're typing data into a cell and have not pressed Enter yet, you can restore the cell to its previous value by clicking the × at the left of the formula bar.)

You can undo a command only if no other command has been issued; that is, you can undo only the last command issued. Some commands do not support any Undo.

Once the Undo command is initiated, the Edit menu changes to show a Redo command. Redo restores whatever was undone.

You cannot undo the Delete command on the File menu or the Delete and Sort commands on the Data menu.

If you are working with a very large worksheet and try to move or copy a range of cells, you may get a message saying that there is insufficient room and that you must choose Continue, Stop, or Undo. When this box appears, always select Stop. Then select a smaller range to move or copy. This protects you in case an undo is later necessary.

DELETING AND INSERTING PARTIAL ROWS AND COLUMNS

Excel permits you to delete a partial row or column. Select the range to delete and choose the Delete command from the Edit menu (or press Ctrl– –). A dialog box will then ask you how you want the space to be filled: by shifting cells left or up. Select the desired option and click OK.

Before deleting an entire row or column, check the rest of the row or column to be sure that no important data will be deleted. Even in deleting partial rows and columns, check to the right or below (depending upon the direction of adjustment) before deletion.

You can use the Insert command in the same way to insert partial rows and columns. Excel displays the same type of dialog box, which asks which way to shift the cells to fill the space.

CREATING A SERIES OF VALUES

Excel's Series command gives you a quick and easy way to enter sequential numbers into columns or rows. For example, the Series command would have been useful when you created the Amortization worksheet in Chapter 8. Column A of that worksheet contains a series of numbers. When you created the worksheet, you had to enter each number into column A sequentially—a laborious job, because there were 48 payments in the example.

To use the Series command, you simply enter the starting value into the first cell of the row or column, select the cell range for the series (including the starting cell), open the Data menu, and choose Series. When you see the Series dialog box, choose whether you want the series in a row or column and choose the series type (as explained below). Then, enter a step value for each increment of the series (the default value is 1). After you've made your selections, click OK and Excel will enter the Series values automatically.

You have a choice of three types of series:

- A **linear series**, in which each entry is increased by a constant amount. For example, a linear series with a starting value of 1 and a step value of 2 would increase 1, 3, 5, and so on
- A **growth series**, in which each entry is multiplied by the step value. For example, a growth series with a starting value of 1 and a step value of 2 would increase 1, 2, 4, 8,

16, and so on. The growth series is useful for calculating compounded interest or growth rates

- A **date series**, in which a date is increased by a unit (day, weekday, month, or year) that you select in the Date unit box in the Series dialog box. For example, to create columnar headings for the months of the year, enter the first month, select the row for the column titles, choose Date, and then select Month

You also can choose a stop value for a series. For example, if you did not know how many rows or columns your series would require, you could select a larger range than you need and enter a specific stop value in the Series dialog box. The series would then terminate at that specified value.

You can use the Series command to enter the data into column A of your Amortization worksheet easily. After you clear column A from row 15 down, follow these steps:

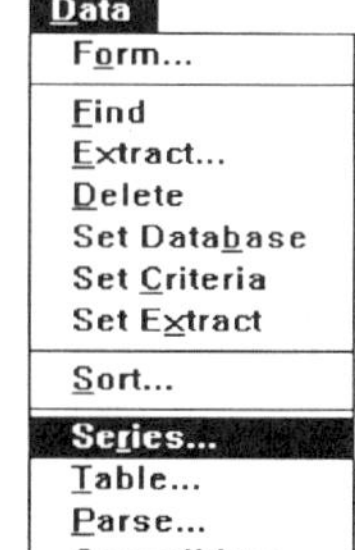

1. Enter the starting value of 1 into cell A15.
2. Select cell A15, open the Formula menu, and choose Goto.
3. Enter A62 into the Reference box, then hold down the Shift key and click OK.
4. Open the Data menu and choose Series.
5. When the Series dialog box appears, leave the default Columns and Linear options selected and click OK.

With just a few clicks, the series is entered into column A.

CHANGING REFERENCE STYLES AND TYPES

Excel gives you the flexibility of changing both the style of cell referencing (from column letter and row number to numbers for both columns and rows) and the type of cell referencing (from absolute to relative and vice versa).

CHANGING REFERENCE STYLES

Some worksheet programs designate rows and columns in a different style than Excel's. They reference a cell's location in R1C1 style—an R followed by the row number and a C followed by the column number—rather than Excel's column letter and row number (A1) style. For example, Figure 14.3 shows the formula (in the formula bar) for cell C15 of the Amortization worksheet in Excel's reference style. Figure 14.4 shows the same formula in R1C1 style. Notice the difference in both absolute and relative addressing. The absolute $B$7 reference in A1 style becomes R7C2—row 7, column 2. The mixed reference B$8 becomes row 8 and one column left (– 1) of the current column, or R8C [– 1].

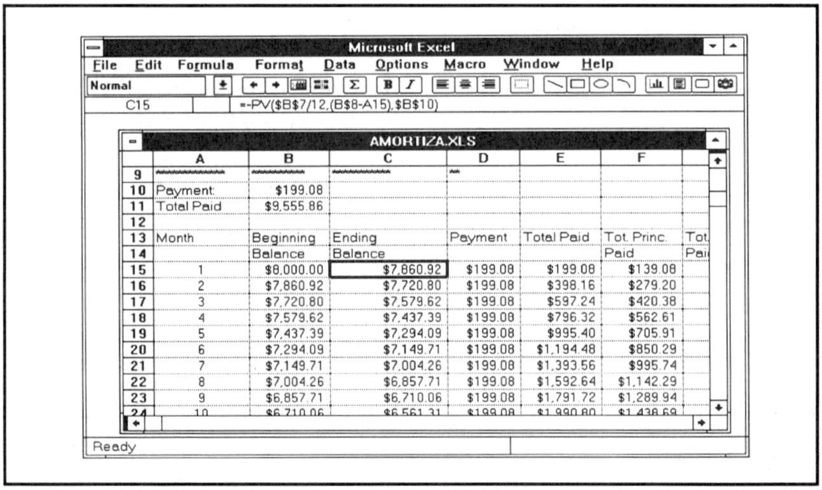

Figure 14.3: A formula in A1 reference style

Some Excel formulas require the use of the R1C1 style.

If you are more familiar with the R1C1 style and would rather have Excel use it, you can change to that style by using the Workspace command on the Options menu.

On the Workspace dialog box, choose R1C1, then click OK. The worksheet's column letters will change into numbers, so that both the rows and columns are referenced by numbers.

Change the worksheet back to Excel's normal referencing style. Select the Options menu, choose Workspace, and click R1C1 to turn the × off.

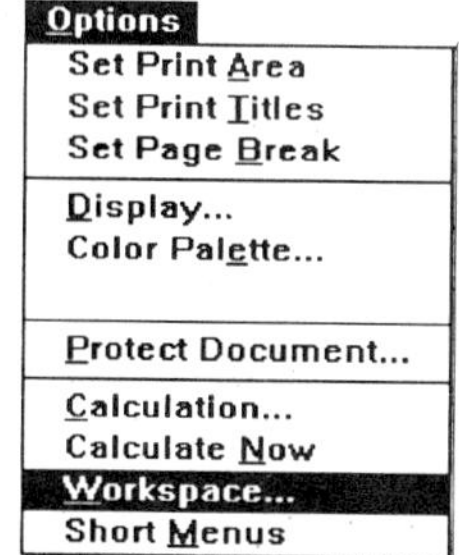

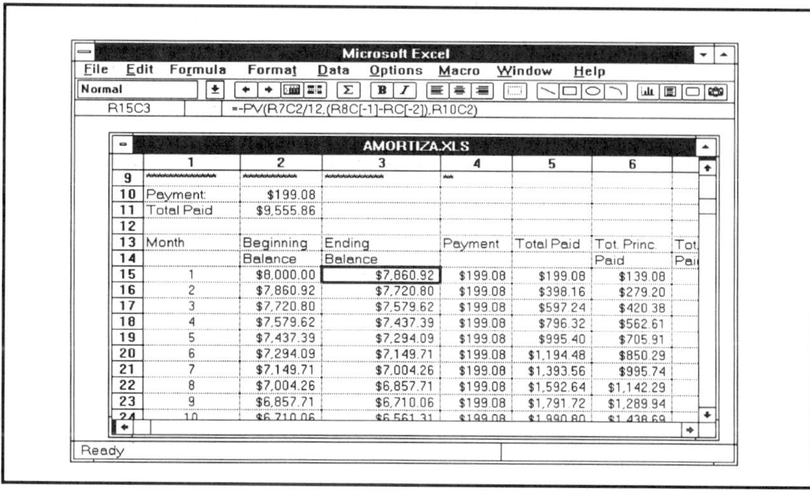

Figure 14.4: A formula in R1C1 style

CHANGING REFERENCE TYPES

There may be times when you need to change the type of cell reference in a formula. For example, when you click a referenced cell to enter it into a formula, it is automatically entered as a relative cell address. You can change this reference easily with the mouse: open the Formula menu and choose Reference. This will toggle the reference between absolute, mixed, and relative.

Formula
Paste Name...
Paste Function...
Reference
Goto...
Find...
Show Active Cell

There are only two points to note before you use the Reference command:

- The formula bar must be active (click the cursor in the formula bar)
- The command changes only the reference to the *left* of the insertion point in the formula bar unless you have selected several references by highlighting them, in which case all addresses are changed

MOVING TO AND FINDING CELLS

The Formula menu lists several commands that let you move quickly to particular cells and find cells that contain specific data.

MOVING TO SPECIFIC CELLS

If you are using a large worksheet, you will occasionally need to move quickly to a particular cell on it. The Goto command on the Formula menu allows you to jump to any specified cell. When you use this command, or press F5, you will see the Goto dialog box. Simply enter the reference to the cell that you want to make active in the Reference box and click OK.

Formula
Paste Name...
Paste Function...
Define Name...
Create Names...
Apply Names...
Note...
Goto...
Find...
Replace...
Select Special...
Show Active Cell
Outline...
Goal Seek...
Solver...

There is an even easier way to move to a particular cell. If there is a cell or cell range on your worksheet that you use often, assign it a name using the Define Name command on the Formula menu (see Chapter 9). Then, when you choose Goto or press F5, you will see that name in the dialog box's list of active names. Double-click the name and you'll move to that cell or cell range immediately.

The Goto command actually has more uses than just getting you to a particular cell quickly: you can use it for range selection, formula entry, or viewing, as well. Let's try a few simple experiments so that you can see for yourself.

First, open your Amortization worksheet and define a name for cell C18:

1. Select cell C18.
2. Open the Formula menu and choose Define Name.
3. Type **Test** into the Define Name dialog box and click OK.

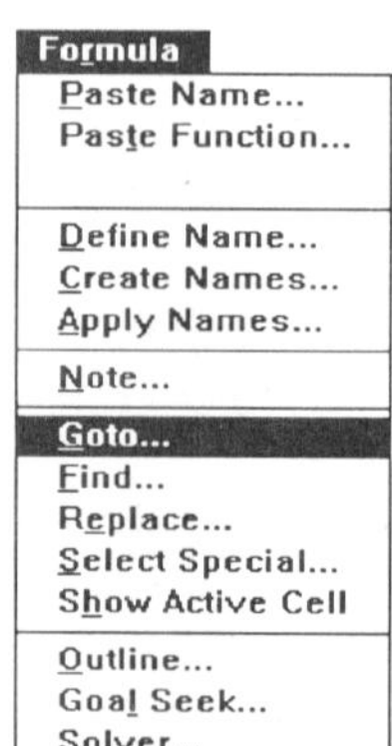

Now, use the Goto command to select a range:

1. Select cell C15.
2. Open the Formula menu and choose Goto or press F5.
3. Hold down the Shift key and double-click **Test** in the Goto dialog box.

You have now selected the entire cell range from C15 to C18. The result is shown in Figure 14.5.

If there is a cell range that you use often, select the entire range and assign a name to it. You can then use the Goto command to select that range quickly.

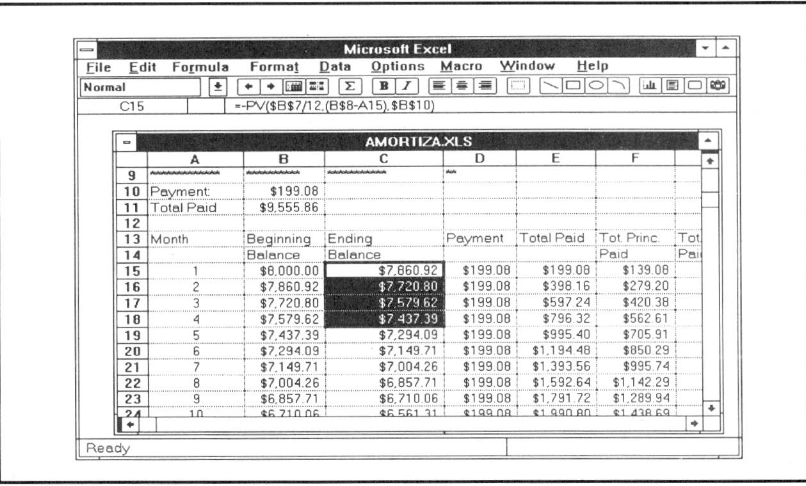

Figure 14.5: Selecting a range with the Goto command

FINDING SPECIFIC CELLS

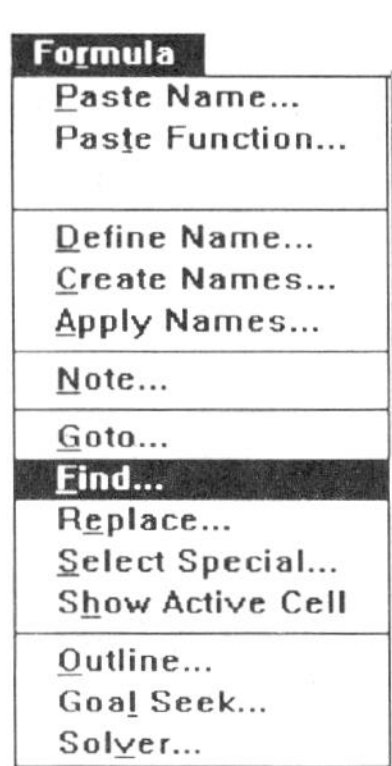

There may be times when you need to find the specific cell that contains a particular value or formula. You can do this by using the Find command on the Formula menu (or pressing Shift–F5).

When you select the Find command, you'll see the Find dialog box. Once you've entered what you want to find in the Find What box, you can have Excel look in formulas or in values, look for the entry as a whole or as part of other entries, and look by columns or by rows.

Here are other features of the Find command:

- If you have a single cell selected when you use the Find command, the entire worksheet will be searched. If you have a range selected, only the range will be searched
- The search will stop when Excel finds the first occurrence
- When entering the search string into the Find What box, you can use the wild-card characters ? and *, where ? represents a single character and * represents a group of characters. You also can use any of the relational operators to specify the search string (see Chapter 4)

- The Look By box is used to specify the direction of the search—either by rows or columns. If you know the approximate location of the cell on a large worksheet, specifying the correct direction here can speed up the search
- The Shift–F5 key is the shortcut key for the Find command. Press F7 to find the next occurrence, or Shift–F7 to find the previous one

As an example, you can use the Find command to locate the cell on your Amortization worksheet that contains the final payment. Follow these steps:

1. Open the Formula menu and choose Find.
2. When the Find dialog box is displayed, enter **48**.
3. Choose Values to indicate that you wish to search in values instead of in formulas (otherwise it would stop on C48).
4. Choose Whole to indicate that you want to skip cells in which the value is a part of a cell's value (otherwise it would stop on E20).
5. Click OK.

The cursor should jump to cell A62, the month cell in the last payment row.

When you've finished editing a worksheet, use the Find command to locate all unresolved references by searching for #REF.

DISPLAYING THE ACTIVE CELL

You can use Show Active Cell command on the Formula menu to find the current active cell. This is particularly useful when you select a cell or cell range, scroll away to view something else in the worksheet, and want to get back to where you were.

REPLACING CELL VALUES

The Replace command on the Formula menu can be used to replace characters in the worksheet or a cell range. Select the replacement range or, if you wish the command to apply to the entire worksheet, a single cell. The first cell in the range should be active. Select Replace from the Formula menu. The dialog box of Figure 14.6 will be displayed. Enter the current value and what it is to be replaced with. Choose Whole to check an entire cell's contents or Part to check for a match on any part of a cell's contents. You may use * and ? wildcards.

Formula
Paste Name...
Paste Function...
Define Name...
Create Names...
Apply Names...
Note...
Goto...
Find...
Replace...
Select Special...
Show Active Cell
Outline...
Goal Seek...
Solver...

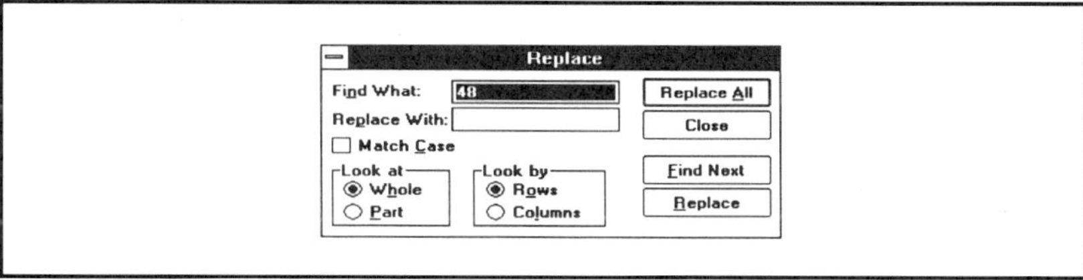

Figure 14.6: Starting a replacement

For global replacement, click Replace All. For selective replacement, first click Find Next to find the next occurrence. Then click Replace to replace the single occurrence. Click Find Next to locate the next occurrence. Replace only applies to the currently active cell. To reverse to a previous occurrence, hold down the Shift key and click Find Next.

To exit, click Close. To undo, select Undo Replace from the Edit menu.

Formula
Paste Name...
Paste Function...
Define Name...
Create Names...
Apply Names...
Note...
Goto...
Find...
Replace...
Select Special...
Show Active Cell
Outline...
Goal Seek...
Solver...

SELECTING THE LAST CELL

Sometimes you may need to find the last cell of a worksheet. This command is useful if you simply want to move quickly to the last cell, but you don't remember its location.

To find the last cell, choose Select Special on the Formula menu. Then choose Last Cell (see Figure 14.7).

CALCULATION OPTIONS

The Calculation command on the Options menu allows you to tell Excel when to recalculate values and when to use iterations.

Figure 14.7: Finding the last cell

CONTROLLING RECALCULATIONS

Normally, whenever you change a value, formula, or name, Excel automatically recalculates all cells that are dependent upon the changed cells. The time required for Excel to recalculate a worksheet depends on the size of the worksheet, the number of dependent cells, and the number of open documents. Because it calculates only the cells that are changed as a result of an edit or addition, Excel is faster than many competitors. If you are entering data on a large worksheet or using tables, however, recalculations can still be time-consuming. You can speed up the data-entry process by using the Calculation command on the Options menu to turn off the calculations until you've entered all the data.

When you use the Calculation command, you will see the Calculation dialog box. Choose Manual to turn off calculations, then click OK.

For some worksheets, you may want Excel to recalculate automatically all values except the tables. If you select this option on the Calculation dialog box, the tables will be recalculated only when you invoke the Table command on the Data menu or Calculate Now on the Options menu.

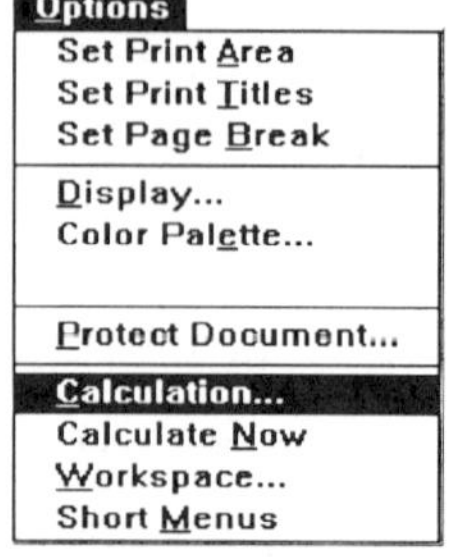

To calculate the worksheet after you have entered all the data, first be sure that the formula bar is not selected, then open the Options menu and choose Calculate Now. If the formula bar is active when you select the Calculate Now command, Excel will evaluate the formula and enter the result (not the formula) into the active cell. You also can select part of a formula and use the Calculate Now command to evaluate only that part.

Remember, you need to use the Calculate Now command only when you have set Excel in the Manual calculation mode or selected Automatic Except Tables. When Excel is in the Automatic calculation mode, the Calculate Now command will do nothing unless the formula bar is active, as described above.

USING ITERATIONS

There may be times when your calculations require you to use formulas that depend upon each other in a circular manner. Excel allows you to perform the worksheet calculations repetitively, or to use *iterations*. Let's try an example so that you can get an idea of how this works. Open an empty worksheet.

Acme Manufacturing had a good year, and the Board decided to pay the employees a bonus. The amount allocated for the bonus payments was five percent of the net profit after the bonuses were subtracted from the gross profit. Let's create a worksheet to help Acme calculate the bonus:

1. Enter the row titles **Gross Profit**, **Bonus**, and **Net Profit** in cells A3, A4, and A6, respectively, and enter **23,500** as the value for Gross Profit (Figure 14.8).
2. Create the names by selecting A3 to B6 and then choosing Create Names on the Formula menu. In the dialog box, choose Left Column, then click OK.
3. Enter the formula for Net Profit as **Gross_Profit – Bonus**.
4. Enter the value of the Bonus as **Net_Profit*5%**.

What happens? You will quickly get the error message shown in Figure 14.9: Cannot resolve circular references.

This message indicates that you have created formulas that depend upon each other. Here, net profit is the gross profit minus the bonus, but you need to know the net profit before the bonus can be calculated. Solution: use iterations to make your calculation.

Continue with the worksheet:

5. Choose OK to cancel the message box, then open the Options menu and choose Calculation.

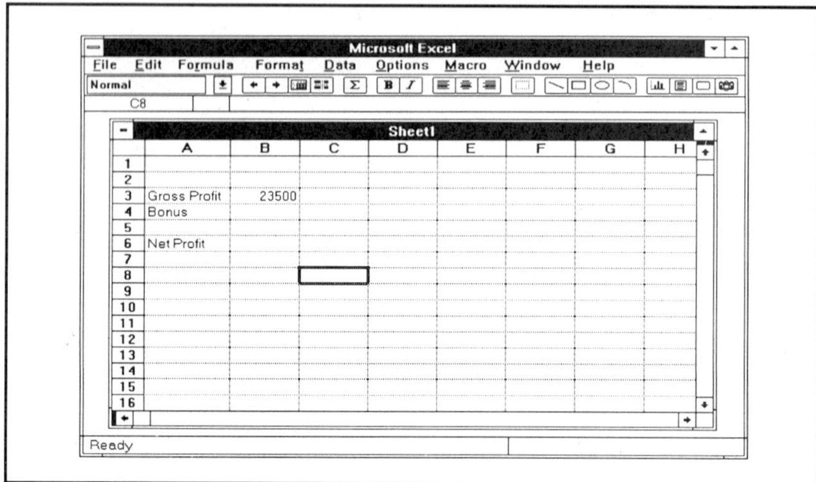

Figure 14.8: The Acme Manufacturing worksheet

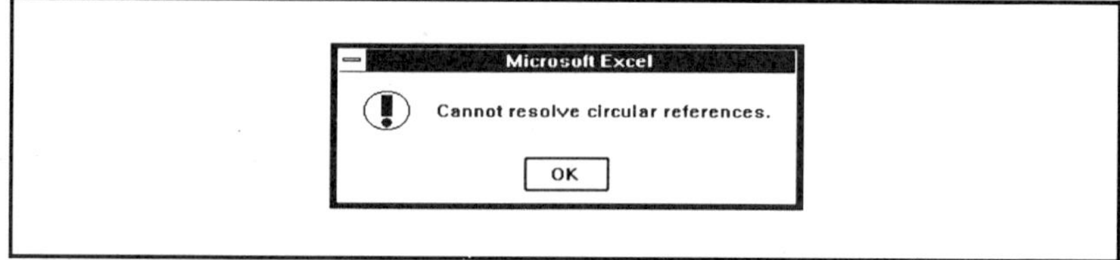

Figure 14.9: The circular reference error message

Here, the resulting values change less and less with each iteration. The iterations are said to converge to a solution. In some examples, the resulting values may change more and more with each iteration. In this case, the iterations diverge, and no real solution is possible. Both the design of the model and the starting values determine whether the solution converges or diverges.

6. When the Calculation dialog box appears, choose Iteration, then click OK, as shown in Figure 14.10).

Excel will repeat the calculations until the net profit and bonus change by 0.001 or less, or until a maximum of 100 iterations have occurred. As shown in Figure 14.10, these limits are set in the Calculation dialog box. The final iteration worksheet, after some numerical formatting, is shown in Figure 14.11.

Excel is much faster than some competitors at doing iterative calculations because it calculates only the cells necessary for resolving the circular reference, instead of taking the time to recalculate the entire worksheet.

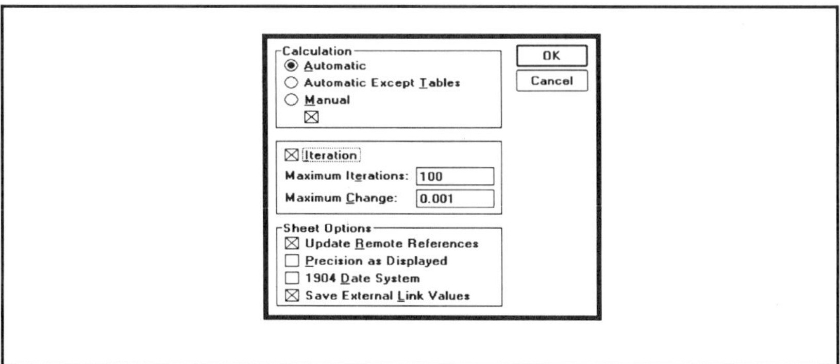

Figure 14.10: The Calculation dialog box with iterations turned on

If you see the Cannot resolve circular references error message and you didn't intend to use circular references, check your equations. The alert box is a warning that you have an error in an equation.

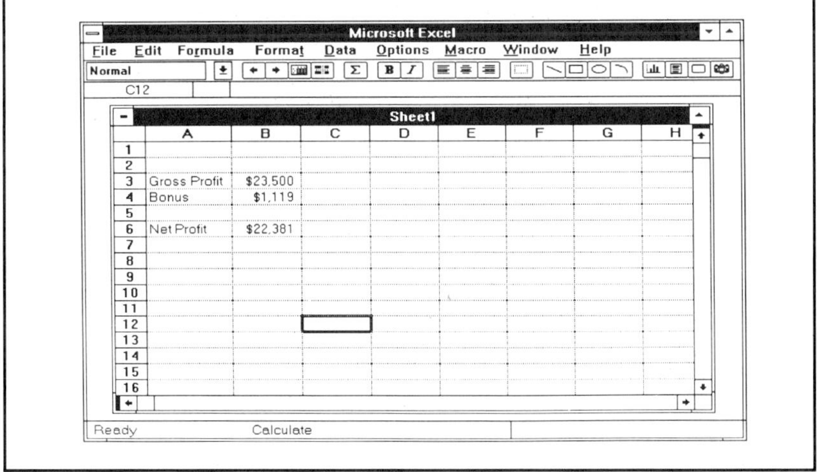

Figure 14.11: The final Acme Manufacturing iteration worksheet

PROTECTING AND HIDING CELLS

Excel allows you to protect cells on your worksheet, so that their contents cannot be changed, and to hide cells, so that their formulas are not displayed in the formula bar.

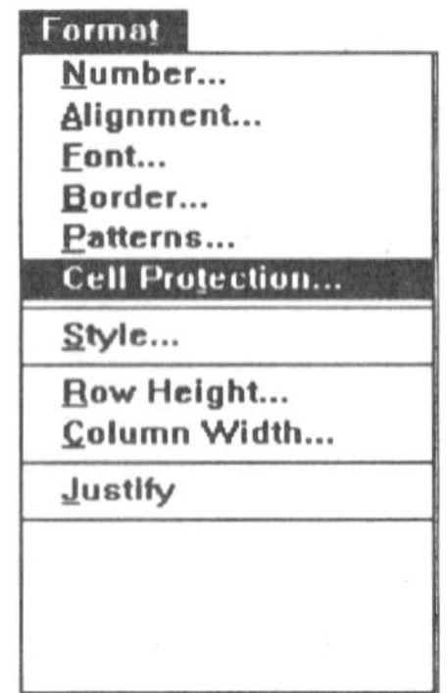

PROTECTING CELLS

The Cell Protection command on the Format menu and the Protect Document command on the Options menu together allow you to protect cells on your worksheets. When you protect cells, you *lock* them so that no one can enter data into them or alter their contents. The usefulness of cell protection is demonstrated by the Amortization worksheet that you created in Chapter 8, in which only three cells were actually used for data entry. All the remaining cells in the worksheet could be protected to prevent them from being altered. Load the Amortization worksheet now.

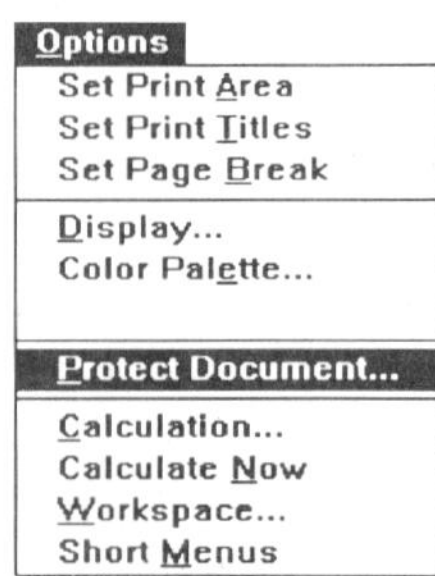

Unless you tell Excel otherwise, when you use the Cell Protection command on the Format menu, *all* the cells of the document are locked after the document is protected. So the general procedure for protecting cells on a worksheet is first to select the cells that should *not* be protected. Then, use the Cell Protection command on the Format menu to unlock these cells by toggling Locked off in the Cell Protection dialog box. Protect the rest of the worksheet by selecting the Protect Document command on the Options menu.

When you use the Protect Document command, you must enter a password. If you forget this password, you will never be able to unlock the protected cells. For this reason *always check the password that you enter before you click OK to be sure that it is what you intended.* Keep a record of your passwords. The exact same word must be entered to unprotect the document.

When you need to unlock a protected cell, the procedure is just the reverse. First, use the Unprotect Document command on the Options menu. Then select the cells that you want to unlock and use the Cell Protection command on the Format menu to unlock them.

When a document is protected, many commands are no longer available for use with that worksheet. The menus change to reflect this—the unavailable commands are no longer highlighted. For example, all the commands on the Format and Data menus, except the Find, Form, and Consolidate commands, are inactive.

To see how cell protection works, try locking all but the data-entry cells on your Amortization worksheet. Follow these steps with that worksheet:

1. Select cells B6 through B8 (the data-entry cells).
2. Open the Format menu and choose Cell Protection.

3. When the Cell Protection dialog box appears, toggle Locked to unlock the cells that you selected. (Remove the × next to Locked to unlock the cells.) Then click OK.
4. Open the Options menu and choose Protect Document.
5. When the Protect Document dialog box appears, enter the password **Secret** (capitalization is important). Notice that only asterisks are displayed as you type in the password. Press Enter or choose OK. Notice that you can protect cells, windows, and objects.

Your Amortization worksheet is now protected. You can enter a new interest rate, principal, or term, but you cannot alter the contents of any other cell. Try to edit the other cells just to see what happens. You will get an alert box with the message:

Locked cells cannot be changed.

If it is ever necessary to alter the formulas or otherwise change the protected areas of your Amortization worksheet, follow the reverse procedure:

1. Open the Options menu and choose Unprotect Document.
2. Enter **Secret** as the password in the Unprotect Document dialog box, then click OK.
3. Select the cells that you want to unlock.
4. Open the Format menu and choose Cell Protection.

Protect as many cells as possible in your document, leaving only the cells that depend upon input data unprotected. This prevents someone from accidentally changing a formula or constant value that may be the basis of important decisions in a worksheet.

If you forget which cells are protected, use the Display command on the Options menu to turn off the grid lines. The unprotected cells will be underlined, as shown in Figure 14.12.

HIDING CELLS

You may wish to prevent a user from seeing the formula used in a particular calculation. You can do this by hiding a cell, using a procedure similar to the one that you use to protect cells. First, select the

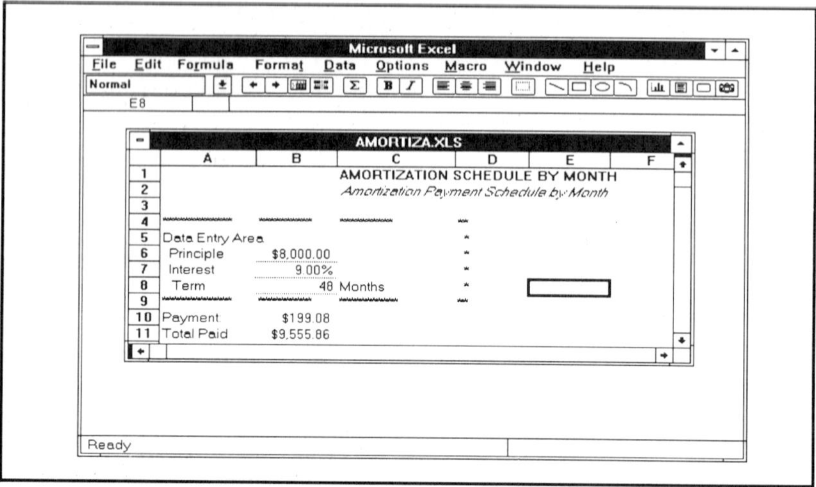

Figure 14.12: The unprotected cells underlined

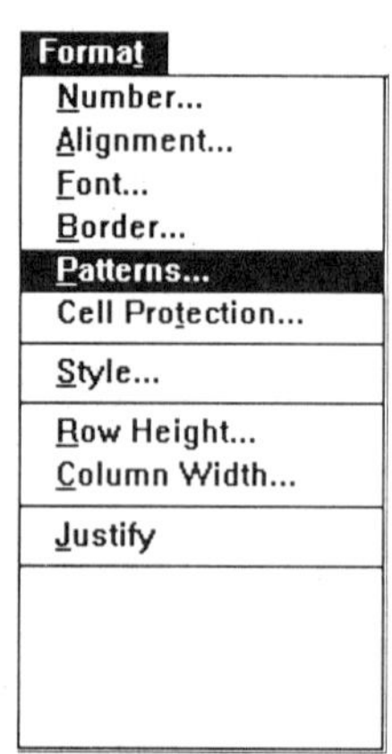

cell or cell range that you want to hide. Then, open the Format menu and choose Cell Protection. When the Cell Protection dialog box appears, choose Hidden. Then click OK. Next, open the Options menu and choose Protect Document. When the Protect Document dialog box appears, enter your password and choose OK. Then, when the hidden cell is selected, its formula will not appear in the formula bar.

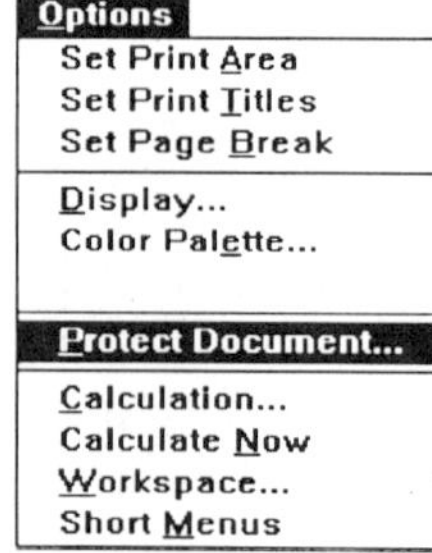

To recover hidden cells, use the Unprotect Document option on the Options menu. Enter your password in the Unprotect dialog box. As with protected cells, you must remember your password or you will never be able to view the formulas again.

Here are a few tips about using hidden cells:

- Hiding a cell doesn't hide the cell value, only the formula used to obtain the value. To hide a cell value, select the cell and format it to a custom picture of ;;
- Hide cells to protect proprietary formulas or hide entire macro sheets from unauthorized viewing
- You *can* omit the need for a password, but if you do so any user will be able to quickly unhide protected cells

CONTROLLING THE NUMERIC PRECISION

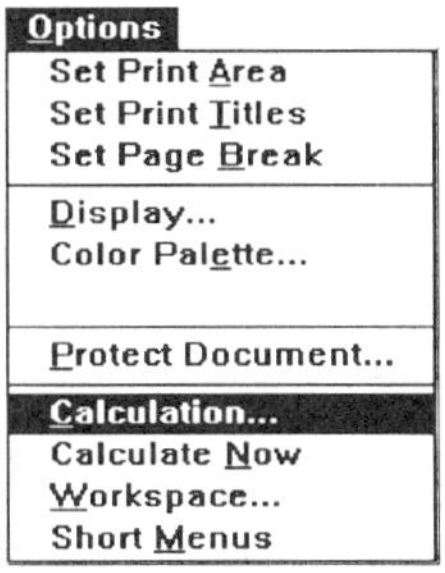

Excel stores all numbers that you enter into your worksheets with 15-digit precision. (*Precision* refers to the number of decimal places to which a value is carried when it is stored or displayed.) Excel performs all calculations with this precision, without regard to how the number is displayed.

You can change the precision for all templates except the General template, which always stores numbers with full precision.

Sometimes you may wish to change this so that Excel stores numbers and performs calculations only with the precision displayed. For example, you may want to change the precision when the results of formulas do not seem to match the numbers used to calculate them.

Options
Set Print Area
Set Print Titles
Set Page Break
Display...
Color Palette...
Protect Document...
Calculation...
Calculate Now
Workspace...
Short Menus

To switch from full precision to the displayed precision, open the Options menu, choose Calculation (see Figure 14.10), choose Precision as Displayed on the dialog box, and click OK. A message explaining that data will permanently lose a degree of accuracy is displayed. Once this option is turned on, data are rounded off to the displayed picture. You cannot recover the former precision. To switch back, open the Options command, choose Calculation, turn off Precision as Displayed, and click OK.

TRANSPOSING LISTS

Excel also supports transposition, which can be useful for rearranging columns and lists. Figure 14.13 shows a worksheet with long names for the column titles. In this form, the column titles are not very readable. If the columns were increased in width, the numbers would be lost on the page in the too-wide columns.

To solve this problem, transpose the list so that the column titles are row titles and the row titles become column titles. Select the entire worksheet, and then choose Copy from the Edit menu to place the worksheet in the Clipboard. Select B6 (an empty cell away from the data) and choose Paste Special from the Edit menu. On the dialog box, click Transpose and All. Then click OK. Adjust the column width of A slightly. The rows and columns are switched and the worksheet becomes more readable (see Figure 14.14). The numbers aren't lost on the page.

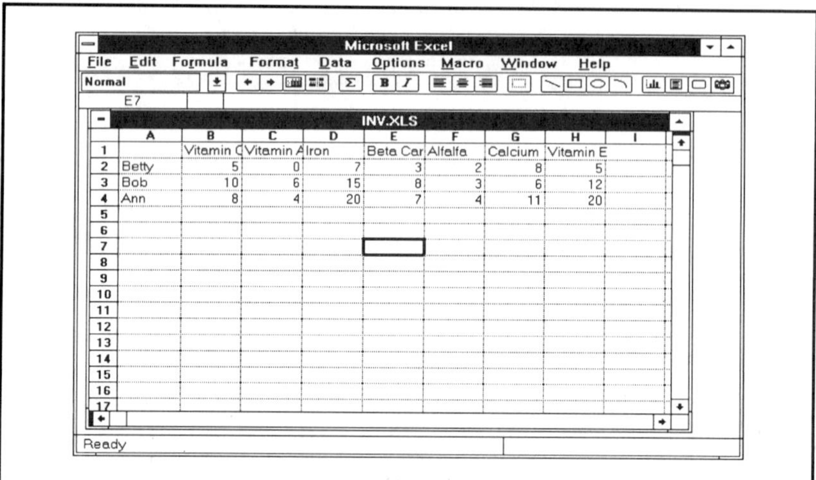

Figure 14.13: A worksheet that needs transposing

Microsoft Excel
File Edit Formula Format Data Options Macro Window Help
Normal
E16
INV.XLS

	A	B	C	D
6		Betty	Bob	Ann
7	Vitamin C	5	10	8
8	Vitamin A	0	6	4
9	Iron	7	15	20
10	Beta Carotine	3	8	7
11	Alfalfa	2	3	4
12	Calcium	8	6	11
13	Vitamin E	5	12	20

Ready

Figure 14.14: The transposed worksheet

Formula integrity is maintained and formulas are adjusted. You also can choose Values when transposing and paste values instead of formulas.

In summary, Excel contains many features that facilitate your worksheet creation and editing. Learning these will make your work easier and faster.

15 Calculating with Arrays

IN SOME APPLICATIONS, YOU MAY WANT TO USE multiple values as an argument for a function, or you may want a function to produce multiple values. Such a list of multiple values is called an *array.*

In all the examples in the previous chapters, you have used only simple functions. In a simple function, each argument refers to a single value—a single cell or a single cell range. For example, the result of the formula =SUM(A1:A11) is the sum of the values from cells A1 through A11—a single cell range. In this chapter, you will learn about Excel's capability of using multiple-value arguments. The basic idea of using an array will be illustrated with a simple example. Then, you will work through a more complex example that clearly shows how an array can make your worksheet calculations much easier.

ENTERING AN ARRAY

Suppose that you have an Inventory worksheet that lists four products, the cost of each, and the quantities on hand, as shown in

Figure 15.1. The extended cost of each product equals the quantity on hand multiplied by the cost. The total inventory value, then, is the sum of the extended costs of the product.

Create this worksheet. Enter the labels for column A and row 5, the title, and the data for rows 6 and 7. Select cells A6 to E9 and choose Create Names from the Formula menu. Choose Left Column and click OK. Enter the formulas to row 9 as shown in Figure 15.2.

Notice that you entered the same formula four times in the Ext Cost row. It would be easier to calculate the total value of the

Microsoft Excel

File Edit Formula Format Data Options Macro Window Help

Normal

E12

SHEET1.XLS

	A	B	C	D	E	F	G
1							
2			INVENTORY				
3							
4							
5		Product A	Product B	Product C	Product D		
6	Qty on Hand	125	215	165	34		
7	Cost	$64.95	$119.50	$91.25	$175.00		
8							
9	Ext Cost	$8,118.75	$25,692.50	$15,056.25	$5,950.00		
10							
11							
12	Total	$54,817.50					
13							
14							
15							
16							
17							

Ready

Figure 15.1: The Inventory worksheet

	A	B	C	D	E
1					
2			INVENTORY		
3					
4					
5		Product A	Product B	Product C	Product D
6	Qty on Hand	125	215	165	34
7	Cost	64.95	119.5	91.25	175
8					
9	Ext Cost	=Qty_on_Hand*Cost	=Qty_on_Hand*Cost	=Qty_on_Hand*Cost	=Qty_on_Hand*Cost
10					
11					
12	Total	=SUM(B9:E9)			

Figure 15.2: The Inventory worksheet formulas

inventory using an array. To do so, type in the following formula for the total in cell B14:

=SUM(B6:E6*B7:E7)

After you have entered the formula from the keyboard, *hold down the Control and Shift keys while you press Enter, or click the Enter box.* This will force Excel to accept the arguments as an array. Clear A9 to E9. As shown in Figure 15.3, the displayed total in cell B14 is still the same as it was in B12 before, but the formula used to calculate that total is different. Before doing anything else, undo the clear using Undo Clear.

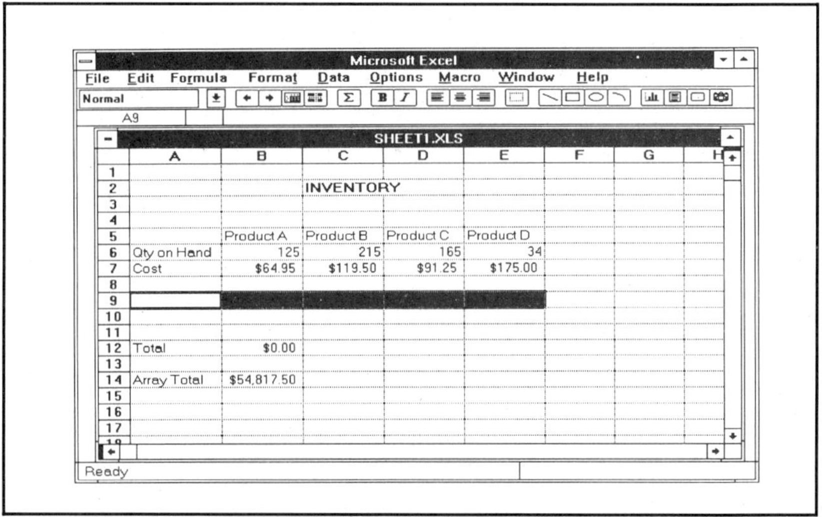

Figure 15.3: Using an array to calculate the total

Examine the formula in B14. Notice that it is exactly as you entered it, except that by using the Shift and Control keys you enclosed it in braces:

{=SUM(B6:E6*B7:E7)}

The values for cell ranges B6 through E6 and B7 through E7 are treated as an array, or list of values. The SUM function multiplied the corresponding values in each list and then summed the products to get the final total. The formula is identical to

B14 = B6*B7+C6*C7+D6*D7+E6*E7

Change any value in row 6 or 7 and the total will change to reflect the new quantity on hand or cost.

Use arrays to speed up data entry. In this example, the use of the array eliminated the necessity of naming the rows, entering the first formula, and then filling right. (You named the rows for the equations in row 9, not for the array in B14.) Only the final total formula was entered, and no names were used with it.

Arrays simplify data entry and save worksheet space. However, they can make your worksheet more difficult to interpret and check.

You also can use range names in an array formula. In the Inventory worksheet, you could enter the formula in B14 as

{=SUM(Qty_on_Hand*Cost)}

Keyboard entry of the braces won't work here; use Ctrl-Shift-Enter instead.

As you just learned, there is a simple technique for entering an array with Excel: after you type a function that operates on an array, hold down the Shift and Control keys while you press the Enter key or click the Enter box. Excel will add braces to indicate that the function contains an array.

Many functions listed in Chapter 8 *require* array arguments. With these functions, it is not necessary to use the Shift and Control keys, because Excel assumes the argument is an array. Later in the chapter, you will use one of these functions.

Save your worksheet as "Invent," as you will need it in the next chapter.

CALCULATING MULTIPLE OUTPUT VALUES

In the previous example, multiple values were used to obtain a single output value. Sometimes you may need multiple output values; that is, the output of the function should be an array as well. To understand how you can use multiple outputs, let's look at the following linear regression example.

Linear regression is often used to project a future trend from known data about the past. For instance, this technique is used by manufacturing operations to project data on future productivity based on changes in the number of employees, working conditions, and other factors. It also can be used by a sales department to plan warehousing, marketing, and sales representation.

Suppose, for example, that your company discovered there was a relationship between the disposable income per person in various areas and the sale of its product. You have information about the disposable income in future years, and you wish to project your sales for these years. This would enable you to plan how much warehouse space is needed, the number of sales representatives to employ, your marketing costs, and other factors. You'll use linear regression to make this projection. In the following example, you'll first do the linear regression using conventional worksheet techniques. Then, you'll do the same linear regression using the more convenient arrays.

Figure 15.4 shows a good example of why linear regression should be done with arrays. Without arrays, *six* columns are needed to perform the calculation. As we shall soon see, arrays can reduce this to *two* columns. Figure 15.5 shows the formulas used, and the values are plotted in Figure 15.6 (the x axis is the disposable income, and the y axis is the sales). As the graph shows, there seems to be a correlation that could be used to plan future sales.

The data for the disposable income and sales are used to calculate the constants for the linear regression. This calculation is done in cells C29 and C30 using the following formulas:

$$\mathrm{b} = \frac{\Sigma xy - \bar{x}\Sigma y}{\Sigma x^2 - \bar{x}\Sigma x}$$

$$\mathrm{a} = y - bx$$

$$y_n = a + bx_n$$

Here, x is the range A11 to A20, y is the range B11 to B20, and $\bar{x}$ represents the average of x (B27).

If you wish to try this, enter the data for the entire worksheet shown in Figure 15.5. You can use the Fill Down command to enter

REGRESS.XLS

LINEAR REGRESSION EXAMPLE

Year	Disposable Income ($K)	Projected Disp. Income ($K)	Sales ($K)	Disp. Income X Sales	Disp. Income Squared	Projected Sales ($K)
1982	$200		$2,350	470000	40000	
1983	$260		$2,500	650000	67600	
1984	$270		$2,400	648000	72900	
1985	$190		$2,390	454100	36100	
1986	$119		$2,360	280840	14161	
1987	$115		$2,260	259900	13225	
1988	$325		$2,575	836875	105625	
1989	$350		$2,550	892500	122500	
1990	$302		$2,503	755906	91204	
1991	$212		$2,475	524700	44944	
1992		$250				$2,453
1993		$275				$2,481
1994		$325				$2,535
Sum	2343		24363	5772821	608259	
Average	234.3		2436.3	577282.1	60825.9	

Value of a = 1.088980185
Value of b = 2181.151943

Figure 15.4: Doing a linear regression the hard way

much of the data, but you will probably still find it cumbersome to use this approach to obtain your projections. Whether you enter the data or not, look over the example.

Now try the same thing using two arrays:

1. Enter the years as column A, as in the previous example. Place the first year in A11 and use the Data Series command on the Data menu to create the column.
2. Place the disposable income in column B for each year. (If you tried the previous example, copy from column C of that worksheet to column B of the new worksheet to create a single column B.)

TEMP.XLS

	A	B	C	D	E	F	G
1		LINEAR REGRESSI					
2							
3							
4							
5							
6							
7	Year	Disposable	Projected	Sales	Disp. Income	Disp. Income	Projected
8		Income	Disp. Income	($K)	X Sales	Squared	Sales
9		($K)	($K)				($K)
10							
11	1982	200		2350	=B11*D11	=B11*B11	
12	1983	260		2500	=B12*D12	=B12*B12	
13	1984	270		2400	=B13*D13	=B13*B13	
14	1985	190		2390	=B14*D14	=B14*B14	
15	1986	119		2360	=B15*D15	=B15*B15	
16	1987	115		2260	=B16*D16	=B16*B16	
17	1988	325		2575	=B17*D17	=B17*B17	
18	1989	350		2550	=B18*D18	=B18*B18	
19	1990	302		2503	=B19*D19	=B19*B19	
20	1991	212		2475	=B20*D20	=B20*B20	
21	1992		250				=$C$30+($C$29*C21)
22	1993		275				=$C$30+($C$29*C22)
23	1994		325				=$C$30+($C$29*C23)
24							
25	Sum	=SUM(B11:B20)		=SUM(D11:D20)	=SUM(E11:E20)	=SUM(F11:F20)	
26							
27	Average	=B25/10		=D25/10	=E25/10	=F25/10	
28							
29		Value of a=	=((E25-(B27*D25))/(F25-(B27*B25)))				
30		Value of b =	=(D27-(C29*B27))				

Figure 15.5: The formulas for the linear regression example

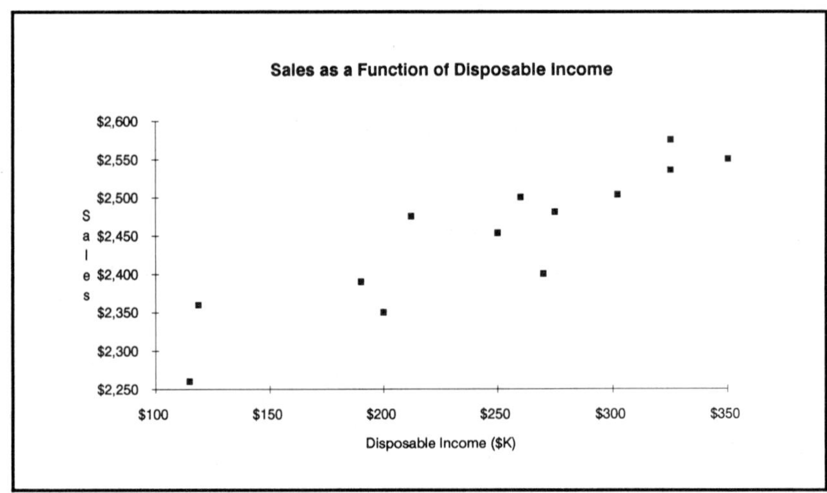

Figure 15.6: The chart of the linear regression

3. Create the Sales column in column C (D in previous example) and enter (or copy) the values for each year.
4. Delete the rest of the worksheet data if you tried the earlier example.
5. Label the columns as shown in Figure 15.7. Add the worksheet title, **LINEAR REGRESSION EXAMPLE**. Disposable Income will be the input array. Sales will be the output array.
6. Enter the first array formula. You will need to use two functions, SUM and LINEST. The LINEST function has two arrays for an input and one array for an output (see Chapter 8). Enter the following formula into cell C21:

   =SUM(LINEST($C$11:$C$20,$B$11:$B$20)*{250,1})
7. Copy the formula in cell C21 into cells C22 and C23 using the Fill Down command, then edit the SUM functions in cells C22 and C23 so that the **250** in the next-to-last argument reads **275** and **325**, respectively—the proper disposable incomes. Your final formulas should look like those shown in Figure 15.7.
8. Format the worksheet (see Figure 15.8) and print it.

The final projected values are the same as those that were obtained the hard way in Figure 15.4, but here they are generated with much less work.

Let's review the array formula that you just used. The LINEST function returns an array of two values: the slope (*m*) and the intercept (*b*) of the line of regression, represented by $y=b+mx$. These are the same constants that you calculated earlier using multiple columns, squares, sums, and averages. Excel does it all with a single function.

The general form of the LINEST function is

LINEST(*y array, x array*)

The *y* array is the known and projected sales (C11:C23). The *x* array is the known and projected disposable income. The LINEST

	A	B	C	D
1		LINEAR REGRESSION EXA		
2		*Using Arrays*		
3				
4				
5				
6				
7	Year	Disposable	Sales	
8		Income	($K)	
9		($K)		
10				
11	1982	200	2350	
12	1983	260	2500	
13	1984	270	2400	
14	1985	190	2390	
15	1986	119	2360	
16	1987	115	2260	
17	1988	325	2575	
18	1989	350	2550	
19	1990	302	2503	
20	1991	212	2475	
21	1992	250	=SUM(LINEST($C$11:$C$20,$B$11:$B$20)*{250,1})	*
22	1993	275	=SUM(LINEST($C$11:$C$20,$B$11:$B$20)*{275,1})	*
23	1994	325	=SUM(LINEST($C$11:$C$20,$B$11:$B$20)*{325,1})	*
24				
25		*Projected Sales		

Figure 15.7: The linear regression example using arrays

REGRESS.XLS

LINEAR REGRESSION EXAMPLE
Using Arrays

Year	Disposable Income ($K)	Sales ($K)	
1982	$200	$2,350	
1983	$260	$2,500	
1984	$270	$2,400	
1985	$190	$2,390	
1986	$119	$2,360	
1987	$115	$2,260	
1988	$325	$2,575	
1989	$350	$2,550	
1990	$302	$2,503	
1991	$212	$2,475	
1992	$250	$2,453	*
1993	$275	$2,481	*
1994	$325	$2,535	*

*Projected Sales

Figure 15.8: The final printout of the regression using arrays

function returns an array of two values: the slope of a regression line that fits the points and the y intercept of the line. This returned array is then used with the SUM function (as in the previous example) to calculate the x value for a known y value. The formula multiplies the first argument of the LINEST function (the slope) by an x value (250) and adds the second part of the LINEST function (the y intercept) multiplied by 1:

$$y \text{ value} = (x \text{ value}) * \text{slope} + (y \text{ intercept}) * 1$$

The 1 is really a dummy constant, and is necessary only to keep both arrays the same size.

You also could try an exponential regression using the LOGEST function. The other functions that require arrays are GROWTH, TREND, COLUMNS, ROWS, and TRANSPOSE. The LOOKUP functions and others (such as MIRR) can also use arrays. Even functions that normally use single-value arguments, such as SUM, can work with array arguments (as you have seen).

Chapter 24 will introduce you to more examples of linear regression and explain how to do a more complex quadratic regression.

CREATING A REGRESSION CHART

The creation of charts is described later in Part 5, but you can take the time now to make the regression graph of Figure 15.6 if you wish. Start with the worksheet of Figure 15.8:

1. Select B11 to C23. Open the Edit menu and choose Copy. This puts the series data in the Clipboard.
2. Open a new chart. Open the File menu and choose New. Choose Chart on the dialog box. An empty chart will be displayed.
3. On the chart menu bar, open the Edit menu and choose Paste Special. In this dialog box choose Categories (X Labels) in First Column. This will map the first column to the category axis and the second column to the value axis. Click on OK.

4. Open the Gallery menu and choose XY (Scatter). Choose the first option for the scatter chart.
5. Add any axis labels or titles desired. To make the *x* axis start at 100, click the axis, open the Format menu and choose Font. Click the Scale button. Specify under Auto, Minimum: 100. Click on OK. Select Attach Text on the Chart menu to add axes labels and a chart title.

ARRAY CONSTANTS

In Chapter 7, you created the cash-flow analysis worksheet that had a parameter file with several constants. These constants served as inputs for formulas used elsewhere in the worksheet. In the same way, you can store an array as a single constant and use it in a formula.

To enter an array constant into an array formula, type the values into the formulas and enclose them in braces ({ }). Separate values in the same row with commas, and separate rows with semicolons. For example, {1,2,3;4,5,6} is an array of two rows and three columns. If the formula produces an array as a result, enter the expression and then press Ctrl-Shift-Enter.

RULES FOR USING ARRAYS

Here are some general rules for using arrays:

- The values of an array must be constant values and not formulas. An array can contain numeric, text, logical, or error values (such as #VALUE!). Text values must be enclosed in quotation marks
- You can use an array with most functions
- When an array is used with a function, the type of values must be consistent with what is required by the function
- When an array formula is entered into a range of cells, the formulas should produce an array that is the same size as the selected cell range

- Relative cell addresses in an array are considered relative to the cell in the upper-left corner of the range. If you copy an array, the relative references will be adjusted
- You cannot type an array that has a mixed number of columns in the rows. For example, {4,9,1;3,4} is illegal
- If an array is used as an argument in a function, all other arguments in the same function should be arrays of the same size
- You cannot edit the individual cells or a constant array
- Excel permits a maximum of 6,500 elements in an array

EDITING AN ARRAY FORMULA

You can enter an array formula into a range of cells in the same way that you enter any formula into a range of cells: hold down the Shift and Control keys while you press the Enter key. There is a difference, however, when you are editing a formula that has been entered into a range of cells. After an array formula is entered into a range, you cannot edit or clear an individual cell or delete rows or columns within that range. The entire cell range must be treated as a unit. You can only select, edit, or clear the entire range.

You can edit an array formula by using the commands on the Edit menu. If you click the cursor on any point in the formula bar, whatever you type will be entered at the cursor location. You also can drag the cursor in the formula bar to mark a range of characters, then use the Cut command to delete the marked characters. Once you have finished editing the formula, clicking the Enter box or pressing the Enter key will complete the entry. (Remember, If you enter a constant array to a range of cells, the individual cells of the array cannot be edited.)

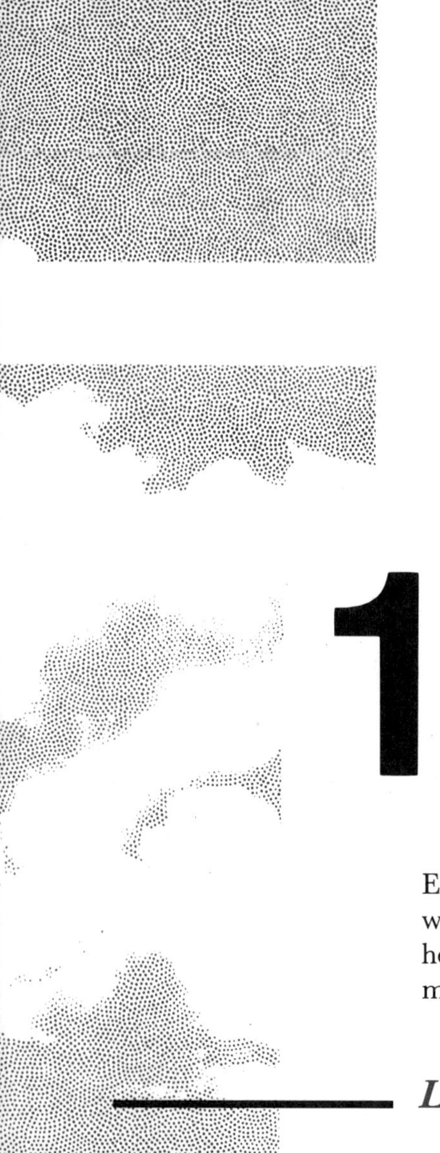

16 Working with Multiple Documents

EXCEL PROVIDES EXTENSIVE SUPPORT FOR WORKING with multiple documents simultaneously. This chapter shows you how to link documents and consolidate documents to create summary worksheets.

LINKING DOCUMENTS

One of Excel's most valuable features is its ability to link documents together. Why is this important? A major corporation could create a complex system of interlinked worksheets that simulates the company's financial flow, then use the model to see what happens as you change various parameters. One financial vice-president told me that the ability to link documents was one of the most important features of the spreadsheet that he uses.

When linking Excel documents, you create a relationship in which a change in one document will automatically affect the other. In

Chapter 3, for example, you created a chart that was linked to a worksheet. When you made any changes in the worksheet, they were immediately reflected in the chart.

You can link cells or cell ranges in two or more documents. This allows you to set up a hierarchical structure of worksheets that will always reflect your most current data.

Using linked worksheets is easier than creating large worksheets that are cumbersome to scroll and update.

Linked documents are useful for:

- Consolidating data from many source worksheets to a single summary worksheet
- Creating different views of the same data
- Creating a large model from several smaller models

In this section, you will learn some basic concepts of linking documents. You will be guided through a simple example, then you will use it to study the more complex aspects of linking documents.

When you link cells in different worksheets, the values in one will change whenever you change the values in the other. This is an easy way to be sure that your associated worksheets are up-to-date without having to enter new data into each. You can link individual cells of worksheets or whole cell ranges.

LINKING SINGLE CELLS

Let's link two worksheets together to see how linking works. In the following example, you'll link one cell in the Sales worksheet that you created in Chapters 10–13 to a cell in a new cash-flow analysis worksheet.

Assume that your Sales worksheet was prepared by the sales department manager of a company. She needs to copy the sales totals for all the regions into a new worksheet that will be used by another department in the company for a cash-flow analysis. The projected sales total will change as the year progresses, and the company's managers want to have the cash-flow analysis worksheet updated automatically to reflect each change.

In this and the more complex examples in the next few chapters, I'll assume that you know the basic procedures. Although you'll be told what to do, I won't include all the steps. If you need help, refer to the chapters in the first part of the book.

After you open your Sales worksheet, which you used in Chapter 13, follow the steps below to create two linked documents:

1. Sort the Sales worksheet in name order if necessary. Add the hyphens in cell B10 and make B11 the sum of B6 through B9. Add the word **Total** in cell A11, and then save this worksheet (see Figure 16.1).

Microsoft Excel — SALES.XLS

	A	B	C	D	E	F	G
1							
2							
3	LAST	FIRST	TARGET	REGION	ACTUAL		
4							
5							
6	East	$682,000	$750,000		1868000		
7	Midwest	$369,000	$395,000				
8	South	$394,000	$320,000				
9	West	$423,000	$428,000				
10		----------					
11	Total	$1,868,000					
12							
13	LAST	FIRST	TARGET	REGION	ACTUAL		
14	Adams	Chuck	$118,000	South	$110,000		
15	Allen	Ellen	$90,000	East	$110,000		
16	Atkins	Lee	$113,000	East	$95,000		
17	Conners	Paul	$142,000	West	$213,000		

Figure 16.1: Adding a total

2. Use the New command on the File menu (or press Shift-F11) to open a new worksheet. Select Arrange All on the Window menu to see both worksheets.
3. Enter the title **Acme Manufacturing** in cell B2 on the second worksheet and **Sales** and **Cost of Goods** in cells A6 and A7, respectively, as the first two row headings (see Figure 16.2). Widen column A for the row titles.
4. Click cell B11 in the Sales worksheet and select Copy from the Edit menu (or press Ctrl-Ins) on that worksheet to place the contents in the Clipboard.
5. Click cell B6 on the new worksheet to indicate that the sales total will be placed in this cell.
6. Select Paste Link from the Edit menu.

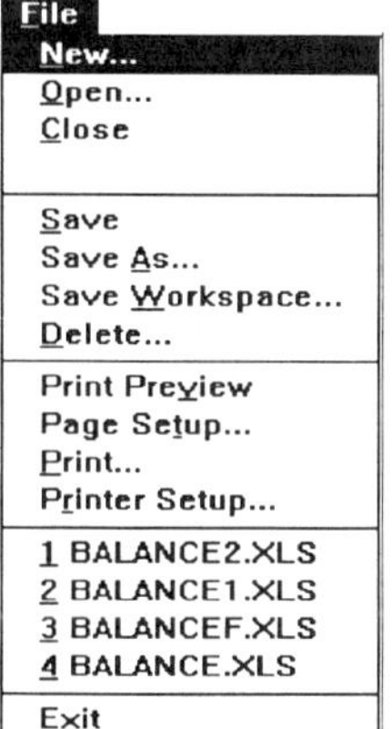

7. The sales total from cell B6 of the Sales worksheet is now in cell B6 of the new worksheet, as shown in Figure 16.3. Format the total in the new worksheet with the Number command on the Format menu.

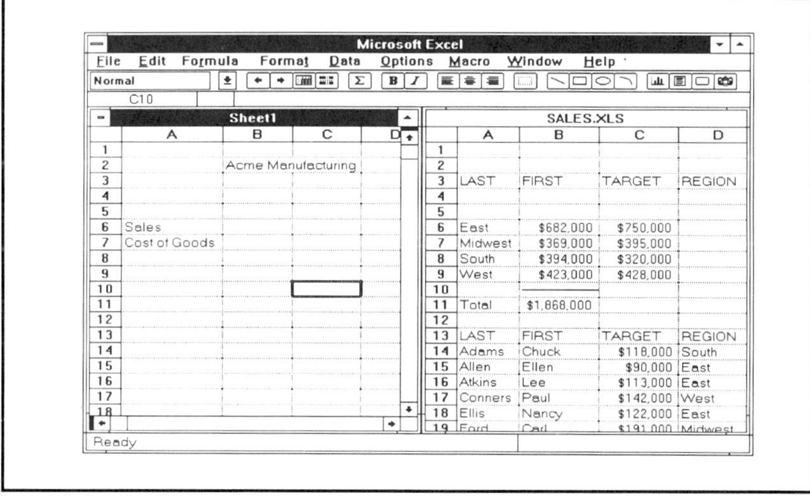

Figure 16.2: Adding labels to the second worksheet

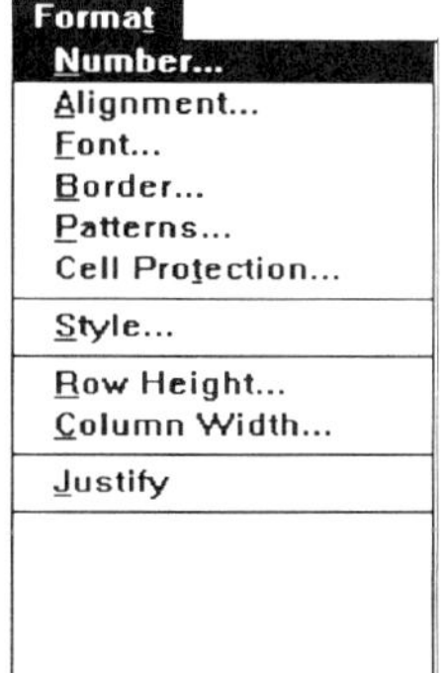

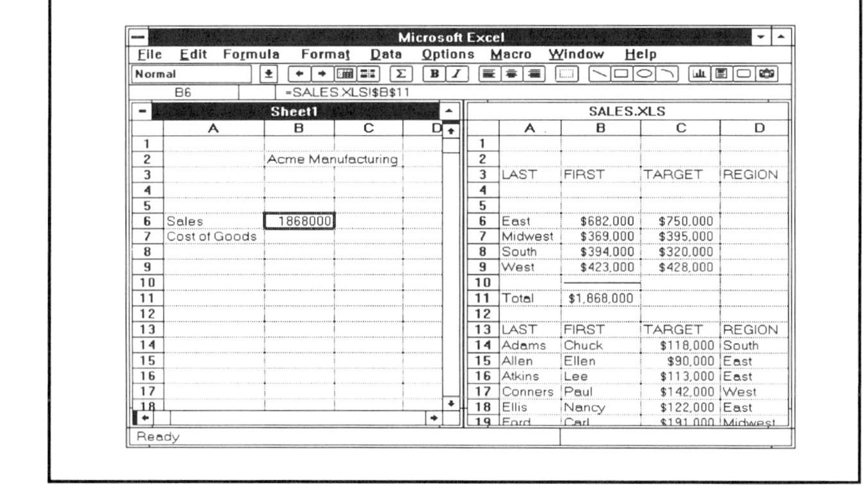

Figure 16.3: The sales total on the second worksheet

Take a few minutes to examine your worksheets. Look at the formula for cell B6 in the formula bar (see Figure 16.3). It contains the linked worksheet's name, an exclamation point, and an absolute reference to cell B11 of the linked worksheet. You could have entered the same formula directly from the keyboard.

Instead of using the Paste command, you could have held down the Shift key and selected Paste Picture Link from the Edit menu to paste the total as a text box in the destination worksheet.

Now experiment with the linked worksheets to see what happens when you make changes. Change one of the Target figures in cells C14 through C28 in the Sales database. You will see the totals change in cell B11 of the Sales database *and* cell B6 of the new worksheet.

DEPENDENT AND SUPPORTING DOCUMENTS

Whenever the values of targets in the Sales worksheet change, the values in the new worksheet also will change. The new worksheet is called the *dependent document,* because the value in at least one of its cells depends upon at least one value in another worksheet. The Sales worksheet, which contains the value for the dependent worksheet, is called the *supporting document.* The dependent worksheet contains an *external reference formula*—a formula that refers to a cell or cell range on the supporting document.

You can create complex and interlinked hierarchical documents that depend upon each other at several levels. You also can link several supporting documents to a single dependent document. For example, our theoretical company could have sales worksheets for several regions and use them as supporting documents for a single company-wide Sales worksheet, which would, in turn, support another dependent document.

To quickly load a group of worksheets that are linked, assign them to a workspace. When you load the workspace, all documents will be opened. (For information on linking charts, refer to Chapter 19.)

Before leaving this section, continue to experiment with the link that you created. What happens, for example, if you save the dependent worksheet, change the values for a target in the supporting worksheet, and then open the dependent worksheet again? Have the values in the dependent worksheet been updated to reflect your change?

LINKING CELL RANGES

In the previous example, you linked a single cell in one worksheet to a single cell in another worksheet. You also can link a range of cells in one worksheet to a range of cells in another worksheet using the same basic procedure.

To link cell ranges, select the range of cells on the dependent worksheet that you want to contain the formulas. Type in or copy the formula, referencing the appropriate cell range on the supporting worksheet. Then hold down the Shift and Ctrl keys and press Enter.

You can try this with the new worksheet if you wish. Find an empty cell in Sheet1 and paste the SUM function to that cell (the Edit menu's Paste Function command). Now select cells B6 to B9 in the Sales worksheet to enter that range as the formula argument. Edit the display in the formula bar as necessary (you'll probably have to erase **number 2**, ...) and press Enter.

MOVING SUPPORTING CELLS

3.0

If you create linked worksheets and then use the Copy or Cut commands to move cells in the supporting worksheet, the relative cell addresses in the formulas will be adjusted properly.

Let's try an example: with your linked Sales and new worksheet open, follow these steps:

1. Select cell B11 on your Sales worksheet.
2. Open the Edit menu and choose Cut (or press Shift-Del).
3. Select cell C11 on the Sales worksheet.
4. Open the Edit menu and choose Paste (or press Shift-Ins).

You'll see that the total on the dependent worksheet is still correct. In other words, the dependent worksheet has been adjusted to refer to the new location of the sales total cell in the supporting worksheet.

Before saving the worksheet, more C11 to B11.

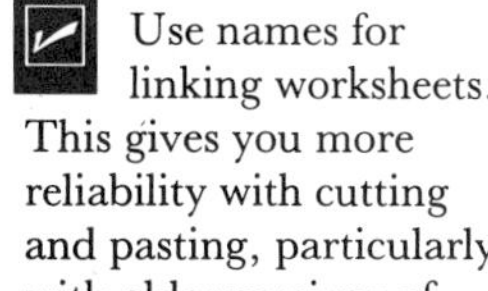

Use names for linking worksheets. This gives you more reliability with cutting and pasting, particularly with older versions of Excel.

SAVING LINKED DOCUMENTS

Saving linked documents is as easy as saving documents that are not linked. Use the Save (F12) or Save As (Shift-F12) commands on the File menu to save each open document. Save any supporting document(s) (in this case, SALES.XLS) before saving any dependent document(s). This ensures that names are not changed in the supporting document. Save the dependent document as SALEST.XLS.

Try keeping all dependent and supporting documents in the same directory. That way they all don't have to be open to be linked. If one document *is* in a different directory, you'll have to open it yourself to keep it linked to the other file(s).

VIEWING AND OPENING LINKED WORKSHEETS

To open a linked document, follow this procedure:

1. Open the dependent worksheet first (SALEST). You will get a message box asking if you wish to update from supporting worksheets (see Figure 16.4). Choose Yes.
2. Once the dependent worksheet is opened, select Links from the File menu. This will display a dialog box showing the name of each supporting document (see Figure 16.5). If all you need is a view, or list, of the supporting documents you can choose Cancel. If you wish to open one or more supporting documents, go to Step 3.
3. Be sure Excel Links is displayed in the Link Type list box.
4. In the Links box, select the documents to open and update. To open multiple documents, hold down the Shift key as you click on the names.

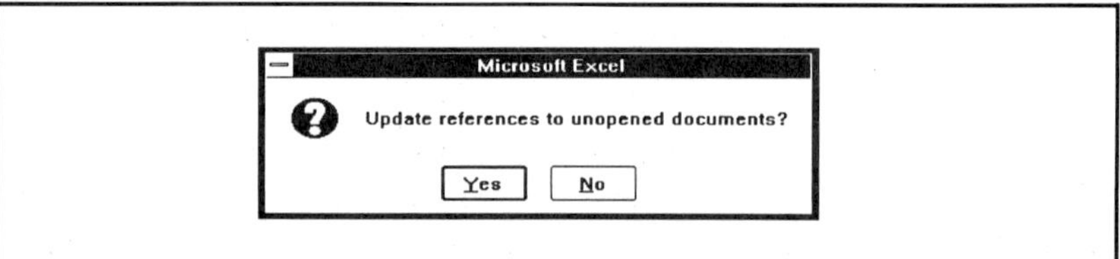

Figure 16.4: The Update References message box

REMOVING DOCUMENT LINKS

To remove the links in a dependent worksheet, you need only remove the references to the supporting document. If you wish to scan a document and be sure that all the links are removed, use the Find command on the Formula menu (or press Shift–F5). Don't use the Find command on the Data menu. Then search the formulas for the name of the supporting worksheet, or search for an exclamation point.

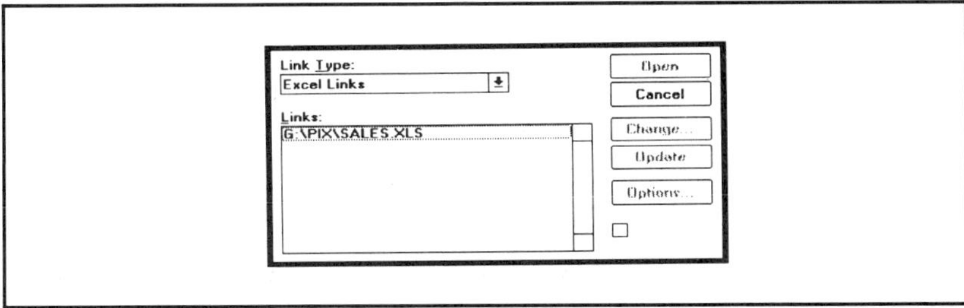

Figure 16.5: Establishing the links

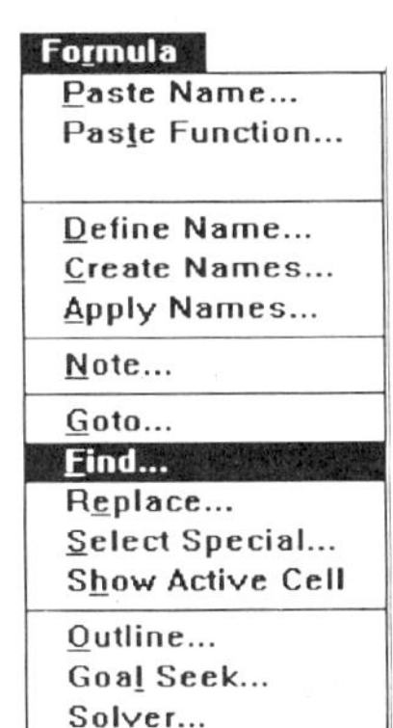

An alternative is to convert the formula or part of the formula referencing the supporting worksheet to a value; for instance, changing the contents in cell B6 from =SALES.XLS!$B$11 to 1,868,000.

REDIRECTING LINKS

You may wish, at times, to redirect a link to another supporting worksheet. You should do this if the supporting document is moved to another directory or changes its name.

To redirect a link:

1. Open the dependent document and choose Links from the File menu.
2. In the Link Type list box, choose Excel Links.
3. In the Links box, select the names of the supporting worksheets whose links you need to redirect.
4. Click on the Change button.
5. On the next dialog box, select the supporting document name, or enter the name with the path in the Copy From File box.
6. Click OK.
7. Repeat for each link you want to change.

LINKING WORKSHEETS WITH ARRAYS

A worksheet that uses array formulas and references can be linked to another worksheet by using external references, just as if it used any other linked formula. To see how this works, link a cell in a new worksheet to the cell that contains the total value in the Inventory worksheet that you created at the beginning of Chapter 15:

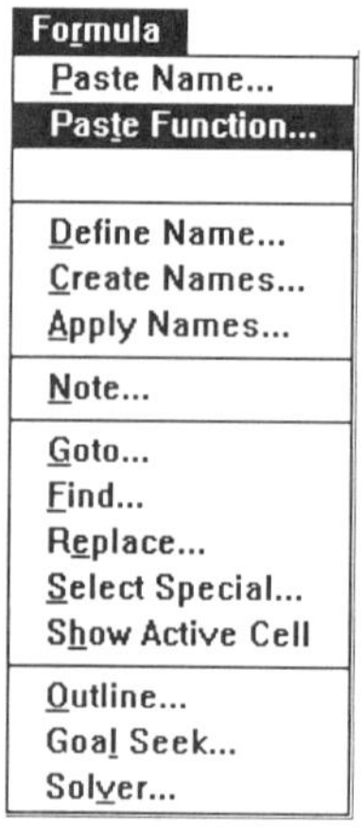

Formula
Paste Name...
Paste Function...
Define Name...
Create Names...
Apply Names...
Note...
Goto...
Find...
Replace...
Select Special...
Show Active Cell
Outline...
Goal Seek...
Solver...

1. Open the Inventory worksheet and be sure the row titles on it are defined as names (see Chapter 9).
2. Open up a new worksheet window and display both windows on the screen.
3. Enter the title **Inventory Summary** in cell B1 of the new worksheet.
4. Select cell B3 in the new worksheet as the cell for the total, open the Formula menu, and choose Paste Function (or press Shift–F3). You'll see the Paste Function dialog box. Be sure Paste Arguments is off. Scroll to the SUM function and double-click it.
5. Click anywhere in the Inventory worksheet, open the Formula menu, and choose Paste Name (or press F3). You'll see the Paste Name dialog box. Double-click Qty_on_Hand.
6. Type an asterisk (*).
7. Press F3 or select the Formula menu and choose Paste Name. Double-click Cost in the Paste Name dialog box.
8. Hold down the Shift and Ctrl keys and press Enter.

Formula
Paste Name...
Paste Function...
Define Name...
Create Names...
Apply Names...
Note...
Goto...
Find...
Replace...
Select Special...
Show Active Cell
Outline...
Goal Seek...
Solver...

The correct total is now in cell B3 of the new worksheet, and the formula is in the formula bar, as shown in Figure 16.6.

USING WORKGROUPS

3.0

Workgroups are useful for permitting you to enter the same data to multiple worksheets at the same time. Using a workgroup reduces keystrokes and the possibility of errors, and saves you time as well. You can use worksheets and macro sheets in the workgroup only (no charts). See Chapter 7 for details on how to create one.

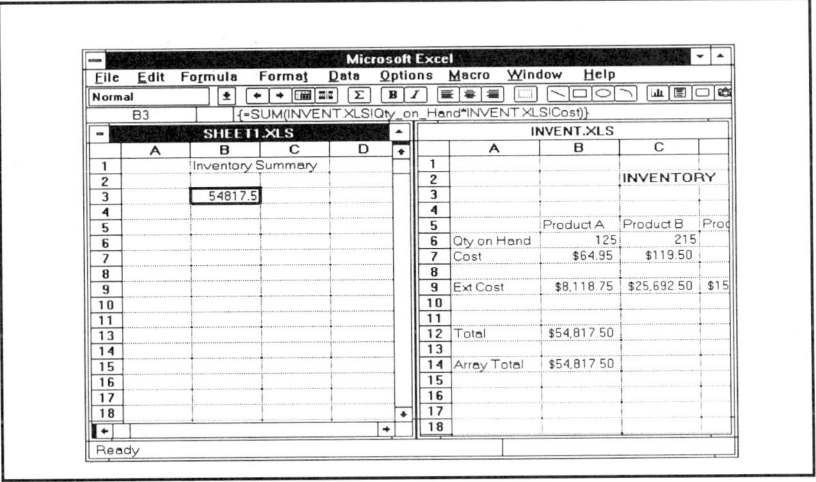

Figure 16.6: Linking an array

CONSOLIDATING WORKSHEETS

3.0

Consolidation is a useful method for summarizing large amounts of data in a single summary worksheet. For instance, monthly or quarterly reports can be easily summarized in yearly reports.

Langer Products (a fictitious company) manufactures a variety of products. They wish to consolidate data for a few years so they can determine how much their sales vary quarterly. Let's look at this example and see how consolidating worksheets can help them.

1. Create each of the three annual Langer worksheets shown in Figure 16.7. Set up the sheets as a workgroup to simplify label entry and keep the entries more accurate (see Chapter 7).
2. Create a fourth worksheet that will contain the consolidated data. Call it "Output." Enter **Qtr1**, **Qtr2**, **Qtr3**, and **Qtr4** into cells B4, B5, B6, and B7, respectively. There are no data in C4 to C7 for the moment. The object here is to consolidate by categories—each quarter, in this case.

3. Select the destination area as B4 to C7 on the Output worksheet.
4. Open the Data menu and select Consolidate. The dialog box shown in Figure 16.8 appears. Reposition the box so that LANG1989 is visible.
5. Click on LANG1989 to make it active, then select cells B4 to C7 as the first source range.

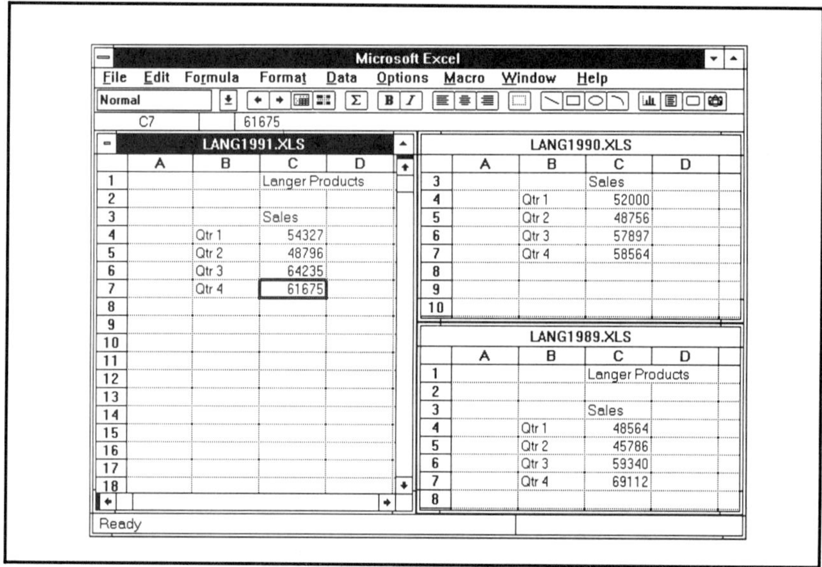

Figure 16.7: The Langer worksheets

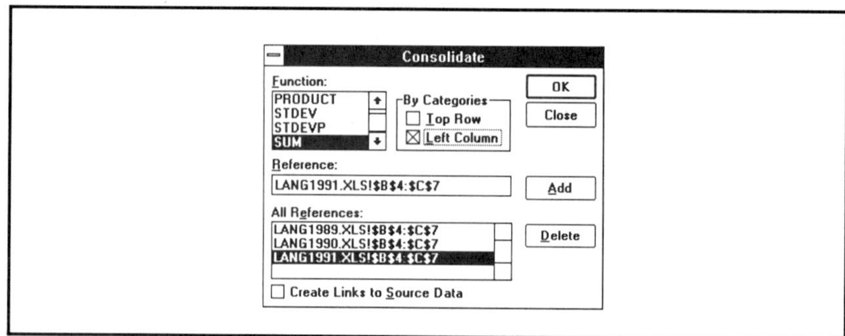

Figure 16.8: The Consolidate dialog box

6. Click on the Add button in the dialog box. The range you selected appears in the All References box.
7. Continue by selecting the similar ranges in LANG1990 and LANG1991, clicking Add each time.
8. Click Left Column in the dialog box, as the labels are in the left column.
9. Select the desired function in the dialog box. SUM is the default function and the one we wish to use here.
10. Click OK.

The consolidated data now appear in Output, with column C showing the total sales for each quarter, summed by year (see Figure 16.9).

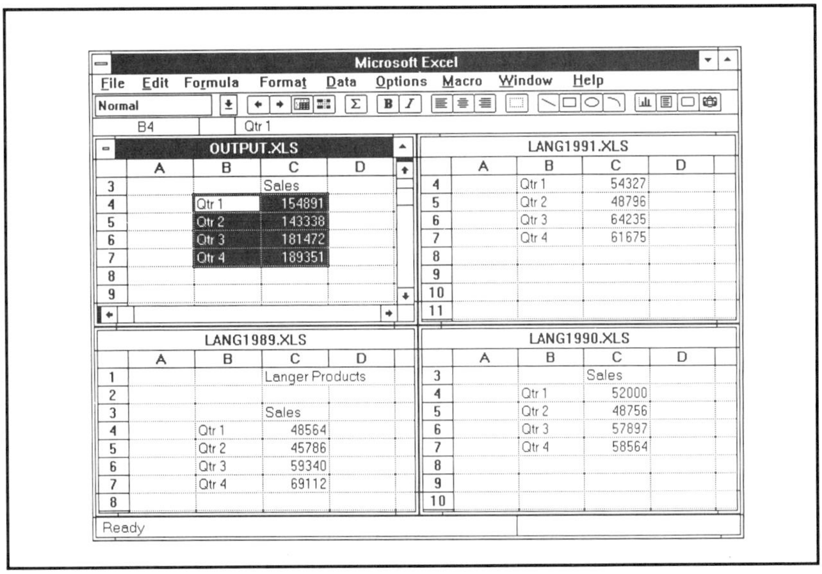

Microsoft Excel

File Edit Formula Format Data Options Macro Window Help

Normal

B4 Qtr 1

OUTPUT.XLS

	A	B	C	D
3			Sales	
4		Qtr 1	154891	
5		Qtr 2	143338	
6		Qtr 3	181472	
7		Qtr 4	189351	
8				
9				

LANG1991.XLS

	A	B	C	D
4		Qtr 1	54327	
5		Qtr 2	48796	
6		Qtr 3	64235	
7		Qtr 4	61675	
8				
9				
10				
11				

LANG1989.XLS

	A	B	C	D
1			Langer Products	
2				
3			Sales	
4		Qtr 1	48564	
5		Qtr 2	45786	
6		Qtr 3	59340	
7		Qtr 4	69112	
8				

LANG1990.XLS

	A	B	C	D
3			Sales	
4		Qtr 1	52000	
5		Qtr 2	48756	
6		Qtr 3	57897	
7		Qtr 4	58564	
8				
9				
10				

Ready

Figure 16.9: The consolidated Langer worksheet

At the moment, the destination worksheet is not linked to the source documents. If the source documents are changed, the output worksheet will not change. To link them, select Consolidate from the Data menu and click on Create Links to Source Data at the bottom of the box.

You can specify consolidation by range or, as we did here, category. You can define up to 255 source areas, and they can be on different worksheets. The source area worksheets need not be open, but they must have been saved. The functions available are SUM (the default), AVERAGE, COUNT, COUNTA, MAX, MIN, PRODUCT, STDEV, STDEVP, VAR, and VARP.

Consolidate by category when possible, as this ensures greater reliability. This also makes the worksheet expressions less likely to change with editing.

You can edit the consolidation by selecting the Consolidate command and editing the reference. You also can add or delete references in the list.

In the reference box you can use wildcards to reference a group of worksheets; LANG19??.XLS!$B$3:$C$7 was used in the previous example to include all three worksheets. You also can use names in references.

Only values are consolidated. Text, formats, and formulas cannot be consolidated.

17 Printing Worksheets

EXCEL INCLUDES MANY FEATURES THAT MAKE IT easy to create presentation-quality reports from your worksheet. You can add headers and footers, define your page breaks, print specific worksheet ranges, print a report with landscape orientation, control the margins, and turn grid lines on and off. This chapter will provide an overview of these and other printing features.

Printing is controlled from three commands on the File menu and four on the Options menu. The File menu commands include Print, Page Setup, and Printer Setup. Those on the Options menu are Set Print Area, Set Print Titles, Set Page Break, and Display.

INTRODUCTION TO EXCEL PRINTING

Excel is a Windows application, which means it uses the Windows environment for printing. The software that controls the printer is called a *printer driver,* and is a part of Windows. If you change printers or add a new one, you install the new printer driver to Windows using the Windows Control Panel utility. Once installed, the printer is available for all Windows application programs, including Excel. Programs that are not Windows applications (such as dBASE IV) do not use the Windows printer drivers and have their own drivers, even when running under Windows. This means if you have a problem with printing, it is normally a Windows problem, not an Excel problem.

The fonts that are available for printing are, like the printer, determined by what you have installed in Windows. A font is a type design or family, such as Helvetica or Times Roman. The same type family is generally available in various styles (normal, bold, italic) and sizes. The font size is a measure of the height of the letters, and is measured in points. There are 72 points in an inch, so a 12-point font is one-sixth of an inch high.

Fonts are installed as two sets of files for each family. One set is for the display, the other for the printer. When you select the Font command on the Format menu to choose the font, there is a Printer Fonts check box in the dialog box. If this box is checked, Excel lists only the printer fonts available. If not checked, Excel lists the display fonts available. You should always be sure that both font sets are installed for each font you use.

Printer fonts are specific for a particular type of printer. Hewlett-Packard LaserJet printers and compatibles can use either cartridge or soft fonts. Cartridge fonts are kept in the printer. You can choose the cartridge you want by inserting it into the printer. Soft fonts are kept on the computer's disk in the size(s) you want, and downloaded to the printer automatically when needed. When you install the printer, you specify the soft fonts available on your computer.

Postscript printers use outline fonts so you don't have to store all font sizes. This is more efficient for storage, but slower as the printer must create the fonts as it prints.

All the information on the fonts and printers available on your system is stored in the Windows WIN.INI file. Use the Windows Notepad program to print this file and see which display and printer fonts are available.

There are many software utilities available for helping you create, edit, and manage fonts. These are useful, since whatever you create is made available for all your Windows programs.

THE FILE MENU PRINTING COMMANDS

The commands on the file menu control most aspects of the final printout:

Page Setup sets up the page image and controls headers, footers, margins, orientation, and whether row and column headings or gridlines are printed. This only affects the current document being printed

Printer Setup selects destination printer, paper type and source, and the resolution. This affects all Windows print jobs

Print Preview gives you a display image of what the printout will look like. You also can control the page image from this command

Print controls text resolution, the page range to print, and the number of copies. You also can choose to print the sheet, notes, or both

You may not use all of these to print a worksheet. For example, you typically may use only Page Setup and Print.

THE PAGE SETUP DIALOG BOX

To control headers, footers, margins, row and column headings, orientation, and gridline printing, use the Page Setup command. The page frame for the current page settings is shown on the worksheet with dotted lines. As you change orientation or margins, the frame will change. Using this frame, you can check what columns and rows will print without having to preview or print the document. All the page-setup settings are saved with the document.

Defining Headers and Footers

A *header* is a line of text that prints at the top of every page. A *footer* is a line of text that prints at the bottom of every page. To set a header or footer, open the File menu and choose Page Setup. When the Page

Setup dialog box (see Figure 17.1) appears, enter the text you want for the header or footer in the Header or Footer box. Then click OK.

Excel defaults to printing the worksheet name as a header and the page number as a footer. To clear these selections, select Page Header or Page Footer (dragging if necessary to select the box contents) and press Delete.

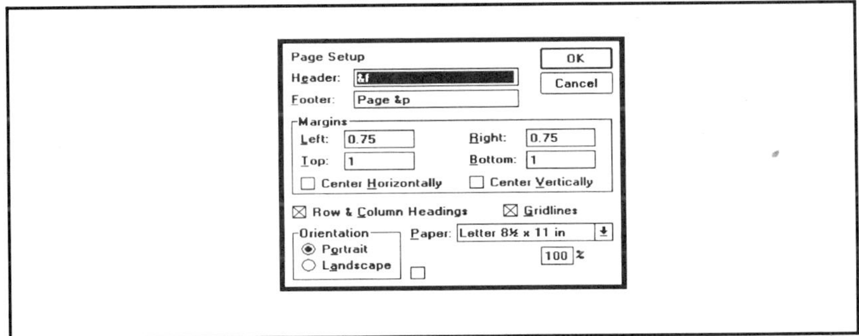

Figure 17.1: The Page Setup dialog box

You can justify headers and footers and include a date, time, and page number. You also can control the style of headers and footers. The control codes that you can use in creating headers and footers are listed in Table 17.1.

Table 17.1: Header and Footer Control Codes

SYMBOL	FUNCTION
&L	Left-justify following characters
&C	Center following characters
&R	Right-justify following characters
&P	Print page number
&P + *number*	Print page number plus *number*
&P – *number*	Print page number minus *number*

Table 17.1: Header and Footer Control Codes (continued)

SYMBOL	FUNCTION
&N	Print total number of pages in document (see text)
&D	Print current date
&T	Print current time
&F	Print the name of the document
&B	Print in boldface
&I	Print in italics
&"*font*"	Print in specified *font*
&*size*	Print in specified font *size*
&S	Print in strikethrough
&U	Print in underline
&&	Print an ampersand

Note: You can combine two or more of these in a header or footer.

Use &N to designate the total number of pages. For example, to print **Page 4 of 12** enter:

Page &P of &N

in the Footer box.

You can combine the control codes for any desired header line. For example,

&L&"Helv"&10Acme Manufacturing&C&P&R&D

prints "Acme Manufacturing" at the left margin in Helvetica font at 10 point, centers the page number, and prints the current date at the right margin.

Try turning off the default headers and footers on your Balance worksheet. Load the worksheet, then open the File menu and choose Page Setup. When the Page Setup dialog box appears, the cursor will be on the Header entry. Press the Delete key, and the Header box will clear. Drag the cursor over the Footer box until it is selected, then press the Delete key again to clear the current footer entry. Click OK and print your worksheet using the Print command.

Setting the Margins

Laser printers normally require at least a half-inch margin at the top, bottom, left, and right.

The margin options permit you to control the amount of space between the paper and the printed area. The margins at the top, bottom, left, and right of the page can be set independently. The margin settings do not affect headers or footers, so margins should be large enough to prevent printing the worksheet over the header or footer.

Clicking on Center Horizontally or Center Vertically controls where the print image is placed on the page.

Setting the Orientation

Set the desired orientation with the Page Setup command. Portrait is the normal orientation (like the way this book is printed); Landscape is for a sideways printout. All Page Setup settings are saved with the worksheet. (The default orientation is set with the Printer Setup command.)

The fonts available for displaying or printing the worksheet probably will change with the orientation, since Portrait and Landscape printing use a different set of fonts. You can use the Fonts command on the Format menu, and click the Printer Fonts check box on, to check the fonts available in the current orientation.

Other Page Setup Options

The Row & Column Headings and Gridlines options indicate whether these will print. The Paper option permits you to choose the paper size. Enlarge and Fit to Page are available only if the selected printer supports these options.

SETTING UP THE PRINTER

Avoid using this to set the print orientation. Printer Setup controls the default orientation, which most users keep at Portrait. Use Page Setup to set the orientation for a particular worksheet.

The Printer Setup command permits you to control the print orientation, the graphics resolution, the type of paper used, the paper source, and the memory and cartridges used with a laser printer.

To change the printer setup, select the Printer Setup command. When the dialog box is displayed (see Figure 17.2), select the type of printer you are using. The dialog box lists all printers installed to Windows that are available.

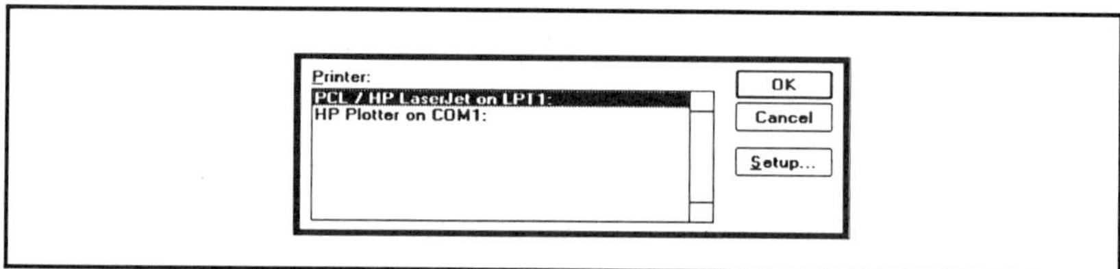

Figure 17.2: The first Printer Setup dialog box

Click the Setup button. A warning box appears, indicating that these options affect the printing of all documents under all applications. Click on OK. On the next dialog box (see Figure 17.3), you can select from the remaining options. This second dialog box is printer dependent; that is, it is a part of the printer driver. It's identical with the one you would see if setting up the printer from the Windows Control Panel.

Click on OK to return to the first dialog box, then click OK again to return to the worksheet.

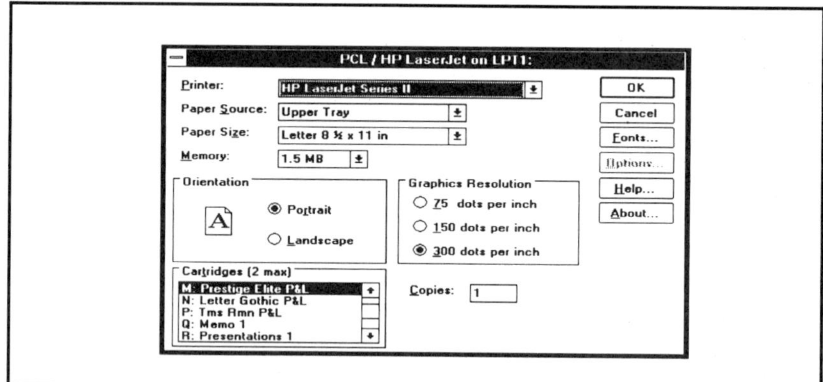

Figure 17.3: The second Printer Setup dialog box

PREVIEWING THE PRINTOUT

The Preview option is particularly useful for seeing how the finished page will look. To turn on the preview mode, select the Preview command. A reduced copy of the first page of the final printout is displayed on-screen (see Figure 17.4). To see an area in more detail, click on the Zoom button (or press *Z*) or move the mouse and click the area of the worksheet to which you wish to zoom (see Figure 17.5). Scroll bars permit you to scroll within the zoomed window. Press *Z* again or click anywhere on the screen to restore the reduced-size view. Click the Next and Previous buttons to move to the next or previous page. Click the Close button to exit the preview mode.

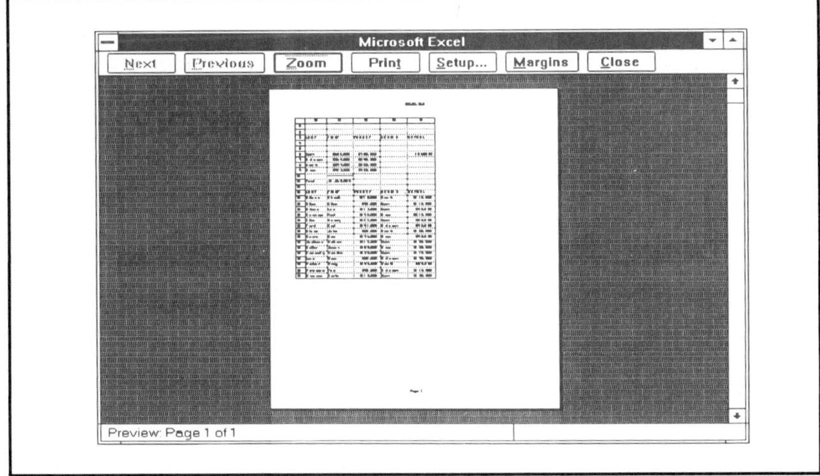

Figure 17.4: A print preview

3.0

Many page and printer-setup commands are available while in the preview mode, making it possible to adjust the page image. For example, to change the margins, click the Margins button. Drag the margin handle at either end of the dotted line while watching the status bar at the bottom of the screen to see the margin setting.

You also can change the column widths in the preview mode. With Margins selected, column handles are displayed at the top of the page over each column. Move the mouse over a column handle and the status bar displays the column width. Drag the column handle to change the width.

Microsoft Excel

Next | Previous | Zoom | Print | Setup... | Margins | Close

2					
3	LAST	FIRST	TARGET	REGION	ACTUAL
4					
5					
6	East	$682,000	$750,000		1868000
7	Midwest	$369,000	$395,000		
8	South	$394,000	$320,000		
9	West	$423,000	$428,000		
10					
11	Total	$1,868,000			
12					
13	LAST	FIRST	TARGET	REGION	ACTUAL
14	Adams	Chuck	$118,000	South	$110,000
15	Allen	Ellen	$90,000	East	$110,000
16	Atkins	Lee	$113,000	East	$95,000
17	Conners	Paul	$142,000	West	$213,000
18	Ellis	Nancy	$122,000	East	$80,000
19	Ford	Carl	$191,000	Midwest	$95,000
20	Glenn	John	$80,000	South	$125,000
21	Harris	Ken	$176,000	West	$95,000

Preview: Page 1 of 1

Figure 17.5: Zooming in on a preview

File
- New...
- Open...
- Close
- Links...
- Save
- Save As...
- Save Workspace...
- Delete...
- Print Preview
- Page Setup...
- Print...
- **Printer Setup...**
- 1 SALEST.XLS
- 2 E:\EX3\BALANCE2.XLS
- 3 E:\EX3\BALANCE1.XLS
- 4 E:\EX3\BALANCEF.XLS
- Exit

To control more features on the page setup, click the Setup button in the preview mode. You will see the Page Setup dialog box, and you can adjust any setup parameters you wish. Choosing OK returns you to the previewed document with the new parameters active.

PRINTING THE WORKSHEET

You initiate printing with the Print command (or by pressing Ctrl-Shift-F12). The Print dialog box (see Figure 17.6) appears. It controls which pages will be printed, the number of copies to print, and gives you some control over the print quality. Modify the desired options and click OK.

File
- New...
- Open...
- Close
- Links...
- Save
- Save As...
- Save Workspace...
- Delete...
- Print Preview
- Page Setup...
- **Print...**
- Printer Setup...
- 1 SALEST.XLS
- 2 E:\EX3\BALANCE2.XLS
- 3 E:\EX3\BALANCE1.XLS
- 4 E:\EX3\BALANCEF.XLS
- Exit

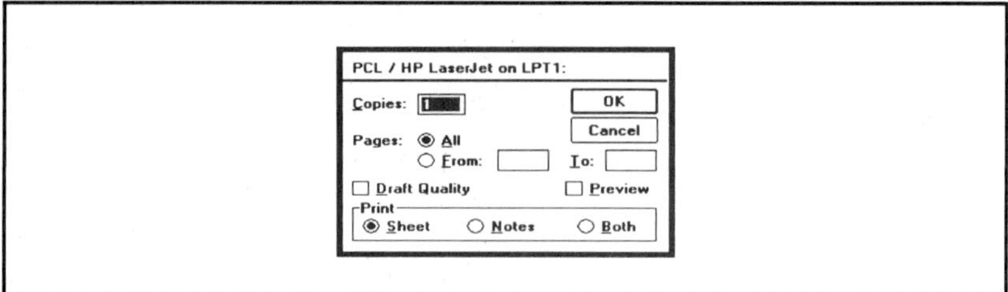

Figure 17.6: The Print dialog box

The following options are available on the Print dialog box:

Draft Quality prints using the printer's built-in character set. The result is generally lower-quality, but faster, printing. Not all printers support such a draft mode

From/To selects which pages to print. Use this option if you make minor changes to a worksheet and need only a part printed. Put the same number in both boxes to print only that page

Copies determines how many copies of the worksheet are printed

Print chooses whether to print document, notes, or both

Preview displays a preview image

THE OPTIONS MENU

The Options menu controls the printing of ranges, titles, break settings, and whether formulas or values are printed.

Options
- Set Print Area
- Set Print Titles
- Set Page Break
- Display...
- Color Palette...
- Protect Document...
- Calculation...
- Calculate Now
- Workspace...
- Short Menus

PRINTING A RANGE

You can, if you like, print just part of a worksheet. This is particularly useful when you're working with only a portion of a very large worksheet.

To print part of a worksheet, first select the range to be printed. Open the Options menu and choose Set Print Area. Excel names the area that you selected as *Print_Area.* You can refer to this area in other commands by using this name in the Define Name and Paste Names commands. To print this area, open the File menu, choose Print, and then choose OK.

Formula
- Paste Name...
- Paste Function...
- Define Name...
- Create Names...
- Apply Names...
- Note...
- Goto...
- Find...
- Replace...
- Select Special...
- Show Active Cell
- Outline...
- Goal Seek...
- Solver...

Subsequent printings will again print this range. To turn off the printing of a range and again print the entire worksheet, use the Define Name command on the Formula menu (or press Ctrl-F3) and delete the *Print_Area* name.

As an example:

1. Select the cell range that you wish to print.
2. Open the Options menu and choose Set Print Area.
3. Open the File menu and choose Print (or press Ctrl-Shift-F12).
4. When the Print dialog box appears, choose OK.

Your printout will contain only the area of the worksheet that you selected. An example of this procedure is included in the section "Printing Formulas" later in this chapter.

You can print a discontinuous range by selecting it and defining it as the print area. Select the first part of the range and press the Control key while you select other areas. (From the keyboard, select one range, press Shift-F8, select the other range(s), and then press Shift-F8 again. Each area will print on a separate page.

If you constantly need to print various range settings from the same worksheet, assign each a different name. Find an empty cell and name it *Print_Area.* Then to print a range named PrintX, use the Define Name command on the Formula menu. Select *Print_Area* as the name and enter = **PrintX** in the Refers To box. This sets the print area to PrintX.

SETTING A PAGE BREAK

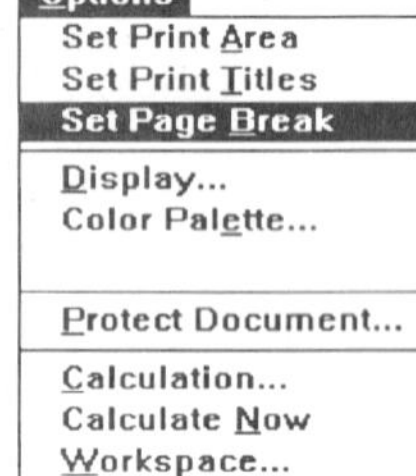

You also can force a page break at any point in the worksheet. To do so, select any cell in the row *before* which you want the page break to come. Then choose Options Set Page Break. The row with the selected cell will be the first row of the next page.

To remove a page break, first select a cell in the row below or to the right of the page break. Choose Remove Page Break.

The Display command determines whether the page breaks are displayed on the worksheet. When turned on, page breaks (both automatic and manual) are marked with a dotted line on the worksheet. In the preview mode, manual page breaks appear darker.

Options
Set Print Area
Set Print Titles
Set Page Break
Display...
Color Palette...
Protect Document...
Calculation...
Calculate Now
Workspace...
Short Menus

Options
Set Print Area
Set Print Titles
Set Page Break
Display...
Color Palette...
Protect Document...
Calculation...
Calculate Now
Workspace...
Short Menus

PRINTING ROW AND COLUMN TITLES

If you print a worksheet that has a few columns but many rows, the column titles will only appear on the first page; subsequent pages of the printout will only contain the data under them. To keep the columns aligned with their respective titles, you would need to paste the pages end to end into one long sheet. Since this is seldom practical, Excel provides a way to repeat the titles on every page of the printout.

Before printing column titles on repeated pages, you need to tell Excel to repeat the titles. Select the row of the worksheet that contains the titles and choose Set Print Titles. Similarly, to repeat row titles on the pages of a large worksheet that extends over many columns, select the column that contains the titles (typically column A) and choose Set Print Titles.

Excel names the title area that you select as *Print_Titles.* You can refer to this area in other commands by using this name. (See Chapter 9 for information on using names.)

If you would now select Print from the File menu, as you normally would to print a worksheet, you would find that Excel prints the column and/or row titles *twice* on the first page of the printout. Can you guess why?

To print the worksheet without this happening, first define a print area that *excludes* the titles by highlighting the relevant cells with the mouse and selecting Set Print Area. Now you can print the worksheet. (Select Print Preview on the File menu first to make sure that the printout will be as you wish.)

Do not use the Display command to turn off row and column headings or the gridlines for printing. These options refer only to the *display.* Use the Page Setup command to turn these features off while *printing.* Also, use Page Setup to set the orientation, not Printer Setup.

PRINTING FORMULAS

You can print the formulas that are used in a worksheet. The basic procedure is simple: display the formulas, and print the worksheet.

1. Open the Options menu and choose Display.
2. When the Display dialog box shown in Figure 17.7 appears, choose Formulas, then click on OK. The formulas are now displayed in each column. Notice that the columns are twice as wide as your regular column setting so that the formulas will fit.

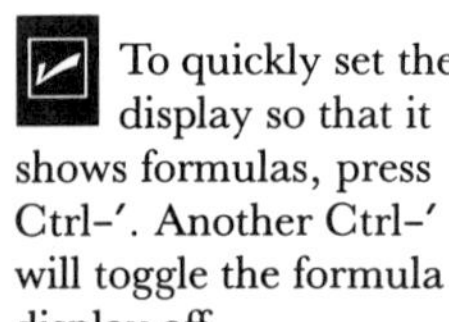
To quickly set the display so that it shows formulas, press Ctrl-′. Another Ctrl-′ will toggle the formula display off.

3. Open the Options menu and choose Set Print Area.
4. Open the File menu, choose Page Setup, and be sure the Row & Column Headings and Gridlines are both selected (see Figure 17.1).
5. Be sure the orientation is set to Landscape, and that the selected font can print in this orientation.
6. Adjust column widths in the worksheet as necessary. In particular, check totals and be sure they fit.
7. Open the File menu and choose Print. On the dialog box displayed (see Figure 17.6), click OK.

Chapters 8 and 13 contain some examples of printouts with formulas.

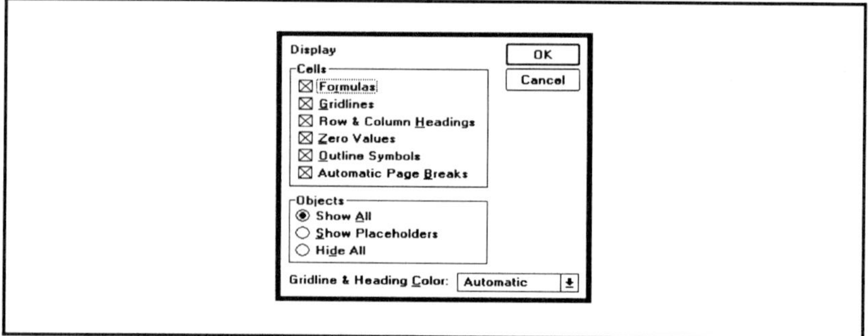

Figure 17.7: The Display dialog box

INSTALLING PRINTERS

At the time you install Excel, you can decide to install one or more printers. When you use the Printer Setup command, you choose from any of the printers already installed.

If you wish to install another printer at a later time, use the Windows Control Panel program. There are four steps:

1. Install the printer driver.
2. Configure the printer (i.e., set the connection).

3. Make the printer active.
4. Set up the printer.

3.0

To use the Control Panel program, open the application's Control menu and choose Run. When the dialog box is displayed, choose Control Panel. When the Control Panel appears, click the Printers icon. Figure 17.8 shows the subsequent dialog box that is displayed.

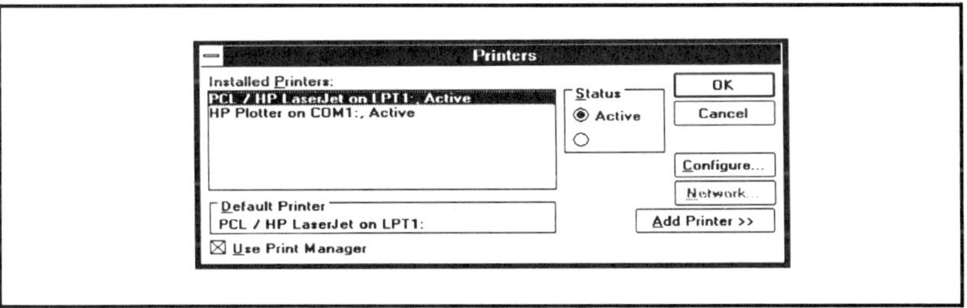

Figure 17.8: Starting the printer installation

To install the driver, you will need the disks that came with Windows. Once you have these disks, click Add Printer on the dialog box. Figure 17.9 shows the next dialog box. Choose the printer to install and click Install. Follow the prompts, and insert the proper printer-driver disk that came with Windows, if prompted for it. Click on OK to return to the first dialog box.

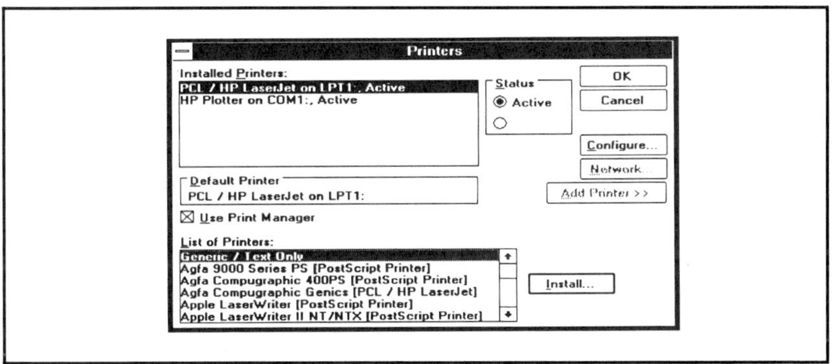

Figure 17.9: Installing the printer driver

The next step is to configure the printer. Click Configure on the first dialog box and select the connection (see Figure 17.10). The first printer (if it is a parallel port printer) is normally assigned to LPT1. Click OK.

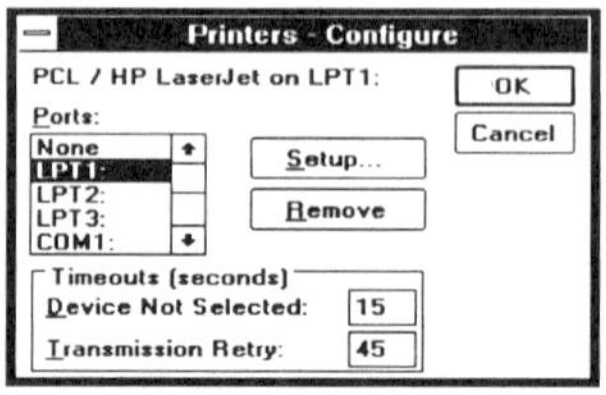

Figure 17.10: Configuring the printer

Now make the printer active. In the first dialog box, select the printer and then click Active. Only one printer can be active on a port at a time.

Finally, set up the printer. Select the printer in the dialog box and then click Configure button. In the Configure dialog box, click the Setup button. The dialog box here is determined by the printer you are using. Figure 17.3 shows the dialog box for a Hewlett-Packard LaserJet Series II. Set the parameters in this box to match your printer. Here the most important parameters are the memory size, cartridges in use, default orientation, and graphics resolution. Then click OK. You can change this at any time by choosing Printer Setup on Excel's File menu.

Click OK to return to the Control menu panel, then close the program from the Control menu and open the Excel program again.

USING THE PRINT MANAGER

Print Manager is a spooler utility program provided with Windows that permits you to continue working with a worksheet while another worksheet is printing, or to share the printer between several programs running under Windows. When using the Print Manager, you actually print to a disk file very quickly, so that Excel is ready to do more work.

Whether Print Manager is used is determined by a statement in the Windows WIN.INI file that contains the option setting:

```
spooler = yes
```

You can edit the WIN.INI file with any editor to turn the spooler option on or off; but there is an easier way—with the Control Panel. Start Control Panel as described in the last section and choose Printers from the panel. At the bottom of the dialog box (see Figure 17.8), choose Use Print Manager to take advantage of it. Then click OK.

If the option is selected to turn the Print Manager on, it will be loaded automatically when a print request is made. The Print Manager icon will then appear at the bottom of the screen. Double-clicking it will display a window for the Print Manager (Figure 17.11). Using this window, you can view the print queue and printing status of several documents.

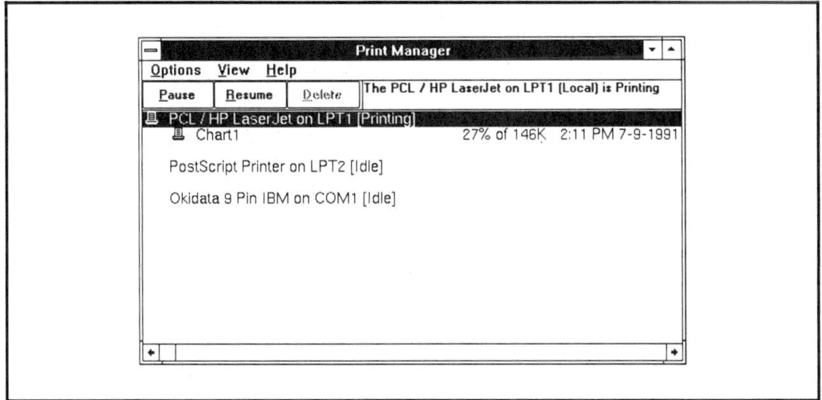

Figure 17.11: The Print Manager window

The Print Manager requires disk space for saving documents to print. In addition, it takes a little longer to get the final document, as the document must first be printed to the disk, then to the printer.

Many users also spool to a buffer box external to the printer. In this case, Print Manager is still advantageous to use because it allows the printer to be shared by several programs when they are in use at the same time.

SPECIAL PRINTING JOBS

Following are some guidelines for printing envelopes, labels, and forms.

PRINTING ENVELOPES

If you are using a dot-matrix printer, envelopes are generally purchased as pinfeed envelope stock and fed to the printer in portrait orientation. With laser printers, you feed normal envelope stock (including company stationery) manually to the printer. Some printers make an envelope tray available as an accessory, but these generally hold only a few envelopes. The envelopes are printed in landscape orientation.

In either case, the best method for printing addresses is to define an area on the worksheet that will be temporarily used to print each address. This is defined as Print_Area, and the Page Setup command is used to define the frame for this area. The paper size is left at the normal letter size, and the margins adjusted to position the address correctly on the envelope. Experiment with paper stock until you get it correct. Once you have this defined, save the worksheet as a template.

Now create a macro (see Part VII) to copy each address in turn to the print area and print it. With some worksheets, you may need to transpose the address to put columnar fields in rows.

PRINTING LABELS

Printing labels is a lot like printing envelopes as far as the worksheet is concerned: define a print area, use the Page Setup command to define the area, and then use a macro to set up the area.

Dot-matrix printers can use pinfeed stock to print the labels as continuous labels. Be sure never to turn the platen backward, as the labels will peel off and stick to the platen. It's very hard to clean the platen in this case.

For laser printers, purchase laser printer labels as sheets. Avery makes a 5261 label with the labels as two-up. This is the best choice for most applications, although it is expensive. You can put these labels in the tray and print them with automatic feed, but be sure the laser printer can handle their thickness. If the printer has a tray that opens at the back to reduce the feed path, use it. Never use labels that are not designed for laser printers, as the heat inside the printer can cause them to stick to the laser printer rollers. If this happens you will need a repair person to get the rollers out, retrieve the label pieces, and clean the rollers. This happened to me once.

PRINTING FORMS

Although you may not have realized it, Excel is a great tool for printing forms and other graphic images. The worksheet grid is ideal for helping you align objects and text. You can turn the grid off for printing or displaying to check the final copy. With the new graphic tools in the tool bar, you can add graphic objects, including text objects. You can draw calendars, organization charts, project charts, and more. They will be presentation-quality and easy to create, edit, and print.

High Impact Presentations with Charts

EXCEL'S CHARTING CAPABILITIES GIVE YOU AN EASY and effective way to illustrate the results of your worksheet and database analyses. Charts convey the full significance of what you are presenting in a concise and persuasive manner. You can use them to show relationships, comparisons, and trends.

Part V shows you how to create a graphic representation of your data with only a few clicks of the mouse. The graphs are dynamically linked to your data—i.e., whenever the data change, your graphs change, too. There is a wide choice of formats and features from which to choose 68 different types of graphs, including three-dimensional formats. You can add arrows, text boxes, legends, and comments to the chart to improve clarity, as well.

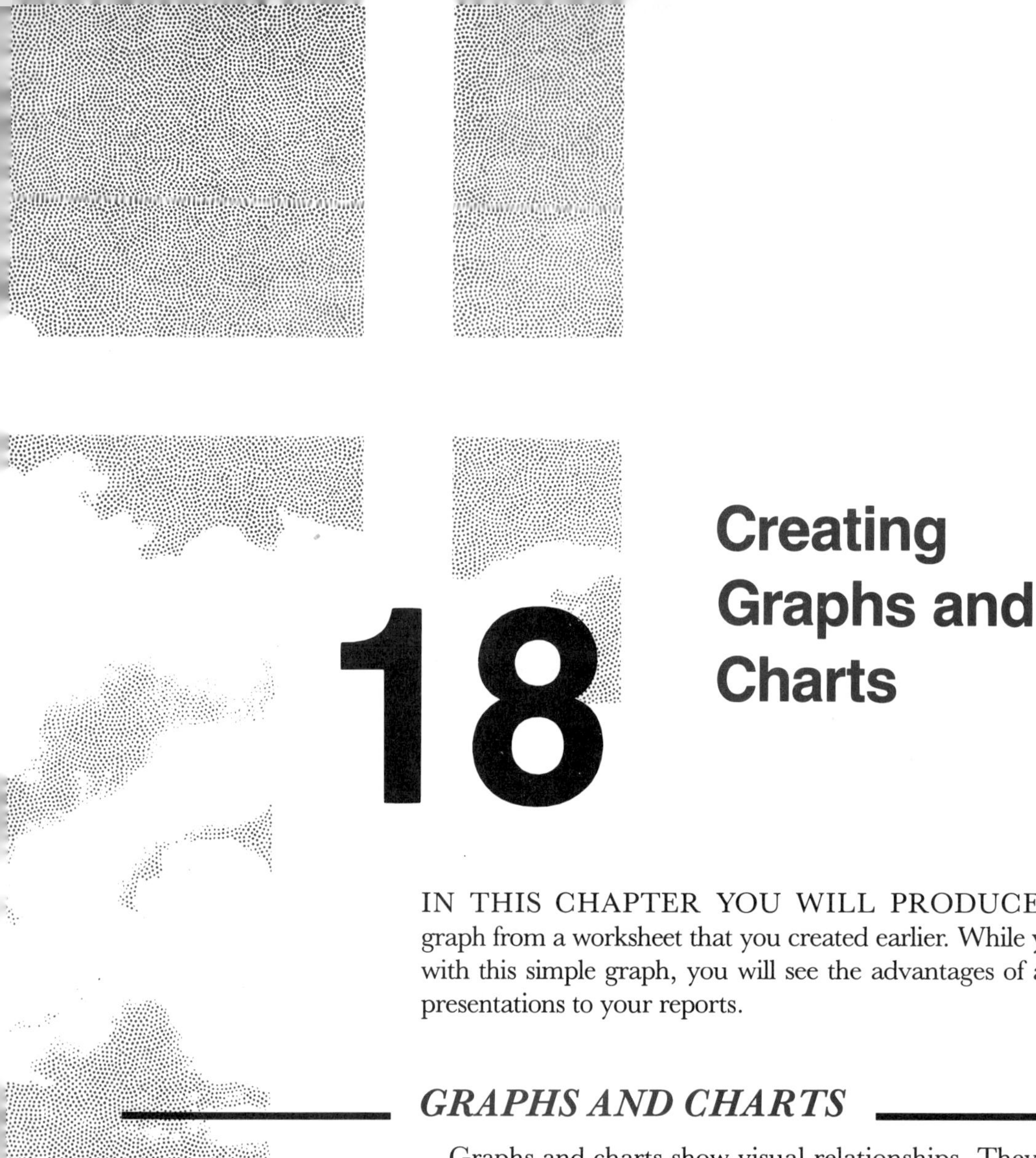

18 Creating Graphs and Charts

IN THIS CHAPTER YOU WILL PRODUCE A SIMPLE graph from a worksheet that you created earlier. While you're working with this simple graph, you will see the advantages of adding graphic presentations to your reports.

GRAPHS AND CHARTS

Graphs and charts show visual relationships. They are especially useful for relaying information to busy people who don't have the time to pore over tables of numbers. Notice how much easier it is to reach conclusions about which regions have better sales and are meeting their targets from the chart in Figure 18.1 than it is to reach these same conclusions from the Sales worksheet.

Although the Excel documentation uses the words "chart" and "graph" interchangeably, I make a distinction between the two terms. A *graph* is a visual presentation of one or more sets of data. A *chart* is a single document that displays graphics. You could create one chart from several graphs.

Figure 18.1 shows the various components of a graph. These components are described below:

- **Axes** are the straight lines used on a graph for measurement and reference. A pie chart has no real axis; all other types have two: the *x* axis (the horizontal line) and the *y* axis (the vertical line). The *x* axis shows the data classification and the *y* axis shows the quantity or unit of measure
- **Markers** are the types of indicators used on a graph to represent the data. A column graph uses vertical bars filled with a pattern for markers. A line graph uses small symbols
- **Tick marks** are the small lines that divide the axes. They are used to indicate categories (for example, quantities or regions) and scales (for example, dollars or another type of measurement)
- **Plot area** is the area bounded by the axes or, in the case of a pie chart, the area within the circle
- **Scale** is the range of values covered by the *y* axis of the chart
- **Legend** shows the symbols and labels used to identify the different types of data on the chart

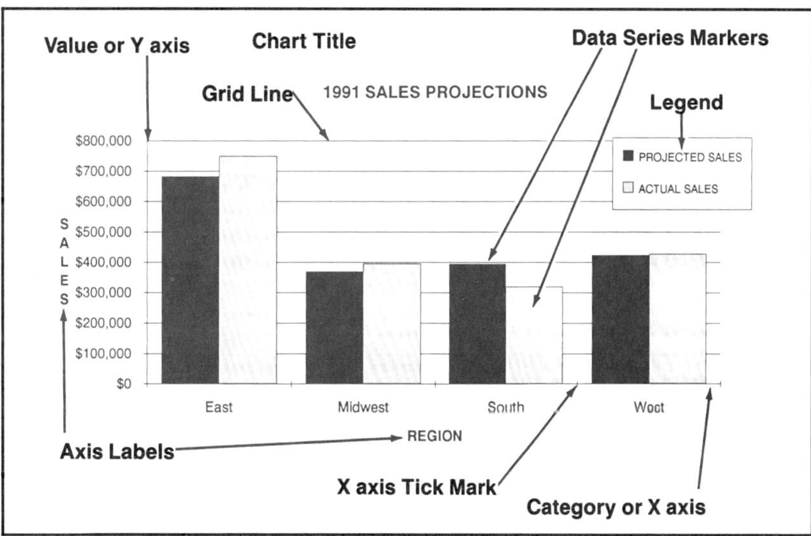

Figure 18.1: The components of a graph

- ***X*-axis** is the title for the *x* axis
- ***Y*-axis** is the title for the *y* axis
- **Chart title** is the title of the chart
- **Grid Lines** are the optional horizontal or vertical lines in the plot area that help the viewer determine the value of a marker

Each marker on a graph represents a data point. A *data series* is a set of related markers. You can plot several data series on a single graph by using different types of markers. Figure 18.1 shows two data series. In a pie chart you can represent only a single data series.

CREATING A CHART

Now you can create a chart. Start Excel and open the Sales worksheet that you created in Chapter 13. To chart the regional sales as a column graph follow these steps:

1. Identify the data series that you want to show on the graph by clicking cell A6 and dragging to cell B9.
2. Press Alt–F1 or F11, or open the File menu and choose New. When the New dialog box appears, choose Chart, then click OK.

You should now see the chart shown in Figure 18.2. Notice that Excel scales the *y* axis automatically, creates the column categories, and labels the columns automatically. You also will see a different menu bar at the top of the screen.

The chart still needs a title and axes labels. You can create these by following the steps below:

1. To add a title, open the Chart menu and choose Attach Text. When the Attach Text dialog box is displayed, click Chart Title, then click OK. Type the title **1991 SALES PROJECTIONS** in the formula bar for the title area now marked on the graph. Press Enter to complete the entry.

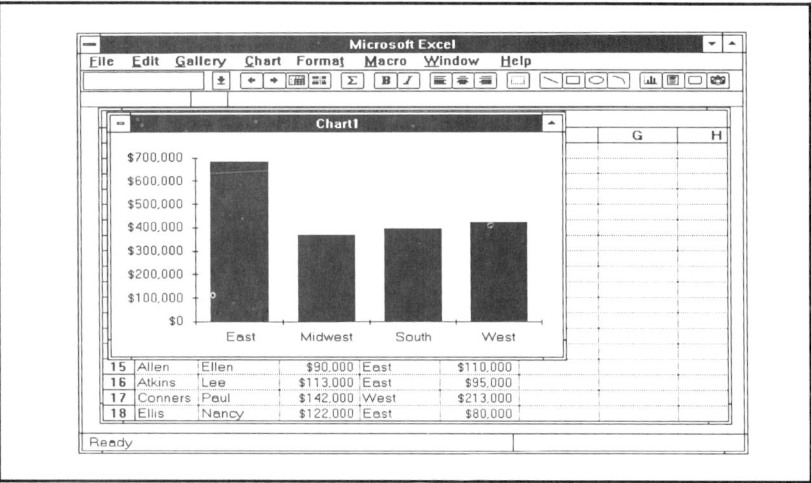

Figure 18.2: The chart after the initial plot

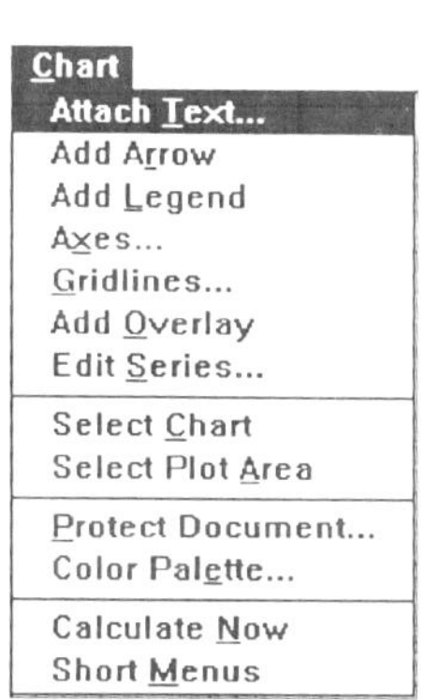

2. To put the title in boldface and larger print, with the title area still selected, choose Font from the Format menu. When the dialog box shown in Figure 18.3 is displayed, choose Helv (or Helvetica or Swiss), 12 points for the size, and Bold in the Style box. Then click OK.
3. To add a label for the *y* axis, open the Chart menu and choose Attach Text. When the dialog box appears, choose Value Axis, then click OK. Type **SALES**. Press Enter to complete the entry (see Figure 18.4).
4. To format the y-axis label, be sure the label is still selected and choose Font on the Format menu. Choose Helv, 10 points, and bold.
5. To add a label for the *x* axis, open the Chart menu and choose Attach Text. Choose Category Axis in the dialog box, then click OK. Type the title **REGION**. Click the Enter box or press Enter to complete the entry. Format the label as with the *y* axis.

When you've finished creating the chart, you can print it. Press Ctrl-Shift-F12 or open the File menu and choose Print. Then click OK in the dialog box.

Be sure Printer Fonts is selected on the dialog box. Select a font, font size, and style available if Helvetica 12 Bold is not available.

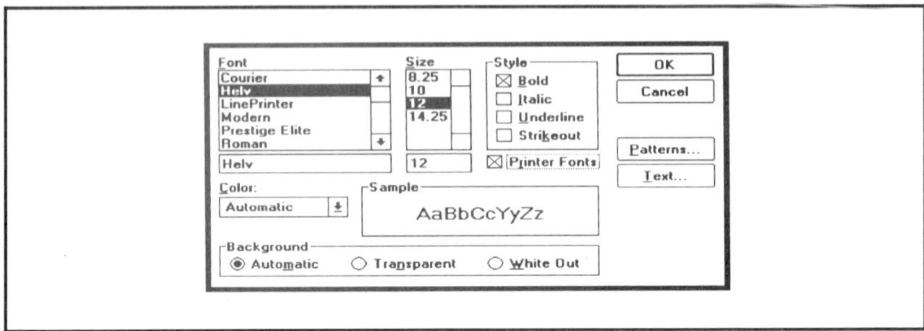

Figure 18.3: Enlarging and boldfacing the title

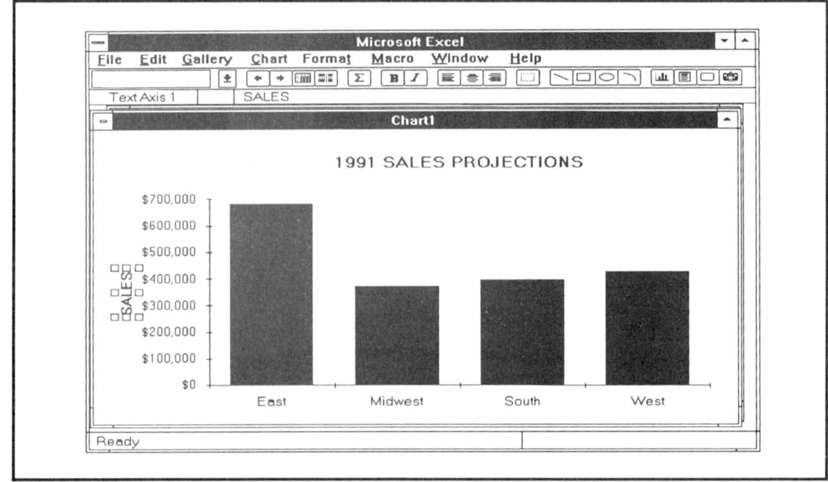

Figure 18.4: Labeling the *y* axis

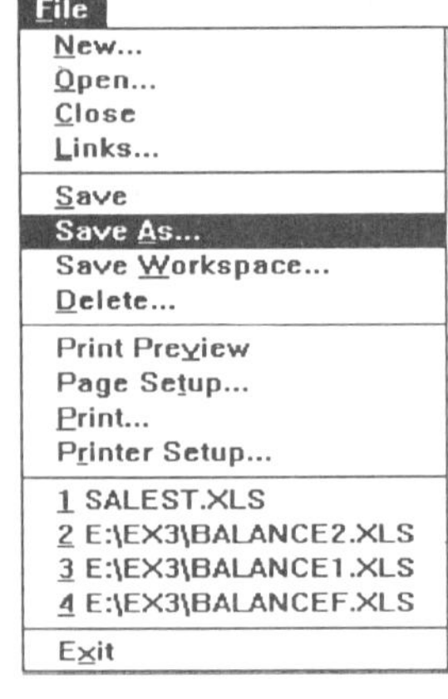

If the printout has problems with the *y*-axis label, remember that it is printing using a landscape font. Try changing it to a portrait font by using the Text command on the Format menu and choosing a Portrait orientation (see Figure 18.5). Figure 18.6 shows the final printout.

You also should save the chart. Press Shift–F12 or open the File menu and choose Save As. In the Save Chart As dialog box, enter **SALES** and click OK. The chart is saved as SALES.XLC.

If you have difficulty fitting the entire graph on the printed page, use Page Setup to set the margins smaller (always keep at least a half inch on laser printers, however). You also can reduce the font size. If you need a small font, use Modern.

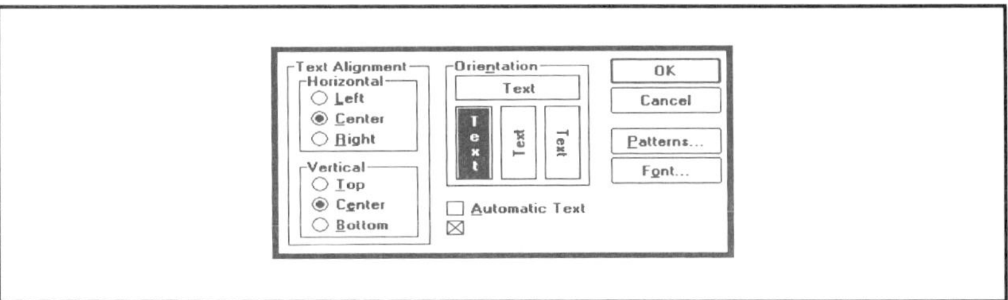

Figure 18.5: Orienting the text

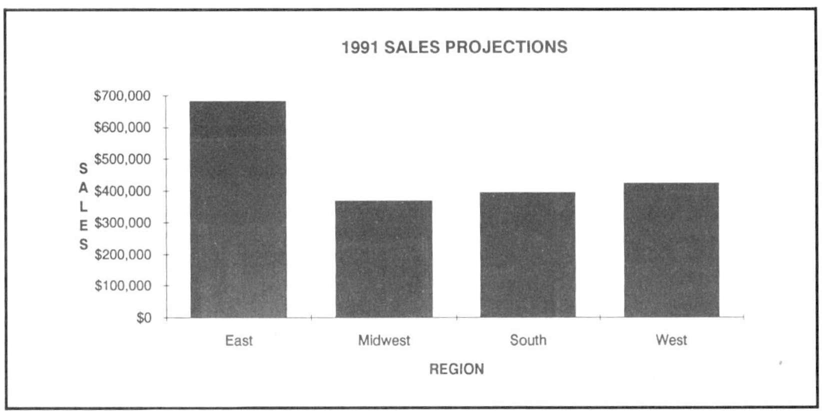

Figure 18.6: The final chart

WORKING WITH CHARTS

Once you have created a chart, you can change its size, data-point values, and category names. Use the Arrange All command under the Window menu to position the windows, then try the following experiments to see how these changes affect your chart:

1. Select the worksheet, then the chart. What happens to the menu bar?
2. Change the width of the chart, then the height, by dragging the borders. What happens? The scaling automatically adjusts and the category labels take two lines if necessary.

Adjust the windows so that you can see the target value for the second person in the eastern region on the database, as well as the chart.

3. To change a data-point value, select cell C14 and change the value to zero. What happens this time? The scaling on the chart changes, and the columns are redrawn, as shown in Figure 18.7. The South bar is smaller.
4. To change a category name, select cell A6 and change the value to "Europe." What happens to the chart? The category labels change, and the chart is redrawn, as shown in Figure 18.8. Since there are no Europe data, there is no column to graph.

As you can see, Excel quickly responds to any changes that you make to the chart or to the worksheet cells that contain the data on which the graph is based. It also can change the chart to an entirely different type just as quickly, as described below.

Before continuing, restore the chart: restore C14 to $118,000, A6 to East, and resize the window so that the chart fills the entire screen.

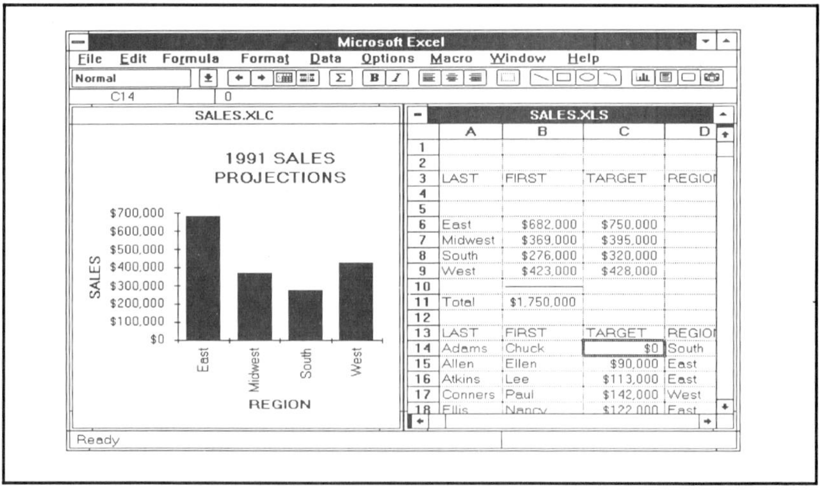

Figure 18.7: Changing a data-point value

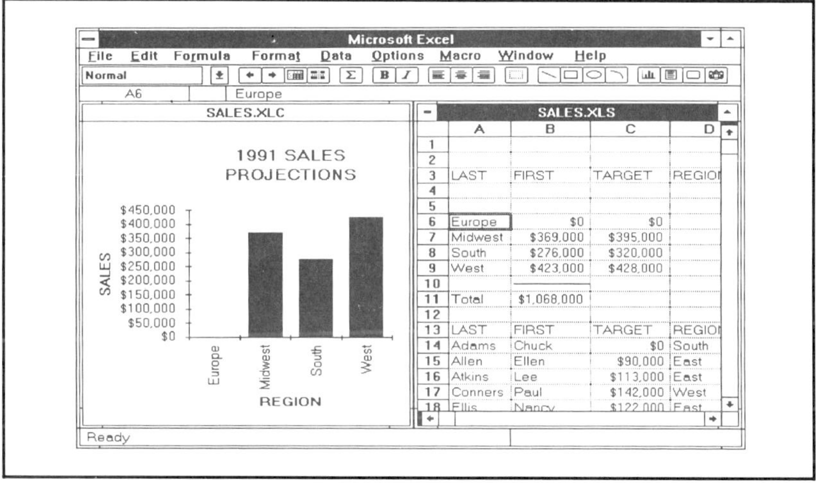

Figure 18.8: Changing a category name

CHANGING CHART TYPES

Once you've recreated the chart, you can practice changing the type, legend, and other features. This is how you would change it into a pie chart:

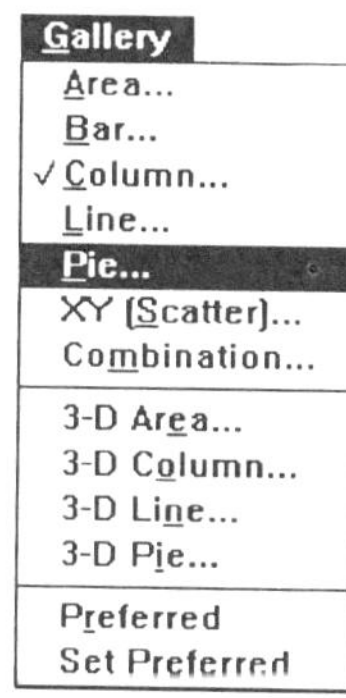

1. Select the chart window, then open the Gallery menu and choose Pie. The Pie dialog box shown in Figure 18.9 is displayed.
2. Double-click box 5 in the lower-left corner of the dialog box (or choose the box and then click on OK). Excel displays a pie chart using the same data that were plotted on your original bar chart.

This pie chart won't print too well on most laser printers, as they print in black and white only. Modify your chart so that it shows patterns for the regions instead of colors. Click on a wedge, open the Format menu, and choose Patterns (Figure 18.10). Click Custom in the area box, open the Foreground list box, and set the color to black. Then open the Patterns list box and choose an appropriate pattern

It is very easy to change a chart type. In creating charts, experiment with different chart types using the Gallery menu to explore different presentation possibilities. Choose the type that best communicates what you wish to say.

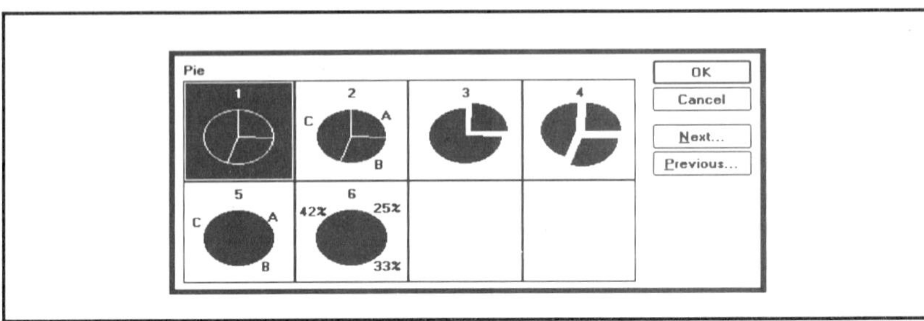

Figure 18.9: The Pie dialog box

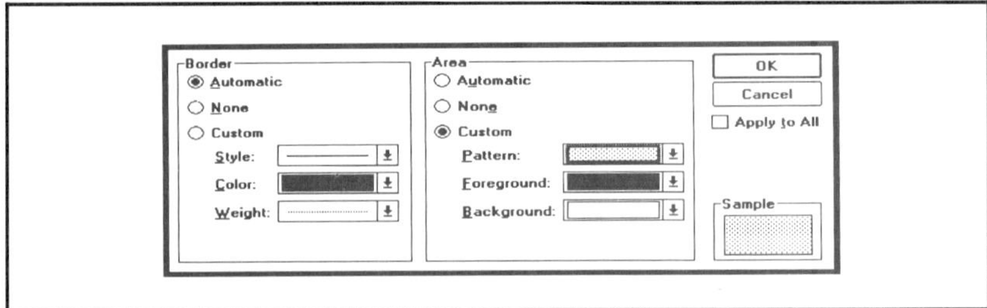

Figure 18.10: Choosing a pattern

for the region. Click OK after you've chosen a pattern for the wedge. Your chart should appear as in Figure 18.11.

Before going on, you may wish to experiment with other options on the various menus on the chart menu bar. Try creating other types of graphs. Be sure when you have finished that you close all windows, but do not save the chart or worksheet again, except under your own name.

DRAWING A CHART ON A WORKSHEET

3.0

You also can draw charts on a worksheet. To try this:

1. Make the original worksheet active. Select the range to chart; for example let's choose the target range. Highlight A6 to A9. Hold down the Ctrl key and highlight C6 to C9.
2. Click the chart tool on the tool bar (see Figure 18.12). Click on the worksheet where you wish the chart to be. Click at

the upper-left corner of the chart and drag down and to the right to size the box for the chart.

3. Set the scales to a smaller font by clicking each axis in turn, selecting the Font command on the Format menu, and choosing the small Modern size.
4. Click the ellipse tool to draw an ellipse around the target figures. Set its fill to None with the Patterns command under the Format menu.
5. Click the line tool to draw a line from the ellipse to the chart. Add the arrowhead by using the Patterns command.

Figure 18.13 shows an example of a chart created this way.

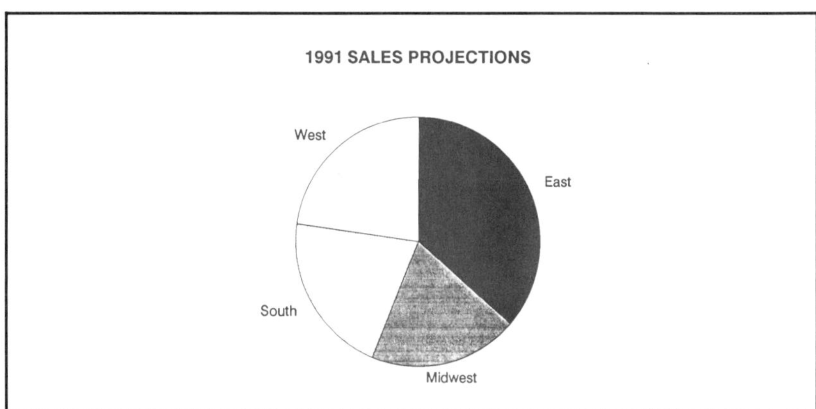

Figure 18.11: The pie chart with patterned wedges

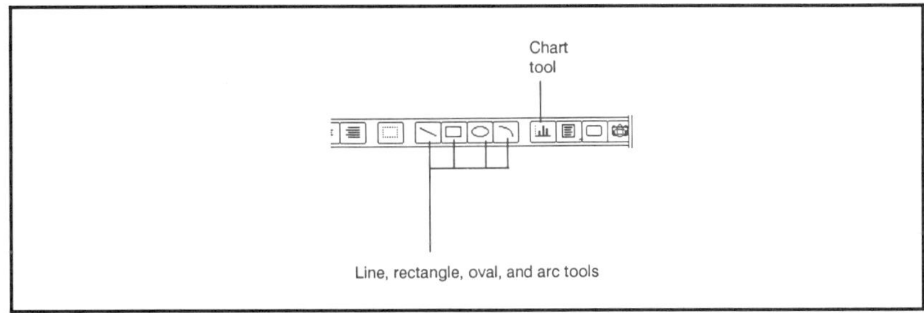

Figure 18.12: The tool bar for worksheet charting

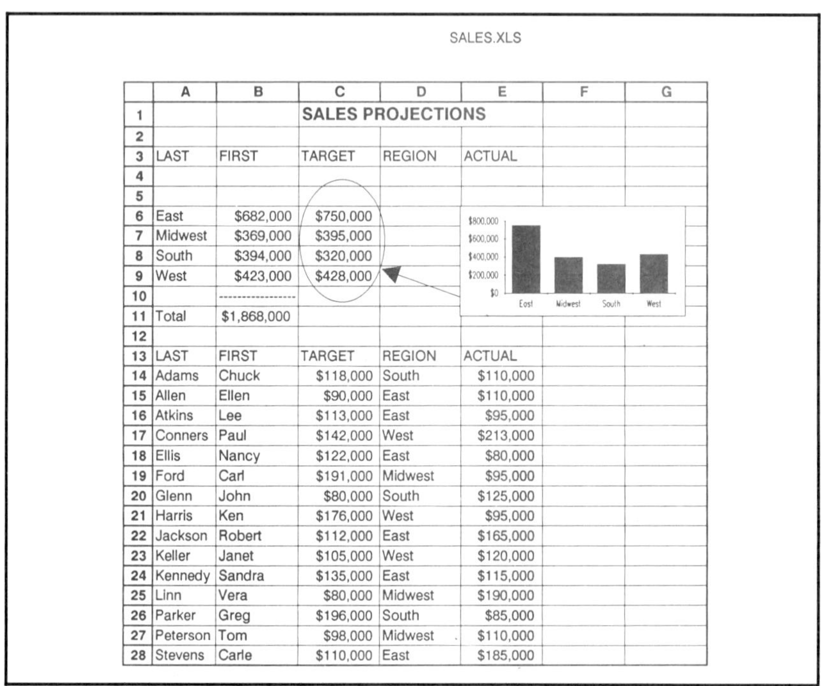
SALES.XLS

	A	B	C	D	E	F	G
1			SALES PROJECTIONS				
2							
3	LAST	FIRST	TARGET	REGION	ACTUAL		
4							
5							
6	East	$682,000	$750,000				
7	Midwest	$369,000	$395,000				
8	South	$394,000	$320,000				
9	West	$423,000	$428,000				
10		----------------					
11	Total	$1,868,000					
12							
13	LAST	FIRST	TARGET	REGION	ACTUAL		
14	Adams	Chuck	$118,000	South	$110,000		
15	Allen	Ellen	$90,000	East	$110,000		
16	Atkins	Lee	$113,000	East	$95,000		
17	Conners	Paul	$142,000	West	$213,000		
18	Ellis	Nancy	$122,000	East	$80,000		
19	Ford	Carl	$191,000	Midwest	$95,000		
20	Glenn	John	$80,000	South	$125,000		
21	Harris	Ken	$176,000	West	$95,000		
22	Jackson	Robert	$112,000	East	$165,000		
23	Keller	Janet	$105,000	West	$120,000		
24	Kennedy	Sandra	$135,000	East	$115,000		
25	Linn	Vera	$80,000	Midwest	$190,000		
26	Parker	Greg	$196,000	South	$85,000		
27	Peterson	Tom	$98,000	Midwest	$110,000		
28	Stevens	Carle	$110,000	East	$185,000		

Figure 18.13: Drawing a chart on a worksheet

19 Advanced Charting Techniques

IN CHAPTER 18, YOU WERE INTRODUCED TO EXCEL'S charting capabilities. This chapter discusses how Excel treats the data series that you chart and how it uses the SERIES function to control what is graphed.

CHART FILE MANAGEMENT

Chart file management is similar to that of worksheet file management. To create a new chart, you define the data range to be charted and then select New Chart on the File menu. Charts are saved with the Save or Save As commands. Templates can be created, as with worksheets, to standardize chart making and reduce the time it takes to create a chart.

WHAT IS A DATA SERIES?

Charts are created from one or more *data series,* which is a collection of data points, each related to the other by some aspect. A *data point* is a single category and related data value. *Data markers* are used to represent the data points on the chart. In a column graph, the data marker is a column; in a line graph, it's a tiny symbol. The Eastern sales, for example, is a single data point in your Sales worksheet.

A data series also could be considered a series of values and a corresponding set of categories. In Figure 19.1, for example, the data series has four data points. The categories are the four regions and the values for the categories are the sales projections.

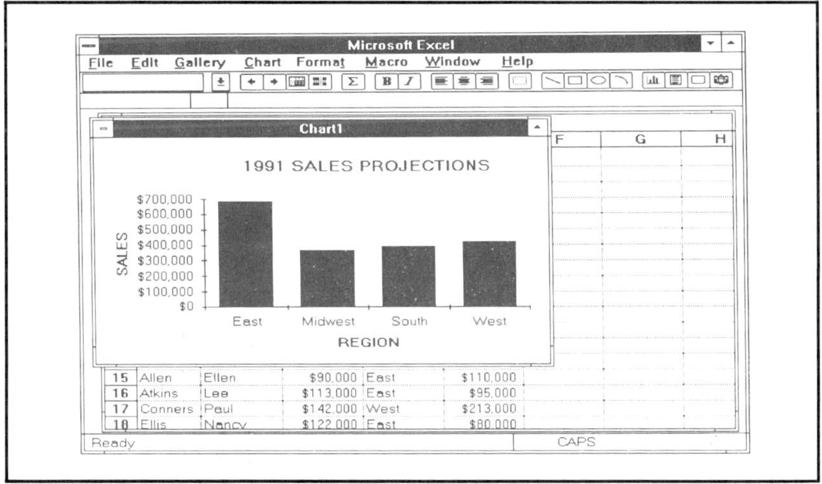

Figure 19.1: A data series with four data points

A data series is always made up of numeric values. Categories can be either text or numeric values. If you do not specify the categories, Excel will assume that they are sequential numbers (1, 2, 3,...).

Charting a data series is very easy:

1. Select the data series on the worksheet that you wish to chart.
2. Open the File menu and select New.
3. Choose Chart in the New dialog box and click OK.

An even faster way is to select the series and press F11.

DATA-SERIES ASSUMPTIONS

Understanding how Excel defines a data series is very important. Figure 19.2 shows some examples of how the data series, names, and categories are defined. When you create a new chart or copy an existing one, Excel makes the following assumptions about the data series:

- If a data series has more rows than columns, the text in the left-most column is used to define the categories, and each column thereafter is assumed to be the data series. The column heading, if selected, is used as the data-series name
- If the data series has more columns than rows, the column headings are used to define the categories, and each row of values is assumed to be the data series. The row heading, if selected, is used as the data-series name
- If the data series is square or the category headings are numeric, Excel does not define any categories for the chart, and each row of values is used as a data series

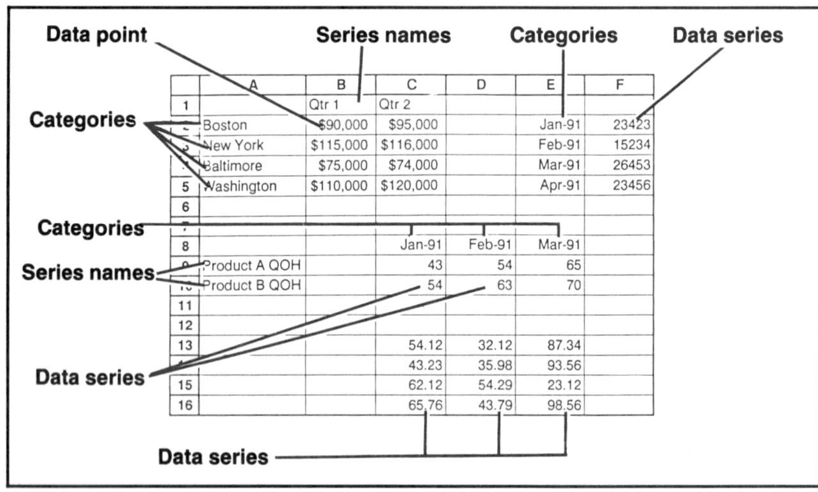

Figure 19.2: Examples of data series, series names, and categories

3.0

If Excel has difficulty defining the series, you will get a dialog box prompt when creating the chart asking how the series should be assumed (Figure 19.3).

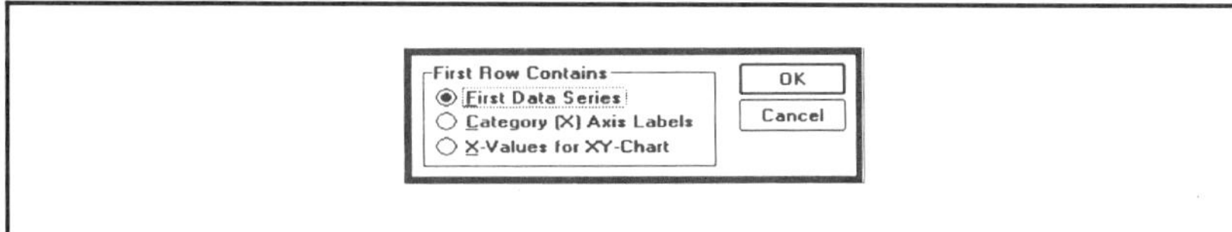

Figure 19.3: Defining the series

CHANGING DATA-SERIES DEFINITIONS

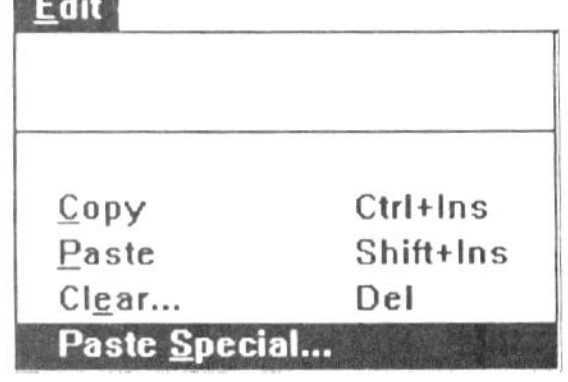

You can change the way that Excel defines a data series by using the Copy command on the worksheet Edit menu, then the Paste Special command on the chart Edit menu. When you choose the Paste Special command, the dialog box shown in Figure 19.4 will appear. The options in this dialog box allow you to define a series of numeric values as your category headings or to switch Excel's normal definitions (see Figure 19.2) so that the chart has more data series than categories. The Values (Y) In box allows you to define whether the pasted values are in a row or column. You can also select whether the series name is in the first row or whether categories are in the first column. If the latter is true, you can choose whether to replace existing categories or not. An example of changing the normal definitions was shown in Chapter 15 in a linear regression chart.

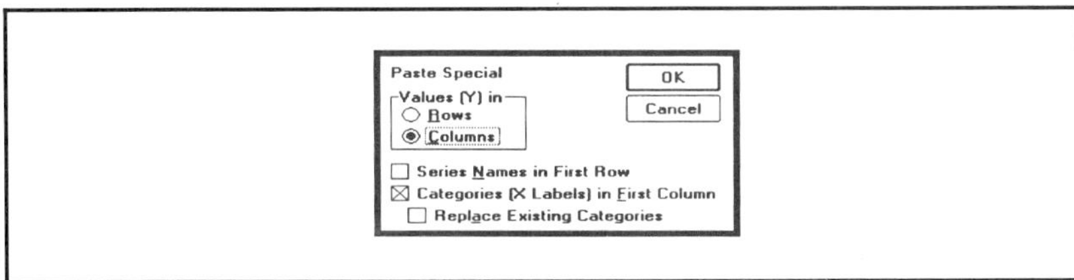

Figure 19.4: Using the Paste Special command

CHARTING DISCONTINUOUS SERIES

If you select A6 to C9 in the Sales worksheet and press F11, you will chart two continuous data series. You can, however, chart discontinuous series. To do so, select the range as you would any other discontinuous range: with the mouse select the first range, then hold down the Ctrl key and select each additional series.

To do it from the keyboard, define the first range and press Shift–F8. The ADD indicator appears in the status bar. Select additional cells or cell ranges. Press Shift–F8 again to turn the indicator off.

Once the ranges are selected, press F11 to create the chart.

ADDING A DATA SERIES TO A CHART

After you've created a chart, you can easily add another data series to it. First, select the values for the new data series on the worksheet. Open the worksheet Edit menu and choose Copy. Click anywhere on the chart to select it. Then, use either the Paste or Paste Special command (as described above) on the chart Edit menu to paste the data series onto the chart.

As an example, let's first create a chart from a single data series, then add another data series to the existing chart. Open the Sales worksheet and create the chart from the first data series:

1. Select cells A6 through B9.
2. Press F11 or open the File menu and choose New Chart. You will see the chart shown in Figure 19.5.

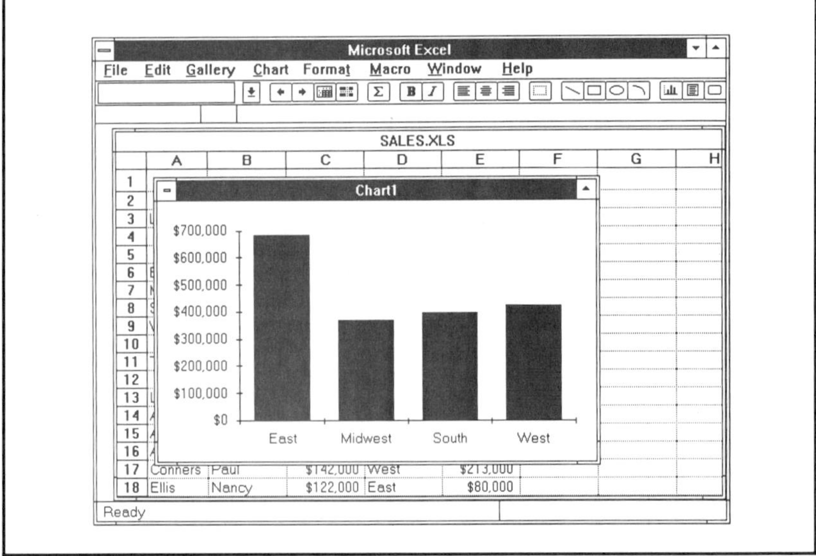

Figure 19.5: Charting a single data series

Now copy and paste the second data series onto this chart:

1. Select cells C6 through C9 on the Sales worksheet.
2. Open the worksheet Edit menu and choose Copy.
3. Select the chart.
4. Open the chart Edit menu and choose Paste.

The final chart is shown in Figure 19.6.

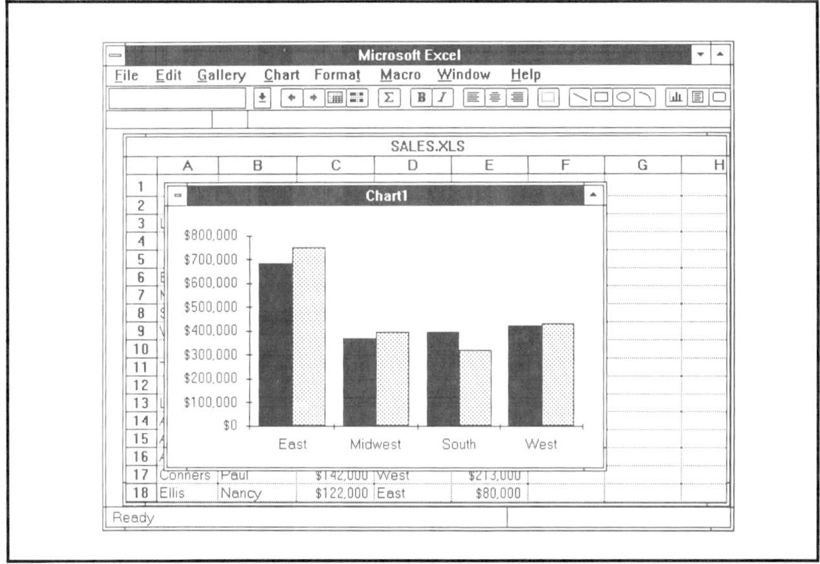

Figure 19.6: The final chart

Using this method, you can continue to copy and paste additional data series onto the chart, either from the same or another worksheet.

THE SERIES FUNCTION

Excel uses the SERIES function to create graphs. This function has four arguments:

- The data-series title, if one exists, in quotation marks
- The category titles, which include the external reference to the supporting worksheet

- The data-series definition, which also includes a reference to the supporting worksheet
- The plot-order value

If you have several data series and include the row or column titles when you select the worksheet area to be graphed, Excel will use the titles for each of the series name arguments automatically. For a single data series, the column or row title is used for the chart title instead. The category titles and the data-series definition arguments are actually arrays and follow the rules for using arrays (see Chapter 15).

You can enter all the SERIES arguments by pointing and clicking, or by typing them in from the keyboard. The function can be edited in the formula bar, just like any other formula. For example, you can enter your data-series title and then point and click to enter the next two arguments.

You can see an example of the SERIES function by clicking any one of the columns on the graph that you just created (see Figure 19.6). The formula bar will display the SERIES function used to create that graph, as shown in Figure 19.7. In this example, the first argument is missing because a data-series title did not exist. The second argument defines categories and the third argument defines the values for the data series. The fourth argument defines the plot order, which equals 1 because this data series is the first one plotted on the graph. The white dots indicate the selected series.

Now click any column of the second series, and the formula bar will display the function with slightly different arguments. The first argument, the data-series title, is omitted as before. The second argument defines the same categories used for the first plot. The third argument defines the cells with the values for the second data series. The plot-order argument has a value of 2, indicating that this is the second plot on the graph.

CHARTS LINKED TO WORKSHEETS

Whenever you create a chart, it is automatically linked to a supporting worksheet. This way, if you change values in a supporting

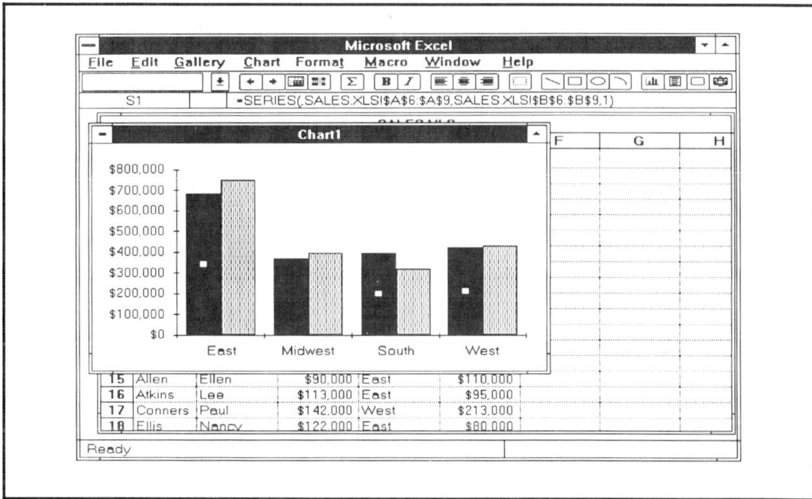

Figure 19.7: The SERIES function for the first data series

worksheet, the chart will be updated to reflect the new values. The procedure for linking charts follows the same rules for linking worksheets:

- When you copy and paste a chart, Excel creates the data-series formulas and external references automatically
- You can block recalculation of a chart by choosing the Manual option in the Calculation dialog box
- External references in a data-series formula should be absolute cell addresses or named references

You can see how a chart and a supporting worksheet are linked by examining the Sales worksheet. Select either of the columns on the chart. You will see the data-series formula in the formula bar with the reference to the worksheet that created the chart. The formula uses a simple external reference. This means that you can open the chart without opening the worksheet and Excel will get the values it needs from the disk.

EDITING A SERIES

3.0

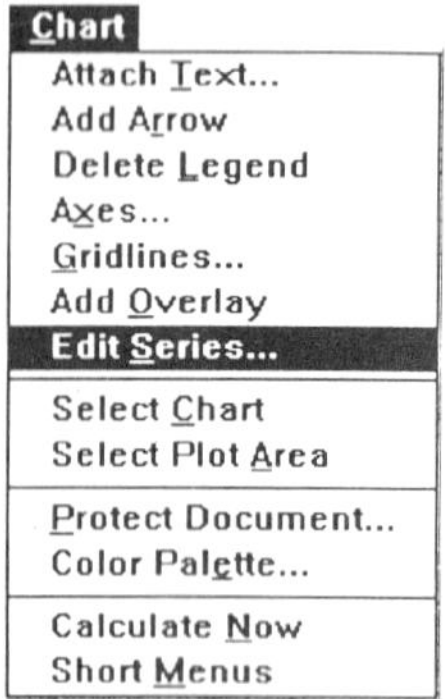

You can edit any series function from the formula bar. Another way to edit or add a series is to use the Edit Series command. Select the series to edit. Open the Chart menu and choose Edit Series. Notice that the *x*-label range and *y*-value ranges are displayed in the dialog box (see Figure 19.8). You can edit either by selecting the series to edit in the Series list box and then editing the respective text boxes.

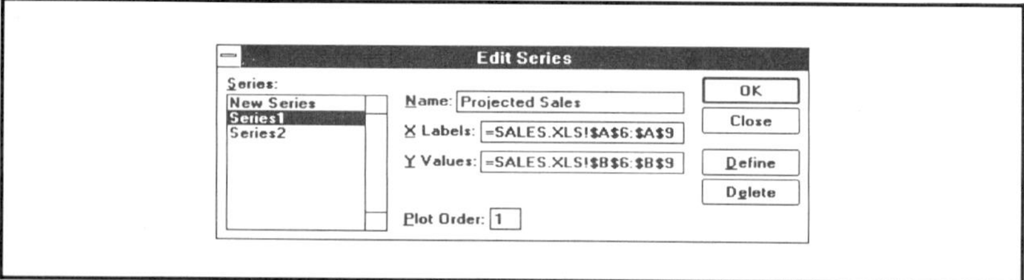

Figure 19.8: Editing a data series

EDITING DATA-SERIES TITLES AND LEGENDS

Now let's add the data series titles and a legend. You will need the series titles for the legend.

There are two ways to add the series titles: you can either edit them with the Edit Series command or use the formula bar directly.

To edit it with the Edit Series command:

1. Select the first series of the chart (dark bar here).
2. Choose Edit Series from the Chart menu.
3. Enter the series name in the Name box as **Projected Sales** (the equal sign and quotation marks are not needed—Excel will add them). See Figure 19.9.
4. Select the second series from the list box and add the name **Actual Sales**.
5. Click OK.

Edit Series
Series:
New Series
Series1
Series2
Name: Projected Sales
X Labels: =SALES.XLS!$A$6:$A$9
Y Values: =SALES.XLS!$B$6:$B$9
Plot Order: 1
OK
Close
Define
Delete

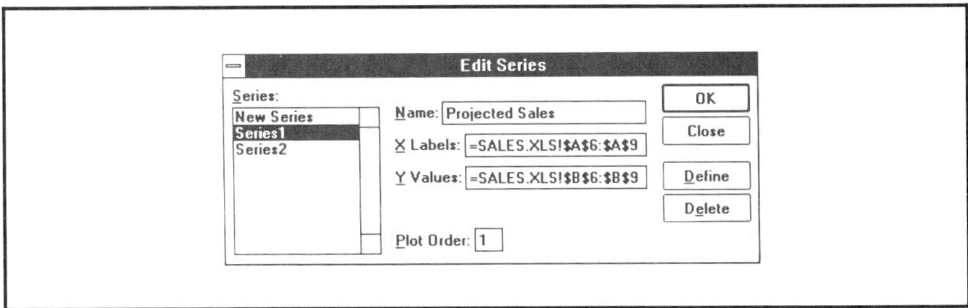

Figure 19.9: Adding a series name

At this time, choose each series in turn and examine the formula bar. The series name has been added to the function (see Figure 19.10).

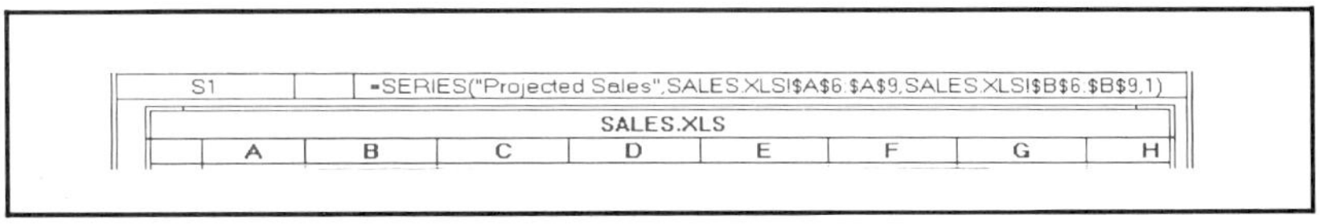

S1
=SERIES("Projected Sales",SALES.XLS!$A$6:$A$9,SALES.XLS!$B$6:$B$9,1)
SALES.XLS
A
B
C
D
E
F
G
H

Figure 19.10: The added series name

You also can add a series name from the formula bar by editing the series in the formula bar directly. To do this, select each series and add it, with quotation marks, in the corresponding formula bar.

Now add a legend that uses the data series names:

1. Open the Chart menu and choose Add Legend. A legend will appear to the right of the chart (Figure 19.11).

CHART1.XLC
$800,000
$700,000
$600,000
$500,000
$400,000
$300,000
$200,000
$100,000
$0
East
Midwest
South
West
Projected Sales
Actual Sales

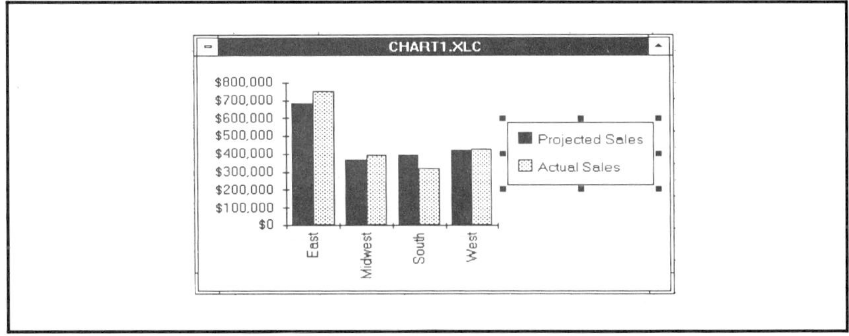

Figure 19.11: Adding a legend

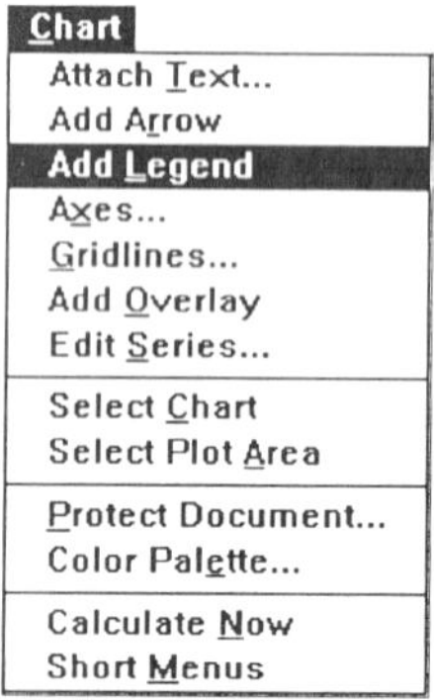

2. Select Format and choose Legend. In the dialog box, choose Bottom and click OK.

The final chart should look like Figure 19.12. Save the chart (select the File menu and choose Save)—you will need it later.

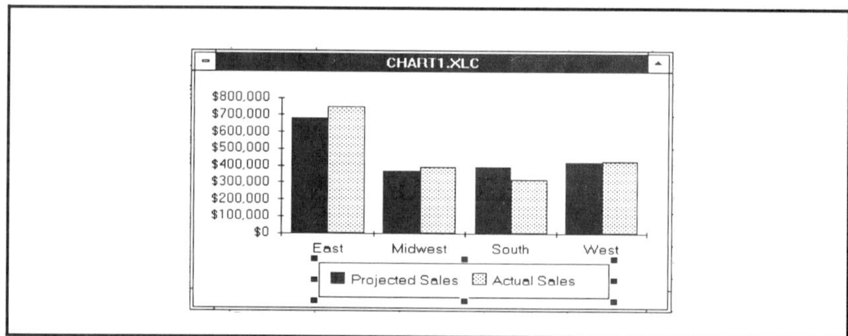

Figure 19.12: The chart after placing the legend

ALTERING THE PLOT ORDER

Excel automatically plots the various data series in the order that you select them. You can alter this plot order by editing the fourth argument in the SERIES function, which is the one that controls the plot order. You also can change the plot order with the Edit Series command.

If you change the plot number to the number of another data series, the other series will be renumbered appropriately. For example, if you changed the plot-order value for the first plot in a graph to 2, Excel would automatically change the plot-order value of the second plot to 1. If you omit the plot number when you enter a formula, the data series will be entered using the next available plot number. After you edit the function and click the Enter box, Excel will redraw the chart and change the legend.

Try changing the plot order on your example chart. Select the first data series and change the last argument of its formula to 2. Click the Enter box, and Excel will redraw the chart. Click the second data series and notice it is now assigned a plot order of 1. Edit the formula for the first data series again so that it is the first series plotted.

3.0

If you wish, you can change the plot order with the Edit Series command. Notice the Plot Order box in this dialog box (see Figure 19.9). You can change this number in the same way to control the plot order.

DELETING A DATA SERIES

3.0

If you wish to remove a data series from a chart, use the following procedure:

1. Select the series from the chart by clicking it.
2. Choose Edit Series from the Chart menu.
3. Select the series you want to delete.
4. Click the Delete button, then click OK.

Here is another way to delete a series:

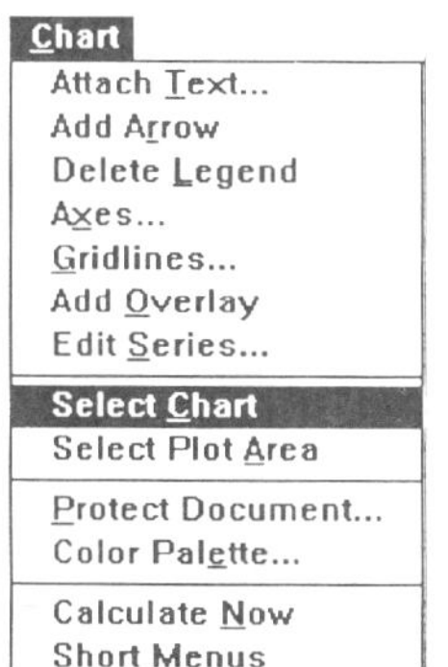

1. On the chart, click the data series that you want to delete. Its formula will appear in the formula bar.
2. Erase the formula with the Backspace key or by using the Cut command on the Edit menu.
3. Press the Enter key or click the Enter box.

The chart will be redrawn without that data series.

You can clear all the data series in a chart by using the following procedure:

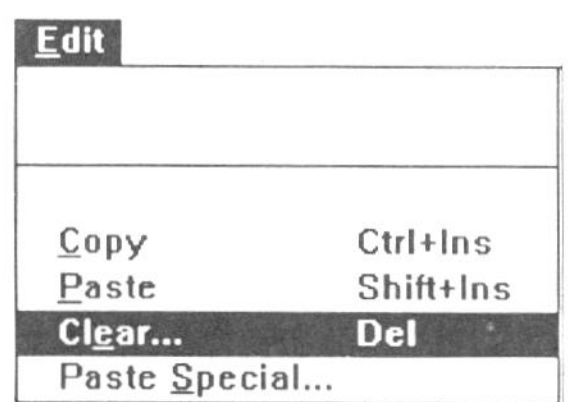

1. Open the Chart menu and choose Select Chart. Markers will appear to show that the entire chart is selected.
2. Open the Edit menu and choose Clear.
3. When the Clear dialog box appears, choose Formulas, then click OK.

The entire chart will clear, but the formats (chart types) will remain. If you copy and paste other data series into the chart, they will be in the format of the previous graph.

COPYING A DATA SERIES

As with worksheets, you can easily copy data from one chart to another. To copy a data series and insert it in another chart, follow these steps:

1. Be sure that the source chart (the one with the data series that you are going to copy) is active.
2. Open the Chart menu and choose Select Chart. The entire chart will be marked.
3. Open the Edit menu and choose Copy. The chart will be marked with dotted lines, as with any other copy operation.
4. Make the destination chart active by clicking it, or open the File menu and choose New to create a new chart.
5. Open the Edit menu and select Paste Special.
6. When the Paste Special dialog box appears, choose Formulas, then click OK.

The data series is copied to the second chart, but the format information (chart type) is not copied. This means that if you copy a data series that was displayed as a column graph into a line graph, the copied data series also will be plotted as a line graph.

CHOOSING THE CHART TYPE

When you change the chart type using either of these methods, *all* the data series plotted on the chart will change to the new type. If you want to change the type of only one data series on the chart, use the overlay method (described next in this chapter), or the Gallery Combination command.

The Gallery menu can be used to change quickly from one chart type to another. There are six basic chart types on the menu: Area, Column, Bar, Line, Pie, and Scatter. Each menu selection, in turn, displays a dialog box from which you can select a subset of the basic type. For example, the dialog box for the column chart type is shown in Figure 19.13.

To change the type of displayed chart, open the Gallery menu and choose the new chart type. When the dialog box for that type appears, choose the new format and click OK. Excel will redraw the chart in the new type.

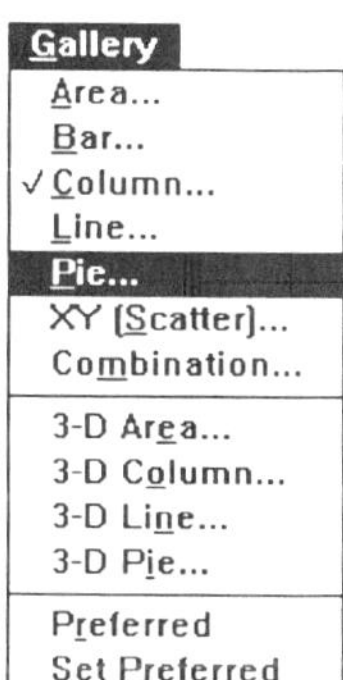

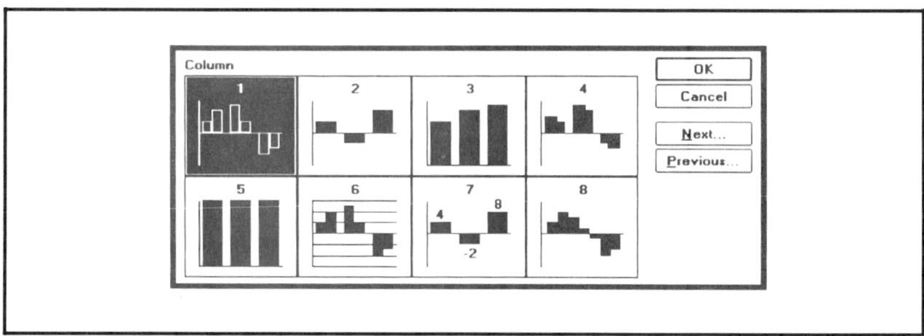

Figure 19.13: Selecting the Column chart type

Another way to change the graph type is to open the Format menu and choose Main Chart. When the dialog box shown in Figure 19.14 is displayed, choose the desired type of chart.

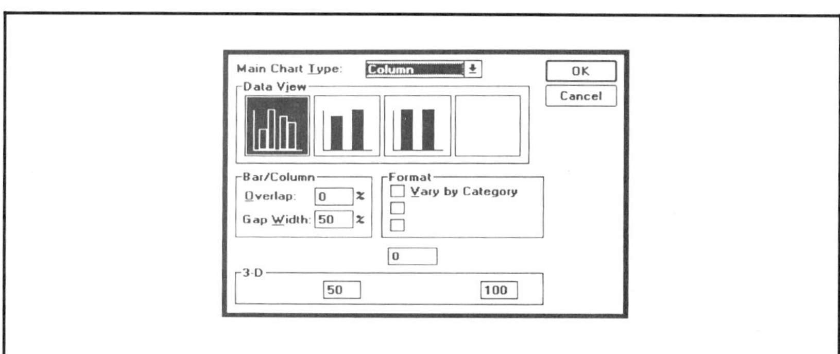

Figure 19.14: The Main Chart Type dialog box

OVERLAYING CHARTS

You can plot two data series in different graph types by overlaying the charts. The overlays can even have different axes.

As an example, let's use the Sales worksheet values and plot the projected sales as a column graph and the actual sales as an overlay line graph. Follow these steps:

1. Open the graph with both data series charted as column types.

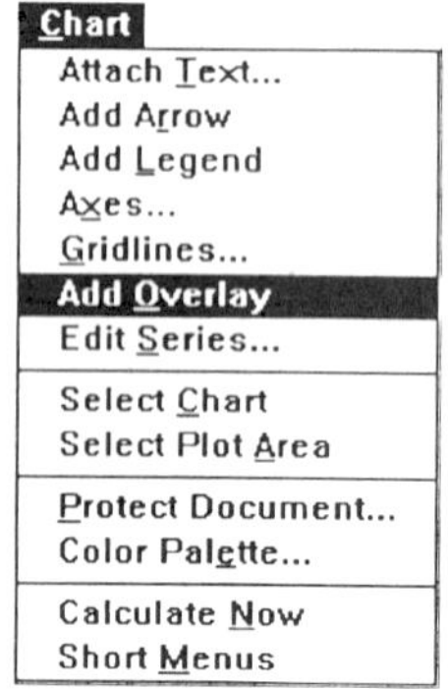

2. Open the Chart menu and select Add Overlay. The second series will show as a line type (see Figure 19.15).
3. If you wish to change the overlay chart type, click Format and choose Overlay. In the dialog box (see Figure 19.16), choose the type.

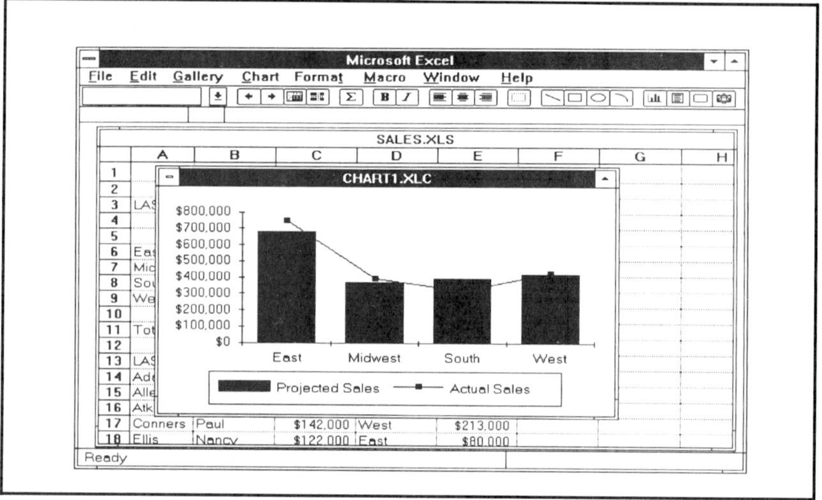

Figure 19.15: Adding an overlay chart

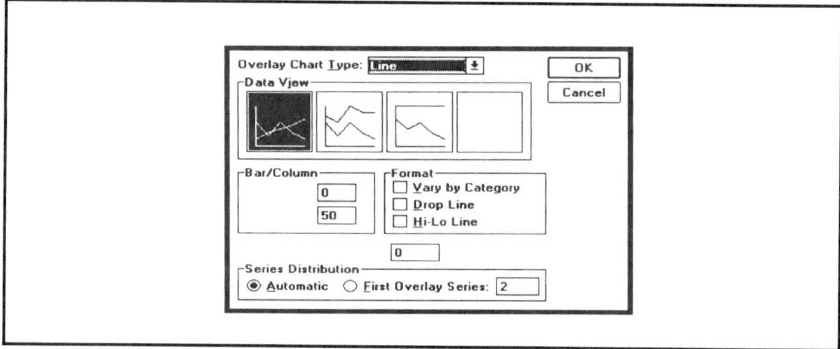

Figure 19.16: The Overlay Chart Type dialog box

Notice that you did not select which data series was the overlay. Excel assumes that the first data series is the main chart type and the second data series is the overlay. You can alter this by editing the plot order in the SERIES function or by using the Overlay command on the Format menu. If there are more than two data series, they will be divided equally between the main and overlay types. If there is an odd number of data series, the extra series will be charted in the main chart type.

Switch the chart back to a single chart by opening the Chart menu and choosing Delete Overlay.

ADJUSTING WORKSHEET VALUES FROM THE CHART

3.0

Excel makes it easy to alter the positions of points on a graph. Simply click on and move a point on-screen, and Excel will change the data in the necessary cell(s) to reflect the new value.

Try this now by copying the Sales chart data (A6 to B9) to an unused area of the worksheet, such as E6:F9. Chart the data. Now try this:

1. Select the new charting range on the worksheet (E6:F9) and make both chart and worksheet visible on the screen.
2. Hold down the Ctrl key and select the bar for the Eastern series. A small black square (or handle) appears at the middle of the top of the bar (see Figure 19.17).
3. Drag the handle downward and watch the Eastern value on the worksheet change to follow the chart.

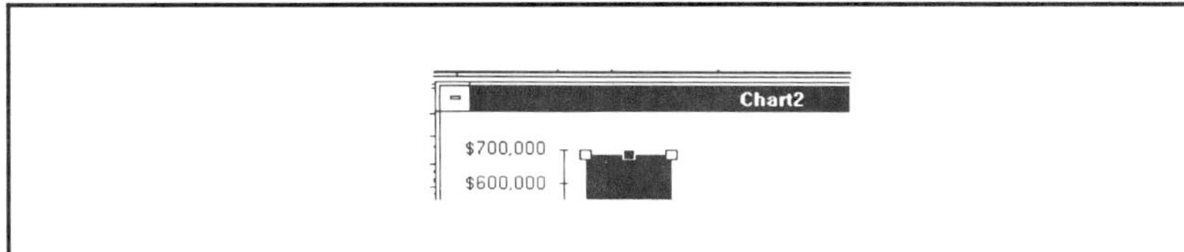

Figure 19.17: The handle to adjust

Now try the same thing with the A6 to B9 range. Create a chart from the range and try to drag the bar. What happens? The charted data are part of the table, and Excel switches to the Goal Seek and displays a dialog box (see Figure 19.18). Enter a cell for the value to adjust, such as C15. The value adjusts to follow the handle. Be sure to adjust a cell with an Eastern region value, or Excel will never be able to find a solution.

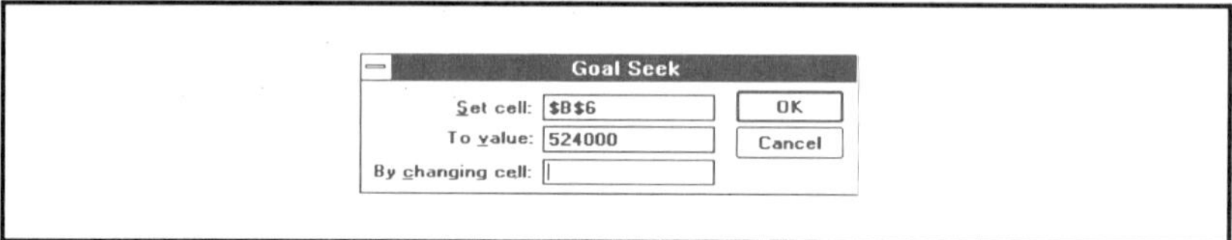

Figure 19.18: Excel in the Goal Seek mode

WORKING WITH EMBEDDED CHARTS

3.0

Charts embedded in a worksheet are created with the chart tool on the tool bar (see Chapter 18). You can activate the charting mode from within the worksheet by double-clicking the chart. The Excel menu will change to the Chart menu and the Chart commands will become active. This permits you to quickly change the chart type and other formatting aspects of the chart that are in the worksheet.

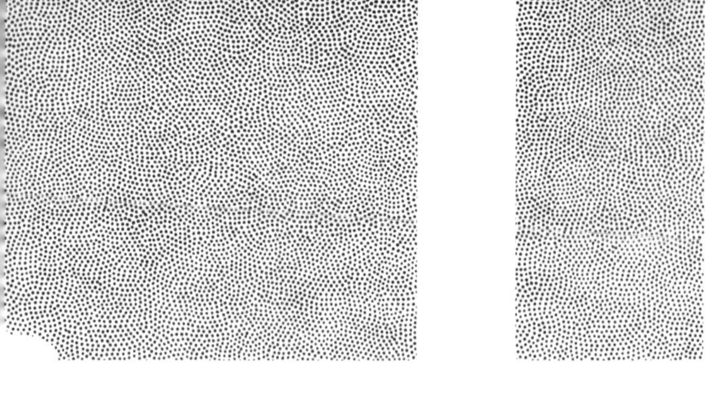

20 Creating High-Impact Charts

WITH EXCEL, YOU CAN DESIGN PRESENTATION-quality charts that communicate ideas quickly and effectively. Excel's charting features are extremely flexible.

This chapter introduces you to some basic principles of charting. You will learn not only how to make charts convey the information and conclusions you wish to communicate, but also some basic design principles and pragmatic aspects of formatting a chart. You also will learn about the details of adding text, legends, and gridlines.

BASIC PRINCIPLES OF CHART DESIGN

Chart design serves two functions, to communicate a single conclusion to the viewer effectively and to be aesthetically pleasing. Communication, however, is ultimately more important than aesthetic design. Communication is also a tricky goal. If you are not careful, you may use your chart as a drunk man uses a lightpost: for support rather than illumination. Be sure your facts are correct, then design your chart to emphasize your conclusions.

Try, as much as possible, to keep a chart simple. Use a single data series if possible, using multiple charts as necessary. If the conclusion depends on showing the relationship of two series, a scatter chart (see "Types of Charts") may be simpler than a chart with two series charted independently. The amount of data on a chart often depends on how it is used. Overheads must be very simple, as the audience generally has little time to see the chart and absorb its message. People who view charts frequently can usually handle a complex one if it is designed properly and is in a printed form that can be digested at leisure.

By taking aesthetics into consideration, you can ensure that a chart catches the reader's attention. This is important for busy people who are information-overloaded and need to see your conclusion quickly.

Keep a chart balanced and use good contrast. Keep a consistent font (don't use one font for the *y* axis and another for the *x* axis) and don't use too many different fonts on a graph. Remember that contrast is often lost when you try to print a color chart on a black and white printer; use patterns to help give the proper contrast.

TYPES OF CHARTS

Excel can create any of 68 types of charts. Your selection should depend upon what you are trying to communicate. Charts can be divided into six general categories:

- **Column graphs** are useful for representing quantitative information, particularly for making comparisons between groups of data. Figure 18.1 shows an example of a column graph
- **Bar graphs** are the same as column graphs, except that they are rotated 90 degrees. The categories are on the vertical axis and the values are on the horizontal axis. Figure 20.1 shows a bar graph that is used to compare sales-forecast figures with actual sales
- **Line graphs** are useful for describing and comparing numerical information, especially for showing trends or changes over time. Figure 20.2 shows a line graph that

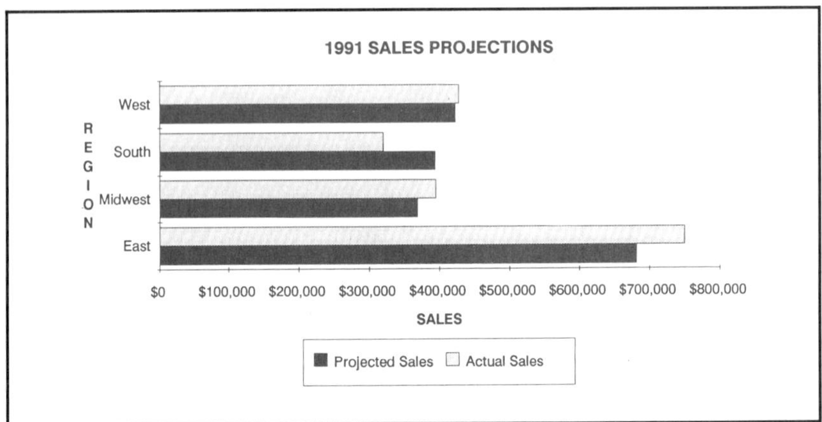

Figure 20.1: A bar graph

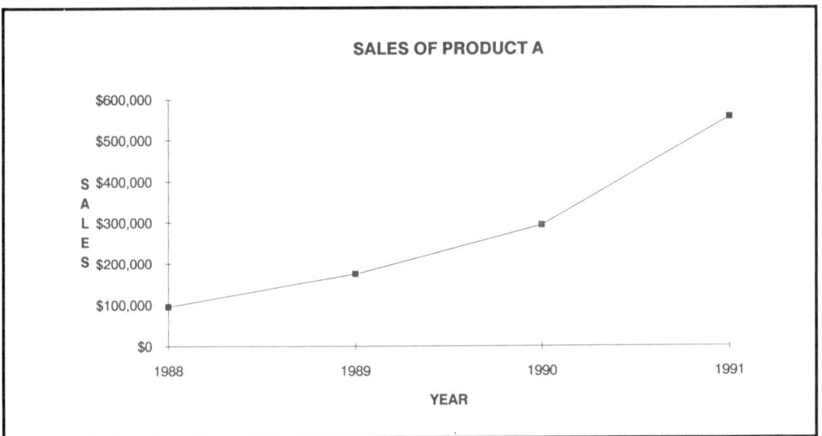

Figure 20:2: A line graph

indicates the growth in sales of a product over a period of time

- **Pie charts** help to show the relationship of quantitative data as they relate to the whole. Figure 20.3 shows a pie chart created from the product A sales data
- **Area graphs** are useful for showing the relative importance of different data. Figure 20.4 shows an area graph that compares the sales of two products over time

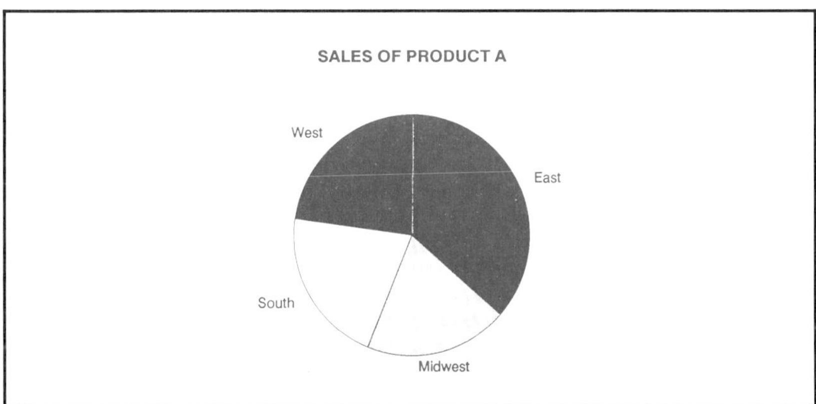

Figure 20:3: A pie chart

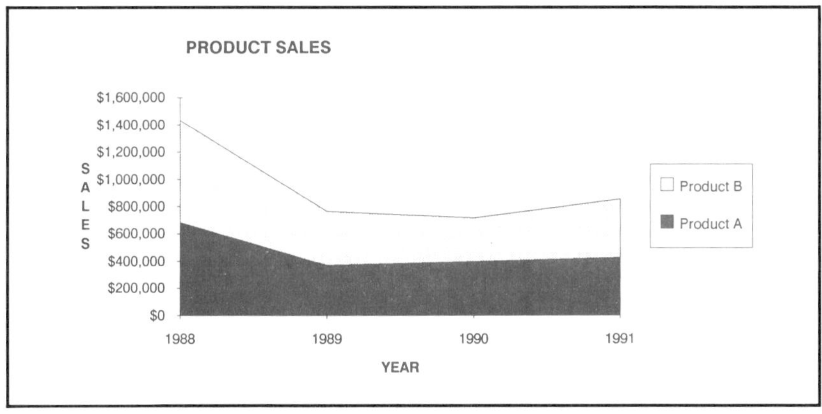

Figure 20:4: An area graph

- **Scatter (or XY) graphs** can show the relationship between two series. The individual data points are marked, but the relationship between these points is left to the observer. Figure 20.5 shows a scatter graph with points showing how disposable income affects sales

3.0 Excel also can draw three-dimensional charts. Figure 20.6 shows a three-dimensional column chart, and Figure 20.7 a three-dimensional area chart. These can give simple data relationships visual interest.

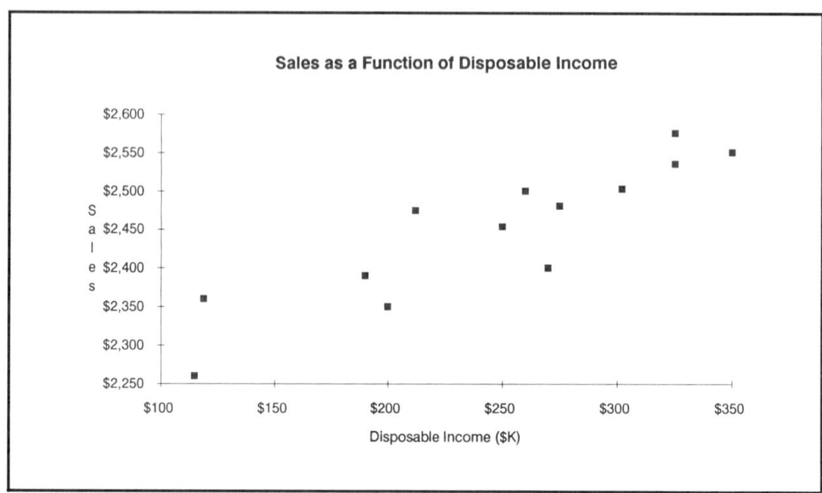

Figure 20:5: A scatter graph

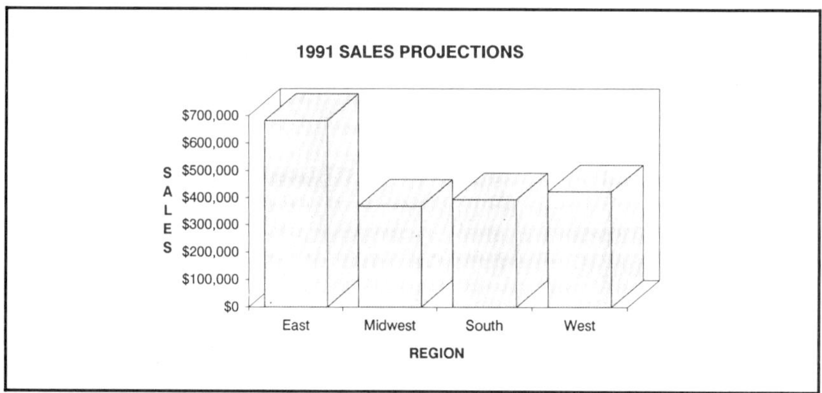

Figure 20.6: A three-dimensional column chart

SETTING THE TYPE

To select the type of chart, choose the general type from the Gallery menu, then choose the specific type from the dialog box.

Selecting the Specific Type

Each selection on the Gallery menu has a dialog box containing a selection of subtypes of that graph. Figure 20.8 shows the eight sub-

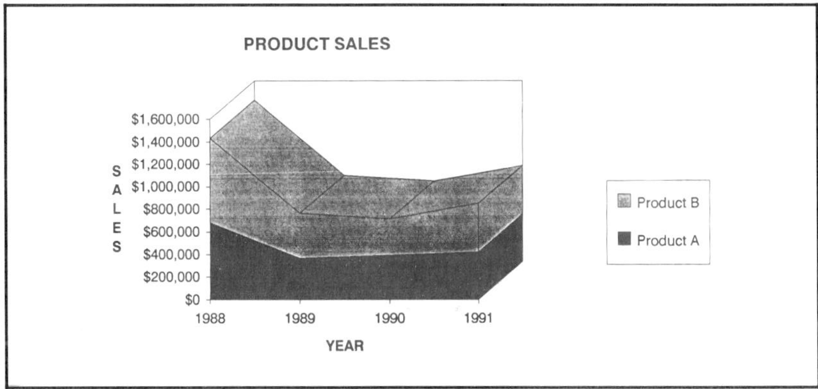

Figure 20.7: A three-dimensional area chart

types for the default column graph:

1. Simple column type, one column for each data point in the series
2. Simple column type, one column per data point, with each column a separate pattern or color
3. Stacked column, values shown proportional as percent of total
4. Overlapping columns. Overlap is set from the Main Chart command on the Format menu
5. 100 percent stacked, each series shown as a percent of the total for the data point

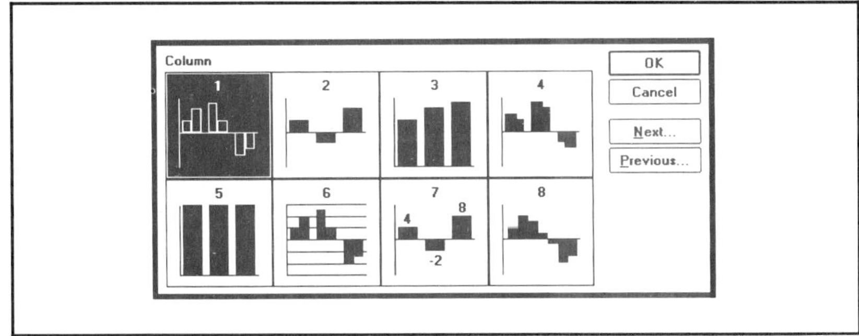

Figure 20.8: Types of column charts

6. Simple column chart with horizontal gridlines
7. Simple column chart with labels
8. Step chart without spaces between columns. Select Main Chart and choose Gap Width to set spacing (default value is 0)

The bar chart is similar, except that only seven options are available (the last column chart variation is not there) and the gridline option shows vertical gridlines.

The line chart has the following variations:

1. Lines and markers
2. Lines only
3. Markers only
4. Lines and markers with horizontal gridlines
5. Lines and markers with horizontal and vertical gridlines
6. Lines and markers with logarithmic scale and gridlines
7. Hi-lo chart with markers (requires two series)
8. Hi, low, close chart (requires three series)

The scatter chart has the following variations:

1. Markers only
2. Markers and lines
3. Markers with horizontal and vertical gridlines
4. Markers with semi-logarithmic gridlines (one axis logarithmic, one axis arithmetic)
5. Markers with log-log gridlines

The area chart has the following options:

1. Simple area chart
2. Area chart showing series as percent of total
3. Area chart with vertical gridlines

4. Area chart with horizontal and vertical gridlines
5. Area chart with labels

The pie chart options are detailed in "Working with Pie Charts."

The combination type permits you to mix two chart types in a chart, with the data series split evenly between the two types. You can choose the types from the Combination dialog box.

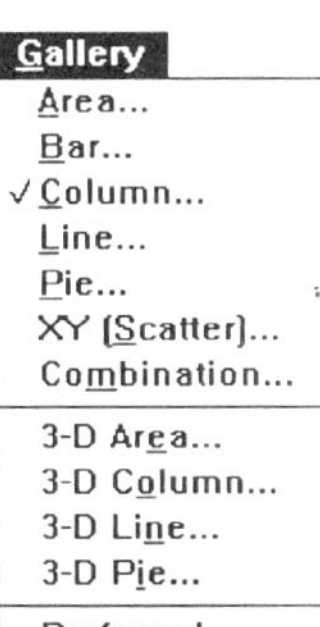

You may create a chart and then decide that the type of graph you selected does not suit the chart's purpose. This is not a problem—you will find it very easy to convert one type of Excel graph to another with only a few clicks of the mouse. You should feel free to experiment with the different types until you've created a chart that communicates what you intended.

Setting the Preferred Type

Gallery
Area...
Bar...
✓Column...
Line...
Pie...
XY (Scatter)...
Combination...
3-D Area...
3-D Column...
3-D Line...
3-D Pie...
Preferred
Set Preferred

If you wish, you can set a preferred chart type that will be used each time you create a chart. By default, Excel draws a column chart; in all examples in this book, the first graph is a column graph. To change the preferred type, first set the active chart to the desired preferred type. Then open the Gallery menu and choose Set Preferred.

After you've selected a chart type as your preferred type, you can still select that type from the Gallery menu, just as you would any other type. You may find it useful to set a preferred type if you are going to alter your chart, but may want to switch back to the earlier type. Before you change the type, save the current one as the preferred type. Then if you need to switch back, select the preferred type from the Gallery menu. This way, you won't have to remember which of the 68 chart types was used for the original chart.

CHART PRESENTATION FEATURES

Excel offers you many options that you can use to improve the appearance of your charts. You can add text at any point in the chart, control the font and size of the text and values, add arrows to emphasize parts of a chart, add titles to axes, change the legend position, and add gridlines. In this section, you'll practice using each of these features on the column chart that shows the projected and actual sales values from the Sales worksheet.

Start with a new chart. Open the Sales worksheet, select A6 to C9 (see Figure 20.9), and press F11 (or choose New Chart on the File menu).

To utilize most of the commands mentioned in this chapter, you need a mouse. For systems without a mouse, use the Move and Size commands on the Format menu to move and resize objects.

WORKING WITH COLOR

Excel makes it easy to change the colors of your charts. With the chart selected, open the Format menu and choose Patterns. Set the foreground color by clicking Foreground in the Area section. Set the background pattern and Border by clicking Pattern and Border respectively.

WORKING WITHOUT COLOR

If you have a color monitor, you know how dazzling a colorful chart can look. If you are in the likely situation of printing charts on a black and white printer, however, you need to design your chart with this in mind. This means carefully using patterns to differentiate data series and choosing symbols for data points.

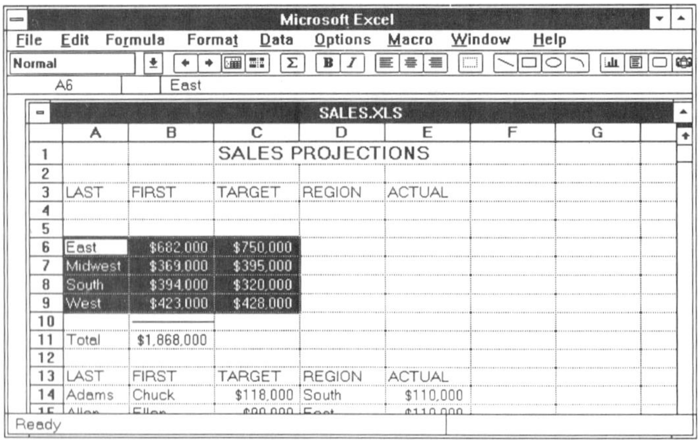

Figure 20.9: Selecting the chart range

For the column chart used so far, follow this procedure:

1. Choose a column for the first data series.
2. Open the Format menu and choose Patterns (see Figure 20.10).
3. Set the area foreground color to black. (This sets the color to Custom.)
4. Set the Pattern as desired. For the first, you might use a solid fill.
5. Click OK.
6. Choose the second data series and set it the same way.

The resulting chart is shown as Figure 20.11.

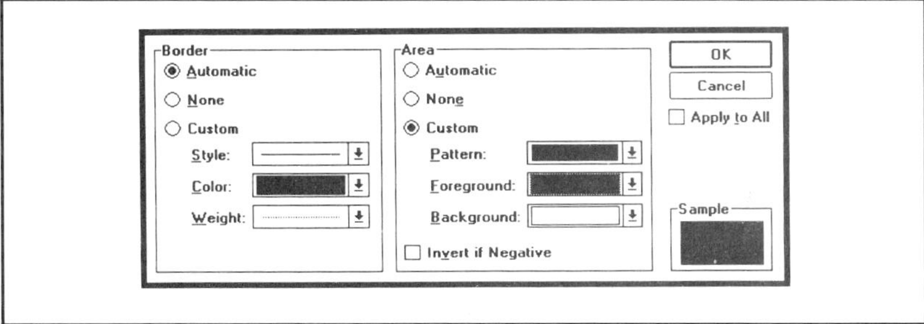

Figure 20.10: Formatting for black and white printing

WORKING WITH TEXT

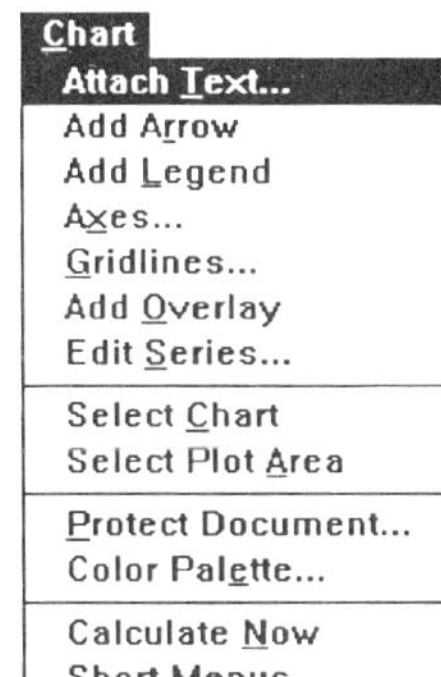

You can add text to any part of a graph. If text is added to a predefined area (axis, data series, data point, or title), it is called *attached text* because it is connected to that specific area. Text that is not associated with any particular part of a graph is called *unattached text.*

Adding a Title

Add a title to your chart as attached text:

1. Open the Chart menu and choose Attach Text.
2. When the Attach Text dialog box appears, select the area to which the text is to be attached. Because we will add a title

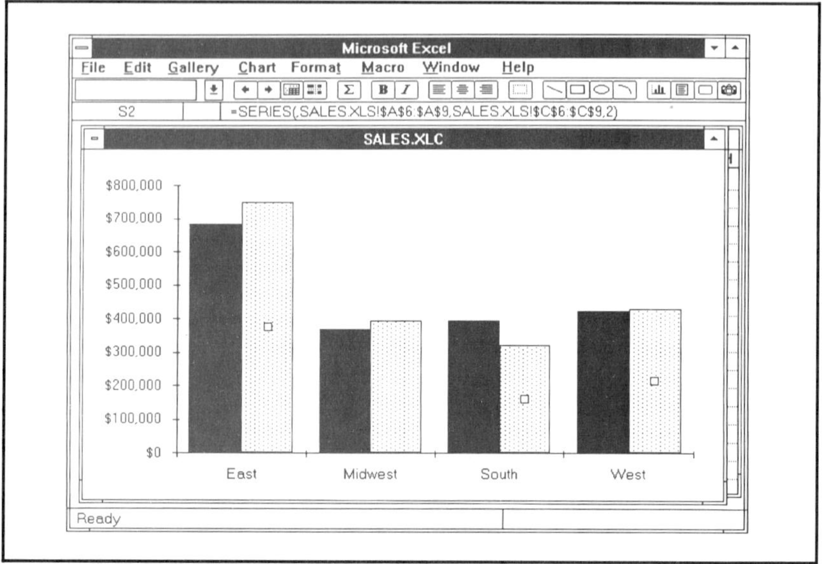

Figure 20.11: The chart after adding patterns

first, choose Chart Title and click OK. There will now be a marker on the chart where the text is to be entered.

3. Enter the text from the keyboard. It will be entered into the formula bar and you can edit it just as you would edit any formula. Enter**1991 SALES PROJECTIONS**.
4. Click the Enter box or press the Enter key. The title will now be displayed on the chart, as shown in Figure 20.12.

Another way to add a title to a chart of a single data series is to add it as a header to the data series in the worksheet. For the Sales worksheet, this would mean cell B5. We can't use that here, however, as it is used for the Table formula. Keep this idea in mind, however, as it is a good way to provide a title from the worksheet. When charting, be sure to select the cell with the title as a part of the charting range.

Adding Unattached Text

Add a subtitle to the chart as unattached text:

1. Click anywhere in the chart outside the title area. Type the subtitle **Target and Actual Sales by Region** on the keyboard. It appears in the formula bar and can be edited.

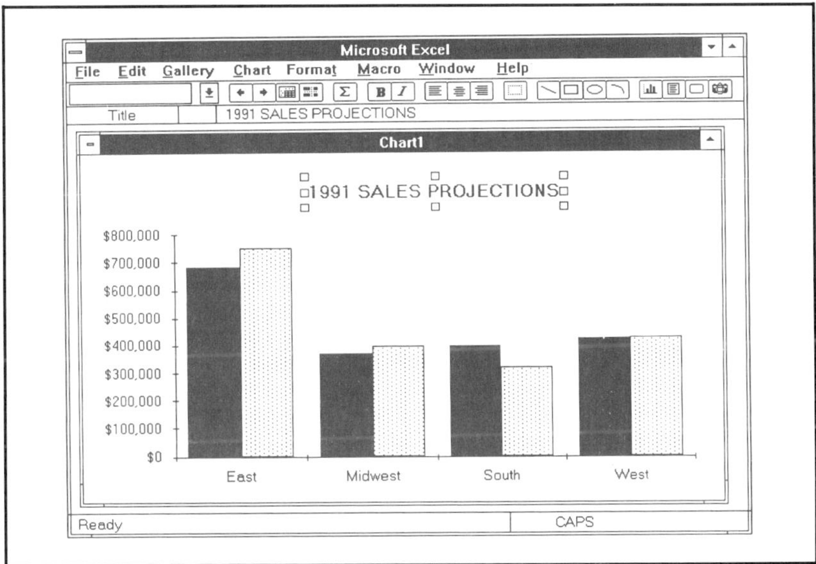

Figure 20.12: Adding the title to the chart

2. Press the Enter key or click the Enter box. The text will be entered approximately in the center of the chart with little boxes (“handles”) around it.
3. Click the text and drag it to a place right below the title. The chart should now look like Figure 20.13.

Unattached text is useful for adding text boxes to arrows. Using the Patterns option on the Format menu, you can add a box (border) around the text. You will see an example of this when we discuss adding arrows.

Adding Axis Titles

You can use the same basic procedure to add a title to either or both axes, as you did in Chapter 18. Figure 18.9 shows how axis titles appear on a graph. To add them, open the Chart menu and choose Attach Text. When the dialog box appears, select the axis that will be titled. Then enter the title from the keyboard and click the Enter box or press enter. Enter **SALES** as the *y*-axis label and **REGION** as the *x*-axis label.

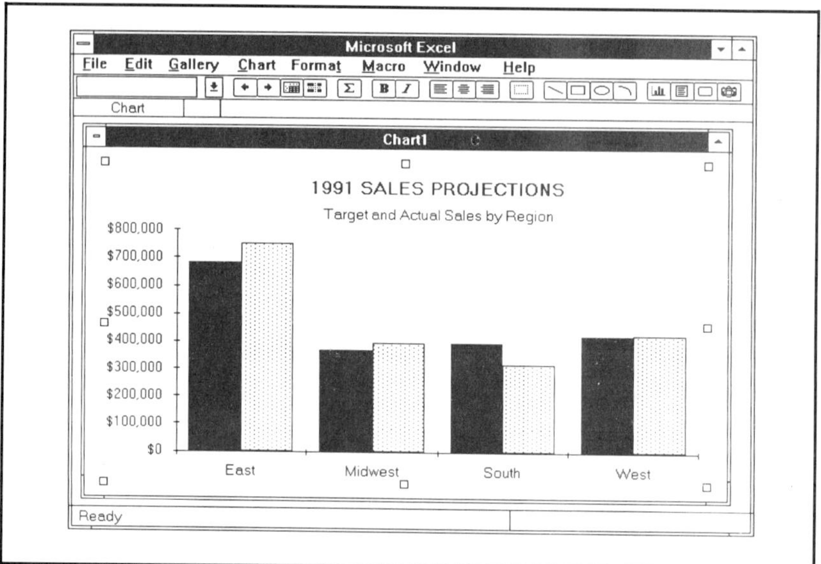

Figure 20.13: Adding the subtitle to the chart

Adding Text to Data Points

You can add text to data points as easily as to other objects. This is a good way to label pie and area charts. To add the label, hold down the Ctrl key and click the data point. Then choose Attach Text from the Chart menu. Choose Series and Data Point and click OK. Type the text and press Enter.

Editing Text

You can easily edit attached or unattached text. Click the text and it will appear in the formula bar. Edit the text there and press Enter to place the edited version on the chart.

Positioning Text

You can position text as you wish, aligning it and setting the orientation. Let's change the orientation of the *y*-axis label:

1. Select the *y*-axis label.
2. Open the Format menu and choose Text.

3. In the dialog box, choose the left-most orientation (see Figure 20.14) and click OK.

You can use this same command to set alignment of unattached text on the worksheet, such as in a text box for an arrow.

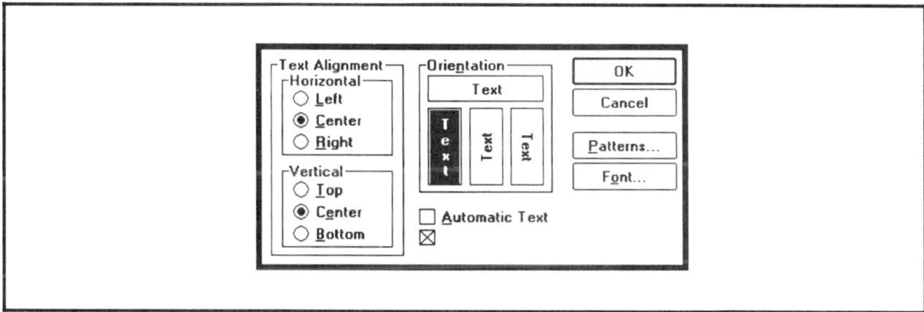

Figure 20.14: Setting the text orientation

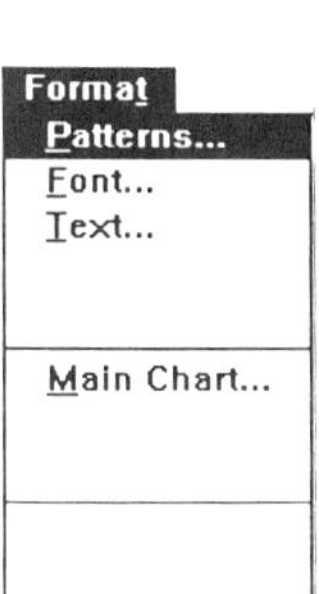

Setting Text Patterns

You can set the pattern of the text: its color, pattern, and border. This enables you, for example, to put a title in a shadow box.

To set the pattern, select the text and then choose Patterns on the Format menu. Choose the desired options in the Patterns dialog box (see Figure 20.10).

Removing Attached and Unattached Text

To remove attached or unattached text, select the text and press Backspace and Enter. For now, leave all text in place.

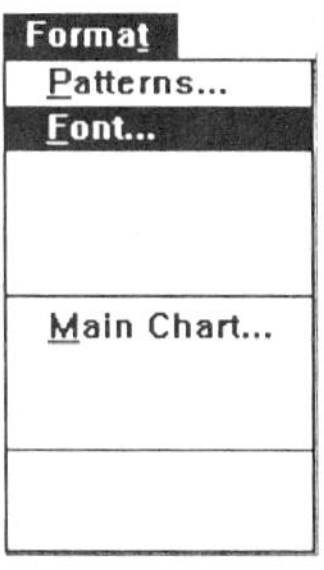

Formatting Text

Excel lets you change the font, size, and style of any text on your chart.

To format both attached and unattached text, first select the text, then use the Font command on the Format menu. Follow these steps to format the title and subtitle of your Sales chart:

1. Click the title, which is the text to be formatted.
2. Open the Format menu and choose Font.

3. When the dialog box shown in Figure 20.15 is displayed, choose Helv, 12, and Bold (this may be the default on your system). Then click OK.
4. Select the subtitle, then select Font again. Choose Helv, 10, and Italic. Click OK.

Your chart should now look like Figure 20.16.

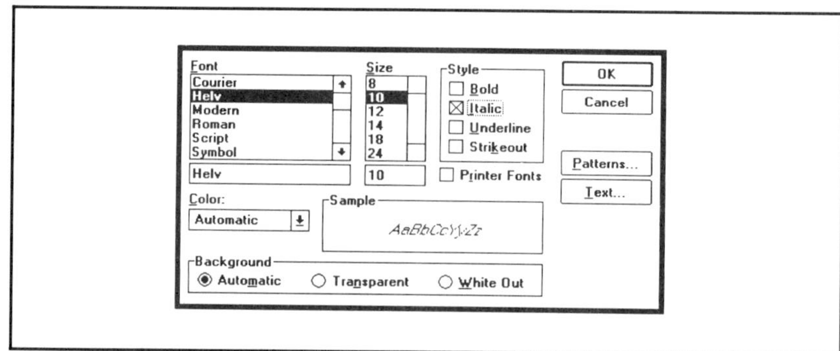

Figure 20.15: The Font dialog box.

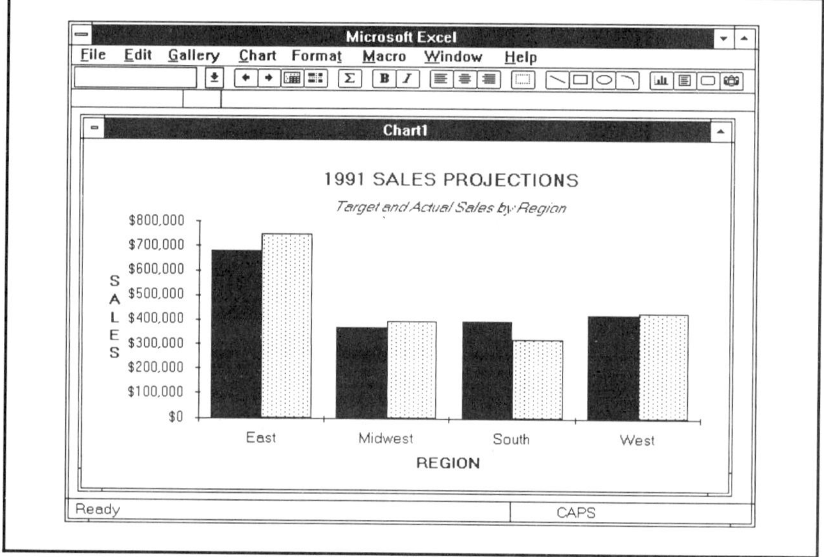

Figure 20.16: The chart after formatting

ADDING AND MOVING LEGENDS

A legend is used to define the symbols and labels in the chart. On a pie chart, it defines the categories. On other charts, it defines the data series. Once you've added a legend to a chart, you can move it and reformat it.

Before adding a legend, be sure that each data series has a name, as the name is used in the legend. To name a series, click it and select Edit Series from the Chart menu. Type the name in the Name box and click OK. In this case, name the first data series **Projected Sales** and the second **Actual Sales**. At this time, the names will not show on the chart.

Chart
Attach Text...
Add Arrow
Add Legend
Axes...
Gridlines...
Add Overlay
Edit Series...
Select Chart
Select Plot Area
Protect Document...
Color Palette...
Calculate Now
Short Menus

To add the legend, simply open the Chart menu and choose Add Legend. Excel will place the legend at the right of the plot area and resize the graph to make room for the legend. The legend shows the markers and names for each data series.

You can readjust the window size if necessary by dragging the legend handles. To reposition the legend, use the Legend command on the Format menu.

Now add a legend to the chart:

1. Open the Chart menu and choose Add Legend. Select the legend.
2. Choose Format on the menu, then choose Legend. When the Legend dialog box is displayed, choose Bottom to move the legend to the bottom of the chart, then click OK.

The last thing you should do with your legend is format it:

1. Click the legend area on the chart to select the legend if it is not already selected.
2. Open the Format menu and select Font.
3. When the dialog box (see Figure 20.15) appears, select Helv, 10, and Italic from the formatting options. Click OK.

Once the legend is created, you can drag it to any chart location. The legend adjusts as necessary to fit areas and can overlay portions of the chart if you wish.

If you want to delete a displayed legend, open the Chart menu and select Delete Legend. (But keep the legend for now.)

FORMATTING GRIDLINES

Gridlines appear on a chart as horizontal and vertical lines at regular intervals in the plot area. They help you to determine the value of a data point. You can add major gridlines (at tick marks), or minor gridlines (between tick marks), or both, and control their thickness.

To add gridlines to a chart, follow these steps:

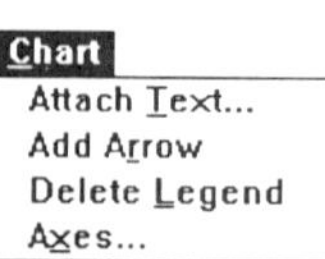

1. Open the Chart menu and choose Gridlines.
2. When the Gridlines dialog box is displayed, choose the type of gridlines you want, then click OK. For the Sales chart, choose Value (Y) Axis: Major Gridlines.

To control the weight of the lines, follow these steps:

1. Click a horizontal or vertical gridline.
2. Open the Format menu and choose Patterns.
3. Select the line weight, color, and style in the Patterns dialog box. Then click OK.

The weight selection in the Patterns dialog box applies to the gridlines, axis, or arrow selected before you invoked the command. Figure 20.17 shows the chart at this point.

FORMATTING AXES

You format either axis. The Scale command on the Format menu lets you control the tick marks, order of the categories, number of categories, scaling, and zero crossing of an axis. To do these things, select the axis, open the Format menu, and choose Scale. You will see a different dialog box, depending on whether you are formatting the *y* axis or the *x* axis.

(Earlier, Figure 20.5 showed a scatter chart with the axis beginning at $100, not the default 0. The Scale command was used to set this.)

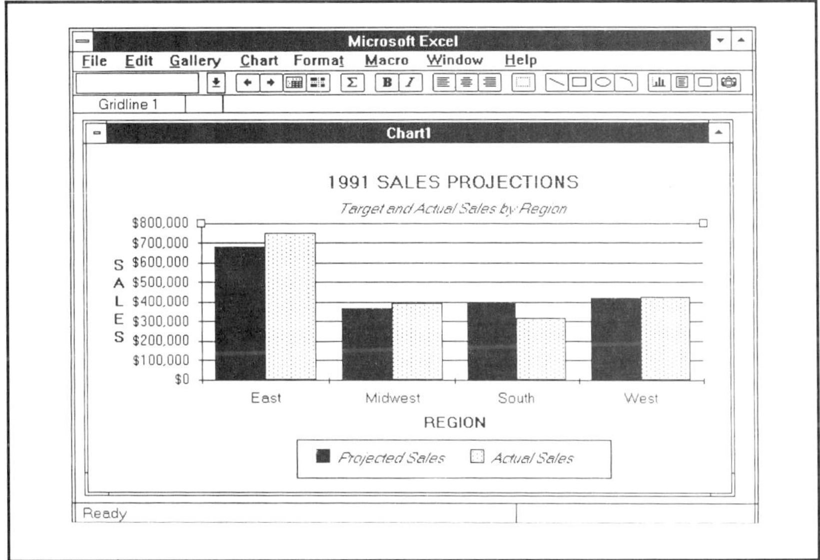

Figure 20.17: Chart with gridlines

You also can change the line weight of an axis. First click the axis, then open the Format menu and select Patterns. When the Patterns dialog box appears, click the line weight and style that you want.

To change the font, size, or style of the tick-mark labels on the axes, click the label on the axis and use the Font command on the Format menu. When the dialog box appears, select the desired format options, then click OK. To change the format of an axis label, click the label, then follow the same procedure.

To turn off the axes (but leave the category and value headings) open the Chart menu and choose Axes. When you see the Axes dialog box, click the × by Category (X) Axis and Value (Y) Axis to remove them from the chart.

FORMATTING A DATA SERIES

You can select a new pattern for a data series, stack two data series, and overlap bar and column charts.

To change the data series marker pattern, select the data series, open the Format menu, and choose Patterns. You'll see a dialog box that gives you your choices for patterns. Select the new pattern and click OK.

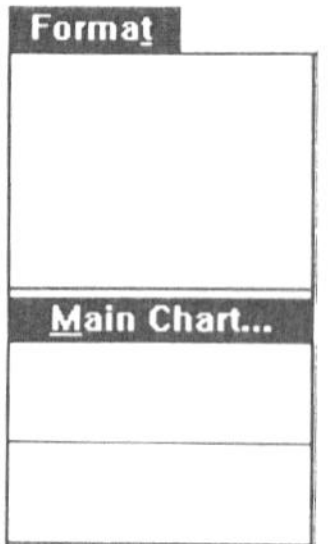

To stack or overlap data series, select the series to set and choose Main Chart or Overlay from the Format menu, depending on whether the series is defined as the main chart or an overlay. The dialog box shown in Figure 20.18 appears. Which items are active depends upon the type of chart you are using. This figure shows the dialog box for a column chart. From this you can adjust the gap between the columns and how the series columns overlay each other. The three-dimensional options control the gap depth and chart depth.

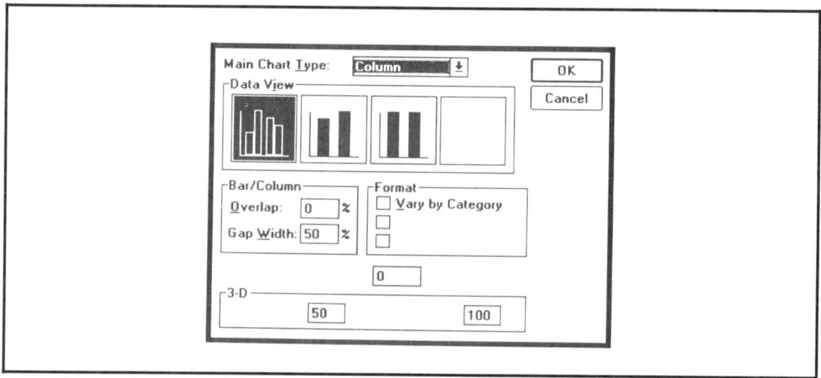

Figure 20.18: Controlling data-series spacing and overlap

ADDING ARROWS

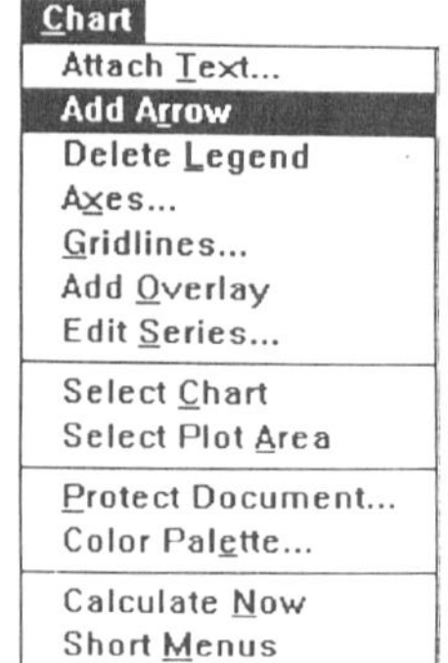

Another one of Excel's presentation features is the ability to add arrows to emphasize any part of a chart. The basic strategy is to utilize the Add Arrow option on the Chart menu to add the arrow, format it, then create an accompanying text box.

Add an arrow to the Sales chart as follows:

1. Open the Chart menu and choose Add Arrow. An arrow will appear on the chart, as shown in Figure 20.19.
2. Position the arrow as you want it (see Figure 20.20). You can resize the arrow by dragging the black box at either end. Move the arrow by clicking it in the middle and dragging it.
3. Use the Patterns command on the Format menu to change the width of the arrow line and the type of arrowhead.

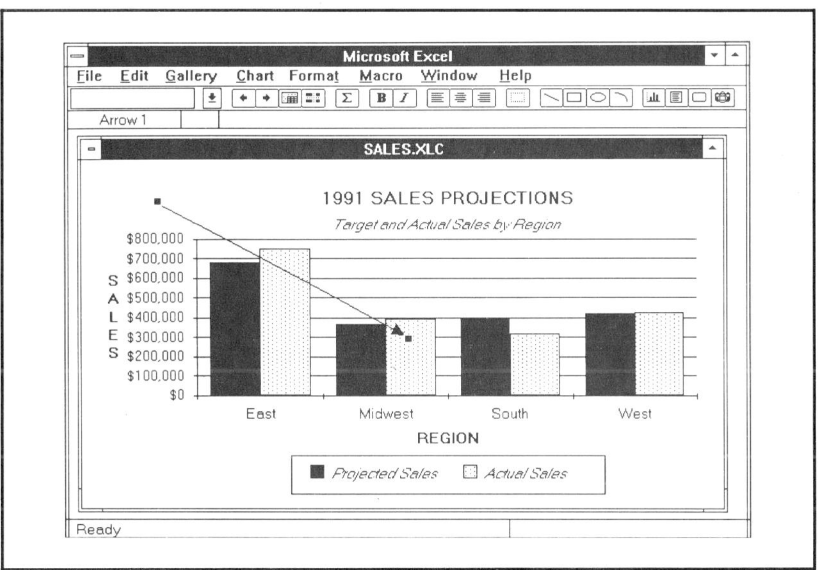

Figure 20.19: Adding an arrow

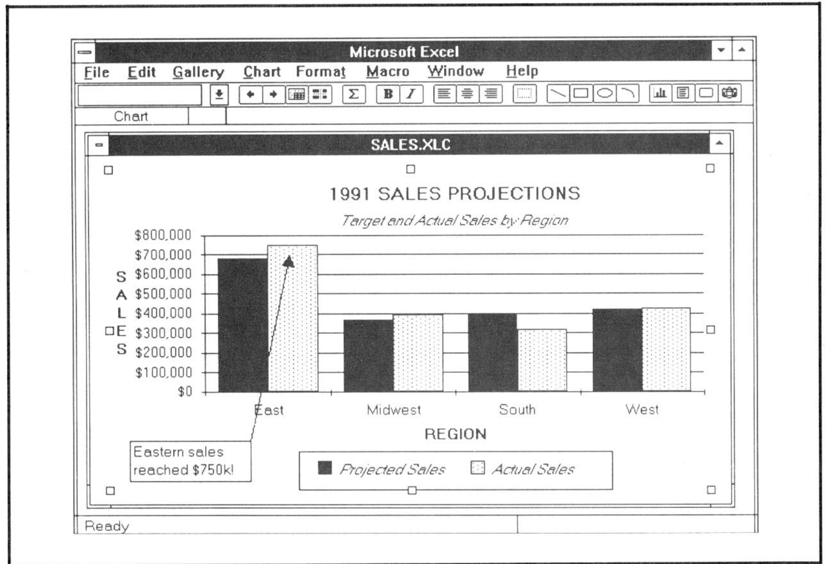

Figure 20.20: Using an arrow for emphasis

4. Type the text as unattached text and position it by dragging. Click the chart, enter **Eastern sales reached $750k!**. Drag the text to the lower left of the window and resize the box by dragging the handles. Word-wrapping is automatic.
5. With the text selected, select the Text option to align it, Font to set the font, and Patterns to add the border (all on the Format menu).

You can repeat this procedure and add as many arrows as you want to any chart.

To delete an arrow, click the arrow, open the Chart menu, and choose Delete Arrow. To delete the text, select it and backspace over the text. Use Patterns to turn the border off.

WORKING WITH PIE CHARTS

A pie chart is different from other chart types since it graphs a single data series *only*. If you select more than one data series on a worksheet and try to create a pie chart, only the first series will be plotted. The legend lists categories instead of data-series titles.

SETTING THE TYPE

The pie chart type is set like any other type. Be sure only a single series is selected, then choose Pie from the Gallery menu. Figure 20.21 shows the displayed pie chart options.

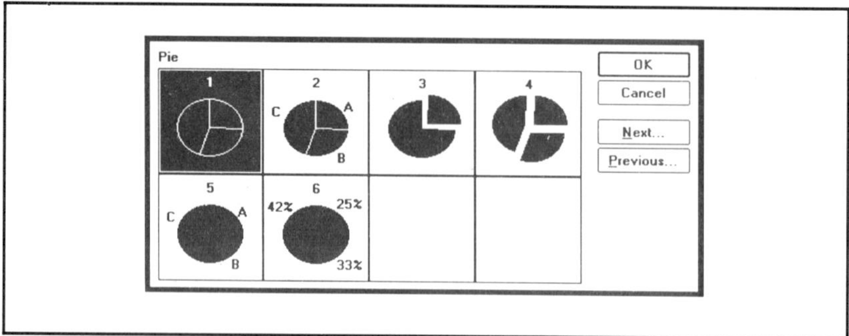

Figure 20.21: The pie chart options

These options can be described as follows:

1. Simple pie chart
2. All wedges have the same pattern and color, and are labeled by category
3. First wedge exploded
4. All wedges exploded
5. Simple pie with category labels
6. Simple pie with values labeled as a percent of the total

You can add custom labels by entering them as unattached text.

MOVING PIE WEDGES

When you *explode* a wedge in a pie chart, you separate it from the rest of the pie, as shown in Figure 20.22. To do this, simply select the wedge and drag it to the desired location.

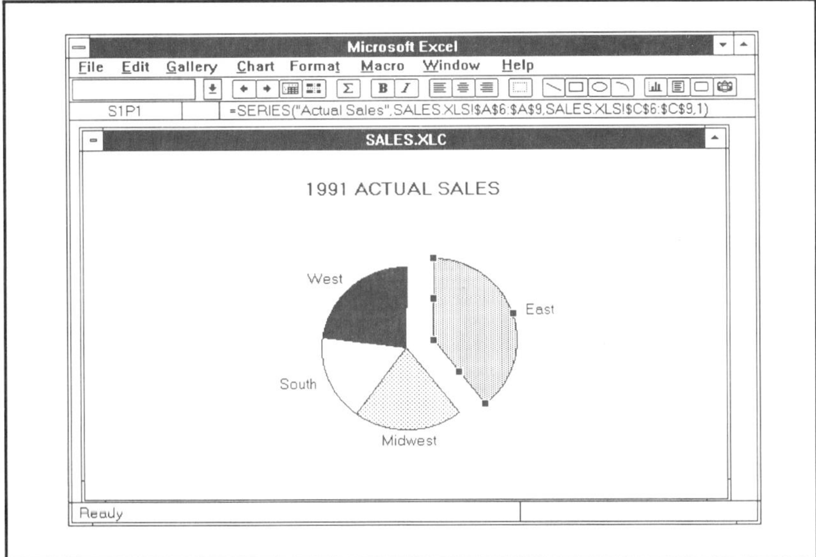

Figure 20.22: A pie chart with an exploded wedge

EXPLORING THREE-DIMENSIONAL CHARTS

3.0

Excel supports three dimensional charting, which is useful for making charts that seem to leap right out of the page. Be sure your new Sales chart is saved, then try a little three-dimensional experimenting with your chart to see how you like it.

To convert the chart to three-dimensional, choose 3-D Column from the Gallery menu. Figure 20.23 shows the resulting chart (you may have to format the *y*-axis label or set the data series pattern again).

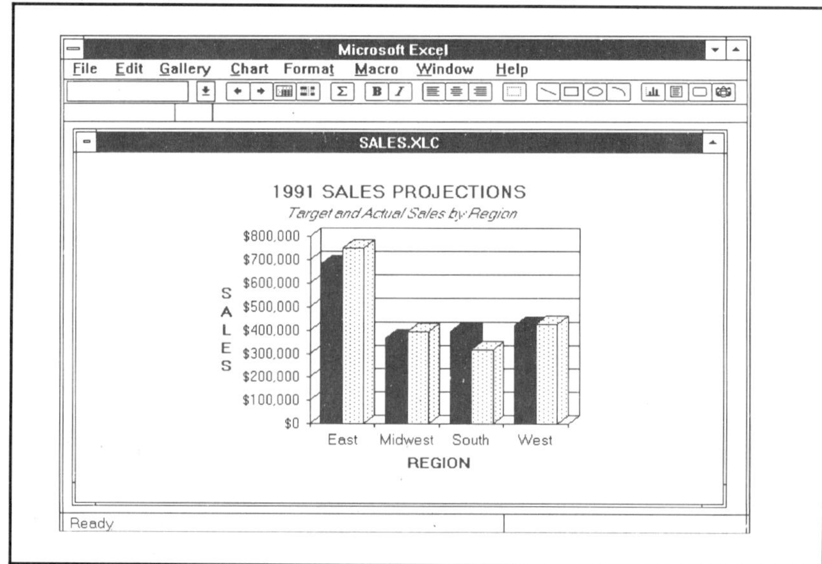

Figure 20.23: The Sales chart as a three-dimensional column chart

To adjust the way you view the chart, choose 3-D View from the Format menu. The available items depend on the type of three-dimensional chart you have. Figure 20.24 shows the displayed dialog box.

- **Elevation:** to change the elevation, click the arrows at the left or enter a value to the Elevation box. This controls your viewpoint of the graph. A value of 0 puts you at eye-level

- **Rotation**: click the rotation arrows or enter a new value in the Rotation box to rotate the view (0 is head-on, 90 is sideways)
- **Perspective**: controls the perspective, making the year plane of the graph smaller
- **Right Angle Axes**: click on to place the axes at right angles (giving you an oblique view). Click off to add perspective to the axes
- **Height**: controls the height of the *z* axis relative to the *x* and *y* axes. It is measured as a percentage of the *x*-axis (base) length. Enter a value greater than 100 to make the chart taller, less than 100 to make it wider

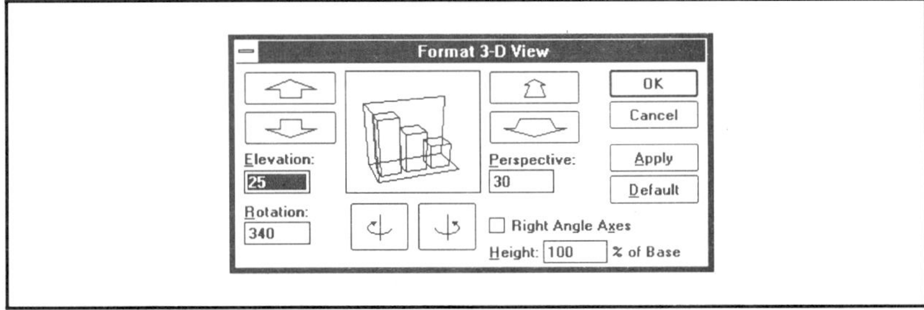

Figure 20.24: The 3-D View dialog box

DESIGNING PICTURE CHARTS

3.0

Excel permits you to import graphics and use them as pictures in creating chart markers. The graphic image for the chart is imported through the Clipboard. For best results, import using the metafile format. This means creating the graphic with software that can create such an image, such as Arts & Letters (Computer Support Corporation). To show how this works, we will use a simplified chart with a single data series (see Figure 20.25). Here is the general procedure:

1. Create the graph in Excel (shown here as a column chart).
2. Minimize Excel and start the graphics program.

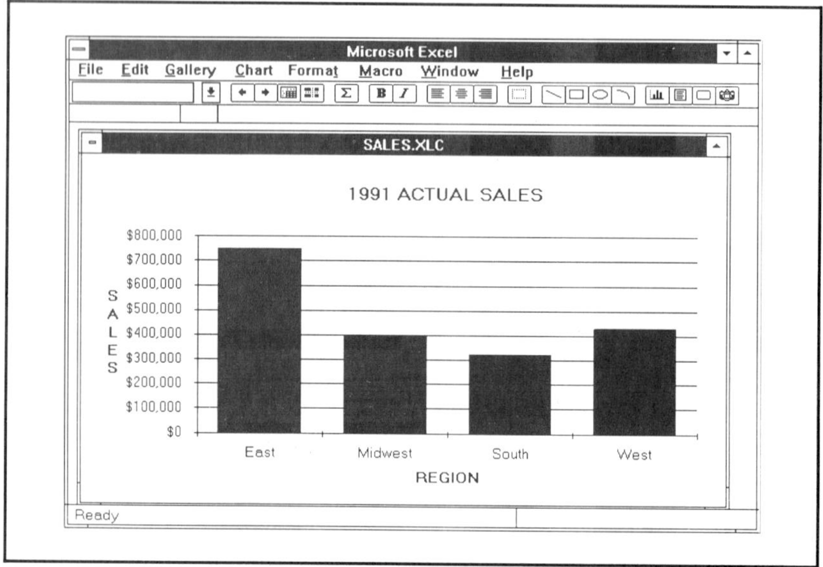

Figure 20.25: The starting chart

3. Create the symbol and copy it to the Clipboard.
4. Minimize the graphics program and restore Excel.
5. Select the data-series marker you wish to change.
6. Choose Paste from the Edit menu. The marker will change to the picture (see Figure 20.26).
7. To change to a stacked marker, use the Pattern command on the Format menu and choose Stacked (see Figure 20.27).

TIPS FOR CHARTING

To recapitulate, here are some basic charting tips:

- Keep charts simple. Use a single data series whenever possible
- If you have a problem fitting a chart on a page, reduce the font (6 point Modern is a good small font). An alternative is to use the Page Setup command on the File menu to change the margins or orientation

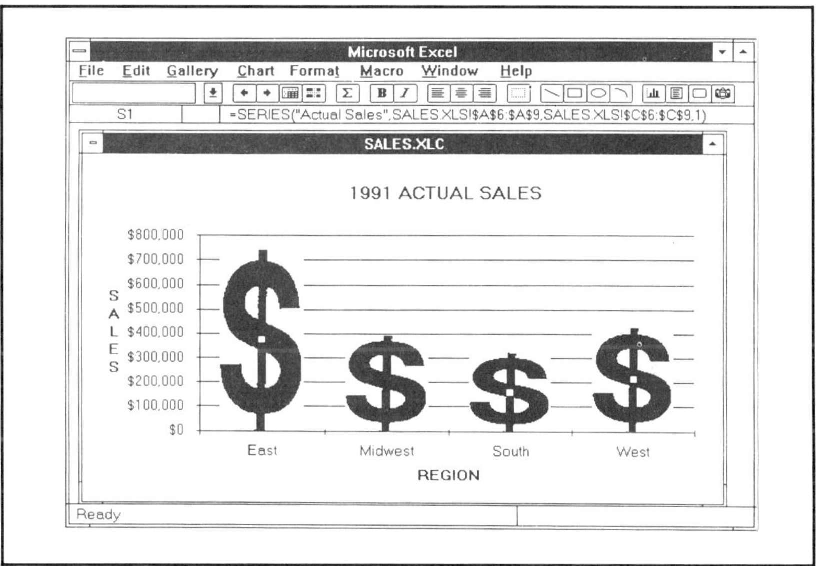

Figure 20.26: Pasting the stretched marker picture

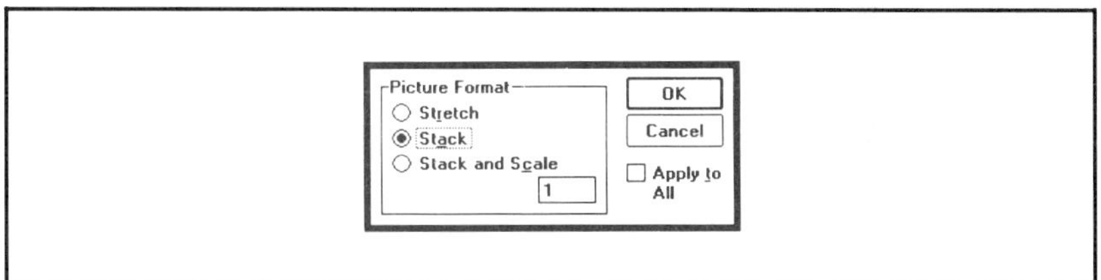

Figure 20.27: Changing to a stacked marker pattern

- Use language that the viewer can understand (e.g., avoid abbreviations unless generally known)
- Remember how the chart will be used—i.e., as an overhead, with text in a document, on the worksheet, or as a stand-alone chart. (Overheads, for example, need larger fonts and thicker lines than other printed charts.)
- Choose the proper chart type. (A line chart, for example, would be inappropriate for comparing sales by region.)
- Set enough contrast to distinguish between data series

VI

Practical Solutions with Excel

NOW THAT YOU'VE GAINED SOME BASIC EXPERIENCE with Excel's features, you are probably interested in using the program to solve problems. Although the application possibilities for Excel are far too numerous for this book, Part VI shows you four of the most common types of applications: data conversion between programs, inventory control, financial management, and trend analysis. You will also be introduced to three of Excel's utilities: the Lotus 1-2-3 Macro Translator, Q + E (which allows you to use Excel with external databases), and the Solver.

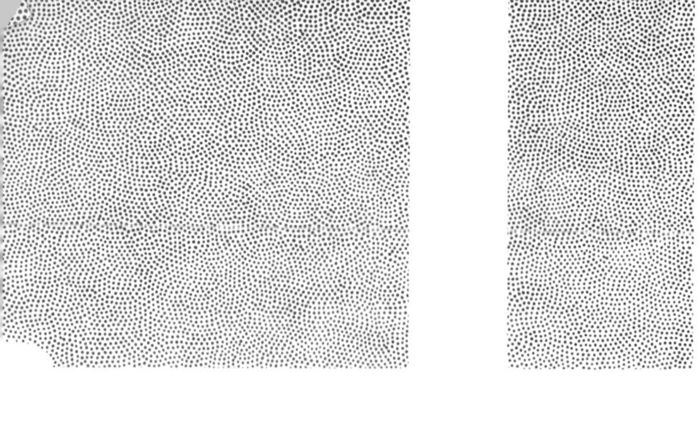

21 Using Excel with Other Software

NOW THAT YOU'VE BECOME FAMILIAR WITH EXCEL, you may want to use it with other software products, such as other spreadsheet programs, word processors, and database managers. You can transfer data from most of these programs to Excel, and vice versa. With some programs, you also can create dynamic links between the application and Excel.

Here are some typical reasons for using Excel with other software:

- You can insert an Excel worksheet or chart into a word-processed document created with Microsoft Word for Windows and *hot-link* the worksheet to the document, so that if it changes, the document will reflect those changes automatically
- If you have several Lotus 1-2-3 worksheets, you can print them with Excel's presentation features and have the print macros in those worksheets converted automatically

- If you have a communications program that runs under Windows, you can link the incoming data to an Excel stock-analysis worksheet automatically
- You can transfer an Excel worksheet you created at home on your Macintosh to an IBM PC you are using at work

The basic techniques for transferring data include using the Clipboard, file transfer using the File menu, creating links, and using embedded objects. This chapter will cover each of these, as well as describe a few related techniques, such as parsing data.

USING THE CLIPBOARD

You've already used the Clipboard to copy data within Excel. Now you can use it to transfer Excel to or from other Windows application programs running under Windows, such as Microsoft Word for Windows, PageMaker, and PowerPoint. You can transfer worksheet ranges, graphic objects, and charts. In addition, you can use the Clipboard to paste graphic objects, such as company logos, to your Excel documents.

Excel supports the following Clipboard formats:

ID	*FORMAT*
BIFF	Microsoft Excel file format
TEXT	Text, tab delimited
CSV	Comma-separated values
SYLK	Symbolic link format
WK1	Lotus 1-2-3 Release 2.0
DIF	Data interchange format
NATIVE	Embedded object
METAFILE	Metafile format (COPY PICTURE)
BITMAP	Bit-mapped format

Data transferred using the Clipboard is static; that is, if you paste some cells to a word-processor document, they won't change if the worksheet changes in the future. If the worksheet does change, you will have to paste the values in the word-processing document again.

COPYING DATA WITH THE CLIPBOARD

To copy a cell range on the worksheet to another application, first select the cell range, then use the Cut, Copy, or Copy Picture command on the Edit menu.

- **Cut** places a copy of the cell range in the Clipboard and removes it from the worksheet
- **Copy** copies the cell range from the worksheet to the Clipboard
- **Copy Picture** copies a picture of the current cell range to the Clipboard

Make the desired window in the destination application active and use the Edit Paste command to copy from the Clipboard to the destination application.

Using these commands with a chart is similar, except that you use the Select Chart command on the Chart menu to select the chart, *then* the Edit menu commands. After the cut or copy, you can run the Windows Clipboard program with the Run command on Excel's Control menu. The Clipboard will not show the data, but only a message about the size of the range in the Clipboard, such as *1R X 4C.* This would mean one row of four columns in the Clipboard (see Figure 21.1).

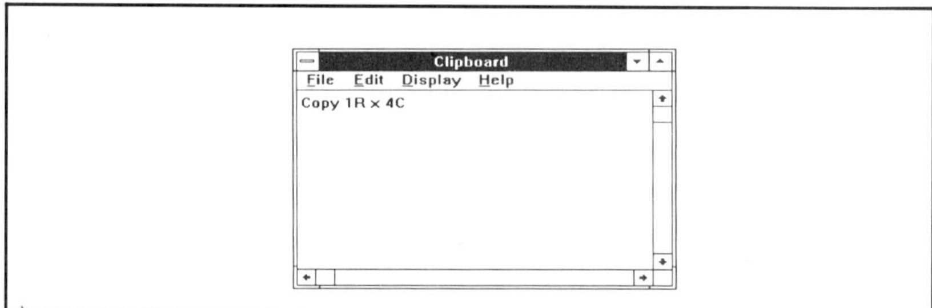

Figure 21.1: Viewing the Clipboard's contents

To use the Copy Picture command, hold down the Shift key and open the Edit menu. Now you'll see the Copy Picture option. A dialog box is then displayed (Figure 21.2 for a worksheet, Figure 21.3 for a chart). Select the desired option(s) and click OK. Copy Picture copies a picture of the selected range to the Clipboard. Viewing the Clipboard would *now* show a full image of the copied cells.

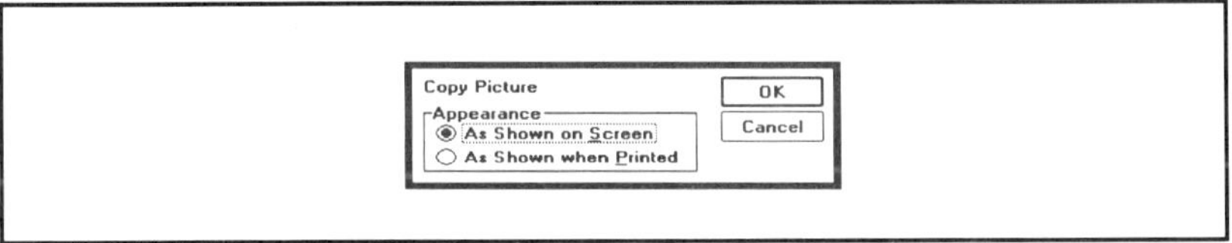

Figure 21.2: The Copy Picture dialog box for a worksheet

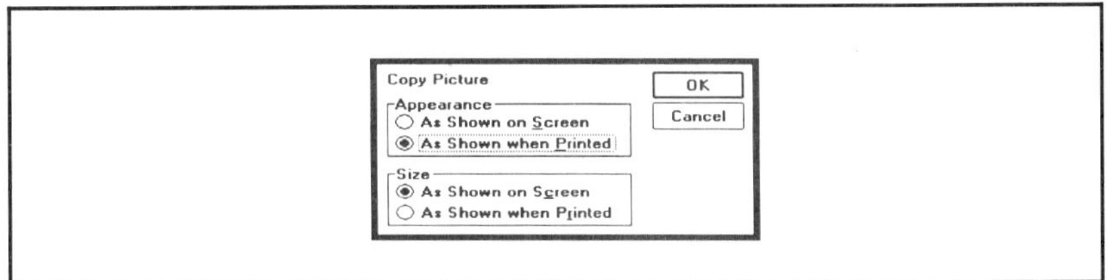

Figure 21.3: The Copy Picture dialog box for a chart

Copy Picture creates a Clipboard image in a metafile format, which has a higher resolution and quality than the Copy command does. This takes up more memory, however, and some applications cannot "receive" this type of image. You can see the difference by pasting both types of images of a chart to a worksheet and printing the worksheet. If an application cannot receive a metafile image, the Paste command of the destination program will be grayed and unavailable, even though the Clipboard has data. This will happen, for example, if you try to paste a metafile image to Windows Paintbrush.

COPYING GRAPHICS

You can copy graphics from other Windows applications to Excel, and vice versa. To copy an Excel object to another program, select the object and then use the Copy command. Switch to the destination program and select Paste.

To copy graphics to Excel (such as a company logo), use a graphics program to put the desired graphic in the Clipboard or the Windows Paintbrush program. To use Paintbrush, open the graphic in Paintbrush as a PCX file. Then select it and use Copy to place it in the Clipboard. Switch to Excel, select the cell for pasting, and use Paste. If the image is inverted, use the Paintbrush Pick menu to reorient the graphic before copying it.

If you have other graphic programs, such as Arts & Letters (Computer Support Corp.) or CorelDRAW (Corel Systems Corp.), you have a lot of flexibility in creating graphics and converting graphics for your Excel documents. Converter programs, such as HiJaak (Inset Systems, Inc.), permit you to convert graphic formats for Excel. Convert the format to PCX, then use Paintbrush to put the image in the Clipboard for Excel.

USING THE CLIPBOARD WITH DOS APPLICATIONS

You can also use the Clipboard with DOS applications when they are running under Windows. DOS applications run either in a window or full-screen mode. If running in a window mode, the familiar Control menu is available, which now also has an Edit option.

To copy to the Clipboard with the mouse, choose Mark from the Control menu, click the start of the area to copy, hold down the Shift key, and drag to select the entire area to copy. Then select Copy from the Control menu to copy it to the Clipboard where it can be pasted.

If you are running in a full-screen mode, press Alt-Spacebar to open the Control menu, then follow the directions for the window mode.

TRANSFERRING DATA USING THE FILE MENU COMMANDS

The File menu has several commands that are useful for transferring Excel worksheet data to or from standard DOS programs, where the Clipboard is limited. *Exporting from Excel* means moving data from Excel to another program. *Importing to Excel* means moving data from another program to Excel.

Excel supports the following file formats:

FORMAT	*DOCUMENT TYPE*
CSV	Comma-separated values
DBF 2	dBASE II
DBF 3	dBASE III
DBF 4	dBASE IV
DIF	Data interchange format (VisiCalc)
Normal	Excel Version 3 format
SYLK	Symbolic link (Microsoft Multiplan, older Excel versions)
Text	ANSI text for Windows, ASCII for OS/2, text for Macintosh
WK1	Lotus 1-2-3 Release 2
WKS	Lotus 1-2-3 Release 1, Lotus Symphony
WK3	Lotus 1-2-3 Release 3
Excel 2.X	Excel Version 2.X

TRANSFERRING EXCEL DATA TO ANOTHER PROGRAM

Use the following general procedure to transfer worksheet data to another program from Excel:

1. Open the File menu and choose Save As.
2. Enter the file name.
3. Click on Options.
4. Select the desired transfer option in the drop-down list of the dialog box.
5. Choose OK to return to the Open dialog box. The proper file extension is now in the file name box.
6. Choose OK.

Copy a worksheet from Excel to a word processor by first saving the Excel worksheet data in text form. Then use the word processor to read this file. When the worksheet is saved in text form, each row becomes a line with the columns separated by tabs. Formatted data is converted to text as it appears on the screen.

When copying from Excel to a dBASE file, first select the database range on the worksheet, open the Data menu, and choose Set Database. Be sure to select the field names. Excel creates a dBASE file with the column titles as the field names. Any existing database file with that name will be overwritten. Be sure to use column titles of ten characters or less, as dBASE is limited to ten characters in a field name. You also must be aware of, and work within, any other dBASE constraints for the version you are using.

TRANSFERRING DATA FROM A PROGRAM TO EXCEL

To read a file of another program to Excel, follow this procedure:

1. Open the File menu and choose Open.
2. Change the file name specifier to *.* (or use the file extension you wish).
3. Choose the correct path.
4. Select the file name in the file list-box and click OK.

The file will load into Excel, which automatically converts the data as necessary. (Excel is smart enough to recognize the various formats.) As the file loads, Excel displays, in the upper left, the format it is reading and the percent of the file read so far.

Before you transfer data from a word processor to Excel, the word-processed file must be in the correct format: each line should end with a carriage return and columns should be separated by tabs. Save the word-processed data as text using the option in your word processor that saves the file in an ASCII or unformatted form. Numeric data in the word processor file will automatically be in a formatted numeric form (for example, $3.43 in the text file will be a numeric $3.43 on the worksheet).

To load text data, use the Open command on the File menu and select Text in the dialog box. Select the delimiting character (command or tab). Select or enter the name of the file to open and click OK. Once the data is loaded, you can add empty rows or columns to move the starting location of the data.

CREATING DYNAMIC LINKS

Another method of transferring data between Windows applications is to use the Windows Dynamic Data Exchange (DDE) facility. This creates *hot links* between the source document with the data and the destination document. For example, if you paste worksheet data into a word-processor document using DDE, any further edits in the worksheet would be reflected in the document. As another example, a communications program could download stock information while you are using an Excel worksheet to analyze it. With dynamic links, the stock prices are in a data area that is common to the communications program and Excel.

Excel provides two methods of supporting DDE. One is with the use of remote references, the second is with the use of macros.

To create a hot link, both documents must be Windows applications and both must support dynamic linking. If a document supports dynamic linking, you will see Paste Links on the Edit menu.

Creating dynamic links is much like creating links between worksheets or a chart and a worksheet (see Chapter 16).

USING MENUS TO CREATE LINKS

The easy way to create links (if the programs support it) is to use the Edit menu of both programs. As an example, let's link a worksheet range in Excel with a document in Microsoft Word for Windows:

1. Make the Excel worksheet active and select the range in the worksheet to copy to the word-processing document.
2. Open the Edit menu and choose Copy.
3. Make the word-processor document active.

4. Place the cursor where you wish the worksheet cells to be inserted.
5. Choose Paste Link from the Edit menu. If it's not there, select Full Menus in the View menu; Paste Link will now be shown.
6. Choose Auto Update.
7. Click OK.
8. Edit the document for column titles or other additions.

Figure 21.4 shows the regional sales figures from the Sales Worksheet (right) linked to a memo (left). If you edit the worksheet, the memo will follow the change.

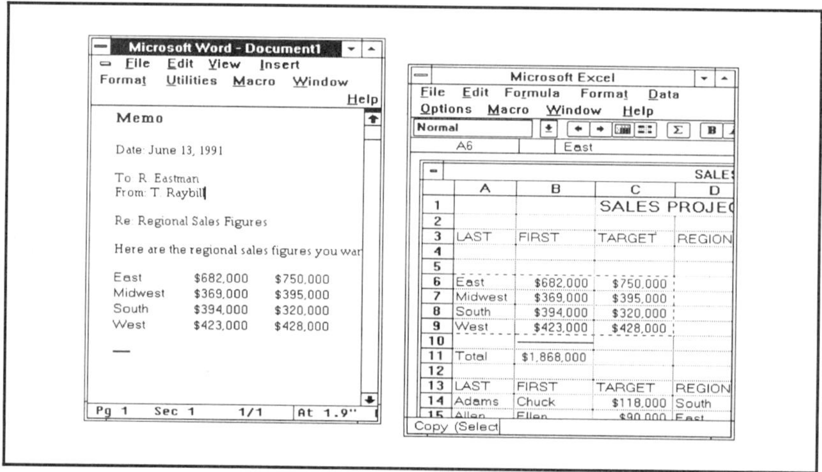

Figure 21.4: Spreadsheet data linked to a memo

As another example, suppose an imaginary communications program called StockPlus were open with its data linked to Excel. Excel contains a database Stock document with records representing the stock and price. Within Excel you could refer to the cell range for a stock that is coded ACM on the document as

=STOCKPLUS | STOCK!ACM

The reference begins with an equal sign, then has the application program name, a vertical bar, the document name, an exclamation point, and the name of the cell, range, field, or data referenced.

This makes it possible to link documents in different application programs, just as you can link two documents in Excel. To create the link, you must first have both applications running under Windows 3.0 or higher. Assume, for example, that a cell in a worksheet is dependent upon a field in the StockPlus program:

Documents being linked must support a data format compatible with DDE.

1. Open the dependent worksheet (the Excel worksheet).
2. Click the supporting application document window (StockPlus).
3. Select the range to link, open the Edit menu, and choose Copy in the supporting document (STOCK).
4. Click the dependent worksheet and the upper-left cell of the destination cell range.
5. Open Edit and either choose Paste Link or type the remote reference. If typing the reference, hold down the Shift and Ctrl keys while pressing Enter. Remote references are entered as array formulas.

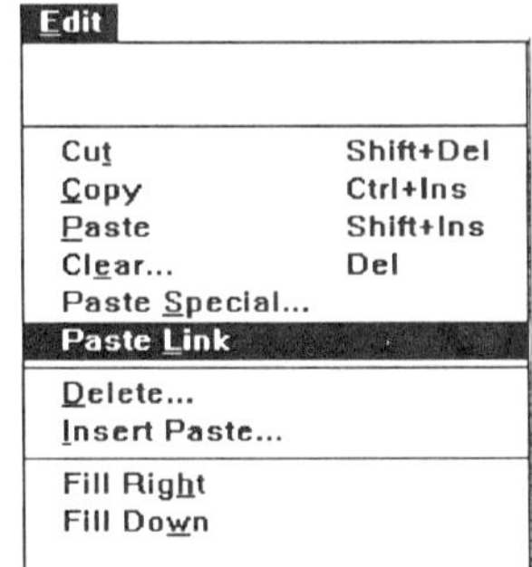

The cells are now linked.

OPENING DOCUMENTS WITH REMOTE REFERENCES

Opening and starting documents with remote references, provided the supporting document is open, is no different than starting documents without remote references. The link is automatically reestablished and the dependent document is updated, if necessary.

If the supporting document is not open and the dependent document is opened, Excel queries whether you wish to reestablish the link. If you choose OK, the supporting application will be loaded (if necessary) and the supporting document opened. If the link can't be established, an error message will appear in the appropriate cell.

SUSPENDING REMOTE REFERENCES

To suspend a link and use only the last values, open the Options menu and choose Workspace. Turn off the Ignore Remote Requests option. Click OK. The dependent cell will then remain locked to its last value. To turn the link back on, click on Ignore Remote Requests again.

USING DDE WITH MACROS

Macros, which will be introduced in Part VII, are another method of transferring data between Windows application programs. With macros you can start another application, send data to it, get data from the application, and even execute commands in the other application.

CREATING EMBEDDED OBJECTS

3.0

Excel supports embedded objects. By selecting an embedded object, you can start another application or mode of the current application.

You have already seen how you can embed a chart in a worksheet. The chart tool creates the chart on the worksheet. If you double-click the embedded chart, the Chart mode starts and the Excel menu changes to that for a chart. The worksheet chart becomes a document window in Excel.

This also works across applications. If you import a chart to Microsoft PowerPoint (Microsoft Corporation) to create a presentation, double-clicking the chart will start Excel with the chart document.

Embedding is different from dynamic linking (DDE) in that no hot link is established. The embedded object is static and doesn't change if the supporting data change. It is, therefore, a quick way to get back to the original document if you need to make edits. In the case of an embedded chart on an Excel worksheet, however, you may wish to establish a hot link to ensure that the chart follows the worksheet data.

If the applications you are using support embedded objects, copying the object is identical to copying any other picture:

1. Open the destination document.
2. Switch to the supporting document and select the object.
3. Use the method for that application to copy the object to the Clipboard (normally the Copy command).
4. Switch to the destination document.
5. Select the area for the object.
6. Open the Edit menu and choose Paste.

The object appears in the destination document. If it is an embedded object in an Excel worksheet, **EMBED** will appear in Excel's formula bar.

EXCEL AND LOTUS 1-2-3

If you already have been using Lotus 1-2-3 or Symphony for your spreadsheets, you can import your Lotus worksheets into Excel, or vice versa. When you transfer in either direction, the cell properties of your worksheet, including values, formulas, format, protection, and any names that you assigned, are converted. However, window properties (such as panes) are not converted. Although the function arguments and their order in Excel are often different from those in Lotus 1-2-3, when you transfer files, Excel automatically converts them. For example, you can take the amortization worksheet that you created in Chapter 8, which has the PMT and PV functions, and transfer it to Lotus 1-2-3, whose functions use different arguments. The Lotus 1-2-3 worksheet will be calculated correctly using the proper formulas.

If the Excel worksheet has a feature that is not supported by Lotus 1-2-3, it cannot be converted correctly. If you plan to do many transfers from Excel to Lotus 1-2-3, avoid using any of Excel's special functions. Appendix D provides more details on how to transfer data between Excel and Lotus 1-2-3.

You also can use Excel's Macro Translation Assistant to translate Lotus 1-2-3 macros to Excel macros. Simple macros will be converted directly. More complex macros probably will need some editing after conversion. To start a macro translation, choose Run from the application's control menu. Select Macro Translator on the dialog box displayed and click OK. Press F1 to get help with the translator.

EXCEL AND OTHER MICROSOFT SPREADSHEETS

Excel also can be used with Microsoft Multiplan, Macintosh Excel, and other products that use the SYLK format. This is a standard format that can be used for transfering data to or from Excel. It is particularly useful for transferring worksheets between different versions of Excel or between Excel versions on the IBM PC and the Macintosh. To save a worksheet in this format, select Save As from the File menu and click Options. Then in the second dialog box, choose SYLK, enter the file name, and click OK. Worksheets already saved in the SYLK format can be read automatically by Excel when you open them.

If an old worksheet won't load with a new version of Excel, save the worksheet from the old Excel version in SYLK format. Then use your new version to load the SYLK-formatted file.

When using the SYLK format, only formulas that can be interpreted by both application software products will be transferred correctly. Formulas specific to either will not be transferred. As with Lotus 1-2-3, data, formulas, formats, and names are transferred within this limitation, but window properties (such as panes) are not transferred. Multiplan does not support arrays and cannot support as large a numeric range as Excel. All Multiplan functions except DELTA and ITERCNT are supported by Excel. Many Excel functions, however, are not supported by Multiplan.

If you experience problems transferring files between Excel and any Microsoft program or version of Excel, revert to the SYLK format (i.e, save the Excel file as a SYLK file).

You also can read a Multiplan worksheet directly with Excel without using the SYLK format. Just open the worksheet in Excel. Excel recognizes it and converts it. The converse, though, is not true. Multiplan will read an Excel worksheet only if it is in the SYLK format.

EXCEL AND DBASE VERSIONS

Excel will export data to dBASE II, dBASE III, and dBASE IV, and can import data from any of these to a worksheet. The conversion is automatic and you do not have to use any special conversion routines or dBASE programs.

Save the worksheet in a normal Excel format as well as the dBASE format. A field name that is too long (and other problems) can prevent the saved database from loading to dBASE. If you save the original form, you can always reload the worksheet and try again.

To export data to dBASE II or dBASE III, first be sure the worksheet area is in a database form. The field names should be in the first row. Use the Set Database command to define the database area on the worksheet. Once it is defined, save it with the Save As command. When the dialog box is displayed, click Options. Select the format desired (DBF 2, 3, or 4). Click Save. The database file is created from the database with the .DBF extension. If any file with the same name currently exists, you will be prompted. If you elect to continue, the file will be overwritten.

When exporting data to dBASE II or dBASE III, some format information will be lost. For example, $3.43 will be saved in the dBASE III file as 3.43. Text fields that are too long may be truncated.

Any data previously in the worksheet area for the database will be overwritten.

To import data from a dBASE II, dBASE III, or dBASE IV file to the worksheet, open the File menu, choose Open, and enter the file name with the .DBF extension in the dialog box. Then click OK. The file will load to the worksheet and the database area will be named Database.

USING THE PARSE COMMAND

On occasion, you may wish to import columnar data and break them out to an Excel worksheet or database. Assume, for a moment, that you downloaded a list of addresses in text form using a communications program. The file is generally in a DOC, PRN, or TXT form. There is a line feed and carriage return at the end of each line. There are no tab separators for the columns. If you display the list using the DOS TYPE command, you see the data in columns.

When you open this file in Excel, in reads the data and places them in a spreadsheet (see Figure 21.5). As there are no tab separators, however, all the data are in column A. It doesn't look aligned here, since Excel defaults to a proportional font. Select column A and set the font to Courier using Font in the Format menu. This removes the proportional spacing. The data are now aligned by columns, but are still all in column A (see Figure 21.6). We wish to break it out so that the first name, last name, address, city, state, and zip are all in separate columns.

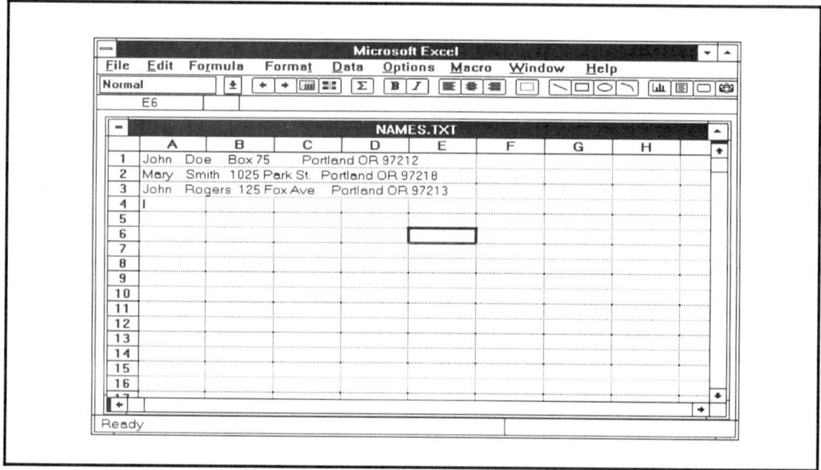

Figure 21.5: Data as initially read

	A	B	C	D	E	F	G	H
1	John	Doe	Box 75		Portland OR 97212			
2	Mary	Smith	1025 Park St		Portland OR 97218			
3	John	Rogers	125 Fox Ave		Portland OR 97213			

Figure 21.6: Data after some fixed-space formatting

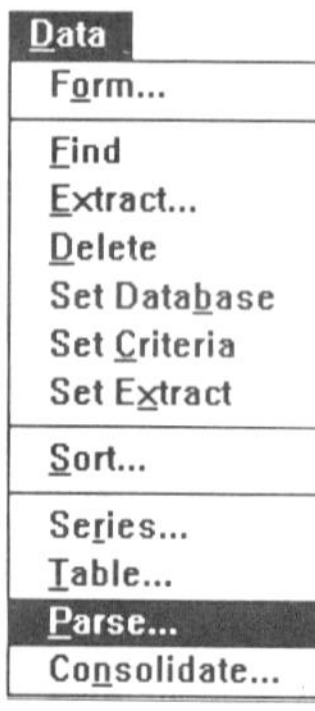

To do this, select all the data in column A, open the Data menu, and choose Parse. Excel displays the first line (see Figure 21.7). Click Guess, and Excel will try to parse the record on its own (see Figure 21.8). Finish the parsing by adding additional brackets after the city and state (see Figure 21.9). Click OK.

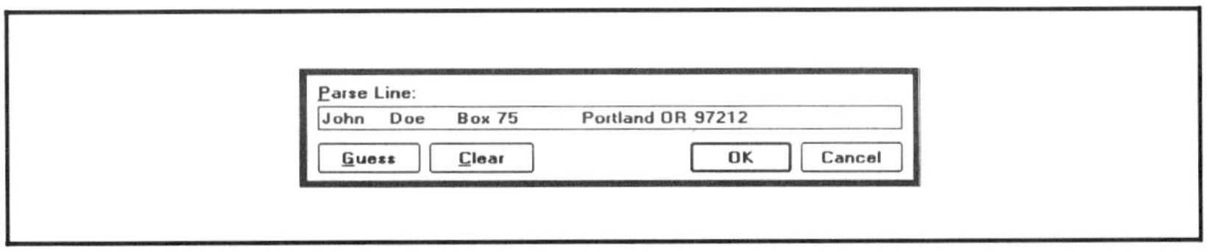

Parse Line:
John Doe Box 75 Portland OR 97212
Guess Clear OK Cancel

Figure 21.7: Starting the parse

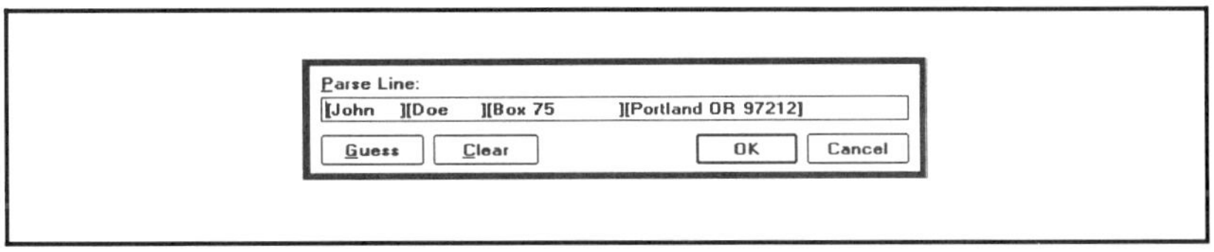

Parse Line:
[John][Doe][Box 75][Portland OR 97212]
Guess Clear OK Cancel

Figure 21.8: Having Excel guess the parsing

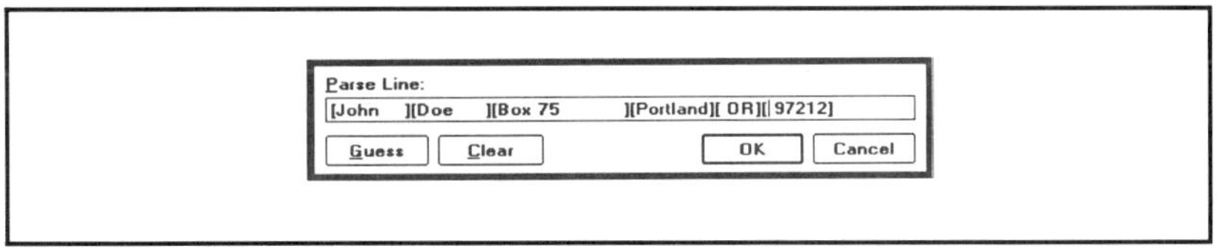

Parse Line:
[John][Doe][Box 75][Portland][OR][97212]
Guess Clear OK Cancel

Figure 21.9: Finishing the parsing manually

Excel will now break all selected records as per the parsed definition, with the first name, last name, address, city, state, and zip code all in separate columns. Widen the columns as necessary (see Figure 21.10).

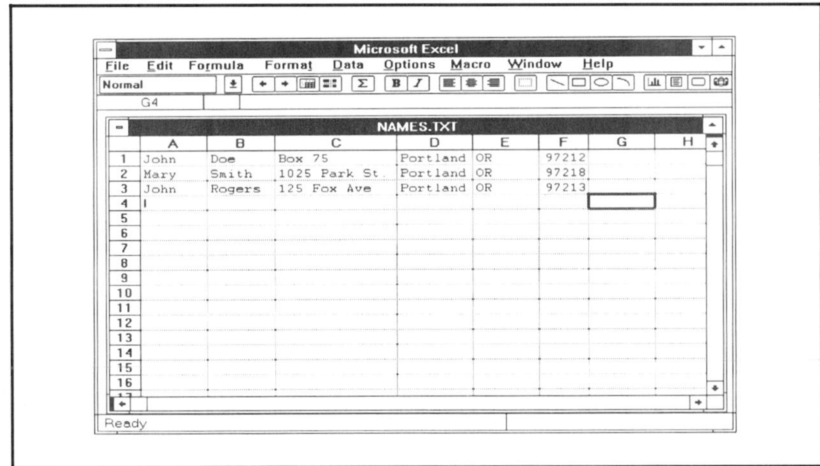

Figure 21.10: The finished worksheet

This method is very useful for converting downloaded reports on a communications system to a dBASE format. Read the report to Excel, parse the records, define a database, and save it as a dBASE file.

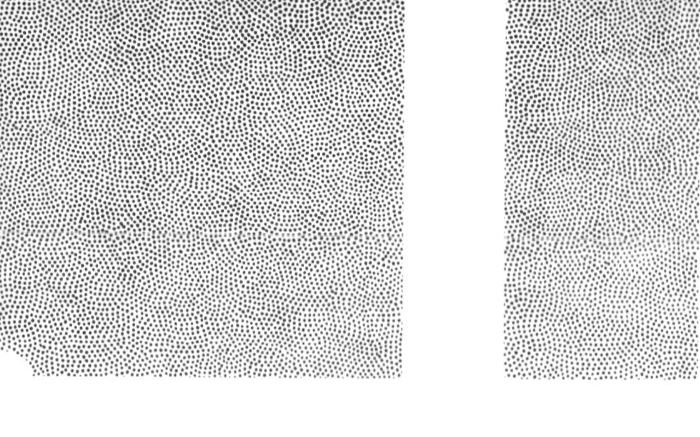

22 Inventory Control and Invoicing

IF YOU HAVE A BUSINESS, YOU KNOW THAT CREATING invoices is a time-consuming chore that is better delegated to a computer. This chapter illustrates the basic concepts of invoicing with Excel. It shows how to create an invoice using an inventory database with multiple price schedules and how to add a tax to the final price, based on a tax-rate table.

CREATING THE INVENTORY DATABASE

One of your first objectives should be to create the inventory database. Fields should include the part or item number, the description, and a column for each price schedule. For inventory control, you may also wish to add fields for the cost, the current quantity on hand (QOH), and the extended cost (quantity on hand times the cost). This permits you to calculate quickly the current value of the inventory.

Create the sample database shown in Figure 22.1. The database starts on row 50 to leave room for the invoice worksheet above (it also could be on a separate worksheet and linked to an invoice worksheet). Each inventory item is a record, entered as a separate row. The prices can either be entered as discrete values or as formula-based prices of another column. Sometimes you may wish to have separate price categories based on the quantity sold. In this example there are only two price categories, Retail and Wholesale. There should be no blanks in this (or any) inventory database, as they can cause incorrect data to be entered in the invoice later.

	A	B	C	D	E	F
50	PARTNO	DESCRIPTION	RETAIL	WHOLESALE	QOH	EXT COST
51	10008	General Purpose Cleaner 1 qt.	$5.00	$4.10	3	$12.30
52	10010	Industrial Cleaner 1qt	$7.25	$5.25	3	$15.75
53	20014	Lecithin	$9.75	$7.05	5	$35.25
54	20031	Zinc	$5.20	$3.50	1	$3.50
55	20042	Alfalfa	$8.75	$6.25	7	$43.75
56	20049	Multi-vitamin	$12.50	$8.50	9	$76.50
57	20051	Iron + Vitamin C	$7.75	$5.10	3	$15.30
58	20061	Beta Carotene	$16.50	$10.75	1	$10.75
59	20081	Vitamin E/Selenium	$10.10	$7.20	3	$21.60
60	20082	Vitamin C (Chewable)	$6.25	$4.10	8	$32.80
61	20083	Vitamin C S/R 500	$6.40	$4.60	8	$36.80
62	20088	Fiber Wafer	$4.50	$3.25	4	$13.00
63	20143	Iron	$8.00	$5.10	4	$20.40
64	20250	Calcium Magnesium	$6.50	$4.50	5	$22.50
65	20310	B Complex	$10.80	$7.50	4	$30.00
66	20810	EPA	$17.50	$12.75	1	$12.75

Figure 22.1: The Inventory database

For the invoicing to work properly, the records need to be in order by part number. You may enter them in any order, but then use the Sort command on the Data Menu to sort by part number. (Remember, do not include the field name when you define the sort range.)

Before leaving this section, you may wish to experiment with the database. You can set up a criteria range and find or extract records based on any criteria.

For the example in this chapter, the invoicing system will not really use this area as a database, but as a lookup table. You do not *need* to name it as a database for the invoicing system to work; however, from the user's perspective naming it as a database is helpful because it permits you to use the Goto command for updating quickly.

You can use the inventory database without sorting on the part number with macros created by using the Data.Find function of the macro language (see Part VII). This adds another degree of complexity, but the capability is there if you need it.

CREATING THE INVOICE

A sample output of the invoice system is shown in Figure 22.2. Begin creating the invoice, using Figure 22.3 as a guide. Fill in everything as shown. You can store a blank form of this invoice as a template on disk and use it for multiple invoices by filling in the areas that change between invoices. The item descriptions, prices, and the extended price columns will be filled in by Excel. For the line items, you enter only the item number and the quantity to ship. The totals will also be calculated automatically.

INVOICE

Remit to:
ABC Health Products
48 Midway Lane
Berkeley, CA 94702

Date:	6/25/91
Invoice #	4023
Tax Code	B
Terms	A

Sold to: John Albert
34 Shady Lane
Berkeley, CA 94702

Ship to: John Albert
34 Shady Lane
Berkeley, CA 94702

Item #	Description	Price	Qty	Ext Price
20143	Iron	$5.10	1	$5.10
20083	Vitamin C S/R 500	$4.60	2	$9.20
20810	EPA	$12.75	1	$12.75
			Subtotal	$27.05
			Tax	$1.89
			Grand Total	$28.94

Figure 22.2: A sample invoice printout

Then fill the item numbers in cells A15 to A17 and place the following function in cell B15:

=LOOKUP(A15,$A$51:$A$66,$B$51:$B$66)

	A	B	C	D	E
1		INVOICE			
2					
3	Remit to:			Date:	6/25/91
4	ABC Health Products			Invoice #	4023
5	48 Midway Lane			Tax Code	B
6	Berkeley, CA 94702			Terms	A
7					
8					
9	Sold to:	John Albert	Ship to:	John Albert	
10		34 Shady Lane		34 Shady Lane	
11		Berkeley, CA 94702		Berkeley, CA 94702	
12					
13					
14	Item #	Description	Price	Qty	Ext Price
15	20143			1	
16	20083			2	
17	20810			1	
18					
19					
20					
21					
22					
23					
24					
25					
26				Subtotal	
27				Tax	
28				Grand Total	

Figure 22.3: The Invoice worksheet

This tells Excel to to look up the value in A15 (the item number) in the range $A$51:$A$66 of the Inventory database and return the corresponding value (the description) found in the range $B$51:$B$66. Excel assumes that the range is sorted. Here the range is our inventory database. Now use the Fill Down command on the Edit menu to copy the function from cell B15 to cells B16 through B25. In doing so, the relative reference to cell A15 will change to reference cells A16, A17, etc. You should now see the item descriptions in column B.

You have one problem at this point. For each row with a blank item number, there appears an =N/A in column B (see Figure 22.4). They appear because there is no value from column A to plug into the LOOKUP function. To eliminate these, modify the function in B15 to include the IF function, using the ISNA function (see Appendix E) to test for the instances of N/A:

=IF(A15 =0," ",LOOKUP(A15,$A$51:$A$66,$B$51:$B$66))

Now copy *this* formula from B15 to cells B16 to B25.

This may be somewhat confusing, so let's look at the basic form of the IF function:

=IF(*condition, value if true, value if false*)

The program uses A15 = 0 as a conditional test for the value in cell A15. If a value in A15 is not found, the first expression is used to evaluate the cell value, leaving cell B15 blank (since there is no second argument in this function). If a value *is* found, the second expression is used to find the cell value.

	A	B
14	Item #	Description
15	20143	Iron
16	20083	Vitamin C S/R 500
17	20810	EPA
18		#N/A
19		#N/A
20		#N/A
21		#N/A
22		#N/A
23		#N/A
24		#N/A
25		#N/A

Figure 22.4: The first attempt to use the LOOKUP function

The next thing you have to do is fill the Price field with a function to find the prices. It is a bit more complicated, because the price depends not only on the item number, but also on the Terms code entered in E6. The term code tells Excel whether to use the retail price or the wholesale price. Enter the following function in C15 (without line breaks):

=IF(A15<>0,IF($E$6="A",LOOKUP(A15,$A$51:$A$66, $D$51:$D$66), IF($E$6="B",LOOKUP(A15,$A$51:$A$66, $C$51:$C$66),0)),0)

If an item number is entered on a line, Excel evaluates the $E$6 ="A" expression. If this condition is TRUE, the next LOOKUP function is used to find the price from the table, using column D. If it is FALSE, the next IF function is evaluated. This tries another condition, and if it is TRUE, activates another LOOKUP function. This time, column C will be used for the prices. Now copy the function from C15 to cells C16 through C25.

Before entering the function for the extended price in column E, name columns C and D "Price" and "Qty", respectively, using Create Names on the Formula menu. Now enter the extended price function in E15:

=IF(AND(A15<>0,Qty<>0),Price*Qty,)

Copy this down through to cell E25.

Now add the tax table (see Figure 22.5) in rows 46–48 of the worksheet. Cell E5 determines which tax rate to use to calculate the tax in E27. The final formulas to enter are listed below:

CELL	*FORMULA*
E26	=SUM(E15:E25)
E27	=LOOKUP($E$5,$B$47:$B$48,$C$47:$C$48)*E26
E28	=E26+E27

	B	C
46	TAX TABLE	
47	A	6.50%
48	B	7.00%

Figure 22.5: The tax table

Now set the alignment, style, and formats for the cells as desired. You should see the worksheet shown in Figure 22.6.

Use the Format command on the Format menu to set the borders. (You can see the borders more easily by using the Display command on the Options menu to turn off the gridlines.) Finally, use the Page Setup to turn off the row and column headings as well as the gridlines on the printed invoice. Print the document. The resulting invoice should look like Figure 22.2.

	A	B	C	D	E
1		INVOICE			
2					
3	Remit to:			Date:	6/25/91
4	ABC Health Products			Invoice #	4023
5	48 Midway Lane			Tax Code	B
6	Berkeley, CA 94702			Terms	A
7					
8					
9	Sold to:	John Albert	Ship to:	John Albert	
10		34 Shady Lane		34 Shady Lane	
11		Berkeley, CA 94702		Berkeley, CA 94702	
12					
13					
14	Item #	Description	Price	Qty	Ext Price
15	20143	Iron	$5.10	1	$5.10
16	20083	Vitamin C S/R 500	$4.60	2	$9.20
17	20810	EPA	$12.75	1	$12.75
18					
19					
20					
21					
22					
23					
24					
25					
26				Subtotal	$27.05
27				Tax	$1.89
28				Grand Total	$28.94

Figure 22.6: The final Invoice worksheet

IMPROVING YOUR INVOICING SYSTEM

This invoicing system is really just a starting point for designing any type of invoice system to meet your needs. A few possible enhancements are listed below:

- You could add a backorder system, checking the quantity ordered against the quantity in inventory
- You could add features to modify the inventory on shipping, keeping the quantities in inventory updated automatically

- You could use the database as a true database, using forms to fill in the invoice cells (see Part III) and eliminating the need to keep the database records sorted
- You could enter the addresses from a database of customers
- You could use the NOW( ) function to automatically enter the date

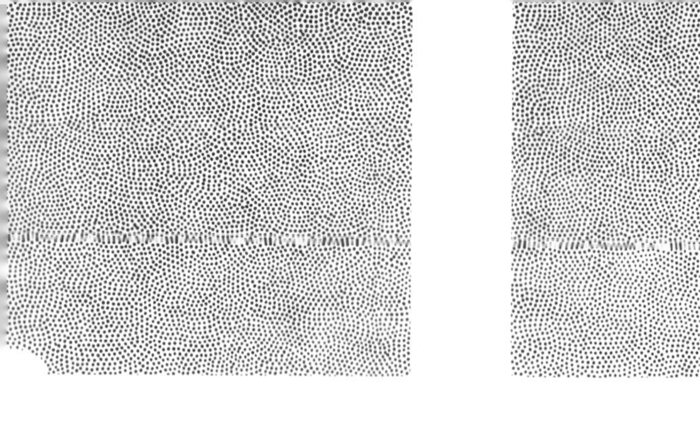

23 Performing Financial Management

ONE OF THE MOST IMPORTANT APPLICATIONS OF any worksheet program is financial management. Using Excel, you can calculate loan payments, make decisions about purchasing or selling investments, and compare investment returns. This chapter will introduce you to Excel's seven basic financial functions: PV, NPV, FV, PMT, RATE, IRR, and MIRR. In almost any business environment today, the knowledge of how to use these types of financial calculations is essential for the success of the business.

THE PRESENT VALUE FUNCTION

The present value function, PV, is used to calculate the present value over time of an investment. This is useful for evaluating a potential investment.

As an example, suppose you have $5000 to invest. A friend offers you an investment plan for your $5000 that will pay $1500 a year for the next five years. Would you take it?

To figure out whether this is a worthwhile investment, you need to compute the present value of the return your friend will give you. The general formula in Excel for this calculation is

=PV(*rate, number_of_periods, payment, future_value, type*)

For the moment, let's ignore the last two arguments, because they are not needed for the example. We need to assume an interest rate for projecting the investment back to the present. Let's assume that nine percent is the current money-market rate at the bank. There are five periods, and the payments are $1500. So you need to set up the following equation (see also Figure 23.1):

=PV(9%,5,1500)

This returns −5834, or $5834, which is the present value of the annual payments. This means that if you were to put the $1500 payments in a bank that paid nine percent interest, you'd end up with the same amount ($8975) as that paid by a bank on a one-time deposit of $5834. Since you are only investing $5000, your friend is offering you a good deal (or at least a better deal than the bank can offer you). The result of the PV function is negative because it represent money that you would *pay.*

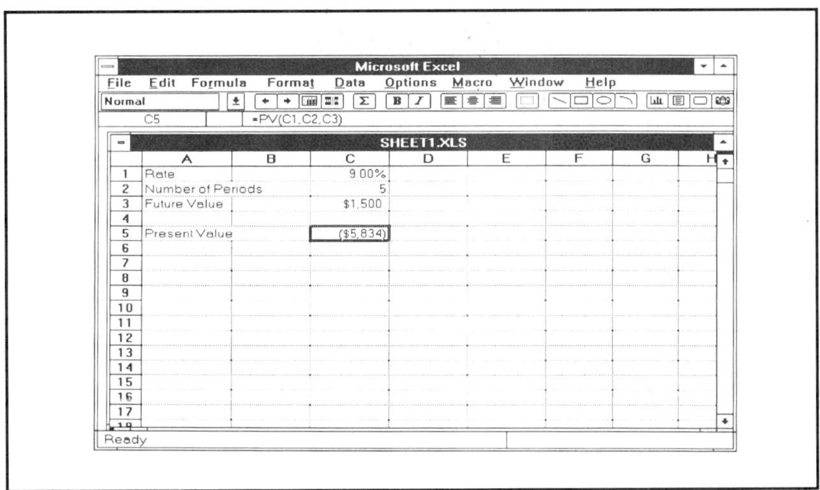

Figure 23.1: The worksheet to calculate the present value

The present value of an investment depends on three factors: the interest rate, the number of periods, and the amount of the payment. The number of periods and the payment values are normally fixed. The interest rate, however, is a variable you can assume. It is the hurdle over which the investment must leap before it becomes attractive, and so is often called the *hurdle rate.* For practical purposes, you generally use the best rate that you could get at the bank.

Now suppose your friend offers you a different plan. Instead of $1500 for each of five years, you could get $8500 at the end of the five years for the initial $5000 investment. Is it still a good deal? Is it better or worse than the last deal?

Now you don't have a payment, but you do have a future value. The interest and the number of periods is the same (note that an extra comma must be inserted to indicate a missing argument):

=PV(9%,5,,8500)

This time the result is –5524. This means that at nine percent interest, you should be willing to invest $5524 now to get $8500 in five years. Since we only have to invest $5000, it is still a good deal. It is not as good as the last offer, but it is still acceptable.

Be sure the interest rate corresponds to the payment period. If you have *x* payments at one-year intervals, make sure you use an *annual* interest rate.

The *type* argument is a flag that indicates whether the payments are made at the beginning or end of the period. If *type* is 1, the payments occur at the beginning of the period. If *type* is 0, the payments are at the end of the period. If the argument is omitted, *type* assumes a default value of 0, and payments are assumed to be at the end of the period.

THE NET PRESENT VALUE FUNCTION

The net present value function, NPV, is similar to the present value function, except that it permits the user to assume unequal payments. If the function returns a value of 0 or greater, the investment is considered a good one.

The NPV function assumes the payment is at the end of the period. You can't change this.

The general form of the function is

=NPV(*rate, inflow 1, inflow 2,... inflow n*)

Let's return to the original problem. The initial investment is an outflow, so it must be represented as a negative number. The returns in subsequent years would be inflows as shown below:

=NPV(9%, –5000,1500,1500,1500,1500,1500)

This returns a value of $766. In using this function, an investment is assumed acceptable if the result is greater than zero. Since this value is greater than zero, the investment is acceptable. Unfortunately, however, this is not the correct answer! The NPV function assumes that all payments are evenly distributed and made at the end of the period. The first cash flow—the initial investment—is assumed to occur one time period from today. Here, the initial inflow (the –$5000) is made at the beginning of the first period. To adjust for this, subtract the initial investment, as shown below, instead of including it as an inflow:

=NPV(9%,1500,1500,1500,1500,1500) – 5000

This gives a result of $834, which is the correct value. This is the most common way to use the NPV function: using the payback values as the inflow values and subtracting the initial investment.

Now you can try it with unequal payments. Assume you still invest $5000, but the return is $1000 the first year, $1600 the next two years, $1700 the next year, and $1800 the last year. To solve this, create a new worksheet and store the return values in cells A1 through A5. You can then use the following calculation in A6:

=NPV(9%,A1:A5)

This returns $873, which indicates that this is a better investment than the fixed payment schedule, as $873 > $834. The inflow arguments represent cash coming back, and, in this case, are positive.

You can use positive or negative values for the inflow arguments. For example, if you pay out more cash later, you can use a negative inflow value for that period.

THE FUTURE VALUE FUNCTION

The future value function, FV, is used to calculate the future value of an investment. It is, therefore, the opposite of PV and NPV. For example, if you are making payments into an IRA or Keogh account, the FV function will tell you the future value of that account.

The general form of the FV function is

=FV(*rate, number_of_periods, payment, present_value, type*)

where *rate* is the interest rate, *number_of_periods* is the number of payments, and *payment* is how much you pay each time. The last two arguments are optional and will be explained later.

Now let's try an example. Assume you are 48 years old and begin an IRA in which you invest $4000 a year. How much will you have when you are 65? The number of payments is 65 – 48, or 17. Assume an interest rate of 11 percent. The equation becomes

=FV(11%,17, -4000)

which returns a value of $178,003.

Because there is no *type* argument in this example, the above calculation assumes a default value of 0, which means that the payments come at the end of the period. If the payments are at the beginning of the period (i.e., you're making your first today), you must set up the equation as follows:

=FV(11%,17, -4000,,1)

With this kind of payment schedule, you will have $197,584 if you take it out when you are 65.

You can use the fourth argument (*present_value*) to indicate a lump-sum investment when two payments are used. For example, if you were creating an IRA with a $5000 investment and you planned no further payments, you would use the following equation:

=FV(11%,17,, −5000,1)

This IRA account would return $29,475 when you reached 65.

You also can combine an initial fixed investment with later payments, as in the following equation:

=FV(11%,17, −4000, −5000,1)

which returns $227,059. The $5000 is the lump-sum amount that a series of future payments is worth now (the present value).

THE PAYMENT FUNCTION

The payment function, PMT, is useful for calculating the payments required to amortize a loan. This is useful when you are borrowing money for a car or house, and you want to calculate the payments you can expect. The general form is as follows:

=PMT(*rate, number_of_periods, present_value, future_value, type*)

Be sure that, if monthly periods are used, you convert the annual interest to monthly interest and convert the years for the payments to months.

For example, assume you are purchasing a $12,000 car at 11 percent interest. Payments are monthly for a five-year period. The resulting formula is

=PMT(11%/12,5*12,12000)

which results in a monthly payment of $261. There are 60 payments (5*12), and the monthly interest for each payment period is 11 percent divided by 12. You can find a more extensive example of this function in the amortization worksheet of Chapter 8.

Again, the *type* argument indicates whether the payments are at the beginning or end of the period.

CALCULATING THE RATE OF RETURN

Sometimes you want to do an inversion of the previous formulas; that is, you want to calculate the rate of return and then compare this rate with the rate of return of other investments. Excel provides three functions for calculating the rate of return.

THE RATE FUNCTION

Assume you are back to the initial problem of lending $5000 with a return of $1500 for the next five years. This time you wish to calculate the rate of return for this investment. This would be the percentage for which the NPV is equal to 0. You need to use the RATE function. The general form for this function is

=RATE(*number_of_periods, payment, present_value, future_value, type, guess*)

For this example you have

=RATE(5,1500, –5000)

which returns a value of 15.24 percent—quite a good investment.

The *future_value* is used to indicate a lump-sum return. For example, if instead of yearly payments you would receive $8500 at the end of five years, the formula would become

=RATE(5,, –5000,8500)

yielding an 11.20 percent return. This would not be as profitable as the previous plan.

Excel uses an iterative process to calculate the rate using a net present-value function. The *guess* argument is used to define a starting point for calculating the interest. Omit the value when starting. If you get a #NUM! returned from the function, try using a *guess* argument as a starting point for the calculations. (It should be a percent.)

THE IRR FUNCTION

The IRR function, like RATE, is used to calculate the rate of return on an investment. Use it to compare different investments and see which one may be the best. IRR is different from RATE in that it can be used with uneven payments (like the NPV). The general form is as follows:

=IRR(*values, guess*)

Notice that there is only one argument for values. The trick, then, is to put the values as a range on the worksheet. The first value in the range is normally negative, indicating the initial payment or investment.

If A1 contains −5000 and each cell from A2 through A6 contains 1500, the formula becomes

=IRR(A1:A6)

and returns 15.24 percent, as before. You can now change any payment value, though, and see the resulting change in the rate of return. You can even make them all zero except the last one, setting the last payment to $8500. That will give you 11.20 percent, the same as in the previous example.

The internal rate of return calculated by RATE or IRR is a commonly used financial statistic. Like the NPV, you can use it to compare financial investments. In the section on the NPV, you learned that an attractive investment is one in which the net present value, discounted at a specified hurdle rate, gives an NPV of 0 or greater. The IRR and RATE functions turn this around. In essence, the internal rate of return is that value for which the NPV is 0.

THE MIRR FUNCTION

The MIRR function gives a modified rate of return of a series of cash flows. The general form is

=MIRR(*values, safe, risky*)

For example, assume you invest $5000 to finance an investment that will return $1400 a year for the next five years. Use the IRR function by entering –5000 in cell A1 and $1400 in cells A2 through A6. Calculate the rate of return as follows:

=IRR(A1:A6)

This results in 12.38 percent. It assumes that the $1400 you get each year is reinvested at the same (12.38) rate. If the returned money is reinvested at a ten percent rate, use the MIRR function:

=MIRR(A1:A6,9%,10%)

which yields 11.31 percent. The first argument is the range of values. The second is the interest you pay for the borrowed money, and the third is the interest you will earn.

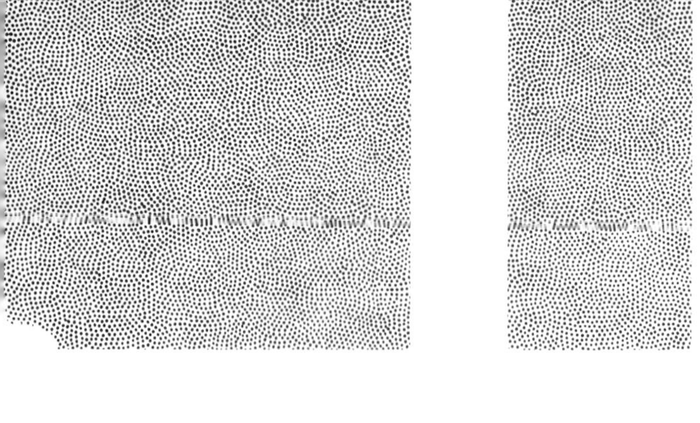

24 Analyzing Trends and Relationships

EXCEL CAN BE VERY USEFUL WHEN YOU NEED TO predict future data based on historical trends and when you want to explore the relationships between variables. Below are some examples:

- A company has tracked sales for several years and wishes to use these data to predict sales in future years
- A city is planning for city roads and wishes to predict future automotive traffic on certain roads based on historical data (traffic records)
- An environmental agency has obtained some data on the local increase in certain types of cancer and the change in air quality in several areas. The agency wishes to calculate the probable relationship of cancer rates with the various air-quality variables
- Educational leaders have tracked the number of local students for several years and wish to use their data to project education resource needs for the future

Predicting future data from current data is called *regression analysis*. Analyzing the relationship of variables is *correlation analysis*. This chapter will look at how you can do both with Excel.

REGRESSION ANALYSIS

The basic goal for any type of regression analysis is to estimate one variable based on one or more related variables. Chapter 15 presented a simple regression analysis. Let's now look at more specific aspects of this type of analysis.

LINEAR REGRESSION

One variable is said to be linearly related to another if an increase or decrease in one causes a proportional increase or decrease in the other. As an example, let's assume we have accumulated 14 years of sales data for a company as follows:

YEAR	SALES ($100K)
1	6.50
2	14.20
3	23.50
4	30.10
5	38.80
6	48.40
7	55.50
8	60.10
9	64.10
10	65.60
11	68.80
12	68.90
13	68.80
14	70.20

For this example the y variable is the sales total, and the x variable is the year. We wish to estimate the value of y corresponding to the x values 15, 16, 17, and 18 (i.e., the next four years). Once you have estimated these values, you can estimate budget values for employment levels, inventory, and the warehouse.

As a start, assume a linear relationship. If this is true, an equation can be found that approximately fits the data of the form:

$$y = a_0 + a_1 x$$

You now need to solve for the values of a_0 and a_1. The resulting curve is said to be the regression curve of y on x, as y is estimated from x; that is, the graph of y as a function of x can be graphed as a straight line.

These constant values can be solved easily with Excel using the LINEST function. The function has two input arguments: the array of y values and the array of x values. It returns an array of two values: a_0 and a_1.

The worksheet for the example is shown in Figure 24.1. Enter the values for A8 to A25 and B8 to B21 as shown. The array function is entered to A31 and B31 as follows:

1. Select A31 and B31.
2. Enter the following equation in the formula bar:

   =LINEST(B8:B21,A8:A21)

3. Hold down the Ctrl and Shift keys while pressing Enter to enter the function as an array.

The slope of the line should now be in A31, and the y intercept should be in B31.

Now enter the formula for the first predicted value in C8:

=$B$31+$A$31*A8

Copy this formula to cells C9 to C25 (Fill Down). This should give you the array of predicted values in column C.

You now need to calculate an R-squared value. This is the number that indicates how well the line fits the data points. The general

	A	B	C
1			
2			
3		LINEAR REGRESSION	
4			
5			
6			
7	YEAR	ACTUAL	PREDICTED
8	1	$6.50	$16.05
9	2	$14.20	$21.09
10	3	$23.50	$26.13
11	4	$30.10	$31.18
12	5	$38.80	$36.22
13	6	$48.40	$41.26
14	7	$55.50	$46.30
15	8	$60.10	$51.34
16	9	$64.10	$56.38
17	10	$65.60	$61.43
18	11	$68.80	$66.47
19	12	$68.90	$71.51
20	13	$68.80	$76.55
21	14	$70.20	$81.59
22	15		$86.63
23	16		$91.67
24	17		$96.72
25	18		$101.76
26			
27	105	683.5	
28		$49	
29			
30	SLOPE	INTERCEPT	
31	5.04153846	11.00989011	

Figure 24.1: The worksheet for the linear regression

equation for this value is

$$\&S(Y_{est} - Y_{avg})^2$$

$$r^2 =$$

$$\&S(Y - Y_{avg})^2$$

You can use the worksheet to calculate this by creating a column for each sum and entering the following equation in the first cell for each:

COLUMN	*TITLE*	*EQUATION*
D	$(Y - Y_{avg})^2$	=(B8 – $B$28)^2
E	$(Y_{est} - Y_{avg})^2$	=(C8 – $B$28)^2

The columnar sums are stored in row 27 (cell B27 contains =SUM(B8:B21)). The average ($B$28) is calculated in column B as the total of that column divided by the number of points in the array (i.e., B27/14). The closer the R-squared value comes to 1, the better the fit of the data to the linear equation represented by the array function. The R-squared value is then E27/D27, or 0.89966, which represents a good fit (see Figure 24.2).

	A	B	C	D	E	F
1						
2						
3		LINEAR REGRESSION				
4						
5						
6						
7	YEAR	ACTUAL	PREDICTED	(Y-Yavg)^2	(Yest-Yavg)^2	
8	1	$6.50	$16.05	1791.10332	1,073.87	
9	2	$14.20	$21.09	1198.64332	768.87	
10	3	$23.50	$26.13	641.174745	514.70	
11	4	$30.10	$31.18	350.491888	311.36	
12	5	$38.80	$36.22	100.429031	158.86	
13	6	$48.40	$41.26	0.17760204	57.19	
14	7	$55.50	$46.30	44.6033163	6.35	
15	8	$60.10	$51.34	127.206173	6.35	
16	9	$64.10	$56.38	233.434745	57.19	
17	10	$65.60	$61.43	281.520459	158.86	
18	11	$68.80	$66.47	399.143316	311.36	
19	12	$68.90	$71.51	403.149031	514.70	
20	13	$68.80	$76.55	399.143316	768.87	
21	14	$70.20	$81.59	457.043316	1,073.87	
22	15		$86.63			
23	16		$91.67			
24	17		$96.72			
25	18		$101.76			
26						
27	SUM	683.5		6427.26357	5782.39254	
28	AVERAGE	48.82142857				
29						
30	SLOPE	INTERCEPT		R squared		
31	5.04153846	11.00989011		0.89966632		

Figure 24.2: Calculating the R-squared value

There is another and simpler method of calculating this R-squared value. There also should be a linear-regression line such that

$$x = b_0 + b_1 y$$

This is the regression curve of x on y. You can use the LINEST function to calculate b_0 and b_1 by simply reversing the arguments in the function used earlier. The R-squared value can then be calculated as

$$r^2 = a_0 * b_0$$

Now chart the two data series (actual and predicted) using the following technique:

1. Select B8 to B21 on the worksheet.
2. Create a new chart and use the Gallery menu to make it a line chart.
3. Select the first option on the Gallery Line dialog box.
4. On the worksheet, select C8 to C25.
5. Copy the series to the Clipboard.
6. Select the chart and paste the series to the chart.
7. Add axis labels and chart title as desired, using Attach Text on the Chart menu.

You should see the graph shown in Figure 24.3. Notice that the points are very close to the line predicted by the linear regression equation, but the scattering of the actual points about the line is not random. Those in the middle are above the line, and those at the end are below the line. The curve of the actual sales line indicates that sales predicted by this linear regression are higher than could realistically be expected from looking at the data for the last few years. This suggests a curved line probably would be a better fit. This alternative will be examined in the next section.

The TREND function is similar to the LINEST function, except that it returns the actual array of values. For example, you could

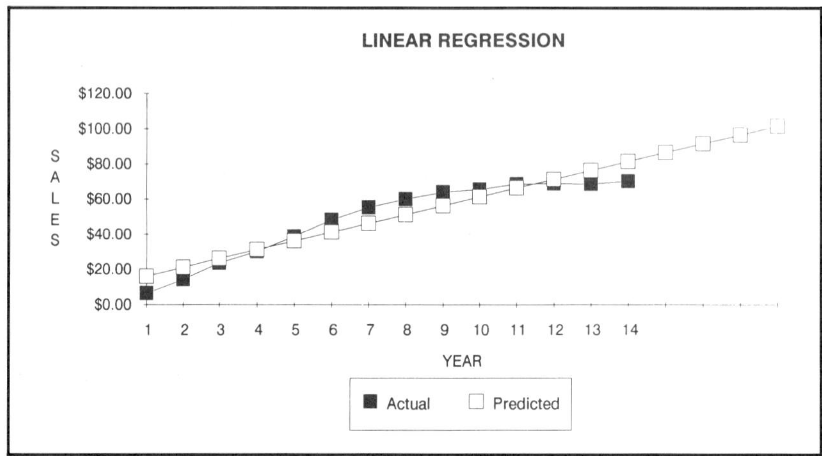

Figure 24.3: The linear regression chart

select C8:C21 as an array, then enter *=TREND(B8:B21,A8:A21)* as an array by holding down the Ctrl and Shift keys while pressing Enter. You will get the same predicted values.

EXPONENTIAL REGRESSION

The same worksheet can be modified easily for an exponential regression. The LINEST function in row 31 is changed to a LOGEST function. The arguments remain the same:

={LOGEST(B8:B21,A8:A21)}

The equation in C8 is changed to

=$B$31*$A$31^A8

This is then copied down column C. Our predicted sales values are now even higher (see Figure 24.4), but are they realistic?

The chart shown in Figure 24.5 shows the new predictions. The predicted sales look good, but do not match up with what could be expected realistically. The actual sales are fairly steady over the last few years. The exponential curve predicts growth that clearly does not fit the data too well. Sometimes (as with population growth curves), however, an exponential regression is quite realistic.

	A	B	C
3		EXPONENTIAL REGRESSION	
4			
5			
6			
7	YEAR	ACTUAL	PREDICTED
8	1	$6.50	$15.72
9	2	$14.20	$18.22
10	3	$23.50	$21.13
11	4	$30.10	$24.50
12	5	$38.80	$28.40
13	6	$48.40	$32.93
14	7	$55.50	$38.18
15	8	$60.10	$44.27
16	9	$64.10	$51.32
17	10	$65.60	$59.50
18	11	$68.80	$68.99
19	12	$68.90	$79.99
20	13	$68.80	$92.74
21	14	$70.20	$107.53
22	15		$124.67
23	16		$144.55
24	17		$167.60
25	18		$194.32
26			
27	SUM	683.5	
28	AVERAGE	48.82142857	
29			
30	SLOPE	INTERCEPT	
31	1.15943025	13.55521499	

Figure 24.4: Predicted sales using the LOGEST function

CURVILINEAR REGRESSION

In the real world, you can often accomplish a good fit by extending the linear regression to include additional terms as necessary:

$$y = a_0 + a_1x + a_2x^2 + a_3x^3 + a_ix^i + \ldots + a_nx^n$$

This is the general form for a curvilinear regression, or a regression in which a curved line that fits the data points is calculated. The

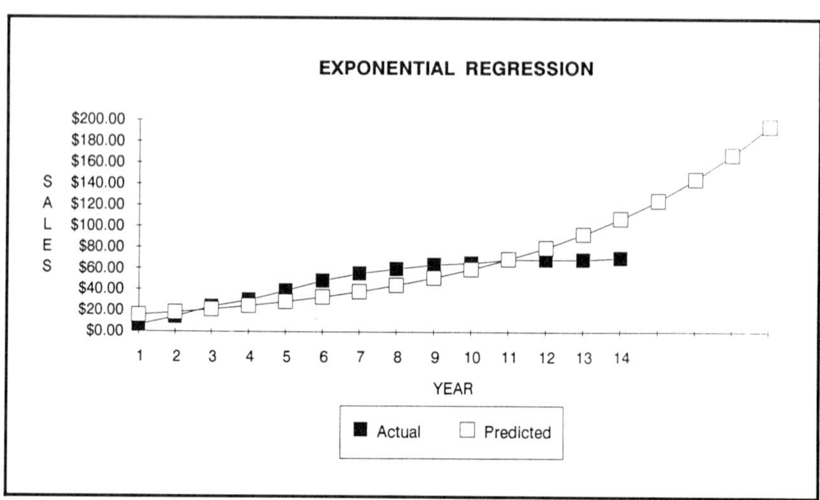

Figure 24.5: The chart of sales using the LOGEST function

calculations aren't for the faint of heart, but the rewards are often well worth including at least the a^2 term, giving a quadratic regression. There is no general function that creates the constants for the equation, so you must calculate them using the following equations:

$$\&SY = a_0 N + a_1 \&SX + a_2 \&SX^2$$

$$\&SXY = a_0 \&SX + a_1 \&SX^2 + a_2 \&SX^3$$

$$\&SX2Y = a_0 \&SX^2 + a_1 \&SX^3 + a_2 \&SX^4$$

The worksheet used to calculate the various coefficients and the resulting R-squared value is shown in Figure 24.6. This gives the following equations:

$$683.5 = 14a_0 + 105a_1 + 1015a_2$$

$$6273.2 = 105a_0 + 1015a_1 + 11025a_2$$

$$65419.6 = 1015a_0 + 11025a_1 + 127687a_2$$

These can be solved to get the following constants:

$$a_0 = -7.3747253$$

$$a_1 = 11.9357692$$

$$a_2 = -0.4596154$$

TREND3.XLS

	A	B	C	D	E	F	G	H	I	J
1										
2										
3		QUADRATIC REGRESSION								
4										
5	Number of degrees of freedom		14							
6										
7	YEAR	ACTUAL	PREDICTED	X^2	X^3	X^4	XY	X^2 * Y	(Y-Yavg)^2	(Yest-Yavg)^2
8	1	$6.50	$4.10	1	1	1	6.5	6.5	1791.10332	1999.8784
9	2	$14.20	$14.66	4	8	16	28.4	56.8	1198.64332	1167.115825
10	3	$23.50	$24.30	9	27	81	70.5	211.5	641.174745	601.4944905
11	4	$30.10	$33.01	16	64	256	120.4	481.6	350.491888	249.8588172
12	5	$38.80	$40.81	25	125	625	194	970	100.429031	64.12313609
13	6	$48.40	$47.69	36	216	1296	290.4	1742.4	0.17760204	1.271689941
14	7	$55.50	$53.65	49	343	2401	388.5	2719.5	44.6033163	23.35863254
15	8	$60.10	$58.70	64	512	4096	480.8	3846.4	127.206173	97.50802899
16	9	$64.10	$62.82	81	729	6561	576.9	5192.1	233.434745	195.9138556
17	10	$65.60	$66.02	100	1000	10000	656	6560	281.520459	295.84
18	11	$68.80	$68.31	121	1331	14641	756.8	8324.8	399.143316	379.6202609
10	12	$68.90	$69.67	144	1728	20736	826.8	9921.6	403.149031	434.6583485
20	13	$68.80	$70.12	169	2197	28561	894.4	11627.2	399.143316	453.427884
21	14	$70.20	$69.64	196	2744	38416	982.8	13759.2	457.043316	433.4724
22	15		$68.25							
23	16		$65.94							
24	17		$62.70							
25	18		$58.55							
26										
27	105	683.5	683.5	1015	11025	127687	6273.2	65419.6	6427.26357	6397.541769
28		$49								
29										
30	SLOPE	INTERCEPT		683.5	=	14	105	1015		
31	5.041538462	11.00989011		6273.2	=	105	1015	11025		
32				65420	=	1015	11025	127687		
33	0.178450749	-1.212220508								
34				a1=	11.9358		Solve for a0			
35				a2=	-0.4596		6607.16667	135.333333	1015	9811.666667
36	0.899666316			a0=	-7.3747		6273.2	105	1015	11025
37							----------	----------	----------	----------
38	R-SQUARED=	0.995375668				#1	333.966667	30.3333333		-1213.333333
39										
40							68139.931	1140.51724	11025	119754.3103
41							65419.6	1015	11025	127687
42							----------	----------	----------	----------
43						#2	2720.33103	125.517241		-7932.689655
44										
45						Mod of #1	2183.45103	198.317241		-7932.689655
46							----------	----------	----------	----------
47							536.88	-72.8		
48										
49							Solve for a2			
50						Mod of #1	1381.93103	125.517241		-5020.689655
51						#2	2720.33103	125.517241		-7932.689655
52							----------	----------	----------	----------
53							-1338.4			2912

Figure 24.6: The quadratic regression worksheet

The following equation is then used in column C to find the predicted values:

$$y = a_0 + a_1 x + a_2 x^2$$

The R-squared value is solved the same way as it is with linear regression. Notice that the R-squared value is now close to 0.995, an extremely good fit.

Here are the column definitions that you should enter:

ROW	*TITLE*	*FIRST CELL EQUATION*
A	YEAR	
B	ACTUAL	(entered)
C	PREDICTED	=$E$36+$E$34*A8+$E$35*A8*A8
D	X^2	=A8*A8
E	X^3	=A8^3
F	X^4	=A8^4
G	XY	=A8*B8
H	$X^2 * Y$	=A8*A8*B8
I	$(Y - Y_{avg})^2$	–(B8 – $B$28)^2
J	$(Y_{est} - Y_{avg})^2$	–(C8 – $B$28)^2

The resulting constants are calculated and stored as follows:

CELL	*CONSTANT*
E34	a1
E35	a2
E36	a0

Here are some of the formulas to enter in the worksheet. All the equations are not shown in Figure 24.7. Row 27, as before, contains

TREND4.XLS

	A	B	C	D	E	F	G	H	I	J
27	=SUM(A8:A21)	=SUM(B8:B21)	=SUM(C8:C21)	=SUM(D8:D21)	=SUM(E8:E21)	=SUM(F8:F21)	=SUM(G8:G21)	=SUM(H8:H21)	=SUM(I8:I21)	=SUM(J8:J21)
28		=B27/C5								
29										
30	SLOPE	INTERCEPT		=B27	=	=C5	=A27	=D27		
31	=LINEST(B8:B21,A8:A21)	=LINEST(B8:B21,A8:A21)		=G27	=	=A27	=D27	=E27		
32				=H27	=	=D27	=E27	=F27		
33	=LINEST(A8:A21,B8:B21)	=LINEST(A8:A21,B8:B21)								
34				a1=	=(D30-F30*E36-H30*E35)/G30		Solve for a0			
35				a2=	=G53/J53		=D30*G31/G30	=F30*G31/G30	=G30*G31/G30	=H30*G31/G30
36	=A31*A33			a0=	=G47/H47		=D31	=F31	=G31	=H31
37							----------	----------	----------	----------
38	R-SQUARED=	=J27/I27				#1	=G35-G36	=H35-H36		=J35-J36
39										
40							=D31*G32/G31	=F31*G32/G31	=G31*G32/G31	=H31*G32/G31
41							=D32	=F32	=G32	=H32
42							----------	----------	----------	----------
43						#2	=G40-G41	=H40-H41		=J40-J41
44										
45						Mod of #1	=G38*J43/J38	=H38*J43/J38		=J38*J43/J38
46							----------	----------	----------	----------
47							=G43-G45	=H43-H45		
48										
49							Solve for a2			
50						Mod of #1	=G38*H43/H38	=H38*H43/H38		=J38*H43/H38
51						#2	=G43	=H43		=J43
52							----------	----------	----------	----------
53							=G50-G51			=J50-J51

Figure 24.7: The equations shown in their cells

the following sums:

Curvilinear Equation Cell Values

CELL	FORMULA
D30	=B27
F30	=C5
G30	=A27
H30	=D27
D31	=G27
F31	=A27
G31	=D27
H31	=E27
D32	=H27
F32	=D27
G32	=E27
H32	=F27

Solving for the a_0 Constant

CELL	FORMULA
G35	=D30*G31/G30
H35	=F30*G31/G30
I35	=G30*G31/G30
J35	=H30*G31/G30
G36	=D31
H36	=F31
I36	=G31
J36	=H31
G38	=G35 – G36

H38	=H35 – H36
J38	=J35 – J36

The actual list is much longer than this, but there is nothing unusual in the calculations. You can use normal algebraic methods to solve the quadratic equation.

Figure 24.8 shows the chart of the quadratic regression. Notice that the curve is now a very good fit, but the sales projections are not as good. The projections actually show a dip in sales. This shows management should begin to take some action to turn things around.

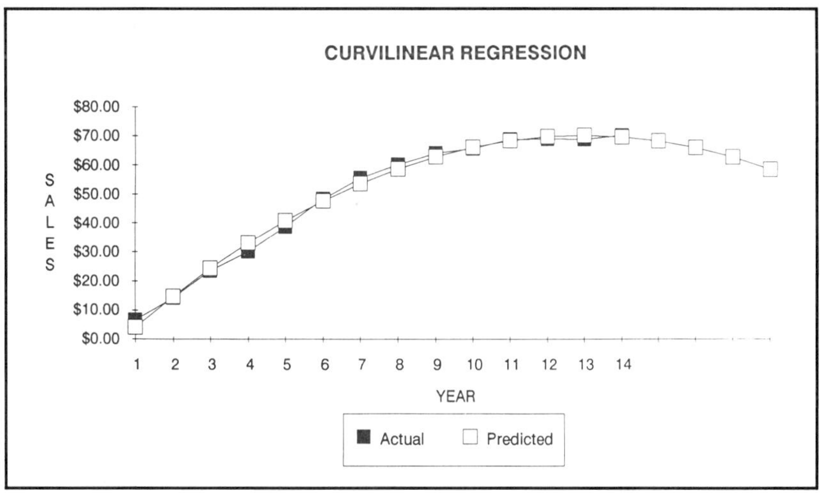

Figure 24.8: The curvilinear regression chart

When inserting or deleting rows in the input array, insert or delete from the *middle* to ensure that the sum formulas in row 27 remain valid.

It is a good idea to use cell references instead of numbers when creating the formulas to solve the equations for the constants. This enables the worksheet to function as a template for other quadratic regressions. For example, the number of samples is stored in C5, permitting it to be used in B28 to calculate the average. This way, you don't have to remember to adjust B28 if rows are inserted or deleted.

You can simplify your work in solving for the constants by modifying the x array so that the sum is 0. (For a 15-element array, you would start at -7.) The second equation can then be solved directly for a_1. There are then only two unknowns, and the other two equations can be solved for the other two constants.

CORRELATION ANALYSIS

In correlation analysis, you try to discover how well an equation describes the relationship between two variables. The problem is closely related to regression analysis. In regression analysis, you try to find a curve that fits the data; in correlation analysis, you are measuring how well the curve fits the data. Indeed, you have already calculated the R-squared value for the examples of this chapter. In correlation analysis, this is called the *coefficient of determination.* The square root of this value is the *coefficient of correlation,* or the measure of the fit of the curve. The value can vary from −1 (negative correlation) to 1 (perfect correlation). A value of 0 indicates no correlation. The general equation for R squared (the coefficient of determination) is the same as in the previous sections:

$$\&S(Y_{est} - Y_{avg})^2$$

$$r^2 =$$

$$\&S(Y - Y_{avg})^2$$

As an example, assume you want to find how much correlation there is between the height of a father and the height of his oldest son. To simplify your work, assume a sample of 14 father-son pairs. Figure 24.9 shows this sample in a worksheet. The fathers are shown as the *x* array, the sons as the *y* array.

The basic worksheet is similar to the earlier examples. The A26:B26 cells contain the array **LINEST(B7:B20,A7:A20)**. The sums are in row 22. The R-squared value is calculated as E22/C22. The coefficient of correlation is the square root of this, or 0.7668.

You also can calculate an error of estimate with the equation

SQRT(SUM(Y − Yest)^2/N)

In this case, the error of estimate is 1.4899 inches. If the sample is large enough, 68 percent of the sample will fall within 1.4899 inches of the regression line. You also will find 95 percent of the sample within twice this distance and 99.7 percent within three times this distance.

	A	B	C	D	E	F
1						
2		CORRELATION ANALYSIS				
3						
4	Number of Samples		14			
5						
6	X	Y	(Y-Yavg)^2	PREDICTED	(Yest-Yavg)^2	(Y-Yest)^2
7	62	66	2.93877551	65.08035714	6.937579719	0.845742985
8	63	66	2.93877551	65.60714286	4.44005102	0.154336735
9	64	65	7.367346939	66.13392857	2.497528699	1.285794005
10	65	68	0.081632653	66.66071429	1.110012755	1.793686224
11	66	65	7.367346939	67.1875	0.277503189	4.78515625
12	66	66	2.93877551	67.1875	0.277503189	1.41015625
13	67	68	0.081632653	67.71428571	0	0.081632653
14	67	67	0.510204082	67.71428571	0	0.510204082
15	68	69	1.653061224	68.24107143	0.277503189	0.575972577
16	68	71	10.79591837	68.24107143	0.277503189	7.611686862
17	69	68	0.081632653	68.76785714	1.110012755	0.589604592
18	70	68	0.081632653	69.29464286	2.497528699	1.676100128
19	71	70	5.224489796	69.82142857	4.44005102	0.031887755
20	72	71	10.79591837	70.34821429	0.907579719	0.424024017
21						
22	938	948	52.85714286		31.08035714	
23		67.7142857				
24						
25	SLOPE	INTERCEPT		Err of Est	1.489975003	
26	0.52678571	32.4196429		R SQUARED	0.588006757	
27				R	0.766815986	
28	0.52678571	32.4196429				

Figure 24.9: Correlation analysis of father-son heights

Before charting, be sure the category column is in ascending order. Here the data were entered in order. If you must sort, select rows 7 to 20. Then select the Sort command and click OK. The values in column A should now be in ascending order. All the rows should have been sorted.

To chart this, select A7:B20. Then open the Edit menu and choose Copy. Open a new chart. The chart area will be blank. Open the Edit menu and choose Paste Special. Choose Categories (X Labels) in First Column and click OK. This will create the first-level graph. Use the Gallery menu to change it to a scatter graph of the default type. Set each data series to start at 61 by selecting each axis in turn and using the Axis command on the Format menu.

Now add the second data series. Select D7:D20 on the worksheet and copy it to the Clipboard. This time use the Paste command to add it to the chart. Open the Chart menu and choose Overlay Chart Type. Choose Line. This will give you a regression line that passes through the scattered points. Add labels, and the resulting graph should look like Figure 24.10. The graph indicates a definite correlation between the height of a father and his oldest son.

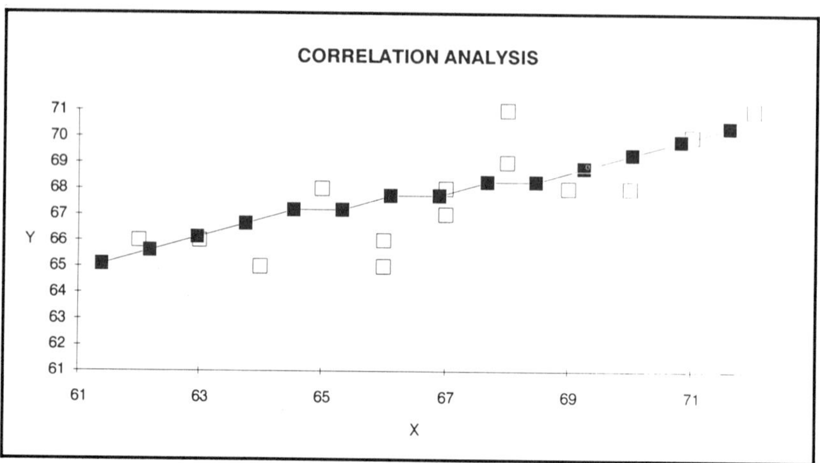

Figure 24.10: Chart of the correlation analysis

The regression analysis only finds a mathematical equation that approximates the existing data. There is no guarantee that future points will fall on the line. The equation defines an observed relationship between two variables. Here are some issues to consider:

- There may really be no relationship between the variables. The observed relationship could be strictly by chance
- The two variables may be two effects of a single cause. For instance, although there may appear to be a positive relationship between local smog and cancer rates, in reality, both factors may be the effects of a single cause—for example, a nearby corporation that produces a pollutant which causes both the smog and cancer
- There may be other causes to consider. Historical data can be used to predict highway traffic in the future for an area. But if a new shopping center is built nearby, don't expect the same equations to work

Excel can be used to analyze trends and supports both regression and correlation analysis. Although linear and exponential regression can be done with Excel's built-in functions, curvilinear regression and correlation analysis require the use of formulas.

25 Using the Q+E and Solver Utilities

THIS CHAPTER FEATURES TWO OF EXCEL'S NEWEST and most powerful utilities: Q+E and the Solver. Q+E is an instrument that allows you to query, sort, format, edit, and generally get the most out of Excel's database ability. The Solver is a useful tool to aid you in conducting what-if analyses and solving for *x,* the variable in often complex equations.

USING Q+E FOR WINDOWS

Q+E (or "Query and Edit") is a Windows application for managing databases. You can use it with dBASE (II, III, and IV), text files, SQL, Oracle, OS/2 Extended Edition, and Excel worksheet files with databases defined.

Excel performs some level of database management, but Q+E can simplify some tasks and do a few things that Excel can't. Use Q+E with Excel when you wish to:

- Use an Excel worksheet with external databases
- Query database files that are linked on common fields

- Process mailing labels
- Link databases with other documents

For the examples in this chapter, we will use Q + E with dBASE files. You won't need dBASE for the examples, since you can create dBASE files with Excel.

OPENING AN EXISTING FILE

To explore Q + E, you can use an existing database file or a worksheet with a database. Create a dBASE file from your Sales worksheet. Open the SALES worksheet in Excel and define the database to include cells A13 through E28. (Use Set Database on the Data menu.) Save the file as SALES.DBF, first clicking the Options button in the dialog box to save it as a dBASE III or IV file. Now minimize Excel to get it out of the way for the moment.

Start Q + E by double-clicking the Q + E icon. Q + E will start and display the blank startup screen. There are two menu options, File and Help, at the extremes of the menu bar.

Open the File menu and choose Open. In the Open dialog box, choose the database name to open. Be sure the source is dBaseFile. Select SALES.DBF and click the Options button. In the Options dialog box, be sure IBM PC is selected as the file character set. Click OK twice. The database will open and be displayed (see Figure 25.1).

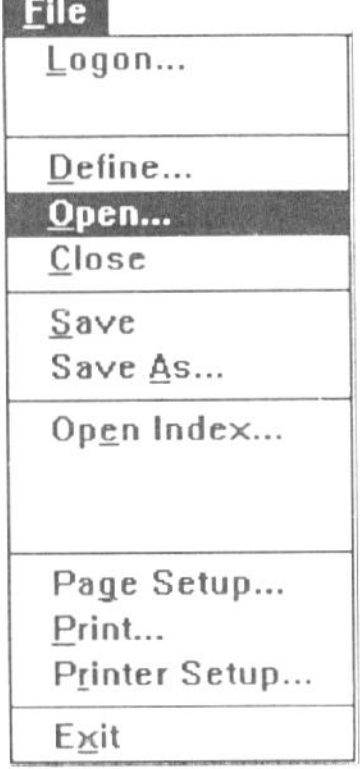

Notice that the database is displayed in a query window (Query1). The title bar indicates that this is a query and displays the query file name. The database name appears in brackets.

With Q + E, you are working with *two* kinds of files: database files and query files. The database file has the data for the queries. The query file defines the database(s) that is used and determines how the data are to be displayed. You can have several query files for a single database or several databases for a single query file. So far, you have opened a single database file. You are starting to create a query window, which eventually will be saved as a query file.

The menu has changed to show the various options:

> File opens and closes the database, opens and saves query files, creates new database files, saves queries (and database structures when creating files), and prints query results

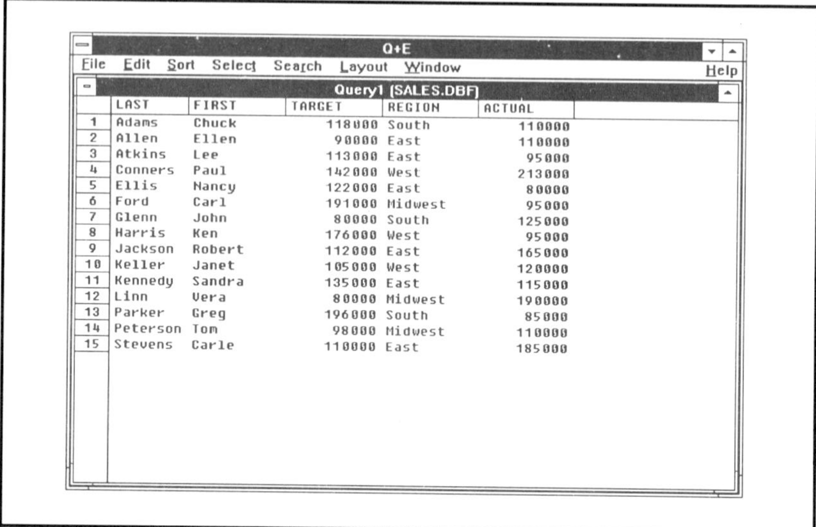

	LAST	FIRST	TARGET	REGION	ACTUAL
1	Adams	Chuck	118000	South	110000
2	Allen	Ellen	90000	East	110000
3	Atkins	Lee	113000	East	95000
4	Conners	Paul	142000	West	213000
5	Ellis	Nancy	122000	East	80000
6	Ford	Carl	191000	Midwest	95000
7	Glenn	John	80000	South	125000
8	Harris	Ken	176000	West	95000
9	Jackson	Robert	112000	East	165000
10	Keller	Janet	105000	West	120000
11	Kennedy	Sandra	135000	East	115000
12	Linn	Vera	80000	Midwest	190000
13	Parker	Greg	196000	South	85000
14	Peterson	Tom	98000	Midwest	110000
15	Stevens	Carle	110000	East	185000

Figure 25.1: The displayed database

Edit edits, moves, and copies data and adds and deletes fields and records

Sort sorts records in a query

Select chooses records from a database that meet a specific condition

Search looks through the database for records containing a specified text string, or takes you to a specific record number

Layout moves, removes, edits, and adds columns; defines fonts and column widths; and calculates summary totals and fields

Window changes windows or gets information about the current query

Help provides information about using Q+E

The Help menu is always available for on-line help. As with Excel, you also can get help by selecting a command and pressing F1.

The database is displayed in columns, with the field names as the column titles. Each record is identified with a record number at the left.

MOVING THE CURSOR AND SELECTING DATA IN A QUERY WINDOW

You select data with the mouse in Q + E in much the same way you do with Excel. Begin by clicking a field to select it. Drag through a range of fields to select them. To select multiple ranges, select the first range and hold down the Ctrl key while selecting other ranges. To select characters in a field, drag through the characters. You also can scroll through a database. (There are no scroll bars in Figure 25.1 because the database does not extend beyond the window.)

To select with the keyboard, you must move the cursor to the starting point and then make the selection. Press these keys to move the cursor:

TO MOVE TO	*PRESS THESE KEYS*
Next field	Tab
Previous field	Shift-Tab
First field	Home
Last field	End
First record	Ctrl-Home
Last record	Ctrl-End
Next record	↓
Previous record	↑

As with Excel, you can press the Ctrl key to select discontinuous ranges. Press PgUp and PgDn to scroll vertically and Ctrl-PgUp and Ctrl-PgDn to scroll horizontally a screen at a time.

To select elements with the keyboard, press these keys:

TO MOVE TO	*PRESS THESE KEYS*
Character to left	Shift-←
Character to right	Shift-→
Entire record	Shift-Spacebar

TO MOVE TO	*PRESS THESE KEYS*
Entire column	Ctrl–Spacebar
Entire window	Shift–Ctrl–Spacebar

To select multiple fields, select the first field, press F8, and use the direction keys to select additional fields. Press F8 again.

To select multiple records, select the first field of the first record and press F8. Use the direction keys to select additional fields in this record. Press Shift–F8 to keep the selection and select additional records. Press F8 again to select multiple fields. When you are through, press F8 again.

PERFORMING BASIC QUERY OPERATIONS

You can edit any field, find a record with a specific field value, go to a specific record, or zoom a field.

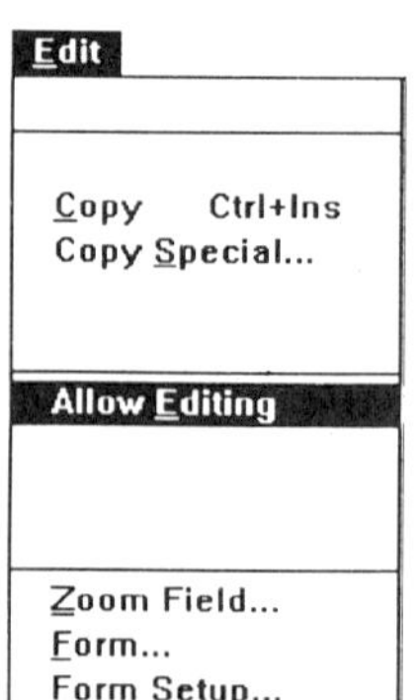

Editing a Record

Field values can be edited from the Edit menu. Select the field (or portion of a field) to edit, then open the Edit menu. Choose Edit Allow Editing. The familiar Cut, Copy, and Paste commands are on the Edit menu. Use them as you would in Excel: Cut removes the selected data to the Clipboard and Copy creates a copy in the Clipboard. Paste moves the data to the new location, even if it is in another Windows application.

Finding a Record

Sometimes you may need to find a record knowing only the value it contains. To initiate this kind of search, use the Find command.

Assume, for example, we wish to find Vera Linn's record in the database.

1. Select any one field in the column on which to execute the query.
2. Choose Find from the Search menu.

3. Enter the value for which you wish to search. Enter **Linn** (see Figure 25.2).
4. Click OK.

The cursor will be sent to the first field that contains the value. You can press F7 or use the Find Next command to find the next matching field. (There is none here.) To find a previous match, use the Find Previous command.

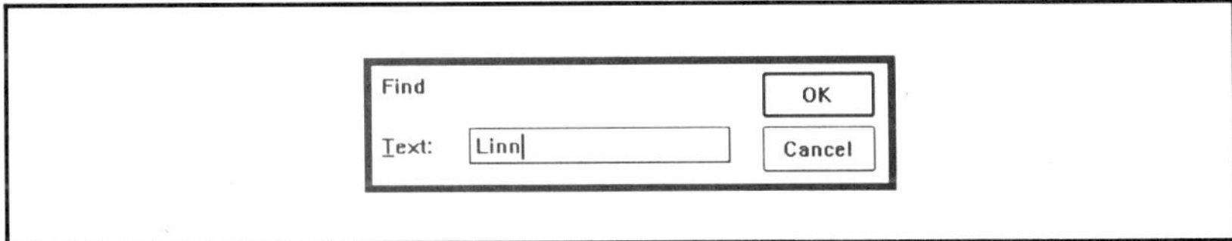

Figure 25.2: Initiating a find

Going to Specific Records

Search
Find...
Goto... F5

To scroll quickly to a specific record in a large database, use the Goto command. For example, to get to record 7:

1. Open the Search menu and choose Goto.
2. Enter the record number to which you wish to go (see Figure 25.3).
3. Click OK.

The cursor will move to record 7.

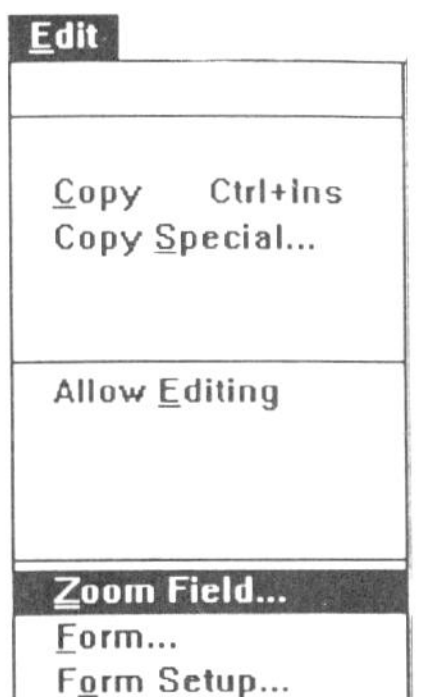

Figure 25.3: Going to a record

Zooming

If a field value is too large for the current column width, it will not fit in the displayed column. To view such a field, choose Zoom Field from the Edit window. The entire field will be displayed in a separate window. You can close the window from its Close box.

SORTING A DATABASE

The database query window defaults to displaying the records in the same order as they appear in the database. You can use the Sort command of the query window to display the records in a different order. Note that this does not change the record order in the database, only the *displayed* order.

The records are now displayed in ascending order based on the Last field. To reorder the display to show the records by Region in ascending order:

1. Select any field in the Region column.
2. Choose Ascending from the Sort menu.

The records are now ordered by region in ascending order. Remember that the database record order is not changed, only the query display.

To reset the display to the normal database order, choose Reset Sort from the Sort menu.

You can sort by multiple columns, as well. Sort on the primary order first, then the secondary. For example, to sort in ascending order by Region and then descending order by Last, sort in ascending order by Region as you just did, then select any entry in the Last field and choose Descending from the Sort menu (see Figure 25.4). Select Show Info from the Window menu to see the current sort order (see Figure 25.5). Choosing Reset Sort will again restore the normal database order.

QUERYING A DATABASE

You can extract records from a database using Q + E by defining a criterion and searching with that criterion. Let's try this now with our database.

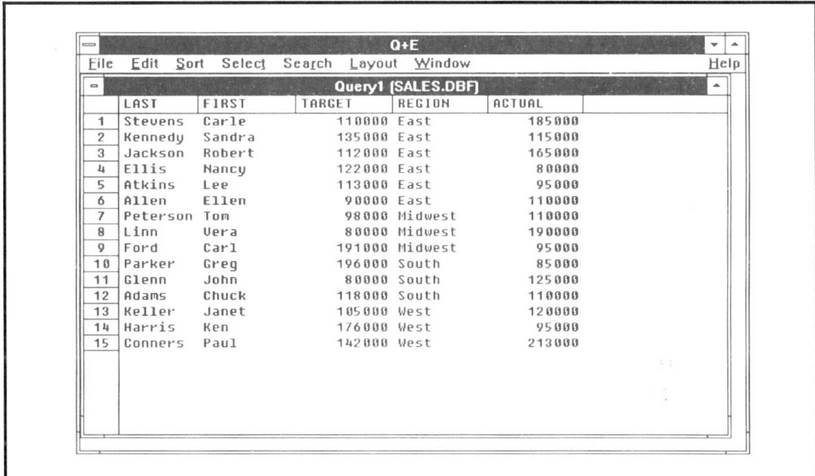

	LAST	FIRST	TARGET	REGION	ACTUAL
1	Stevens	Carle	110000	East	185000
2	Kennedy	Sandra	135000	East	115000
3	Jackson	Robert	112000	East	165000
4	Ellis	Nancy	122000	East	80000
5	Atkins	Lee	113000	East	95000
6	Allen	Ellen	90000	East	110000
7	Peterson	Tom	98000	Midwest	110000
8	Linn	Vera	80000	Midwest	190000
9	Ford	Carl	191000	Midwest	95000
10	Parker	Greg	196000	South	85000
11	Glenn	John	80000	South	125000
12	Adams	Chuck	118000	South	110000
13	Keller	Janet	105000	West	120000
14	Harris	Ken	176000	West	95000
15	Conners	Paul	142000	West	213000

Figure 25.4: An example of a multiple sort

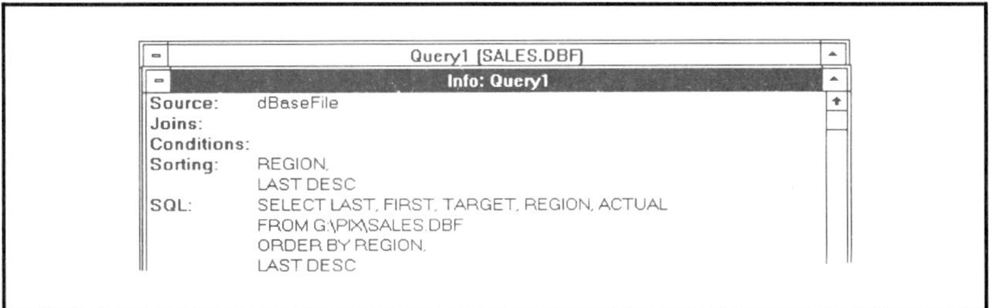

Figure 25.5: Examining the sort order

Selecting by a Single Condition

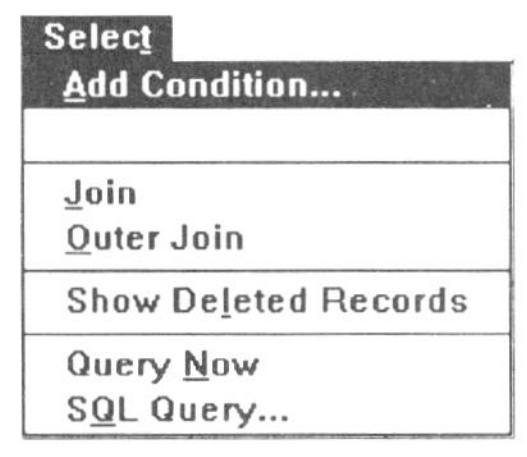

As an initial example, try searching by a single condition. Let's find all records with a target value greater then $100,000.

1. Select any entry in the field used for the criteria. In this case, select any value in the Target column.
2. Choose Add Condition from the Select menu.
3. In the dialog box (see Figure 25.6), choose Greater Than as the operator and enter **100000** in the Value box at the bottom.

4. Click OK.

The query window will change and now show only those records with a target value greater than $100,000.

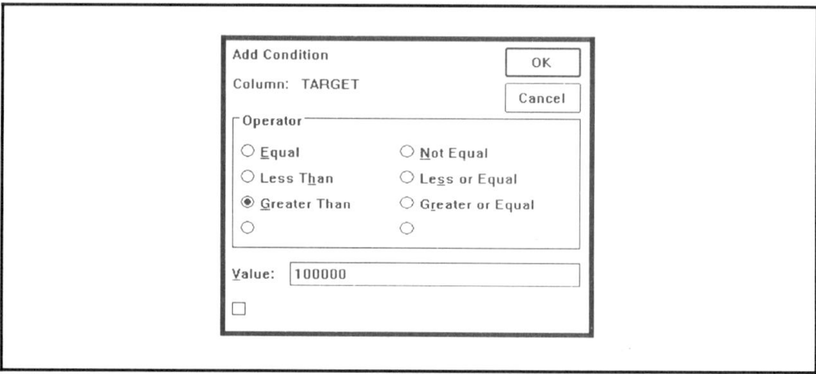

Figure 25.6: Specifying a single criterion

If you are searching through a text field, you can use wildcard characters to match text patterns. In this case, the Like operator becomes available in the Add Condition dialog box. You can use the asterisk (*) to match any character(s) and a question mark (?) to match a single character. For example, **R*** will match any field that starts with an *R*, and ***T** will match any field that ends with a *T*. Specifying **R?B** will match on any three-character value that starts with *R* and ends with *B*.

Selecting by Multiple Conditions

To select on multiple conditions, first specify the first condition. The window will change to reflect the records that match that condition, as in the last example. Now choose Add Condition from the Select menu again. Notice that the dialog box has now changed (see Figure 25.7), permitting you to specify whether the new condition should be "ANDed" or "ORed" with the previous condition (see Chapter 11). Leave it at the default AND. Choose Less Than as the operator and enter **150000** in the Value box. Click OK. The query window now shows only those records with target values greater than $100,000 *and* less than 150,000.

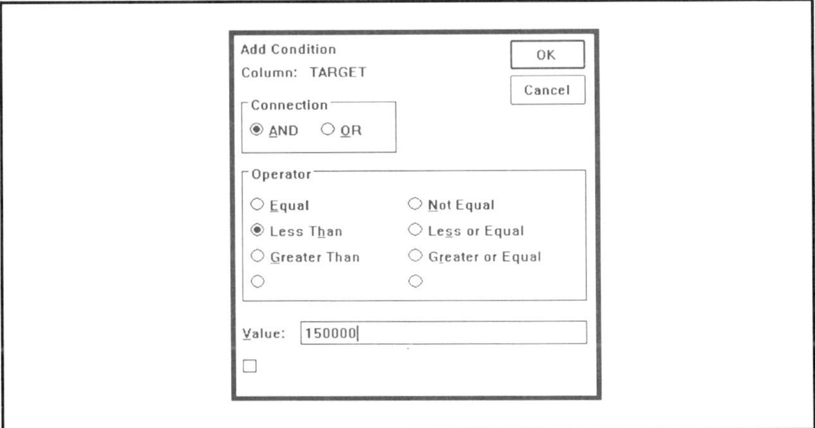

Figure 25.7: Selecting by a second condition

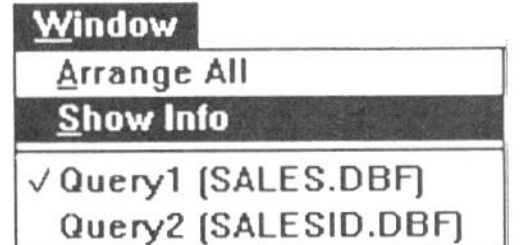

Viewing the Condition

To view the current criteria setting, choose Show Info from the Window menu. The Show Info window (see Figure 25.8) displays the current criteria.

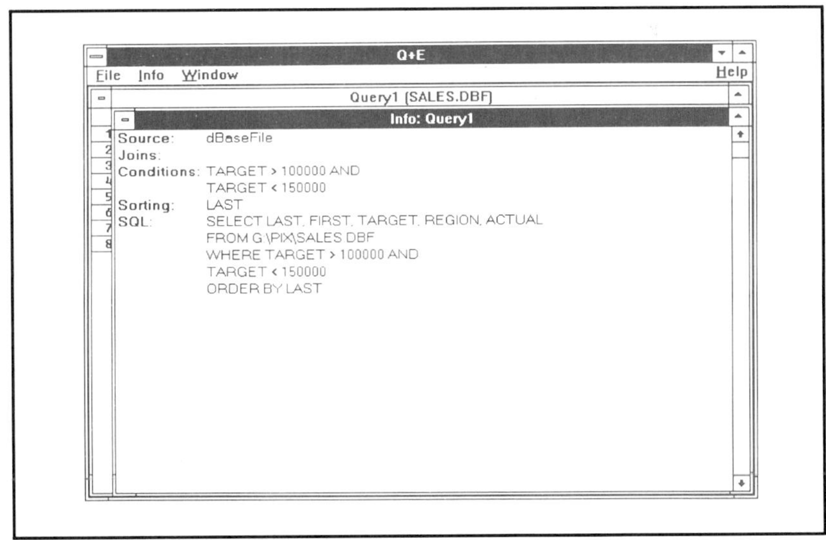

Figure 25.8: Viewing the current criteria setting

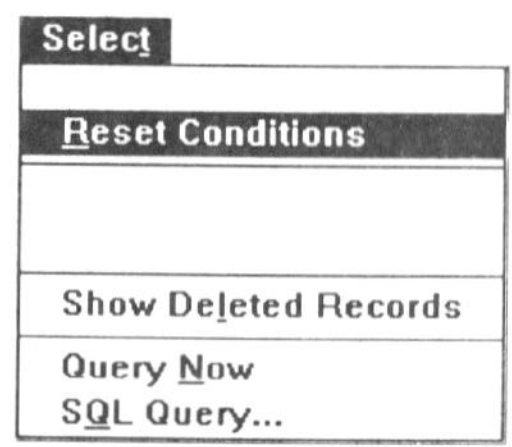

Resetting the Database Display

To restore the default display of all records in the database, choose Reset Conditions from the Select menu. The entire database will again be displayed.

Saving the Query

When using Q + E, you are working with two types of files: database and query files. The database file is opened from a query file or, if no query file exists, with the Open command. As you edit the file, it is automatically updated.

To save the current query under a new name, choose Save As from the File menu. Enter the file name for saving and click OK. Notice that you can't change the directory here. A query file is always saved in the same directory as the database.

To save a query under the current query name displayed in the window title bar, choose Save from the File menu.

FORMATTING THE DATABASE

You use the Layout menu to format the database: i.e., change column widths, change headings, move columns, change the font, and set the formatting.

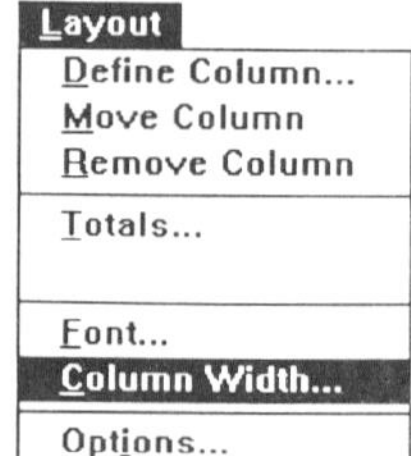

Changing the Column Width

To change a column's width, you can use the mouse or the Layout menu. With the mouse you can drag the column separator, as in Excel. From the Layout menu, you can choose Column Width. Enter the desired width and click OK.

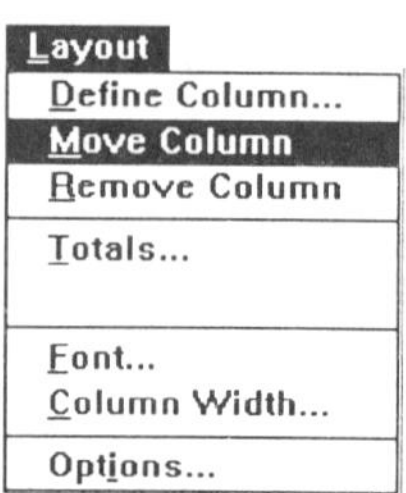

Changing the Column Heading

To change a column heading, double-click the current heading. In the dialog box enter the new column heading and click OK.

Moving Columns

To move a column, first choose the column to move. Then choose Move Column from the Layout menu. Point to the new location and click, or use the arrow or Tab keys to move the column to the new location.

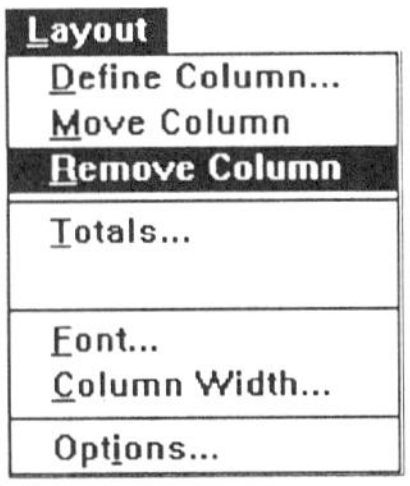

Layout
Define Column...
Move Column
Remove Column
Totals...
Font...
Column Width...
Options...

Removing Columns

To remove a column, select the column to remove and choose Remove Column from the Layout menu. This does not delete the data from the database, but only removes the data from the query form.

To restore a column, select Define Column and choose the column to restore (see Figure 25.27 for an example and dialog box).

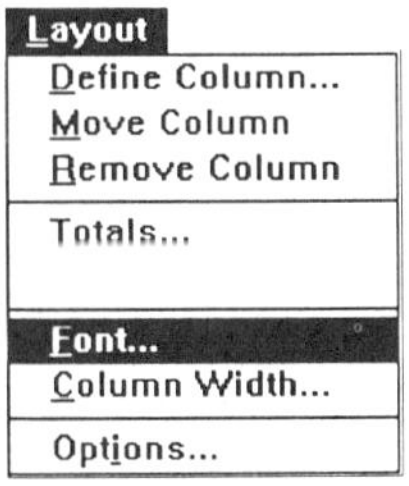

Layout
Define Column...
Move Column
Remove Column
Totals...
Font...
Column Width...
Options...

Changing the Font

To change the character font, select the fields and choose Font from the Layout menu. As in Excel, you can choose the font, size, and style you wish from the dialog box.

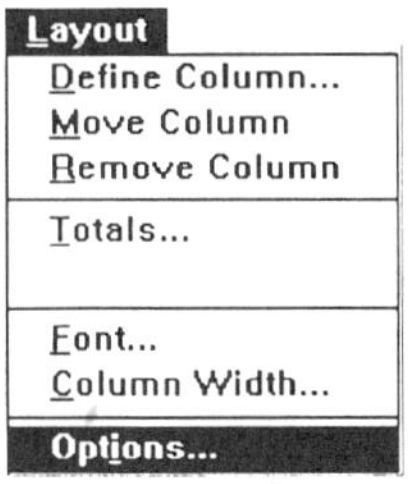

Layout
Define Column...
Move Column
Remove Column
Totals...
Font...
Column Width...
Options...

Setting the Picture

Q + E doesn't provide much formatting control over the picture, unlike Excel's Number command on the Format menu. The picture defaults to that set by the Control Panel program in Windows. To change this, use Control Panel to set the International or Country settings.

You can specify whether the thousands separator is to be used. Select Options on the Layout menu to turn the separator off or on.

If you need more picture control than this, you can link the results to a worksheet and use the formatting control of Excel to print your output.

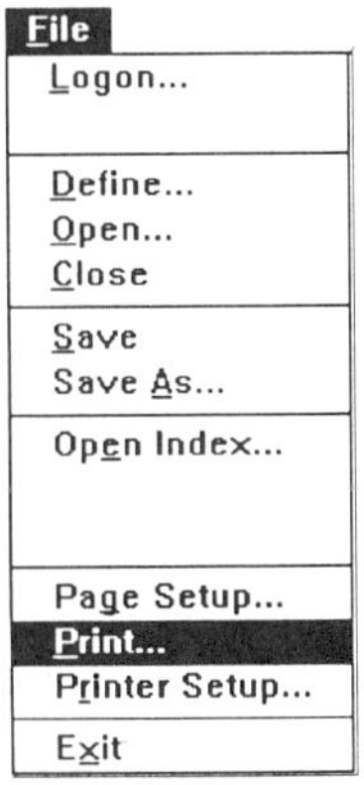

File
Logon...
Define...
Open...
Close
Save
Save As...
Open Index...
Page Setup...
Print...
Printer Setup...
Exit

PRINTING THE RESULTS

You can print the results of a query much as printing a worksheet. Select Page Setup from the File menu to define the page, and Printer Setup to set up the printer. Then select Print to print the worksheet.

CREATING NEW DATABASE FILES

You also can use Q + E to create a new database file using the Define command on the File menu. After the basic file structure is defined, it is saved as a database file using Save As. You can then open a query window to add records to the new file.

Some database systems, such as SQL systems, save the data in tables. In this chapter we will refer to a table as a database.

Creating a Database from an Existing Database

Now let's create a new database for the employees, transferring the names in the current database to a new file. We want to copy the Last and First fields from the Sales database to a new Salesid database, then add fields for the employee address: Address, City, State, Zip, and Phone. Follow this procedure:

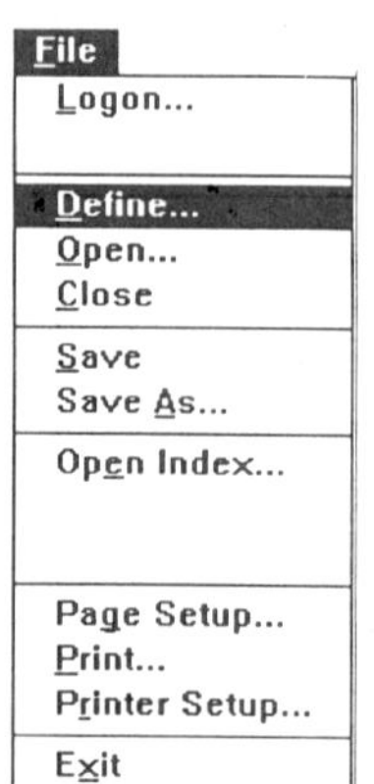

1. Open the File menu and choose Define. The Define dialog box will open (see Figure 25.9).
2. Enter the old database name (Source is dBaseFile) as **SALES** and click OK.
3. A new database window is opened with the structure of the current Sales database (see Figure 25.10). Each row represents one field in the new database. The columns are as follows:

FIELD_NAME	Name of the field
TYPE	Type of field (Character, Numeric, Logical, Memo)

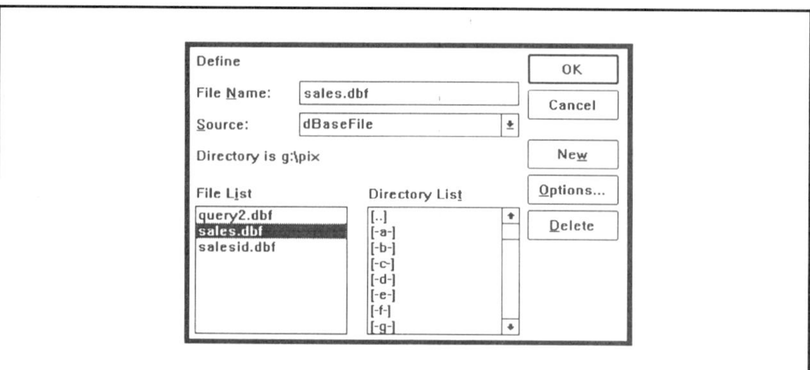

Figure 25.9: Defining a new database

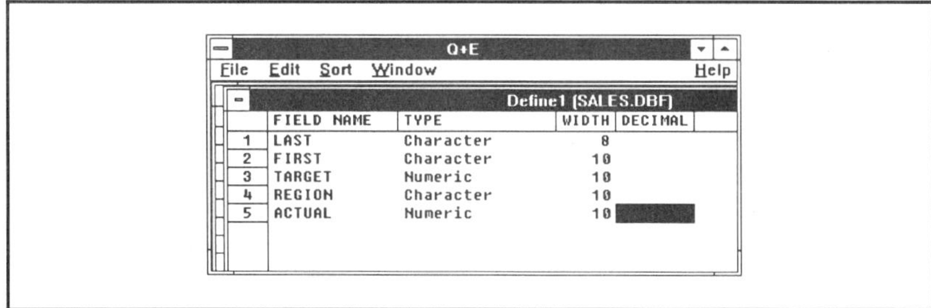

Figure 25.10: The Define database window

WIDTH	Width of the field
DECIMAL	For dBASE numeric fields, the number of decimal places

4. Delete the Target, Region, and Actual fields by selecting rows 3–5 and choosing Delete Fields from the Edit menu (see Figure 25.11).
5. Enter the first new field by selecting a cell in row 1 and choosing Add Before in the Edit menu.
6. Enter **ID**.
7. Tab to the Type column. A pop-up menu defines available data types (see Figure 25.12). Choose Character (or type a *C*).
8. Tab to the next column and enter **5** for the width.
9. Select the First field (i.e., row 3) and choose Add After in the Edit menu.
10. Enter the Address, City, State, and Zip fields as shown in Figure 25.13. Enter the correct type and width for each, too.

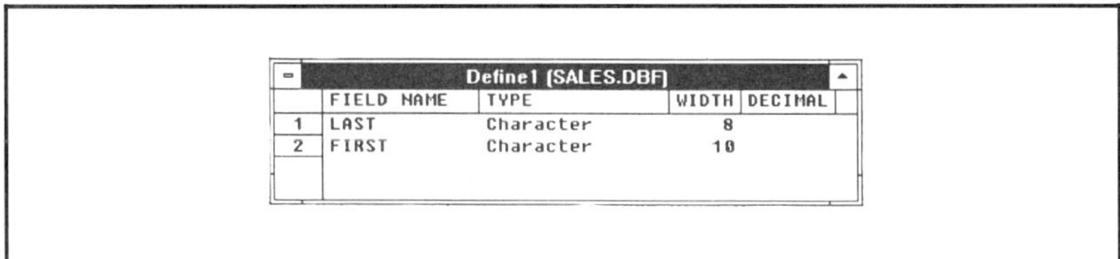

Figure 25.11: Deleting the unused fields

11. Save the database as SALESID. The extension is added automatically. Click the Options button to select from several options, if desired (see Figure 25.14). Choose OK.

The database structure is saved and now you can open a query window on the new structure (by selecting Open on the File menu).

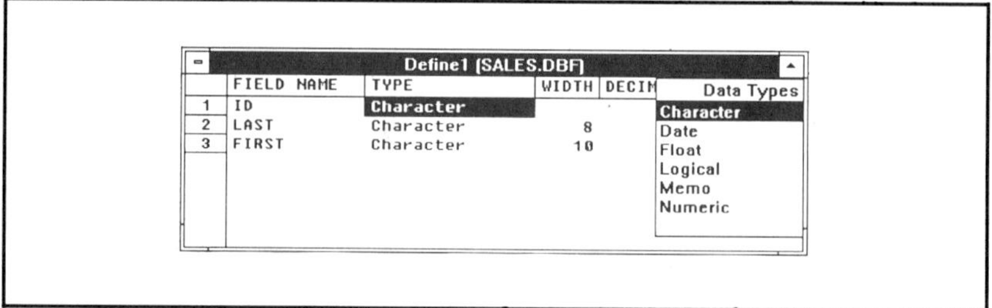

Figure 25.12: Choosing the data type for a new field

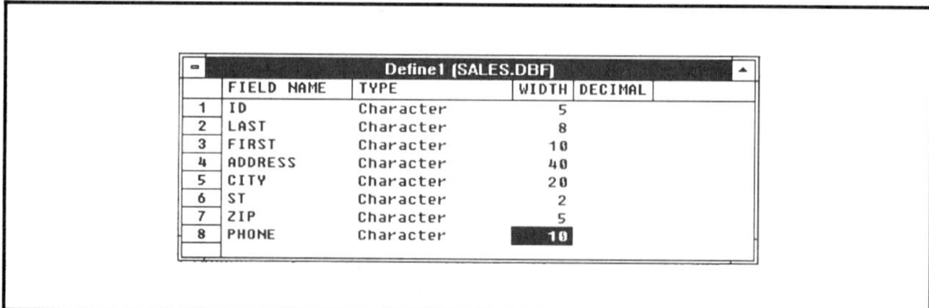

Figure 25.13: Entering the new fields

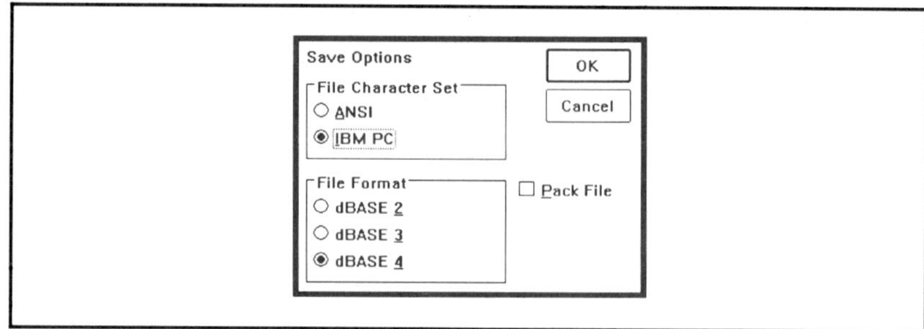

Figure 25.14: Setting the Save options

Creating a New Database

To create a new database with new fields, start as though you were using an existing database. Choose Define from the File menu, but then click the New button on the dialog box. Enter all the fields for the database. Finally, save the database. To add records, open a query form on the database.

EDITING RECORDS IN A DATABASE

You can edit existing records, add new records, and delete records in a database.

To edit records, first open the database. Choose the proper source (dBaseFile here) and select the file name (SALESID). The file will open with a default query form. Any data in the database will be displayed. In this case, the Last and First fields have already been copied from our Sales database.

It is not necessary to save the database after editing. You are entering the data directly to a database with the query form. In fact, you can't save an open database (you can only close it). You can, however, save the query form.

Editing Records Using the Menu

You can edit directly on the query form. Select each ID field and enter an ID number. Enter the remaining data, as shown in Figure 25.15. The first address is Box 75, Jackson, MS 39205. The second is 1602 S. Blount, Raleigh, NC 27610. You need a few addresses, but phone numbers are not needed for this exercise.

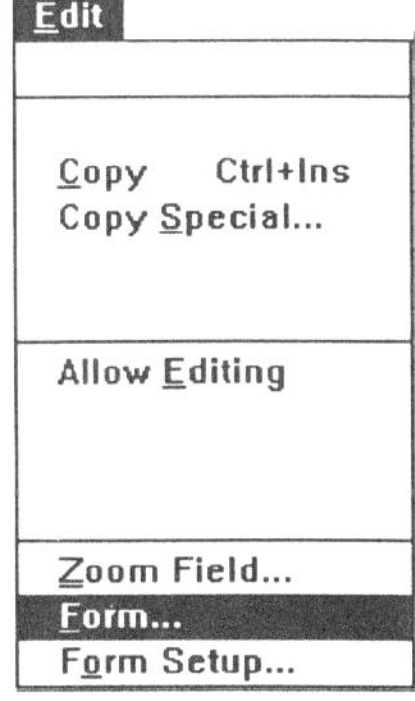

Editing Records with a Form

To edit records with a form, choose Form from the Edit menu or double-click the record number. Edit the entries in the form (see Figure 25.16). Notice that this is easier than directly editing records with many fields, since the entire record's entries are displayed. Use the scroll bar or arrow keys to move through the record. Press the Tab key to move across the fields. Press ↑ and ↓ to move across records. Exit the form mode by clicking the Exit button.

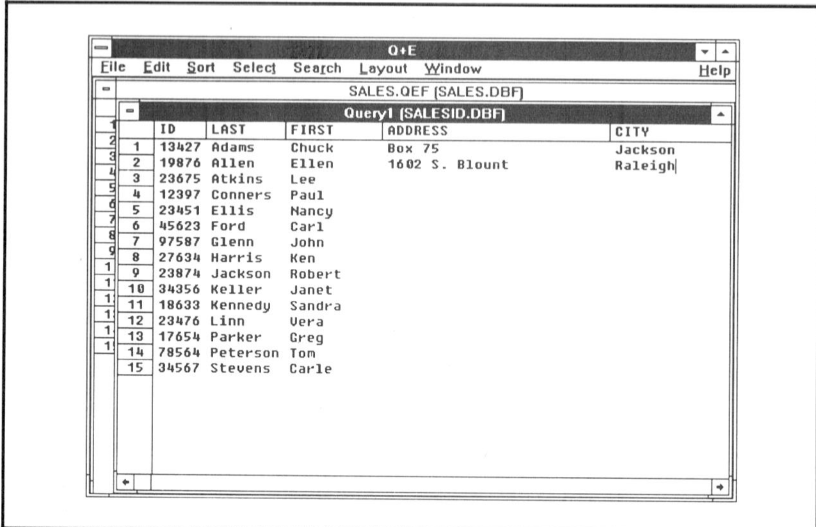

Figure 25.15: Adding data to a database

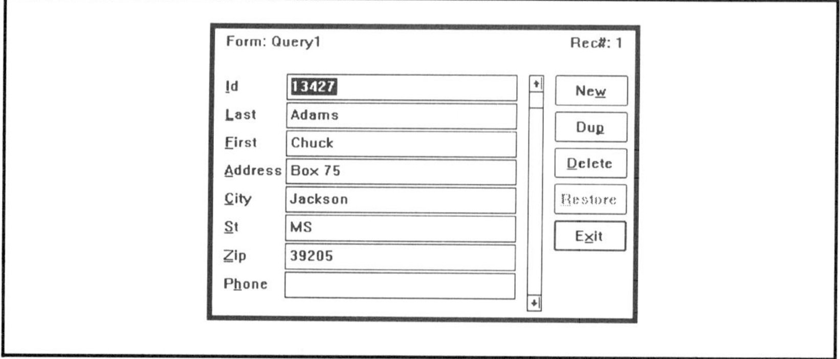

Figure 25.16: Using a form to edit records

To edit a form, choose Form Setup from the Edit menu (see Figure 25.17). Enter the number of columns for the form, the fields per column, and the maximum width for a form field. Then click OK.

Adding Records

To add a new record from the menu, select Add Record from the Edit menu. To use a form to add a record, select Form and click the New button. Then enter the data for the record.

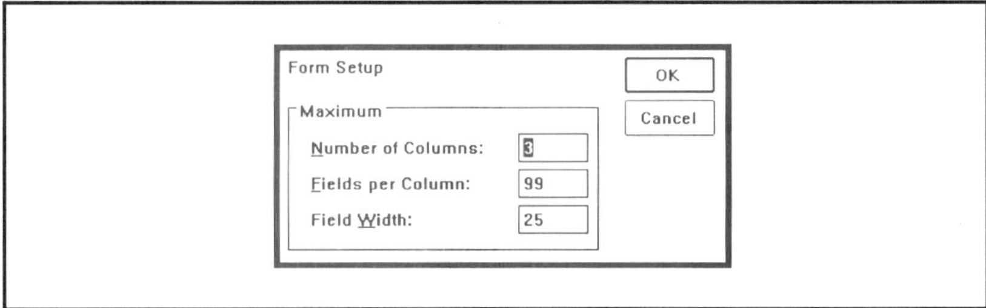

Figure 25.17: Modifying a form

To add records by copying records, select the record to copy by clicking the record number and choosing Copy. Then select Paste Append. The record is added at the end of the database.

You can duplicate existing records by choosing the record to duplicate, selecting Form, and clicking the Dup button.

Deleting Records

To delete a record, select the record and choose Delete from the Edit menu. You can undo the deletion with the Undo command. You also can delete a record with a query form by selecting the record, selecting Form, and clicking Delete. If you delete with a form, you cannot undo the deletion.

Updating the Query Window

As you edit a query form, records are not resorted or checked against the criteria again. To update the query window after editing, choose Query Now from the Select menu.

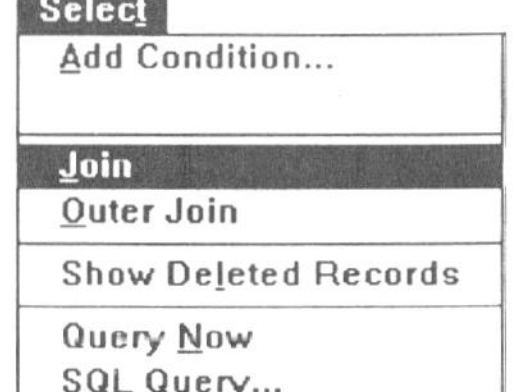

WORKING WITH MULTIPLE FILES

One advantage of Q + E over Excel, when working with databases, is that Q + E supports relational database management; that is, you can join multiple files on common fields.

To see how this works, open both the Sales and Salesid databases in Q + E. Now join them on the common Last field, making it possible to see the employee IDs in the Sales query. Here's the procedure:

1. Be sure both databases are open. Choose Arrange All from the Window menu so you can see both at once.
2. In the source window (SALESID), choose the column for the field that has the common value (Last).
3. In the destination window (SALES), choose the same column.
4. Be sure the destination window is active, and choose Join from the Select menu.

The destination window now shows the fields of both databases. Clean up the display by deleting and moving columns:

1. Remove all but the ID, SALES.LAST, SALES.FIRST, REGION, TARGET, and ACTUAL columns by selecting the columns to delete and choosing Remove Column from the Layout menu.
2. Move the ID column to the first column position by selecting it, choosing Move Column, and then clicking the first column in the query.
3. Using the same procedure, move the REGION column so that it comes after SALES.FIRST.

Figure 25.18 shows the query form at this point. Both database names are displayed in the query window's title bar, and they are linked on the common Last field.

You can create complex joins with Q+E, with many databases and fields linked. Fields can be joined in a one-to-one or one-to-many relationship. The above example is a one-to-one join: one record in a database is joined to a single record in another. In a one-to-many join, one record in one database is joined to many records in another. To see an example of a one-to-many, assume that an inventory database of parts has notes in another database, with the database files linked by part number. There may be several notes for a part. You can link the files in the same way, and the query will show all related notes.

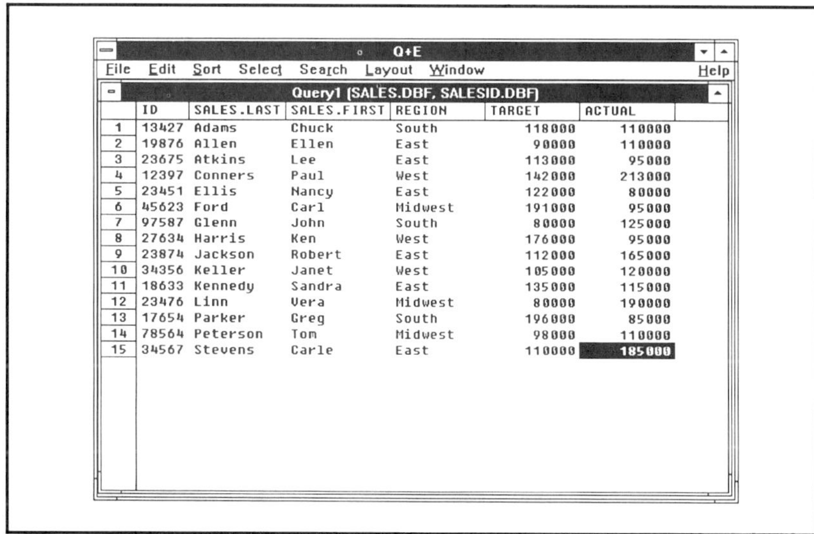

	ID	SALES.LAST	SALES.FIRST	REGION	TARGET	ACTUAL
1	13427	Adams	Chuck	South	118000	110000
2	19876	Allen	Ellen	East	90000	110000
3	23675	Atkins	Lee	East	113000	95000
4	12397	Conners	Paul	West	142000	213000
5	23451	Ellis	Nancy	East	122000	80000
6	45623	Ford	Carl	Midwest	191000	95000
7	97587	Glenn	John	South	80000	125000
8	27634	Harris	Ken	West	176000	95000
9	23874	Jackson	Robert	East	112000	165000
10	34356	Keller	Janet	West	105000	120000
11	18633	Kennedy	Sandra	East	135000	115000
12	23476	Linn	Vera	Midwest	80000	190000
13	17654	Parker	Greg	South	196000	85000
14	78564	Peterson	Tom	Midwest	98000	110000
15	34567	Stevens	Carle	East	110000	185000

Figure 25.18: Linking files on common fields

The Join command shows the records of the destination database only if a matching record exists in the source database. If you wish to see all records of the destination database (even if there is no matching source record), select Join Outer.

CREATING SUMMARY FIELDS

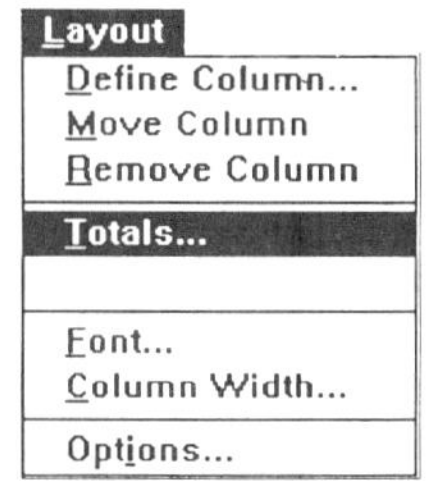

You can use Q + E to calculate column totals or other summary data. To calculate summary data, select the columns to use and choose Totals from the Layout menu. Choose the type of summary data desired (see Figure 25.19) and then click OK. Figure 25.20

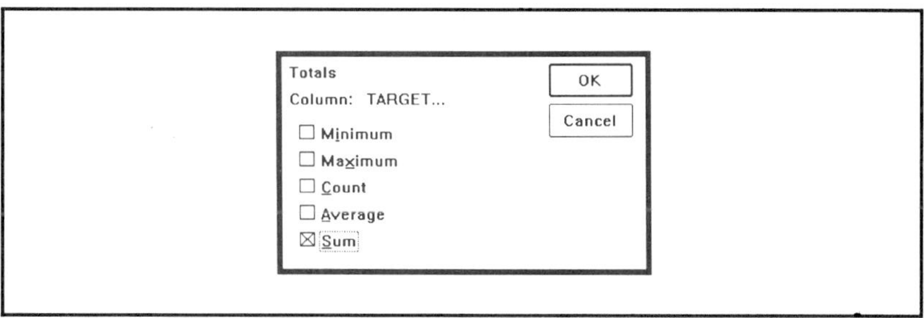

Figure 25.19: Selecting summary data

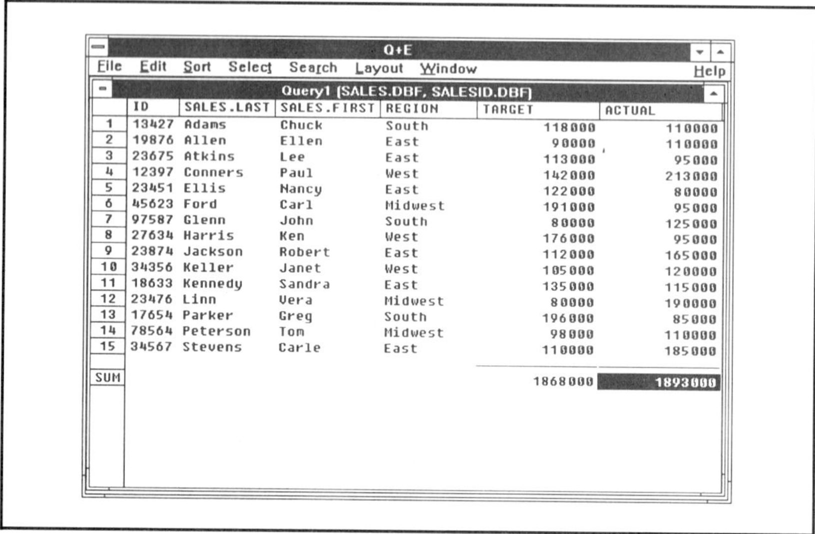

Q+E

File Edit Sort Select Search Layout Window Help

Query1 (SALES.DBF, SALESID.DBF)

	ID	SALES.LAST	SALES.FIRST	REGION	TARGET	ACTUAL
1	13427	Adams	Chuck	South	118000	110000
2	19876	Allen	Ellen	East	90000	110000
3	23675	Atkins	Lee	East	113000	95000
4	12397	Conners	Paul	West	142000	213000
5	23451	Ellis	Nancy	East	122000	80000
6	45623	Ford	Carl	Midwest	191000	95000
7	97587	Glenn	John	South	80000	125000
8	27634	Harris	Ken	West	176000	95000
9	23874	Jackson	Robert	East	112000	165000
10	34356	Keller	Janet	West	105000	120000
11	18633	Kennedy	Sandra	East	135000	115000
12	23476	Linn	Vera	Midwest	80000	190000
13	17654	Parker	Greg	South	196000	85000
14	78564	Peterson	Tom	Midwest	98000	110000
15	34567	Stevens	Carle	East	110000	185000
SUM					1868000	1893000

Figure 25.20: The query after summing target and actual values

shows the query after Sum is selected. You can make multiple selections.

CREATING CALCULATED FIELDS

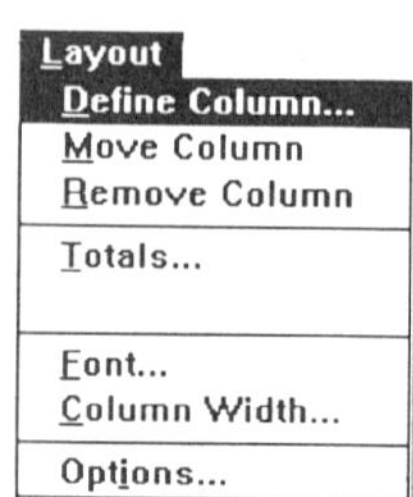

You also can create calculated fields in a query. Open the inventory database used in the invoice system example in Chapter 22. Open it as an Excel worksheet (Source is ExcelFile) within Q + E. Q + E will select the database and display it. Delete the EXT COST column by selecting it and choosing Remove Column from the Layout menu. Now add the column from Q + E:

1. Choose Define Column from the Layout menu.
2. In the Define Column dialog box, enter the heading and expression for the column (see Figure 25.21). Click OK.
3. The new EXT COST column is added to the query form (see Figure 25.22).

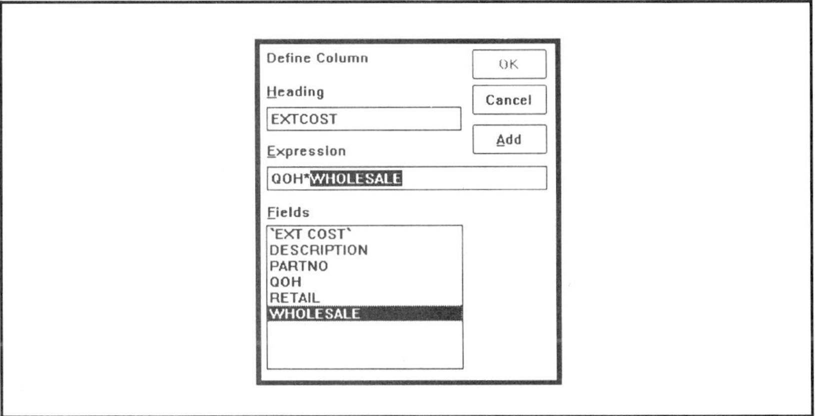

Figure 25.21: Adding a calculated field

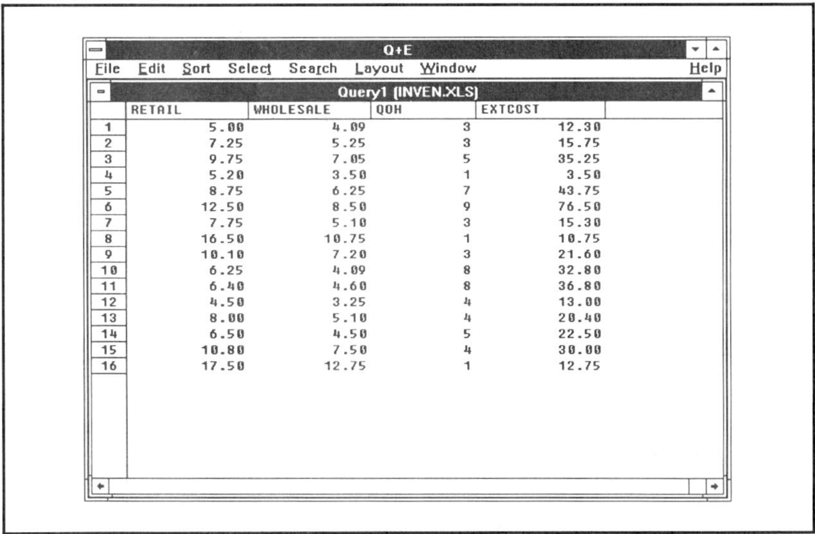

	RETAIL	WHOLESALE	QOH	EXTCOST
1	5.00	4.09	3	12.30
2	7.25	5.25	3	15.75
3	9.75	7.05	5	35.25
4	5.20	3.50	1	3.50
5	8.75	6.25	7	43.75
6	12.50	8.50	9	76.50
7	7.75	5.10	3	15.30
8	16.50	10.75	1	10.75
9	10.10	7.20	3	21.60
10	6.25	4.09	8	32.80
11	6.40	4.60	8	36.80
12	4.50	3.25	4	13.00
13	8.00	5.10	4	20.40
14	6.50	4.50	5	22.50
15	10.80	7.50	4	30.00
16	17.50	12.75	1	12.75

Figure 25.22: Part of the query after adding the calculated field

MAKING MAILING LABELS

Excel is not too good at printing mailing labels. But Q + E makes it simple. Let's try it with the Salesid file:

1. Open a query form on the SALESID database (using Open on the File menu).

2. If two or more fields are to be used in a single label line, move the columns to the line order you will need. In this case, move First before Last in the query form. (Use Move Column on the Layout menu).
3. Select the field(s) for the first line of the database by dragging the cursor over First and Last. Release the Ctrl key.
4. Keep the first selection active and hold down the Ctrl key while dragging the cursor over the fields for the next line (ADDRESS). Release the Ctrl key.
5. Hold down the Ctrl key again and drag the cursor over CITY, STATE, and ZIP for the third line. Release the Ctrl key.
6. Save the file as SALES. Choose MailingLabels from the pull-down Destination list box.
7. Click Options and see the dBASE expression for the label (see Figure 25.23). Edit as necessary.
8. Click OK twice.

The mailing label file is created. Use it as a mailmerge file with any word processor. (See the form-letter instructions in your word-processor documentation.)

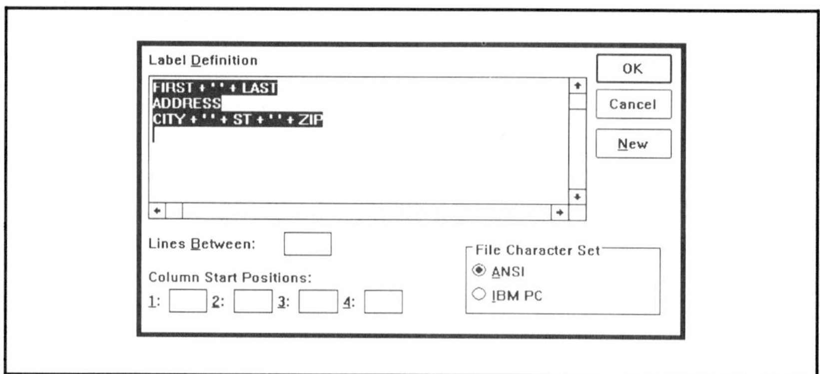

Figure 25.23: Editing the label definition

USING Q + E WITH OTHER APPLICATIONS

Q + E supports the Clipboard and DDE (see Chapter 21), making it easy to link input data to other sources (spreadsheets, communication programs, etc.) and the results of a query to other programs (spreadsheets, presentation programs, word processors, etc.).

Using the Clipboard

To copy data through the Clipboard, select the data and use Cut or Copy to place it in the Clipboard. Then paste it in the destination application. In the same way, you can paste data through the Clipboard from another application to Q + E.

You also can use Copy Special in Q + E to copy data to the Clipboard for another program. When you choose this command, a dialog box appears, permitting you to choose what you wish to copy. Here you can choose to include column headings, record numbers, link formulas, SQL Text for Excel 2.X (includes the SELECT statement in SQL), or to link data (see below). Click OK.

Linking Data

One valuable feature of Q + E is its ability to link field values to other programs. This means that as long as the database file is open, the field values in that file echo data input from another program. In the same way, an output document (word-processor letter or presentation slide) can always contain the latest data from the database. Data links can be created only with Windows application programs that support DDE.

The linking techniques are identical to those described in Chapter 16 for worksheets and in Chapter 21 for DDE.

Linking from Q + E to Another Application Data in Q + E can be linked from Q + E to another application such as a cell in Excel or a document in Microsoft Word for Windows. To create the link, select the information to link and choose Copy. To select special options, use Copy Special. Open the dependent document, select the destination, and choose Paste Link. Be sure to save both the query and document to preserve the link. Once this is done, the dependent document values will always follow those of Q + E.

Linking from Other Applications to Q + E You can link Q + E to another document, making the Q + E query the dependent document. For example, to link a query file result to an Excel document:

1. Open the worksheet document and the Q + E query.
2. Select the records and fields to copy in the Q + E query window.
3. Select Copy (or Copy Special for special copying) from the Edit menu.
4. Choose the starting cell for the paste in the Excel worksheet.
5. Select Paste Link from the Edit menu.

Figure 25.24 shows the result of pasting the names of the database into the worksheet. Notice that the worksheet formula indicates that this is an array. If entered manually, you would need to press Ctrl-Shift-Enter.

USING EXCEL WITH EXTERNAL DATABASES

Q + E can be used with databases external to Excel. Modifying Excel for external database support involves nothing more than

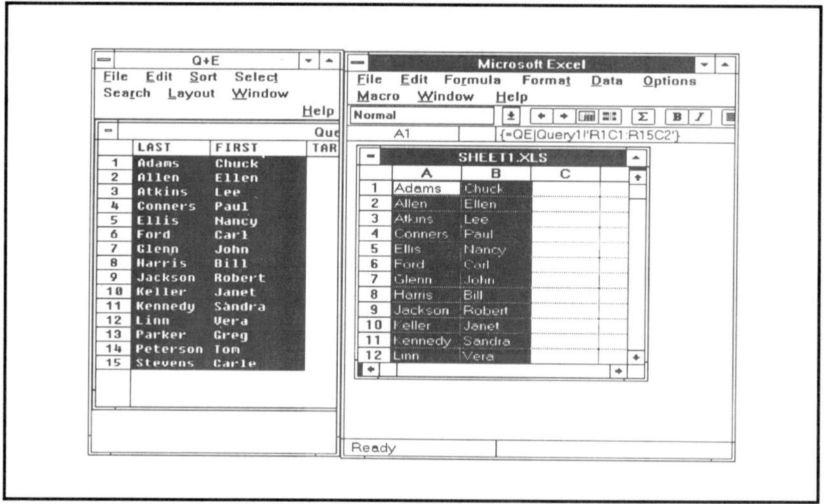

Figure 25.24: The pasted database names

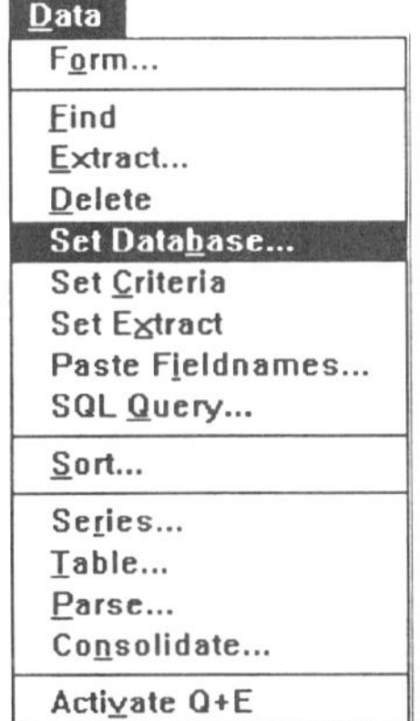

If you wish Excel to always start with database support, move the QE.XLA file to the \EX\XLSTART directory.

executing a single macro:

1. Start Microsoft Excel.
2. Open the File menu and choose Open.
3. Choose QE.XLA from the \EX\XLSTART\ QEMACRO directory (from the EX directory, click XLSTART, then QEMACRO).

Once the macro sheet is open, you will see three new commands on the Data menu:

COMMAND	*FUNCTION*
Paste Fieldnames	Selects field names from database files for criteria and extract ranges
SQL Query	Extracts results of an SQL SELECT statement
Activate Q + E	Starts the Q + E program

In addition, the other Data menu commands have been modified to support external databases:

COMMAND	*FUNCTION*
Set Database	Connects to an external database
Set Criteria	Defines criteria range
Set Extract	Defines extract range
Extract	Extracts data that meet the criteria
Delete	Deletes data that meets the criteria

Opening a Database

To open an external database:

1. Select Set Database. Click the External Database button and then click OK.
2. In the next dialog box (see Figure 25.25), select the file type and name. In the Source box, determine the type of

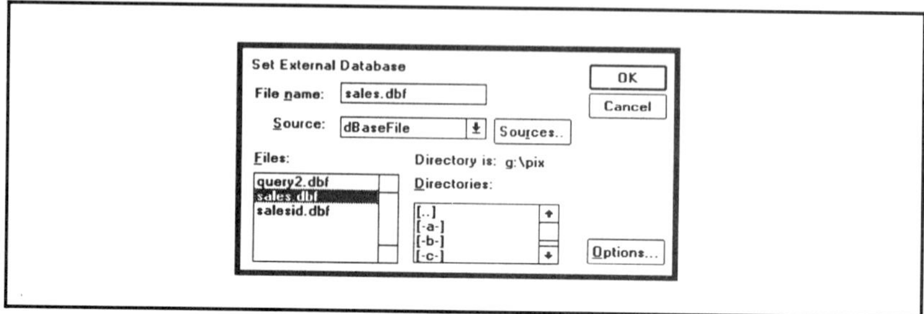

Figure 25.25: Choosing the database name

database file by choosing dBaseFile. If the source is not displayed on the list, click the Sources button to log onto an external source.

3. Choose the directory in which you stored SALES.DBF earlier in this chapter.
4. Choose SALES.DBF. Click Options for additional options, as in Q + E.
5. Click OK and you are returned to the first dialog box. The Change and Add buttons are active now. Click the Add button if you wish to join another database.

To open a database on the worksheet, select the database and choose Set Database from the Data menu, as you would with an external database. Choose Current Selection on the dialog box, then click OK.

To change the database selection, use Set Database, too. Click Change to change the current external database definition, Add to join another database, or Current Selection to switch to the worksheet database.

Extracting from an Internal Database

To extract a criterion, you must open the database and paste the fields to the worksheet. Open the Sales worksheet and try this with the SALES.DBF database:

1. Select the cell for the first field name and choose Paste Fieldnames from the Data menu. Choose G6 on the worksheet.

2. A dialog box opens with the database fields (see Figure 25.26). Select the field names from the list box and click Paste. To paste all field names to the worksheet in the current order, click Paste All. To paste field names in a different order, click the Order Fields button.
3. When pasting fields in a different order, the dialog box expands (see Figure 25.27). To add a field, choose the field in the Available Fields list and click Add. You also can insert a field name anywhere in the output list by choosing the field to add in the Available Fields list. Then choose the field below which you wish to insert the new field and click Add. Clicking Remove removes a field from the output list, and Clear All clears the output list. Select All places all field names in the output list. Click Select All, then Paste.

You can then define a criteria range or extraction range with the list.

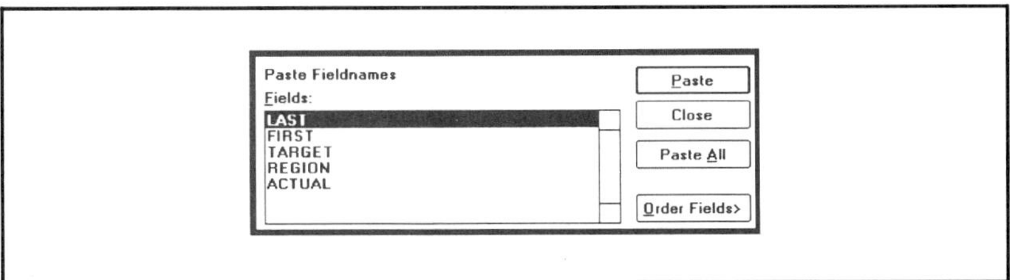

Figure 25.26: Pasting the field names

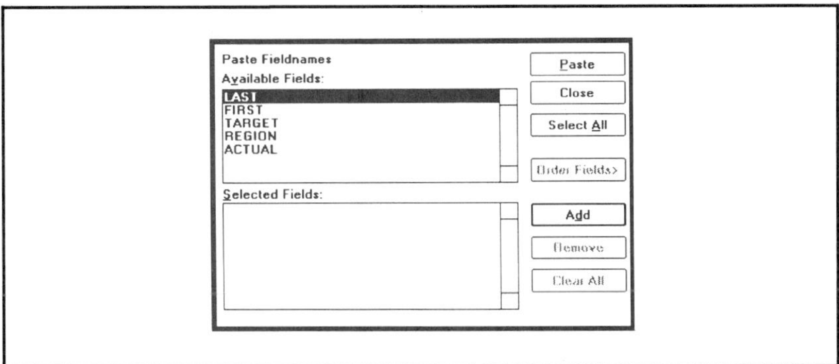

Figure 25.27: Pasting ordered field names

Extracting from an External Database

Using criteria and performing extractions from an external database is identical to doing so from an internal database. Copy the field names you wish to use to the specified area and use Set Criteria or Set Extract. With extraction, you can use a joined file by opening both database files with Set Database. Once this is done, the extracted data will contain the fields of both databases. Here is the procedure summary for extractions:

1. Open the database (or databases) with Set Database.
2. Select all the field names with Paste Fieldnames.
3. Define the criteria and extraction ranges with Set Criteria and Set Extract.
4. Enter the criteria.
5. Initiate the extraction with Extract.

Now try an extraction with the external Sales database.

1. Copy G6:K6 to G10 to get another range (see Figure 25.28).
2. Define the criteria range by selecting G6:K7 and selecting Set Criteria on the Data menu.
3. Define an extraction range by selecting G10:K23 and selecting Set Extract.
4. Enter a criteria by entering **West** into cell J7.
5. Select Extract on the Data menu.
6. On the extraction dialog box, click OK.
7. On the next dialog box, choose whether the records are linked or not. Choose Unlinked and click Paste.

The extracted database is then entered to the worksheet (see Figure 25.29).

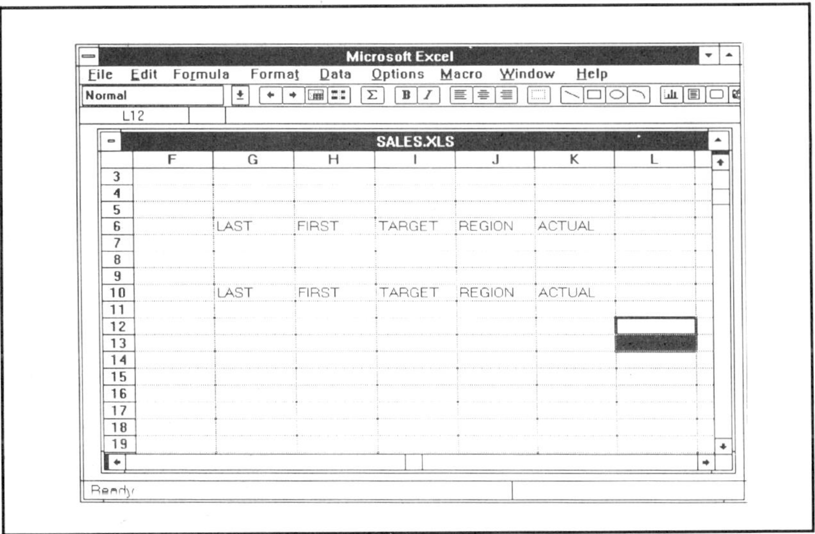

Figure 25.28: The pasted field names

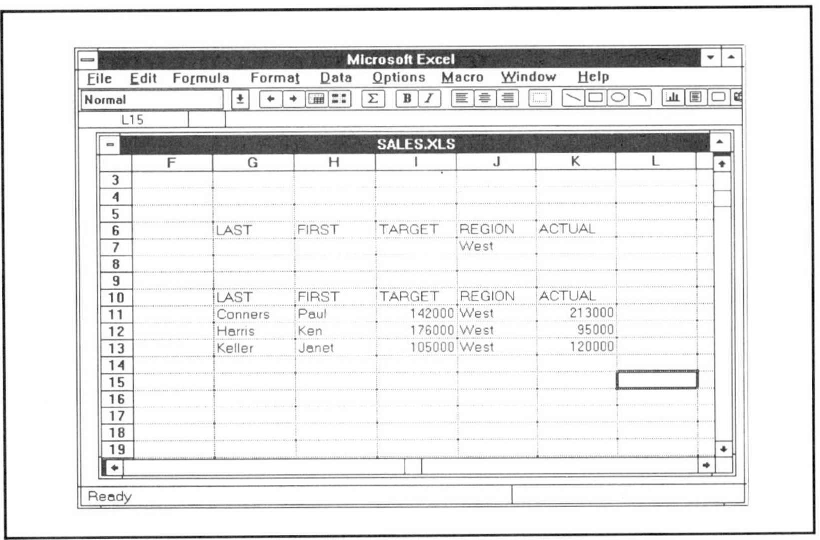

Figure 25.29: The extracted database

CALCULATING WITH THE SOLVER

The Solver is a tool for what-if analysis that is included with Excel. Here are some examples of uses for the Solver:

- You have a cash-flow worksheet (as in Chapter 7) and you wish to plan how much to spend on marketing to maximize sales. This assumes that you know the relationship between sales and marketing costs. An example is shown in the Solver manual and the worksheet is included with the Solver
- You have a series of simultaneous equations to solve (as in the trend analysis example of Chapter 24)
- You need to work backward from a goal to find input variables, given a number of constraints. A simplified example was shown in Chapter 8 with the amortization schedule

Solver can solve complex interrelationships among variables, even when equations don't exist and you need to use lookup tables.

To see how Solver works, let's first try a simple example. To really show its power, we will then show a more complex example.

THE AMORTIZATION SCHEDULE

Let's use Solver with the amortization schedule from Chapter 8, setting a goal for the size of the payment and trying to find how much principal you can afford at a given interest rate. (In Chapter 8 you did this using the Goal Seek command on the Formula menu.) To start, load the Amortization worksheet. Then follow these steps:

1. Open the Formula menu and choose Solver. A dialog box is displayed. You can move the dialog box around the screen by dragging the title bar as necessary.
2. In this case, we simply want to solve for a payment of $150 in B10. We want to find the principal we can afford at this payment and the fixed 9 percent interest. Click in the By Changing Cells box in the dialog box, then click B6 to enter the absolute reference in the box (see Figure 25.30).

3. Click Add to enter a constraint.
4. In the next dialog box (see Figure 25.31), click B10 to enter that cell in the Cell Reference box.
5. From the pull-down list in the middle of the dialog box, choose = as the operator.
6. Click or tab over to Constraint, then enter **150** in the dialog box. Click OK.
7. Click Solve. (Don't click OK here, or the dialog box will close and nothing will happen.)

Solver will initiate execution. Once the Solver has finished, it will display a dialog box saying that it has found the values (see Figure 25.32), and that you can choose whether to accept the new values. Choose OK. The final constant values will be displayed on the worksheet (see Figure 25.33).

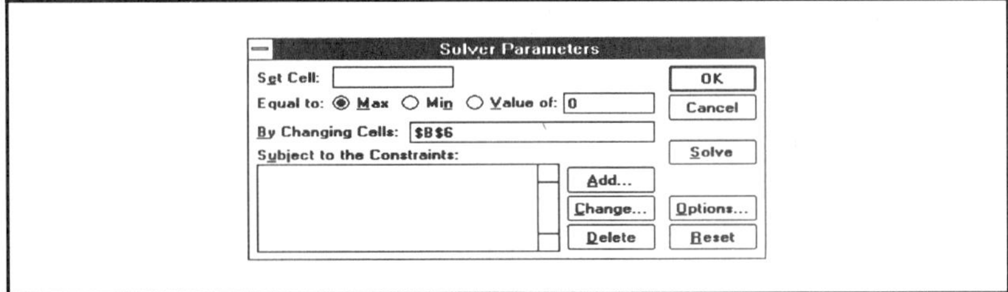

Figure 25.30: Defining the cell to change

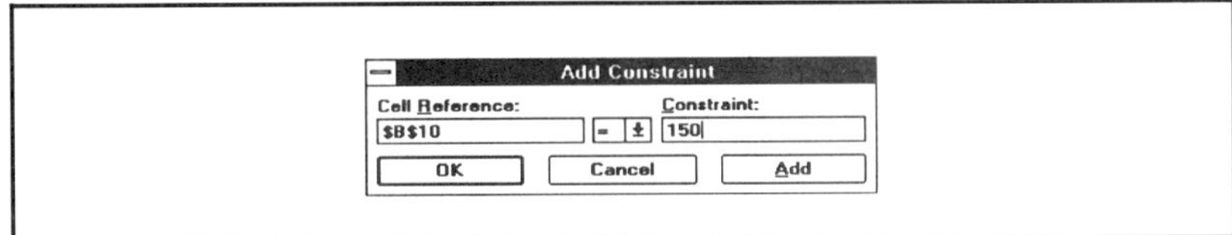

Figure 25.31: Adding the constraint

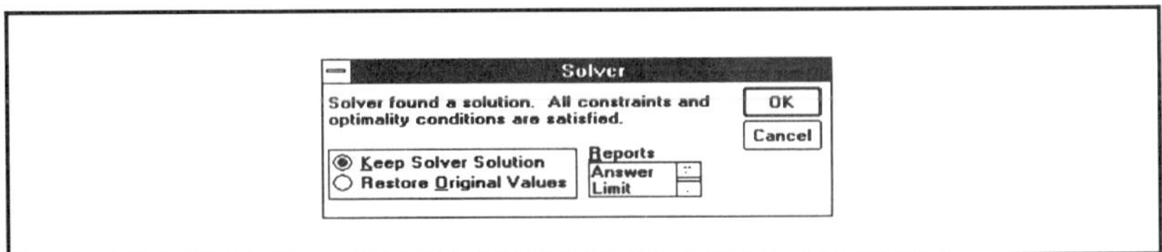

Figure 25.32: The Solver prompt after a solution is found

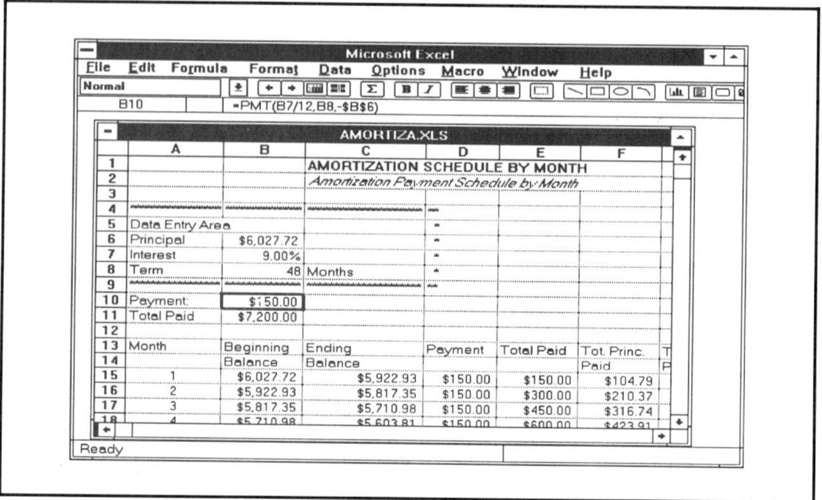

Figure 25.33: The final worksheet

SOLVING QUADRATIC EQUATIONS

In Chapter 24 you did a curvilinear regression (see Figure 24.6) by solving a series of simultaneous equations of the form

$$683.5 = 14a_0 + 105a_1 + 1015a_2$$

$$6273.2 = 105a_0 + 1015a_1 + 11025a_2$$

$$65419.6 = 1015a_0 + 11025a_1 + 127687a_2$$

to find the values for a_0, a_1, and a_2. Once these values were found, you could find any y value in the series by using the equation

$$y = a_0 + a_1x + a_2x^2$$

Unless you were very brave, however, you probably didn't try the entire worksheet. Solver makes this easier.

Let's see how. First, open a new worksheet and enter **a0**, **a1**, and **a2** in cells A1, A2, and A3, respectively. Cells B1 through B3 should hold the constants. For now, enter zero in these. Select Define Name on the Formula menu to name cell B1 as A0, B2 as A1_ and B3 as A2_. Because A1 and A2 are cell locations, you have to add an underline after them when naming cells B2 and B3.

Set up the equations in B5 to C5 as shown in Figure 25.34. (Cells B1:B3 should be 0 at this time.) Now you are ready to start:

1. Select Solver from the Formula menu. Move the dialog box to the bottom of the screen so you can see the rest of the worksheet (click on the title bar and drag).
2. Click in the By Changing Cells box, then select cells B1 through B3 on the worksheet. Excel enters $B$1:$B$3 automatically.
3. Click the Add button to get the Add Constraint dialog box. (Move it to the bottom of the screen, as well.) Select cell B5 and choose = as the operator. Click in the Constraint box, then select cell C5. Notice that Excel automatically enters absolute addresses.
4. Click the Add button to add two more constraints: $B$6 = $C$6 and $B$7 = $C$7. After you enter the second constraint, click OK to get back to the Solver Parameters dialog box.

Figure 25.35 shows the Solver Parameters dialog box after it is set up for this problem. Click Solve and the constant values will appear in B1:B3, as shown in Figure 25.34.

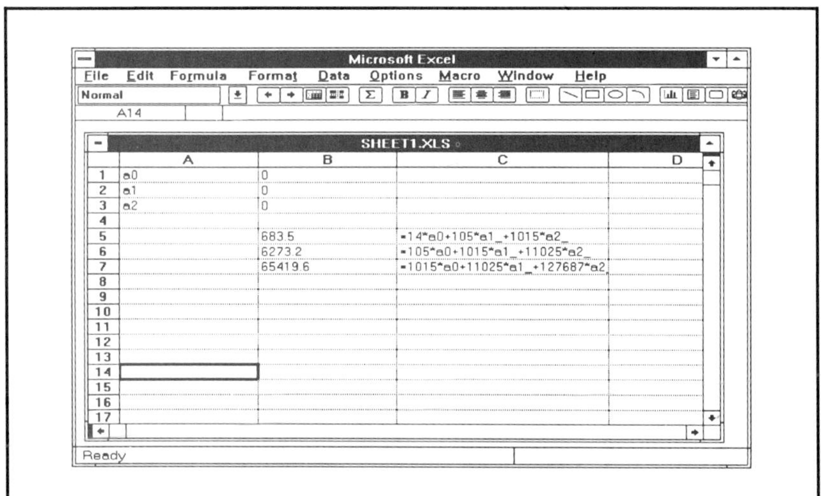

Figure 25.34: Solving a quadratic equation

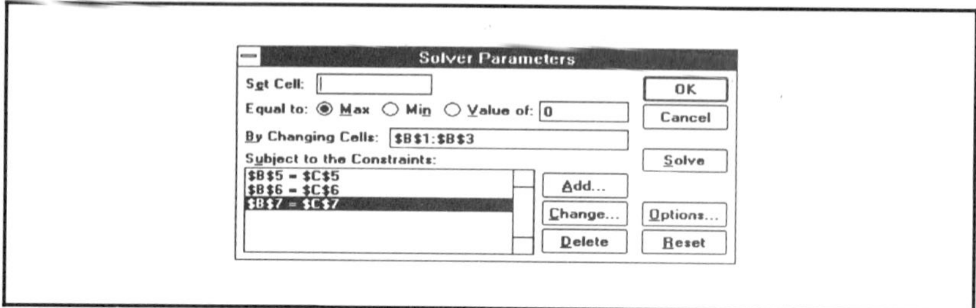

Figure 25.35: The Solver Parameters dialog box

Solver uses iterative calculations based on the principles of numerical analysis to find a solution. The iteration process stops when a solution is found that satisfies the limits defined by the Options dialog box. As with Excel iterations, the assumption is made that the solution converges. There is also a time limit imposed on the solution. If you have trouble finding a solution:

- Be sure the definitions are correct
- Try different starting values. (Zeroes were used in the previous example.)
- Be sure you have a converging solution
- Change the options. For example, checking Assume Linear Model may not be a valid assumption

Using the Solver is similar to the goal-seeking example of Chapter 8, but notice you have more options here:

- You can choose to define the goal as setting a cell to a specific value or as maximizing or minimizing a cell
- You can set multiple constraints and choose their operators
- You can solve multiple problems on a worksheet

When you save your worksheet, the last Solver solution is attached to the worksheet and saved with it. If you do multiple Solver solutions, however, only the last one is saved with the worksheet. If you used Solver to solve several problems on the worksheet, save the problem model on the worksheet. To do so, select an empty range on the worksheet and click Save Model in the Solver Options dialog box.

VII

Powering up with Macros

A MACRO IS A SERIES OF EXCEL COMMANDS THAT performs a specific action. In effect, macros permit you to write and name your own application programs using worksheet commands, as well as create your own functions. For this reason, macros are generally considered one of the most important features of any worksheet program.

Although macros are a part of many worksheet products, Excel's macros have three major distinctions: they are easy to use, they don't take up worksheet room (since they're saved on separate macro sheets), and they extend Excel's command language.

Excel provides the capability of creating two types of macros: command macros and function macros. In Chapter 26 you learn when to use command macros and how to create them. Chapter 27 introduces you to the use of function macros, and Chapter 28 provides some insights on more advanced macro techniques, such as debugging, creating custom menus, and designing your own dialog boxes. The available Excel macro language functions are comprehensively listed in Appendix E.

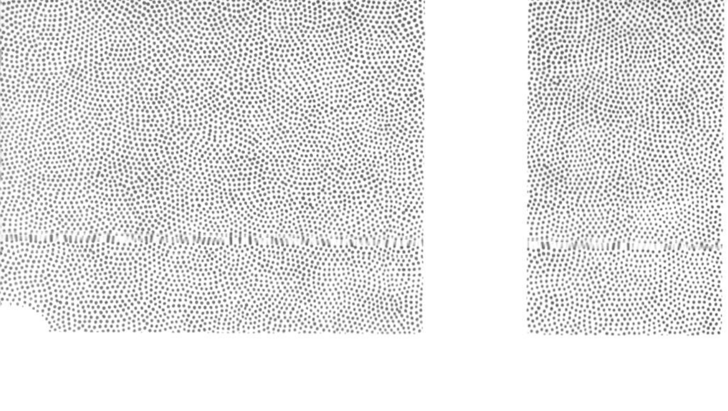

26 Introduction to Macros: The Recorder

EXCEL ALLOWS YOU TO CREATE TWO TYPES OF macros: command macros and function macros. In this chapter, you will learn when to use command macros and how to create them. Excel's recorder makes creating simple command macros very easy. Function macros will be discussed in Chapter 27.

COMMAND MACRO USES

A *command macro* is a series of commands that accomplishes a desired action. The commands are stored as a single program, which can be executed as often as necessary.

Command macros are used primarily when it is necessary to repeat a complex series of steps many times. Should you find yourself repeating certain Excel operations frequently, chances are that you should consider using a command macro. Here are some examples of applications you might use frequently:

- Putting headings in a worksheet
- Creating schedules for financial calculations

- Entering the labels of a frequently-used worksheet
- Simplifying a task (or tasks) for someone else with a minimum of Excel experience
- Creating forms for data entry, custom dialog boxes, or a custom menu
- Doing a complex series of calculations with proprietary equations

Command macros also can simplify and improve the accuracy and efficiency of a task that must be completed within a tight schedule. For example, suppose that a series of annual reports must be prepared from data that will not be available until a few days before the annual meeting. Weeks before the meeting, you could create macros to produce the final report from dummy data. Once the actual data are available, the same macros could be used by almost anyone to create the final reports in a very short time.

As another example, assume a bank sets up a very complex worksheet for making decisions on granting loans to businesses. The five-year history of the business is entered, and Excel uses this to make projections for the next five years, based on assumptions about several variables, such as interest rates. Two worksheets are created: the history worksheet and the projection worksheet. The worksheets are linked using Excel's linking abilities. Macros are used to set up the link and to prompt the user for input. These worksheets can then be used at various bank locations by people who have little experience with Excel. When Excel is started, a menu worksheet can be displayed automatically, guiding the user through the entire problem-solving process with macros.

You can do just about anything with a macro that you can do directly on the worksheet: open new worksheets, create charts, create and paste names, display dialog boxes for entry, or select and print worksheets. You also can do a few things with macros that you can't do with the normal Excel commands, such as create input dialog boxes and data-entry forms or custom menus.

Here are some more applications for command macros:

- Creating a calendar for the month

- Creating a weekly schedule with the date and day of the week as headers
- Doing mail-merge letters or envelopes from a database of addresses
- Creating a new application-oriented menu for a user who has had little Excel experience and doesn't know how to use the default Excel menus
- Doing financial schedules

3.0

Excel 3.0 allows you to put a button on the worksheet (like a dialog box button) and attach your text and macro to it. For example, a button could say **Print**; clicking it would print the worksheet. You also can attach macros to any graphic object, even invisible objects. For example, you can attach a hidden object to a cell and then activate a macro (for example, to display help) by clicking the cell.

WHAT IS A MACRO?

Briefly examine the macro example in Figure 26.4, which you will create later. You should recognize many commands on the Macro1 sheet because they match the menu options you have already used. Don't worry about understanding them now; just keep the following ideas in mind:

- Although it is not obvious here, each macro has a name. The first cell in the macro is named by the user, and that becomes the name of the macro
- The commands are listed in a vertical column. They are executed starting at the named cell and continue downwards until the macro function RETURN, HALT, or GOTO is reached. A RETURN or HALT terminates the macro execution. GOTO causes a branching to its argument. (Macro functions are described in Chapter 27.)

COMMAND MACROS VERSUS TEMPLATES

Templates, which you have already used, are useful for simplifying repetitive tasks. There is a big difference, however, between a template and a command macro. A template is a blank form that has some formats already specified. You fill in the blank form to create a worksheet. Templates are useful for many applications and should be used whenever possible. Macros, however, permit automatic execution of Excel commands, with prompts for input. An example will clarify this.

Assume you run an advertising agency in which employees are working on jobs for several clients during the course of the day. For each period of the day, employees need to keep track of which client they were working for and the job category (since categories are billed at different rates).

You could create a blank time sheet and save it as a template; however, employees would still need to fill in information, such as their names and the date. In addition, they might enter invalid categories accidentally or neglect to fill in certain time slots if, for instance, they couldn't remember the category or preferred not to say what they did during that time. Finally, with a template the user is still required to know how to use Excel.

Using a macro permits you to automate the entire process. The macro could prompt for the employee's code and the input information. The employee's name could then be obtained from a lookup table using the code. The macro could also look up categories, reject invalid entries, and calculate totals based on category rates. It could be designed to block the possibility of any time slot being left empty. Finally, it could print the time sheet automatically. The user wouldn't have to know anything about Excel except how to load the worksheet and answer the prompts.

CREATING A COMMAND MACRO

There are two ways to create a command macro with Excel: using the recorder and entering the macro manually. The recorder is the easiest method but is less flexible than manual entry. In this chapter you will learn the recorder method. The manual entry of command macros is discussed in Chapter 28.

There are four steps to create a command macro using the recorder:

1. Opening the macro sheet and setting the range.

2. Recording the program.
3. Naming the macro.
4. Saving the macro sheet.

Suppose that you are a manager at Acme Manufacturing. You have created many quarterly reports that all use the same heading, as shown in Figure 26.1. You've decided to take advantage of Excel's macro capabilities and create a macro that will add the heading to the quarterly report worksheet. The following sections describe how to create this command macro.

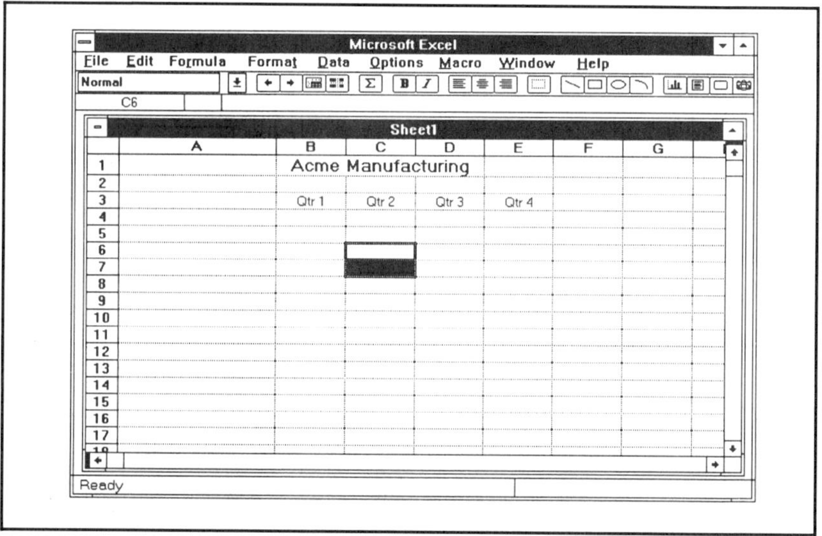

Figure 26.1: The standard heading for your quarterly reports

OPENING THE MACRO SHEET AND SETTING THE RANGE

The macro you create will be recorded on a separate macro sheet, which is much like any Excel worksheet. First, open a regular worksheet. Then follow these steps to open the macro sheet and set the range for the macro:

1. Press Ctrl–F11 or select New from the File menu. Choose Macro Sheet and click OK. A new document titled

"Macro1" will open on the screen. (The menu bar has not changed. The row and column headings are the same, too. Notice, however, that the columns are much wider than they are on a typical worksheet document. This permits you to see the formulas you enter in their entirety. The Display command on the Options is set to display formulas automatically, but you can switch this back to show data if necessary. Here, however, you are interested in the formula, not the result.)

2. Arrange the windows so you can see column A of the macro sheet and columns A to F of the worksheet (see Figure 26.2). You will only use A–E of the worksheet, but column A will be widened later.

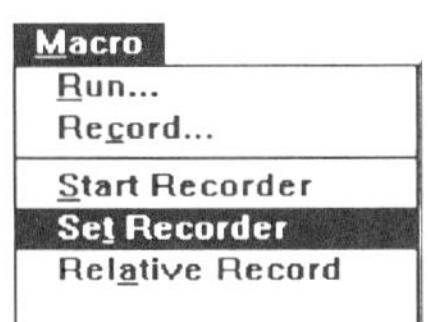

3. Set the macro range by clicking the column A designator on the macro sheet (Macro1). Open the Macro menu and choose Set Recorder.

4. Open the Macro menu again. You will want to record absolute references. This means that the next-to-last menu item should read **Relative Record**. In this case, clicking the menu item would switch you to relative recording. If the

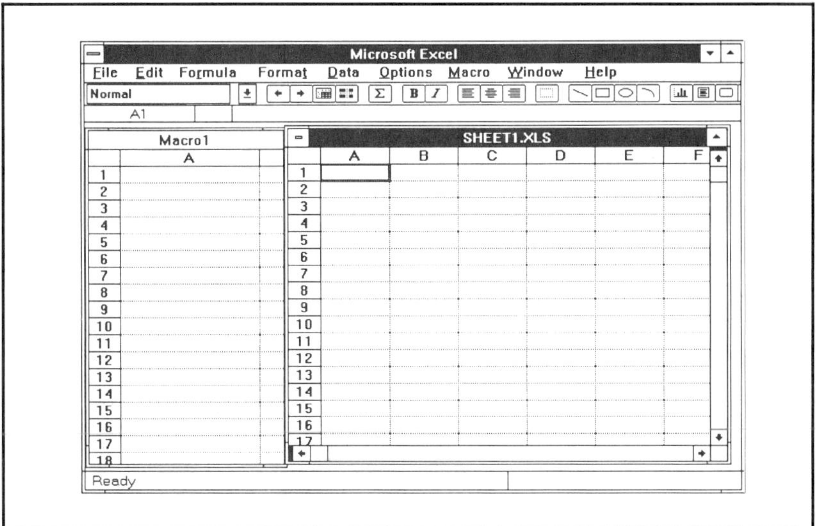

Figure 26.2: The Macro and Worksheet windows

last item reads **Absolute Record**, click it to record absolute references. (The menu item now reads **Relative Record**.)

If you select a column designator or a single cell in a column, Excel assumes that the *entire* column is the recorder range. If you select two or more cells as the range, Excel assumes that only the *selected* range is the recorder range. If the macro recording attempts to exceed this range, a message will be displayed, as shown in Figure 26.3. Select a larger range and continue recording.

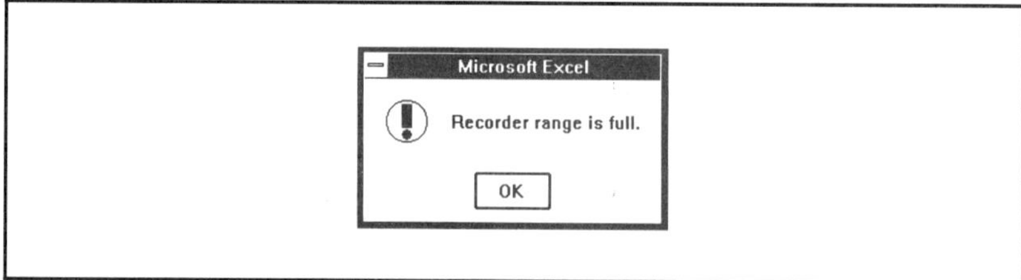

Figure 26.3: Recorder Range Full message

RECORDING THE PROGRAM

Now you must turn on the recorder and then actually perform the task that you want the macro to accomplish. Click on the macro sheet to make it active. Open the Macro menu and choose Start Recorder. A Recording message appears on the status line. As you execute the steps to create the heading, you will see each step recorded in the macro sheet. Carry out the steps that you want the macro to execute:

1. Make the worksheet active, then select cell C1.
2. Enter the title **Acme Manufacturing**.
3. Widen column A on the worksheet by selecting column A, opening the Format menu, and choosing Column Width. When the dialog box appears, change the width of column A to 20 characters and click OK.
4. Enter the column titles by selecting cell B3 and dragging the cursor to cell E3. Enter the column titles shown in Figure 26.1.

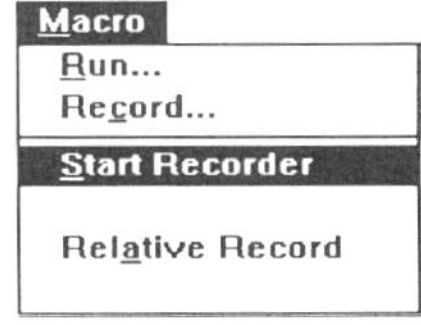

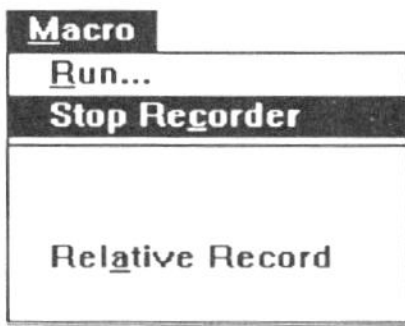

After recording a macro, Excel automatically sets a new range as the next completely empty column on the macro sheet. Defined ranges are saved with the macro sheet. If a column is defined as a macro range, Excel will begin recording in the cell where the last =RETURN() is located (and will record over it).

5. Center the titles by selecting B1 to E3, opening the Format menu, choosing Alignment, and double-clicking Center.
6. Put the title in boldface print by selecting cell C1, opening the Format menu, and choosing Font. When the dialog box appears, click Helv, 12 points, Bold, and then click OK.

Now stop the recorder by opening the Macro menu and choosing Stop Recorder.

If you make a mistake during entry, correct it; your correction will be recorded in the macro automatically. You also can click the Cancel button on the formula bar to clear an entry before it is entered on the macro sheet.

Widen the first column of the macro sheet so that you can see the commands. Your macro sheet should now look like Figure 26.4. Notice that your commands have been stored in column A using a special language. Column A contains a series of formulas that look much like the formulas you have used before. They contain functions from the Excel macro language. Like any functions, these have arguments. The SELECT function selects the cell(s) specified in the argument, and the FORMULA function is used to enter data into a specified cell or

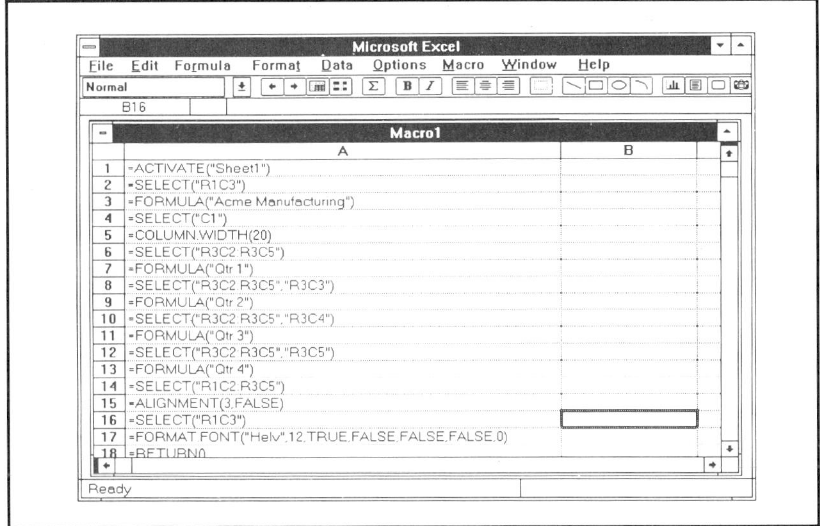

Figure 26.4: The Macro worksheet after recording various commands

cell range. Compare each function in the column with your actions described above.

In any macro, the recorded statements may be of four types:

- Action statements move the cursor, format, and do any menu activities
- Assignment statements assign a value to a variable
- Control statements, such as those that use the IF function, control which statements are executed based on a specified condition
- I/O statements receive keyboard information from the user based on a prompt or display message

You also may have comments, the macro name, and other features in your macro. In Chapter 28, you will learn more about how to use Excel's macro language.

NAMING THE COMMAND MACRO

The macro has now been recorded, but it must be assigned a name before you can use it. You could assign it a keystroke sequence as well as a name so that you can start it with that keystroke.

Follow these steps to name your macro:

1. Select the macro sheet.
2. Select the first cell in the macro commands (i.e., cell A1).
3. Open the Formula menu and choose Define Name. You will see the dialog box shown in Figure 26.5. Notice that the familiar box now has some new options that apply only to macros, and that the Refers To box references $A$1, the first cell of the macro commands. The cursor is in the Name box.
4. Enter the name **HEADING** in the Name box. Do not click OK yet.
5. In the Macro box, click Command Key to indicate that you are creating a command macro.

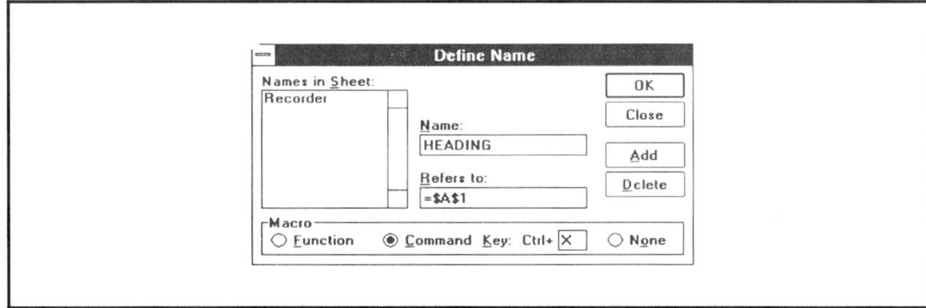

Figure 26.5: The Define Name dialog box for command macros

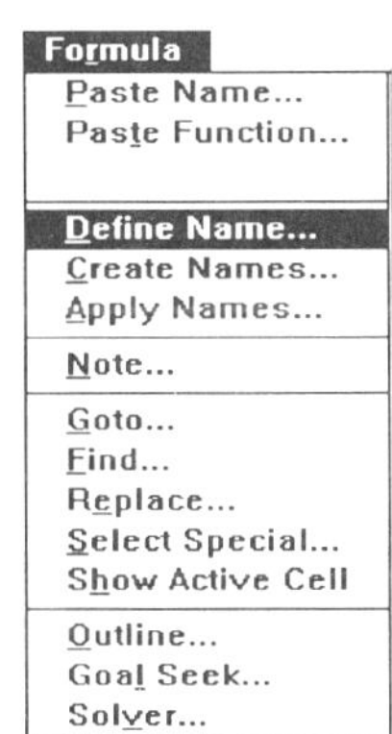

Name macros using the same rules for naming functions: use underlines instead of spaces if the name has more than one word.

6. Tab to the Ctrl + box. Hold down the Shift key and enter **X**. (The Shift key is necessary only because an uppercase *X* is desired.) The key you enter here is the "hot key" to activate the macro. You can use any key from *A* to *Z* or *a* to *z*.
7. Click OK.

You have now named your command macro and defined a keystroke sequence that you can use to execute it.

SAVING THE COMMAND MACRO

The macro that you created is not associated with any worksheet or chart document; it must be stored as a separate macro document. You must save the macro sheet after it is created if you want to use the macro later on or with other worksheets.

Follow these steps to save your command macro:

1. Select the macro sheet.
2. Open the File menu and choose Save As.
3. When the dialog box appears, enter the name **HEADING**.
4. Click OK.

You can store any number of macros in a single macro document. That way, whenever you open that document, all the command macros stored with it will be available for your use.

EXECUTING YOUR COMMAND MACRO

You can use either of two methods to execute your HEADING macro:

- Execute it from the Run command of the Macro menu
- Press the hot-key sequence from the keyboard

However, before you use either method, the macro sheet that contains the macro must be open.

Before you start, clear your worksheet by selecting the entire worksheet (click the box at the upper-left of the sheet) and pressing Ctrl–Del).

To execute your command macro using the Macro menu, follow these steps:

1. Be sure that the worksheet is clear and selected.
2. Open the Macro menu and choose Run.
3. The dialog box shown in Figure 26.6 is displayed (note the short-cut key just before the name). Double-click the macro name HEADING.

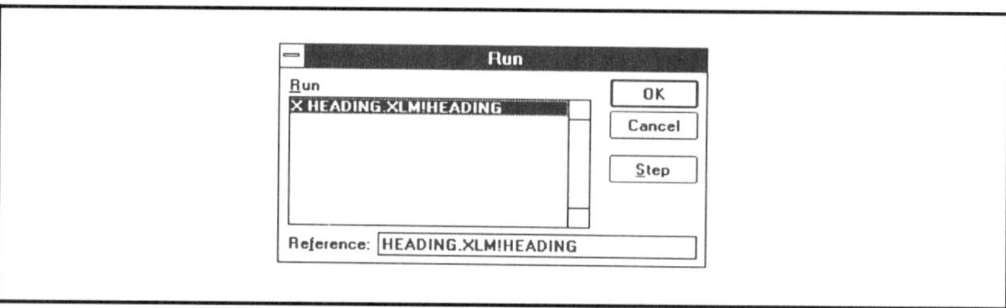

Figure 26.6: The Run dialog box

Excel will execute the macro and the heading will be entered onto the worksheet. Your worksheet should look like Figure 26.1.

To execute a command macro from the keyboard, first clear the worksheet area. Then hold down the Control key and press the key that you assigned to the macro (Shift–*X* for this example). The macro will be executed to create the worksheet heading shown in Figure 26.1.

QUICK RECORDING

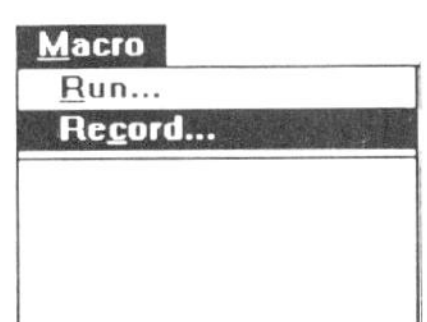

A quick way of recording a macro is to open the Macro menu on the worksheet and choose Record. If no macro sheet is opened, Excel opens a new sheet (such as Macro1), sets a range, and prompts for a name for the macro to be recorded (see Figure 26.7). Recording starts immediately.

If a macro sheet is already opened and a range set, Excel uses that sheet and range. If no range is set, recording starts in the next blank column.

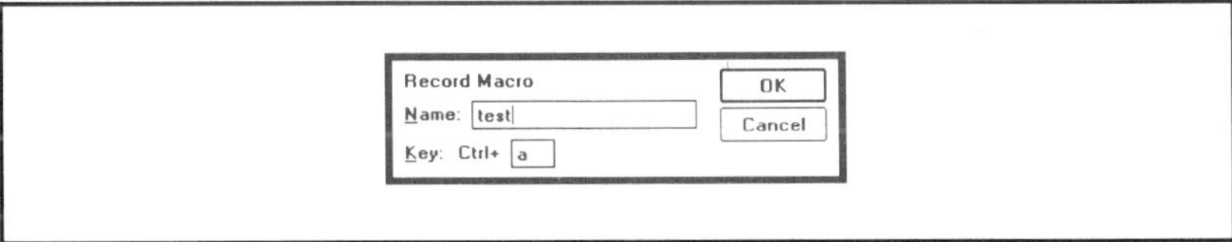

Figure 26.7: Quick recording of a macro

EDITING A MACRO

Edit the macro sheet just like any other Excel document: change arguments, delete or insert rows, etc. Experiment by making the following changes in your macro sheet:

1. Change the width of column A to 25 characters.
2. Put the title in italics instead of boldface by changing the style command to read:

```
=FORMAT.FONT("Helv",12,FALSE,
TRUE,FALSE,FALSE,0)
```

Now, execute your new command macro.

Edit the macro name. To change the name or keystroke sequence, follow these steps:

1. Select the macro sheet.
2. Select the first cell of the macro.
3. Open the Formula menu and choose Define Name.

4. When the Define Name dialog box appears (see Figure 26.5), click the macro's name.
5. Edit the name in the Name box or the keyboard code in the Macro box.
6. Click OK.

You can easily add new entries to the end of an existing macro. If you turn the recorder on after selecting a range that already has entries, the previous entries will not be deleted. Instead, Excel temporarily removes the =RETURN( ) at the end. The new entries are added, and the =RETURN( ) is appended at the end. If this is not what you want, redefine the recorder range first or begin entries *after* the previous =RETURN( ).

Be careful when editing macros that you do not insert a blank cell in other macros on the same worksheet. For example, you might insert a row to add a new line to a macro; at the same time, however, this could open a new blank cell in every macro in other columns.

USING COMMAND MACROS

This chapter is intended only as a brief introduction to command macros. Here are some basic rules and tips for recording macros:

- Be sure that you think through what you are trying to accomplish before you enter the commands. You may wish to make a dummy run to test the sequence before you record it. In this way, you can avoid entering errors or unnecessary steps into the macro sheet
- Generally, the first step after you start recording is to activate the worksheet and position your cursor at the desired point on the worksheet. Don't forget to start the recorder, *then* position the cursor
- Don't be afraid to use macros. Anytime you find yourself repeating a command sequence, save it as a command macro

- Make the macros as readable as possible. Using presentation features, such as style and border control without gridlines, can aid readability
- Put the name of the macro in the first named cell of the macro (see Figure 27.2 in Chapter 27)
- Put many macros on one macro sheet, each with its own name. You can then use the macro sheet as a library, opening it when you first load Excel and using it with many worksheets during the day
- Document your macros: add comments to clarify what the macro is doing. The best place for comments is in the column to the immediate right of the macro column

27 Utilizing Function Macros

EXCEL'S FUNCTION-MACRO CAPABILITY PERMITS you to create your own functions, thereby extending the function library that is already a part of Excel. You can decide which arguments are needed in your functions and which results are to be returned in the worksheet cell. Once you create a function macro, it will be on the function list of the Paste Function command and you can include it in worksheet formulas, just as you would use any other Excel function.

Excel's built-in functions can be used for most standard applications. Here are some examples of functions you may wish to create:

- Functions for numeric conversion, as from English to metric units
- Special functions with lookup tables, such as a function to look up the UPS Zone and shipping cost based on a zip code
- Special functions used in a scientific or engineering speciality

In this chapter, you will learn how to create function macros. You'll find a complete list of the macro language functions in Appendix F.

FUNCTION MACRO USES

A *function macro* is essentially a user-defined function. It calculates an output dependent variable (or array) from one or more independent input variables (or arrays). As explained in Chapter 8, a function is an abbreviation for a formula. A function also can be defined as an operator, similar to a symbol operator, such as + or −. It contains one or more arguments that are used to calculate a result. When you create a function macro, you define the arguments and formulas to calculate the results.

You should create function macros whenever you need to use special formulas many times in several worksheets. If you use function macros, you don't have to remember the formulas to get your results. All you need to remember is the name of the function and the type and order of the arguments.

CREATING A FUNCTION MACRO

Create a simple function macro that converts a temperature from centigrade to Fahrenheit. There are four steps to create a function macro:

1. Defining the formulas and arguments.
2. Entering the function.
3. Naming the macro.
4. Saving the macro sheet.

DEFINING FORMULAS AND ARGUMENTS

The formula for the temperature-conversion function is

$$b = (9/5) \times a + 32$$

where *b* equals the temperature in degrees Fahrenheit and *a* equals the temperature in degrees centigrade. The function will have the name "Fahrenheit" and contain one input argument for the temperature in metric units.

ENTERING THE FUNCTION MACRO

To create the function macro, first open a macro sheet by pressing Ctrl–F11 or selecting New from the File menu, choosing Macro Sheet, and clicking OK. This will open a blank macro sheet. Function macros must be entered manually—you cannot use the recorder.

Now, follow these steps to enter the Fahrenheit function macro:

1. Enter the function macro title **FAHRENHEIT** into cell A1, as shown in Figure 27.1. Widen column A to 12 characters.
2. In cell A2, define the input argument for the function using the ARGUMENT macro-language function. Enter **=ARGUMENT("centigrade")**, including the quotation marks with the argument name.
3. In cell A3, define your formula: **=(9/5)*centigrade + 32**.
4. In cell A4, use the RETURN macro-language function and reference the cell on the macro sheet that contains the result by typing **=RETURN(A3)**.
5. Add the relevant comments in column B, as shown in Figure 27.1.

When entering a function macro, keep in mind the following rules:

- Excel's macro-language functions must be preceded by an equal sign, as with any other function
- In the macro-language functions, the names of the values for the input arguments are enclosed in quotation marks (because they are text strings), using ARGUMENT statements. They must be listed in the same order as they are to be entered in the function

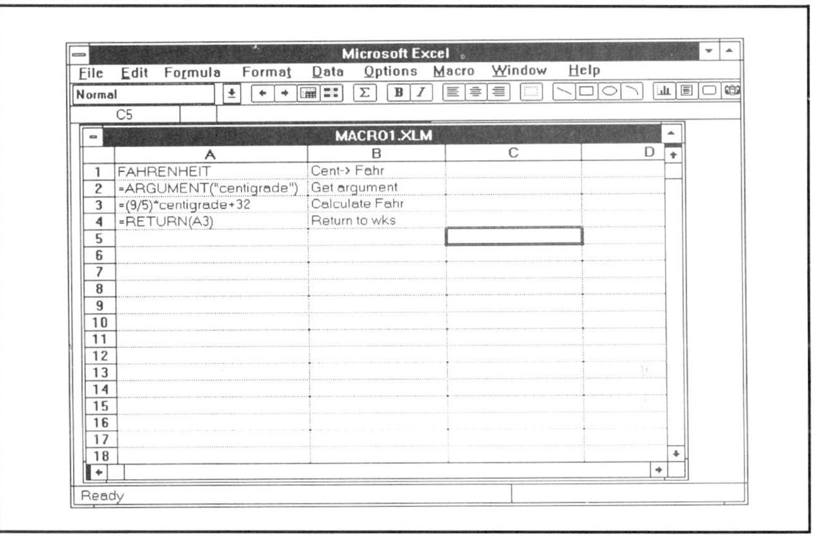

Figure 27.1: Entering the function macro

Include comments in function macros. If the macro is entered to column A, use column B to comment on your macro. For instance, specify the arguments, results, and the calculations.

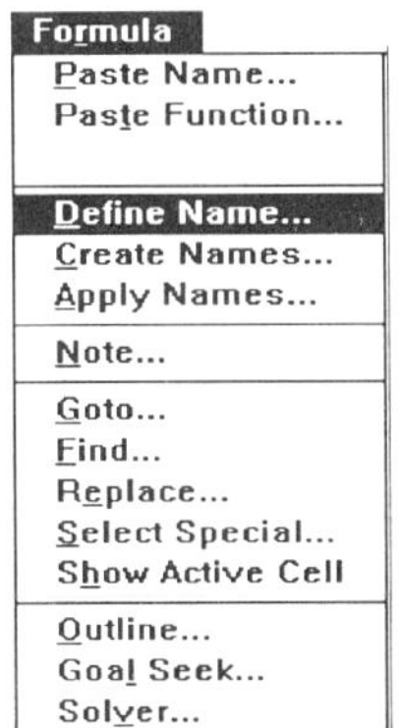

- In the formulas, the names of the input arguments are not enclosed in quotation marks (because they are variable names)

NAMING THE FUNCTION MACRO

The next step is to assign a name to the function macro:

1. Be sure that the first cell of the macro sheet is selected.
2. Open the Formula menu of the macro sheet and choose Define Name.
3. When the Define Name window appears, the name **FAHRENHEIT** from the first cell is displayed in the Name box, as shown in Figure 27.2.
4. Select Function in the Macro box and click OK.

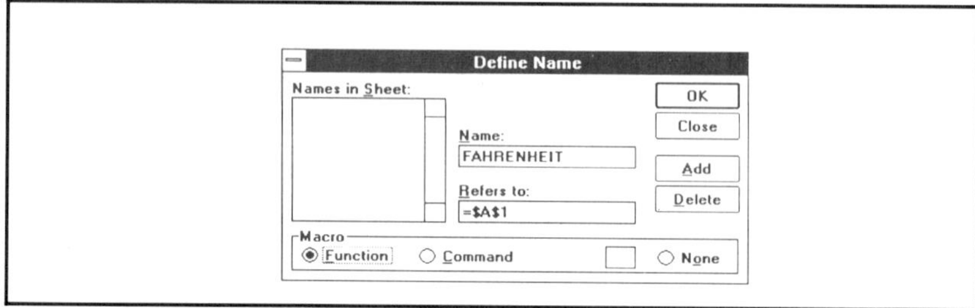

Figure 27.2: The Define Name window for function macros

SAVING THE FUNCTION MACRO

Before you use this function macro, save the macro sheet by following these steps:

1. Select the macro sheet.
2. Open the File menu and choose Save As.
3. When the dialog box appears, enter the name **FAHR**.

USING FUNCTION MACROS

Once you've defined a function macro, you can use it in formulas on a worksheet, just as you would use any other function. Let's use the Fahrenheit macro to see how a function macro works:

1. Create the simple worksheet shown at left in Figure 27.3. Enter the row titles **Centigrade** and **Fahrenheit** in cells A2 and A3, respectively. Widen column A to 10 characters. Enter **80** in cell B2.
2. Now enter the formula:
   a. Select cell B3.
   b. Open the Formula menu and choose Paste Function.
   c. Scroll to the end of the list in the dialog box (drag the scroll box to the bottom) and click the name of your new function, as shown in Figure 27.4. Turn off Paste Arguments and click OK. The formula for cell B3

should now appear in the formula bar, as shown in Figure 27.5.

d. If necessary, click to place the cursor between the parentheses in the formula bar, then click cell B2 on the worksheet. This will enter B2 as the argument to the function in B3, which means entering 30 in the FAHRENHEIT function.

e. Click the Enter box or press Enter. The result **176** is displayed in cell B3, as shown in Figure 27.5.

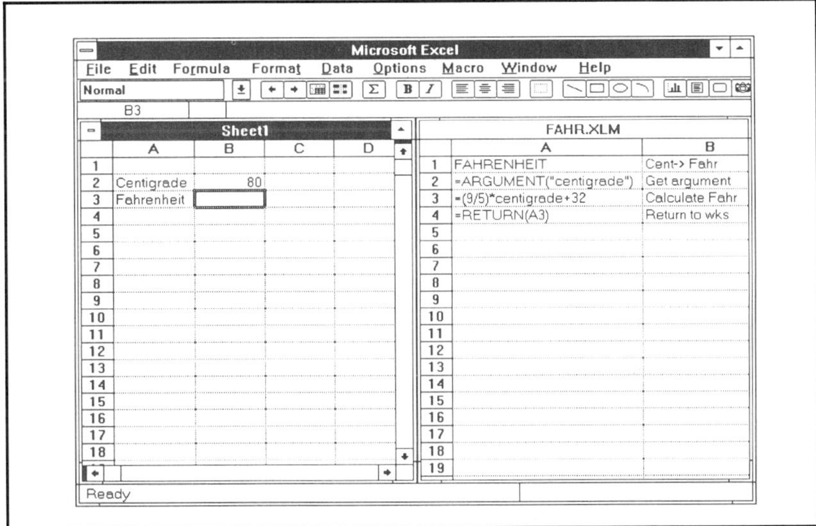

Figure 27.3: The Fahrenheit worksheet

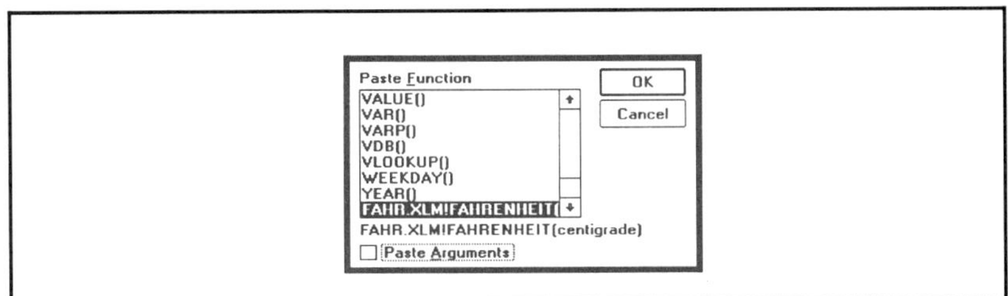

Figure 27.4: The Paste Function dialog box

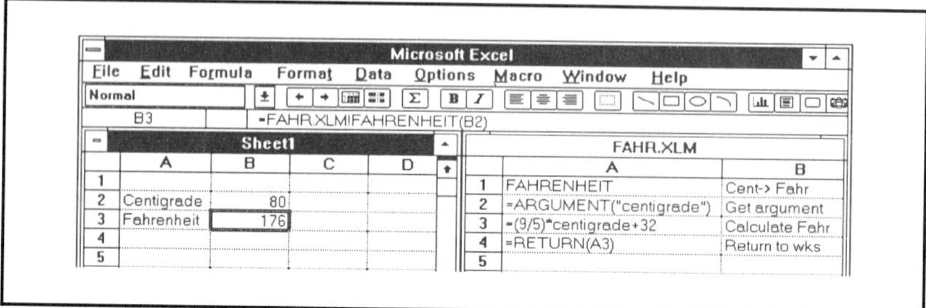

Figure 27.5: Entering the formula

Experiment with your new worksheet—enter a few different values into cell B2 and watch the results change in cell B3.

PUTTING A FUNCTION MACRO IN A TABLE

Here is the procedure for using your Fahrenheit macro in a table:

1. Create two columns, A and B, for the temperatures. In row 5, labelthe first column **Centigrade** and the second column **Fahrenheit**, as shown in Figure 27.6. Widen column B to 10 spaces.

Figure 27.6: Using a function macro in a table

2. In cell A7, enter the first centigrade temperature to be used: **0**.

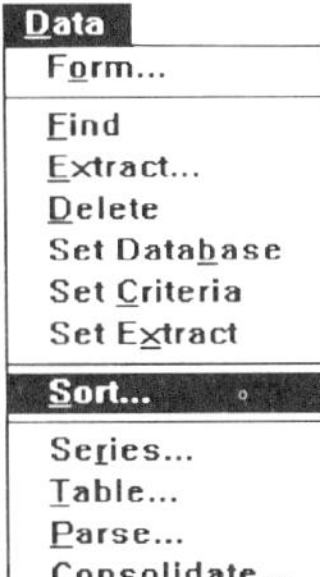

3. Use the Series command on the Data menu with a step value of 5 and a stop value of 100 to fill in the rest of column A to 100 degrees.
4. Put the formula that references the Fahrenheit macro in cell B7. To do this, select cell B7, open the Formula menu, and click Paste Function. When the Paste Function dialog box (see Figure 27.4) appears, select your new FAHRENHEIT function, turn off Paste Arguments, and click OK. Next, click between the parentheses in the formula bar, if necessary, and then click cell A7 to indicate that this is the input cell for the argument. Finally, click the Enter box.

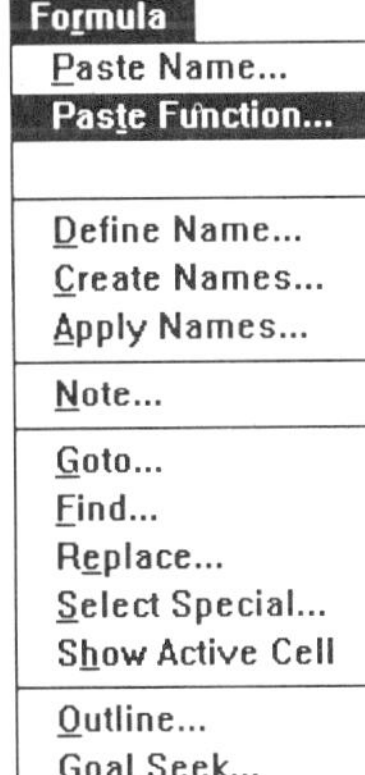

5. Select the range for the table by clicking cell A7 and dragging to cell B27.
6. To set up the table, open the Data menu and choose Table. When the Table window appears, click Column Input Cell, select cell A7, and then click OK.

Excel will then apply each input centigrade temperature to cell A7, use this as an input to the FAHRENHEIT formula in cell B7, and then put the results in column B. Figure 27.7 shows the worksheet with the calculated values.

THE ARGUMENT AND RESULT FUNCTIONS

As you have seen in the example above, Excel's ARGUMENT and RESULT macro language functions can be used to control the types of input and output values calculated by your function macro.

THE ARGUMENT FUNCTION

The ARGUMENT function passes values from the worksheet to the function. In the previous example, the ARGUMENT function contained a single argument. You can use an additional argument to

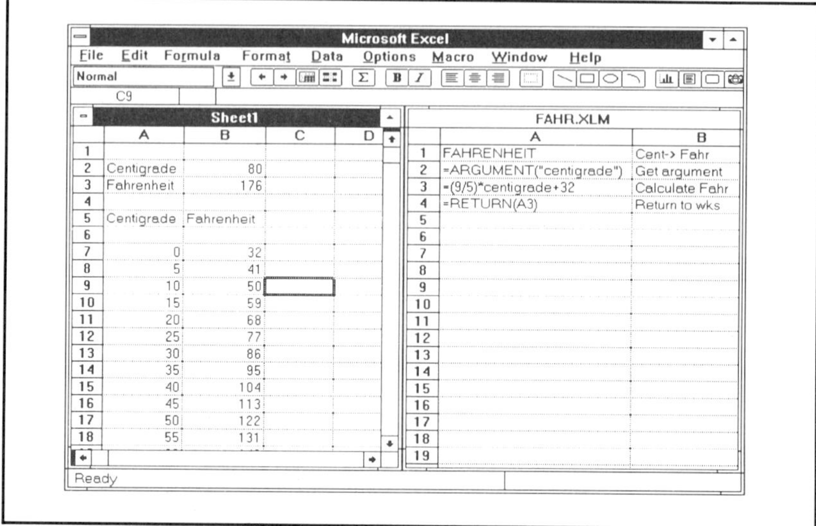

Figure 27.7: The worksheet after the table calculation

control the type of value passed. This optional second argument is primarily used to ensure that the proper argument type is always included in a function macro. Another purpose of the second argument is to permit the use of arrays as arguments.

The form of the function with the second argument is

=ARGUMENT(*name, type*)

where *type* is one of the following numbers:

TYPE VALUE	*REQUIRED ARGUMENT*
1	Numeric
2	Text
4	Logical
8	Reference
16	Error
64	Array

If the input value for the function is not of the proper type, Excel will try to convert it. If the value cannot be converted, Excel will return the error value #VALUE! without executing the function. The *type* argument values can be combined to permit the entry of several data types. If the argument is omitted, Excel uses 7 (1 + 2 + 4) as a default value, which permits the entry of numeric, text, or logical values.

There is a third form of the ARGUMENT function as well:

=ARGUMENT(*name, type, ref*)

Here, *ref* is used to refer to a specific cell on the macro sheet. You can then use formulas on the macro sheet to refer to the input value by a name or by a cell reference. For example, on your Fahrenheit macro sheet, you could change cell A2 to read:

```
=ARGUMENT("centigrade",1,A5)
```

and change the formula in cell A3 to read:

```
=(9/5)*A5+32
```

The formula still works. The third argument, A5, refers to a cell on the macro sheet. Try this and you'll see that the centigrade value from the worksheet is entered into cell A5 on the macro sheet, which is used as the input cell for the formula.

When you are defining a function, you can include several arguments. Each is specified in a separate cell of the macro worksheet, using the ARGUMENT function. As an example, suppose we wish to create our own PMT function and call it PMTX. The built-in PMT function uses five arguments. To calculate the payments for borrowing $24,000 at 15 percent for three years, for instance, you would use

=PMT(.015/12,360,24000,,0)

The last two arguments are not used (the fourth is omitted and the fifth is zero).

You could, however, write your own function using only three arguments and calculating the interest in the macro, using the macro shown in the Macro4 window of Figure 27.8. This uses three input values to calculate a single output value.

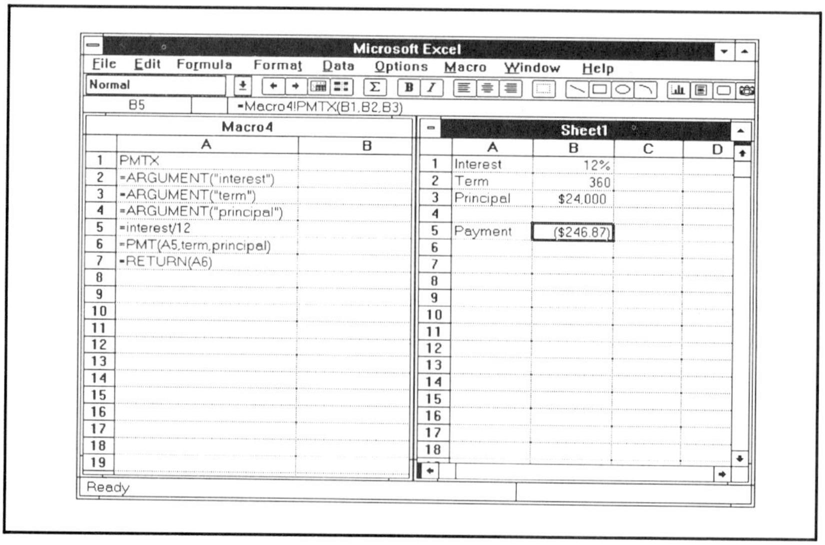

Figure 27.8: Defining a function macro that uses multiple input values

In a similar way, you can use arrays as inputs to a function or have a function return an array value.

It is also possible to create function macros that use no input arguments. An example might be a function that prompts for a value, then returns the value to the program.

THE RESULT FUNCTION

You can use the RESULT function to indicate the type of returned value in the same way that you use the ARGUMENT function to control the input value. The function takes the form

=RESULT(*ref, type*)

The numeric values for *type* are the same as those for the ARGUMENT function. If the result of the function is of a type different than the one defined, Excel will try to convert it. If Excel cannot do this, it will return the error value #VALUE!.

The RESULT function is not the same as the RETURN function. RESULT should be used as the first formula in your function macro on the macro sheet.

As with the ARGUMENT function, you can use the second argument of the RESULT function to accept an array as the output. Just be sure that you use the proper type value for an array. You also can combine values so that your output is several types of data. For example, a value of 71 (1 + 2 + 4 + 64) would permit numeric, text, logical values, or arrays.

COMMAND MACROS VERSUS FUNCTION MACROS

You have now seen how to create two types of macros: the command macro and the function macro. When should you use one instead of the other?

Command macros are generally used to automate tasks that involve a sequence of commands. No arguments are passed to the function and no value is returned. They can be created with the recorder or entered manually to a macro sheet.

Function macros are used much like other functions, and return a value to a cell based on a defined procedure. They cannot be created with the recorder.

Command macros and function macros are compared in Table 27.1.

Table 27.1: Command Macros vs. Function Macros

Command Macros	Function Macros
Perform actions	Are used as part of formulas to return values based on a defined procedure
Do not have arguments	Have arguments. You can pass values to a function
Do not return a value	Can return a value

Table 27.1: Command Macros vs. Function Macros (continued)

Command Macros	Function Macros
Can be recorded with the recorder	Can't be recorded with the recorder
Are initiated with the Macro Run command or with a defined keystroke	Are part of formulas in cells

28 Advanced Macro Techniques

MACROS ARE ONE OF THE MOST IMPORTANT features of a spreadsheet program. Excel supports the most extensive macro library available in any spreadsheet product—as well as features never before available in this type of product, such as dynamic menus and dialog boxes. Learning to use macros gives you an important pathway to taking advantage of the full potential of Excel.

Let's look as some of Excel's advanced macro features. Someone with a minimum of experience with Excel can create command macros easily by using the recorder. You cannot, however, create very complex macros this way. To create more advanced command macros, you must use Excel's macro language. If you are designing an application, you probably will need to use the recorder and enter macros manually.

This chapter covers the following topics:

- Using both relative and absolute cell addressing in macro sheets
- Writing interactive macros

- Using control structures
- Debugging the macros you create
- Organizing your macro sheets
- Deciding when to use the recorder and when to enter macros manually
- Creating macros that automatically start when a document is opened, or when you start Excel
- Creating macros that start given special conditions (times, key-presses, and error conditions)
- Creating custom pull-down menus
- Creating custom dialog boxes
- Attaching macros you create to buttons on the worksheet or to other graphic objects, including invisible objects

Appendix E is a directory of the Excel macros.

Before beginning this chapter, be sure that you have used the recorder to create a few command macros.

RECORDING CELL REFERENCES

You may want to include both relative and absolute cell references in your macros. Excel's recorder can handle both types of cell addressing.

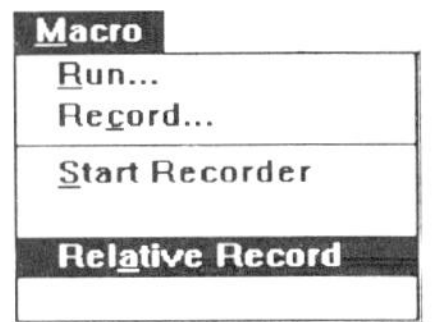

To switch the mode of cell addressing, open the Macro menu. If **Relative Record** is displayed, this means that Excel is set to record absolute addresses; selecting Relative Record will switch you to relative recording. If **Absolute Record** is on the menu, Excel is set to record relative addresses. You normally should record absolute addresses (so **Relative Record** is displayed).

The recording *mode* can be set only after the recording *range* has been set.

You can switch from relative to absolute cell addressing and back at any time while you are recording; the final macro can be a mixture of both types. However, once the macro is recorded, the references cannot be switched by using a command on the Macro menu; you have to edit the macro sheet instead.

WRITING MACRO PROGRAMS

When you create macros, it is often better to record a simple version of the macro first, then insert the extra steps without the recorder.

You may need to create a command macro with some special features that cannot be added using the recorder. Typical examples include interactive macros and macros that contain branches and loops. To create macros with these features, you will need to write your own macro sheet or alter an existing one. In this section, you will learn more about these programming techniques.

CREATING INTERACTIVE MACROS

There may be times when you want your command macro to stop during execution and obtain an input value from the user, then continue. This is called an *interactive macro.* Interactive macros can be used for very simple tasks as well as for complex programs, such as creating advanced macro sheets automatically. The user has to enter only the data needed at the proper steps. Remember, however, that the development of complex macros takes quite a bit of time.

There are three ways to make an Excel macro interactive:

- With the INPUT function
- With the question-mark form of a command
- With the ALERT function

The first step when creating a macro that generates the initial labels is usually to select the worksheet. This ensures that if the cursor is on any other window, the macro output is directed to the worksheet.

Let's take an example and try each of these methods.

In this example, you will create a simple interactive macro that inserts a worksheet heading containing the starting and ending months, which the user specifies. You record the basic macro, then modify it to make it interactive.

To start, create a macro that will generate the worksheet shown in Figure 28.1 using the recorder. Follow these steps (refer to Chapter 26 if you need help):

1. Clear the worksheet you now have, if necessary (select it and press Ctrl-Del).
2. Open a macro sheet and set the recorder (column A of the worksheet).
3. Start the recorder and select the worksheet.

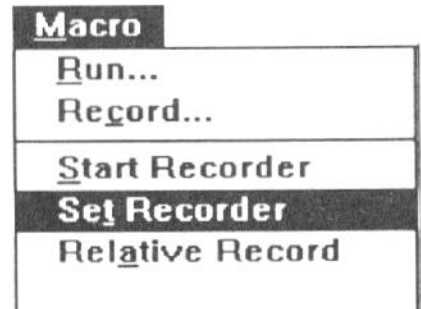

4. Select cell C1, enter the title, and put it in Helv, 12 points, and boldface print.
5. Expand column A to 20 characters by using the Column Width command on the Format menu.
6. Enter **Jan-91** in cell B3.

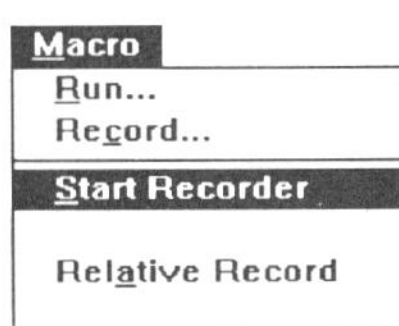

7. Enter the remaining months by selecting columns B–M of row 3 and choosing Series on the Data menu. Then select Month in the Date Unit box of the Series dialog box (see Figure 28.2). Click OK.
8. Center the data in the first three rows.
9. Stop the recorder.

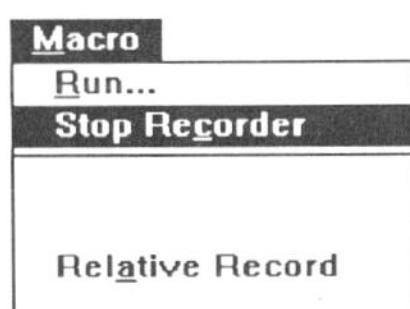

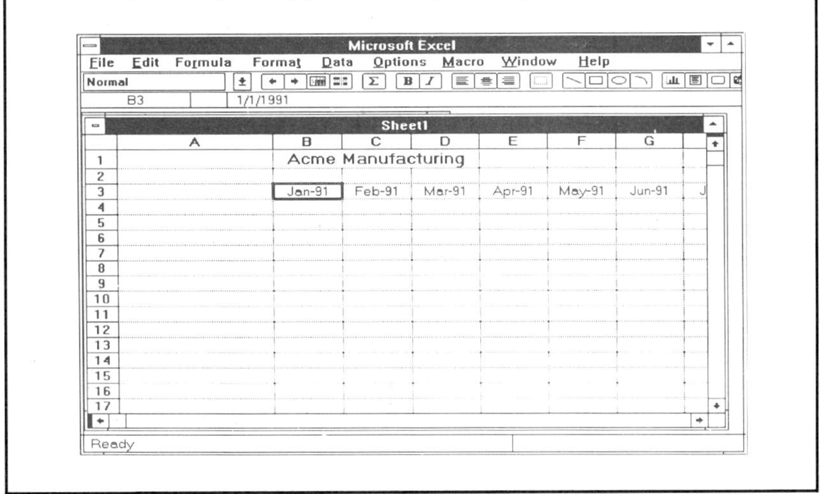

Figure 28.1: The worksheet after executing the interactive command macro

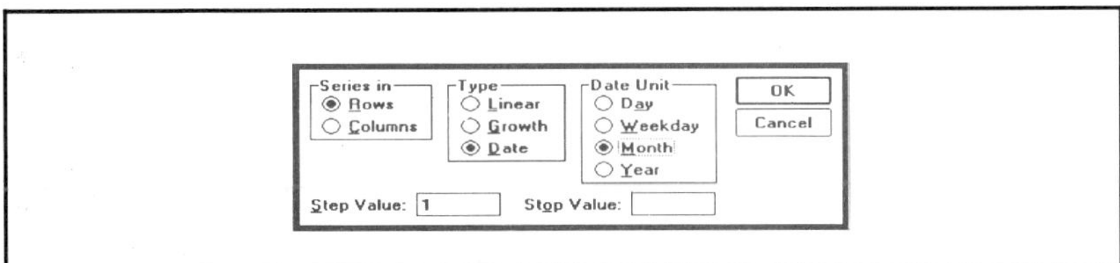

Figure 28.2: The Series dialog box

10. Name the macro by selecting cell A1 of the macro sheet, choosing Define Name in the Formula menu, and entering **Title**.

The final macro sheet should look like Figure 28.3. Save and run the macro to be sure that it works.

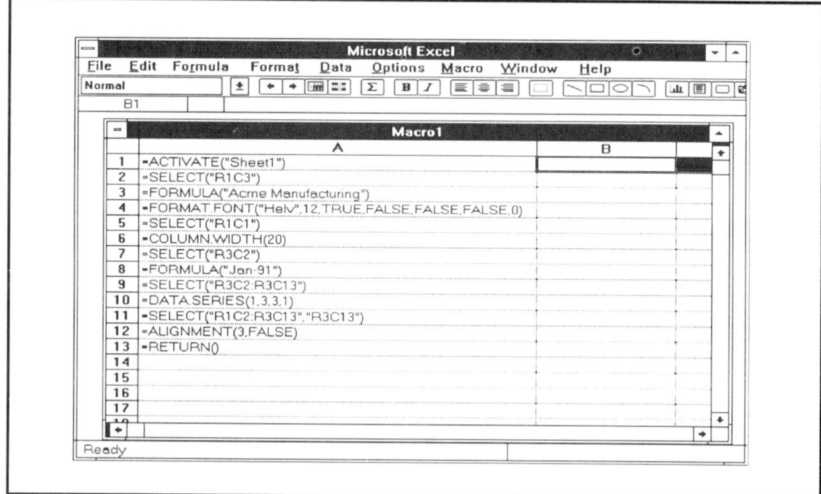

Figure 28.3: The macro sheet

You will now modify this macro sheet to make the command macro interactive in the three different ways mentioned at the beginning of this section.

The INPUT Function

You can replace any of the macro sheet's existing function arguments with the INPUT function. Then, when the macro reaches that function, it will stop and ask for the input value. The form of the INPUT function is INPUT(*prompt, type, title*). Its arguments represent the following:

- *Prompt* is the message to be displayed to the user in the window
- *Type* is an integer that represents the type(s) of input numbers that can be accepted (see Chapter 27)

- *Title* is the name of the window. If *title* is omitted, it is assumed to be "Input"

Now, edit cell A8 (or FORMULA("Jan-91") on the macro sheet) so that it reads

=FORMULA(INPUT("Enter the starting date",1))

The 1 indicates that the input is a constant.

Repeat the macro execution. The program will stop and display the Input window. Enter the starting date **nov-91** and click OK. Column B on the worksheet is now headed by **Nov-91**, and the remaining headings are automatically generated as increments of that date, as shown in Figure 28.4. Repeat this exercise, entering letters that don't form a valid month abbreviation, such as **Apl**. What happens?

Sheet1

	A	B	C	D	E	F	G	
1		Acme Manufacturing						
2								
3		Nov-91	Dec-91	Jan-92	Feb-92	Mar-92	Apr-92	M
4								
5								
6								

Figure 28.4: The worksheet after entering a date in the input window

The Question-Mark Command Form

Another method for obtaining input is to use the *question-mark form* of the command. Most macro language commands that produce a dialog box use a question-mark form. When a macro gets to that command it stops and automatically displays the command's dialog box.

To specify the ending month in the heading that your macro creates and thereby control the number of columns printed when the macro is executed, you need to use the Series dialog box. Cell A10 on the macro sheet (see Figure 28.3) contains the DATA.SERIES command. Replace it with

=DATA.SERIES?( )

Now execute your macro again with Nov-91 in the first cell. After you have filled in the Input window and clicked OK, you will see the Series dialog box. Click Month, enter a stop value of **Jan-92**, and click OK. Your worksheet will be printed with only three columns.

The ALERT Function

A third way to obtain input during a macro execution is to create an alert box using the ALERT function. The form of the ALERT function is =ALERT(*text, type*), where *type* is a value for the type of icon and buttons to display and *text* is the prompt to display in the box. The values available for *type* are listed below:

TYPE	*ICON*	*BUTTONS*
1	? (caution)	OK, Cancel
2	* (note)	OK
3	! (stop)	OK

After the DATA.SERIES? command in cell A10 of your macro sheet, insert a new line (select the row, open the Edit menu, and choose Insert). On this line, add the following:

=ALERT("Are you having fun?",1)

The last argument indicates that a question mark is to be used. Now execute your macro one last time. The program will stop and display an alert box, as shown in Figure 28.5. Click OK to continue the macro. If you click Cancel, the function will return a logical value of FALSE. In this case, the macro execution continues, because the return value is not tested.

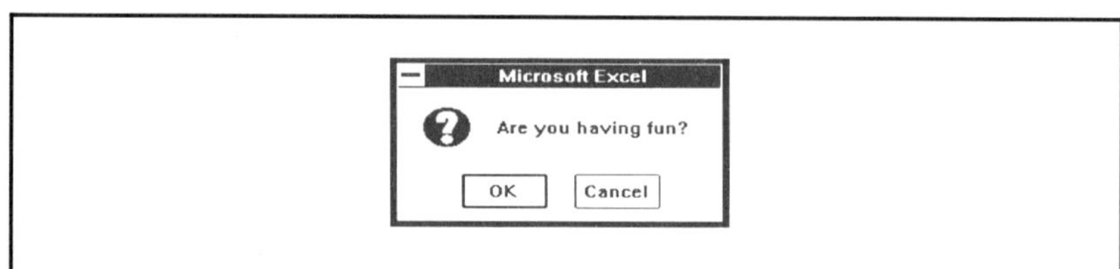

Figure 28.5: Using an Alert box

MAKING DECISIONS WITH CONTROL STRUCTURES

There are two types of control structures you can add to your macro programs: conditional structures (branches) and iterative structures (loops).

Using Conditional Structures

Conditional structures are those in which a program can choose one of several groups of statements to execute, based on the value of a control expression (see Figure 28.6).

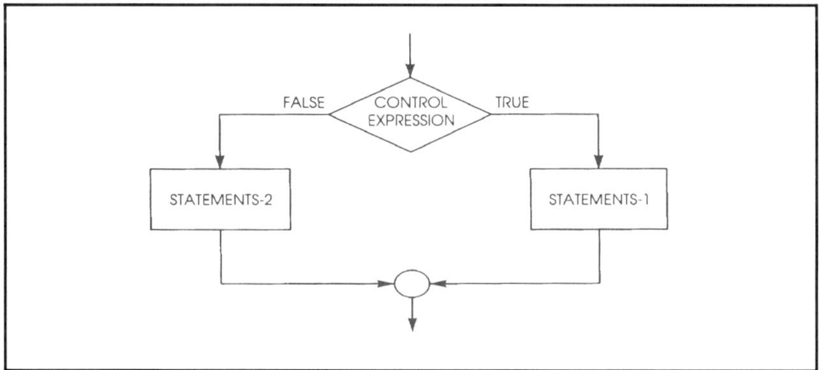

Figure 28.6: A schematic of the conditional structure

One of the simplest types of conditional structure is the IF statement, in which a group of statements are executed if a statement is true. For example, you could use the ROWS function in cell A1 of the macro sheet to return the number of rows in a range selection. It would have the following form:

=ROWS(SELECTION( ))

Later in the program, the macro could examine this value and make a decision based on the number of rows specified. For example, the command

=ALIGNMENT(IF(A1 =1,3,2))

would adjust the alignment according to the number of rows. If there were one row, the ALIGNMENT function would use 3, and the display would be centered. If not, the ALIGNMENT function would use 2, and the display would be left-justified. The first value applies if the IF function is true; the second, if the function is false (see Appendix E).

You can combine the IF function with the GOTO function to control the order in which the commands in the program are executed. For example, the command

=IF(A2 = 1,GOTO(A13))

would cause the program go to cell A13 if the value in cell A2 were 1.

You also can use Boolean operators (AND, OR, and so on) to combine conditions. For example, the command

=IF(AND(A2 = 1,A3 = 1),GOTO(A13))

would cause the program go to cell A13 only if both cells A2 and A3 contained a value of 1.

Be careful not to confuse IF and GOTO. IF is an Excel function, and returns a value based on a condition. GOTO is a macro function, and defines the cell from which the next program statement will be read.

The GOTO function can even be used to branch to another macro and, when that macro is completed, return to the calling macro to continue.

You also can create a block of functions, executing one part of the block if the control expression is true and another part if it is false. The general form with macros is:

=IF(*conditional expression*)

=*statements–1*

=ELSE( )

=*statements–2*

=END.IF( )

Iterative Structures

The iterative structure, or loop, permits the program to execute a group of control statements a specified number of times or for as long as a control expression is true (see Figure 28.7). The control expression is tested at the beginning of the loop.

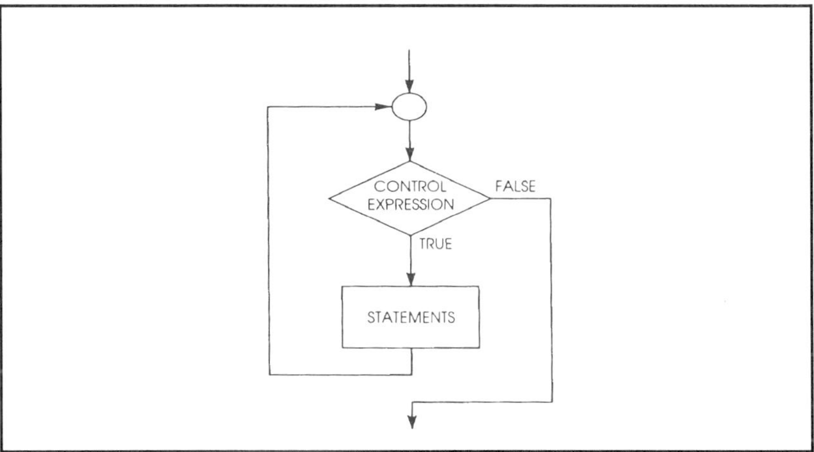

Figure 28.7: A schematic of the iterative structure

Placing labels in the left column (A), macro statements in the middle column (B), and documentation in the right column (C) permits you to name the cells using the Create Names command on the Formula menu.

You can create iteration structures using the IF function. To do so, you must first set a variable in a cell to an initial value using the SET-.VALUE function. For example, the command

=SET.VALUE(A25,1)

in cell A2 would put the value of 1 in cell A25 on the macro sheet. Inside the loop, the following would be entered:

=SET.VALUE(A25,A25+1)

This increases the value in A25 each time it is executed.

When the macro is invoked, the value of that cell will increase by 1 each time the above statement is encountered. You can then have the macro test the condition after the value in cell A25 is increased, and determine whether it should remain in the loop, by using the following command:

=IF(A25<=25,GOTO(A3))

Be sure that you loop back *after* the SET.VALUE function.

An example of a loop is the function that calculates the greatest common denominator (GCD) of two numbers, as shown in Figure 28.8. Noticethat two columns are used for the macro. The Create Names command on the Formula menu is used to define the cells (select A5:B13 for naming, and use row titles). Define B1 as a macro name (function macro) using GCD. The function expression in B3 is =(MACRO1!GCD(B1,B2)).

You also can use the FOR function in a FOR...NEXT form to create a loop. This function has the following form:

=FOR(*counter_text, start_num, end_num, step_num*)

where

- *counter_text* defines a counter variable that monitors the number of times the loop has been executed
- *start_num* defines the starting value of *counter_text*
- *end_num* defines the value for *counter_text* beyond which the loop stops
- *step_num* defines the increment value of *counter_text* for each loop cycle

For changing a cell range, the FOR.CELL...NEXT form is a better alternative:

=FOR.CELL(*ref_name, area_ref, skip_blanks*)

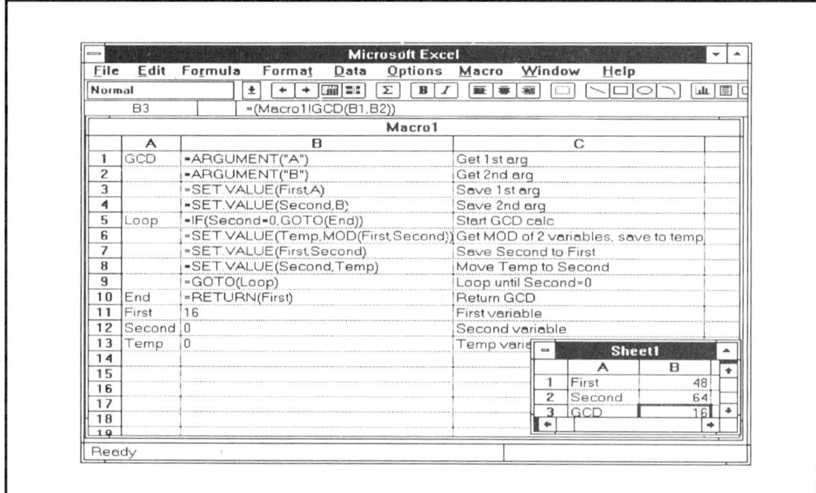

Figure 28.8: A macro that calculates the GCD of two numbers

where

- *ref_name* is the text name of a cell in the range being operated on
- *area_ref* references a range to be operated on (default is the current range)
- *skip_blanks* is a logical value that defines whether blank cells should be skipped (default is FALSE)

Another function supported by Excel permits WHILE loops and has the general form:

=WHILE(*control expression*)

statements

=NEXT( )

The statements section must change the value of the control expression, or else the loop will never terminate.

Figure 28.9 shows the GCD function using a WHILE loop.

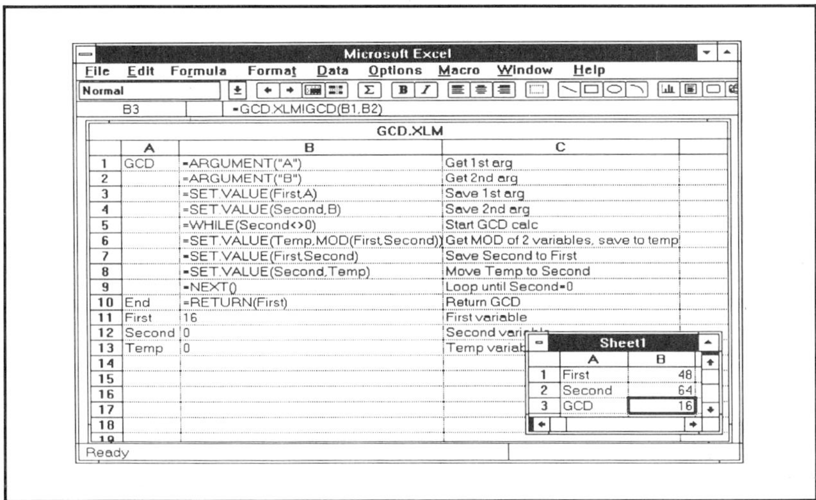

Figure 28.9: The GCD function with a WHILE loop

INTERRUPTING A MACRO EXECUTION

You can interrupt the execution of a macro, just as you would interrupt a printing, by pressing Escape. The dialog box shown in Figure 28.10 is then displayed. This box shows the current cell to be calculated on the macro sheet and has four buttons: Halt, Step, Continue, and Goto. The Halt button terminates the macro execution, the Continue button continues the execution, and the Goto button branches you to a cell you specify in a separate dialog box. The Step button displays the Single Step window shown in Figure 28.11. You can use this window to check a macro that doesn't work properly one step at a time.

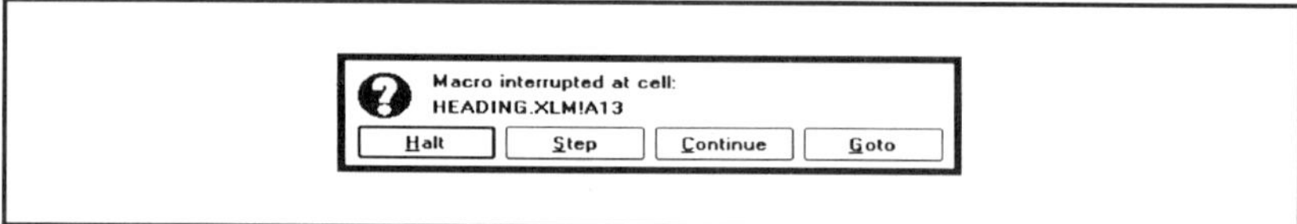

Figure 28.10: The dialog box displayed when you interrupt a macro

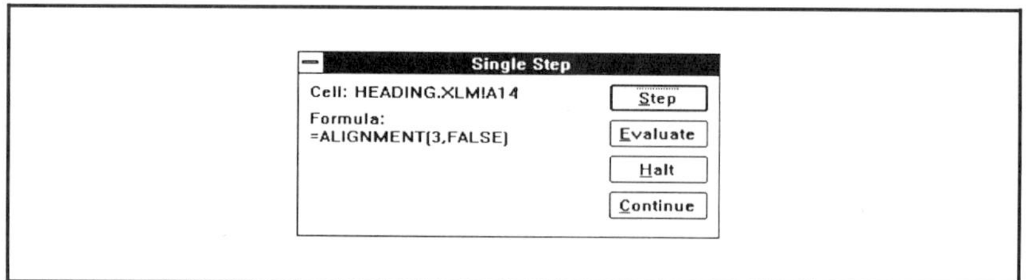

Figure 28.11: The Single Step window

USING MACRO SHEETS

With many other spreadsheet products, a macro is stored on the actual worksheet with which it is used and can be run only with that worksheet open, unless you copy the macro into another worksheet. Because macros are entered into a remote area of the worksheet, the resulting worksheet is quite large and requires a lot of computer memory. Excel's macros, on the other hand, are stored in separate macro sheets and can be used with any worksheet open. You should, however, be careful when creating links or using names as external references on macro sheets, because these features do need specific worksheets open in order to run.

Use the GET.FORMULA function to get the contents of a cell on a worksheet as it would appear in the formula bar. The general form is:

=GET.FORMULA(*reference*)

If the cell contains an expression, it is retrieved in text form. You also can use this function to obtain a value from a worksheet cell, or even from macro sheets.

To get a value from the active worksheet, place an exclamation point before the cell address. GET.FORMULAS(!A12), for example, gets the value from A12 of the active worksheet. This permits you to create generic macros that will work with many worksheets.

When designing a macro to work with a specific worksheet, be sure to use the worksheet name to prevent possible macro misuse (e.g., GET.FORMULA (SALES!$B$11)).

MACRO DESIGN TECHNIQUES

Here are some suggestions for designing your macros:

- Plan your macros first. Write out the procedure as a flow diagram. Break complex or long macros down into a hierarchical system of smaller macros. The main routine should be short, with a collection of subroutines. Each subroutine, in turn, can call others. Macros should be short and simple, calling other macros as necessary. Each macro should perform a single function
- Use descriptive names for your macros that have a meaning in the context of the problem you are solving
- Document your macros. Write comments for each step
- For a command macro, record as much as possible using the recorder. Then insert steps as necessary to do what additional work needs to be done. This minimizes errors

- Trap errors using ARGUMENT and RESULT functions to be sure that the correct data types are passed to and from a function. Check for FALSE returns from functions. Create an error subroutine that is called when an error is sensed, and pass an error code to the routine. Use the ERROR function to customize this
- Generalize your macros by using the INPUT function to prompt the user for information
- Test macros with parallel testing; that is, first use data for which you know the results
- Anticipate the types of errors that may occur with user input and try to trap these: e.g., invalid dates, out-of-range data, no data entry
- Check for FALSE and error codes on return from functions. Use the ERROR macro function to customize this
- Always save your macro before testing it
- To simplify your work, create libraries of common macros that you use. Put the command macros that you use frequently on a single macro sheet, assign it a name, and then use this with other programs as a library. This will save you development time. (What's more, you know that they already work!)

MACRO SPEED TIPS

Almost all macros can be improved. The Excel macro language is quite diverse, and there are generally several ways of accomplishing the same objective.

Here are a few techniques to keep macro execution fast:

- Use the ECHO function to turn off screen updating (use ECHO(FALSE)). This will speed up many macros by a factor of ten. Screen updating is automatically turned back on when the macro terminates
- Turn off automatic calculations. Do the calculation just before printing

- Hide the macro sheets you are using. You can do this with HIDE( ) or by saving the macro in a hidden state. To save a macro in a hidden state, select Hide from the Window menu, then save the sheet
- Use external references instead of ACTIVATE. For example, here is a slow version of a program:

  ```
  =ACTIVATE("Sheet1")
  =SELECT("R3C3")
  =FORMULA(" =2 +3")
  =ACTIVATE("Sheet2")
  =RETURN( )
  ```

  Here is the fast version:

  ```
  =FORMULA(" =2 +3","Worksheet1!R3C3")
  =RETURN( )
  ```

- Minimize the use of file operations (such as OPEN and SAVE commands)
- Keep dialog boxes simple. Complex dialog boxes take longer for Excel to create
- Minimize the use of names. Use SET.VALUE in assignment operations (for example, SET.VALUE(X,4) instead of X =4). SET.VALUE is up to two times faster than SET.NAME on a macro sheet
- When possible, use SET.VALUE instead of FORMULA to change the contents of a cell on the macro sheet; it's about three times faster
- For loops, using a cell as a counter with SET.VALUE may be faster than using FOR...NEXT or WHILE...NEXT loops
- Use SET.NAME instead of DEFINE.NAME; it's about twice as fast
- Minimize loop operations
- Minimize the use of text operations. Manipulate references as references rather than text. When possible, use

OFFSET, ROW, and COLUMN instead of TEXTREF and REFTEXT

- CUT, COPY, and PASTE operations are relatively slow. Use them only with large ranges of cells. For smaller selections, use the FORMULA command in a loop with external references or use the SET.VALUE command

In addition, you can make macros *seem* faster by distributing *waits* (periods of seeming inactivity) over several operations and through background processing. Dead screens (blank or no activity) make any wait seem longer. Keep the user informed of what is happening with dialog boxes.

Note that adding names does not slow down macro execution. Names improve macro reliability as well as minimize problems caused by rearranging the worksheet. Names are enclosed in quotation marks only when the text, rather than the current value of the name, is important.

DEBUGGING MACROS

Here are a few tips to prevent bugs from entering your macros:

- Save macros frequently as you develop them
- If you experience problems in creating a macro, try to simplify what you are doing and then build to the complex. Use the recorder to build the basic part of the macro, then add the decision controls and other enhancements manually. If you already have a complex macro that has problems, try to break out the troublesome part and test it separately
- Put the STEP function in the macro where you wish to test a result
- For debugging purposes, use the Display command on the Options menu to make the macro sheet temporarily display values instead of formulas
- Use the recorder to enter the basic components of a command macro, then add to it

- The default ARGUMENT and RETURN modes do not pass arrays (see Chapter 27). Be sure to put the 64 type value in if you are passing an array
- Keep ECHO on
- Use comments liberally
- Try to anticipate the types of errors you may encounter
- Use the Paste Function command to eliminate function name misspellings

SPECIAL MACRO TECHNIQUES

Excel permits you to modify existing Excel menus, create special menus, run macros automatically upon opening documents, create dialog boxes, and carry out many other special operations with macros that cannot be performed with normal Excel commands. This section is a review of some of these techniques.

CREATING MENUS

With Excel, you can modify the existing menu bars and drop-down menus, or even create your own menus. As an example, assume a company approaches a bank for loans periodically. The bank needs a spreadsheet system for analyzing these requests. You could create a system in which the data about the company is first entered into a historical worksheet that contains the last four years of the company's financial data. A projections worksheet is then opened and linked to both this historical worksheet and an assumption worksheet (with interest rates and other variables). From these, the projections worksheet calculates the next four years of financial data for the company. This worksheet system could be used at bank branches by users who have little or no experience with Excel. In addition, chances of mistakes could be minimized by automating as much of the process as possible.

Consider using a batch file to automatically start Excel. Macros could automatically load and start, displaying a menu. Only those options you wanted available to the user would be displayed. The

Such a system is *really* locked in. As long as the macro sheet is open in this example, there is no File or Edit menu—or any other familiar Excel command. This protects the user from making mistakes, but once the macro is executed the user is locked into the new menu.

macro sheet would be hidden; the user would be essentially locked into a closed system.

Excel contains six menu bars: the main menu bar for the worksheet and macros, the Chart menu bar, a short form of each of these (when the Short Menus option is selected), a special menu bar for worksheets when a file is not open, and a menu bar for the help system. You can modify any one of these or create your own. In this example, we will create a completely new menu bar.

The macro worksheet for creating this menu is shown in Figure 28.12. The main macro is in cells A11:A14. The ADD.BAR() function creates a new menu bar, but does not display it. The cell value will be the next menu ID number that is available.

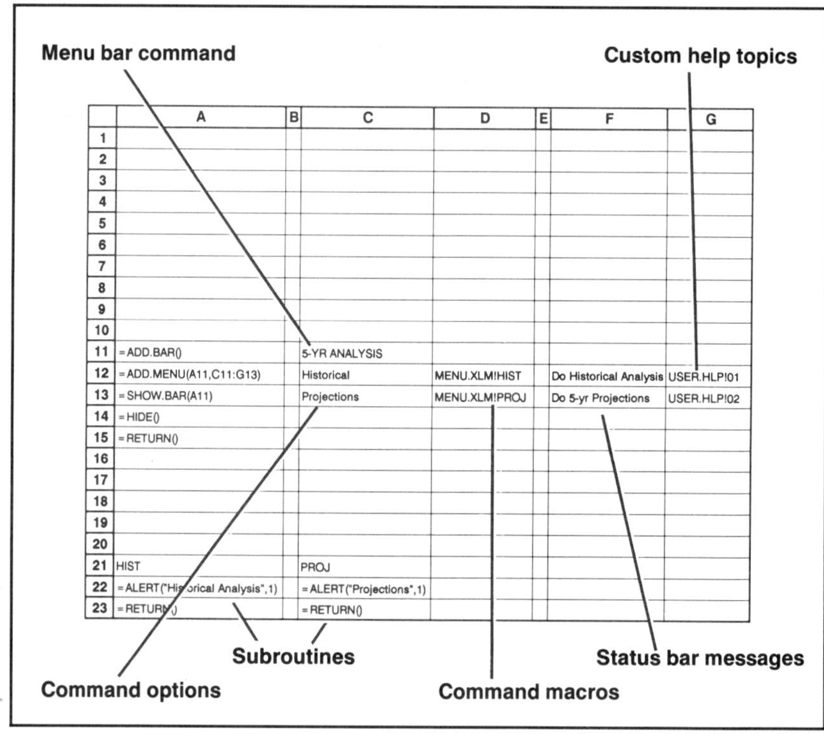

Figure 28.12: The macro sheet for a menu description

Excel has six built-in menu bars with IDs. The IDs for the internal Excel menus are as follows:

ID	*MENU*
1	Worksheet and Macro menu, full
2	Chart menu, full
3	Nil menu (no documents open)
4	Info window menu
5	Worksheet and Macro menu, short
6	Chart menu, short

In this case, we are inserting a new menu bar with an ID of 7. The ADD.MENU( ) function creates an option on this menu bar. The function form is

ADD.MENU(*bar_ID,menu_ref,position*)

The *bar_ID* for the bar is the menu ID to which the function refers (7 in this case). The *menu_ref* argument references a cell range that defines the menu (here, C11:G13). The *position* argument is new with Excel 3.0, and optionally defines the menu position.

Cell C11 in Figure 28.12 contains the title of the pull-down menu. Below it are the various menu commands. Column D defines a command macro that is initiated by each option. Column F defines a text line that will be displayed in the Status area when that command is selected. Column G contains pointers to the custom help-topics that are available. Use the Define Name command on the Formula menu to name A11, A21, and C21 by their contents.

The programs run by the menu are subroutines, one starting in A21 and the second in B21. At the moment they only display alert boxes, but in the final program they will activate their appropriate routines.

If you wished to use an existing menu and add a new command option to it, you would use the function

ADD.COMMAND(*bar_id, menu_pos, menu_ref,position*)

where *bar_id,* as before, references the menu to be modified. The *menu-_pos* argument defines which menu bar selection is to be modified, starting from the left. You can use either the menu name, such as Edit, or the numeric position (Edit is 2). The *menu_ref* argument, as before, defines the menu command. You can use a single hyphen in the first column to define a separator bar.

Other functions that are useful for creating and displaying menus are

FUNCTION	*ACTION*
DELETE.MENU(*bar_id, menu_pos*)	Deletes a menu bar
DELETE.COMMAND(*bar_id, menu_pos, cmd_pos*)	Deletes a command on a menu
RENAME.COMMAND(*bar_id, menu_pos, cmd_pos, name*)	Renames a menu command
ENABLE.COMMAND(*bar_id, menu_pos, cmd_pos, state*)	Shades a command. If *state* is TRUE, the command is not shaded; if it is FALSE, the command is shaded
CHECK.COMMAND(*bar_id, menu_pos, cmd_pos, state*)	Checks a command. If *state* is TRUE, the command is checked; if FALSE, it is not checked.
GET_BAR( )	Returns ID of current menu bar (see Appendix E)

EXECUTING MACROS AUTOMATICALLY

You can use macro commands to run a macro whenever a worksheet is opened, whenever a particular command is executed, at a specific time you define, in response to a particular keystroke, whenever an error occurs, or on encountering a specified condition in another document.

In this example, we wish the menu macro to run automatically when a document is opened. In this case, we could make it possible for the bank to create a batch file that opened a blank worksheet. To select a macro for automatic execution when a worksheet is opened:

1. Make the document active. Select the first cell of the macro.
2. Open the Formula menu and choose Define Names.
3. Enter the macro name as **AUTO_OPEN**. You can use any name that begins with AUTO_OPEN, such as AUTO_OPEN_ONE. Verify that the reference is correct and click OK.

Here are some notes and tips on using AUTO_OPEN macros:

- If you ever wish to open the document without running the macro, hold down the Shift key while clicking OK when opening the document
- Be sure the macro is saved before testing. In this example, you won't be able to save the macro once it's been executed
- Be sure the macro is tested before naming it AUTO_OPEN
- If a document with an automatic macro is opened from within a macro, the automatic macro will not execute

If you wish to create a macro that executes automatically when a document is closed, name it "AUTO_CLOSE". Holding down the Shift key while choosing Close will close the document without executing the macro.

Here are the Excel functions that support automatic macro execution under other conditions:

CONDITION	*MACRO FUNCTION*
At a particular time	ON.TIME
When a particular key is pressed	ON.KEY
On an error condition	ERROR
On a macro interruption	CANCEL.KEY

CONDITION	*MACRO FUNCTION*
On a change in linked data	ON.DATA
When a window is activated	ON.WINDOW
When document is recalculated	ON.RECALC
On Command	(Use customized menus, as in the last example)

Sometimes you may wish to load and execute a macro sheet when Excel is started. To do this, place the macro file in the EXCEL\XLSTART directory. Then, when you start Excel, it will open the document and execute any AUTO_OPEN macro.

CREATING DIALOG BOXES

You are already familiar with the dialog boxes that are a part of many commands. You can also create your own dialog boxes that can be called from macros. These can be used for almost any type of input and are much more versatile than the Input box or direct entry to a cell.

As an example, look again at the Sales worksheet used in Chapters 10–13. Let's create a dialog box to use with the worksheet for entering records. Figure 28.13 shows this new dialog box. Notice that you now have more control over data entered: the user can select from only one of the four boxes.

To create the dialog box, start the Dialog Editor from the Program Manager's Excel group. An application window is displayed with three menu options (File, Edit, and Item) and an empty dialog box. We will use this editor to create the entry form.

Select Info from the Edit menu to see the current box dimensions. Turn off any auto options and enter the new values as:

X	150	postion to start dialog box
Y	42	position to start dialog box
Width	305	width of dialog box
Height	237	height of dialog box

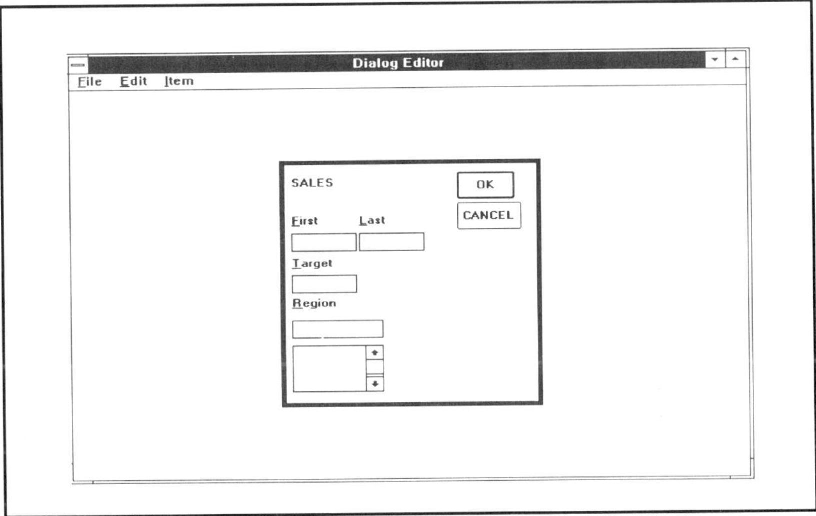

Figure 28.13: A customized dialog box

Click OK. The new dialog box frame is displayed in its new size.

Enter each item (or Control) for the dialog box, as follows: choose the item from the Item menu, place it where you wish on the frame, and then select Info on the Edit menu to enter specific information about the item. You can use Clear on the Edit menu to remove any object you need to delete. Following these steps, add each of the objects shown in Figure 28.14.

Object	Item (Control)	X	Y	Width	Height	Text	Init/Result
Title	Text	8	12	96	18	SALES	
FIRST label	Text	8	51	80	12	&First	
LAST label	Text	90	51	80	12	&Last	
FIRST entry	Edit box (Text)	8	70	80	18		FIRST
LAST entry	Edit box (Text)	90	70	80	18		LAST
TARGET label	Text	8	94	80	12	&Target	
TARGET entry	Edit box (Integer)	8	113	80	18		0
REGION label	Text	8	135	112	12	&Region	
REGION entry	Edit box (Text)	8	159	112	18		East
REGION list	List box (Standard)	8	185	112	48	REGION	1
OK button	OK button	212	8	72	28	OK	
CANCEL button	Cancel button	212	40	80	28	CANCEL	

Figure 28.14: The dialog box particulars

Once the dialog box is created, select it (choose Select Dialog on the Edit menu) and choose Copy to copy the dialog box to the Clipboard. (Notice there is no Save As or Save on the File menu; you place the dialog box on the worksheet through the Clipboard.) Minimize the Dialog Box Editor to get it out of the way, and load the Sales worksheet. Select cell F12 on the worksheet as the starting point for the dialog box description and choose Select Paste. Add the column titles in row 11, as shown in Figure 28.15. Enter the text in M13:M16 and define this range as REGION using Define Names on the Formula menu. The worksheet should look like Figure 28.15.

	F	G	H	I	J	K	L	M
11	TYPE	X	Y	DX	DY	TEXT	INIT/RESULT	
12		150	42	305	237			
13	5	8	12	96	18	SALES		East
14	5	8	51	80	12	&First		West
15	5	90	51	80	12	&Last		Midwest
16	6	8	70	80	18		FIRST	South
17	6	90	70	80	18		LAST	
18	5	8	94	80	12	&Target		
19	7	8	113	80	18		0	
20	5	8	135	112	12	&Region		
21	6	8	159	112	18		East	
22	15	8	185	112	48	REGION	1	
23	1	212	8	72	28	OK		
24	2	212	40	80	28	Cancel		

Figure 28.15: The dialog box description

The column heads used here are the same as those used to create a data form. They are as follows:

- TYPE is a code for the type of dialog-box element or *control* (see Table 28.1)
- X and Y are the coordinates for the upper-left corner of the control, as measured from the upper-left corner of the dialog box. The horizontal units are 1/8 the width of one character in the system font. The vertical units are 1/12 the height of one character
- DX and DY are the size of the control. They are measured in the same units as X and Y
- TEXT indicates how to display the text. An ampersand prefix indicates that the first letter should be underscored. (This is a "hot key": pressing Alt and the underlined letter accesses the control quickly.) For list-box controls, this column specifies the range for the list M13:M16

- INIT/RESULT is the column that contains the default value that is displayed for the control. After the dialog box function is executed, it contains the returned value. For a list box, it contains the number of the default item in the box and returns the number of the item selected

Table 28.1: Dialog Box Controls

TYPE	CONTROL	COLUMN	DESCRIPTIONS
1	Default OK button	TEXT	The text to appear on the button
2	CANCEL	TEXT	The text to appear on the button
3	OK button	TEXT	The text to appear on the button
4	Default CANCEL Button	TEXT	The text to appear on the button
5	Text	TEXT	The text to display
6	Text box	TEXT	(not used)
		INIT/RESULT	Initially, the default value for the box; after the box is displayed, the returned value
7	Integer box	TEXT	(not used)
		INIT/RESULT	Initial integer value, returns integer entered
8	Number box	TEXT	(not used)
		INIT/RESULT	Initially, the numeric value; returns the numeric value entered
9	Formula box	INIT/RESULT	The formula with the cell value and the result of the formula
10	Reference box	INIT/RESULT	The reference with the cell value and that of the reference cell
11	Option button group	INIT/RESULT	The number of the Option button selected in the subsequent group (see type 12)
12	Option Button	TEXT	The name of the button
13	Check box	INIT/RESULT	TRUE to turn on the check box, FALSE to turn it off

Table 28.1: Dialog Box Controls (continued)

TYPE	CONTROL	COLUMN	DESCRIPTIONS
14	Group box	TEXT	The text to appear at the top of the group box
15	List box	TEXT	A reference for the items in the list box
		INIT/RESULT	The Number of the initial item; returns the number of the item selected
16	Linked list box	TEXT	A reference for the items in the list box
		INIT/RESULT	The number of the initial item; returns the number of the item selected
17	Icon	TEXT	1 to display a question mark, 2 to display an asterisk, 3 to display an exclamation point
18	Linked file	TEXT	(ignored)
	List box	INIT/RESULT	(ignored)
19	Linked Drive and Directory list box		Permits altering the directory
		TEXT	(ignored)
		INIT/RESULT	(ignored)
20	Directory text	TEXT	(ignored)
21	Drop-down list box	TEXT	Reference to items in the list
		INIT/RESULT	Number of selected list item
22	Drop-down combination edit/list box	TEXT	Reference to items in the list
		INIT/RESULT	Number of selected list item

You can use no more than 64 controls, 32 items that take or return arguments, 4 list boxes, and 1,024 text characters in each dialog box that you design.

To activate the new dialog box, open a macro sheet and create a new macro:

```
=DIALOG.BOX(SALES.XLS!$F$12:$L$24)
=RETURN( )
```

Use the correct name of your document in the DIALOG.BOX function as the first argument. Name the macro and execute it. You will then see a form displayed (see Figure 28.16) for data entry. Fill out the form and then click OK.

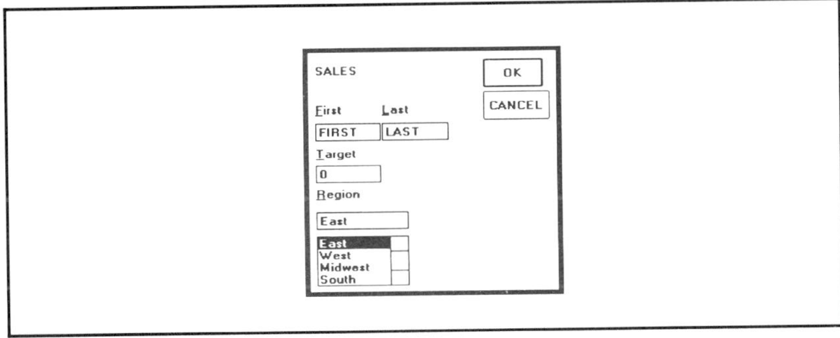

Figure 28.16: The final dialog box as displayed

After you return from the form, the values you entered will be in cells L16, L17, L19, and L21. These values can be used by the rest of the macro. For example, for a macro to add a record you would copy the values to the bottom of the database. For an edit macro, you would copy the values to edit to cells L16, L17, L19, and L21 as the starting values, use the form, and then copy the new values back. For the list-box control, the selected item will be returned in the text control immediately before it. The number 1 in cell L22 indicates that the first list-box value will be highlighted when the box is displayed.

Dialog boxes can be activated from the Form command of the Data menu using this method:

1. Create the dialog box with the editor.
2. Copy it to the worksheet.
3. Select the dialog box area and name it DATA_FORM.

Now, if you select Form from the Data menu, you will see your new dialog box. There is one serious limitation, however: you can use only text, buttons, and edit box controls. You can't use list boxes, as in the example here.

3.0

ACTIVATING MACROS WITH BUTTONS

You can place pushbuttons (or other graphic objects) on a worksheet and attach macros to them. As an example, let's add a button to the Sales worksheet so that a user can print the worksheet by clicking this button.

Load the Sales worksheet and try this procedure to add the pushbutton:

1. Open a macrosheet and enter the macro you wish to use. For the print macro, enter:

   ```
   PRINTER
    =PRINT(1,,,1,,,,,)
    =RETURN( )
   ```

   Name the macro PRINTER using the Define Name com- on
   mand on the Formula menu. Define it as a command macro.

2. Make the worksheet active. Click the button tool on the worksheet and drag from the upper-left corner of the area in which you wish to place the button. For a square button, hold down the Shift key as you drag. To align the button with the grid, hold down the Ctrl key as you drag. Excel places a button with the default name at that location and prompts for a macro name using an Assign Macro box.
3. Select the name for the macro in the dialog box (see Figure 28.17). Click OK.
4. Edit the text in the button by dragging over the text and entering the desired text. Enter **Print**. You can format the text using the Format menu, if you wish (see Figure 28.18).

To print the worksheet, simply click the button!

If you wish to assign a macro to a graphic object that is not a button, click the object, then choose Assign To Object from the Macro menu. Choose the macro name and click OK.

If you wish to edit the macro assignment, hold down the Ctrl key and click the object. Choose Assign to Object from the Macro menu and edit the assignment in the dialog box.

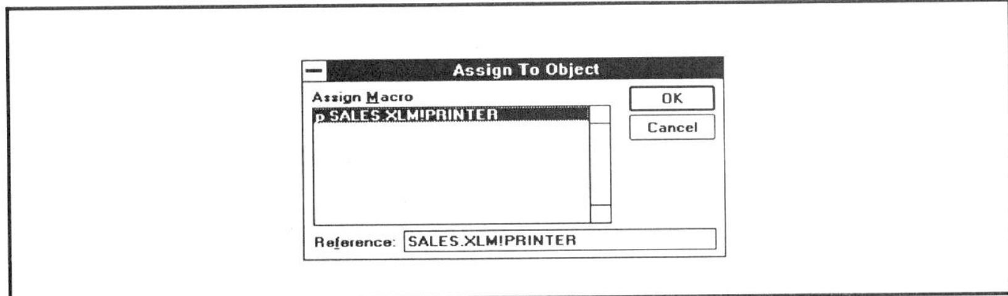

Figure 28.17: Assigning a macro to an object

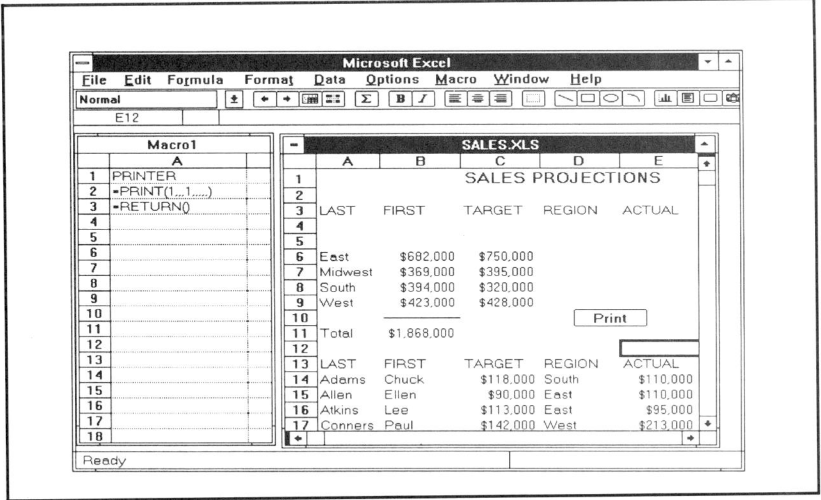

Figure 28.18: The final worksheet with a button

To attach a macro to an invisible object, create the object and assign the macro to it. Then select the object and use the Patterns command from the Format menu to set the border to None and set the Fill as invisible. Use this method for attaching macros to specific cells—create the object at the cell location, attach the macro, and make the object invisible.

A Glossary

Absolute reference A reference to a specific cell or group of cells on a worksheet. An absolute cell reference does not change with moving or copying. In the A1 format, an absolute reference is designated by a dollar sign before both the row and the column, such as $A$5. In the R1C1 style, an absolute reference is just written out as R#C#; for example, R1C5 is an example of an absolute cell reference written in this style.

Active cell The selected cell in which any current keyboard entry would be stored. The active cell is always indicated with a heavy border. The formula bar always shows the contents of the active cell.

Active window The window that is currently selected.

Alignment The position of text or a value in a cell. Alignment can be left, right, or centered.

Argument The value used as input to a function to calculate an output value.

Array A two-dimensional set of values, normally arranged in rows and columns.

Attached text Text created with the Attach Text command on the chart menu and connected to a specific object on the chart: title, axis, legend, and so on.

Axes The straight lines used on the graph for measurement and reference. A pie chart has no real axis; other types have two.

Border The line around an area on a worksheet or chart.

Cancel box The small box with an × in the formula bar. Clicking this box discards any changes you have made to a cell using the formula bar.

Category A name associated with a numeric value in a data series. Each data point in a series has a category name and a value.

Cell The basic unit of the worksheet used for storing values, formulas, and text; also the intersection of a row and column.

Chart One or more graphs displayed in a single document.

Chart format The basic information that defines how a data series is plotted.

Chart object Any part of the chart: axes, markers, lines, legend, plot area, chart, arrows, unattached text, and so on.

Chart style The basic type of chart used. Excel has six basic chart types: area, bar, column, line, pie, and scatter. Several of these have a three-dimensional version.

Circular references Two or more formulas that depend upon each other for results.

Client area (See *Work area.*)

Cluster On a chart, a group of bars or columns in the same category.

Constant value Anything entered to a cell that is not a formula.

Control menu A menu activated by clicking the Control-menu box (see below). The application Control menu is used to close Excel, resize or move the application window, maximize or minimize Excel, and activate programs that run with Excel. Control menus can close, resize, move, or maximize the document.

Control-menu box A small box in the upper left of the Excel application window and on each document that opens the Control menu.

Criteria A test used to find, extract, or delete records in a database.

Database An organized collection of data about one or more records. Each record takes up a row in the database. Information about each record is recorded in fields, or columns.

Database range That part of a worksheet that contains the database—both records and field headers. It is defined with the Set Database command.

Data form A type of dialog box used for updating and searching an Excel database.

Data point A chart category with a corresponding numeric value.

Data series A collection of data points, each related to the other in some respect.

Dependent document Any document in which one or more cells contain a reference to another worksheet (the *supporting document*).

Descriptors The indicators at the top and left of the display area that indicate the rows and columns. At the left of the worksheet are the row descriptors, and at the top are the column descriptors.

Dialog box A window or box that is used in Excel and other Windows application programs for user input. On a menu, the names of commands that activate dialog boxes and with an ellipsis. You can also create dialog boxes for data input in a macro.

Document Any worksheet, chart, or macro sheet, either active or saved to the disk.

Dynamic Data Exchange (DDE) A method of accessing a common data area in Windows that can be shared by several Windows application programs.

Embedded object An object that, if selected, opens the creating application. A chart on a worksheet is an embedded object.

Enter box The small box with a ✓ in the formula bar that is clicked to complete an entry or edit.

Excel macro language A special group of functions used for writing programs in Excel.

External reference A reference to a specific cell or group of cells, normally on another worksheet. The reference format consists of the worksheet name, an exclamation point, and the cell reference. You can also refer to the currently active worksheet as an external reference by including an exclamation point before the cell reference. This is useful in macros that must refer to cells in several worksheets generically.

Extract To copy from a database records that meet specific criteria.

Field Any column of data in a database.

Font A specific design of text.

Format Information that controls how the contents of a cell will be displayed. It consists of a picture, style, alignment, font, and font size.

Formula A mathematical arrangement of one or more values, cell references, names, functions, and operators that produce a value.

Formula bar An area below the menu bar that displays the contents of the active cell.

Function An abbreviation of a formula. A function produces an output value (or values) from a specified input. (Some functions require no input value.)

Graph A visual representation of one or more data series. It includes the plotted area, labels, legends, and comments.

Gridlines Optional horizontal or vertical lines on a chart to help you determine the value of a marker.

Input cell The cell that holds each of a series of input values used to create a table.

Label In a chart, text used to identify that part of the chart.

Legend The symbols with corresponding labels that are used to identify the different series of data on the chart.

Link A defined relationship between two documents in which a formula in a dependent document references a cell in a supporting document.

Lock To protect a cell so that its contents cannot be altered.

Macro A collection of functions that can be executed to produce some specified result.

Macro sheet A worksheet used to store macros.

Main chart The primary graph on a chart.

Marker A type of indicator used on a graph to make a data point. In a column chart, each column is a marker.

Mixed reference A reference that consists of both absolute and relative addresses.

Outlining A type of structure that permits you to control the level of the worksheet rows and columns that are displayed. Collapsing an outline, for example, permits you to omit detail rows on a worksheet temporarily.

Overlay chart A second graph that is plotted in the same chart window as the main chart.

Pane A subdivision of a worksheet window.

Picture One or more characters used to format a number, time, or date in a cell.

Plot area The area bounded by the axes or, in the case of the pie chart, the area within the circle.

Precision The number of decimal places to which a value is stored or used in calculations.

Print area That part of the worksheet that is printed when you invoke the Print command.

Protect To prevent the contents of a cell, cell range, or worksheet from unauthorized or unnecessary access.

Q + E A utility provided with Excel for interfacing with external databases. It can query and extract from databases based on a criterion.

Range One or more highlighted cells.

Record Any row of data in a database range.

Relative reference A reference to a cell or group of cells located relative to the reference on a worksheet. A relative reference changes with moving or copying. In the A1 format, a relative reference is designated by the column letter and row number, such as A5. In the R1C1 style, a relative reference is written to reflect the cell's location relative to the reference's location. An example of such a relative reference would be R[2]C[2], meaning two rows down and two columns to the right of the reference's location.

Scale The range of values covered by the *y* axis on the chart.

Solver A utility provided with Excel for supporting what-if simulations.

Split bar The small black rectangle at the top of the vertical scroll bar and the left of the horizontal scroll bar used to separate a window into panes.

Status area An area at the bottom of an Excel window that displays the current status of the program.

Style The appearance of the font on the worksheet (bold, italic, etc.).

Supporting document Any document in which one or more cells are referenced by another worksheet (the *dependent document*).

Table A range of cells that contains the results of applying a series of values to an input cell.

Tickmarks Divisions of an axis used to indicate categories or scale.

Title bar A bar at the top of the application window that contains the program name (Microsoft Excel) and at the top of each document displayed in the work area that contains the current file name.

Tool bar An optional bar displayed with a worksheet that can simplify some worksheet operations and supports adding and editing graphic objects on the worksheet.

Unattached text Text on a chart that is not attached to any object and can be moved.

Wildcard Special characters used to stand for any character(s) in text. The question mark (?) is used to represent any single character; the asterisk (*) represents a group of characters.

Work area The area in the Excel window that displays documents and other program-related features (such as the status area, formula bar, and so on). It is also called the client area.

Worksheet A grid of cells 256 columns wide and 16,384 cells long to which you can enter formulas and values.

***X* axis** The horizontal (or category) chart axis.

***Y* axis** The vertical (or value) chart axis.

B Speed Tips

EXCEL RUNS FASTEST UNDER WINDOWS 3.0 OR LATER in a 386 Enhanced mode. Using several megabytes of extended memory will minimize disk swapping, which slows down Excel, so if you are expanding your system and want speed to be a priority, buy more memory.

Periodically, you should defragment each disk drive using a compression utility such as PC Tools Compress (Central Point Software) or Norton Utilities Speedisk (Symantic). This ensures that all the sectors of each file are physically adjacent on the disk and speeds up disk access.

To maximize the speed of Windows and Excel in the 386 Enhanced mode, install a permanent *swap file.* This is a hidden file that is installed on the disk as an extension of memory. The 386 Enhanced mode is the only mode that supports a permanent swap file. The file is installed at a fixed location on the disk, and Windows can bypass DOS in accessing this file, which thus permits higher access speeds. To install the permanent swap file, first defragment the disk, then start Windows in Real mode (type **WIN /r** at the DOS prompt). Choose Run from the File menu and enter **SWAPFILE**. Windows displays the recommended size. Choose Create. Then exit Windows and restart Windows in the 386 Enhanced mode.

Another way to improve the speed of Excel is to install a *disk cache.* A disk cache is a buffer area in memory with appropriate controls that manage the transfer of data to and from the disk. Database managers that use a lot of disk reading and writing need large caches. Excel isn't that demanding, but a good disk caching program can help speed up things. Windows includes its own, which can be installed by adding the following line in the CONFIG.SYS file:

SMARTDRIVE caches only when reading the disk, and offers no special advantage when writing. Other products cache when reading *and* writing, such as PowerCache +1.25 (Intelligent Devices Corporation) and PC-Kwik 2.00 (MultiSoft Corporation).

DEVICE = SMARTDRV.SYS 512 256

Microsoft's SMARTDRIVE is for computers that have a hard disk and extended (512K) or expanded (256K) memory. The first number is the cache size (in kilobytes) assigned to the cache upon booting DOS. The second number defines the *minimum* size of the cache in kilobytes. You may wish to explore some commercial disk-cache programs. Many are faster than the Windows version and will work with Windows 3.0.

If you are using DOS 4 or later, you may find speed is improved by using FASTOPEN, a utility included with DOS. This keeps part of the disk directory in memory, minimizing access to the directory portion of the disk. To use this utility, include the following line in the CONFIG.SYS file:

INSTALL = FASTOPEN.EXE C: = –100

where the number is the number of disk directory entries to maintain in memory.

Windows is a multitasking system. You can speed execution by closing or suspending applications you are not using. Printing in the background will also slow down Excel.

Here are some speed tips specifically for Excel:

- Turn off automatic calculations with the Calculate command on the Options menu. Do the calculation just before printing, using Calculate Now or by pressing F9
- For faster recalculation, calculate only the active worksheet by pressing Shift–F9

- Hide the documents you are temporarily not using. Hiding a macro sheet, for example, keeps it available but makes the screen faster. You can do this with the HIDE( ) function or by saving the macro in a hidden state.
- Avoid performing operations (such as Cut or Copy) on an entire row or column. These take more Clipboard space and require more time than operations performed on only the relevant cells
- Use a macro sheet that automatically loads with frequently used macros. Then add an Auto_Open macro to it to block the loading of Sheet1 when you open a file. Keep the macro in the EXCEL\XLSTART directory to automatically load and execute. Give the macro sheet any name you wish, but select Define from the Formula menu first to name $A$1 as Auto_Open. An example would be:

  ```
  Auto_Open
  =HIDE( )
  =OPEN?( )
  =IF(A3 =TRUE,GOTO(A6))
  =NEW(1)
  =RETURN( )
  ```

  This hides the macro sheet and displays a dialog box to open a file. If you cancel, Sheet1 will be loaded
- Select the worksheet names at the bottom of the File menu to load recently used worksheets
- Keep templates of frequently used worksheets. Keep custom pictures in the templates, as well as your custom styles
- Explore creative font management to speed printing. For example, a Microsoft Z cartridge with Helvetica 10 is fast, but trying to download it as a soft font from the computer helvetica for landscape printing is slow. Printing the document in portrait mode, in this case, is definitely faster
- Place tables on a separate worksheet to control their recalculation better

C Installation Tips

Before altering WIN.INI, always create a backup. In this way, if you do make a mistake you can always get home again.

WINDOWS CONTAINS A WIN.INI FILE THAT DEFINES the system parameters for the Windows environment. When you install Excel, this file is modified to contain the system parameters for the Excel application program. The Windows Control Panel also modifies this file.

You can edit the WIN.INI file at any time to customize your system, using the Windows Notepad or any editor. You should not, however, use a word processor to modify the file unless the word processor can save the new file in ASCII format. This means saving the file as text only, without any formatting codes.

Now let's take a look at a typical WIN.INI file. We won't look at the entire file, but a few parts are very relevant for Excel:

```
[windows]

load = clock,winfile,carl.crd

run =
```

```
[Extensions]
.
.
.
xls = excel.exe ^.xls
xlc = excel.exe ^.xlc
xlw = excel.exe ^.xlw
xlm = excel.exe ^.xlm
xlt = excel.exe ^.xlt
xla = excel.exe ^.xla
.
.
.
[fonts]
Helv 8,10,12,14,18,24 (VGA res) = HELVE.FON
Courier 10,12,15 (VGA res) = COURE.FON
Tms Rmn 8,10,12,14,18,24 (VGA res) = TMSRE.FON
Symbol 8,10,12,14,18,24 (VGA res) = SYMBOLE.FON
Roman (All res) = ROMAN.FON
Script (All res) = SCRIPT.FON
Modern (All res) = MODERN.FON
Small Fonts (VGA res) = f:\fonts\smalle.fon
Helv 36 (VGA res) = f:\fonts\helv36e.fon
Helv 6,7 (VGA res) = TMSR7E.FON
Tms Rmn 36 (VGA res) = f:\fonts\tmsr36e.fon
ITCZapfDingbats 6,7,8,10,12,14,18,24 (VGA
res) = f:\fonts\zd24e.fon
Tms Rmn 6,7 (VGA res) = f:\fonts\tmsr7e.fon
```

```
[HPPCL,LPT1]
.
.
.
FontSummary=e:\win\FSLPT1.PCL
sfdir=C:\PCLFONTS
SoftFont1=C:\PCLFONTS\TRPR0060.PFM,C:\PCLFONTS\
TR060RPN.USP
SoftFont2=C:\PCLFONTS\TRPB0060.PFM,C:\PCLFONTS\
TR060BPN.USP
SoftFont3=C:\PCLFONTS\TRPI0060.PFM,C:\PCLFONTS\
TR060IPN.USP
SoftFont4=C:\PCLFONTS\TRPR0080.PFM,C:\PCLFONTS\
TR080RPN.USP
SoftFont5=C:\PCLFONTS\TRPB0080.PFM,C:\PCLFONTS\
TR080BPN.USP
SoftFont6=C:\PCLFONTS\TRPI0080.PFM,C:\PCLFONTS\
TR080IPN.USP
SoftFont7=C:\PCLFONTS\TRPR0100.PFM,C:\PCLFONTS\
TR100RPN.USP
SoftFonts=7
.
.
.
[Microsoft Excel]
Options=119
Maximized=1

[Embedding]
Graph=Business Graphs from PowerPoint Graph, Graph,
PPtGraph.exe, picture
```

```
ExcelWorksheet = Worksheet created by Microsoft Excel,Excel
Worksheet,Excel.exe, picture
ExcelChart = Chart created by Microsoft Excel,Excel
Chart,Excel.exe, picture

[Q + E]
connect = dBASEFile
NoLogon = dBaseFile,TextFile,ExcelFile
Maximized = 0
AsciiOem = 0

[QEDBF]
Extension = DBF
IndexExtension = NDX,MDX

[QETXT]
Extension = CSV

[QEXLS]
Extension = XLS
```

You'll find that the file is divided into sections, each with some type of [*xxx*] heading that defines a section, and then a list of lines of the form:

parameter = value

Each line sets a certain parameter to a value or text string. You can edit parameter values, add new parameters, or delete parameters.

At the beginning of the list is a collection of parameters under [windows]. *Load* defines programs that are automatically loaded as icons upon starting Windows. You can put Excel here if you wish

Excel to be started in Windows as an icon. Be sure to add the full path name and file extension as:

load = d:\excel\excel.exe

The *run* parameter defines any program automatically started with Windows. Putting Excel here will not only load it, but start it as well.

Further down under **[extensions]**, you find a parameter list that defines which program is started when you select a data file. This list is automatically modified when you install Windows, and permits you to start Excel with a document by choosing that document from the Windows File Manager.

Under **[fonts]**, you will find the display fonts that are installed in Windows and available to Excel. These are added when you install Windows, but if you add new fonts to Windows this list will be modified. In this example, some fonts were added when Microsoft PowerPoint was installed, and these new fonts are available to Excel.

Further down you will find a section for your printer. If you have installed any soft fonts for that printer, they will be listed here.

You should also find a section specifically for Microsoft Excel, along with a Q+E section. In the Excel section, *Maximized* determines whether Excel is maximized upon starting. Set the parameter to 0 to make this happen. Other options generally need not be changed.

You should also find an EXCEL.INI file in your windows directory. It contains basic startup information used by Excel, for example:

```
[Microsoft Excel]
Options = 87
Options3 = 1
Maximized = 1

[Recent File List]
File1 = G:\PIX\GCD.XLM
File2 = G:\PIX\DIALOG.XLS
File3 = G:\ML\PRIZM.XLS
```

```
File4 = D:\XLS\SALES.XLS

[Init Commands]

solver = 1,Formula,Sol&ver...,'E:\EX3\XLSTART\SOLVER\
SOLVER.XLA'!STUB,,,Find feasible or optimal solution to
worksheet model,EXCELHLP.HLP!1700
```

Notice that this file defines the last parameters used by Excel. It can be modified by an editor as well, but the same rule applies as to WIN.INI—save the current file first.

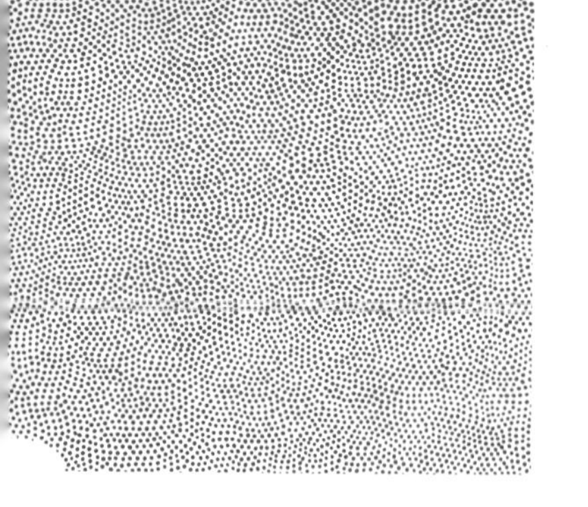
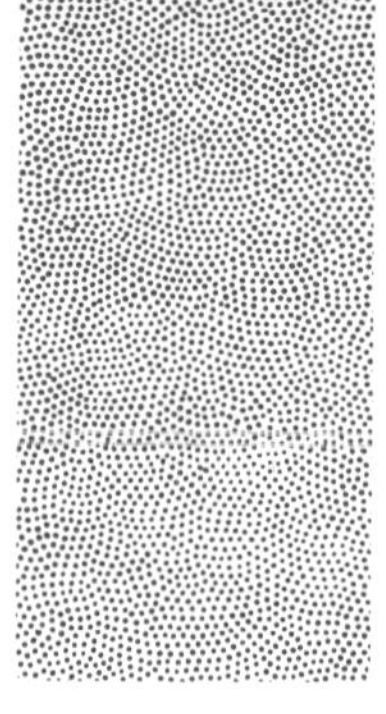

D Using Excel with Lotus 1-2-3

WHEN A FILE IS TRANSFERRED IN EITHER DIRECTION between Lotus 1-2-3 (Lotus Development Corporation) and Excel, the following items convert:

- Cell values, formulas, and formats
- Names

The following do not convert:

- Window properties
- Macros
- Lotus charts to Excel graphs

Although many functions in Lotus have a different order of arguments, they will still convert, and the worksheet will operate properly when transferred in either direction. See Chapter 21 for information about how to convert files. Here are some additional notes:

- Some Lotus formulas cannot be converted; you will be alerted by a dialog box when these are encountered. Some Excel functions are not in Lotus
- Lotus uses logical functions in a different way than Excel. For example, the Lotus expression:

  IF(A25<5#AND#A25>25,"","Entry not in 5–25 range")

  becomes this in Excel:

  IF(AND(A25<5,A25>25),"","Entry not in 5–25 range")
- Excel permits the use of text as constants in formulas; Lotus does not. Any Excel formula containing a text argument or operand will not convert

DATA ENTRY DIFFERENCES

With Excel, you first select the cells, then choose the command. With Lotus, the opposite is true. Excel has the advantage of permitting you to do several operations on the same selection. You can also select multiple and discontinuous ranges.

Lotus uses the first typed character of a cell entry to determine whether the entry is a value or text. Excel looks at the *entire* cell contents before making a decision. For example, *1-2-3* is considered a numeric entry for Lotus and a text entry for Excel. This means that Excel can interpret an address entry that begins with a number as a text string; Lotus cannot.

When defining a range of cells, Excel uses a semicolon in the same way that Lotus uses a double period. Lotus equations start with an ampersand. Excel begins them with an equal sign. Thus, @SUM(A8..A14) in Lotus is =SUM(A8:A14) in Excel.

When reading a Lotus worksheet, Excel automatically takes care of these differences.

FUNCTIONS

Most Lotus and Excel functions are identical, but you will find some that differ in name or how they are used. For financial functions, Excel considers anything you pay out to be a *negative* cash flow.

For this reason, some financial functions return negative values. For Lotus, the same functions return *positive* values.

Lotus defines the LOOKUP functions slightly differently, too, with the offset beginning at 0 instead of 1.

Use caution as well with the order of the arguments. In some cases, Excel orders them differently than Lotus. This is particularly true of financial functions.

FORMATTING

In converting, the formatting information will be maintained as much as possible. In converting from Excel to Lotus, the alignment for text cells is maintained; all nontext cells will be right-aligned.

MISCELLANEOUS

Excel emphasizes presentation-quality reporting with both worksheets and charts. If you have been using a particular Lotus worksheet and want to add some graphic elements to it, set it up with Lotus and use Excel to create the final image: i.e., import the final worksheet to Excel and add the extras there.

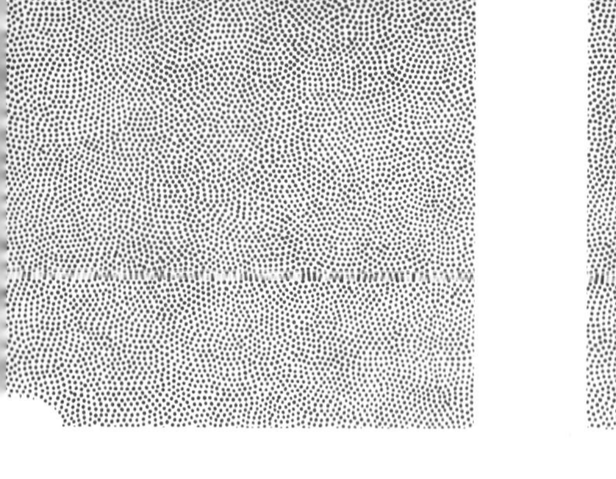
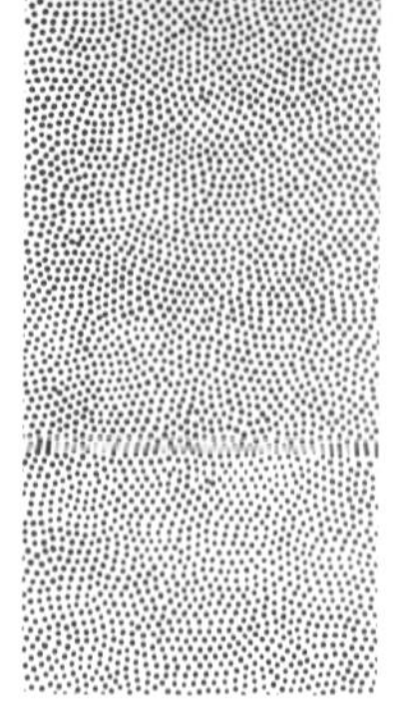
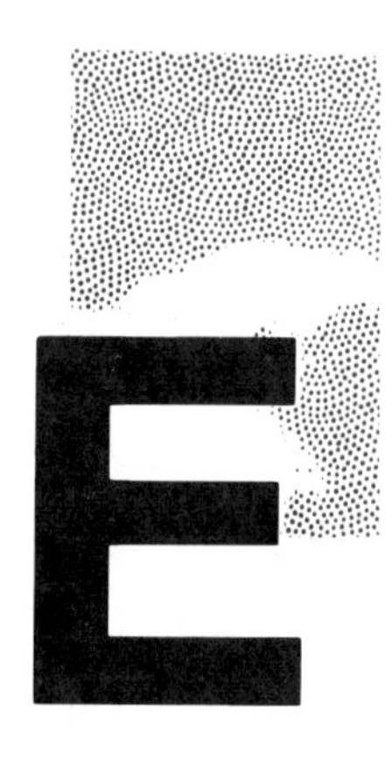

E The Macro Language Function Directory

THIS APPENDIX LISTS EACH OF THE MACRO functions that are available to the Excel user. The functions are in alphabetical order, with each listing giving the argument(s), menu-equivalent commands, action, and one or more examples, where helpful. Macro-function arguments fall under the same categories as those of other functions: text, numeric, logical, reference, error, and array.

For each listing, the question-mark equivalent (if available) displays the command's dialog box, from which you can choose the desired options.

Certain macro commands are provided in PC Excel for compatibility with Macintosh Excel. Although not generally used in Excel for Windows, they enable you to import macro sheets from the Macintosh so that they function properly on an IBM PC. These macros are indicated in this appendix by the phrase, "Included for compatibility with Macintosh Excel"; the PC-Excel–equivalent command is shown as well. Although these Macintosh commands are supported by Excel for Windows, you should use the PC Excel version of the command when writing macros—unless they must operate on both systems—since it generally provides more options.

The typographical conventions used in this appendix are as follows: required arguments appear in ***bold italics***; optional arguments appear in *plain italics*. Text arguments are indicated with the suffix *text*; when entered, they must be enclosed in quotes (" "). Menu options are separated by a →. Thus "Formula→Define Name" means "the Define Name command in the Formula menu."

A1.R1C1(*logical*)

Menu Equivalent: Options→Workspace R1C1

Action: Switches display mode to A1 if *logical* is TRUE. Switches display mode to R1C1 if *logical* is FALSE.

Example: =A1.R1C1(TRUE) switches display mode to A1.

ABSREF(***ref_text, ref***)

Menu Equivalent: None.

Action: Returns an absolute reference defining cells that have a relative relationship to *ref*, as specified by *ref_text*. *Ref_text* must be an R1C1-style relative reference. (OFFSET is a preferred function for this.)

Example: =ABSREF("R[-1]C[-2]",C4) equals A3.

ACTIVATE(*window_text, pane_no*)

Menu Equivalent: Window→*window_name*

Action: Activates the window defined by *window _text,* and *pane_no* is the pane.

Example: =WINDOW("Sheet1") activates Sheet1.

ACTIVATE.NEXT( )

ACTIVATE.PREV( )

Menu Equivalent: None.

Action: Activates the next/previous window.

The SELECTION function returns the selected range; ACTIVATE.CELL returns the active cell in that range.

ACTIVE.CELL( )

Menu Equivalent: None.

Action: Returns reference to active cell in the selection.

Example: The function =SET.NAME("Cost",ACTIVE.CELL ( )) assigns the name "Cost" to the currently active cell.

ADD.ARROW( )

Menu Equivalent: Chart→Add Arrow

Action: Adds an arrow to the active chart.

ADD.BAR(*bar_number*)

Menu Equivalent: None.

Action: Creates a new and empty menu bar in the system. If *bar_number* is already used, restores the previous menu bar associated with *bar_number*.

Example: See Chapter 28.

ADD.COMMAND(*bar_number, menu_pos, menu_ref, position*)

Menu Equivalent: None.

Action: Adds a command bar defined by *menu_ref* on the sheet to the menu at *menu_pos* in menu-bar number *bar_number*:

BAR_NUMBER	*MENU BAR*
1	Worksheet and macro sheet menu bar (full menus)

BAR_NUMBER	*MENU BAR*
2	Chart menu bar (full menus)
3	Null menu bar (the menu when no documents are open)
4	Info menu bar
5	Worksheet and macro sheet menu bar (short menus)
6	Chart menu bar (short menus)

Position indicates the placement of the bar. Commands are added above the specified position. If not specified, the command is put at the bottom.

Example: See Chapter 28.

ADD.MENU(*bar_number, menu_ref, position*)

Menu Equivalent: None.

Action: Adds a menu described in *menu_ref* on the sheet to *bar_number*. The optional *position* argument specifies the placement. The new menu is placed at the left of the specified position. If omitted, the menu is placed at the end.

Example: See Chapter 28.

ADD.OVERLAY( )

Menu Equivalent: Chart→Add Overlay

Action: Adds an overlay to the active chart.

ALERT(*text, type*)

Menu Equivalent: None.

The type 1 alert box can be used to give the user a choice between two options.

Action: Displays an alert box with the message *text*. The box can be one of the three following types:

TYPE	ACTION
1	Caution alert with the ? icon and both the OK and Cancel buttons
2	Note alert with the "i" (information) icon and the OK button
3	Stop alert with the ! icon and the OK button

Example: =ALERT("Number must be less than 10",2) displays a note-alert box with **Number must be less than 10** in it.

ALIGNMENT(*type*,*wrap*)

ALIGNMENT?(*type*,*wrap*)

Menu Equivalent: Format→Alignment

Action: Aligns the selected cells to the *type* format:

TYPE	FORMAT
1	General
2	Left
3	Center
4	Right
5	Fill

The *wrap* argument specifies whether text is to be wrapped in the cell. The default is FALSE.

Example: =ALIGNMENT(3) centers the selected cells.

APP.ACTIVATE(*title_text*, *wait_log*)

Menu Equivalent: (Control) Run

Action: Activates *title_text*. If *wait_log* is TRUE, Excel must be loaded first; if it is FALSE or omitted, the named application loads immediately.

APP.MAXIMIZE( )

Menu Equivalent: (Control) Maximize

Action: Maximizes the application window.

APP.MINIMIZE( )

Menu Equivalent: (Control) Minimize

Action: Minimizes the application window.

APP.MOVE(*x_number, y_number*)

APP.MOVE?(*x_number, y_number*)

Menu Equivalent: (Control) Move

Action: Moves the window to the specified location. The question-mark form of the command does not display a dialog box but permits moving with the mouse or keyboard.

Example: =APP.MOVE(100,150) moves the Excel window so that there are 100 points from the left edge of the screen to the left edge of the window and 150 points between the top edge of the screen and the top edge of the window (1 point equals 1/72 of an inch).

APP.RESTORE( )

Menu Equivalent: (Control) Restore

Action: Restores the active window.

APP.SIZE(*x_number, y_number*)

APP.SIZE?(*x_number, y_number*)

Menu Equivalent: (Control) Size

Action: Resizes window to *x_number, y_number*. The question-mark form does not display a dialog box. The window is resized with the keyboard or mouse.

Example: =APP.SIZE(200,250) sizes the window to be 200 points wide and 250 points high (1 point equals 1/72 of an inch).

APPLY.NAMES(*name_array,* *ignore, use_rowcol, omit_col, omit_row, name_order, append*)

APPLY.NAMES?(*name_array, ignore, use_rowcol, omit_col, omit_row, name_order, append*)

Menu Equivalent: Formula→Apply Names

Action: Searches for the definition(s) of a name or names in *name_array* in the formulas and replaces the definition(s) with the name(s).

APPLY.STYLE(*style_text*)

APPLY.STYLE?(*style_text*)

Menu Equivalent: Format→Style

Action: Applies the specified style to the selected cell(s).

ARGUMENT(*name_text,* *type*)

ARGUMENT(*name_text, type,* ***ref***)

Menu Equivalent: None.

Action: Permits passing arguments to a macro. For each argument of a macro, there must be one ARGUMENT function in the macro. ARGUMENT functions must come before any other formulas in the macro except the RESULT function. If you use the form ARGUMENT(*name_text, type*), then *name_text* refers to the value passed in the macro. If you use the form ARGUMENT(*name_text, type, ref*), the value is passed to *ref* (on the macro sheet), and *name* refers to the cell where the value is stored. The former must be used if the value to be passed is a reference.

The value of *type* determines what types of values Excel will accept for the argument. If the value passed is not the correct type, Excel will attempt to convert it. If it cannot be converted, Excel will return the error value #VALUE!.

TYPE	*ARGUMENT TYPE ACCEPTED*
1	Number
2	Text
4	Logical
8	Reference
16	Error
64	Array

You can combine these for multiple types. For example, a value of 3 for *type* would permit a number or text to be accepted. If *type* is omitted, a default value of 7 will be assumed. This permits numbers, text, or logical values. *Type* must be specified to use arrays or references.

Example: See Chapter 27.

ARRANGE.ALL( )

Menu Equivalent: Window→Arrange All

Action: Rearranges displayed windows in work area.

ASSIGN.TO.OBJECT(*ref*)

ASSIGN.TO.OBJECT?(*ref*)

Menu Equivalent: Macro→Assign to Object

Action: Assigns a macro to be run when the object is clicked.

ATTACH.TEXT(*attach_to_number*, *series_number*, *point_number*)

ATTACH.TEXT?(*attach_to_number*, *series_number*, *point_number*)

Menu Equivalent: Chart→Attach Text

Action: Attaches text to title, axis, or series. The value of *attach_to_number* defines what the text is attached to:

ATTACH_TO_NUM	*ATTACHES TEXT TO*
1	Title
2	Value (*y*) axis, or value (*z*) axis on 3-D charts
3	Category (*x*) axis, or series (*y*) axis on 3-D charts
4	Series or data point or category (*x*) axis on 3-D charts
5	Overlay value (*y*) axis, or series or data point on 3-D charts
6	Overlay category (*x*) axis

If a series or data point is specified, the *series_number* argument defines the series and the *point_number* argument defines the point.

ATTRIBUTES(*comment_text, auto_share*)

ATTRIBUTES?(*comment_text, auto_share*)

Menu Equivalent: File→Object Attributes (only if you are using NewWave by Hewlett-Packard).

Action: Sets file object attributes (NewWave only).

These are for a 2-D chart.

AXES(*x_main, y_main, x_over, y_over*)

AXES?(*x_main, y_main, x_over, y_over*)

These are for a 3-D chart.

AXES(*x_main, y_main, z_main*)

AXES?(*x_main, y_main, z_main*)

Menu Equivalent: Chart→Axes

Action: Turns the display of an axis on or off. The arguments correspond to those of the dialog box.

BEEP(*number*)

Menu Equivalent: None.

Action: Sounds the built-in tone, specified by *number*, from 1–4. Useful for alerting the user after a specified action is completed.

BORDER(*outline, left, right, top, bottom, shade, outline_color, left _color, right_color, top_color, bottom_color*)

BORDER?(*outline, left, right, top, bottom, shade, outline_color, left_color, right_color, top_color, bottom_color*)

Menu Equivalent: Format→Border

Action: Creates the specified border on the currently selected cells. The first five arguments are numbers specifying the line types corresponding to the line styles in the dialog box. *Shade* corresponds to that option on the box. The color arguments are numbers specifying the color.

Example: =BORDER(1,0,0,0,0) draws an outline around the currently selected cells.

BREAK( )

Menu Equivalent: None.

Action: Interrupts the execution of a FOR...NEXT or WHILE ...NEXT loop.

BRING.TO.FRONT( )

Menu Equivalent: Format→Bring To Front

Action: Puts the selected objects on top of others.

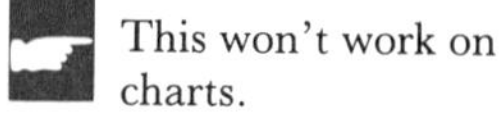
This won't work on charts.

CALCULATE.DOCUMENT( )

Menu Equivalent: Options→Calculate Document

Action: Calculates the active document.

CALCULATE.NOW( )

Menu Equivalent: Options→Calculate Now

Action: Initiates a calculation on all open documents.

CALCULATION(***type***, *iteration, number_of, change, update, precision, date_1904, calc_save, save_values*)

CALCULATION?(*type, iteration, number_of, change, update, precision, date_1904, calc_save, save_values*)

Menu Equivalent: Options→Calculation

Action: Specifies the type of calculation to use. There are three types:

TYPE VALUE	*CALCULATION TYPE*
1	Automatic
2	Automatic except tables
3	Manual

The arguments are as follows:

- *Iteration* is a logical value where TRUE indicates checked and FALSE indicates not checked

- *Number_of* and *change* are numbers representing the maximum number of iterations and the maximum amount of change respectively
- *Update* represents the Update Remote Reference check box *Precision* represents the Precision as Displayed check box *Date_1904* represents the 1904 Date System check box
- *Calc_save* is the Recalculate Before Save check box*Save_values* represents the Save External Link Values check box

Example: =CALCULATION(2,FALSE) sets the calculation type to automatic except for tables.

CALLER( )

Menu Equivalent: None.

Action: Gives the reference of the cell containing the function that called the current macro. If the function was part of an array formula in an array of cells, CALLER( ) gives the reference of the range. This is useful in a macro if the calculation depends on the location or size of the calling reference.

Example: =ROWS(CALLER( )) returns the number of rows in the calling reference.

CANCEL.COPY( )

Menu Equivalent: Equivalent to pressing Escape.

Action: Cancels marquee on a range after a cut or copy operation.

CANCEL.KEY(*enable, macro_ref*)

Menu Equivalent: None.

Action: Disables macro interruption.

CELL.PROTECTION(*locked, hidden*)

CELL.PROTECTION?(*locked, hidden*)

Menu Equivalent: Format→Cell Protection

Action: Specifies cell protection or hiding on the selected range. *Locked* and *hidden* are logical values where TRUE is checked and FALSE is not checked.

CHANGE.LINK(*old_link, new_link,* *type_of_link*)

CHANGE.LINK?(*old_link, new_link, type_of_link*)

Menu Equivalent: File→Links

Action: Changes a link between worksheets.

CHECK.COMMAND(*bar_number, menu_pos, command_pos, check*)

Menu Equivalent: None.

Action: Adds or removes a check mark from beside the command in position *command_pos* on the menu *menu_pos* in bar number *bar_number*.

CLEAR(*parts*)

CLEAR?(*parts*)

Menu Equivalent: Edit→Clear

Action: Clears the specified cell range. There are four possible values for *parts*:

PARTS	*CLEARS*
1	All
2	Formats
3	Formulas
4	Notes

Example: =CLEAR(1) clears everything from the cell range.

CLOSE(*save_logical*)

Menu Equivalent: File→Close

Action: Closes currently active window. If *save_logical* is TRUE, the document is saved first if altered; if it is FALSE, the document is not saved; if the function is omitted, the user is prompted.

CLOSE.ALL( )

Menu Equivalent: File→Close All

Action: Closes all unprotected windows.

COLOR.PALETTE(*file_text*)

COLOR.PALETTE?(*file_text*)

Menu Equivalent: Copy Colors From option in Options→Color Palette dialog box.

Action: Copies color palette from open document to active document.

COLUMN.WIDTH(*width, ref, standard, type_number*)

COLUMN.WIDTH?(*width, ref, standard, type_number*)

Menu Equivalent: Format→Column Width

Action: Changes the width of currently selected columns. The new width will be *width*. If *ref* is specified, it changes the width of the columns containing *ref* to *width*. *Ref* should be an external reference to the current sheet or an R1C1 reference in a text style (in quotation marks). *Standard,* if checked, sets the column to standard width. *Type_number* specifies other options (1 = Hide, 2 = Unhide, 3 = Best Fit).

Example =COLUMN.WIDTH(16) changes the currently selected column(s) to a width of 16.

=COLUMN.WIDTH(16,!$B:$C) changes the width of columns B and C to 16.

COMBINATION(*type*)

COMBINATION?(*type*)

Menu Equivalent: Gallery→Combination

Action: Selects the combination chart type from the menu. *Type* is a number that corresponds to a format in the gallery.

Use the SELECT function first to select a range at least as large as the total number of rows and columns to consolidate.

CONSOLIDATE(*source_refs, function_number, top_row, left_col, create_links*)

CONSOLIDATE?(*source_refs, function_number, top_row, left_col, create_links*)

Menu Equivalent: Data→Consolidate

Action: Consolidates data from multiple ranges on multiple worksheets to a range on a single worksheet.

COPY( )

Menu Equivalent: Edit→Copy

Action: Copies the selected cells or data series to the Clipboard.

COPY.PICTURE(*appearance, size*)

Menu Equivalent: Edit→Copy Picture (with Shift)

Action: Copies selection to the Clipboard as a picture.

- *Appearance* must be the number 1 or 2, with the following meanings:

  1 copy as shown on the screen

  2 copy as how it will be printed

- *Size* applies only to a chart and has the following meanings:
  1 copy using the same size as the window displaying the chart
  2 copy as how it will be printed

CREATE.NAMES(*top_row, left_column, bottom_row, right_column*)

CREATE.NAMES?(*top_row, left_column, bottom_row, right_column*)

Menu Equivalent: Formula→Create Names

Action: Creates names using row or column headings. Arguments must be logical values, with TRUE indicating checked and FALSE indicating not checked.

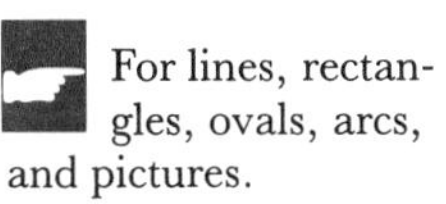
For lines, rectangles, ovals, arcs, and pictures.

CREATE.OBJECT(***object_type***, ***ref_1***, *x_offset1, y_offset1, ref_2, x_offset2, y_offset2*)

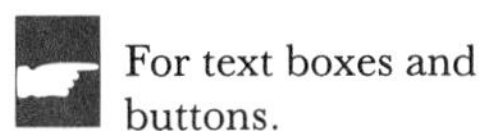
For text boxes and buttons.

CREATE.OBJECT(***object_type***, ***ref_1***, *x_offset1, y_offset1,* ***ref_2***, *x_offset2, y_offset2, text*)

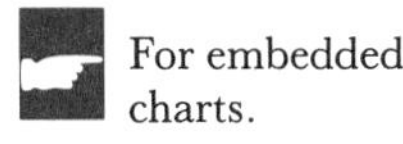
For embedded charts.

CREATE.OBJECT(***object_type***, ***ref_1***, *x_offset1, y_offset1, ref_2, x_offset2, y_offset2, xy_series*)

Menu Equivalent: None.

Action: Draws an object on the worksheet or macro sheet from *ref1* to *ref2* with the specified offset (in points, 1/72 of an inch). Text boxes and buttons are labeled with text. The *xy_series* argument is used for embedded charts (as on a worksheet) and specifies how the series is arranged in the chart:

XY_SERIES	*RESULTS*
0	Displays dialog box if selection is unclear
1	First row/column is the first data series (default)

XY_SERIES	*RESULTS*
2	First row/column contain the category (*x*) axis labels
3	First row/column are *x* values; created chart is an XY (scatter) chart

The *object_type* argument specifies the object to draw:

OBJECT_TYPE	*OBJECT*
1	Line
2	Rectangle
3	Oval
4	Arc
5	Embedded chart
6	Text box
7	Button
8	Picture (using camera tool)

CUSTOM.REPEAT(*macro_text, repeat_text, record_text*)

Menu Equivalent: None.

Action: Creates a custom Edit→Repeat command. *Macro_text* references a macro to run when Edit→Repeat is chosen. It can be a name or macro-cell reference.

CUSTOM.UNDO(*macro_text, undo_text*)

Menu Equivalent: None.

Action: Creates a custom Edit→Undo command. *Macro_text* references a macro to run when Edit→Undo is chosen. It can be a name or macro-cell reference.

CUT( )

Menu Equivalent: Edit→Cut

Action: Deletes the selected range from the sheet.

DATA.DELETE( )

DATA.DELETE?( )

Menu Equivalent: Data→Delete

Action: Deletes the records from the database that meet the specified criteria.

DATA.FIND(*logical*)

Menu Equivalent: Data→Find and Data→Exit Find

Action: The value of *logical* determines the action. If *logical* is TRUE, Excel attempts to find a record that meets the specified criteria. If *logical* is FALSE, Excel attempts an Exit Find.

DATA.FIND.NEXT( )

DATA.FIND.PREV( )

Menu Equivalent: Equivalent to pressing ↓ or ↑ after the Data→Find command has been chosen.

Action: Finds the next and previous records in the database that match the specified criteria.

DATA.FORM( )

Menu Equivalent: Data→Form

Action: Displays a data form for modifying or searching a database.

DATA.SERIES(*series_in, type, date_number, step, stop*)

DATA.SERIES?(*series_in, type, date_number, step, stop*)

Menu Equivalent: Data→Series

Action: Creates a data series in the selected range. There are two choices for the *series_in* argument:

SERIES_IN	*OPTION*
1	Rows
2	Columns

The three choices for the *type* argument are as follows:

TYPE	*OPTION*
1	Linear
2	Growth
3	Date

The four choices for the *date_number* argument are below:

DATE_NUMBER	*OPTION*
1	Day
2	Weekday
3	Month
4	Year

Step and *stop* are numbers indicating the stepping and stopping points for the series.

Example: =DATA.SERIES(2,1,,1,) creates a linear series in the selected column.

DEFINE.NAME(***name_text***, *refers_to, type, key, hidden*)

DEFINE.NAME?(*name_text, refers_to, type, key*)

Menu Equivalent: Formula→Define Name

Action: Defines a name for a cell range. The arguments are defined as follows:

name_text	Text value for macro name
refers_to	If an external reference, refers to cells named. If omitted, selected range is assumed. If a number, text, or logical value, assigns the name to the value
type	Defines the macro type: 1 is a function, 2 is a command, 3 is no macro (macro sheet only)
key	Defines the letter to activate the command. It must be in quotation marks, as in "Z" (macro sheet only)

Examples: =DEFINE.NAME("TEST"," =R1C2") assigns the name "TEST" to cell B1.

=DEFINE.NAME("INCOME",SELECTION( )) assigns the name "INCOME" to the currently selected range.

=DEFINE.NAME("QTY"," =R1C2:R6:C2") assigns the name "QTY" to the range B1:B6.

DEFINE.STYLE(*style_text, number, font, alignment, border, pattern, protection*)

DEFINE.STYLE?(*style_text, number, font, alignment, border, pattern, protection*)

Menu Equivalent: Format→Style Define

Action: This macro is used to set a selected range to a defined style. This command has seven forms, depending on the aspect of the style being set and how the command is used. Consult Excel's function manual for more information. The above form is used to set a style by example. *Style_text* is the name of the style, and the other arguments correspond to the options of the dialog box.

DELETE.ARROW( )

Menu Equivalent: Chart→Delete Arrow

Action: Deletes the selected arrow.

DELETE.BAR(*bar_number*)

Menu Equivalent: None.

Action: Deletes the custom menu *bar_number*.

DELETE.COMMAND(*bar_number, menu, command_pos*)

Menu Equivalent: None.

Action: Deletes the command in position *command_pos* on the menu *menu* in menu *bar_number*.

Example: The expression =DELETE.COMMAND(Income, "Reports","Income Report") removes the Income Report command from the Reports menu on a custom menu bar created by the ADD.BAR function in a cell named "Income."

DELETE.FORMAT(*format_text*)

Menu Equivalent: Format→Number (Delete)

Action: Deletes custom *format_text* from the list of formats (or pictures) in the Format Number dialog box. You cannot use this to delete Excel's built-in pictures.

Example: =DELETE.FORMAT("#,##0.00") deletes the custom-designed number formatting scheme #,##0.00 from the list.

DELETE.MENU(*bar_number, menu_pos*)

Menu Equivalent: None.

Action: Deletes the menu *menu_pos* in bar number *bar_number*.

DELETE.NAME(*name_text*)

Menu Equivalent: Formula→Define Name (Delete)

Action: Deletes *name_text* from the name list.

Example: =DELETE.NAME("QTY") deletes the name "QTY" from the current list.

DELETE.OVERLAY( )

Menu Equivalent: Chart→Delete Overlay

Action: Deletes an overlay from a chart.

DELETE.STYLE(*style_text*)

Menu Equivalent: Format→Style Delete

Action: Deletes the style *style_text* from a worksheet. You can only delete styles from the active document.

DEMOTE(*rowcol*)

DEMOTE?(*rowcol*)

Menu Equivalent: None—equivalent to clicking the demote button.

Action: Demotes the selected rows or columns from the outline. If *rowcol* is 1 or omitted, rows are demoted. If *rowcol* is 2, columns are demoted.

In the SET.NAME function and others, references are not converted to values automatically. In such cases, the DEREF function must be used.

DEREF(*ref*)

Menu Equivalent: None.

Action: Returns the value of the cells in *ref*. If *ref* is a single cell, it gives the value in that cell. If *ref* is a range, an array of values is returned.

Example: =SET.NAME("QTY",DEREF(B2)). Here, DEREF converts the reference to cell B2 to its value. The SET.NAME function then sets QTY to that value.

DIALOG.BOX(*dialog_ref*)

Menu Equivalent: None.

Action: Displays the dialog box described by *dialog_ref* on the macro or sheet (see Chapter 28).

DIRECTORY(*path_text*)

Menu Equivalent: None.

Action: Sets the current drive and directory to path *path_text* and returns the name of the new directory as text. Use with the Open and Save As functions to set the correct directory.

DISABLE.INPUT(*logical*)

Menu Equivalent: None.

Action: Blocks all input from the keyboard (except for dialog boxes) and mouse if *logical* is TRUE. Used with DDE. Be sure to turn keyboard input back on before leaving the macro.

For controlling the screen display.

DISPLAY(*formulas, gridlines, headings, zero, color, reserved, outline, page_breaks, object_number*)

DISPLAY?(*formulas, gridlines, headings, zero, color, reserved, outline, page_breaks, object_number*)

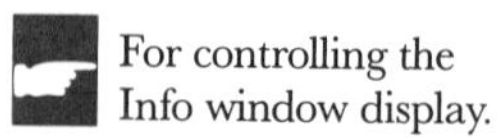

For controlling the Info window display.

DISPLAY(*cell, formula, value, format, protect, names, precedents, dependents, note*)

Menu Equivalent: Options→Display (first and second functions). Info menu (third function), displayed with the F1 key.

Action: *First two functions:* Changes the display form. The arguments refer to the check boxes in the dialog box, with TRUE indicating checked and FALSE indicating not checked.

Third form: Corresponds to commands with the same name on the Info menu.

Example: =DISPLAY(TRUE,TRUE,FALSE) turns on formulas and gridlines but not row or column headings.

DOCUMENTS(*type_number*)

Menu Equivalent: None.

Action: Returns a horizontal text array of the currently opened documents in alphabetical order. Using the INDEX function, you can then select a document name from the array to use as an argument in another function. If *type_number* is 1 or omitted, the function returns all except add-in documents. If it is 2, add-in documents are returned only. If it is 3, all documents are returned.

Example: =DOCUMENTS( ) might equal {"Sheet1","Sheet2"}.

DUPLICATE( )

Menu Equivalent: None.

Action: Duplicates a selected object.

ECHO(*logical*)

Menu Equivalent: None.

Action: Turns screen updating off (*logical* = FALSE) or on (*logical* = TRUE) during macro execution. Macros run faster when updating is off.

EDIT.COLOR(***color_number***, *red_value*, *green_value*, *blue_value*)

EDIT.COLOR?(***color_number***, *red_value*, *green_value*, *blue_value*)

Menu Equivalent: Options→Color Palette Edit

Action: Defines a custom color for any one of the 16 color palette boxes. *Color_number* must be from 1 to 16. Other arguments can be from 0 to 255, and specify the amount of each color added.

Example: =EDIT.COLOR(2,0,0,0) sets the second color-palette box to black.

EDIT.DELETE(*direction*)

EDIT.DELETE?(*direction*)

Menu Equivalent: Edit→Delete

Action: Removes the selected range from the sheet. *Direction* must be a number: 1 shifts cells left to adjust, 2 shifts cells up, 3 deletes an entire row, and 4 deletes an entire column.

Example: =EDIT.DELETE(1) deletes the range and shifts cells left. The same command deletes the entire current row if the row heading is selected.

EDIT.REPEAT( )

Menu Equivalent: Edit→Repeat

Action: Repeats the last Edit command, if available.

EDIT.SERIES:(*series_number, name_ref, x_ref, y_ref, z_ref, plot_order*)

EDIT.SERIES?(*series_number, name_ref, x_ref, y_ref, z_ref, plot_order*)

Menu Equivalent: (Chart) Edit→Series

Action: Creates or edits a data series on a chart. The arguments correspond to the options on the dialog box. To delete a series, use the SELECT and FORMULA macro functions.

Example:

```
=SELECT("S2")
=FORMULA(" ")
```

deletes the second series.

EDITION.OPTIONS(***edition_type***, *edition_name, ref, option*)

EDITION.OPTIONS?(*edition_type*, *edition_name*, *ref*)

Menu Equivalent: None.

Action: Sets the options or performs actions on the specified publisher or subscriber. With DOS or OS/2, permits canceling a publisher or subscriber created in Microsoft Excel for the Macintosh (see Excel Function Reference for more details).

ELSE( )

Menu Equivalent: None.

Action: Use with IF...ENDIF in control structures to support branching.

ELSE.IF(*logical_text*)

Menu Equivalent: None.

Action: Use with IF...ENDIF in control structures to support branching. Supports nested structures.

EMBED(*object_type*)

Menu Equivalent: None.

Action: This function is displayed in the formula bar when an embedded object is selected. It cannot be entered to a worksheet or entered as a macro.

ENABLE.COMMAND(*bar_number, menu_pos, command_pos, enable*)

Menu Equivalent: None.

Action: Enables or disables the command in position *command_pos* on the menu *menu_pos* in menu bar *bar_number*.

END.IF( )

Menu Equivalent: None.

Action: Ends a control structure for conditional branching.

ERROR(*logical, ref*)

Menu Equivalent: None.

Action: Turns macro error checking on or off, and optionally defines a macro to run on an error condition. If *logical* is TRUE, error checking is turned on. If an error is encountered during the macro execution, the control branches to *ref*. If *ref* is omitted, a dialog box is displayed upon finding an error. If *logical* is FALSE, errors in the macro are automatically ignored and execution continues. *Ref* tells the macro to run if *logical* is TRUE.

EXEC(*program_text, window_number*)

Menu Equivalent: None.

Action: Starts the program *program_text* in a window type defined by *window_number* (1 is normal, 2 is minimized (default), and 3 is maximized).

Example: =EXEC("NOTEBOOK.EXE",3) loads the NOTEBOOK program and displays it in a maximized window.

EXECUTE(*channel_number, execute_text*)

Menu Equivalent: None.

Action: Carries out the command *execute_text* in the application defined by *channel_number*.

EXTRACT(*unique*)

EXTRACT?(*unique*)

Menu Equivalent: Data→Extract

Action: Extracts records from the database based on the specified criteria. If *unique* is TRUE, only unique values are extracted.

FCLOSE(*file_number*)

Menu Equivalent: None.

Action: Closes the file specified by *file_number*.

FILE.CLOSE(*save_logical*)

Menu Equivalent: File→Close

Action: Closes document of the active window. If *save_logical* is TRUE, file is saved. If omitted, a dialog box is displayed for saving if the file has been changed.

FILE.DELETE(*document_text*)

FILE.DELETE?(*document_text*)

Menu Equivalent: File→Delete

Action: Deletes *document_text* from the disk. If *document_text* is not on the disk, you will have to enter the name in a dialog box. In the question-mark form, you can use wildcard expressions when entering the name.

FILES(*directory_text*)

Menu Equivalent: None.

Action: Returns a horizontal text array of file names in the directory specified by *directory_text*. Use the COLUMNS function to count the number of entries or the TRANSPOSE function to convert to a vertical column of names.

Example: The function =FILES("S") returns the names of the files on the current directory starting with the letter *S*.

FILL.DOWN( )

FILL.LEFT( )

FILL.RIGHT( )

FILL.UP( )

Menu Equivalent: Edit→Fill Down, Edit→Fill Left, Edit→Fill Right, and Edit→Fill Up

Action: Fills the selected range with the value in the first cell of the range. Multiple ranges can be selected.

FILL.WORKGROUP(*type_number*)

FILL.WORKGROUP?(*type_number*)

Menu Equivalent: Edit→Fill Workgroup

Action: Fills the contents of the active worksheet's selected area to the same area in all worksheets of the workgroup. Use this function to fill the identical range of cells on all worksheets at once. *Type_number* defines what to fill (1 = All, 2 = Formulas, 3 = Formats).

FONT(*name_text, size_number*)

FONT?(*name_text, size_number*)

Menu Equivalent: None.

Action: Sets font for Normal style. (Included for compatibility with older versions of Macintosh Excel.)

FOPEN(*file_text, access_number*)

Menu Equivalent: (None—this is not File→Open)

Action: Opens the file specified by *file_text*. *Access_number* specifies the manner in which it is opened: 1 = read/write, 2 = read only, and 3 = create *and* read/write. It returns the file number. Close with FCLOSE. Unlike with OPEN, the file is not loaded into memory. FOPEN establishes a channel with the file for exchanging information with it.

FOR(*counter_text, start_number, end_number*, *step_number*)

Menu Equivalent: None.

Action: Starts a FOR...NEXT iterative structure (loop).

FOR.CELL(*ref_name*, *area_ref, skip_blanks*)

Menu Equivalent: None.

Action: Starts a FOR.CELL...NEXT iterative structure (loop). The instructions in the loop are repeated over a range of cells, one cell at a time. There is no loop counter.

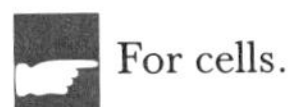

For cells.

FORMAT.FONT(*name_text, size_number, bold, italic, underline, strike, color, outline, shadow*)

FORMAT.FONT?(*name_text, size_number, bold, italic, underline, strike, color, outline, shadow*)

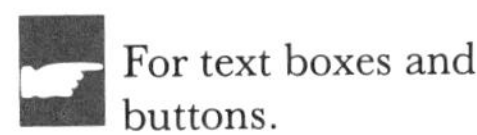

For text boxes and buttons.

FORMAT.FONT(*name_text, size_number, bold, italic, underline, strike, color, outline, shadow, object_ID_text, start_number, char_number*)

FORMAT.FONT?(*name_text, size_number, bold, italic, underline, strike, color, outline, shadow, object_ID_text, start_number, char_number*)

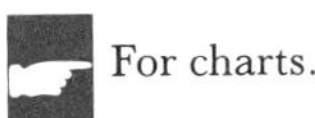

For charts.

FORMAT.FONT(*color, backgd, apply, name_text, size, bold, italic, underline, strike, outline, shadow*)

FORMAT.FONT?(*color, backgd, apply, name_text, size, bold, italic, underline, strike, outline, shadow*)

Menu Equivalent: Format→Font

Action: Applies fonts to the current selection. The arguments correspond to those in the dialog box. The *outline* and *shadow* options are not available for fonts with Excel for Windows; they are provided for

Macintosh compatibility. To shadow and outline fonts in Excel for Windows, a character set with those features must be installed as a separate font.

FORMAT.LEGEND(*position_number*)

FORMAT.LEGEND?(*position_number*)

Menu Equivalent: Format→Legend

Action: Sets the position and orientation of the legend on a chart indicated by *position_number* and returns TRUE (1 = Bottom, 2 = Corner, 3 = Top, 4 = Right, 5 = Left).

FORMAT.MAIN(*type_number, view, overlap, gap_width, vary, drop, hilo, angle, gap_depth, chart_depth*)

FORMAT.MAIN?(*type_number view, overlap, gap_width, vary, drop, hilo, angle, gap_depth, chart_depth*)

Menu Equivalent: Format→Main Chart

Action: Formats the main chart. The *type_number* argument corresponds to the type of chart:

TYPE_NUMBER	*CHART TYPE*
1	Area
2	Bar
3	Column
4	Line
5	Pie
6	XY (Scatter)
7	3-D Area
8	3-D Column
9	3-D Line
10	3-D Pie

The *view* argument has a value of 1–4 and corresponds to one of the four views in the dialog box:

CHART TYPE	*VIEW 1*	*VIEW 2*	*VIEW 3*	*VIEW 4*
Area	Overlapped	Stacked	Stacked 100%	
Bar	Side-by-side	Stacked	Stacked 100%	
Column	Side-by-side	Stacked	Stacked 100%	
Line	Normal	Stacked	Stacked 100%	
Pie	Normal			
XY (Scatter)	Normal			
3-D Area	Stacked	Stacked 100%	3-D layout	
3-D Column	Side-by-side	Stacked	Stacked 100%	3-D layout
3-D Line	3-D layout			
3-D Pie	Normal			

The other arguments correspond to the options on the dialog box.

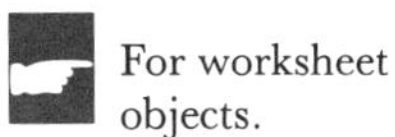
For worksheet objects.

FORMAT.MOVE(*x_offset, y_offset, reference*)

FORMAT.MOVE?(*x_offset, y_offset, reference***)**

For chart items.

FORMAT.MOVE(*x_pos, y_pos*)

FORMAT.MOVE?(*x_pos, y_pos***)**

Menu Equivalent: Format→Move (only for charts); equivalent to moving an object with the mouse.

Action: For worksheet objects, moves the upper-left corner of the object to a position specified by *x offset* and *y offset*, measured in points (1/72 of an inch) from the upper-left corner of the *reference* cell (or A1 if omitted).

For chart items, moves the base of the selected item to a position specified by *x_pos* and *y_pos*, measured in points from the base of the object to the lower-left corner of the window.

Example: =FORMAT.MOVE(20,25,!$C$3) moves the object 20 points horizontally and 25 points vertically offset from cell C3.

FORMAT.NUMBER(*format_text*)

FORMAT.NUMBER? (*format_text*)

Menu Equivalent: Format→Number

Action: Sets the formatting scheme or picture of the selected cells to *format_text*.

FORMAT.OVERLAY(*type_number, view, overlap, width, vary, drop, hilo, angle, series_dist, series_number*)

FORMAT.OVERLAY(***type_number,*** *view, overlap, width, vary, drop, hilo, angle, series_dist, series_number*)

Menu Equivalent: Format→Overlay

Action: Formats the overlay chart. *Type_number* can be from 1 to 6, and corresponds to the first six types of the FORMAT.MAIN function. The value of *view* can be from 1 to 3, as defined by FORMAT-.MAIN. The other arguments correspond to those in the dialog box. *Series_dist* specifies automatic or manual series distribution (1 = automatic and default, 2 = manual). *Series_number* specifies the first series in the overlay chart.

For worksheet objects, relative.

FORMAT.SIZE(*x_offset, y_offset,* ***reference***)

FORMAT.SIZE?(*x_offset, y_offset, reference*)

For worksheet objects and chart items, absolute.

FORMAT.SIZE(*width, height*)

FORMAT.SIZE?(*width, height*)

Menu Equivalent: Format→Size (only for charts), or the same as sizing an object with the mouse.

Action: The first two functions size the selected object, according to *x_offset* and *y_offset,* which specify the width and height, respectively, of the object and which are measured in points (1/72 of an inch) from the lower-right corner of the object to the upper-left corner of *reference.*

The last two functions size the selected object as per *width* and *height,* both measured in points.

FORMAT.TEXT(*x_align, y_align, orient_number, auto_text, auto_size, show_key, show_value*)

FORMAT.TEXT?(*x_align, y_align, orient_number, auto_text, auto_size, show_key, show_value*)

Menu Equivalent: Format→Text

Action: Formats the selected text as defined by argument check boxes. *X_align* is a number from 1 to 3 specifying the horizontal alignment (1 = Left, 2 = Center, 3 = Right). *Y_align* specifies the vertical alignment (1 = Top, 2 = Center, 3 = Bottom). *Orient_number* sets the orientation (0 = Horizontally, 1 = Vertically, 2 = Upward, 3 = Downward). The other buttons correspond to the options in the Format→Text dialog box.

FORMULA(*formula_text, ref*)

Menu Equivalent: None.

Action: Inserts *formula_text* in the active cell or in a reference.

Examples: =FORMULA(5) enters 5 to the active cell.

=FORMULA(INPUT("Enter: ",0),P20) prompts for a formula to enter into cell P20.

FORMULA.ARRAY(*formula_text, ref*)

Menu Equivalent: None.

Action: Inserts *formula_text* as an array to the active range or *ref*. It is equivalent to entering an array formula while pressing Control-Shift-Enter.

FORMULA.CONVERT(*formula_text, from_a1, to_a1, to_ref_type, rel_to_ref*)

Menu Equivalent: None.

Action: Changes the reference style and type of formula between A1 and R1C1 modes and absolute and relative. *Formula_text* is the formula, entered as text. *From_a1* is a logical value that specifies whether *formula_text* is A1 or R1C1 (TRUE = A1). *To_a1* is a logical value specifying the destination reference style (TRUE = A1). *To_ref_type* specifies the type of returned reference (1 = Absolute, 2 = Absolute row, relative column, 3 = Relative row, absolute column, 4 = Relative). *Rel_to_ref* is an absolute reference that specifies to which cell the relative references are relative.

Examples: =FORMULA.CONVERT(" =B2 +B6",TRUE, TRUE,1) converts =B2 +B6 to =$B$2 +$B$6.
=FORMULA.CONVERT(" =B2 +B6",TRUE,FALSE,1) converts =B2 +B6 to =R2C2 +R6C2.

FORMULA.FILL(*formula_text, ref*)

Menu Equivalent: None.

Action: Inserts *formula_text* in each cell of the currently selected range or the cell *ref*. It is the equivalent of entering a formula while pressing the Ctrl key.

Example: If B1:B6 is selected, =FORMULA.FILL(4) enters 4 in each cell of the range.

FORMULA.FIND(*find_text, look_in, look_at, look_by, dir_number, match_case*)

FORMULA.FIND?(*find_text, look_in, look_at, look_by, dir_number, match_case*)

Menu Equivalent: Formula→Find

Action: Searches for a formula or value in the current sheet. The *find_text* argument is the text for which to search. The *look_in* argument has three choices:

LOOK_IN	TYPE OF SEARCH
1	Formulas
2	Values
3	Notes

The *look_at* argument has two choices, depending upon whether you are matching a whole cell or a part of a cell:

LOOK_AT	MATCH TYPE
1	Whole
2	Part

The *look_by* argument has the following choices:

LOOK_BY	SEARCHES BY
1	Rows
2	Columns

Dir_number specifies direction (1 = Forward, 2 = Backward or previous) and *match_case* specifies whether the case should be matched.

Example: =FORMULA.FIND("6",2,1,1) searches the sheet for the first cell with the value of 6 and makes the cell active if found.

FORMULA.FIND.NEXT( )

FORMULA.FIND.PREV( )

Menu Equivalent: Equivalent to F7 and Shift-F7, respectively.

Action: Finds the next or previous cells on the sheet that match the search criteria.

FORMULA.GOTO(*ref, corner*)

FORMULA.GOTO?(*ref, corner*)

Menu Equivalent: Formula→Goto (or pressing F5)

Action: Goes to the cell referenced as *ref*. *Ref* can be a name or external reference (using A1- or R1C1-style referencing). *Corner* is a logical value that specifies whether to scroll the window so that *ref* appears in the top-left cell of the active window.

Example: If A2 is "INCOME", the following are all equivalent:

=FORMULA.GOTO(!$A$2)

=FORMULA.GOTO("R2C1")

=FORMULA.GOTO("INCOME")

=FORMULA.GOTO("!INCOME")

FORMULA.REPLACE(***find_text, replace_text,*** *look_at, look_by, active_cell, match_case*)

FORMULA.REPLACE?(*find_text, replace_text, look_at, look_by, active_cell, match_case*)

Menu Equivalent: Formula→Replace

Action: Replaces text with the specified text. The options match those of the dialog box.

Example: =FORMULA.REPLACE("TOO","TWO") replaces *TOO* with *TWO* in the entire document.

FPOS(***file_number,*** *position_number*)

Menu Equivalent: None.

Action: Positions the document *file_number* at the position *position-_number*. *File_number* is the file ID number returned by the FOPEN command.

FREAD(*file_number, number_chars*)

Menu Equivalent: None.

Action: Reads *number_chars* from the document *file_number*, starting at the current position. *File_number* is the file ID number returned by the FOPEN command.

FREADLN(*file_number*)

Menu Equivalent: None.

Action: Reads the next line from the document *file_number*. *File_number* is the file ID number returned by the FOPEN command.

FREEZE.PANES(*logical*)

Menu Equivalent: Option→Freeze Panes or Option→Unfreeze Panes

Action: Freezes or unfreezes the top or left panes on the active sheet that were split by a previously executed SPLIT function.

FSIZE(*file_number*)

Menu Equivalent: None.

Action: Returns the number of characters in the document *file_number*. *File_number* is the file ID number returned by FOPEN.

FULL(*logical*)

Menu Equivalent: Equivalent to maximizing the current document window or restoring it. Also equivalent to Ctrl–F10 (full size) and Ctrl–F5 (previous size) or double-clicking the title bar.

Action: Controls the size of the displayed window. If *logical* is TRUE, Excel makes the displayed window full-size. IF *logical* is FALSE, Excel returns the active window to its previously smaller size.

FWRITE(*file_number, text*)

Menu Equivalent: None.

Action: Writes *text* to the document *file_number,* starting at the current position.

FWRITELN(*file_number, text*)

Menu Equivalent: None.

Action: Writes *text* with a carriage return and line feed to the document *file_number,* starting at the current position.

GALLERY.3D.AREA(*type_number*)

GALLERY.3D.AREA?(*type_number*)

Menu Equivalent: Gallery→3-D Area

Action: Converts the currently displayed chart to a 3-D Area form. *Type_number* is a number that must correspond to a valid format in the gallery.

GALLERY.3D.COLUMN(*type_number*)

GALLERY.3D.COLUMN?(*type_number*)

Menu Equivalent: Gallery→3-D Column

Action: Converts the currently displayed chart to a 3-D Column form. *Type_number* is a number that must correspond to a valid format in the gallery.

GALLERY.3D.LINE(*type_number*)

GALLERY.3D.LINE?(*type_number*)

Menu Equivalent: Gallery→3-D Line

Action: Converts the currently displayed chart to a 3-D Line form.

Type_number is a number that must correspond to a valid format in the gallery.

GALLERY.3D.PIE(*type_number*)

GALLERY.3D.PIE?(*type_number*)

Menu Equivalent: Gallery→3-D Pie

Action: Converts the currently displayed chart to a 3-D Pie form. *Type_number* is a number that must correspond to a valid format in the gallery.

GALLERY.AREA(*type_number*, *delete_overlay*)

GALLERY.AREA?(*type_number*, *delete_overlay*)

Menu Equivalent: Gallery→Area

Action: Converts the currently displayed chart to an Area form. *Type_number* is a number that must correspond to a valid format in the gallery. *Delete_overlay* is a logical argument that defines whether overlay charts are to be deleted.

GALLERY.BAR(*type_number*, *delete_overlay*)

GALLERY.BAR?(*type_number*, *delete_overlay*)

Menu Equivalent: Gallery→Bar

Action: Converts the currently displayed chart to a Bar form. *Type_number* is a number that must correspond to a valid format in the gallery.

GALLERY.COLUMN(*type_number*, *delete_overlay*)

GALLERY.COLUMN?(*type_number*, *delete_overlay*)

Menu Equivalent: Gallery→Column

Action: Converts the currently displayed chart to a Column form. *Type_number* is a number that must correspond to a valid format in the gallery.

GALLERY.LINE(*type_number*, *delete_overlay*)

GALLERY.LINE?(*type_number*, *delete_overlay*)

Menu Equivalent: Gallery→Line

Action: Converts the currently displayed chart to a Line form. *Type_number* is a number that must correspond to a valid format in the gallery.

GALLERY.PIE(*type_number*, *delete_overlay*)

GALLERY.PIE?(*type_number*, *delete_overlay*)

Menu Equivalent: Gallery→Pie

Action: Converts the currently displayed chart to a Pie form. *Type_number* is a number that must correspond to a valid format in the gallery.

GALLERY.SCATTER(*type_number*, *delete_overlay*)

GALLERY.SCATTER?(*type_number*, *delete_overlay*)

Menu Equivalent: Gallery→Scatter

Action: Converts the currently displayed chart to a Scatter form. *Type_number* is a number that must correspond to a valid format in the gallery.

GET.BAR(*bar_number, menu, command*)

Menu Equivalent: None.

Action: The second function returns the name or position number of a specified command on a menu. Use this one with functions that add, delete, or alter menu commands. *Bar_number* is the number of the menu bar (see ADD.COMMAND). *Menu* is the menu where the command is (either the name in quotes or the number—menus are numbered from left to right, beginning with 1). *Command* is either the name or number of the command you want returned (the top command on a menu being 1).

If you do not use *any* arguments, the function returns the number of the active menu bar. Use this form in macros when you need to know which menu bar is active, so that you can refer to it in other functions.

GET.CELL(*type_number*, *ref*)

Menu Equivalent: None.

Action: Returns the information about the location, contents, and formatting of the cell in the upper-left corner of *ref*. There are 40 possible values for *type_number*, depending on what information is needed (see the Excel function manual).

GET.CHART.ITEM(*x_y_index*, *point_index*, *item_text*)

Menu Equivalent: None.

Action: Returns the vertical or horizontal position of a point on a chart item. If *x_y_index* is 1, the horizontal coordinate is returned. If 2, the vertical coordinate is returned (see the Excel function manual).

GET.DEF(*def_text*, *document_text*, *type_number*)

Menu Equivalent: None.

Action: Returns as text the name for a particular area. *Def_text* can be a reference, value, or formula (anything you can name) in *document_text*. *Type_number* specifies the type of names returned (1 = Normal and default, 2 = Hidden only, 3 = All).

GET.DOCUMENT(*type_number*, *name_text*)

Menu Equivalent: None.

Action: Returns information about the document named *name_text*. The type of information returned depends on the value of *type_number* (see Excel Function Reference for a list of these 44 numbers).

GET.FORMULA(*ref*)

Menu Equivalent: None.

Action: Gives the contents of the upper-left cell of *ref* as it would appear in the formula bar. Formulas returned in R1C1 format.

Example: =GET.FORMULA(!A1) returns 5 if A1 contains 5.

GET.LINK.INFO(*link_text, type_number, type_of_link, ref*)

Menu Equivalent: None.

Action: Returns information about the specified link. *Link_text* is the path name of the link. *Type_number* specifies the type of information desired. If *type_number* is 1, function returns 1 if link is set to automatic. If *type_number* is 2, returns date of last edition as a serial number, or #N/A if *link_text* is not a publisher or subscriber. *Type_of_link* specifies the type of link you want information about:

TYPE_OF_LINK	*LINK TYPE*
1	n/a
2	DDE link
3	n/a
4	Outgoing NewWave link
5	Publisher
6	Subscriber

Reference specifies the cell range (in R1C1 format) of the publisher or subscriber that you want information about.

GET.NAME(*name_text*)

Menu Equivalent: None.

Action: Gives the definition of *name_text* as it would appear in the Refers To box of the Define Name command. The definition is in a text form. If the name contains references, they are returned in R1C1 style.

Example: If NET is defined as =SALES – COST, =GET.NAME-(!NET) returns "=SALES – COST".

GET.NOTE(*cell_ref, start_char, count_char*)

Menu Equivalent: None.

Action: Returns *count_char* characters from the note attached to *cell_ref* starting at *start_char*. Use to move the contents of a note to a cell, text box, or another note.

GET.OBJECT(***type_number,*** *object_ID_text, start_number, count_number*)

Menu Equivalent: None.

Action: Returns information about a specified object, based on *type_number*. There are 40 types of information categories defined (see the Excel function manual).

GET.WINDOW(***type_of_info,*** *name_text*)

Menu Equivalent: None.

Action: Returns information about the window named *name_text*. See the Excel function manual for available type categories.

GET.WORKSPACE(***type_of_info***)

Menu Equivalent: None.

Action: Returns information about the workspace. See the Excel function manual for available type categories.

GOAL.SEEK(***target_cell, target_value, variable_cell***)

GOAL.SEEK?(*target_cell, target_value, variable_cell*)

Menu Equivalent: Formula→Goal Seek

Action: Calculates the values that are necessary to achieve a specific goal. Arguments are those of the Goal Seek dialog box.

GOTO(*ref*)

Menu Equivalent: None.

Action: Directs macro to branch to upper-left cell of *ref*. *Ref* can be an external reference to another macro sheet.

Example: =IF(ISERROR($A$5),GOTO($C$4),) says that if cell A5 contains an error value, the macro should go to cell C4, otherwise go to the next line in the macro.

GRIDLINES(*x_major, x_minor, y_major, y_minor, z_major, z_minor*)

GRIDLINES?(*x_major, x_minor, y_major, y_minor, z_major, z_minor*)

Menu Equivalent: Chart→Gridlines

Action: Controls visibility of major and minor gridlines. Arguments are logical values that correspond to the dialog box check-boxes.

GROUP( )

Menu Equivalent: Format→Group

Action: Creates a single object from a group of selected objects. Returns object identifier for the group.

HALT(*cancel_close*)

Menu Equivalent: None.

Action: Terminates execution of all macros. If macro is called by another macro, that macro is also terminated. If *cancel_close* is TRUE in an Auto_close macro, Excel halts the macro but does not close the document. If FALSE (or omitted), the macro is halted and the document closed.

HELP(*file_text!topic_number*)

Menu Equivalent: Same as pressing F1.

Action: Initiates help. Displays a help message specified by *file_text!topic_number,* which is a reference to a topic in a text file.

Example: =HELP("HELP.TXT!99") displays Help topic 99 from the file HELP.TXT.

HIDE( )

Menu Equivalent: Window→Hide

Action: Hides the active window. Hiding windows will speed up macro execution.

HIDE.OBJECT(*object_ID_text, hide*)

Menu Equivalent: None.

Action: Hides or displays the specified object. *Object_ID_text* is the name or number of the object. If *hide* is TRUE, it is hidden. If FALSE, it is displayed.

Example: =HIDE.OBJECT("arc 1",TRUE) hides the object named "arc 1."

HLINE(*number*)

VLINE(*number*)

Menu Equivalent: None.

Action: Scrolls the active window *number* rows (VLINE) or columns (HLINE). *Number* can be positive (forward scroll) or negative (backward scroll). *Number* should be an integer.

Example: =VLINE(9) scrolls the active window down 9 rows.

HPAGE(*number*)

VPAGE(*number*)

Menu Equivalent: None.

Action: Scrolls the active window *number* windows horizontally (HPAGE) or vertically (VPAGE). *Number* must be an integer but can be positive (scroll forward) or negative (scroll backward).

Example: =HPAGE(1) scrolls the active window horizontally one window forward.

HSCROLL(*column_number, col_log*)

VSCROLL(*row_number, row_log*)

Menu Equivalent: None.

Action: Scrolls the active window horizontally or vertically to the specified column or row. It is the equivalent of dragging the scroll box. *Column_number* and *row_number* should either be percentages less than 100 or fractions.

Examples: =HSCROLL(64/256) scrolls to column BL, the 64th column (out of 256).

=VSCROLL(25%) scrolls to row 4096—because 4,096 is one-fourth of 16,384, the total number of rows.

INITIATE(*app_text, topic_text*)

Menu Equivalent: None.

Action: Opens a DDE channel to an application and returns the number of the channel. *App_text* is the DDE name of the application you want to access. *Topic_text* is the name of the document or database record in the application that you want to access.

Example: =INITIATE("WORKS","BOOK") opens a DDE channel to the Microsoft Works document named "BOOK."

INPUT(*prompt_text, type, title_text, default, x_pos, y_pos*)

Menu Equivalent: None.

Action: Displays a dialog box with title *title_text* and prompt *prompt-_text*, to which the user can enter input (values, text, etc.). The box also contains the OK and Cancel buttons. When you click the OK button or press Enter, the function gives the value you entered. If you click Cancel or press Esc, the function gives the logical value FALSE. If you omit *title_text*, the title INPUT is assumed. *Type* defines the type of value that the function returns:

TYPE	*RETURNED*
0	Formula
1	Number
2	Text
4	Logical
8	Reference (absolute)
16	Error
64	Array

Example: =INPUT("Enter the current interest rate: ",1) displays a dialog box with the title "INPUT" and prompt, **Enter the current interest rate**, which awaits a numeric entry.

INSERT(*direction*)

INSERT?(*direction*)

Menu Equivalent: Edit→Insert

Action: Inserts rows or columns in the sheet. *Direction* must be a number: 1 shifts cells to the right to adjust, 2 shifts cells down, 3 shifts an entire row, and 4 shifts an entire column. If you have just cut or copied to the Clipboard, this command inserts from the Clipboard.

Example: =INSERT(1) inserts a range of cells and shifts cells to the right.

JUSTIFY( )

Menu Equivalent: Format→Justify

Action: Rearranges the text of the left column of a range so that all cells in the range display text of the same width.

LAST.ERROR( )

Menu Equivalent: None.

Action: Returns the reference of the cell where the last macro sheet error occurred. Use with the ERROR function to locate errors.

LEGEND(*logical*)

Menu Equivalent: Chart→Add Legend and Chart→Delete Legend

Action: If *logical* is TRUE, a legend is added to the chart. If FALSE, the current legend is deleted.

LINKS(*document_text, type_number*)

Menu Equivalent: None.

Action: Returns a horizontal array of the names of all worksheets referred to by external references in *document_text* as text values. You can then select individual names from the array for other functions using the INDEX function. *Type_number* defines the type of documents to return:

TYPE_NUM	*RETURNS*
1	Excel link (default)
2	DDE link
3	n/a
4	Outgoing NewWave link
5	Publisher
6	Subscriber

Example: If the chart called SALES.XLC is open and contains some data series that refer to two worksheets called SALES.XLS and FUTURE.XLS, this function will open both worksheets:

=OPEN.LINKS(LINKS("SALES.XLS"))

LIST.NAMES( )

Menu Equivalent: Formula→Paste Names (Paste List)

Action: Pastes the name list into the document.

MAIN.CHART(*type, stack, 100, vary, overlap, drop, hilo, overlap%, cluster, angle*)

MAIN.CHART?(*type, stack, 100, vary, overlap, drop, hilo, overlap%, cluster, angle*)

Menu Equivalent: Format→Main Chart

Action: Changes the basic type of the main chart. This function is replaced in Excel 3.0 by FORMAT.MAIN, and is included here for compatibility only.

MAIN.CHART.TYPE(*type_number*)

Action: This function is included for compatibility with Macintosh Excel. Equivalent to FORMAT.MAIN in Excel 3.0 or later.

MERGE.STYLES(*document_text*)

Menu Equivalent: Format→Style Merge

Action: Merges styles from *document_text* to the active document.

MESSAGE(*logical, text*)

Menu Equivalent: None.

Action: Displays the message *text* in the status bar if *logical* is TRUE. If *logical* is FALSE, the message is removed. This macro function is useful for displaying a message to the user about what a macro is doing.

Example: =MESSAGE(TRUE,"Sorting the database...") displays the message Sorting the database... (when another macro runs).

MOVE(*x_number, y_number, window_text*)

MOVE?(*x_number, y_number, window_text*)

Menu Equivalent: Equivalent to moving a window by dragging its title bar or using the Move command.

Action: Moves *window_text* to *x_number, y_number*. The origin is in the upper-left corner of the screen. *Window_text* must be a window name in the form of text. If *window_text* is omitted, the active window is moved. You can also specify the Clipboard for moving (by typing **"Clipboard"**). To move the Clipboard, it must be available.

NAMES(*doc_text, type_number*)

Menu Equivalent: None.

Action: Returns a horizontal text array of all names that are defined in the document *doc_text*. *Type_number* defines the name types displayed (1 = Normal and default, 2 = Hidden, 3 = All). The function is like LIST.NAMES, but returns names to the macro sheet instead of the worksheet for further macro operations.

NEW(*type, xy_series*)

NEW?(*type, xy_series*)

Menu Equivalent: File→New

Action: Opens a new sheet, chart, macro sheet, or template. *Type* must be a number that indicates the type to open:

TYPE	OPENS
1	Sheet
2	Chart
3	Macro Sheet
4	International macro sheet
Quoted text	Template

The *xy_series* argument is used with charts to define how the data are arranged in the chart:

XY_SERIES	RESULT
0	Displays dialog box
1	First row/column is first data series (default)
2	First row/column is the category (*x*) axis labels
3	First row/column is *x* values; scatter chart is created

Example: =NEW(3) opens a new macro sheet.

NEW.WINDOW( )

Menu Equivalent: Window→New Window

Action: Opens a new window on the current document.

NEXT( )

Menu Equivalent: None.

Action: Ends a FOR...NEXT loop.

NOTE(*add_text, cell_ref, start_char, count_char*)

NOTE?( )

Menu Equivalent: Formula→Note

Action: Replaces *count_char* in a note attached to *cell_ref* with *add_text,* starting at *start_char*. NOTE( ) deletes note attached to active cell. Returns number of last character in the cell.

OBJECT.PROTECTION(*locked, text_lock*)

Menu Equivalent: Format→Object Protection

Action: Changes protection status of the selected object. *Locked* is a logical value that determines whether the selected object is locked, and is TRUE if the object is to be locked. *Text_lock* applies to objects with text (buttons and text boxes) and is TRUE to lock the text.

OFFSET(***reference, rows, columns,*** *height, width*)

Menu Equivalent: None.

Action: Returns a reference of a specified *height* and *width,* offset from another *reference* by a specified number of *rows* and *columns*.

ON.DATA(*document_text, macro_text*)

Menu Equivalent: None.

Action: Starts the macro specified by *macro_text* whenever another application sends new data to the document specified by *document_text*. To turn off ON.DATA, omit the second argument.

ON.KEY(***key_text,*** *macro_text*)

Menu Equivalent: None.

Action: Executes the macro specified by *macro_text* when *key_text* is pressed.

Example: =ON.KEY(" +^R","CHART.XLM!CHART") executes the CHART macro in CHART.XLM when Shift, Control, and *R* are pressed.

ON.RECALC(*sheet_text, macro_text*)

Menu Equivalent: None.

Action: Runs macro *macro_text* whenever *sheet_text* is recalculated.

ON.TIME(***time, macro_text***, *tolerance, insert_logical*)

Menu Equivalent: None.

Action: Runs macro *macro_text* at *time*. *Tolerance* is the time and date (as a serial number) that defines how long you are willing to wait and still have the macro run. Use *insert_logical* to turn off a previously set TIME macro. If TRUE (or omitted), macro runs at *time*. If FALSE, the macro is turned off.

ON.WINDOW(*window_text, macro_text*)

Menu Equivalent: None.

Action: Starts the macro *macro_text* whenever *window_text* is activated.

OPEN(***file_text***, *update_links, read_only, format, prot_pwd, write_res_pwd, ignore_rorec, file_origin*)

OPEN?(*file_text, update_links, read_only, format, prot_pwd, write_res_pwd, ignore_rorec, file_origin*)

Menu Equivalent: File→Open

Action: Opens *file_text*. *Update_links* is used to control the updating of external references (0 = no updating, 1 = update external, 2 = update remote, 3 = update external and remote, default). If *read_only* is TRUE, changes can't be saved. *Format* specifies whether values in a text file are to be separated by tabs (1) or commas (2). *Prot_pwd* is the password (text) to unprotect a protected file. *Write_res_pwd* is the password (text) to open a read-only file with full write privileges. *Ignore_rorec* is a logical value that controls whether the read-only recommended message is displayed. *File_origin* specifies the origin of a text file (1 = Macintosh, 2 = Windows, 3 = DOS or OS/2).

OPEN.LINKS(*documents1_text*, *documents2_text,...*, *read_only, type_link*)

OPEN.LINKS?(*documents1_text*, *documents2_text,...*, *read_only, type_link*)

Menu Equivalent: File→Links

Action: Opens the documents specified (as text) that are linked to the current document. The document names can be generated with the LINKS function. *Read_only* specifies whether the file is read only. *Type_link* specifies the type (1 = Excel, 2 = DDE, 4 = NewWave outgoing, 5 = Subscriber, 6 = Publisher).

Example: If the chart SALES is open and refers to a sheet called SALES, this function opens the sheet:

```
=OPEN.LINKS(LINKS("SALES"))
```

OUTLINE(*auto_styles, row_dir, col_dir, create_apply*)

Menu Equivalent: Formula→Outline

Action: Creates an outline and automatically defines settings. The arguments correspond to the dialog box check-boxes. *Create_apply* is a number that corresponds to the Create button and the Apply Styles button (1 = Create outline with current settings, 2 = Apply outlining styles to the selection based on the level).

OVERLAY(*type*, *stack, 100, vary, overlap, drop, hilo, overlap%, cluster, angle, series, auto*)

OVERLAY?(*type, stack, 100, vary, overlap, drop, hilo, overlap%, cluster, angle, series, auto*)

Menu Equivalent: Format→Overlay in Excel versions 2.2 or earlier, which is still supported. Use FORMAT.OVERLAY for formatting the overlay in Excel 3.0 or later.

Action: Sets the type and format of the overlay chart.

For worksheets and macro sheets.

PAGE.SETUP(*header, footer, left, right, top, bottom, headings, gridlines, h_ctr, v_ctr, orient, paper_size, scaling***)**

PAGE.SETUP?(*header, footer, left, right, top, bottom, headings, gridlines, h_ctr, v_ctr, orient, paper_size, scaling***)**

For charts only.

PAGE.SETUP(*header, footer, left, right, top, bottom, size, h_ctr, v_ctr, orient, paper_size, scaling***)**

PAGE.SETUP?(*header, footer, left, right, top, bottom, size, h_ctr, v_ctr, orient, paper_size, scaling***)**

Menu Equivalent: File→Page Setup

Action: Both types of functions set up either a worksheet (macro sheet) or chart for printing. *Header* and *footer* must be text. *Left, right, top,* and *bottom* are numbers that specify the relevant margins. *Headings* and *gridlines* correspond to the dialog-box check boxes and are logical values—TRUE if checked, FALSE if not checked. *Size* is a number (1 = Screen size, 2 = Fit to page, and 3 = Full page.) Other options correspond to options on the Page Setup dialog box. For more details, see the Excel function manual.

Example: =PAGE.SETUP("Sales-1991",Page&p,0.75,0,0.75, 1,1,TRUE,TRUE,2,5) sets up the chart to carry the heading "Sales-1991," have page numbers in the footer, have a 3/4" left and top margin and 1" bottom margin, be centered horizontally and vertically on the page, and be printed in landscape mode on legal-sized paper.

PARSE(*parse_text***)**

PARSE?(*parse_text*)

Menu Equivalent: Data→Parse

Action: Parses the input data stream. *Parse_text* is the parse line.

PASTE( )

Menu Equivalent: Edit→Paste

Action: Pastes from the Clipboard to the current location.

PASTE.LINK( )

Menu Equivalent: Edit→Paste Link

Action: Pastes copies data into destination cells and establishes a link with the source cells.

PASTE.PICTURE( )

Menu Equivalent: Edit→Paste Picture

Action: Pastes a picture of the Clipboard contents to the worksheet at the active cell location. There is no linking.

PASTE.PICTURE.LINK( )

Menu Equivalent: Edit→Paste Picture Link or the camera tool on the tool bar.

Action: Pastes a linked picture of the Clipboard contents to the worksheet at the active cell location.

Worksheet-to-worksheet form.

PASTE.SPECIAL(*paste_number, operation_number, skip_blanks, transpose*)

PASTE.SPECIAL?(*paste_number, operation_number, skip_blanks, transpose*)

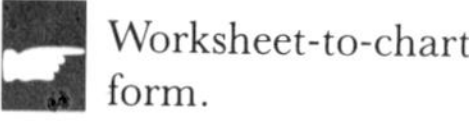

Worksheet-to-chart form.

PASTE.SPECIAL(*rowcol, series, categories, replace*)

PASTE.SPECIAL?(*rowcol, series, categories, replace*)

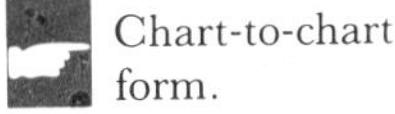
Chart-to-chart form.

PASTE.SPECIAL(*paste_number*)

PASTE.SPECIAL?(*paste_number*)

Menu Equivalent: Edit→Paste Special

Action: The worksheet function pastes from a worksheet to a worksheet, where *paste_number* is a number:

PASTE_NUMBER	WHAT TO PASTE
1	All
2	Formulas
3	Values
4	Formats
5	Notes

Operation_number specifies any operation desired (1 = None, 2 = Add, 3 = Subtract, 4 = Multiply, and 5 = Divide). Other arguments are logical values and correspond to the check boxes on the dialog box.

The chart function pastes values in rows if *rowcol* is 1, and in columns if it is 2. If *series* is TRUE, the contents of the first cell of each row is used as the name of the data series. If FALSE, it is used as a data point. If *categories* is TRUE, the contents of the first row or column is used as the chart categories. If FALSE, it is used as a data series. *Replace* corresponds to the Replace Existing Categories check box.

When using the chart-to-chart function, *paste_number* defines what to paste (1 = All, 2 = Formats, 3 = Data series).

For cells.

PATTERNS(*a_pattern, a_fore, a_back*)

PATTERNS?(*a_pattern, a_fore, a_back*)

For lines (arrows) on worksheets or charts.

PATTERNS(*l_auto, l_style, l_color, l_weight, h_width, h_length, h_type***)**

PATTERNS?(*l_auto, l_style, l_color, l_weight, h_width, h_length, h_type***)**

For text boxes, rectangles, ovals, arcs, and pictures.

PATTERNS(*b_auto, b_style, b_color, b_wt, shadow, a_auto, a_pattern, a_fore, a_back, rounded***)**

PATTERNS?(*b_auto, b_style, b_color, b_wt, shadow, a_auto, a_pattern, a_fore, a_back, rounded***)**

For chart plot areas, bars, columns, pie slices, and text labels.

PATTERNS(*b_auto, b_style, b_color, b_wt, shadow, a_auto, a_pattern, a_fore, a_back, apply***)**

PATTERNS?(*b_auto, b_style, b_color, b_wt, shadow, a_auto, a_pattern, a_fore, a_back, apply***)**

For chart axes.

PATTERNS(*l_auto, l_style, l_color, l_wt, t_major, t_minor, t_label***)**

PATTERNS?(*b_auto, b_style, b_color, b_wt, t_major, t_minor, t_label***)**

For chart gridlines, high-low lines, drop lines, lines on a picture line chart, and picture bar, column, and 3-D column charts.

PATTERNS(*l_auto, l_style, l_color, l_wt, apply***)**

PATTERNS?(*l_auto, l_style, l_color, l_wt, apply***)**

For chart data lines.

PATTERNS(*l_auto, l_style, l_color, l_wt, m_auto, m_style, m_fore, m_back, apply***)**

PATTERNS?(*l_auto, l_style, l_color, l_wt, m_auto, m_style, m_fore, m_back, apply***)**

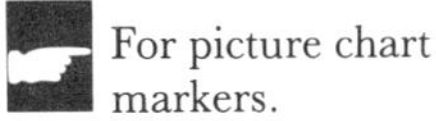
For picture chart markers.

PATTERNS(*type, picture_units, apply*)

PATTERNS?(*type, picture_units, apply*)

Menu Equivalent: Format→Patterns

Action: Changes the appearance of a selected object in a chart. The arguments correspond to those of the dialog box (see the Excel function manual).

PLACEMENT(*placement_type*)

Menu Equivalent: Format→Object Placement

Action: Specifies how the selected object is attached to the cells beneath it. *Placement_type* defines the relationship (1 = Moved and sized with cells, 2 = Moved with cells, 3 = Not moved or sized with cells).

POKE(*channel_number, item_text, data_ref*)

Menu Equivalent None.

Action: Sends the data referenced by *data_ref* to the item specified by *item_text* in the application connected to channel *channel_number*. The channel number is returned by the previously run INITIATE function.

PRECISION(*logical*)

Menu Equivalent: Options→Calculation (Precision as Displayed)

Action: Sets the precision of the calculation. If *logical* is FALSE, calculations are made to full precision. If *logical* is TRUE, calculations are to the displayed precision only. This may permanently alter the data.

PREFERRED( )

Menu Equivalent: Gallery→Preferred

Action: Changes the displayed chart to the default or preferred format.

PRINT(*range, from, to, copies, draft, preview, print_what, color, feed*)

PRINT?(*range, from, to, copies, draft, preview, print_what, color, feed*)

Menu Equivalent: File→Print

Action: Prints the sheet, chart, or macro sheet. The arguments correspond to the same arguments in the dialog box. *Range* is a number: 1 = Print all, 2 = Print a range. *From* and *to* specify the range limits. *Copies* is the number to print. For *feed*, 1 = Continuous and 2 = Cut sheets. The *print_what* argument specifies what to print (1 = Document, 2 = Notes, 3 = All).

Example: =PRINT(1,,,1,1) prints one copy of the entire sheet as a continuous form.

PRINT.PREVIEW( )

Menu Equivalent: File→Print Preview

Action: Previews the page and page breaks of the document to print.

PRINTER.SETUP(*printer_text*)

PRINTER.SETUP?(*printer_text*)

Menu Equivalent: File→Printer Setup

Action: Sets up the printer for printing. *Printer_text* name should be exactly as it appears in the File→Printer Setup dialog box.

Example: =PRINTER.SETUP("HP LaserJet + on LPT1") sets up the Hewlett-Packard LaserJet+ printer on port LPT1.

PROMOTE(*rowcol*)

PROMOTE?(*rowcol*)

Menu Equivalent: Equivalent to clicking the promote button.

Action: Promotes the selected rows or columns in an outline. If *row-col* is 1 or omitted, rows are promoted. If 2, columns are promoted.

PROTECT.DOCUMENT(*contents, windows, password, objects*)

PROTECT.DOCUMENT?(*contents, windows, password, objects*)

Menu Equivalent: Options→Protect Document and Options→ Unprotect Document

Action: Turns document protection on or off, with arguments corresponding to the dialog box check boxes. To protect a document, the first two arguments should be TRUE. To unprotect, both should be FALSE.

QUIT( )

Menu Equivalent File→Exit

Action: Quits Microsoft Excel.

REFTEXT(*ref, a1*)

Menu Equivalent: None.

Action: Converts the reference *ref* to an absolute reference in the form of text. Use this to operate on references with text functions.

This is an advanced function and should only be used by expert programmers.

REGISTER(***module_text, procedure_text, type_text,*** *function_text, argument_text*)

Menu Equivalent: None.

Action: Makes the specified dynamic link library available and returns the number identifying the code for use by the CALL and UNREGISTER functions. *Module_text* specifies the name of dynamic link library that contains the procedure you want to access. *Procedure_text* defines the name of the procedure. *Type_text* specifies the data type of the return value and the number and data types of the arguments (see the Excel function reference for details). The last two arguments define, respectively, the name of the function you are creating and its argument(s).

RELREF(*ref1, ref2*)

Menu Equivalent: None.

Action: Gives the reference of *ref1* relative to the upper-left cell of *ref2*. The reference is returned in text in the R1C1-style.

Example: =RELREF(A1,D4) yields R[-3]C[-3].

REMOVE.PAGE.BREAK( )

SET.PAGE.BREAK( )

Menu Equivalent: Options→Set Page Break and Options→Remove Page Break

Action: Sets or removes a page break at the indicated cell.

RENAME.COMMAND(*bar_number, menu_pos, command_pos, name_text*)

Menu Equivalent: None.

Action: Assigns the name *name_text* to the command in position *command_pos* on the menu *menu_pos* in the menu bar number *bar_number*.

REPLACE.FONT(*font, name_text, size_number, bold, italic, underline, strike, color, outline, shadow*)

Menu Equivalent: Format→Font

Action: Replaces a current font with a new font in older versions of Excel. Included for compatibility. Use FORMAT.FONT function in Excel Version 3.0 and later.

REQUEST(*channel_number, item_text*)

Menu Equivalent: None.

Action: Requests an array of information specified by *item_text* from the application connected to the channel specified by *channel_number*.

RESTART(*level_number*)

Menu Equivalent: None.

Action: Removes *level_number* RETURN statements from the stack. If *level_number* is omitted, all RETURN statements are omitted.

Example: Suppose that macro *C* is called by macro *B*, which in turn is called by macro *A*. Then =RETURN(1) in *C* will return execution directly to macro *A*.

RESULT(*type*)

Menu Equivalent: None.

Action: Defines the type of value that is to be returned by the function. The RESULT function is optional except when references or arrays are returned. If used, it must be the first function in the macro. *Type* defines the type of value returned:

TYPE	*VALUE*
1	Number
2	Text
4	Logical
8	Reference
16	Error
64	Array

Example: =RESULT(64) returns an array.

RETURN(*value*)

Menu Equivalent: None.

Action: Terminates the macro execution and, optionally, returns values to the calling program or macro. If *value* is to be returned, its type is specified by the RESULT function, which, if used, must be the first function in the macro. The *value* argument can be used only with function macros.

ROW.HEIGHT(*height_number, ref, standard_height, type_number*)

ROW.HEIGHT?(*height_number, ref, standard_height, type_number*)

Menu Equivalent: Format→Row Height

Action: The rows in *ref* are changed to height *height_number* in points (1/72 of an inch). *Type_number* permits you to hide, unhide, or set the height to best fit (1 = Hide, 2 = Unhide, 3 = Best fit). If *standard_height* is TRUE, *height_number* is ignored.

RUN(*ref, step*)

RUN?(*ref, step*)

Menu Equivalent: Macro→Run

Action: Initiates a macro execution defined by *ref*. *Ref* should be an external reference to a macro on a macro sheet or an R1C1-style external reference on a macro sheet. *Step* is a logical value and, if TRUE, permits single stepping the macro. If FALSE, or omitted, the macro is run normally.

Example: =RUN(MACROS.XLM!Heading) runs the macro normally, beginning at the upper-left cell of the range named "Heading."

SAVE( )

Menu Equivalent: File→Save

Action: Saves the current sheet under its current name.

SAVE.AS(*file_text, type, passwd_text, backup, write_res_pwd, read_only_rec*)

SAVE.AS?(*file_text, type, passwd_text, backup, write_res_pwd, read_only_rec*)

Menu Equivalent: File→Save As

Action: Saves the sheet using the name *file_text*. *Type* is a number that defines the saved format as follows:

TYPE	FORMAT
1	Normal
2	SYLK
3	Text
4	WKS
5	WK1
6	CSV
7	DBF2
8	DBF3
9	DIF
11	DBF4
15	WK3
16	Microsoft Excel 2.*X*
17	Template
18	Add-in macro
19	Text (Macintosh)
20	Text (Windows)
21	Text (DOS, OS/2)
22	CSV (Macintosh)
23	CSV (Windows)
24	CSV (DOS, OS/2)
25	International macro
26	International add-in macro

Types 10 and 12–14 are not defined. Worksheets can use all but 18, 25, and 26. Charts can use 1, 16, and 17. Macro sheets can use 1–3, 6, 9, and 16–26. Other arguments correspond to the dialog box options. *File_text, passwd_text,* and *write_res_pwd* are text. *Backup* and *read_only_rec* are logical values.

Example: =SAVE.AS("Sales",1) saves the file as "Sales" in the Normal format.

SAVE.NEW.OBJECT(*object_name_text*)

SAVE.NEW.OBJECT?(*object_name_text*)

Menu Equivalent: File→Save New Object (only if you are using NewWave by Hewlett-Packard).

Action: Saves a copy of the current object under the name you specify.

SAVE.WORKSPACE(*name_text*)

SAVE.WORKSPACE?(*name_text*)

Menu Equivalent: File→Save Workspace

Action: Saves the current workspace—opened documents, their position on-screen and status, preferred chart formats, and workspace display settings.

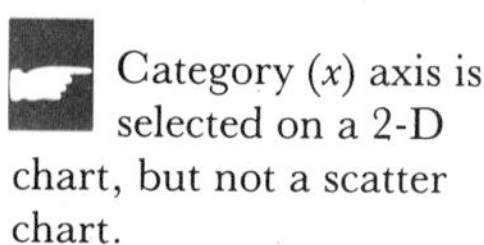

Category (*x*) axis is selected on a 2-D chart, but not a scatter chart.

SCALE(*cross, cat_labels, cat_marks, between, max, reverse*)

SCALE?(*cross, cat_labels, cat_marks, between, max, reverse*)

Value (*y*) axis selected on a 2-D chart, or *x* or *y* (value) axis selected on a scatter chart.

SCALE(*min_number, max_number, major, minor, cross, log, reverse, max*)

SCALE?(*min_number, max_number, major, minor, cross, log, reverse, max*)

Category (x) axis selected on a 3-D chart.

SCALE(*cat_labels, cat_marks, reverse, between*)

Series (y) axis selected on a 3-D chart.

SCALE(*series_labels, series_marks, reverse*)

Value (z) axis selected on a 3-D chart.

SCALE(*min_number, max_number, major, minor, cross, log, reverse, min*)

Menu Equivalent: Format→Scale

Action: Formats the scale. The arguments match those of the corresponding dialog box (see Excel Function Reference for more details).

Cells on a worksheet or macro sheet.

SELECT(*selection_ref, active_cell_ref*)

Worksheet and macro sheet objects.

SELECT(***object_ID_text***, *replace*)

Chart form.

SELECT(***item_text***, *single_point*)

Menu Equivalent: Equivalent to selecting cells or objects with the mouse.

Action: The first function applies to a worksheet or macro sheet and selects the cells referenced by *selection_ref* and makes *active_cell_ref* the active cell. *Selection_ref* should be either a reference to the active worksheets (such as !B1:B3 or !Income) or an R1C1-style reference in text form (such as "R[– 2]C[– 1]:R[2]C[3]"). If you omit *selection_ref*, the selection is not changed. *Active_cell_ref* should be a reference to a single cell inside of *selection_ref* either on the current sheet or as an R1C1-style reference. If *active_cell_ref* is relative, it is assumed to be relative to the currently active cell. If *active_cell_ref* is omitted, it is assumed to be the upper-left cell of *selection_ref*.

The second function applies to selecting objects, where *object_ID-_text* is the text that identifies the object and *replace* is a logical value which specifies that previously selected objects are included in the selection. If TRUE (default), only the current object is selected.

The third function applies to a chart and selects the object specified by *item_text*. If *single_point* is TRUE, a single point is selected.

Examples: =SELECT(!Sales,!A5), =SELECT("Oval1"), or SELECT("S1P2",TRUE). The third one selects the second point in the first series of a chart.

SELECT.CHART( )

Included for compatibility with Macintosh Excel. Same as the third form of SELECT in Excel for Windows.

SELECT.END(*direction_number*)

Menu Equivalent: None.

Action: Moves the active cell in the next block edge in the direction specified by *direction_number* (1 = Left, 2 = Right, 3 = Up, and 4 = Down).

SELECT.LAST.CELL( )

Menu Equivalent: Equivalent to Formula→Select Special and selecting the Last Cell option.

Action: Makes the last cell of the sheet the active cell.

SELECT.PLOT.AREA( )

Included for compatibility with Macintosh Excel. Same as SELECT("Plot") in Excel for Windows.

SELECT.SPECIAL(*type_number*, *value_types*, *levels*)

SELECT.SPECIAL?(*type_number*, *value_types*, *levels*)

Menu Equivalent: Formula→Select Special

Action: Selects cells with the specified characteristics. *Type_number* identifies the dialog box option:

TYPE_NUMBER	DESCRIPTION
1	Notes
2	Constants
3	Formulas
4	Blanks
5	Current region
6	Current array
7	Row differences
8	Column differences
9	Precedents
10	Dependents
11	Last cell
12	Visible cells only (outlining)
13	All objects

Value_types identifies the types of selection (1 = Numbers, 2 = Text, 4 = Logical values, 16 = Error values). These values can be added to select multiple types (e.g., 6 = text and logical values).

Levels specifies how precedents and dependents are selected (1 = Direct only, 2 = All levels). It is available only when *type_number* is 9 or 10. The default is 1.

SELECTION()

Menu Equivalent: None.

Action: Returns the reference of the currently selected cells or object.

Example: If the current sheet is SALES and the cells B1 to B3 are selected, then =REFTEXT(SELECTION( )) gives SALES-.XLS!R1C2:R3C2.

SEND.KEYS(***key_text***, *wait_log*)

Menu Equivalent: None.

Action: Sends the keys specified by *key_text* to the active applications, just as if they were typed at the keyboard. *Wait_log* is a logical value that determines whether the macro should wait until actions from *key_text* are completed. If TRUE, the macro waits.

SEND.TO.BACK( )

Menu Equivalent: Format→Send To Back

Action: Places selected objects behind other objects.

SERIES(*name_ref*, *categories*, ***values***, ***plot_order***)

Menu Equivalent: None.

Action: Represents the active data series in a chart. You cannot use it as a function in a macro sheet. To edit a series, use EDIT.SERIES.

SET.CRITERIA( )

Menu Equivalent: Data→Set Criteria

Action: Assigns the name "Criteria" to the currently selected range.

SET.DATABASE( )

Menu Equivalent: Data→Set Database

Action: Assigns the name "Database" to the currently selected range.

SET.EXTRACT( )

Menu Equivalent: Data→Set Extract

Action: Assigns the name "Extract" to the currently selected range.

SET.NAME(*name_text, value*)

Menu Equivalent: None.

If *value* is to be the value of a referenced cell, you must use the DEREF function.

Action: Defines a name on the macro sheet as a specified value. *Name_text* must be a text value for the name to be assigned. *Value* can be a number, text, logical, error value, array, or a reference.

Examples: =SET.NAME("One",1) assigns the name "One" to the value 1.

=SET.NAME("Qty",DEREF(A3)) assigns the name "Qty" to the value in A3 on the macro sheet.

SET.PAGE.BREAK( )

See REMOVE.PAGE.BREAK( ).

SET.PREFERRED( )

Menu Equivalent: Gallery→Set Preferred

Action: Sets the current chart format as the preferred format.

SET.PRINT.AREA( )

Menu Equivalent: Options→Set Print Area

Action: Defines the current selection as the sheet area to be printed with the File→Print command.

SET.PRINT.TITLES( )

Menu Equivalent: Options→Set Print Titles

Action: Defines the current selection as the text that will be used as page titles when the sheet is printed.

SET.UPDATE.STATUS(*link_text, status, type_of_link*)

Menu Equivalent: None.

Action: Sets the update status of a link to automatic (*status* = 1) or manual (*status* = 2). *Link_text* is the full path name of the link, as displayed in the Links dialog box. *Type_of_link* defines the type (2 = DDE, 4 = Outgoing NewWave).

SET.VALUE(*ref, values*)

Menu Equivalent: None.

Action: Changes the value of the cells specified by *ref* to *values*. Formulas are not changed. Used for loop control during macro execution. *Ref* must be a reference to cells on the macro sheet. If *ref* is a range, *values* should be an array of the same size.

Example: =SET.VALUE(D5,3) sets the value in D5 of the macro sheet to 3.

SHARE( )

Menu Equivalent: Edit→Share (only if you are using NewWave by Hewlett-Packard).

Action: Places a shared view of the selection on the Clipboard.

SHARE.NAME(*range_text*)

Menu Equivalent: Edit→Share (only if you are using NewWave by Hewlett-Packard).

Action: Places a shared view of *range_text* on the Clipboard.

SHORT.MENUS(*logical*)

Menu Equivalent: Options→Short Menus

Action: Sets the menu display to short or full menus. If *logical* is TRUE or omitted, Excel uses short menus. If FALSE, full menus are used.

SHOW.ACTIVE.CELL( )

Menu Equivalent: Formula→Show Active Cell or Ctrl-Backspace

Action: Scrolls sheet until active cell is visible.

SHOW.BAR(*bar_number*)

Menu Equivalent: None.

Action: Displays the menu bar specified by menu bar ID number *bar_number*.

SHOW.CLIPBOARD( )

Menu Equivalent: Equivalent to running the Clipboard from Windows Control Panel.

Action: Displays contents of the Clipboard in a new window.

SHOW.DETAIL(*rowcol, rowcol_number, expand*)

Menu Equivalent: None.

Action: Expands or collapses detail under the specified expand or collapse button. If *rowcol* is 1, the function operates on rows; if 2, on columns. *Rowcol_number* specifies the row or column to expand or collapse. If *expand* is TRUE, the function expands; otherwise it collapses. If omitted, the row or column changes state (collapsing if already expanded and vice versa).

SHOW.INFO(*enable_log*)

Menu Equivalent: Window→Show Info

Action: If *enable_log* is TRUE, the command activates the Info window. If the current window is the Info window and *enable_log* is FALSE, the command activates the document linked to the Info window.

SHOW.LEVELS(*row_level, col_level*)

Menu Equivalent: None.

Action: Displays the specified number of row and column levels of the outline. At least one of the arguments must be specified. *Row_level* defines the number of row levels to display, and *col_level* defines the number of column levels to display.

SIZE(***x_number, y_number***, *window_text*)

Menu Equivalent: (Control) Size; equivalent to changing the size of a window by dragging.

Action: Changes the size of the specified window. The lower-right corner is moved until the window is the size defined by *x_number* and *y_number*. If you omit *window_text,* the current active window is resized.

SORT(***sort_by, 1st_key, order1***, *2nd_key, order2, 3rd_key, order3*)

SORT?(*sort_by, 1st_key, order1, 2nd_key, order2, 3rd_key, order3*)

Menu Equivalent: Data→Sort

Action: Sorts the specified range in the order defined by the arguments. There are two *sort_by* options:

SORT_BY	***ORDER***
1	Rows
2	Columns

and two orders:

ORDER	***DIRECTION***
1	Ascending
2	Descending

1st_key, *2nd_key*, and *3rd_key* are external references to the current sheet or R1C1-style references in text. You may also wish to use the DEREF function to define a key.

Examples: =SORT(1,"R12C1",1) sorts the selected rows, using R12C1 as a key, in ascending order.

If C11 on the sheet contains the text "Target," this function sorts the sheet by target values:

=SORT(1,DEREF(!$C$11),1)

SPLIT(*col_split, row_split*)

Menu Equivalent: (Control) Split

Action: Splits the active window.

STANDARD.FONT(*font_text, size_number, bold, italic, underline, strike, color, outline, shadow*)

Menu Equivalent: None.

Action: In earlier versions of Excel, this set the standard font. For Excel 3.0 or later, use DEFINE.STYLE or APPLY.STYLE. The arguments are the same as for FORMAT.FONT.

STEP( )

Menu Equivalent: None.

Action: Permits calculating a macro one step at a time and is useful for debugging. When the STEP function is encountered in a macro execution, the calculation stops and displays a dialog box that defines the next cell to calculate and the formula in that cell. You can then click Step in this box to execute the next macro cell and stop again, click Evaluate to calculate part of the formula, click Halt to interrupt the macro, or click Continue to run without single-stepping.

STYLE(*bold, italic*)

STYLE?(*bold, italic*)

Included only for compatibility with older versions of Excel. Equivalent in Excel for Windows to FORMAT.FONT.

SUBSTITUTE(*text, old_text, new_text, instance_number*)

Menu Equivalent: None.

Action: Substitutes *new_text* for *old_text* in *text* for instance *instance_number.*

TABLE(*row_input, column_input*)

TABLE?(*row_input, column_input*)

Menu Equivalent: Data→Table

You can use the DEREF function to define cells.

Action: Creates a table in the selected range. Both *row_input* and *column_input* should be external references to single cells on the active sheet, or R1C1-type references in text form.

Example: In the SALES example of this book, cell D4 was used as a column input to define a table. This could also be done as follows:

=TABLE(,"R4C4")

If D3 contained the heading "Criteria" as the name for D4, you could also use the following:

=TABLE(,DEREF(!D$3))

TERMINATE(*channel_number*)

Menu Equivalent: None.

Action: Closes the DDE channel *channel_number* set up by the INITIATE function.

TEXT.BOX(*add_text, object_ID_text, start_number, number_chars*)

Menu Equivalent: None.

Action: Replaces characters in a text box with *add_text.*

TEXTREF(*text, a1*)

Menu Equivalent: None.

Action: Converts *text* to an absolute reference. If *a1* is TRUE, *text* is assumed to be in the A1-style reference. If FALSE or omitted, the R1C1-style is assumed.

UNDO( )

Menu Equivalent: Edit→Undo

Action: Undoes the previous command.

UNGROUP( )

Menu Equivalent: Format→Ungroup

Action: Separates a grouped object into its components.

UNHIDE(*window_text*)

Menu Equivalent: Window→Unhide

Action: Unhides the specified window.

UNLOCKED.NEXT( )

UNLOCKED.PREV( )

Menu Equivalent: Pressing Tab or Shift-Tab.

Action: Moves the active cell to the next or previous unlocked cell in a protected sheet.

UNREGISTER(*register_number*)

Menu Equivalent: None.

Action: Removes dynamic link library or code resource previously registered by the REGISTER function.

UPDATE.LINK(*link_text, type_of_link*)

Menu Equivalent: File→Links Update

Action: Updates a link to another document. *Link_text* defines the full path as defined in the dialog box. *Type_of_link* is a number that defines the type of link to update (1 or omitted = Excel, 2 = DDE, 4 = Outgoing NewWave).

VIEW.3D(*elevation, perspective, rotation, axes, height%*)

VIEW.3D?(*elevation, perspective, rotation, axes, height%*)

Menu Equivalent: Format→3-D View

Action: Specifies the view of a 3-D chart. The arguments correspond to the items in the dialog box.

VLINE(*number*)

See HLINE.

VOLATILE( )

Menu Equivalent: None.

Action: Specifies that the current function is volatile; that is, it is recalculated each time any cell in the worksheet is recalculated. In a macro, it must immediately follow the RESULT or ARGUMENT functions.

VPAGE(*number*)

See HPAGE.

VSCROLL(*row_number, row_logical*)

See HSCROLL.

WAIT(*serial_number*)

Menu Equivalent: None.

Action: Suspends execution of the macro until the time specified by *serial_number*.

WHILE(*logical_test*)

Menu Equivalent: None.

Action: Starts a WHILE...NEXT loop.

WINDOWS(*type_number*)

Menu Equivalent: None.

Action: Returns an array of text values that are the names of all active windows on the screen. You can then use the INDEX function to select from the array. *Type_number* specifies the types of windows to include (1 = All except add-in documents, 2 = Add-in documents only, 3 = All). The default value, if omitted, is 1.

Example: =WINDOWS( ) gives {"Sheet1", "Sheet2"}.

WORKGROUP(*name_array_text*)

Menu Equivalent: Window→Workgroup

Action: Creates a workgroup, where *name_array_text* is a list of open, unhidden worksheets and macro sheets for the workgroup.

WORKSPACE(*fixed, decimals, r1c1, scroll, status, formula, menu, remote, entermove, underlines, tools, notes, nav_keys, menu_key_action*)

WORKSPACE?(*fixed, decimals, r1c1, scroll, status, formula, menu, remote, entermove, underlines, tools, notes, nav_keys, menu_key_action*)

Menu Equivalent: Options→Workspace

Action: Sets the Excel workspace. The options correspond to those on the dialog box.

INDEX

A

D

F

M

T

W

FREE CATALOG!

Mail us this form today, and we'll send you a full-color catalog of Sybex books.

Name ______________________________

Street ______________________________

City/State/Zip ______________________________

Phone ______________________________

Please supply the name of the Sybex book purchased.

____

How would you rate it?

____ Excellent ____ Very Good ____ Average ____ Poor

Why did you select this particular book?

- ____ Recommended to me by a friend
- ____ Recommended to me by store personnel
- ____ Saw an advertisement in ______________________________
- ____ Author's reputation
- ____ Saw in Sybex catalog
- ____ Required textbook
- ____ Sybex reputation
- ____ Read book review in ______________________________
- ____ In-store display
- ____ Other ______________________________

Where did you buy it?

- ____ Bookstore
- ____ Computer Store or Software Store
- ____ Catalog (name: ______________________________)
- ____ Direct from Sybex
- ____ Other: ______________________________

Did you buy this book with your personal funds?

____Yes ____No

About how many computer books do you buy each year?

____ 1-3 ____ 3-5 ____ 5-7 ____ 7-9 ____ 10+

About how many Sybex books do you own?

____ 1-3 ____ 3-5 ____ 5-7 ____ 7-9 ____ 10+

Please indicate your level of experience with the software covered in this book:

____ Beginner ____ Intermediate ____ Advanced

Which types of software packages do you use regularly?

____ Accounting
____ Amiga
____ Apple/Mac
____ CAD
____ Communications
____ Databases
____ Desktop Publishing
____ File Utilities
____ Money Management
____ Languages
____ Networks
____ Operating Systems
____ Spreadsheets
____ Word Processing
____ Other ____________________ (please specify)

Which of the following best describes your job title?

____ Administrative/Secretarial
____ Director
____ Engineer/Technician
____ President/CEO
____ Manager/Supervisor
____ Other ____________________ (please specify)

Comments on the weaknesses/strengths of this book: ____________________

PLEASE FOLD, SEAL, AND MAIL TO SYBEX

SYBEX, INC.
Department M
2021 CHALLENGER DR.
ALAMEDA, CALIFORNIA USA
94501

SEAL